Praise for *UFOs a*

"Rich Dolan's meticulous research takes us behind the headlines into the archives to document the interplay between the UFO subject and the National Security apparatus . . . a must-read for serious students of the field."

—H. E. Puthoff, Ph.D., director, Institute for Advanced Studies at Austin

"Destined to become a true classic . . . packed with information . . . [Dolan] is a skilled writer whose style never bores . . . [he] has done Ufology a major service."

—Nick Redfern, UFO Magazine (U.K)

"This book marks a true watershed in Ufology . . . one of the most important books ever written in this field. Dolan has settled, once and for all, any question about the importance of the UFO to the national security apparatus of the United States. This book promises to have tremendous staying power and become truly influential as time passes. Read it today and get an advanced look at what everyone will be thinking a few years from now."

—Val Germann, UFO researcher and writer

"Dolan's research provides facts to substantiate the claims that the UFO phenomenon has always been global; that UFOs are actual objects; that the actual number of UFO sightings exceeds any official total; and that official government investigators found that some people were actually seeing alien beings."

—John Schuessler, MUFON UFO Journal

"This is the best history of the UFO phenomenon in one volume that I have ever read."

—Loy Lawhon, UFO researcher, columnist, and former MUFON investigator

UFOs

and the National Security State

RUSSELL TARG EDITIONS

UFOs and the National Security State by Richard M. Dolan

The Heart of the Internet by Jacques Vallee, Ph.D.

Studies in Consciousness/Russell Targ Editions

Mental Radio by Upton Sinclair

An Experiment with Time by J. W. Dunne

Human Personality and Its Survival of Bodily Death by F. W. H. Myers

Mind to Mind by René Warcollier

Experiments in Mental Suggestion by L. L. Vasiliev

Mind at Large edited by Charles T. Tart, Harold E. Puthoff, and Russell Targ

Dream Telepathy by Montague Ullman, M.D., and Stanley Krippner, Ph.D., with Alan Vaughan

Distant Mental Influence by William Braud, Ph.D.

Thoughts Through Space by Sir Hubert Wilkins and Harold M. Sherman

The Future and Beyond by H. F. Saltmarsh

Mind-Reach by Russell Targ and Harold Puthoff

The Secret Vaults of Time by Stephan A. Schwartz

Some of the twentieth century's best texts on the scientific study of consciousness are out of print, hard to find, and unknown to most readers; yet they are still of great importance, their insights into human consciousness and its dynamics still valuable and vital. Hampton Roads Publishing Company—in partnership with physicist and consciousness research pioneer Russell Targ—is proud to bring some of these texts back into print, introducing classics in the fields of science and consciousness studies to a new generation of readers. Upcoming titles in the Studies in Consciousness series will cover such perennially exciting topics as telepathy, astral projection, the after-death survival of consciousness, psychic abilities, long-distance hypnosis, and more.

UFOs

and the National Security State

Chronology of a Cover-up 1941–1973

REVISED EDITION

RICHARD M. DOLAN

Foreword by Jacques F. Vallee, Ph.D.

HAMPTON ROADS
PUBLISHING COMPANY, INC.

Cover design by Bookwrights Design
Cover painting by Ingo Swann
Photo of cover painting by Bob Sasson

Hampton Roads Publishing Company, Inc.
1125 Stoney Ridge Road
Charlottesville, VA 22902

434-296-2772
fax: 434-296-5096
e-mail: hrpc@hrpub.com
www.hrpub.com

If you are unable to order this book from your local
bookseller, you may order directly from the publisher.

Call 1-800-766-8009, toll-free.

Library of Congress Catalog Card Number: 2001099307

ISBN 1-57174-317-0

10 9 8 7 6 5 4 3

Printed on acid-free paper in Canada

To Michael and Elaine:

the reason it matters.

Table of Contents

Foreword

The important book you are about to read is the first comprehensive study of the U.S. government's response to the intrusion of UFO phenomena in American skies over the last fifty years. While several historical studies of the controversies surrounding the reports have been conducted, the military and intelligence implications have, until now, remained in a state of confusion.

As a longtime student of the phenomenon, I can testify to the complexity of the data Richard Dolan had to decipher. The U.S. Air Force itself, overtly the main contender in this drama, never attempted to compile a comprehensive history of its own files on the matter. When I reviewed the 11,000 cases in the air force files between 1963 and 1967, the military had no index of that data. The most cogent participants, such as Capt. Edward Ruppelt and professor J. Allen Hynek, did write about what they had done but they left many undocumented areas. Interested outsiders picked up the pieces of the various projects, and presented personal interpretations of what had happened. Understandably, the result was a vibrant mélange of facts, fiction, and subjective interpretations, which has led to the wildly conflicting theories the media love to exploit.

Even the White House was unable to reconstruct the full picture when President Jimmy Carter instructed NASA to undertake a review of UFO information in the late seventies. A Washington wag described the space agency's reaction to this presidential order as "a flurry of alarmed paralysis." At the height of the Carter effort a small group of us from various research institutes and universities volunteered to help. I vividly recall a meeting I had with a high-level official at the Office of Science and Technology Policy, across the street from the White House in September 1977. I tried to convey to him that we had experts all across the U.S. who were ready, willing, and able to get involved in NASA's review of the phenomenon if they were given a green light. He listened to me sympathetically but expressed discouragement about what he saw as "an impossible political situation." Discussion turned to the fact that the CIA and the air force, as well as several other agencies, must have entire file cabinets filled with reports from their own people, if only because the phenomenon is known to trigger the kinds of sensors that have been deployed to detect enemy threats during the Cold War. I was told there was plenty of data all right, collected by the military and intelligence community, but it "never saw the light of day." The White House might force some of it to be released, he told me, but that might not advance the problem: "Those guys twist everything to suit their own political schemes. It's like pulling teeth to get data, and you never know if they tell you the truth."

Into this murky world of deception and confusion Richard Dolan has now cast a welcome light. But it will take a sustained effort along the lines he has pioneered if we hope to validate the facts, uncover the motives, and reconstruct the patterns. In order to conduct this analysis it is very important to take notice of what is *not* there: the missing parts of the overall puzzle. What is not there constitutes a world of heroic complexity and immense proportion.

I had a vivid example of this fact, on a much smaller scale, when I unearthed a secret letter from a Battelle scientist named Cross, who had written to the CIA at the time of the Robertson panel in 1953. (I have referred to this document in my previous books as the "Pentacle Memorandum.") To this day there are ufologists who claim the letter was unimportant. Yet there are indications it may represent the point of major bifurcation when the most serious part of the official study plunged underground while Blue Book continued as a public relations exercise, the visible effort by the military to gather UFO reports from American citizens.

The experience of tracking down that single document makes me appreciate the delicate nature and the sheer difficulty of the task undertaken by Richard Dolan in compiling the present book.

The Cross letter was significant because it implied that a group of specialists working in the shadows on the most massive UFO study to date had the power to keep critical information from a prestigious national security panel. Furthermore, they had another plan, a brilliant project of far-reaching implication which they proposed to implement as a way of getting to the heart of the phenomenon. I had a copy of that letter. It was stamped "Secret." I knew its exact origin. Yet all the efforts I made to unearth an official copy from the air force or the National Archives through the Freedom of Information Act failed to yield results. It is finally through Congress that I obtained clearance to release the text. The process has given me a sobering view of the ability of the bureaucracy to hide the truth for decades, occasionally using the colorful community of UFO believers itself as an unwitting tool as it covered its tracks. To this day, I am convinced that historians of the phenomenon have remained blind to some of the implications. It is my hope that books like the present one can stimulate a renewed effort to get at the truth.

Like the "missing mass" that astronomers are trying to locate in the far reaches of our universe, the UFO phenomenon rests on an ocean of dark matter, deep secrets, and forgotten wars fought only in shadows. Not all of it had to do with the kind of objects the American public imagines UFOs to be. Some of the warriors seemed to have understood, early on, that if UFOs existed as a genuine new phenomenon of intelligent origin, this fact did not necessarily mean they were from outer space. And other warriors may have decided that the belief in the reality of UFOs could be twisted, exploited, and bent to obscure political ends. They may have planted false UFO stories to hide real experiments. They may have disguised helicopters as flying saucers, or lied to witnesses at sites where advanced prototypes had crashed, never to be divulged again. No wonder even White House officials get confused when they try, years later, to reassemble the facts.

As we ponder the implications, we are led, inexorably, to a much larger issue. As anyone learns who has become a naturalized United States citizen, the rock upon which American democracy is built is "an informed citizenry." Without full information, how would you know how to vote? And if you didn't know how to vote, could you still pretend you lived in a democracy?

In the last fifty years the various branches of the military and intelligence community in the United States have so clouded the reports of the UFO phenomenon that the citizenry has been left not just uninformed but indeed misinformed. This may not have been the intent, but it is indeed the result. Those who truly care about democracy are justified in asking that the government come clean about what it knows and—most importantly perhaps—*what it doesn't know* about a phenomenon of such far-reaching consequences for our science and our society.

All efforts to break open the mystery so far have made the assumption that the "big secret" merely involves extraterrestrial spacecraft put together with metal and rivets. This partial view is supported by the many instances in which UFOs have been seen by pilots, photographed, and tracked on radar. Yet modern physical theory opens up a much wider, richer spectrum of hypotheses for objects that might blink in and out of perception, impact the consciousness of witnesses, accelerate without creating sonic booms, change shape, and merge with one another dynamically. Concepts of higher dimensionality, once on the fringes of physics, have entered the mainstream of science. Given what we know about the universe today, it is irrational to assume it can be described with only three dimensions of space and one dimension of time.

The UFO witnesses are telling us they have experienced objects of vast complexity that challenged their sense of reality. Such observations are anomalous in the narrow sense of the classical physics we learn in school, but they may help build a conceptual framework for the physics of the twenty-first century. It is all the more important then, as Richard Dolan points out, to make a precise assessment of what the most reliable witnesses have observed, and to seriously start looking for the missing parts of this famous puzzle. UFOs have been with us since the beginning of recorded history. Could they be trying to tell us who we are, and what true place we are destined to occupy in the universe?

—by Jacques F. Vallee, Ph.D.

Preface

When I originally undertook to edit this book for its release by Hampton Roads, I believed it was perhaps too long and intimidating for many readers. Therefore, I decided to tighten the book throughout, eliminate some redundancies of description, and shorten it by about 150 pages.

The result has been both less and more than I expected. As for length, this new edition is only shorter by about fifty pages, but it has several changes from the original that make it substantially different. Every chapter has been edited, although the bulk of the changes are in the first half of the book. The most significant are:

Some paring down of non-UFO-related activities by the American military and intelligence apparatus. This is not complete by any means, and certainly enough remains to place UFO policies and activities within an appropriate context.

Streamlining and clarification of the crash at Roswell; more thorough analysis of the Maury Island and MJ-12 controversies.

More complete analysis of some documents from late 1947, including a correction regarding the Schulgen Memo and a better study of the "Soviet angle."

Expanded coverage of the Mantell case of 1948, Secretary of Defense James Forrestal, astronomer J. Allen Hynek, Thomas Townsend Brown, and anti-gravity research from the 1950s.

Improving the footnoting so as to cite primary documents whenever possible. Not having done this adequately the first time had been a major regret.

Throughout, I took the opportunity to improve organization whenever possible, add new and relevant information, and always keep the reader's best interest in mind.

—Richard M. Dolan
Rochester, New York, 2001

Acknowledgments

While writing this book, I was fortunate to discuss this topic with hundreds of individuals who provided observations, insights, and invaluable support. I am grateful to all of them. In addition, several people took the time to read various parts of the book in progress. They, too, have my gratitude: Duane Abrams, Nancy Arrington, Sally Campbell, Jim DeFelice, Lisa Dolan, Dr. Juan Dura, Dr. Ted Farcasin, Joan Marg, Debra Scacciaferro, Marsha Schneider, Art Schneider, Annette Sullivan, Christopher Thomas, and William Sherwood. For the second edition of this book, several other attentive readers provided invaluable support and insight: Dr. Gary Alevi, Dr. Michael Altfeld, Don and Vicky Ecker, Joe Firmage, Leslie Kean, Dr. Hal Puthoff, Clifford Stone, Whitley and Anne Strieber.

There remain a few individuals who provided assistance and guidance of a special sort.

Christopher Rozzi, Rochester, New York's premier used-book dealer, a man who hunted down crucial resources I could obtain nowhere else, and who provided his own substantial knowledge of the UFO phenomenon in many personal conversations, and as a reader.

Russell Targ, pioneering physicist and author, whose support was instrumental in enabling me to write a second edition of this book.

Frank DeMarco, my editor at Hampton Roads Publishing, a consummate reader's advocate who combined a probing mind with a skillful editorial touch.

Dr. Edgar Mitchell, astronaut and interested reader, who was gracious and kind enough to lend his time to my book.

Dr. Stuart Campbell, mentor and friend, my first and best teacher in the discipline of history, and who, as in all matters, gave his critical eye and valuable insights.

Val Germann, UFO analyst extraordinaire, whose essays sparked my interest in this subject, and whose friendship, conversations, and services as a reader have been of great value to me.

Dr. Jacques Vallee, who was kind enough to write the Foreword to this second edition.

Richard T. Dolan, my father. Every child needs his father's encouragement and support; I am fortunate to have received it my entire life, including during the course of this project.

Barbara Dolan-Rice, my mother. She is a constant inspiration, and her ever-practical nature provided some of the best insights of all of my readers, thus proving the adage: Always Listen to Your Mother.

Karyn Dolan, my wife and partner in everything I do. She survived it all: my consuming obsession with this project, the late hours, the many difficult days and weeks it demanded. Throughout, she supported, prodded, asked myriad questions, and listened beyond any reasonable expectation. She read carefully and with precision, never failing to offer thoughtful suggestions, all of which strengthened this book. It is an especially extraordinary accomplishment, considering that she gave birth not once, but twice, during the writing of this book.

Even the best insights from a legion of perceptive readers, however, cannot overcome all the limitations inherent in a work such as this, which are my responsibility alone.

Introduction

In formal logic, a contradiction is the signal of defeat; but in the evolution of real knowledge it marks the first step in progress toward victory.

—Alfred North Whitehead

It is a mistake to believe that a science consists in nothing but conclusively proved propositions, and it is unjust to demand that it should. It is a demand only made by those who feel a craving for authority in some form and a need to replace the religious catechism by something else, even if it be a scientific one.

—Sigmund Freud

There is a skeleton in every house.

—Anonymous

THE PROBLEM OF UFOS

The UFO problem has involved military personnel around the world for more than fifty years, and is wrapped in secrecy. Over the years, enough pieces of the puzzle have emerged to give us a sense of what the picture looks like. I have tried to use these pieces to construct a clear, historical narrative, focusing on the national security dimensions.

Because this subject is so widely ridiculed, it is important to stress why it is worthy of serious attention. Stories of strange objects in the sky go far back in time, but the problem received little attention until the Second World War.

At that time, military personnel from Allied and Axis countries reported unconventional objects in the sky, eventually known as foo fighters. In retrospect, this development is not so surprising. First, human aviation had become widespread for the first time. Above the clouds, thousands of pilots suddenly had the kind of visibility never before possessed. A second reason was the invention of radar, which extended the range of human vision by electronic means. Most investigators during the war assumed the odd sightings were related to the war itself, the product of anomalies related to their new technologies of detection, or perhaps enemy experimental aircraft.

With that in mind, one might have expected such sightings to vanish after the war's end in 1945. Instead, they increased. In Europe in 1946, then America in 1947, people saw and reported objects that could not be explained in any conventional sense. Wherever sightings occurred, military authorities dominated the investigations, and for perfectly understandable reasons. Unknown objects, frequently tracked on radar and observed visually, were flying within one's national borders and, in the case of the United States, over sensitive military installations. The war was over. What was going on here?

During the UFO wave of 1947, American military and intelligence organizations conducted multiple, simultaneous investigations of these sightings. Although the air force was officially charged with investigating them, it was never the only game in town. Every service was involved. The FBI investigated UFOs for a while, and by 1948 at the latest, the CIA initiated an ongoing interest.

Initially, some Americans feared that the Soviet Union might be behind the "flying saucer" wave. This possibility was studied, then rejected. At a time when the world's fastest aircraft approached the speed of 600 mph, some of these objects exceeded—or appeared to exceed—1,000 mph. What's more, they maneuvered as no aircraft could, including right-angle turns, stopping on a dime, and accelerating instantly. Could the Soviets really have built something like *that?* If so, why fly them all over America and Western Europe? To experts, the idea seemed far-fetched at best, and fifty years later, their conclusion stands. Could the objects, then, have been American? The possibility was studied and rejected for the same reasons. It was not credible to American investigators that their military had secretly discovered a hypersonic antigravity technology.

Options quickly narrowed. Either this was something real and alien, or it was something "conventional" but as yet unknown or unexplained. But what could explain the strong appearance of metallic craft performing the impossible? By the end of 1947, a contingent of analysts at the Air Technical Intelligence Center (ATIC) at Wright-Patterson Air Force Base believed that UFOs were extraterrestrial. By the summer of 1948, this team prepared an "Estimate of the Situation," stating the extraterrestrial thesis that landed on the desk of Air Force Commander Hoyt Vandenberg. As the story goes (there are no official papers proving this, only the statements of several insiders), Vandenberg rejected it, either for lack of proof or because it did not state his desired conclusion. Either way, he made it clear that the air force would not accept speculation about extraterrestrials as a solution to UFOs.

Of course, people continued to see these things and wondered what they were. In the summer of 1952, for instance, UFO sightings were so frequent and often of such high quality that some in the air force actually wondered whether an invasion was under way. With some help from the secret CIA-sponsored Robertson Panel of January 1953, the air force improved censorship over the problem. Still, it never quite went away. Civilian organizations began to collect and analyze interesting UFO reports. Moreover, the air force had backed itself into a corner by committing itself to monitoring UFOs as a possible national security threat. Those who criticized the air force's dismissive statements about UFOs—and there were many such people—frequently asked, if saucers posed no threat to national security, and existed only in the imagination, why did the air force create Project Blue Book to study the reports?

Then came the great UFO wave of 1965 and 1966, when the air force could no longer hide behind weather balloons and swamp gas, nor withstand public scrutiny. As a result, it funded a scientific study of UFOs by the University of Colorado, known to history as the Condon Committee, to "settle" the matter. After two years, the committee concluded that UFOs were not worthy of scientific study. Critics replied that the study's conclusions did not match its own data. The committee certainly had bad blood among its own members, which resulted in the removal of the "pro-UFO" contingent midway through the project. It appeared to many that the project's leadership had been set on a negative conclusion from the beginning. Rumors spread about control over the committee, either by the air force or CIA.

As messy as the Condon Committee was, it enabled the air force to close Blue Book. In December 1969, the air force announced it was no longer investigating UFOs. The major civilian investigative organizations soon declined, and people who saw UFOs had scarcely anywhere to turn.

Let us pause to assess the situation. By the mid-1940s, America's intelligence apparatus had reason to believe that there were artifacts in the skies that did not originate from America, Russia, Germany, or any other country. These objects violated some highly sensitive military airspace, and did not appear to be natural phenomena. One may presume that the affected national security authorities made it an immediate obsession to determine the nature and purpose of these objects, and we may infer that the issue *probably* became a deep secret by 1946, or 1947 at the latest.

Some will dismiss this as one of the many conspiracy theories dotting America's landscape. The very label serves as an automatic dismissal, as though no one ever acts in secret. Let us bring some perspective and common sense to this issue. The United States comprises large organizations—corporations, bureaucracies, "interest groups," and the like—which are conspiratorial by nature. That is, they are hierarchical, their important decisions are made in secret by a few key decision-makers, and they are not above lying about their activities. Such is the nature of organizational behavior. "Conspiracy," in this key sense, is a way of life around the globe.

Within the world's military and intelligence apparatuses, this tendency is magnified to the greatest extreme. During the 1940s, while the military and its scientists developed the world's most awesome weapons in complete secrecy, the UFO problem descended, as it was, into their laps. Would they be interested in unknown objects snooping around their restricted airspace? Would they want to restrict the information they acquired? The available evidence, contained within this book, indicates an affirmative response.

If we assume, then, the existence of a UFO conspiracy, we may ask, where is it? Is there a central control group, for example, managing the problem? Perhaps yes, perhaps no. It is possible, even plausible, that no one holding public office today knows what is going on. It may be that a UFO control group existed at one time within the Department of Defense or the CIA, but there is no absolute reason why such a situation must exist today. Not only is secrecy within those circles axiomatic, but information is so highly compartmentalized that it is easy to imagine how various strands of UFO information could fall into dozens of semi-isolated domains.

Clearly, within the military, secrecy remains the rule regarding UFOs. Despite claims of noninterest, the military continues to respond to reports of unidentified flying (and underwater) objects. But military personnel would be foolish in the extreme to be caught discussing this with the public. The military's "Oath upon Inadvertent Exposure to Classified Security Data or Information" is taken by all personnel exposed to classified information of any kind, and is binding for life, under all circumstances. When you sign this oath, in the words of 133rd Airborne Wing Officer James Goodell:

> . . . you sign away your constitutional rights. You sign a piece of paper saying that if you violate your security agreement . . . without a trial, without the right of appeal, you're going to go to the Leavenworth federal penitentiary for twenty years. That's a real big incentive to keep your mouth shut.[1]

The military has taken the UFO issue deep undercover. For the last thirty years, requests to the air force or other government bodies about UFOs have elicited the same response:

> From 1947 to 1969, the air force investigated Unidentified Flying Objects under Project Blue Book. The project, headquartered at Wright-Patterson Air Force Base, Ohio, was terminated December 17, 1969. Of a total of 12,618 sightings reported to Project Blue Book, 701 remained "unidentified."

The decision to discontinue UFO investigations was based on an evaluation of a report prepared by the University of Colorado titled, "Scientific Study of Unidentified Flying Objects," a review of the University of Colorado's report by the National Academy of Sciences, previous UFO studies, and Air Force experience investigating UFO reports during the 1940s, '50s, and '60s.

As a result of these investigations, studies, and experience gained from investigating UFO reports since 1948, the conclusions of Project Blue Book were: (1) no UFO reported, investigated, and evaluated by the air force was ever an indication of threat to our national security; (2) there was no evidence submitted to or discovered by the air force that sightings categorized as "unidentified" represented technological developments or principles beyond the range of modern scientific knowledge; and (3) there was no evidence indicating that sightings categorized as "unidentified" were extraterrestrial vehicles. . . .

Since the termination of Project Blue Book, nothing has occurred that would support a resumption of UFO investigations by the air force. . . .

Such is the unchanging, official truth about UFOs.[2]

OFFICIAL CULTURE VS. UNOFFICIAL CULTURE

Some things are true, and some things are officially true.

In 1937, Joseph Stalin authorized the first Soviet census in a decade. Based on growth estimates of the 1920s, he expected a total near 170 million. Unfortunately, the numbers came in at 156 million, and Stalin was none too pleased. Rather than inquire as to what happened to the 14 million missing souls, Stalin devised a simpler solution: he had most of the census takers shot, the rest sent to the Gulag. Two years later, a more amenable 1939 census counted 170 million, which became the official number.

Anyone who has lived in a repressive society knows that official manipulation of the truth occurs daily. But all societies have their many and their few. In all times and all places, it is the few who rule, and the few who exert dominant influence over what we may call official culture. While Stalin's solution to his census problem was extreme, all elites take care to manipulate public information to maintain existing structures of power. It's an old game.

Like everywhere else, America has its topics that are too sensitive to discuss openly without distressing some powerful interest. UFOs have always been such a topic, as seen by the combination of official denial, extreme secrecy, public ridicule, and widespread popular belief connected to it. Officially, UFOs do not exist, and are only discussed in public as a kind of joke, or perhaps a piece of cultural kitsch. Yet, some three-quarters of Americans believe in them. Why this disparity? After all, most Americans believe in God, and there is no official ridicule associated with that belief. Could it be that a belief in UFOs is—however odd this may at first seem—slightly subversive?

THE REDMOND, OREGON, INCIDENT

There are many examples in this book that illustrate the disparity between official and unofficial truth about UFOs. Here is one: the Redmond, Oregon, UFO case.

Shortly before dawn on September 24, 1959, Police Officer Robert Dickerson was driving through the streets of Redmond, Oregon, when he saw a large, bright object descend over the city, stop abruptly, and hover at two hundred feet. The object was low enough that nearby treetops glowed. Minutes later, Dickerson drove to the Federal Aviation Administration office at the Redmond airport. Meanwhile, the object rapidly moved to an area northeast of the airport and once again hovered. Its color had changed from bright white to reddish-orange. Through binoculars, Dickerson and others perceived it as flat and round; tongues of "flame" occasionally extended from its edge.

At 5:10 A.M., the FAA reported the object to the Seattle Air Route Control Center, which relayed the message to Hamilton Air Force Base in California. At 5:18 A.M., six F-102 jet fighters were scrambled from Portland to intercept. Witnesses were still watching the hovering object when the jets roared over Redmond. As the aircraft approached, the object squelched its "tongues of flame," emitted a fiery exhaust, shot up into the air at an incredible speed, and disappeared into the clouds at fourteen thousand feet. It was so close to the path of the jets that one of the pilots swerved to avoid hitting it. Another jet, caught in the turbulence of the tremendous exhaust, nearly lost control. One pilot, using gunsight radar, continued the chase, but the object abruptly changed course—an event that was tracked by radar at Klamath Falls Ground Control Intercept—and the pilot gave up. For two hours afterward, the unknown object continued to register on radar, performing high-speed maneuvers at altitudes between six thousand and fifty-four thousand feet.

The pilots immediately received an intelligence debriefing and were ordered not to discuss the matter, even among themselves. But hundreds of Redmond citizens had heard the jets, some had seen the interceptors, and a few had made reports about the unknown object. Forced into an explanation, the air force said the flight was a routine investigation caused by false radar returns. Excitable witnesses probably imagined the glow.

Word soon leaked out, however, that the FAA was checking for abnormal radioactivity where witnesses saw the object hover and "blast off." This made it difficult for people to swallow the air force explanation. Why would the

FAA check for abnormal radiation if the whole event was illusory? As a result, the air force changed its solution: the object everyone had seen was probably a weather balloon. It did not bother to explain how a weather balloon could outdistance jets flying at 600 mph.

When offering this explanation, the air force did not know that the nation's leading civilian UFO group—the National Investigations Committee on Aerial Phenomena—had obtained certified copies of FAA logs. This was an unexpected coup, as the FAA logs described the UFO and its maneuvers in great detail, including its evasion from the interceptors. The logs also included air force confirmations of radar tracking, scrambling of Portland jets, and a report from Klamath Falls.

When this information became public, the air force promptly denounced the FAA for issuing false information and maintained its balloon answer. After more pressure from NICAP and several legislators, however, the air force finally announced the "true" explanation: the witnesses had seen the planet Venus.[3]

THE NATIONAL SECURITY STATE

"We think we're Luke Skywalker," says a friend of mine, "when we're actually Darth Vader." America is a country with a bad conscience, nominally a republic and free society, but in reality an empire and oligarchy, vaguely aware of its own oppression, within and without. I have used the term "national security state" to describe its structures of power. It is a convenient way to express the military and intelligence communities, as well as the worlds that feed upon them, such as defense contractors and other underground, nebulous entities. Its fundamental traits are secrecy, wealth, independence, power, and duplicity.

1. Secrecy

Nearly everything of significance undertaken by America's military and intelligence community in the past half-century has occurred in secrecy. The undertaking to build an atomic weapon, better known as the Manhattan Project, remains the great model for all subsequent activities. For more than two years not a single member of Congress even knew about it, although its final cost exceeded the then-incredible total of $2 billion. During and after the Second World War, other important projects, such as the development of biological weapons, the importation of Nazi scientists, terminal mind-control experiments, nationwide interception of mail and cable transmissions of an unwitting populace, infiltration of the media and universities, secret coups, secret wars, and assassinations all took place far removed not only from the American public, but from most members of Congress and a few presidents. Indeed, several of the most powerful intelligence agencies were themselves established in secrecy, unknown by the public or Congress for many years.

2. Wealth

Since the 1940s, the U.S. Defense and Intelligence establishment has had more money at its disposal than most nations. In addition to official dollars, much of the money is undocumented. From its beginning, the CIA was engaged in a variety of off-the-record "business" activities that generated large sums of cash. The connections of the CIA with global organized crime (and thus de facto with the international narcotics trade) has been well established and documented for many years.[4] In addition, the CIA maintained its own private airline fleet which generated a tidy sum of unvouchered funds primarily out of Asia. Indeed, much of the original money to run the American intelligence community came from very wealthy and established American families, who have long maintained an interest in funding national security operations important to their interests.

3. Independence

In theory, civilian oversight exists over the U.S. national security establishment. The president is the military commander-in-chief. Congress has official oversight over the CIA. The FBI must answer to the Justice Department. In practice, little of this applied during the period under review. One reason has to do with the secrecy: the compartmentalization of information within military and intelligence circles. "Top Secret" clearance does not clear one for all Top Secret information. Sensitive information is available on a need-to know basis. Two CIA officers in adjoining rooms at the Langley headquarters can be involved in completely different activities, each ignorant of the other's doings. Such compartmentalization increases not only secrecy, but independence from the wrong (i.e., official) kinds of oversight.

A chilling example of such independence occurred during the 1950s, when President Dwight Eisenhower effectively lost control of the U.S. nuclear arsenal. The situation deteriorated so much that during his final two years in office, Eisenhower asked repeatedly for an audience with the head of Strategic Air Command to learn what America's nuclear retaliatory plan was. What he finally learned in 1960, his final year in office, horrified him: half of the Northern Hemisphere would be obliterated.

If a revered military hero such as Eisenhower could not control America's nuclear arsenal, nor get a straight answer from the Pentagon, how on earth could Presidents Truman, Kennedy, Johnson, or Nixon regarding comparable matters?

4. Power

Secrecy, wealth, and independence add up to power. Through the years, the national security state has gained access to the world's most sophisticated technology, sealed off millions of acres of land from public access or scrutiny, acquired unlimited snooping ability within U.S. borders and beyond, conducted overt or clandestine actions against other nations, and prosecuted wars without serious media scrutiny. Domestically, it maintains influence over elected officials and communities hoping for some of the billions of defense dollars.

5. Duplicity

Deception is a key element of warfare, and when winning is all that matters, the conventional morality held by ordinary people becomes an impediment. When taken together, the examples of official duplicity form a nearly single totality. They include such choice morsels as the phony war crisis of 1948, the fabricated missile gap claimed by the air force during the 1950s, the carefully managed events leading to the Gulf of Tonkin resolution, or, as illustrated in the following pages, the many deceptions practiced regarding the UFO issue.

The UFO cover-up (precisely the right phrase) is one secret among many within the American national security state. Like other areas within its domain, the UFO problem has been handled secretly, with great deception, and with significant resources. The secrecy stems from a pervasive and fundamental element of life in our world, that those who are at the top of the heap will always take whatever steps are necessary to maintain the status quo.

CAN THEY REALLY COVER THIS UP?

UFO skeptics often ask, "Do you really think the government could hide something like this for so long?" The question itself reflects ignorance of the reality that secrecy is a way of life in the national security state. Actually, though, the answer is yes, and no.

Yes, in that cover-ups are standard operating procedure, frequently unknown to the public for decades, becoming public knowledge by a mere roll of the dice. But also no, in that UFO information has leaked out from the very beginning. It is impossible to shut the lid completely. The key lies in neutralizing and discrediting unwelcomed information, sometimes through official denial, other times through proxies in the media.

The severity of military orders is certainly a major incentive to secrecy. In addition, the history of the U.S. media shows unsettling developments, not least of which is penetration by the intelligence community. By the early 1950s, the CIA had cozy relationships with most major media executives in America. The most significant of these were with the *New York Times*, *Washington Post*, *Christian Science Monitor*, *New York Herald-Tribune*, *Saturday Evening Post*, *Miami Herald*, Time-Life, CBS News, Scripps-Howard Newspapers, Hearst Newspapers, the Associated Press, United Press International, the Mutual Broadcasting System, and Reuters. In addition, the CIA had major ownership over many proprietary publications throughout Europe, Asia, and the Americas. By the early 1970s, the agency admitted to having working relationships with over four hundred American journalists. Consider the possibilities with four hundred strategically placed people throughout the mainstream media. There is evidence that this relationship continues.[5]

The result is effective news management. Without question, the mainstream media have supported government propaganda about UFOs. From 1947 onward, while the air force worked to remove the UFO problem from the public domain, the media helped it to ridicule the subject. The release of every major air force and CIA statement about UFOs has, without exception, been met by uncritical media acquiescence. It is true that the decade of the 1990s brought a different kind of media openness about UFOs than existed in decades, due to the recognition that money can be made. The net result, however, is a very mixed bag. At the same time that such television networks as *A&E* and *Discovery* have provided fairly serious documentaries on the subject, UFOs have essentially become an adjunct of pop culture. Moreover, serious treatment by the major networks has remained nonexistent.[6]

SCIENTIFIC QUESTIONS

In the conclusion of the University of Colorado Report on UFOs, physicist Edward U. Condon asked with evident annoyance, if aliens are really here, why haven't they presented themselves? The whole question, he wrote, "would be settled in a few minutes if a flying saucer were to land on the lawn of a hotel where a convention of the American Physical Society was in progress, and its occupants were to emerge and present a special paper to the assembled physicists . . . ."[7]

If there are aliens here, they do not appear to be interested in announcing themselves to us. Is it yet possible to prove the issue? Are there hypotheses that can be tested? Can "believers" somehow produce the proof that skeptics continually demand?

What would constitute proof? Many people have videotaped UFOs. Some are hoaxes, while others appear to be genuine. Is it possible to prove one is genuine? What about consistent witness testimony? Perhaps persuasive in a court of law, but provable in the court of science? What about radar/visual cases, such as the Redmond, Oregon, case described earlier, in which a UFO was observed visually and tracked on radar? Certainly compelling to someone who was there, but . . . proof?

We must ask not only what constitutes proof, but who would be authorized to deem it so? Certainly, an acknowledgment of aliens would have to come from a major spokesperson of official culture—a message from the president, perhaps. In other words, the matter may be more political than scientific. UFO evidence derived from a grassroots level is unlikely to survive its inevitable conflict with official culture (fifty years of failure have borne this out). An acknowledgment about the reality of the UFO phenomenon will only occur when the official culture deems it worthwhile or necessary to make it. Don't hold your breath.

As a result, the easiest thing to do with UFO evidence is to ignore it, which is what most people do. Much harder is to confront it honestly, whether this means accepting or debunking it. That is, accepting into one's worldview something as "far out" as extraterrestrials is not easy for many people, especially when one's official culture finds little more than ridicule in the subject. The problem with most skeptical arguments against alien visitation is that, quite simply, they fail to look at the UFO evidence. They appear plausible at first, but usually fall apart when presented with a few good reports. (When all else fails, a committed skeptic can always retreat to the final line of defense: claiming the event was hoaxed.)

The most common of the theoretical complaints are:

Granted that there may be intelligent life elsewhere in the universe, interstellar travel is still impossible. The distances between stars are too vast to travel.

J. Allen Hynek, longtime consultant to the air force's Project Blue Book, had an expression for this kind of attitude: "It can't be; therefore, it isn't." It is true that the distances of interstellar space are so vast as to make travel appear to be impossible. No person could survive a ten-thousand-year interstellar journey, considering our current technologies.

The most common rejoinder is that perhaps a breakthrough in propulsion technology is possible, and that perhaps we can somehow surpass or bypass the speed-of-light obstacle, like the *Enterprise* at warp eight. Physicists scoff at the idea, except those who are now working on it. Is it at least possible that someone else might already have gotten further on this problem? The claims of thousands of eyewitnesses point to revolutionary propulsion methods of UFO craft.

Even dismissing breakthroughs in propulsion technology, however, recent developments in just two areas—artificial intelligence and biotechnology—will bring revolutionary developments within the next century. Many in those fields believe it will be possible to create an artificially intelligent organism. Perhaps, having found a twin to Earth somewhere out there, an artificially intelligent organism could make the long journey. Or why even use an organism when one could equip the ship itself with artificial intelligence?

If we can plausibly imagine ourselves finding another planet with features similar to our own, and sending an intelligent probe there, how likely is it that someone else has already done the same to us? There are many unknown variables, to be sure, but the prospect cannot be denied.

Why haven't they announced themselves?

This was Condon's question. After all, the landing of an alien vessel on the White House lawn would settle matters. The question, however, assumes some kind of parity between humans and any others who may arrive. A human scientist studying a band of gorillas would not introduce herself to the dominant male with a view toward establishing diplomatic relations (although she might interact with some or all gorillas in some manner). Perhaps open relations with aliens are not possible, or at least less practical than we typically imagine. Or perhaps the prospect promises too many headaches for them. We just don't know.

Besides, if one takes seriously the thousands of reports and claims of alien abduction, it appears that aliens have made their presence known. They have done so, however, covertly, in a manner that bypasses all official channels of our civilization—an act of extreme subversion.

Aren't people really seeing experimental or classified aircraft?

The question is valid. There are objects being tested and flown today of staggering technology. The fabled *Aurora* craft, an open secret flown out of Area 51 in Nevada, possesses extraordinary speed, maneuverability, and stealth capabilities, and is rumored to incorporate revolutionary principles in propulsion technology. Regarding the early years, CIA historian Gerald Haines argued recently that most UFO sightings in the 1950s and 1960s were actually of classified aircraft such as the U-2 and SR-71 spy planes.[8] There is no doubt that some of those UFO reports were of these aircraft. A closer inspection of the facts, however, reveals his claim to be specious. The U-2, for instance, did not fly until 1955. Its altitude was typically eighty thousand feet, and it flew straight as a string. It did not hover, nor accelerate instantly, nor land vertically, nor do any of the other things thousands of witnesses attributed to UFOs. The same can be said for the rest of America's cutting-edge technology of the cold war. It should be added that, even today, experimental technology does not appear to be the explanation for the majority of good UFO reports, but such a discussion exceeds the scope of this book.

Infrastructure questions.

Where is the infrastructure of this alien civilization that can produce such incredible technology and enormous vessels? Or, if UFO reports are to be taken seriously, there must be thousands, or even millions, of aliens already here—how can that be? Good questions, surely, but which—like many of the others—are guilty of the same mistake: trying to place us inside the enlarged heads of these aliens. Such questions presume that we can somehow think for them and imagine what their civilization can be like. They are too theoretical. It is one thing to discuss the likelihood or impossibility of space travel, quite another to examine and explain a few good UFO reports.

POSSIBLE DIMENSIONS OF THE UFO PROBLEM

So, how serious is the UFO problem? Are aliens really among us? If so, what do they want?

Keeping this discussion completely factual, we can acknowledge that the UFO phenomenon has always been global. It is not, as some Americans continue to believe, a uniquely American phenomenon, or restricted to the southwestern states. By no means. Sober, reliable people of all sociological strata have reported unconventional objects throughout North and South America, Europe, Africa, Asia, Australia, Antarctica, all the world's major bodies of water, and even outer space.

UFOs are also actual objects, not simply atmospheric phenomena. This is not to say that some atmospheric phenomena have not been mistakenly believed to be flying saucers, but that the core of difficult UFO cases is of actual objects of apparently unconventional design (e.g., disc-shaped), and capable of incredible speeds and maneuverability. When an object is seen visually, is tracked clearly on radar, and when pilot after pilot is adamant that what he saw was a real object, it is reasonable to conclude that we are dealing with something real.

It is also true that from the 1950s and beyond, people around the world have been claiming to see alien entities. Now, it is certainly possible that they were mistaken. It is interesting to note, however, that such people have frequently been interviewed by civil and military authorities, and typically have been considered honest. In late 1954, for example, hundreds of witnesses in France and the rest of the Mediterranean region, as well as South America, claimed to see short alien beings. The witnesses were men, women, youths, elderly, doctors, professors, mechanics, homemakers, and peasant farmers. Several cases left significant landing traces. Were these people hoaxing? Not according to the authorities who investigated them. Were they delusional? If so, what caused such widespread and similar delusions? Was it a case of mass hysteria? If so, it was an event that cut across national and language barriers among people who knew little about UFOs to begin with.

There is also no doubt that the actual number of UFO sightings vastly exceeds any official total. Hynek believed the difference to be a factor of ten. That, of course, was when people had somewhere to report their sightings. I can add that, in the final twelve months of writing this book, I encountered about thirty people who volunteered UFO sightings to me, without any solicitation on my part. In every case, the witnesses never reported what they saw to any authority, and in most cases told either no one, or perhaps a close friend. How many people have seen a UFO, but not reported it? I believe the answer is, *lots*.

This is a widespread phenomenon affecting many people, generating high levels of interest, taking place in near-complete secrecy, for purposes unknown, by agencies unknown, with access to incredible resources and technology. A sobering thought, and cause for reflection.

SOURCES AND DOCUMENTATION

Bodies need bones; history needs facts. In the course of this study, some seemingly outlandish claims are made; how do I back them up?

In preparing this book, I have drawn from three basic groups of sources.

1. Previously classified documents released through the Freedom of Information Act.

The Freedom of Information Act was a completely unforeseen development to those involved in UFO secrecy during the 1940s, 1950s, and 1960s. The Act was passed in 1966, but gained some teeth only in the aftermath of Watergate and Vietnam. By the mid-1970s, many citizens filed FOIA requests regarding government involvement with UFOs, and obtained information that confirmed extreme interest in UFOs.

2. Primary sources (e.g., books) from people involved in UFO research at the time.

Many of the primary sources from the mid-1940s to the mid-1960s are hard to come by. Still, with some effort, it is possible to track down the key sources. There were three organizations of the period that collected significant UFO data. They are: (1) Project Blue Book (formerly Projects Sign and Grudge), which was conducted by the United States Air Force; (2) the Aerial Phenomena Research Organization (APRO), a global organization founded by Jim and Coral Lorenzen; and (3) the National Investigative Committee for Aerial Phenomena (NICAP), led by retired Marine Corps Major Donald Keyhoe. The records of these organizations are not especially accessible. Blue Book's records are available for a fee at the National Archives in Washington, D.C. APRO's records were never published in a systematic form and have been unavailable for years. NICAP's files ended up at the Center for UFO Studies in Chicago, but have never been published.

There are books that have made use of the above sources. Many Blue Book cases were distilled by Air Force Captain Edward Ruppelt and astronomer Allen Hynek. Ruppelt headed Blue Book in the early 1950s; his *Report on Unidentified Flying Objects* (1956) derived heavily from Blue Book files and was amplified by his account of military and government attitudes toward the UFO problem. Hynek wrote two books based on his twenty years of affiliation with Blue Book. In addition, the complete list of Blue Book unknowns is available at several Internet sites.[9] Two Internet sites with complete listings of Blue Book unknowns are available.[10]

Much of APRO's work was published in the many books of its founders, Jim and Coral Lorenzen. All are valuable and most are difficult to find. Many NICAP reports are available through the extremely rare *UFO Evidence*, which NICAP published in 1964. Besides this, the writings of NICAP director Donald Keyhoe contain a wealth of information. It surely helped that Keyhoe was friend and associate to prominent figures in the American military and intelligence community.

It is true that Keyhoe and the Lorenzens made their share of mistakes, and Hynek's writings are often self-serving and coy (until his "conversion" to the UFO cause during the mid-1960s, Hynek was held in low regard by many UFO researchers for his servility to the air force). Still, these writers offered some of the best information we will ever have on this period. Read with care, they and other early writers about UFOs remain indispensable sources of information.

3. Contemporary scholarship.

There is quite a lot of good scholarship on this subject, in book form and on the Internet. While most of it is not historical writing, per se, it remains valuable. For years, the best genuine history of the subject was *The UFO Controversy in America* (1975), by Temple University historian David Jacobs. Its two major drawbacks are its time of publication, which preceded the great release of UFO data through FOIA, and its paucity of information about the U.S. intelligence community. Jerome Clark's three-volume *UFO Encyclopedia* is another important resource for the serious reader. Although I disagree with some interpretations offered by Clark, his work is valuable. Other useful books are indicated in the bibliography.

The waters of UFO research are deep, and I have tried not to lose my footing. Throughout, I have been careful never to veer far from established facts. I am reminded of the saying, "we are never as radical as reality itself." Thus, while some of my conclusions are more conservative than what others may think justified, they are just as often more radical.

FINAL REMARKS AND CONCERNS

I am confident that I have followed through on my intention to adhere to the facts. Where I have speculated, I have tried to make this clear. Throughout, I have tried to serve as a useful guide through the maze of UFO reports and policy. If nothing else, this topic deserves a respectable history.

Even if UFOs were to turn out to be a unique form of mass hallucination (which they will not), this study will still have value for its review of how the U.S. national security apparatus handled the problem. If there are other answers, then this book should clarify some of the key patterns involved.

Unfortunately, those patterns leave little cause for optimism regarding either the problem or its response. Americans are in a bad enough state trying to struggle through the ordinary smoke of their official culture. How can they be expected to assess the implications of the UFO problem? They can begin only by recognizing that secrecy over UFOs exists, and that this secrecy is part of a broader policy of control and deception. It is a bad omen that our civilization, beleaguered as it is by its own doing, has not faced this problem squarely.

Chapter 1

Prologue: To 1947

He who desires to reform the government of a state, and wishes to have it accepted and capable of maintaining itself to the satisfaction of everybody, must at least retain the semblance of the old forms; so that it may seem to the people that there has been no change in the institutions, even though in fact they are entirely different from the old ones. For the great majority of mankind are satisfied with appearances, as though they were realities, and are often even more influenced by the things that seem than by those that are.

—Niccolo Machiavelli, *Discourses on Livy*, Chapter XXV

UFOs Before World War Two

It is quite possible that UFOs have existed for millennia. A steady stream of reports—stories might be a better word—appears through the centuries, some of them suggestive of modern reports. Of course, most of these stories were not about spaceships, although some of them were. Rather, people interpreted what they saw in the terms and concepts they knew best: they saw fiery wheels or chariots in the sky, conversed with fairy folk, or had visions of God, angels, and demons.[1] While the accounts are certainly worth collecting, there is not much we can do with them other than reflect on the possibilities they suggest. Ultimately, they remain just stories.

Toward the end of the nineteenth century, the number of these stories spiked upward. Whether this means that more weird events were really taking place, or simply that more people were noticing them, is anybody's guess. Even today, some of these reports make for interesting reading. The *London*

1

Times of September 26, 1870, for example, described a strange elliptical object that crossed the face of the moon. In November 1882, astronomer E. W. Maunder, a member of the Royal Observatory staff at Greenwich, noted "a strange celestial visitor" in his observational report. Others also saw this object, which they described as torpedo- or spindle-shaped. Years later Maunder said the object looked exactly like a zeppelin, except that there were no zeppelins in 1882.[2] Sightings were widespread for the rest of the decade, occurring in Mexico, Turkey, Nova Scotia (a five-minute sighting in which shipmates saw a huge red object rise from the ocean, pause, and fly off rapidly), New Zealand, the Dutch East Indies, and elsewhere.

In 1897, the United States experienced the first modern wave of sightings. These were the "airships" which first appeared in San Francisco in late 1896 and moved eastward.[3] Thousands of people, including astronomers, saw them, which typically had lights (usually red, green, or white), moved slowly, and seemed to be under intelligent control. Sometimes voices could be heard, whether in English or something unintelligible. On a few occasions, people claimed to see their occupants, and even to speak with them. Such outlandish sightings got some press. The *New York Herald-Tribune* described a sighting in Chicago on April 9, 1897, that lasted from 8 P.M. until 2 A.M.:

> Thousands of amazed persons declared that the lights seen in the northwest were those of an airship, or some floating object, miles above the earth. . . . Some declared that they could distinguish two cigar-shaped objects and great wings.

Two giant searchlights apparently illuminated the object. Other, far stranger, incidents occurred. Explanations included many of the standard culprits of later ages: mass hallucination and hysteria, experimental aircraft (private, not military), opium-induced dreams, hoaxes, or all of the above.

The 1897 airship sightings were the most remarkable of the pre-1940s era. But other noteworthy UFO events also took place, including one in western China in 1926 by the party of explorer Nicholas Roerich. In his book, *Altai—Himalaya*, Roerich described the sighting as an "interesting occurrence." As he related, his party noticed a high-flying shiny object. The group brought "three powerful field glasses" and watched a "huge spheroid body shining in the sun, clearly visible against the blue sky, and moving very fast." Roerich and his party were certain they saw something real. What was it? What would be flying like that in the western China desert—in 1926? No answer ever emerged.[4]

These early reports are intriguing, but offer few avenues for further research. UFOs appeared sporadically, elicited minimal response from the public and authorities, and were promptly forgotten. One wonders, in any event, what kind of response would have been possible?

The Second World War changed all this. Before the war, airplanes were scarce and radar nonexistent—by the war's end, both were global. In other words, it became much, much easier to detect strange aerial phenomena after 1940. Since military personnel were the main users of radar and airplanes, they might naturally be expected to encounter more UFOs than the average person—and they most certainly did. Let us take a moment to review some key developments of the American military and national security establishment.

THE NATIONAL SECURITY CONNECTION

When UFO skeptics claim that hiding something as significant as alien visitation is impossible, they should study some of the secrets that *were* kept for many, many years. A veritable secrecy industry exists in the modern world, complete with its own standard operating procedures and tricks of the trade.

The granddaddy of all secret projects was the Manhattan Project, the program to design and build an atomic bomb during the Second World War. More than any other program, it helped to forge the American military-industrial establishment, and served as a model for future secret projects. One of its key contributions was its secret—or black—budget. When President Roosevelt learned that such a weapon might be feasible, the best guess was that it would cost $100 million. The actual cost ballooned to a mammoth $2.19 billion, over twenty times the original estimate. Getting that much money through traditional means (i.e., congressional approval) raised the dual problem of asking Congress to authorize outlays that were unprecedented while at the same time alerting the enemy to the Allies' most important military weapon. The money, therefore, had to be hidden from Congress. Roosevelt told his science advisor, Vannevar Bush, he could draw upon hidden funding, "a special source available for such an unusual expense." Most of the money for the project was disguised in two line items in the military budget, and the rest was buried in other appropriations. The secrecy of the Manhattan Project was so remarkable that when the scientists at Los Alamos laboratory exploded an atomic device on U.S. soil in July 1945, the most decisive scientific achievement in human history, no one in the country knew a thing.[5]

The Manhattan Project showed that the U.S. defense establishment could keep a secret. There were several others, such as its research into biological weapons, the interception of domestic cable transmissions, the wiretapping and bugging of First Lady Eleanor Roosevelt, and much more. But the military had no monopoly when it came to spying against American citizens. Indeed, no organization had the kind of open-ended mandate bequeathed to the Federal Bureau of Investigation. In 1940, Roosevelt authorized the FBI, directed by the obsessively paranoid J. Edgar Hoover, to engage in electronic eavesdropping against political spies, saboteurs, or merely suspicious individuals. This order became the basic document that permitted later presidents to wiretap. Thirty-five years later, Attorney General Levi testified that the FBI installed 2,465 microphones (bugs) against American citizens from 1940 to 1975, nearly all of which required break-ins. This total derives only from the FBI files that remained intact after Hoover's death in 1972—much had been destroyed. Hoover also systematically collected blackmail information against members of Congress, a substantial and secret effort that lasted for decades.[6]

Compared with the wartime activities of the military or FBI, the birth of the Office of Strategic Services (OSS) might seem a humble affair. It was not. Forerunner to the CIA, the OSS owed its existence to the great failure of American intelligence: the bombing of Pearl Harbor. Roosevelt established it on June 13, 1942, and placed Gen. William "Wild Bill" Donovan at its head. The mission of the OSS was to gather intelligence, but it soon became famous for its success in special operations, just as the CIA did in the post-war period. The OSS earned its romantic reputation from a long list of wartime successes, including its work with resistance movements in France, Italy, Greece, Yugoslavia, and elsewhere.[7]

The OSS successes prompted Donovan in late 1944 to plan the creation of an American central intelligence authority headed by himself. Hoover, however, saw the plan as a threat to his own ambitions (at the time, he was running intelligence operations throughout the Western Hemisphere). Hoover obtained copies of Donovan's memo and leaked them to a *Chicago Tribune* reporter in January 1945. End of plan. Donovan also faced opposition from the Joint Chiefs of Staff, which pigeonholed his plan. The OSS was an upstart, and with so many competitors in the American intelligence community, the birth of the CIA was no foregone conclusion.

Secretive, competitive, lawbreaking, and at times paranoid—into precisely this world was the UFO problem thrust. The very organizations of the new national security apparatus became those groups responsible for dealing with UFOs. Often the same people were involved, a pattern that recurs throughout the scope of this study.

Closely related to the world of intelligence was the world of science. The Second World War changed forever the relationship of professional scientists to the state. Shortly after its conclusion, half of all scientists and technical personnel in America were working for the Defense Department. The result was not only the most incredible leap in weapons development in human history, but a leap in power for scientists themselves. Men who had had to scrape for money in the 1930s now found themselves in positions of prestige, often above that of military leaders.[8]

"Power scientists" were actively involved not only in the Manhattan Project and other secret projects such as Paperclip (which imported German scientists after the war), but in the UFO problem. Scientific names that cropped up in connection with one project were often tied to another. Names like Bush, Berkner, Bronk, Teller, Sarnoff, Page, Robertson, and Goudsmit would soon intersect with the UFO problem at some key juncture, and all were involved in other projects involving extreme levels of secrecy, always in close collaboration with military groups.

It is a matter of significance that such men of science, power, and secrecy would become interested in the problem of unidentified flying objects.

FOO FIGHTERS

Even today, little is known about foo fighters, the bizarre aerial phenomena encountered by pilots of all countries during the war. Still, researchers over the years have collected enough information to describe some strange goings-on. Perhaps the earliest foo fighter report, a tame affair, dates from September 1941. In the early morning hours of a clear night out in the Indian Ocean, a sailor aboard the SS *Pulaski*, a Polish vessel converted for the British military, saw "a strange globe glowing with greenish light about half the size of the full moon as it appears to us." He alerted a gunner, and the two watched the object as it followed them for the next hour.[9]

A not-so-tame incident occurred in Los Angeles on February 25, 1942. That night, a number of unidentified craft flew over the city and seemingly caused a blackout. At least a million residents awoke to air raid sirens at 2:25 A.M., and U.S. Army personnel fired 1,430 rounds of antiaircraft shells to bring down what they assumed were Japanese planes. But these were *not* Japanese planes. George Marshall wrote a memorandum to President Roosevelt about the incident, which remained classified until 1974. Marshall concluded that conventional aircraft were involved, probably "commercial sources, operated by enemy agents for purposes of spreading alarm, disclosing locations of antiaircraft positions, and slowing production through blackout." Despite the barrage of American antiaircraft fire, none of these "commercial" planes were brought down, although several homes and buildings were destroyed, and six civilian deaths were attributed to the barrage. Considering the carnage, the military's explanation was meager. U.S. Navy Secretary Knox even denied that any aircraft had been over the city; he called the incident a false alarm due to war nerves. The local press, needless to say, did not take this very well. The *Long Beach Independent* noted that: "There is a mysterious reticence about the whole affair and it appears some form of censorship is trying to halt discussion of the matter." It is noteworthy that for thirty years, until the release of the Marshall memorandum, the Department of Defense claimed to have no record of the event.[10] Five years before Roswell, the military was already learning to clamp down on UFOs.

The very next day after "The Battle of Los Angeles," the crew of the Dutch Cruiser *Tromp* in the Timor Sea saw "a large, illuminated disc approaching at terrific speed." The object circled above the ship for three or four hours, then flew off at an estimated speed of 3,000 to 3,500 mph. Obviously, the officer on duty could not identify the object as any known aircraft.[11]

Many similar, baffling sightings occurred throughout the war. An RAF bomber over Zuider Zee in Holland in March 1942 saw a luminous orange disc or sphere following the plane, about one hundred or two hundred yards away. The tail gunner fired some rounds—no effect—and the object departed at 1,000 mph. On August 12, 1942, a U.S. Marine sergeant in the Pacific saw a formation of about 150 objects, no wings or tails, wobbling slightly, not Japanese planes. He called it "the most awe-inspiring and yet frightening spectacle I have ever seen in my life."[12] On August 29, 1942, an Army Air Corps control tower operator named Michael Solomon in Columbus, Mississippi, saw two round reddish objects descend near the AAC flying school, hover, accelerate, and speed away.[13]

Such sightings continued through 1943 and 1944. In November 1944, a B-17 pilot in Austria reported being paced by an amber-colored, disc-shaped object. In January 1945, a pilot with the 415th Night Fighter Squadron was followed by three red and white lighted objects which followed his evasive maneuvers. In France that month, an American pilot reported being paced by an object at around 360 mph before it "zoomed up into the sky." In March 1945, while in the Aleutian Islands, fourteen sailors aboard the U.S. attack transport *Delarof* saw a dark sphere rise out of the ocean, follow a curved trajectory, and fly away after circling their ship.[14]

The last significant foo fighter sighting occurred in the Pacific, and nearly brought down an American plane. On August 28, 1945, less than three weeks after the atomic bombings and Japanese surrender, twelve 5th Air Force intelligence specialists aboard a C-46 flew toward Tokyo in advance of the occupation forces. As the plane approached Iwo Jima at ten thousand feet, the crew saw three teardrop-shaped objects, brilliantly white—"like burning magnesium"—and closing on a parallel course to the plane. The navigational needles went wild, the left engine faltered and spurted oil, the plane lost altitude, and the crew prepared to ditch. Then, in a close formation, the objects faded into a cloud bank. At that moment, the plane's engines restarted, and the crew safely flew on. One of the plane's passengers was future UFO researcher Leonard Stringfield.[15]

One would expect that events such as these warranted an investigation, and that is what they received. There were at least two official American investigations of foo fighters. The U.S. 8th Air Force, under the command of General James Doolittle, conducted a study, although no copy of it has come to light. The report is said to have concluded that the sightings were possibly Axis experimental weapons, static electricity charges, misidentification of ordinary sights, or some kind of "mass hallucination." The young OSS also investigated the phenomenon. At first its investigators believed the sightings to be German experimental craft, but soon discounted that theory. Donovan and his staff apparently settled on the notion that the objects, if that is what they could be called, were unusual but harmless. The *New York Times* published a story on foo fighters on January 2, 1945, under the title, "Balls of Fire Stalk U.S. Fighters in Night Assaults over Germany." The article suggested German "sky weapons" as the culprit. None of the American investigators knew that the Germans and Japanese had encountered the same unusual phenomena, and had explained them as secret Allied weapons.[16]

It is not known whether American interest in foo fighters continued after the war. Quite possibly, foo fighters got lost in the shuffle. After all, no casualties resulted, and none of the objects showed clearly hostile activity. Much can get lost in something as big as the Second World War. But it remains puzzling that over fifty years later, no one really knows what the military or OSS thought about the strange foo fighters.

For a while after the war, stories of foo fighters remained submerged, the subject of discussion among veterans who had encountered them but not talked about openly. During the 1950s, the well-connected UFO investigator Maj. Donald E. Keyhoe collected foo fighter reports and said that "hundreds" of foo fighters were encountered by American, British, German, and Japanese pilots. One of his sources claimed to have a dozen or so reports that Pacific gunners fired at strange objects circling their ships.[17] Considering what little about foo fighters has slipped out, such reports could well be true. Unfortunately, we will probably never know. Reports like Keyhoe's and Stringfield's lack official sanction, and for that reason elicit mere shrugs and smiles from the military and press—that is, when they are not simply ignored, which is the rule.

GHOST ROCKETS

The puzzling foo fighter sightings of the war had scarcely ended when a new wave of aerial sightings took place. In the spring of 1946, the Scandinavian countries began witnessing an impressive spectacle of luminous objects zipping through their skies, night after night, and at times during the day. Sweden remained the center of action throughout, with additional heavy activity in Finland, Norway, and Denmark. By late summer, the phenomenon had spread throughout Europe and beyond, to places such as Portugal, France, Tangier, Italy, Greece, and even India. Witnesses eventually numbered in the tens of thousands. This was a serious development, and indications are that the American military watched it closely.

Many sightings were of elongated, cigar-shaped objects. On May 24, 1946, at 2 A.M., for example, several Swedish witnesses saw a wingless cigar-shaped object, a scant three hundred feet above the ground, spurting "bunches of sparks" from its tail. The object moved at the speed of an ordinary airplane. On the thirty-first, just before noon, a wingless, huge metallic cigar was seen moving rapidly at about one thousand feet altitude.[18] From these kinds of descriptions, the objects acquired the name of "ghost rockets." It soon became clear, however, that these could not be conventional rockets. In the first place, they left no exhaust trail. Second, they were almost always silent. Third, many of them moved too slowly to be rockets. Fourth, they were often seen in formation, breaking formation, maneuvering, or hovering. Finally, the longest trajectory recorded by observers was one thousand kilometers: this was three times the range of the German V rockets. Strange rockets, for sure.

Still, the Swedes, Americans, British, and other interested parties (which included just about everybody) looked into the possibility that these were Soviet missiles of some sort, constructed with the help of *their* cache of German scientists from Peenemünde, home of the V rockets. Even then, most investigators realized this was unlikely, but few could rule it out completely.

Americans were most likely to blame the Soviets. On July 11, 1946, a member of the American Embassy in Stockholm actually saw a ghost rocket and sent a telegram to Washington:

One landed on beach near Stockholm . . . without causing any damage and, according to press, fragments are now being studied by military authorities. . . . If missiles are of Soviet origin as generally believed (some reports say they are launched from Estonia), purpose might be political to intimidate Swedes . . . .[19]

This is an important development: here is a clear statement that fragments were collected and studied. Who had them, and what were they? If the fragments were not Soviet, perhaps they were from a meteor, as some have later asserted.[20] Still, conclusive evidence remains lacking.

Many people assumed the ghost rockets were meteors. On July 19, the French newspaper *Resistance* wrote about them as "bright meteors traveling at fantastic speeds across [Swedish] skies." However, on July 25, a Swedish defense staff spokesman told newspapers, "[That] they are meteors in every case is a theory which has been rejected without further ado." Two days later, a French newspaper described the objects as rocket-propelled projectiles and said that over five hundred of them had been seen over Sweden since the beginning of July. The sheer number of occurrences suggested a serious national security concern.[21]

Needless to say, the ghost rockets were *the* topic of conversation in Sweden. On August 8, the chief of Swedish Air Defense, Gen. Nils Ahlgren, stated that some of the objects were seen at low altitudes, many maneuvered in half-circles, and most appeared to come from the south. On August 11, the Swedish military issued a press release acknowledging that the objects had become a common occurrence. A *New York Times* article described Stockholm as "near the boiling point."[22] On the thirteenth, it reported that "the Swedish General staff . . . described the situation as 'extremely dangerous,' and it is obvious that Sweden no longer is going to tolerate such violations." The General staff noted, for example, that they received more than a thousand reports of "rocket bombs" from the night before and that very morning. One astronomer evidently saw one such "bomb." It was at least ninety feet long, he said, exploded without a sound only a mile and a half away, and gave "a terrific light" that "for a moment blinded me. No fire, no smoke or sparks were noticeable."[23]

On August 13, American General James Doolittle and David Sarnoff arrived in Stockholm. Doolittle, it will be recalled, had recently headed the American 8th Air Force's investigation of foo fighters, a fact unknown to the public. Doolittle said he was in Sweden merely as a private citizen on behalf of his new employer, Shell Oil Company. Sarnoff, of RCA, was one of the world's leading electronics experts, a pioneer in radio and television, and had been a brigadier general during the war. Upon consulting with the highest Swedish authorities on the ghost rockets, they learned that some objects had been tracked on radar. Unfortunately, little else is known about the Doolittle-Sarnoff trip or what conclusions they reached. What is clear, though, is that soon after their arrival, the Swedish government clamped down on ghost rocket information. That, in turn, coincided with an upsurge in interest by prominent Americans. The *New York Times,* for example, mentioned that American Undersecretary of State Dean Acheson was personally interested in the matter, although he maintained that the U.S. government was never consulted officially on the subject. Were Doolittle and Sarnoff "loose cannons," acting on their own? This seems doubtful. Most likely, Doolittle and Sarnoff were acting on behalf of the U.S. government under the cover of private citizens.[24]

On the fifteenth, Swedish authorities disclosed that they came upon a fragment of metal less than three inches long and with letters on it. If this ever helped to solve the mystery, the answer is not publicly known. A week later, on August 22, Sweden's defense staff announced it had obtained radar results, and that they would soon identify the source and nature of the rockets. In the meantime, they issued a ban of information "limited to any mention of where the rockets have been seen to land or explode." In Norway, where the activity was only slightly less intense, the Norwegian General staff asked the press not to mention any appearance of the "rockets" over Norwegian territory, but instead to report them to the Intelligence Command of the High Command. The Danish military soon followed suit.[25]

Let us pause for a moment to reflect on the significance of rockets that were "seen to land." Invading one's airspace was serious enough, but *landings*—if these were indeed controlled landings—were a problem of an entirely different magnitude. In the first place, it would rule out natural phenomena. Second, it would point to piloted craft, assuming we are talking about human technology—in 1946, an object that landed had to be piloted. But what human agency could have piloted these objects? No viable candidates ever emerged. What did the military authorities think about this? We do not know.

While the Swedes, Norwegians, and Danes investigated and clamped down, Britain and America provided assistance. On August 23, British radar experts, back from Sweden, submitted secret reports to the British government on the origin of the rockets. Their conclusion: the objects were not of Soviet origin. The scientific advisor to MI6, Prof. R. V. Jones, found it doubtful that "the Russians were supposedly cruising their flying bombs at more than twice the range that the Germans had achieved." On September 9, the British Air Ministry's Directorate of Intelligence (Research) summarized the main features of the ghost rocket phenomenon and included eight types of sightings. Some Americans remained steadfast in their belief that the ghost rockets were a Russian ploy to intimidate the Swedes. On August 29, the American Embassy in Stockholm sent a Top Secret message to the State Department in Washington:

> While over eight hundred reports have been received and new reports come daily, Swedes still have no tangible evidence. Full details of reports thus far received have been forwarded to Washington by our military and naval attaches. My own source is personally convinced some foreign power is actually experimenting over Sweden and he guesses it is Russia.[26]

Within Sweden, explanations were conventional. Some scientists blamed mass hallucinations, others meteorological balloons, others were openly puzzled. Although, inevitably, the rockets became the butt of jokes, no one mentioned extraterrestrials. UFO researcher Jacques Vallee pointed out that "there does not seem to have been one single voice suggesting that the objects seen in 1946 might have been of interplanetary origin."[27]

Sightings slowed down in September, but also spread to new places. Reliable witnesses continued to see cigar-shaped objects with flames projecting from the tail, traveling at the speed of a normal or slow airplane, and giving off little noise except for an occasional slight whistling. In France on September 6, two luminous globes were seen flying in a straight line. The witnesses said the objects were not a shooting star or plane. That same day, a photograph of one of the Swedish ghost rockets was published in the *Daily Telegraph*.[28]

The objects appeared over Greece. Projectiles were seen over Macedonia and Salonika, and one appeared to fall into the sea, according to Greek Prime Minister Tsaldaris. Living in Greece was Dr. Paul Santorini, a physicist of world renown: he had helped to develop radar, fuses for the atomic bomb, and the

Nike missile guidance system. According to a statement Santorini made in 1967, the Greek government was seriously alarmed by the presence of the ghost rockets over its territory, initially believing them to be Russian missiles. He claimed that the Greek army supplied him with a team of engineers to investigate the problem. The team's conclusion: the ghost rockets were neither Russian nor missiles. Before long, U.S. military officials pressured the Greek army commanders into silence. In Santorini's words, "before we could do any more, the Army, after conferring with foreign officials, ordered the investigation stopped." Santorini himself was closely questioned by U.S. scientists from Washington. He later reaffirmed this statement to UFO researcher Raymond Fowler.[29]

Back in Sweden, on October 10, the Swedish defense staff officially announced its failure to explain the ghost rockets. After four months of inquiring into approximately one thousand ghost rocket reports—a number much smaller than the actual total of sightings—they said that 80 percent were some form of "celestial phenomena" such as meteors. The rest had clear, unambiguous evidence that could not be explained as natural phenomena, nor as Swedish aircraft, nor imagination on the part of the observer. At least two hundred of the "rockets" were tracked on radar, and these were definitely not the V-type missiles used by the Germans during the war. Beyond that, the Swedes gave no clues as to what they believed the objects to be.[30]

The Soviets repeatedly denied they had been behind the ghost rocket sightings. Of course, the denial would be expected whatever the truth of the matter, but no evidence linking the ghost rockets to the Soviets has ever emerged.

So ended the ghost rocket mystery, except for one addendum. On December 1, 1946, a Swedish report that remained classified until 1983 noted that

approximately one hundred impacts have been reported, together with fragments from thirty of these. All have been investigated by the Defense Research Institution. It has been impossible to make certain that any of the objects originated as parts of projectiles or rockets; they have generally been attributed to other sources.

The committee admitted it failed to learn the nature of the rockets.[31] Thus, the mystery did not so much conclude as stall out.

DEUTSCHLAND ÜBER ALLIES

There is nothing to show that the ghost rockets sprung from Soviet or German technology. Still, over the years, a few people have continued to speculate that UFOs resulted from Nazi war technology.[32] The theory is based on frail evidence, loose interpretation of known facts, and a great deal of specu-lation. The Germans had been working on some advanced aviation technology. Their V-1 and V-2 rockets are well known. Indeed, one of those crashed in Sweden in 1944, which let the secret out in the first place. They experimented with a disc-shaped airframe, although it led to no break-throughs, and even developed the first rocket-powered fighter plane, the Me-163, which was effective but limited in supply. Less can be said for the famed Horten flying wing design, which never made it to production (more on this later). This German technology cannot account for the vast numbers of UFO reports, nor for the reported characteristics of the observed objects.

Still, there are connections between Nazi scientists and UFOs. Not only were Nazi scientists involved in the cutting edge of American aviation and propulsion technology in the years after 1945, but many of them worked at installations that became indelibly associated with UFOs, such as Wright-Patterson Air Force Base and White Sands Proving Ground. The project that brought these scientists, engineers, and spies into the United States became known as Paperclip. It was an exceptionally well-orchestrated web of propa-ganda and lies that hid their Nazi past. Military intelligence even succeeded in bringing the press on board for assistance.

Within the world of intelligence, the cold war started before World War Two ended. OSS officers such as Allen Dulles realized the importance of obtaining Nazi spies with Soviet expertise. With OSS/CIA money, they recruited the bulk of Hitler's *Abwehr* intact. For years, in fact, this organiza-tion actually reigned as the dominant intelligence service in West Germany, *before* it was even legally constituted. Thus, an illegal, foreign-funded group held more power than the official West German intelligence organization.[33]

Scientists, however, were the real prize. The competition was intense—Americans, Soviets, British, French, and even Argentines scrambled for scientists. Several were kidnapped, despite everyone's denials. These German scientists, the most prominent of them being rocketry genius Wernher von Braun, were years ahead of Allied scientists in a number of areas, including aircraft design and chemical/biological weapons. There remained the small matter that many of them were ardent Nazis, some wanted for war crimes. But the U.S. military intelligence falsified their records before putting them to work. We can assume other countries did likewise.[34]

Army intelligence (G-2) countered dissent against the project through wiretaps and domestic spying, and it soon became necessary for the army to lie to the State Department on a regular basis. The press promoted a sanitized version of the project to the American public. In late November 1946, the War Department issued a five-page press release favorably describing how German scientists were helping Americans at Wright Field. In December, *Life* and *Newsweek* gave the story national coverage. The Nazi past of many of the scientists escaped notice, as did the strong undercurrent of hostility many

Americans at Wright Field had toward these "former" Nazis. All in all, it was perfectly orchestrated War Department propaganda posing as news. Paperclip continued as part of American policy through the 1950s and even into the 1960s, albeit in a more limited fashion. Congress and the public knew nothing about it for decades.[35]

COMING TO AMERICA

After the Second World War, much effort went into reorganizing the American national security establishment. In September 1945, Ferdinand Eberstadt, upon Navy Secretary James Forrestal's request to study various military merger proposals, recommended a "complete realignment of our governmental organizations to serve our national security." Truman believed he was doing his part when in the same month he disbanded the OSS, scattering OSS personnel throughout the Departments of State and War. No doubt Hoover was gleeful.[36]

However, Truman soon developed second thoughts about his OSS decision. In January 1946, he created a National Intelligence Authority (comprised of the Secretary of State, Secretary of War, Secretary of the Navy, and Chief of Staff) and, under it, a Central Intelligence Group (CIG)—the direct forerunner of the CIA. To head the CIG, Truman swore in old friend Rear Adm. Sidney Souers as the nation's first director of central intelligence (DCI). The CIG's mission was to "coordinate" information, and its operation was as modest as it was secret: it had no spies, no legal power, and was not financed by lawful appropriations, but rather with funds secretly diverted from the armed forces budgets.[37]

CIA historian Thomas Powers called the CIG "something of a joke." Certainly, compared with its later growth it was. But from humble beginnings, the CIG grew rapidly. On June 10, 1946, Hoyt Vandenberg, the army's former director of intelligence, replaced Souers as head of CIG. By the year's end, he enlarged CIG's staff and won the right to collect intelligence in Latin America (although the ever-jealous Hoover denied him use of the FBI's agents or files). By the end of 1946, the CIG also obtained the authority to engage in psychological warfare and conduct covert operations. We know that some policy makers regarded the ghost rockets as Soviet psychological warfare. It is plausible that covert action policy was, at least in part, a response to the ghost rockets.[38]

The resurrection of the OSS was not the only facet of wartime continuity. In September 1945, the army's Signal Security Agency used a combination of arm-twisting and calls to patriotism to persuade ITT, RCA, and Western Union to continue its wartime cable intercept program, code-named Shamrock. This was a massive operation (albeit unknown to Congress) to intercept foreign *and domestic* cable transmissions. It targeted companies, governments, and private citizens, with or without grounds for suspected espionage. The army implemented it by physically scanning the text of cables made available by the three companies, and by directly monitoring international telephone and cable traffic. After the war, the participating companies conveyed their fears to Forrestal. After all, this was wholly illegal. Forrestal assured them that the Administration would soon introduce legislation to legalize the program. True to his word, he floated the idea to several members of Congress, but got nowhere. Such technicalities, however, did not end Operation Shamrock, which continued in extreme secrecy for the next thirty years. Truman appears not to have known about it, and certainly no other president until Nixon knew. The implications are well worth pondering.[39]

By the end of 1946, much of America's "invisible government" was in place, just in time to respond to a steady increase in domestic UFO sightings. There had been at least one interesting American UFO sighting during the ghost rocket period. On August 1, 1946, Capt. Jack E. Puckett was flying a C-47 transport plane thirty miles from Tampa, Florida. Suddenly, he and his copilot saw a large object speeding toward them on a collision course. The object had a long cylindrical shape, which Puckett described as "twice the size of a B-29 bomber." He claimed to see a row of portholes. The object trailed a stream of fire half its length, and disappeared at the incredible speed of 1,500 to 2,000 mph.[40]

The defense establishment was secretly receiving UFO reports from its military no later than January 1947. On January 16, 1947, an army air force plane had a long chase over the North Sea at twenty-two thousand feet. A classified memo wrote that "the unidentified craft appeared to take efficient, controlled evasive action." A month later, in the afternoon of February 28, 1947, an air force jet pilot, a Lieutenant Armstrong, flying thirty miles north of Lake Meade, Nevada, saw a formation of five or six white discs at an altitude of six thousand feet. Throughout the spring of 1947, sightings of disc-like objects occurred sporadically throughout the United States, including at least one that was observed through a theodolite (a small telescope that pivots in two directions to give accurate sighting angles, and is used for accurate tracking of airborne objects). Several of these sightings were later investigated by the FBI and air force intelligence.[41]

On May 1, 1947, Rear Adm. Roscoe H. Hillenkoetter replaced Hoyt Vandenberg as DCI. Hillenkoetter was an Annapolis graduate who spoke three languages, had been at Pearl Harbor, and had set up an intelligence network for Adm. Chester W. Nimitz. He was also a friend and Annapolis classmate of future UFO researcher Donald E. Keyhoe. One of the interesting, ignored tidbits of American history is the fact that, from 1957 until 1962, Hillenkoetter sat on the board of directors of the country's leading civilian UFO organization, the National Investigative Committee on Aerial Phenomena (NICAP). For some reason, historians of American national security and the cold war do not find this interesting. Why, we may ask, did a CIA director who held the post for three years—during some of the most dramatic moments of the cold war— become interested in NICAP, and even make public statements regarding the need to end UFO secrecy? Was Hillenkoetter "eccentric"? Was he spreading disinformation? Was he sincere? What did he know about UFOs? Professional historians, taking the road most traveled, do not ask these questions, or indeed any questions regarding Hillenkoetter and UFOs, even though the most cursory review of the man's career clamors for such treatment.

SUMMARY

A process began during the war years which gained momentum during 1946 and 1947. This concerned the ability of human beings to detect and do something about an age-old phenomenon: UFOs. Such a development required the growth of a large and technologically sophisticated national security apparatus. After all, until the 1940s, the only way to detect UFOs had been by looking up at the sky. Moreover, there had been nothing one could *do* about such things. By the war's end, this was no longer the case. On the contrary, the emerging cold war required extreme diligence by the United States, the Soviet Union, and the other major militaries of the world to monitor their national borders against unauthorized intrusions.

By mid-1947, the reorganization and expansion of America's national security apparatus was well under way, and a fair portion of this remained covert. It should not be surprising, therefore, that the UFO problem emerged within the American military before it became a public issue. Yet, on the eve of the Kenneth Arnold sighting, no one could have foreseen just how big the UFO problem would become.

Chapter 2

Saucers in the Skies: 1947

The first rule in keeping secrets is "nothing on paper."
—CIA Director Richard Helms

CRESCENDO

In the summer of 1947, flying saucer mania spread across America. Millions of people read about strange objects that were seen throughout the country and seemed to defy the standard rules of flight. Were flying saucers some odd, unknown natural phenomenon? Were they mechanical objects, and if so, whose? A communist stratagem? War nerves? Hoaxes? A new fad? Rubbish? Everyone wondered, no one knew.

Before Kenneth Arnold sparked the flying saucer frenzy on June 24, there had been a steady buildup of odd things in the sky. On June 2, 1947, a UFO sighting occurred at Rehoboth, Delaware, which the air force investigated. Not much is known about it: the case is missing from the Blue Book files, although in theory Blue Book was the comprehensive repository of unidentified sightings reported to the air force. The air force also investigated a Weiser, Idaho, report from June 12, describing two strange, fast-moving objects. Around noon on the twenty-first, residents of Spokane, Washington, reported eight disc-shaped objects about the size of a house, said to be flying at around 600 mph. The objects then fell with a "dead leaf" motion, landing on the shore of the Saint Joe River in Idaho before ten witnesses. On the twenty-third, in Cedar Rapids, Iowa, a railroad engineer saw ten shiny, fluttering disc-shaped objects in a line high in the sky. That same day, pilot

Richard Rankin saw a formation of ten objects in Bakersfield, California, flying north. They, too, seemed to be disc-like, with a diameter of about one hundred feet, flying in formation at a good speed, anywhere from 300 to 600 mph. Dick Rankin was a respected pilot with over seven thousand hours of flight-time experience. His sighting remains unidentified.[1]

These sightings, all by civilians, eventually gained some publicity. But the series of sightings which began that month at the Oak Ridge nuclear facility in Tennessee remained unknown to the public for years. Oak Ridge was the atomic testing facility for the Atomic Energy Commission, housing some of the world's most sophisticated technology. In 1947, nuclear technology was cutting edge, and the U.S. government severely restricted access to it. Violating the airspace over Oak Ridge was a very serious matter. And yet *something*, according to a declassified FBI document, without authorization flew over Oak Ridge that June (another FBI document mentioned July). This object was photographed by a civilian employee, a resident engineer with Air Material Command. A 1949 FBI memo to Hoover discussing this noted that at least twenty-four copies of the photograph had been made, and said that an unnamed source asked the employee to recover all of them and bring them to air force intelligence. He complied. According to the FBI document, the witness "further stated that [blacked out] had appeared extremely concerned over the matter and seemed quite emphatic that the matter should be given no more publicity than was absolutely necessary."

UFO sightings over Oak Ridge continued with great frequency during the late 1940s and beyond. A number of them were radar and visual cases, although the radar and visuals were reported from different locations. The events caused great concern at the FBI Field Office in Knoxville, the U.S. Third Army, and the Atomic Energy Commission's security division at Oak Ridge. A classified FBI report from November 1950 listed a recent spate of sightings over the facility in a chronological summary.[2]

THE FLOODGATES OPEN

The skies were becoming busy, yet all was quiet. The dam broke on June 24. On that day, pilot and businessman Kenneth Arnold from Boise, Idaho, was flying near Mount Rainier, Washington, in search of a downed C-46 Marine transport and a sizable reward. He saw a "tremendously bright flash" and noticed a formation of nine bright, extremely fast objects moving along in a column. He was startled because he saw no tail on the objects. At first he thought they must be experimental jets and that the air force was using camouflage to hide the tails. He said "they flew in a definite formation" but "backward" (with the first craft elevated more than the others). "Their flight was like speed boats on rough water" or "like a saucer would if you skipped it across water." He estimated their size to be about one hundred feet in diameter. Arnold was struck by how fast the objects seemed to be moving, so he decided to measure their speed as they passed between Rainier's peak and another peak he knew to be fifty miles away. They covered this distance in one minute and forty-two seconds—a speed of 1,700 mph! Arnold could not accept his own calculations, the speed was just too fast. He reworked his calculations, allowing for all possible errors, and arrived at the still-incredible speed of 1,200 mph. In 1947, no flying craft could reach much more than half that speed.

Arnold gave up on the C-46, flew to Yakima, and told his story. One pilot said, "It's just a flight of those guided missiles from Moses Lake." Arnold was unconvinced and flew on to Pendleton, Oregon, unaware that someone at Yakima had telephoned ahead to report his strange encounter. When he arrived, a large crowd on hand for an air show was waiting for him. A discussion followed, and Arnold warmed to the idea of guided missiles. Speaking to the *East Oregonian*, he was "fairly convinced that it was some new government invention along the line of guided missiles."

The next day, the *East Oregonian* ran the first flying saucer story under the headline "Impossible! Maybe, But Seein' Is Believin', Says Flier." The story hit the AP wire and made page one of the Chicago *Daily Tribune*. The phrase "saucer-like" quickly became "flying saucers," and Arnold was flooded with phone calls and requests for interviews. Kenneth Arnold's sighting has never been explained satisfactorily, although UFO debunker Donald Menzel tried to do so several times.

As people began talking about flying saucers, it became apparent that Arnold's sighting had not been the first. In fact, there were many other sightings from the twenty-fourth, most from the Pacific Northwest. Within the hour of Arnold's sighting, an Oregon prospector named Fred Johnson saw five or six "round, metallic-looking discs" through a telescope over the Cascade Mountains. As they circled overhead, they disrupted his compass needle. Johnson insisted he had not heard of the Arnold report, which was not broadcast until early evening. He later wrote about the incident to the air force and was interviewed by the FBI, which judged him "very reliable."[3]

The day after Arnold's sighting, people in Kansas City, Oklahoma City, and Pueblo, Colorado, reported sightings of "flying discs." All of these involved several objects flying in loose formations. Sightings were also being made in Canada, Australia, and New Zealand. On June 27, Army Air Force Public Relations Officer Captain Tom Brown stated the army had "no idea what they are."[4] In mid-afternoon of the twenty-eighth, an army air force pilot in an F-51 flying near Lake Meade, Nevada, saw a formation of five or six circular objects off his right wing. That same day, four air force officers (two pilots and two intelligence officers) from Maxwell AFB in Montgomery, Alabama, saw a bright light traveling across the sky. It zigzagged with bursts of high speed.[5] On June 29, at White Sands Proving Ground in New Mexico, a naval rocket expert, Dr. C. J. John, along with two fellow scientists, saw a silvery disc. He reported the sighting to the army with the observation:

> We noticed a glare in the sky. We looked up and saw a silvery disc whirling along. We watched the thing for nearly sixty seconds and then it simply disappeared. It didn't go behind the mountain range. At one time it was clearly visible, and then it just wasn't there.[6]

The next day, a navy officer flying near the Grand Canyon at thirty thousand feet saw two gray, circular objects diving at "unconceivable" speed. The objects looked about ten feet in diameter and seemed to land about twenty-five miles south of the canyon.[7]

A mere week after the Arnold sighting, flying saucers seemed to be engulfing America. The Pacific Northwest had the heaviest concentration of activity. Newspaper coverage of flying saucers was intense, and interesting sightings occurred into July. On the first of the month, an Albuquerque Chamber of Commerce official saw a "disc-like, bluish object following a zigzag path in the northwestern sky" over New Mexico. Another report from New Mexico came from the Navajo reservation in the northwestern part of the state. Flying saucer reports came from the east, too. Meteorologist E. E. Unger, who ran the U.S. Weather Bureau at Louisville, Kentucky, believed he saw one. In eastern Canada, four people on Prince Edward Island saw objects "traveling at great speed high in the sky." One witness described them as "shapeless, but glistening in the sunlight."[8]

On July 3, an astronomer in South Brookville, Maine, saw a UFO about one hundred feet in diameter. Air Material Command publicly explained it as birds or insects, although the air force's Project Grudge later listed the sighting as an "unusually well-supported incident" with no explanation. That evening in Denver, several people reported seeing "projectiles" variously described as "too fast for an airplane and not fast enough for a falling star," "not moving at all," and "traveling at great speed."[9]

Activity increased yet more on Friday, July 4. One sighting that occurred near Boise, Idaho, received a great deal of attention, since the objects were witnessed by Capt. Edward J. Smith and his copilot, Ralph Stevens, of United Airlines. Smith was a highly regarded pilot with much experience in the air. While en route to Portland, Smith and Stevens saw nine disc-like objects. Smith's stature prompted an FBI investigation into the sighting, which credited him as reliable. In Portland, many people, including police officers, saw a large number of UFOs in the middle of the afternoon, in formation and alone. In Redmond, Oregon, a car full of people saw four disc-shaped UFOs streak past Mount Jefferson. In Seattle, a Coast Guard yeoman took the first publicly known photograph of a UFO, a circular object moving against the wind. The photo showed a round dot of light.[10]

MAKING SENSE OF IT

It is easy to see why flying saucers elicited such strong interest. Here were clearly seen objects that did not look like airplanes, and often moved at incredible speeds. Were they even real? If so, what could they be? The most widely discussed possibilities were experimental military craft (Arnold's initial opinion), experimental civilian-designed craft, foreign (e.g., Soviet) craft, atmospheric and meteorological phenomena, and mass hysteria. No one wrote about aliens.

It is reasonable to assume that so many well-observed strange sightings would be of interest to the U.S. military. Publicly, however, the military's attitude was varied. A July 3 article said the Air Research Center at Wright Field was looking into the matter, "and all service intelligence agencies are at work on them." According to the army spokesman, "If some foreign power is sending flying discs over the United States, it is our responsibility to know about it and take proper action." The next day, an army air force spokesman discounted the secret weapon theory—nothing in America's possession could have caused the sightings. He dismissed the Arnold sighting as not realistic enough to deserve further study, and dismissed the whole flying saucer phenomenon. Perhaps the whole thing was meteorological. Air Material Command, he noted, was trying at this moment to determine that very possibility.[11]

Behind the public facade, however, the military wondered about more serious implications. After reviewing what documents he could find a few years later, Capt. Edward Ruppelt, who for several years managed the air force's Project Blue Book, believed the air force during this time established "a project to investigate and analyze" all UFO reports. He described their attitude as "a state of near panic." Donald Keyhoe later obtained military sources who told him that the air force at this time ordered its pilots "to down a UFO for examination, by shooting, or by running and bailing out." We know that the army air force, the Army Counter Intelligence Corps (CIC), and the FBI were all doing a great deal of field work regarding UFOs, interviewing witnesses and trying to determine just what these things were.[12]

Within this context, let us move on to the most controversial event in the entire history of the UFO phenomenon, the crash at Roswell, New Mexico.

ROSWELL, ROSWELL!

The debate over what crashed at Roswell has monopolized UFO researchers for a generation.[13] Something certainly fell from the air and crashed outside Roswell, New Mexico, during the summer of 1947. The date is disputed, but the leading candidates have generally been June 14, July 2, and July 4. Some have even placed the date in May. On Saturday, July 5, sheepherder Mac Brazel, foreman of the Foster ranch seventy-five miles from Roswell, found crash debris. Accounts have varied as to how widely this debris was scattered. Brazel discovered metal, plastic-like beams, lightweight material, foil, and either string or "stringlike material." Some of the material seemed unusually lightweight and strong. Brazel spoke with his nearest neighbors, the Proctors, but they were too busy to visit his field. It appears that at some later point Brazel showed them some fragments, which he had tried—and failed—to cut or burn.

On Sunday, July 6, Brazel brought some of the material to Roswell to show Sheriff George Wilcox. Wilcox sent two deputies out to the ranch and notified the Roswell Army Air Force base. At RAAF, Col. William Blanchard, the commanding officer of the 509th Bomb Group, ordered air intelligence officer Captain (later Major) Jesse Marcel to investigate. The 509th was one of the nation's elite units, and the only military group in the world with atomic capability. Marcel, accompanied by Army CIC Capt. Sheridan Cavitt and Cavitt's subordinate, Master Sgt. Lewis S. Rickett, visited Wilcox's office and spoke with Brazel. They then accompanied Brazel back to the Foster ranch, where they arrived late that night. This issue is somewhat confusing because for many years Cavitt denied having been to the debris field. But not only was he there, so was Rickett, who gave details to researchers such as Friedman and Mark Rodighier. Meanwhile, it took an interview with Air Force Colonel Richard Weaver in 1994 to elicit a confirmation from Cavitt that he, too, had been at the debris field.

After these men left Wilcox's office, the sheriff's two deputies returned to Roswell without finding the debris field, although they claimed to see a burned area in one of the pastures, where the sand had been turned to glass. Military police arrived at Wilcox's office and collected the wreckage Brazel had left there.

On Monday, July 7, Lt. Gen. Nathan Twining, commander of Air Material Command (AMC), flew unexpectedly to Alamogordo Army Air Field, New Mexico, then made a side trip to Kirtland AFB in Albuquerque. He remained in the area until July 11, although reporters initially had been told that Twining was "probably" in Washington, D.C. Meanwhile, Gen. Carl Spaatz, commander of the army air forces, was vacationing in the state of Washington. One wonders how much of a vacation it could have been. According to the *New York Times*, five P-51 Mustangs of the Oregon National Guard were flying over the Cascade Mountains on an airborne alert—they were searching for the mysterious flying discs. Spaatz told reporters that he knew nothing about the saucers or of the plans to search for them.[14] Whether by coincidence or design, two of the nation's most important air force generals just happened to be in the nation's two leading UFO hot spots.

Regarding the Twining visit, it should be noted that a declassified document from June 5, 1947, stated that Twining, Gen. Benjamin Chidlaw, and a few other high-level brass were scheduled to attend a three-day temporary duty status at Sandia Base in Albuquerque for a Bomb Commanders Course. This took place between July 8 and July 11. Visitor logs and secretary calendars indicate that this group did take the course. But Twining was also scheduled for a trip to Boeing at this time, which he had to cancel. In a July 17 letter to a Boeing executive, Twining referred to a "very important and sudden matter that developed here." Since Twining had not received confirmation of his clearance to attend the conference at Sandia until July 3, it is possible that this is what he was referring to. It is also likely, however, that the Roswell crash received his immediate attention.

Let us now follow Jesse Marcel's experience, as he related thirty years later. On Monday morning (the day Twining flew to New Mexico), Brazel took Marcel and Cavitt out to the debris field. According to Marcel, the field was three-quarters of a mile long, and two to three hundred feet wide. A gouge in the field extended for four or five hundred feet, "as if something had touched down and skipped along." The debris was as thin as newsprint, but incredibly strong. Marcel said that one soldier later told him that the metal was unbendable and could not be dented, even with a sledgehammer. Marcel also found foil that, when crumpled, would unfold itself without any sign of a wrinkle, and I-beams with odd symbols on them and a pink/lavender coloration. The beams flexed slightly but would not break.

Marcel concluded that the debris was "definitely not a weather or tracking device, nor was it any sort of plane or missile. . . . It was something I had never seen before, or since . . . it certainly wasn't anything built by us."

Marcel and Cavitt collected debris at Brazel's ranch for most of the day. According to many accounts, including that of Roswell skeptics, Lewis Rickett drove out with Cavitt at some point. After filling Cavitt's vehicle, Marcel told Cavitt to go on ahead and meet him back at Roswell AAF. He then filled his own vehicle and, late at night, began his drive back to the base. On the way, however, he made a stop at his house at 2 A.M. He woke up his wife, Viaud, and his son, Jesse, Jr., showed them the debris, and identified it as part of a flying saucer.

Marcel and Cavitt arrived at RAAF the morning of Tuesday, July 8, with two carloads of debris. Blanchard notified the Eighth Air Force headquarters in Fort Worth and ordered Marcel to go there with the debris and meet with Gen. Roger Ramey. At this point both Marcel and Blanchard believed they had obtained pieces of the mysterious flying discs. At around noon, Blanchard ordered Public Information Officer Lt. Walter Haut to issue a press release stating this. Haut gave the release to Frank Joyce at radio station KGFL, who sent it to Western Union, radio stations, and newspapers. It reached the AP wire by 2:26 P.M.; at that point, all hell broke loose throughout Roswell and, we may assume, up the military chain of command.[15] The *Roswell Daily Record*, an evening paper, carried three stories about the crash, all on the front page. The main statement: "The intelligence office of the 509th Bombardment group at Roswell Army Air Field announced at noon today that the field has come into possession of a flying saucer."[16]

Meanwhile, Marcel arrived with the debris at Ramey's office. What happened next is disputed. According to Marcel, the two left the office, then came back. Marcel swore that *this* time, the debris was different, that it had been changed. In its place was a ripped-apart weather balloon scattered on the floor. Nonsense, maintained the air force. Ultimately, we are left with Marcel's word on the matter versus that of the air force.

Ramey brought in the Associated Press, which broke the story—only three hours after the original RAAF press release—that the Roswell flying disc was nothing more than a weather balloon. Ramey also appeared on a local Fort Worth-Dallas radio station to announce that Marcel and the officers at Roswell had been fooled by a weather balloon.[17]

The FBI followed the events in Roswell. An FBI teletype labeled "Urgent" and headed "Flying Disc—Information Concerning" was sent shortly after the Ramey press conference to J. Edgar Hoover and Strategic Air Command in Cincinnati. Following Ramey's lead, the author of the teletype said it was all just a balloon—sort of. The message stated that:

> Major Curtain, HQ Eighth Air Force, telephonically advised this office that an object purporting to be a flying disc was recovered near Roswell, New Mexico, this date. The disc is hexagonal in shape and was suspended from a balloon by a cable, which balloon was approximately twenty feet in diameter. [Blacked out] further advised that the object found resembles a high-altitude weather balloon with a radar reflector, but that telephonic conversation between their office and Wright Field had not [blacked out] borne out this belief. Disc and balloon being transported to Wright Field by special plane for examination. Information provided this office because of national interest in case [blacked out] and fact that National Broadcasting Company, Associated Press, and others attempting to break story of location of disc today . . . .[18]

An important memo, for sure. Of particular interest is the phrase: "telephonic conversation between their office and Wright Field had not [blacked out] borne out this belief." Not borne out the belief that this object was a high-altitude weather balloon?

By July 9, newspapers were reporting that the Roswell disc was just a weather balloon. Mac Brazel, under military guard for several days, had meanwhile been led back into town under military escort. Contrary to his initial claim, he was now telling reporters that he found the wreckage on June 14, but continued to maintain it was no weather balloon.[19] Meanwhile, a poll among Roswell residents revealed that most thought that experimental military tests were behind the saucer sightings, slightly fewer blamed mass hysteria, while most of the rest attributed them to natural phenomena. The army baked it, the press served it, the public ate it.

For the next thirty years, the Roswell incident became a nonevent, forgotten by everyone except the residents. In 1978, while in Baton Rouge, UFO researcher Stanton Friedman heard a story that Maj. Jesse Marcel, retired from the air force and living nearby, had once handled the wreckage of a UFO. Friedman interviewed Marcel, reexamined the stories about Roswell, found other witnesses, and concluded that there had been a cover-up of "cosmic Watergate" proportions. His research became the basis of the 1980 book *The Roswell Incident*, cowritten by Charles Berlitz and William Moore.

In 1988, the Center for UFO Studies (CUFOS) in Chicago sponsored a team to find the crash site, recover any remaining debris, and interview surviving witnesses. Three years later the key members of that team, Kevin Randle and Don Schmitt, published their conclusions in the book *UFO Crash at Roswell*. Not only had the military recovered a UFO at Roswell, they asserted, they also retrieved alien bodies. In 1992, Friedman and Don Berliner coauthored *Crash at Corona*, which argued that the government recovered not one but two saucers in July 1947, along with seven dead extraterrestrials and one that was still alive. The first crashed at Corona (near Roswell) after a midair accident that showered debris on the Foster ranch, the second on the Plains of San Augustin. Randle and Schmitt wrote a Roswell sequel in 1994, which disputed the San Augustin crash story, moved the date from July 2 to July 4, and argued that alien bodies were taken to RAAF, examined, sealed in a crate, and taken to a hangar and flown to Andrews AFB in Washington, D.C., at 2 A.M. on Monday, July 7.

ROSWELL: MORE WITNESSES

By the 1990s, many of the main alleged witnesses to the Roswell events were dead. But some were not, and others, such as the children of the deceased, claimed to possess relevant information gotten from their parents. A brief synopsis of the accounts from some of the more noteworthies follows, with the proviso that judging the credibility of these claims is sometimes difficult but, alas, part of the package.

Lewis S. Rickett

Lewis Rickett, a Counter Intelligence Corps NCO based in Roswell, was not only at the crash scene with Cavitt and Marcel, but claimed to have escorted Dr. Lincoln La Paz on a tour of the crash site and surrounding area. La Paz was a world-renowned meteor expert from the New Mexico Institute of Meteoritics. Rickett's description of the debris was consistent with that of other witnesses. According to him, La Paz was "to find out what the speed and trajectory of the thing was." La Paz flew over the area and found a spot where the sand had been turned glasslike, which he believed was caused by a landing and takeoff. He also apparently spoke to a number of the local witnesses and decided that there had been several objects.[20]

General Arthur Exon

On or around July 9, 1947, according to future Brigadier General Arthur Exon, then stationed at Wright Field in Ohio, various aircraft from Roswell arrived. Although Exon did not see any bodies, he did hear rumors about them. Nor did he participate in analyzing the metal that arrived, but he later claimed to talk with friends who did the work and who indicated to him that the material was "extraordinary." Exon soon flew over the Roswell sites and saw obvious gouges in the terrain and tire tracks over two distinctive sites.[21]

William Brazel

Bill Brazel was the son of Mac Brazel. Although his father died before the Roswell resurgence, Bill offered his own account of events. In 1947, he was living in Albuquerque, but returned to run the ranch when his father was taken into custody. According to Bill (and other witnesses), this lasted for about a week, during which time Mac was seen on the streets of Roswell with a military escort. Afterwards, Mac repudiated his initial story.

Bill Brazel offered a description of the crash wreckage that corresponded with Marcel's account. He claimed to have found various types of debris, including something similar to balsa wood, except that it would not whittle or break. Another type of debris looked like heavy-gauge fishing line—this, too, could not break. The last type of material was similar to tinfoil or lead foil, except that the foil would unfold and straighten out after being crumpled up.

Bill also claimed that sometime after the crash, he discussed the foil with some friends in a Corona bar. Then, in his words, "lo and behold, here comes the military out to the ranch, a day or two later." They told him they had learned of his possession of "some bits and pieces" of debris, and wanted him to relinquish them. They reminded him that his father had turned over everything that he had found. The younger Brazel gave up the pieces. The men told him that they "would rather you didn't talk very much about it."[22]

Glenn Dennis

Glenn Dennis was a mortician in Roswell in 1947. His employer provided mortuary services for Roswell Army Air Field. Dennis claimed that in early July he received several phone calls from the Roswell AAF mortuary officer, who was more of an administrator than a mortuary technician. The officer wanted to know about chemical solutions and hermetically sealed caskets, including how small they came. That evening, Dennis took a GI accident victim to the base infirmary. He walked the injured GI inside, then drove around to the back to see a nurse he had recently gotten to know. According to Dennis, the nurse warned him that he should not be there, that he was going to get himself killed. Almost immediately, a "big, red-headed colonel" said "what's that son of a bitch doing here?"

Dennis was quickly escorted off the base and told, "you open your mouth and you'll be so far back in the jug they'll have to shoot pinto beans [into you] with a bean shooter." Dennis also told Stanton Friedman that he spoke with the nurse again the following day, who told him there had been three little bodies—two were badly mangled, one was in fairly good condition. The nurse swore him to secrecy and was soon transferred to England. Later, Dennis said, he heard that the nurse had been killed in a plane crash. The identity of the nurse has never been established.[23]

Barbara Dugger

Barbara Dugger was the granddaughter of Roswell Sheriff George Wilcox. She claimed that her grandmother, Inez (the wife of George Wilcox), said that after the incident, military police told the Wilcox couple that the entire family would be killed if they ever talked about it. Inez said George Wilcox had gone out to the site, saw a big burned area, debris, and "four space beings" with large heads and suits "like silk." One of the beings was alive. According to Dugger: "if she [Inez] said it happened, it happened."[24]

Frank Joyce

Joyce worked at the Roswell radio station in 1947. He claimed that during the frenzy of activity in town, the station received a phone call from someone identifying himself as an officer at the Pentagon. According to Joyce:

> . . . this man said some very bad things about what would happen to me. He was really pretty nasty. Finally, I got through to him. I said, "You're talking about a release from the U.S. Army Air Corps." Bang, the phone went dead, he was just gone.

That evening, Joyce received a call from Mac Brazel, who said the station had not gotten his story right. Joyce invited Brazel to the station. He now claimed that the debris was from a weather balloon. Joyce commented that this story differed quite a lot from Brazel's earlier claim about the little green men, to which Brazel is supposed to have said, "No, they weren't green." Joyce had the feeling Brazel was "under tremendous pressure."[25]

Witnesses to the Transport of Debris.

Loretta Proctor's brother, Master Sgt. Robert Porter, was a B-29 flight engineer with the 830th Bomb Squadron. Porter claimed to have flown

26

Roswell debris to Fort Worth and that one officer said they were parts of a flying saucer. On board were Lt. Col. Payne Jennings (deputy commander of Roswell) and Major Marcel.

First Lt. Robert Shirkey was assistant operations officer of the 509th Bomb Group. Shirkey said that he saw part of the loading process that transported the debris to Fort Worth, "carrying parts of the crashed flying saucer."

Robert Slusher, a staff sergeant assigned to the 393rd Bomb Squadron, corroborated Shirkey's account. Slusher said he was on board a B-29 that carried a single crate from Roswell to Fort Worth, which he described as twelve feet long, five feet wide, and four feet high. The contents of the crate seemed to be sensitive to air pressure, since the plane flew at the unusually low altitude of four to five thousand feet (rather than the standard twenty-five thousand for a B-29). Unlike the cabin, which could be pressurized, the bomb bay (where the crate was stowed) could not be pressurized. This suggests the crate was carrying something other than metal. Slusher also believed the flight to be unusual in that it was a hurried flight, ordered with little advanced notice; he also reported rumors that the crate had debris from the crash.

Another witness to the transport of debris was Robert Smith, a member of the First Air Transport Unit, which operated Douglas C-54 Skymaster four-engined cargo planes out of RAAF. Smith helped load crates of debris into the aircraft. He described seeing many armed guards, something unusual at Roswell, and "a lot of people in plainclothes all over the place." There were quite a few crates to load, and the whole process took six to eight hours. He claimed to have seen a small piece of foil that would not crease.[26]

The foregoing account of witnesses is by no means exhaustive, but should give an indication that, by the 1990s, the air force was in danger of losing control of the Roswell story.

ROSWELL: THE SKEPTICS EXPLAIN

By 1993, New Mexico Representative Steven Schiff, under pressure from his constituency, requested information from the Pentagon about the Roswell crash. The response was not exactly expeditious. Schiff accused the Pentagon of "stonewalling," called its lack of response "astounding," and said he was "clearly getting the runaround." As a result, he asked the General Accounting Office, Congress's investigative arm, to prepare a report on the status of government records related to the Roswell incident. In July 1995, the GAO issued its report, "Results of a Search for Records Concerning the 1947 Crash Near Roswell, New Mexico." The GAO reported that, incredibly, all administrative records of Roswell Army Air Field from March 1945 through December 1949 were inexplicably destroyed, as were all outgoing messages from October 1946 through December 1949. These were permanent records that should not have been destroyed. In the words of the report, "our search of government records was complicated by the fact that some records we wanted to review were missing and there was not always an explanation." As Schiff put it, "documents that should have provided more information were destroyed. The military cannot explain who destroyed them or why." No explanation or follow-up ever occurred.[27]

For nearly fifty years, the air force had maintained that the crash at Roswell had been nothing other than a downed weather balloon. In July 1995, it released "The Roswell Report: Fact Versus Fiction in the New Mexico Desert." The air force now modified its weather balloon explanation. A balloon *did* cause the crash, but this was no ordinary balloon. "Its real purpose was to carry classified payloads for a top secret U.S. Army Air Forces project. The project's classified code name was Mogul." Mogul was designed to assist the U.S. military in detecting signs of Soviet nuclear explosions—in other words, to learn when Russia got the bomb. It had a 1A priority classification, the highest available.[28]

The report introduced Charles Moore, a scientist who worked on Mogul in 1947, as its key witness. Moore explained that Mogul involved launching trains of balloons that carried acoustical equipment designed to monitor Soviet nuclear tests. The balloons were equipped with corner reflectors to track them more easily by radar. The reflectors were put together with beams made of balsa wood and coated with Elmer's-type glue to strengthen them. A toy company that manufactured the reflectors had reinforced the seams with leftover tape that Moore recalled had "pinkish-purple, abstract, flower-like designs," markings, according to the report, that Major Marcel could have misinterpreted as hieroglyphics.

The air force report claimed "with a great degree of certainty," that Mogul flight Number 4, launched on June 4, 1947, was the actual debris mistaken for a flying saucer. The report gave three reasons for this conclusion.

1. Descriptions of the debris provided by Brazel, Cavitt, and Mogul scientist Dr. Albert Crary (who kept a diary of the launches), as well as the photos of the debris in Ramey's office, "were consistent with the components of a Mogul service flight. . . ."

2. Brazel's statement of July 8, 1947, that he found debris on June 14, "obviously eliminating any balloons launched in July."

3. Only two flights launched in June were unaccounted for, Numbers 3 and 4. Of these, Number 3 did not have unorthodox corner reflectors. Flight #4, launched on June 4, was tracked to within twenty miles of the Foster ranch before it disappeared from the radar scopes in mid-June.

Of these three reasons, only the first is an actual reason, as the other two work entirely within the structure provided by the first. That is, the entire air force Mogul explanation rests upon accounts by Brazel (as reported on July 8), Cavitt (a loyal CIC officer known to be hostile to the UFO explanation), and Crary's diary. All other evidence—and there is a lot of it—was ignored. If one does not accept the June 14 crash date, as many do not, the air force explanation falls.

The original air force explanation made no mention of alien bodies, although many Roswell residents claimed either to have seen bodies or heard about them secondhand. The air force representative explained the omission simply: "It seemed rational to us that since we proved there were no UFOs, it automatically meant no aliens." In the summer of 1997, amid the mayhem in Roswell marking the fiftieth anniversary of the crash, the air force issued its second official report on the crash. The air force now indicated that, during the 1950s, it had conducted experiments that involved dropping dummies from high-altitude balloons to study the results of the impact. Witness descriptions of the "aliens" somewhat matched the characteristics of the dummies: bluish skin coloration and no ears, hair, eyebrows, or eyelashes. The air force dummies, however, were all six feet tall. The air force maintained that people who saw these dummies probably mistook them for aliens. As for the apparent incongruity of the dates, the air force contended that the sheer span of time made it difficult for people to remember exact dates.[29]

Let us, with efficient dispatch, look at the combined air force argument more closely.

1. In neither report did the air force make any attempt to interview still-living witnesses of the 1947 events.

2. The air force ignored its own experts, such as Lt. Col. (Ret.) Raymond A. Madson, a project officer on Project High Dive, who told the Associated Press that there is no way the dummies could be confused with aliens. Each dummy had a reward notice, and were stamped as property of the U.S. Air Force.

3. The air force ignored the fact that no dummies fell near the Roswell crash site.

4. The dummy tests were known to the public through extensive air force publicity at the time, a fact the air force mentioned.

5. The description of Mogul's apparatus in no way fits with the consistent description of Roswell wreckage by the people who say they were there. Can one truly consider glue-treated balsa-wood sticks to have the toughness and durability ascribed to the Roswell wreckage? Were Marcel, Brazel, Blanchard, Wilcox, and the rest unable to identify rubber, tinfoil, and balsa wood debris?

6. A Mogul balloon was not large or heavy enough to have caused the kind of widespread remains and incisions into the ground that witnesses ascribed to the Roswell crash.

7. Neither report tried to answer why the army incarcerated Brazel, interrogated him for a week, and held him incommunicado. Brazel's detention by the military was corroborated by his family, friends, neighbors, Roswell base provost marshal, and Wilcox's family.

8. Other Mogul launches did not exhibit the level of security that Roswell witnesses attributed to the crash recovery. For example, Mogul flight #7, launched July 2, 1947, crashed off course. Before the balloon train could be recovered, some of the balloons were stolen by civilians. In this case, however, no military squad was sent to round up the thieves.

Another example was Mogul #6, launched June 7. Albert Crary noted in his diary that rancher Sid West found the remains of this balloon train and payload. West easily identified the balloon and knew immediately who to contact. The next day, two men associated with Mogul came by to pick it up.

Considering that Mogul #4—the supposed Roswell object—was simply an unlisted test flight, carrying no classified equipment, it is strange that so many witnesses should have attested to such stringent security around it.

ROSWELL: CONCLUSIONS

Roswell has been the Holy Grail of UFO research. It has offered hope to those seeking to prove a UFO cover-up, but has yet to deliver the goods. In retrospect, Roswell's hammerlock on public discussion about UFOs has been unfortunate. Through the lens of the pop media, the Roswell case has become a kind of litmus test for the legitimacy of the entire UFO phenomenon. The case for the UFO is much broader and stronger than a fixation on Roswell warrants. While Roswell debate is important on its own merits, it has brought an unmerited sense of finality to the UFO debate in general.

Another problem with placing all of one's chips on Roswell is the unlikelihood that the true nature of the crash will ever be established—*to the satisfaction of all concerned parties*. Heated though the Roswell argument has become, there is just not enough proof to establish beyond any reasonable doubt either of the two main contentions: (1) that an extraterrestrial object (with alien bodies) crashed, or (2) that the crash resulted from debris of a balloon of some sort. Ultimately, Roswell will probably always have more evidence than proof, lots of witness testimony but no smoking gun.

One thing we can say with reasonable certainty: claims to have "closed the case" are greatly premature, based on slender evidence, wrapped in the cloak of official sanction, and given widespread circulation by the mass media. In such an environment, it is unrealistic to presume that we will ever get to the bottom of the mystery. We may form opinions about what we *think* happened, but we would be wise to refrain from claiming to *know* much of anything, except that the military deceived the public about it for fifty years, and probably continues to do so.

A final observation that often goes unnoticed: the Roswell crash occurred amid one of the greatest UFO-sighting waves in modern history. While the case must stand or fall on its own merits, isolating it from its historical context has been an all-too-common mistake.

OTHER SIGHTINGS

The Roswell crash not only followed a rash of interesting sightings, it preceded one. On Sunday, July 6, as the events in Roswell were still unfolding, a sergeant in Birmingham, Alabama, saw several dim, glowing lights speed across the sky, and photographed one of them. The same day, a B-25 crew saw a bright, disc-shaped object below their aircraft. At Fairfield-Susan AFB in California, a pilot saw a strange object "oscillating on its lateral axis" shoot across the sky in a few seconds. In southern Wyoming, an aviation engineer also saw an oval-shaped UFO.[30]

On Monday the seventh, a young man named William H. Rhodes of Phoenix, Arizona, took two photographs of a flying saucer, which were published two days later on the front page of the *Arizona Republic*—right next to the article debunking the Roswell crash. The photographs did not appear in any other newspapers, but Rhodes was soon visited by an FBI agent and an Intelligence officer from Hamilton Field, California. At their request he gave them his pictures, which he never saw again. In early 1948, Rhodes was asked to come to Wright-Patterson Field for an interview—he declined—and was soon afterward interviewed for a second time at his home. Years later, publisher Raymond Palmer erroneously charged that the army had picked up all sixty-four thousand copies of the newspaper's July 9 edition and destroyed the plates. The paper humorously rebutted his claim. After conceding his mistake, Palmer said he had heard the story from a Phoenix resident, and asked the paper for a copy of the edition or a front page photostatted from the back issue file. He never heard from them. For the rest of his life, Palmer continued to think "that Rhodes photographed the real thing, and that the air force felt it was necessary to quiet the whole matter."[31]

While Roswell buzzed with activity, claims, and denials, an extraordinary series of sightings occurred in California's Mojave Desert, at Muroc Air Field (now Edwards AFB). Ruppelt called it "the first sighting that really made the

air force take a deep interest in UFOs." This is unlikely, but there is no denying that the events there concerned the air force.

On July 8, 1947, at Muroc, four separate sightings by a number of officers
and technicians took place. Each involved circular or disc-shaped UFOs seen
at 9:30 A.M., 11:50 A.M., 12:00 noon, and 3:50 P.M. The first is by far the best-
known. Several pilots on the ground saw two silver-colored, spherical or
disc-like UFOs maneuvering over the base, circling tightly at eight thousand
feet at speeds of 300-400 mph—rather fast maneuvering. According to the
report, the "objects in question were not, repeat, were not, aircraft." Nor were
they balloons, since the objects were traveling against the wind. They simply
flew off and disappeared. Very soon afterward, the witnesses saw another
object "traveling in circles." One witness said, "I have been flying in and have
been around all types of aircraft since 1943, and never in my life have I ever
seen anything such as this."

Somewhat later, at 11:50 A.M., a crew of technicians saw a white-aluminum
object with a distinct oval outline descending and moving against wind. Then
at noon, an air force major at the field saw a thin metallic object climb, oscil-
late over the field, dive down to ground level, and rise again. The event was
simultaneously observed by a test pilot (a captain) at Rodgers Dry Lake, a
secret test base. The final sighting occurred as an F-51 pilot saw a flat object
"of light-reflecting nature" pass over his plane. There were no known aircraft
in the area at that time.

Over fifty years later, the public explanation of the sightings—"probably"
research balloons—remains not credible. Balloons are incapable of 300 mph
speed and the tight circles reported. The Muroc incident continues to provide
evidence for military knowledge, interest, and secrecy regarding UFOs.[32]

ENTER THE FBI

On July 9, 1947, the day that Roswell debris probably arrived at Wright
Field, Brig. Gen. George F. Schulgen, chief of the Requirements Intelligence
Branch of the Army Air Force Intelligence, requested FBI assistance in the
problem of the flying discs. Army intelligence claimed the objects were not
army and navy craft.[33] The next day, July 10, an FBI memo titled "Flying
Discs" sent in the request, suggesting the discs could be a "communist-
inspired plan to induce mass hysteria." Appended to the memo were
comments by Assistant Director David M. Ladd, Clyde Tolson, and Hoover.
Ladd recommended that the bureau not assist, since many sightings were
found to be "pranks." Tolson wrote, "I think we should do this." Hoover
wrote, "I would do it, but before agreeing to it we must insist upon full access

to discs recovered. For instance, in the La. case the army grabbed it and would not let us have it for cursory examination."[34]

The location of "La" has never been certain. Fawcett and Greenwood attributed the reference to a Blue Book case of July 7, from Shreveport, Louisiana (La.), which involved a hoaxed flying saucer (a sixteen-inch aluminum disc with the inscription "Made in USA"). Another researcher offered the possibility of the town Laborcita in New Mexico. That town sits on the main Highway 28 near the intersection with Highway 380, which leads to White Sands Proving Grounds and then to Roswell. The distance to Roswell, however, is over 150 miles, making a Roswell connection appear unlikely.[35]

By the end of July, Schulgen assured Hoover that the FBI would have full access to any crashed discs. There was no hint that the discs were anything other than of terrestrial manufacture. On July 30, Hoover agreed to give full FBI cooperation in the investigation of flying discs. His main concern seems to have been that the discs might be made by subversive individuals, or those "desirous of seeking personal publicity, causing hysteria, or playing a prank."[36]

Even before Hoover's formal approval, the FBI interviewed many prominent UFO witnesses, including E. J. Smith and Kenneth Arnold. By the end of July, the FBI/Army Intelligence Report concluded:

(a) This "flying saucer" situation is not all imaginary or seeing too much in some natural phenomena. Something is really flying around. (b) Lack of topside inquiries, when compared to the prompt and demanding inquiries that have originated topside upon former events [such as the Swedish ghost rockets of 1946], give more than ordinary weight to the possibility that this is a domestic project about which the President, etc., know.[37]

We may ask what domestic project would account for the wave of 1947, but come up empty.

Throughout August, the FBI assisted the air force in investigating flying saucer sightings. The two jealous organizations had a rocky relationship. A September 3 letter from Air Defense Command Headquarters implied that the FBI was only good for "relieving the numbered air forces of the task of tracking down all the many instances which turned out to be ash can covers, toilet seats, and whatnot." The memo reached an FBI agent in San Francisco who sent it up the chain, where it soon reached Hoover. On September 27, Hoover notified the air staff assistant chief that the FBI would "discontinue all investigative activity regarding the reported sightings of flying discs." Four days later, the FBI formally ended its cooperation with the air force, although it continued to investigate UFOs.[38]

MEDIA CLAMPDOWN

These documents remained classified for nearly thirty years, unavailable for an informed public to judge. Meanwhile, people relied on newspapers and radio, which continued to ply their trade on behalf of the national security establishment. After the middle of July, flying saucers disappeared with astonishing rapidity from mainstream journalism, unless to appear as the subject of ridicule. The *New York Times* published a tongue-in-cheek editorial dismissing flying saucers, while *Life* magazine compared UFOs to the Loch Ness Monster. By now, as historian David Jacobs noted, "newspaper reporters automatically placed any witness who claimed to see something strange in the sky as in the crackpot category."

According to Ruppelt, the few members of the press who did inquire into the air force attitude toward flying saucers "got the same treatment that you would get today if you inquired about the number of thermonuclear weapons stockpiled in the U.S.'s atomic arsenal." Thus—a very important point to consider—there was no independent investigation of UFOs to compete with the military monopoly.

An August Gallup poll reported that 90 percent of the adult population had heard of flying saucers; most considered them to be illusions, hoaxes, secret weapons, or other explainable phenomena; a small number believed them to be from outer space.[39] Interesting sightings continued to occur, however, several of which involved U.S. military personnel. Sometime during the summer, a navy commander saw a disc-shaped UFO over the airport in Pittsburg, Kansas. In Media, Pennsylvania, an air force pilot reported a disc hovering and speeding away.[40]

An interesting case was related by the Signal Corps of the Alaska Communication System to the commanding general of the 4th Air Force in San Francisco. The report stated:

> Capt. Jack Peck and his copilot, Vince Daly, have stated that on August 4, 1947, they sighted and followed a flying saucer northwest of Bethel, Alaska. This object was bigger than the Douglas DC-3 they were flying, crossed their course at right angles to them. It was flying at an altitude of one thousand feet. They swung in behind it and followed it at an air speed of one hundred seventy miles per hour, but it was out of sight in four minutes. They state the object was smooth surfaced and streamlined with no visible means of propulsion whatever.

The report emphasized the excellent reputation of Captain Peck and added that "no one here doubts in the least but that he actually saw this object." The sighting report was forwarded to Air Defense Command.[41]

U.S. military personnel in Guam reported two objects—"small, crescent-shaped, and traveling at a speed twice that of a fighter plane"—flying in a zigzag motion over Harmon Field on August 14 at 10:40 A.M. The objects flew westerly at 1,200 feet and disappeared into clouds. A few seconds later, a single object, possibly one of those just seen, emerged from clouds and proceeded west.[42] Later that week, an air force major at Rapid City AFB in South Dakota saw "approximately twelve objects flying a tight diamond-shaped formation." The objects were elliptical-shaped, silent, and glowed yellow-white. The official air force evaluation: birds. On August 19, in Twin Falls, Idaho (near the sighting six days earlier), residents and police saw a group of twelve strange objects "flying in formation over the city . . . at terrific speed." The air force explained this, too, as birds.[43]

Within the higher levels of the military, there was—Ruppelt again—"confusion to the point of panic." A few senior officers in the Pentagon probably knew what was going on at ATIC. Overall, "the UFO security lid was down tight."[44]

General Schulgen was not one of those officers in the know, but wanted to be one. At the end of July he decided to make a direct request to the Air Material Command, which housed the labs and resources best able to identify the flying saucers. He prepared an "Estimate of the Situation" (not the famous Estimate of 1948), which concluded that the discs were mechanical aerial objects, and probably part of a highly classified U.S. project. Schulgen then sat on this document for a month. He sent it to Twining's office at AMC in late August, along with a request for information about flying saucers.[45] Before we consider Twining's response, we must review the Maury Island affair.

THE MAURY ISLAND SAGA

The Maury Island affair shows a singular interest by U.S. intelligence agencies in flying saucers. The most complete account about it came from Kenneth Arnold, who investigated the events and wrote about them at length in his 1952 book, *The Coming of the Saucers.*[46] The air force stated the case was a hoax, and Ruppelt concurred in his book. In the 1990s, however, several researchers began revising their conclusions about the case, based on a careful reading of Arnold's account and renewed investigations.

The incident was said to have occurred on June 21, 1947. Harold A. Dahl, a log salvager on Maury Island (situated in Puget Sound between Tacoma and Seattle) who helped the local Harbor Patrol Association, was out on the bay with his son, dog, and two crewmen. He saw six large, metallic, doughnut-shaped aircraft, about one hundred feet in diameter and two thousand feet overhead. Five objects circled around one that seemed to be in trouble and losing altitude. Dahl heard no sound, and saw no motors, propellers, or means of propulsion. The objects had large, round portholes on the outside and a dark, continuous, "observation" window toward the bottom and inside. As Dahl took three or four photographs, one craft moved toward the center, apparently to help the troubled craft. A dull explosion followed, and the troubled craft ejected a stream of light metal which "seemed like thousands of newspapers," then ejected a heavier and darker type of metal, similar to lava rock. After this, the craft lifted slowly and drifted out over the Pacific Ocean, disappearing from sight. Dahl said the heavy material damaged his boat, killed his dog, and injured the arm of his son, requiring a trip to the hospital. He described the event to a man he described as his supervisor, Fred L. Crisman, estimating that twenty tons of material had fallen.

Actually, Fred Crisman was an intelligence agent, formerly of the OSS and soon to be of the CIA, who specialized in internal "disruption" activities. This fact was unknown for many years, then suspected, then finally proven with the discovery of certain CIA documents. More on that in a moment.

Dahl also claimed that the next morning an ordinary-looking man in a black suit arrived at his house and invited him to breakfast. This was not as unusual as it might seem. Many lumber buyers called on people in Dahl's business to buy salvaged logs. Dahl followed him to a diner, ordered breakfast, and listened in astonishment as the man related Dahl's entire experience from the day before, all in precise detail. "What I have said is proof to you," said the man, "that I know a great deal more about this experience of yours than you will want to believe." He warned Dahl not to discuss the experience. Dahl considered the man to be a crackpot and mailed some fragments to Raymond Palmer, a Chicago publisher of the paranormal.

Around July 22, 1947, Palmer wrote to Kenneth Arnold, mentioning the Maury Island case, and asked whether Arnold would look into it and send back some fragments. Arnold did not think Palmer was especially "cranked up." He had merely asked Arnold to check into it during one of his routine flights to the area. On July 25, two representatives of military intelligence of the Fourth Air Force, Lt. Frank M. Brown and Capt. William Davidson, visited Arnold, and told him to contact them "if anything of an unusual nature" came to his attention. Despite his growing interest, Arnold wavered on Maury Island until Palmer wired him two hundred dollars through Western Union on the twenty-seventh. It should be remembered that army intelligence was then using Western Union as part of Operation Shamrock.

On Tuesday, July 29, 1947, Arnold took off from a private cow pasture in Boise, headed for Tacoma. Only his wife knew of his exact plans. A few of his friends knew he was going but not when, and he did not file a flight plan. En route, he had another, lesser known, UFO sighting, of about twenty small objects moving at a "terrific rate of speed." Arnold took movie pictures of them, which turned out poorly, then landed at La Grande Airfield, Oregon, where he phoned aviation editor Dave Johnson about the sighting, and mentioned it to some Eastern Air Lines crew members. By dusk, he reached Tacoma and phoned around for a room. He assumed this would be difficult, as Tacoma's housing shortage made hotel rooms scarce. When he called the city's most prominent hotel, the Winthrop, he learned to his surprise that a room and bath were already reserved for "Kenneth Arnold." Who had known about his arrival, he wondered, and how?

Arnold arrived at the hotel that night and found Harold A. Dahl in the phone book. After some determined prodding by Arnold, Dahl visited Arnold that night, then took Arnold to his "secretary's" home to see some fragments, one of which served as an ashtray. Arnold said it looked like simple lava rock. No, said Dahl, this was the stuff that hit his boat, and Crisman had a box of it in his garage. The next morning, Arnold met with Dahl and Crisman, who claimed to have had an independent flying saucer sighting. Arnold asked Dahl for the photographs and Crisman for the fragments. Feeling that something was wrong but distrusting his ability to evaluate the situation, Arnold then called his friend, pilot E. J. Smith ("Smithy") who had also witnessed a flying saucer. Smith arrived that day, cross-examined Dahl and Crisman, but could not trip them up. The two investigators then decided that Smith would stay in Arnold's room, and that they would see everything the next morning, including Maury Island.

That evening, Arnold received a telephone call from Ted Morello of United Press, who informed him that some "crackpot" had been calling his office, telling him everything that had happened in Arnold's hotel room the entire day. Arnold was stunned. He initially suspected Dahl or Crisman of leaking information, until Morello quoted conversations Arnold had had with Smith when they were alone. The two spent the next hour looking for a microphone in their room.

On the morning of Thursday, July 31, Crisman and Dahl brought heavy fragments and some white metal. The lava-like pieces were unusually heavy, smooth on one side, and slightly curved. On the other side they looked as though they had been subjected to extreme heat. The white metal had square rivets as opposed to the standard round ones, but seemed normal otherwise. It did not match Dahl's original description. Regarding the photographs, Dahl said he had given the camera with its film to Crisman, who now could not find it, but would try in the afternoon.

Although Arnold smelled a hoax, he decided to call his acquaintances Brown and Davidson from Hamilton Air Force Base. Perhaps the Communists were involved, he thought. It struck Arnold as odd that Brown refused to take his call on base, and called back from an off-base phone. The two officers quickly left for Tacoma. Before their arrival, Ted Morello phoned again. His informant had been calling from a pay telephone, for about fifteen to twenty seconds each time, with the latest news that Brown and Davidson were on their way in a B-25. Dahl and Crisman were both present at the time of this call, and Morello said the voice had not changed. That would seem to rule them out as the caller. By now, Arnold and Smith were "at a point of nervous tension." Brown and Davidson arrived in the late afternoon, and the five men (Dahl had left) talked until 11 P.M., at which time Crisman offered to go home and retrieve another box of fragments. No thanks, said the officers, they were no longer interested. Anyway, they had to return for Air Force Day the next morning. Every plane on the base, including their newly overhauled B-25, had to be ready for maneuvers. Crisman, undeterred, still left to get his fragments.

One might wonder why on earth Crisman left to get more fragments when many pieces of both types were lying on the hotel room floor. He returned just in time with his new fragments, stuffed into a large cereal box, and put them into the army vehicle. Arnold thought they appeared rockier and less metallic than the other fragments, but he no longer cared. He had gotten the matter to the competent military authorities and wanted out. After Brown and Davidson left, Ted Morello called again, revealing everything that had taken place in Arnold's room, courtesy of the informant.

At 1:30 A.M., Brown and Davidson's plane exploded and crashed, some twenty minutes after taking off. Also aboard were an army hitchhiker and engineer who survived. According to their account, the two officers had loaded a heavy cardboard box. Shortly after takeoff, the left engine caught fire, the emergency fire-fighting system failed, and Brown ordered the two men to parachute. For the next ten minutes, they watched the burning plane continue to fly. The army blamed the crash on the loss of an exhaust collector ring on the left engine, but could not answer why Brown and Davidson failed to signal distress or bail out.

Arnold and Smith learned the news the next morning. Arnold called Palmer (speaking to him for the first time), and offered to refund his money. Keep the money, said Palmer, but mail me some fragments. After a visit to Morello, who warned them to leave town, the pilot-investigators took a trip to see Dahl's damaged boat and talk again with Crisman, who said "I don't know what could have happened to those pictures."

They gave up on seeing Maury Island and talked briefly with reporter Paul Lance in their hotel lobby. Lance's article appeared later that day in the *Tacoma Times* titled, "Sabotage Hinted in Crash of Army Bomber at Kelso," with the sub-headline, "Plane May Hold Flying Disc Secret." Lance wrote that the *Times's* mysterious informant had said the plane was sabotaged or shot down to prevent the shipment of flying disc fragments to Hamilton Field, California. Twelve hours before the army released the official identification, the informant correctly identified Davidson and Brown.

Dahl told Arnold and Smith that Crisman had left and would be gone "for a few days." Morello then called. His informant said that Crisman boarded an Army bomber and was flying to Alaska. It turned out that an army flight *was* leaving from Tacoma's McChord Field to Alaska, but no passenger list was available. Morello said his paper's normally excellent channels of obtaining data "drew a blank" with McChord, as did attempts to trace the informant's calls. He did confirm that the B-25 had been under military guard "every minute it was at the field." Morello told Arnold and Smith, "you're involved in something that is beyond our power here to find out anything about. . . . I'm just giving you some sound advice. Get out of this town until whatever it is blows over." Yet they remained, mistakenly assuming that military intelligence would want to speak with them. They spent the next day sitting around "like a couple of dead ducks."

Finally, on August 3, Smith reached a Major Sander of army intelligence at McChord Field. Sander came and said he was "positive" they had been victims of a hoax. Even so, he took the fragments for analysis—just to be thorough—leaving none for Arnold or Smith. Sander made the empty promise that they would know the official evaluation in two weeks. He then drove the two to a smelting lot. Arnold thought it odd that Sander knew just which road to take, and that he stopped exactly at pieces of slag similar to their own. Arnold "thought [Sander] must have been there before." From inside the car, it initially appeared that Sander had been right. But after examining the pieces, Arnold believed they looked like the material Crisman gave Davidson and Brown, not like the original fragments. Unfortunately, Sander did not allow Arnold or Smith to take out any original fragments from the truck for comparison. Thus, while Crisman and Dahl's story "did not ring completely true . . . for some reason we couldn't convince ourselves it was all as simple as the Major put it."

Still, the two pilots were relieved to be done. They checked out of the Hotel Winthrop, trying but failing to find Dahl's house one last time. Arnold then flew home to Boise and continued his efforts to reach Dahl, but could not track him down.

On August 7, 1947, the Seattle FBI office interrogated Crisman and Dahl, and soon announced the affair had been a hoax, and that the two had also been the mysterious informants. They supposedly offered Palmer their exclusive story for money—something Palmer vehemently denied. The fragments mailed by Dahl, said the FBI, were not from a flying saucer. Palmer, by the way, claimed that the fragments were stolen from his office shortly thereafter. Before they were stolen, he had sent them out for analysis. The results, he said, indicated they were neither slag nor natural rock. One may ask, why would someone break into his office to steal some slag samples, anyway?[47]

Behind the scenes, the matter was not so clearly settled. J. Edgar Hoover wrote the following week: "It would also appear that Dahl and Crisman did not admit the hoax to the army officers. . . ." In response, the FBI special agent in charge from Seattle answered:

> Please be advised that Dahl did not admit to Brown that his story was a hoax but only stated that if questioned by authorities he was going to say it was a hoax because he did not want any further trouble over the matter.[48]

Crisman is the key to this event. We now know a great deal about him, little of which was available to the early researchers. Crisman, for instance, was a member of the OSS during the war, flew fighter planes over the Pacific, and served as a liaison officer with the British RAF. Later, he wrote to Palmer's magazine that he had been hit by a "ray gun" in a cave in Burma. After the war, Crisman was supposedly discharged from the military, but actually entered a special Internal Security School. There is evidence linking him to Project Paperclip shortly before the Maury Island affair. Then, sometime around the Maury Island incident, he was brought to the newly formed CIA as an "extended agent" specializing in internal disruption activities. During the Korean War, he sent secret reports to the CIA regarding military officers, and later did the same regarding company officials while working for Boeing. New Orleans District Attorney Jim Garrison, while reinvestigating the Kennedy assassination, subpoenaed Crisman (who denied to a grand jury that he was any kind of agent). Crisman was closely connected to Clay Shaw, Garrison's main target. Shaw, like Crisman, was a member of the OSS and had many ties to the murky world of intelligence and crime. It was later suggested—in the 95th Congress at the Hearings Before the Select Committee on Assassinations—that Crisman was one of the three tramps at Dealy Plaza.[49]

UFO researchers from Ruppelt to Jacobs to Clark have dismissed the Maury Island incident as a hoax. The standard line is that Crisman and Dahl, under interrogation, had confessed that they made up the whole story in hopes of selling it to Palmer.[50] But this is based primarily on statements obtained by the FBI which show all the signs of having been coerced (or otherwise strongly encouraged). Moreover, this assessment does not take into account Crisman's history with the CIA.

That a CIA agent was pulling some strings regarding the Maury Island incident changes the complexion of the case entirely. Note that Crisman ended up with nearly all the material Dahl found, that he switched it with old scrap to present to Brown and Davidson, and that he obfuscated during the entire time Arnold was in Tacoma. If this were a hoax, what kind of hoax was he pulling, and why would a CIA agent be doing it? Might it be more probable that Crisman's job was to maintain control over a real event?

In addition to focusing on Crisman, we are bound to ask other questions. First, who was spying on Kenneth Arnold? Several organizations could have done this, but the one with the easiest means to do so was the Army Signal Security Agency (the precursor to the National Security Agency). Shamrock was already in place and theoretically could have been used to follow Arnold through a combination of telephone taps, bugs, and personal surveillance. The FBI is another candidate. It had, after all, interviewed both Arnold and Smith in mid-July, and also engaged in the necessary illegal activities.

Who was the mysterious informant? If we believe Morello, that the voice never changed, then Crisman and Dahl must be ruled out. The informant immediately knew about the flight of Brown and Davidson to Tacoma. How could this have been Dahl or Crisman, when both were with Arnold during the call from Morello? And how did the informant know about the particulars of Brown and Davidson's death? A military informant, perhaps someone from within McChord, seems most likely.

The Maury Island incident shows all signs of being investigated by multiple agencies (CIA, FBI, army, and private individuals) with competing motives. Poor Brown and Davidson stumbled into this mess and never made it out. Paul Lance may also have been a victim. Almost immediately after writing the key article on Maury Island, he died in mid-August 1947. Arnold stated years later that "the cause of his death was not clear. It was laid to meningitis, but this should have been easy to establish. However, he lay on a slab in the morgue for about thirty-six hours while the pathologists apparently hemmed and hawed."[51] Arnold himself described what appeared to be dangerous tinkering with his aircraft upon leaving Maury Island for home. Had he not noticed this, he said, he could easily have crashed.

Two more interesting facts bear comment. First, an internal FBI memo dated August 6, 1947, referred to one of the men who died in the B-25 crash as a "CIC Agent." That is, Counter Intelligence Corps, the job of which was to examine and counter enemy (or possible enemy) intelligence. Recall that Brown and Davidson had visited Arnold a week earlier, asking him to send along any new UFO information he collected. Thus, someone charged the CIC with collecting UFO reports. Right from the beginning, UFOs were handled within the classified world—quite logically, one might add—as potentially hostile.[52]

Second, the executive summary of the 1994 air force report on Roswell divulges something with possible relevance to this case. The air force author was refuting Vandenberg's involvement in the Roswell crash by referring to allegations that he was near Roswell on July 7. In fact, claimed the air force, Vandenberg was involved in a "flying disc" incident at that time, but not at Roswell. (Air Force General Nathan Twining, of course, was near Roswell, a fact discussed earlier in this book.) Rather, he was busy with an incident that "involved Ellington Field, Texas, and the Spokane (Washington) Depot." Vandenberg, in other words, was checking into an event that had presumably occurred earlier, and involved the state of Washington (albeit on the other side of the state). This might be a reference to a different event, but the next remark is suggestive of official comments concerning Maury Island: "after much discussion and information gathering on this incident, it was learned to be a hoax." At the very least, Vandenberg's role as a secret investigator of UFO reports speaks volumes about the perceived importance of this topic to the people at the top.[53]

Unfortunately, Kenneth Arnold was out of his depth in this investigation. He was an honest and intelligent man (he later was a candidate for lieutenant governor of Idaho). But Arnold failed to check into the basic starting points of inquiry, such as Maury Island itself, the alleged witnesses who accompanied Dahl, Dahl's son, the doctor who allegedly treated his arm, or the story about Dahl's dog. Arnold's preoccupation with finding the boat blinded him from pursuing more fruitful avenues of investigation.

Arnold distrusted Fred Crisman (a sign of good instincts), but he seems to have believed Dahl to be sincere, if slow-witted and phlegmatic. Could Dahl have been telling the truth? The description Dahl gave to Arnold of his sighting at Maury Island happens to coincide with the description of a UFO event that took place in Brazil in the 1950s. Such a similarity does not automatically validate the sighting, but it remains possible that Harold Dahl saw what he claimed to see. For many years after, Dahl lived in the state of Washington as a "self-employed surplus dealer," quietly out of the public view. According to 1990s Maury Island researcher Ken Thomas, he maintained to the end that the event had been real. Harold Dahl died in 1982 at the age of seventy.[54]

NATIONAL SECURITY REORGANIZATION

Amid the flying saucer mayhem, the U.S. government passed the National Security Act on July 26, 1947. This created a unified National Military Establishment (NME), a National Security Council (NSC) and a Central Intelligence Agency (CIA). The reorganization had been in the making for several years. The investment of time was not wasted—at least from the perspective of the policymaking elite—as the Act was, by far, the century's most significant overhaul of the country's national security apparatus. It unified the armed services under the authority of a Secretary of Defense, and scrapped the old, more honest, title of Secretary of War. James Vincent Forrestal, former Secretary of the Navy, became the nation's first SecDef.

Forrestal himself had done much to sabotage the authority of the new position. As navy secretary, he favored continued independence of that service. Largely due to his efforts, each service secretary—the army, the navy, and the newly established air force—gained the right to appeal to the president regarding crucial issues, such as budget allotments. The Act therefore exacerbated interservice rivalries. Forrestal wanted a coordinating, not executive, role for the position of Secretary of Defense. To his eventual chagrin, he now acquired it.[55]

The National Security Act also established a Central Intelligence Agency. It prohibited the CIA from any "internal security functions," that is, from spying operations in the United States. But it contained a huge loophole (written by future DCI Allen Dulles) enabling the CIA "to perform such other functions and duties related to intelligence affecting the national security as the

National Security Council may from time to time direct." This quickly translated into carte blanche to carry out nearly any mission it wished, wherever it
wanted, without scrutiny from Congress or, when necessary, the president.

Although the CIA still had no operational spending authority, this was
quickly overcome through a variety of subterranean enterprises conducted
globally. Intelligence agencies need money, and lots of it. If one wishes to raise
private armies for secret wars around the world, or remove intractable
national leaders determined to forge policies independent of U.S. wishes, then
huge amounts of money become a necessity. Initially, much of the CIA's
money seems to have come from wealthy Americans. (As future CIA Operations Chief Frank Wisner put it, in obtaining money for secret ventures "it is
essential to secure the overt cooperation of people with conspicuous access to
wealth in their own right," in other words, people who are rich.)[56] Soon,
however, the CIA's money came from two basic sources: Congress (e.g., legitimate taxes, classified amounts of which were distributed to the agency) and
its ever-growing number of private ventures, not all of which, to put the matter mildly, were legal.

THE TWINING LETTER

By this time, Schulgen's letter had reached the desk of Gen. Nathan Twining, head of Air Material Command (AMC). On September 23, 1947,
Twining wrote a classified, now famous, letter regarding the flying discs. He
noted that the discs were "real and not visionary or fictitious." They may possibly be natural phenomena, he wrote, such as meteors. But:

> the reported operating characteristics such as extreme rates of climb, maneuver-
> ability (particularly in roll), and action which must be considered evasive when
> sighted . . . lend belief to the possibility that some of the objects are controlled
> either manually, automatically, or remotely.

He went on to list the common descriptions of the objects:

> (1) Metallic or light-reflecting surface; (2) Absence of trail, except in a few
> instances when the object apparently was operating under high performance
> conditions; (3) Circular or elliptical in shape, flat on bottom and domed on top;
> (4) Several reports of well-kept formation flights varying from three to nine
> objects; (5) Normally no associated sound, except in three instances a substantial
> rumbling roar was noted; (6) Level flight speeds normally above 300 knots are
> estimated.[57]

Twining recommended that Air Force Headquarters "issue a directive
assigning a priority, security classification and code name for a detailed
study of this matter." He also ordered that the best UFO reports be

sent to the following places: the Joint Research and Development Board; the Office of Scientific Research and Development; the National Advisory Committee on Aeronautics; and the Atomic Energy Commission. Each of these offices had strong links with Vannevar Bush.

Twining's letter stated that no wreckage of a flying disc had been recovered. This point has been used by some skeptics as evidence against the reality of the Roswell crash. Here was Twining, head of an organization that *would* be in a position to know, and who was right next door to Roswell in early July, saying it did not happen. This is one possibility, although it contains its own problems. It assumes that the branches of the American military, the American intelligence community, and the American government somehow acted seamlessly together toward a common goal. Frequently, they did not. Twining may not have told Schulgen all he knew. If, for example, a UFO had been recovered, Twining would have had good cause to state exactly the opposite. Any project to gather UFO data would have to function on a need-to-know basis. Writing about crashed discs would not exactly help the cause of secrecy, and therefore control over the problem. Twining might have been telling all he knew, *or not*. The researcher must decide which alternative is more likely, based upon the available facts.

Twining did state that UFOs were *not* secret American craft. This came as a surprise to Schulgen, who expected the reply that there was nothing to the affair, that everything was under control. Instead, Twining wrote that the phenomenon was unexplained and warranted further study. Again, one might ask whether he was hiding the fact that UFOs really were U.S. experimental craft. Fifty years later, the answer clearly is no. The U.S. had no craft in 1947, experimental or otherwise, that could duplicate the reported maneuvers of flying saucers. When Twining wrote his letter, Chuck Yeager had not yet broken the sound barrier (he did it the next month at Muroc Field). Why would Twining tell Schulgen to keep studying flying saucers if they were simply classified American craft? If there were good reasons for doing so, none have emerged.[58]

Twining's letter, a crucial document in UFO policy, received no official acknowledgment for twenty years. Yet, because of it, the air force soon created its first formal UFO investigatory body, Project Sign.

MJ-12: YES OR NO?

We now enter a topic as rancorous and disputed as the Roswell controversy. In December 1984, filmmaker Jaime Shandera received an unmarked package in the mail, containing an undeveloped roll of film. Along with his friend, UFO researcher William Moore, the two had the film developed. The photographs were of documents that looked like a secret briefing paper for then-president-elect Dwight Eisenhower, dated November 18, 1952.

The documents stated that flying saucers were the product of an extraterrestrial civilization, that several flying saucers had crashed (including at Roswell) and come into the possession of the U.S. government, and that the U.S. had one of the aliens in custody for some time before it died. The documents claimed that President Truman had established a top secret control group to deal with the UFO problem, called MJ-12, on September 24, 1947. The group's original members were CIA Director Adm. Roscoe Hillenkoetter, Dr. Vannevar Bush, Secretary of Defense James Forrestal, Gen. Nathan Twining, Gen. Hoyt Vandenberg, Dr. Detlev Bronk, Dr. Jerome Hunsaker, Sidney Souers, Gordon Gray, Dr. Donald Menzel, Gen. Robert Montague, and Dr. Lloyd Berkner. Included was a memorandum from President Truman, addressed to James Forrestal, which established the group. It was dated September 24, 1947, and stamped "TOP SECRET" and "EYES ONLY." It read as follows:

Memorandum for the Secretary of Defense

Dear Secretary Forrestal:

As per our recent conversation on this matter, you are hereby authorized to proceed with all due speed and caution upon your undertaking. Hereafter this matter shall be referred to only as Operation Majestic Twelve.

It continues to be my feeling that any future considerations relative to the ultimate disposition of this matter should rest solely with the Office of the President following appropriate discussions with yourself, Dr. Bush, and the Director of Central Intelligence.

[signed] Harry Truman

It is not known with certainty who sent the film, but the strongest evidence points to members of the U.S. intelligence community, specifically ten or so individuals from the air force Office of Special Investigations (AFOSI) at Kirtland AFB. In his UFO research, William Moore had already been in contact with several intelligence people at the base, including Master Sergeant Richard Doty, a special agent with OSI. This group informed Moore that they opposed UFO secrecy, and would assist him in his research by leading him to key documents. Unfortunately, the group members were skilled disinformation and psy-ops specialists, a fact that throws the legitimacy of the documents into doubt.

Few have denied that the documents look impressive. They looked authentic enough to get the attention of many who would be in a position to know. Former CIA Chief of Operations Richard Bissell, for example, commented,

"The document certainly looks authentic. On the basis of the material you have sent me, I personally have little doubt that it is authentic." Others who seem to concur are former Truman administrative assistant David Stowe and former National Security Council planning and board member Robert R. Bowie.[59] Even Roswell debunker Kal Korff was surprisingly easygoing on the MJ-12 documents. At best, he said, there was only *circumstantial* evidence supporting their authenticity. Not a ringing endorsement, but certainly not a definitive refutation, either.[60]

Research on the documents proved very interesting. Moore enlisted the help of Stanton Friedman, who spent many hours at the Truman and Eisenhower libraries, checking dates and other relevant information. Friedman learned quite a lot. First, that the Truman library archives confirmed that September 24, 1947, happened to be the only day that Truman and Vannevar Bush met between May and December. Forrestal was also present at the meeting, and had met with Bush for a half hour beforehand (Friedman believed this was when the two prepared the memorandum.) As for the meeting with Truman, there were "no indications in the archives to say what was discussed." Friedman also found supporting information for the other key date, November 18, 1952. On that day, Eisenhower received a forty-three-minute national security briefing on matters that are still classified, during which Gen. Nathan Twining was present.[61]

The Eisenhower briefing documents appear to have been prepared on an R. C. Allen machine, which was manufactured in the 1940s. The typewriter and typeface used for the Truman memorandum is a matter of dispute. Friedman argued that it was prepared on a Remington P4 from the 1940s, a machine also used by Bush for his memoranda. This reinforced Friedman's belief that Bush prepared the memorandum. Other typewriter experts have suggested the memorandum was prepared using either a Ransmayer and Rodrian 664 (no manufacture dates offered) or an Underwood UP3A, which was manufactured from 1933 until 1946. Kevin Randle, who argued strenuously against the authenticity of the MJ-12 documents, spoke to an expert who believed the memo typeface was most consistent with a Smith Corona P102 (a "slam dunk," said the expert), which was used on typewriters only after 1966. Randle challenged Friedman, Moore, and Shandera to produce their experts, which they did not do, and which led him to charge that the experts probably never existed.[62]

An especially controversial point about the document was its mention of Harvard astronomer Donald Menzel as a member of MJ-12. For decades, Menzel was the world's leading UFO debunker. Could Menzel really have belonged to a group like MJ-12? It seemed like a bad joke. To the surprise of all, however, Friedman soon learned that Menzel was closely tied to the American intelligence community as a cryptologist, and had a long-standing association with the National Security Agency (NSA). A 1960 letter from Menzel to President-elect John F. Kennedy mentioned his Top Secret clearance and "some association" with the CIA. In the 1970s Menzel wrote that he "was a consultant with Top Secret Ultra Clearance to the National Security Agency."[63] Menzel and Vannevar Bush were also friends from the early days of the war. Randle argued that these discoveries proved nothing, as "almost any scientist who was alive and working during the early 1940s was probably involved in some sort of work for the government." But this misses Friedman's point that Menzel was at the top of that power pyramid.

Many people, including UFO debunker Philip Klass, criticized the dating style of the documents, such as "07 July, 1947," which was never a standard military format. Neither the comma nor the initial zero should have been included, and certainly not for a presidential briefing paper to a five-star general. Klass also discovered that the style of dating happened to be a type used by Moore himself in several letters to Klass! That would seem to clinch it, except that (a) Moore also used several other dating styles, and (b) Friedman found a wide range of dating styles in the archives, including the day, month, comma, year format. Moreover, the format was common in France, where Hillenkoetter had served for some time. Friedman also emphasized that dating formats of the time were not set in stone. His opponents, such as Joe Nickell and John F. Fischer, countered that no one has found any other documents, whether from Hillenkoetter or anyone else, containing the extra zero *combined with* the anomalous comma.[64]

Friedman brought the MJ-12 documents, along with about twenty other documents written by Hillenkoetter, to a notable linguist, Dr. Roger W. Wescott of Drew University. Wescott said there was no compelling reason to regard any of these communications as fraudulent or to believe that any of them were written by anyone other than Hillenkoetter himself. That statement holds for the controversial presidential briefing memorandum of November 18, 1952.

Randle countered that Wescott's expertise was in linguistics, not in the examination of questioned documents. Indeed, Wescott later realized he had stepped into "a hornet's nest" and stated that, while he thought its fraudulence unproved, he "could equally well have maintained that its authenticity is unproved."[65]

The main argument against the documents' authenticity, and the one which swayed most UFO researchers, concerned Truman's signature. Klass found that it matched a letter in the Truman archives: a xeroxed letter written by Truman to Bush on October 1, 1947. Thus, it appeared that the forger simply tacked a real signature on to a fake letter. The discovery of tampering was enough to turn most seasoned researchers away.

Surprisingly, not everyone was persuaded that this meant the documents were faked. In the first place, the identical signature was found on a copy of a document addressed to, of all people, Vannevar Bush. A careful study of the

UFOs and the National Security State

signatures shows the MJ-12 signature to be much stronger than the copy it supposedly came from (the signature on Truman's letter to Bush is thin and broken in places). If the MJ-12 signature was forged or copied, how could it have come from the document found by Klass (the original of which, incidentally, has never been found)? It may be that both signatures are from the same missing source.

Where could the original signature be? If the MJ-12 memorandum were legitimate, it would have gone to Forrestal, to whom it was addressed. It is plausible that Bush, as the other person attending the meeting, had an unsigned copy of the memorandum. By the time of the 1952 briefing, however, Forrestal was long dead, and the original memorandum might have been unavailable. Bush might have been asked to submit his copy, along with an original signature of Truman's. He could logically have used his letter of October 1, 1947.[66]

If the above scenario seems far-fetched, consider the hoax alternative. In all likelihood the hoaxer, such as Doty or others at AFOSI, would have had to have access to the original signature of the 10/1/47 letter from Truman to Bush, either in Bush's possession or elsewhere. No evidence to that effect has ever turned up. The hoaxer would also have had to know about the precise schedules of Forrestal, Bush, and Truman, or else have made some very lucky guesses.

Friedman, whatever else one could say about him, was a man who did his homework. He countered that the signature on the Truman memorandum was *not* an exact match with the one on the document addressed to Vannevar Bush. The height-width ratios of the letters are (ever so) slightly different. Also, was it realistic to expect that Truman, who signed thousands upon thousands of documents, should not be found to have many close matches? With these and other counterarguments, the debate continued.

After such a prolonged controversy, most UFO researchers have concluded the MJ-12 documents are fake. There is no provenance for the documents, they contain many questionable elements, and the likely sources (Moore, Doty, AFOSI) do not inspire confidence. Assuming this is true, it still remains unclear how someone not from Truman's inner circle of power would have known some of the information contained within the documents. And of course it is worth asking, why fake them? For profit? (If so, whose?) Dissimulation? A joke?

Regardless of the veracity of the MJ-12 documents themselves, evidence has surfaced to justify the belief that an organization *something like MJ-12* did exist. Such evidence is presented at various points in this book.

A brief word about another document in the MJ-12 controversy: the Cutler-Twining Memo. In 1985, Friedman learned about the impending declassification of some materials of possible interest at the Modern Military Branch of the National Archives. He soon found several Top Secret UFO documents, including one dealing with the 1955 sighting by Sen. Richard Russell. He notified Moore and Shandera about the archives, and they flew to Washington. Recently, the two had been receiving odd postcards, one of which included the return address of "Box 189, Addis Ababa, Ethiopia." Within a few days, they had gone through over a hundred boxes and found about seventy-five pages that looked worthwhile. Shandera then found a piece of paper between two files in Box 189. The document was a July 14, 1954, memo from Robert Cutler, special assistant to President Eisenhower, addressed to Gen. Nathan Twining. It read:

> Memorandum for General Twining. Subject: NSC/MJ-12 Special Studies Project. The President has decided that the MJ-12 SSP briefing should take place *during* the already scheduled White House meeting of July 16, rather than following it as previously intended. More precise arrangements will be explained to you upon arrival. Please alter your plans accordingly. Your concurrence in the above change of arrangements is assumed. Robert Cutler, Special Assistant to the President.

The memo was a carbon copy in blue ink on old onionskin, watermarked paper. It had a red pencil mark through the security marking in the upper right corner. The watermark of the paper indicated the company name, Fox Paper, which (it was learned) manufactured this type of paper only between 1953 and the early 1970s. Moreover, the paper was not available by retail, but sold only to major customers, in particular, the government. Regarding the memo itself, the language, style, format, and typeface closely matched with other memos by Cutler.

Critics pointed out several problems. First, the document was unsigned, prompting UFO researcher Barry Greenwood to argue that the memo could have been faked, then planted in the newly available archives. The hoaxer could then have ordered a copy of the document from the National Archives, which would carry the official declassification stamp. Friedman said this was an impossibility, "given how archives operate." Besides, he said, it was discovered that Cutler was in Europe at the time of the memo, and therefore obviously could not sign it. As to why he might allow an unsigned memo to leave his desk, Cutler had left explicit instructions prior to his departure to Europe to James Lay (executive secretary of the NSC) and Lay's associate, J. Patrick Coyne, to "keep things moving *out* of my basket."[67]

Another problem was that the pica typeface seemed wrong. UFO debunker Philip Klass actually challenged Friedman to produce authentic White House letters or memos by Cutler or Lay between 1953 and 1955 which used a typeface identical in size and style to the Cutler-Twining memo. Klass offered Friedman $100 for each verified document, to a maximum of $1,000. Friedman immediately found and mailed twenty, then another fourteen the following month. He received his $1,000.

For most researchers, the clincher was the statement by the Military Archives Division, which issued a ten-point list of problems with the memo in an official letter dated July 22, 1987. Some of these points were closely related, but essentially they were: the document was not correctly filed; no government researcher was able to find any other information on MJ-12; the classification "Top Secret Restricted Information" (marked on the document) did not come into use at the NSC until the Nixon administration; the memo did not bear an official government letterhead or watermark, nor did it match the paper Cutler used at the time; no records were found of an NSC meeting on July 16, 1954; a search of NSC Meeting Minutes from July 1954 did not uncover any mention of MJ-12 or Majestic; another memo was found which indicated that NSC members would be called to a civil defense exercise on July 16, 1954; the Eisenhower Library found no entry in President Eisenhower's appointment books containing an entry for a special meeting on that date which might have included a briefing on MJ-12.[68]

Friedman had answers to these, as well. For example, the statement that the memo's watermark and paper differed from what Cutler used, he argued, was based on a limited sampling. After Friedman pointed out a number of copies done on onionskin paper with differing watermarks, the Division changed its statement. Regarding the assertion that there were no NSC meetings on July 16, 1954, Friedman replied that the memo did not specify that the briefing would take place during an NSC meeting, but an "already scheduled meeting." And so on.[69]

Despite the attacks from what might be called "mainstream" ufology, Friedman has retained many loyal defenders. For years, the situation has been reminiscent of a disputed boxing title, with both groups claiming to be the legitimate arbiter of evidence. No definitive resolution appears likely soon, regarding either MJ-12 or the Cutler-Twining memo.

SOVIET OR SOMETHING ELSE?

By late fall of 1947, the question "do UFOs exist?" was not at issue to analysts at ATIC. Nor were they expecting natural phenomena to explain the mystery. It was clear that objects were being seen, that they appeared to be of exceptional technological sophistication, and that their movements indicated intelligent control. The question was, "who do they belong to?"

As if to reinforce the immediacy of the problem, two cigar-shaped UFOs were seen near Dayton, Ohio, on October 20—very close to Wright-Patterson AFB and ATIC, where the air force's UFO investigation was centered. The air force comments on the sighting were as follows:

Impossible to draw definite conclusions. Extremely unlikely they were fireballs, but if one were to stretch the description to its very limits and make allowances for untrained observers, he could say the cigarlike shape might have been an illusion caused by rapid motion. . . . This investigator does not prefer that interpretation, and it should be resorted to only if all other possible explanations fail.[70]

That became the official explanation.

On October 28, Brigadier General Schulgen, chief of the air force's Air Intelligence Requirements Division wrote a five-page report based on a summary of flying saucer characteristics supplied him by Twining's letter from the previous month. Schulgen's report, titled "Draft of Collection Memorandum," listed what he called the "current intelligence requirements in the field of flying saucer type aircraft." Taken together with Twining's letter and the rest of the year's documentation, it shows that America's military leaders considered UFOs to be something extraordinary and a matter of great national security.[71]

The memo revealed many details about UFOs as seen by military personnel. It noted that "flying saucer" type aircraft had been reported "by many observers from widely scattered places, such as the United States, Alaska, Canada, Hungary, the Island of Guam, and Japan. This object has been reported by many competent observers, including USAF rated officers. Sightings have been made from the ground as well as from the air." The performance characteristics were described much as Twining described them in September, only in much greater detail:

(a) Relatively flat bottom with extreme light-reflecting ability; (b) absence of sound except for an occasional roar when operating under superperformance conditions; (c) extreme maneuverability and apparent ability to almost hover; (d) a plan form approximating that of an oval or disc with a dome shape on the top surface; (e) the absence of an exhaust trail except in a few instances when it was reported to have a bluish color, like a diesel exhaust, which persisted for approximately one hour. Other reports indicated a brownish smoke trail that could be the results of a special catalyst or chemical agent for extra power; (f) the ability to quickly disappear by high speed or by complete disintegration; (g) the ability to suddenly appear without warning as if from an extremely high altitude; (h) the size most reported approximated that of a C-54 or Constellation type aircraft; (i) the ability to group together very quickly in a tight formation when more than one aircraft are together; (j) evasive action ability indicates possibility of being manually operated, or possibly by electronic or remote control devices; (k) under certain power conditions, the craft seems to have the ability to cut a clear path through clouds—width of path estimated to be approximately one-half mile. Only one incident indicated this phenomenon.

Schulgen's memo, which surfaced in 1985, contained a paragraph implying credence in the extraterrestrial hypothesis:

While there remains a possibility of Russian manufacture, based upon the perspective thinking and actual accomplishments of the Germans, it is the considered opinion of some elements that the object may in fact represent an interplanetary craft of some kind. . . . The presence of an unconventional or unusual type of propulsion system cannot be ruled out and should be considered of great interest.

During the late 1990s, UFO researcher Robert Todd obtained a fresh copy of the Schulgen memo which did not contain the above paragraph. Instead, that passage read as follows:

This strange object, or phenomenon, may be considered, in view of certain observations, as long-range aircraft capable of a high rate of climb, high cruising speed (possibly subsonic at all times) and highly maneuverable and capable of being flown in very tight formation. For the purpose of analysis and evaluation of the so-called "flying saucer" phenomenon, the object sighted is being assumed to be a manned aircraft, of Russian origin, and based on the perspective thinking and actual accomplishments of the Germans.

Rather different from considering the ET hypothesis, leading the UFO research community to declare the original to be a fake. The authentic memo, while not considering the extraterrestrial hypothesis, gives great detail about the objects seen, and leaves no doubt that they were truly extraordinary, as this description shows:

Construction
(a) Type of material, whether metal, ferrous, non-ferrous or nonmetallic;
(b) Composite or sandwich construction utilizing various combinations of metals, metallic foils, plastics, and perhaps balsa wood or similar material;
(c) Unusual fabrication methods to achieve extreme light weight and structural stability.

Arrangement
(a) Special provisions such as retractable domes to provide unusual observation for the pilot and crew members; (b) Unusual features or provisions regarding the opening and closing of doors.

Landing Gear
(a) Indicate type of landing gear—whether conventional, tricycle, multiple wheel, etc. or of an unconventional type such as tripod or skid.

Powerplant
(a) (3) Nuclear propulsion (atomic energy). Atomic energy engines would probably be unlike any family type of engine, although atomic energy might be employed in combination with any of the above types (piston, jet). Aircraft would be characterized by lack of fuel systems and fuel storage space.
(b) The powerplant would likely be an integral part of the aircraft and possibly not distinguishable as an item separate from the aircraft.

Schulgen's thinking was that the Soviets could well be behind the UFO mystery. He analyzed at great length the possibilities of Soviet manufacture of a German flying wing design from the recent war, in particular, the work of the Horten brothers, whose work was under contract to the Luftwaffe. Immediately following the memo, American military investigators followed up to check on the Horten brothers and any other European leads that might point to the Soviet manufacture of flying saucers. By December, both brothers were found, along with a number of other leading-edge German aviation experts, but after extensive questioning, the Americans found nothing to connect the Soviets—or anyone else, for that matter—to the flying saucer phenomenon. Schulgen's speculations had seemingly reached a dead end.[72]

The same dead end appears to have been reached at ATIC, which was studying recent German aeronautical research, assisted in large measure by the presence of German aviation experts at Wright Field. The aerodynamicists at ATIC, Wright Field's Aircraft Laboratory, and the Aeromedical Laboratory of the air force concluded that (1) no known aircraft could do what UFOs were reported to be doing; (2) even if such an aircraft could be built, the human body could not survive the violent maneuvers that were reported; and (3) no known material could withstand the loads of the reported maneuvers, nor the heat caused by the high speeds. For this reason, a certain significant number of analysts (we do not know how many) believed it probable that flying saucers were interplanetary. The evidence seemed to rule out everything else. A memo from this period asked, "Why couldn't these people, whoever they might be, stand these horrible maneuver forces? Why judge them by earthly standards?"[73]

ESTABLISHING PROJECT SIGN

By the end of 1947, ATIC had received 156 UFO reports and was settling down to a routine of studying reports of flying saucers. On December 30, 1947, the air force established the Project Sign. Known to the public as Project Saucer, Sign's role was to serve as the official air force investigation of UFOs. As we have seen, investigating such things was not a new activity, but Sign gave flying saucers an official status within the military bureaucracy. Studies continued to be centered at Wright Field under the auspices of ATIC. The project carried a 2A restricted classification (1A being the highest), but the memorandum creating Sign stated that, when necessary, higher security classifications could be applied. Sign's function was to:

> collect, collate, evaluate, and distribute to interested government agencies and contractors all information concerning sightings and phenomena in the atmosphere which can be construed to be of concern to the national security.[74]

Throughout these first few years of ATIC's investigation of UFOs, percentages of unknowns remained fairly high, usually between 15 and 20 percent. In later years, as we shall see, the air force systematically cooked the books, reducing unidentifieds by explanatory methods that were absurd. In the early period, some analysts took their task more seriously. Ruppelt explained the standards that would qualify a sighting as unknown:

> the observer was not affected by any determinable psychological quirks and that after an exhaustive investigation the object that was reported could not be identified. To be classed as an unknown, a UFO report also had to be "good," meaning that it had to come from a competent observer and had to contain a reasonable amount of data.[75]

The rigorous screening of reports helped to account for the relatively high percentage of unknowns, despite the many official "explanations" that strained the limits of credulity. And with such a high percentage, it is small wonder that military secrecy and deception were paramount to handling the UFO problem.

But the investigation of flying saucers did not begin and end at ATIC. The army and navy were both receiving UFO reports; by no means did all of them end up for study at Wright Field. Where were the reports going? At least some UFO reports were going into CIA files as early as 1948. Years later, Hillenkoetter told Donald Keyhoe that the CIA began at this time to keep "a close watch" on the UFO problem, and even on the air force investigation.[76]

Publicly, talk about flying saucers was in the opposite vein. Air force officials continued to deny any serious interest in flying saucers. Academia and the media helped out. In late December 1947, astronomer C. C. Wylie, at an AAAS conference, suggested that flying saucers were an example of national mass hysteria. Press ridicule of UFOs remained intense, and newspaper articles that printed UFO reports were scarce. Yet, it often happened that when a reporter went out to interview someone who had seen a UFO, military intelligence agents had been there first and gotten the story, complete with sketches. Many people had apparently been warned not to talk too much.[77]

By the end of 1947, the discrepancy between truth and *official truth* in the matter of UFOs had already become a wide gulf. Over the years, it would become wider.

Chapter 3

Managing the Problem: 1948 to 1951

All evidence and analysis indicate that reports of unidentified flying objects are the result of (1) misinterpretation of various conventional objects; (2) a mild form of mass hysteria and war nerves; (3) individuals who fabricate such reports to perpetuate a hoax or to seek publicity; (4) psychopathological persons.

—1949 air force press release

. . . it is quite evident to the Intelligence Officers who interviewed these men that they had certainly seen some very unusual object which they could not identify but was just as certainly not any conventional type of aircraft.

—1950 CIA report

. . . inquiries in this matter should be made in such a manner as not to indicate air force interest.

—1950 air force memo on retrieving
UFO movie footage from a civilian

PROJECT SIGN BEGINS WORK

For the first half of 1948, Project Sign studied UFO reports and analyzed evidence at Wright-Patterson AFB. Many of the reported objects were domed discs or cigar-shaped, maneuvered in formation, accelerated swiftly, and made reversals in flight. The Sign team, however, never agreed fully on the nature of these reports. Factions existed, variously believing UFOs to be nonsense, foreign technology, interplanetary spaceships, public psychosis, or a fad spawned by postwar nerves. The idea that this might derive from German technology had not died out, based on an army memorandum dated January 21, 1948, which essentially repeated the thesis and verbiage of the Schulgen memo, and stressed the need to continue investigating leads that flying saucers might be Soviet in origin.[1]

On January 7, 1948, one of the earliest and most controversial UFO cases occurred in the history of the U.S. military, and ended in the death of an experienced fighter pilot. At 1:20 P.M., a large object was seen by the commanding officer and others at Godman AFB, Kentucky. Personnel described it alternatively as a bright disc-shaped object, round, and cone-shaped. The object was still visible at 2:30 P.M., when a flight of P-51s flew by the base. Capt. Thomas Mantell, the flight commander, was asked to look into it, if his mission allowed. Accompanied by two other planes, he tried to intercept the object. After climbing to fifteen thousand feet, his fellow pilots turned back because they were not equipped with oxygen. Nor was Mantell. Known to others as a cautious man, he nevertheless kept going.

At about 2:45 P.M., Mantell reported, "I have the object in sight above and ahead of me, and it appears to be moving at about half my speed or approximately 180 miles an hour." When asked to describe it, he replied, "It appears to be a metallic object, and it is of tremendous size." At about 3:15 P.M., or about thirty minutes after he first sighted the object, Mantell made his last contact with the base: "Directly ahead of me and slightly above, and is now moving at about my speed or better. I am trying to close in for a better look." He told one of the pilots that he would climb to twenty thousand feet and if no closer would abandon chase. Mantell's plane soon went into a downward spiral and crashed, almost certainly after he lost consciousness from lack of oxygen.

Mantell's description of the object was not fully declassified until 1985. Thus, the air force explanation that he had mistakenly chased the planet Venus initially went unchallenged, despite the seeming implausibility of the answer. No one in the air force seems to have believed it. The encounter, for instance, had been in the midafternoon, several hours before sunset. Also, Mantel had obviously not described a celestial object. A review of the case in late 1948 concluded, "It is apparent . . . that the object sighted . . . was not the planet Venus. Therefore, this sighting must be considered as unexplained." Note that Mantell's description of the object as a "metallic object" of "tremendous size" came well before his crash, thus presumably before a lack of oxygen would have impaired his judgment.

In 1952, the air force, under continuing media pressure about the incident, ordered Blue Book chief Edward Ruppelt to reopen the case. Ruppelt learned that beginning in late 1947, the navy had secretly been launching high-altitude photographic reconnaissance Skyhook balloons from Clinton County Air Field, in Wilmington, Ohio. The balloons were large, with a diameter of about one hundred feet, and could move along jet streams at the speeds indicated by Mantell, and often flew at sixty thousand feet or higher. Ruppelt noted that on the same day as Mantell's sighting, many witnesses in Ohio, Tennessee, and Kentucky had reported an object that could have been a balloon. He checked the weather and wind patterns for the day and concluded that Mantell's object *could* also have been a Skyhook balloon. That was good enough for the air force, which announced the balloon explanation to the public. The only nagging problem was that Ruppelt was unable definitely to establish that a balloon launch was made that day.

It is possible that the object was a Skyhook balloon, but the case has certain features which leave one wondering. Years after Ruppelt left the air force, Blue Book files indicated there were still no Skyhook plots available, although by then such plots should have long since been declassified.

Clifford Stone, a twenty-year U.S. Army veteran, has informed me that a navy colleague of his checked the Office of Naval Research for Skyhook balloon plots. The man said that ONR records indicated there was definitely no launch of a Skyhook balloon from at least January 6 to January 8, 1948, but also that probably none had been launched since late December 1947. No reason was given for the lack of precision in this matter. If true, however, it throws doubt on a likely Skyhook launch of January 7. Of course, the matter cannot be settled until someone publishes the actual records.

It is also intriguing or coincidental that one of the other UFO sightings of January 7, 1948 came from none other than Clinton Army Air Field, where Skyhook balloons were launched. From 7:20 P.M. to 7:55 P.M., base personnel with field glasses studied an object that initially looked like an aircraft in trouble. It "seemed to be pretty high in the air," appeared to change color from white to red, to hover and then move "with great speed." During rapid descents, it appeared in the form of a cone or upside-down triangle. When it climbed, it seemed to turn itself right side up. A "green mist" was seen following the object, which headed southwest rapidly and disappeared at about 7:55 p.m. It so happened that Venus did set in the southwest that evening at about that time, and the air force therefore concluded that this had caused the confusion. Seen through the Earth's lower atmosphere, Venus can create odd illusory effects. Moreover, while all of the personnel explicitly stated that the object was too bright to be a star, none of them mentioned the possibility of Venus in their report, or seemed aware of its presence. Still, the heading of Venus (245 degrees) was not exactly where the personnel placed the object (210 degrees). The precision with which base personnel noted the object's location and behavior leave just enough doubt that some other explanation might be the answer. One thing seems clear: it was not a Skyhook balloon. If nothing else, the sighting shows how complex analyzing a typical UFO report can be.[2]

During February and March, there was talk within Air Material Command about authorizing a comprehensive plan to intercept UFOs. Indeed, Col.

Howard M. McCoy, chief of intelligence for AMC, sent a proposal to Air Force Headquarters to station fighter aircraft at all bases on a continuous alert status for just this purpose. The proposal was rejected on March 3 as not feasible. In the first place, said Headquarters, the outlay of aircraft and personnel would be too great. Second, proper interception was not considered possible, "except by accident," without complete radar coverage, which was beyond the capability of the air force. Finally, Headquarters doubted the ability of air force pilots to follow up effectively from the many civilian reports that would be expected from such a scenario.[3]

On March 17 and 18, the Air Force Scientific Advisory Board met at the Pentagon for briefing and conference. Colonel McCoy was present and spoke briefly on the subject of UFOs:

> This can't be laughed off. We have over three hundred reports which haven't been publicized in the papers from very competent personnel, in many instances. . . . We are running down every report. I can't even tell you how much we would give to have one of those crash in an area so that we could recover whatever they are.[4]

McCoy's statement contains two main points of interest. First, that the subject of UFOs was serious, despite public statements to the contrary. There can be no question that McCoy was speaking the truth in this matter. Second, that no crash debris had been recovered. An interesting statement, especially considering that it was at Wright Field where alien bodies were supposedly kept, according to some defenders of the crashed disc theory. As chief of intelligence at Wright Field, McCoy would seem to be in a position to know whether or not such notions were true. Recall Gen. Arthur Exon's statements that rumors of alien bodies circulated throughout Wright Field immediately following the Roswell crash. All one can say is that McCoy told members at this meeting that nothing had been found. The statement may or may not have been truthful, and may or may not have been based on good information. We simply do not know.

Shortly after this meeting, on April 5, another important incident occurred over White Sands Proving Ground in New Mexico. A team of navy missile trackers and a scientist tracked a UFO for several minutes as it streaked across the afternoon sky in a series of steep climbs and incredible maneuvers. The object appeared to be disc- or oval-shaped, and about one-fifth the apparent size of the full moon. Most amazing was the object's speed, which theodolites measured to be as fast as 18,000 mph.

As a result, Dr. Joseph Kaplan, a member of the Air Force Scientific Advisory Panel, secretly visited the area on April 27 and 28. Kaplan was charged with reviewing the UFO situation and, if necessary, recommending appropriate scientific measures. He spoke with people at the Kirtland AFB Office of Special Investigations, AEC's Sandia Base, Dr. Lincoln La Paz, and "several security personnel at Los Alamos." He decided that UFOs were "of extreme importance and should be investigated scientifically."[5]

THE SUMMER CRISIS OF 1948

As spring became summer, sightings increased and the situation reached a dramatic climax. Sometime in the summer of 1948 (exact date unknown), there occurred a remarkable UFO encounter by the U.S. and Canadian air forces at Goose Bay, Labrador. The account was later reported to NICAP by Air Force Maj. Edwin A. Jerome (Ret.), a former command pilot and air provost marshal for eight years. A high-ranking inspection team that included several generals was visiting the base radar facilities when a radar operator picked up a target on his scope moving at the incomprehensible speed of 9,000 mph. The generals assumed that the American equipment was way off calibration. But nearby Canadian facilities had obtained the same radar return. The inspecting officers were "appalled" over such a coincidence and attributed the sighting to a meteor. Jerome, involved in writing the intelligence report, discounted this because of the object's altitude (a constant sixty thousand feet) and speed. The following day, both radars reported an object hovering over the base at forty-five thousand feet moving at 10 mph. The official explanation was that they were probably "high-flying seagulls."[6]

In late July came two sightings of a brilliant, rocket-like object which shook the analysts at Project Sign. On July 20, the Netherlands government reported to the USAF that a wingless, cigar-shaped object with two decks of windows was seen flying rapidly on four separate occasions at The Hague.[7] Then, on July 24, at 2:45 A.M, an Eastern Air Lines DC-3 had a near-collision with an object of the same description near Montgomery, Alabama. The pilots, C. S. Chiles and J. B. Whitted, as well as one passenger, said the object rushed straight at them, then veered to the right of the airliner, emitted a long gust of red exhaust, and either shot up into the clouds or vanished. The pilots were adamant that the object was not a meteor. An hour before, a similar object was seen by a ground maintenance crewman at Robins AFB in Georgia, who was certain the object was no meteor.

The Pentagon showed little outward interest, identifying the object as a weather balloon. Behind the public facade, the air force took a strong interest. Ruppelt said it disturbed the Project Sign team more than the Mantell incident had. The official explanation soon became "unknown," but the members of the Project Sign team believed they identified this one—as extraterrestrial. The qualifications of the witnesses, the incredible description of what they saw, and the up-close-and-personal nature of the sighting itself led them to endorse the extraterrestrial hypothesis as the most logical for the existence of UFOs.

Allen Hynek conceded the faint possibility that the object seen might have been a fireball, but candidly called this "far-fetched." Within a few years, however, the air force took this reed for its explanation. The pilots never agreed with it. Years later, they spoke at length with UFO researcher Dr. James McDonald, who was impressed by the detail they gave so many years after the fact. Hynek himself doubted the fireball explanation. Throughout his career, he believed that the sighting had no apparent astronomical explanation.[8]

"THE ESTIMATE OF THE SITUATION"

After the dramatic Chiles-Whitted sighting, the members of Project Sign prepared an "Estimate of the Situation." No copy of this has ever surfaced. Throughout the 1950s and 1960s, the air force flatly denied its existence. However, Ruppelt claimed to see one of the 1948 originals, as did Air Force Maj. Dewey Fournet, who prepared an affidavit in the late 1950s that confirmed the document's existence. Several researchers have looked for this document. UFO researcher Jan Aldrich, who searched Directorate of Intelligence and ATIC documents at the National Archives II, estimated that perhaps 40 percent of the material was withdrawn at its time of declassification in 1987. "Everyone had a say on withdrawal," he wrote, "CIA, DOD, USN, British Government, etc."

Regarding the Estimate itself, Ruppelt wrote:

> The situation was the UFOs; the estimate was that they were interplanetary! When the estimate was completed, typed, and approved, it started up through channels to higher-command echelons. It drew considerable comment but no one stopped it on its way up.

The Top Secret Estimate then reached Air Force Chief of Staff Gen. Hoyt S. Vandenberg, who rejected it. A group from ATIC went to see Vandenberg to reinforce their argument, but to no avail. Ruppelt said that some months later the report was completely declassified and "all but a few copies" were burned. Aldrich wrote that Ruppelt's stated method for the destruction of the documents—declassification and burning—is incorrect procedure, and why he said it, "a mystery."

The report was also said to have concluded that aliens were making a full-scale observation of the Earth, but that attack did not seem imminent. Officials decided to maintain secrecy until they gathered more information. Ruppelt told Keyhoe privately, "The general said it would cause a stampede. . . . How could we convince the public the aliens weren't hostile when we didn't know it ourselves?"

A policy change ensued. At Project Sign, the ET hypothesis lost prestige. Everyone involved in writing the report was reassigned. Flying saucers were now to be explained in a more "down to earth" fashion.[9]

All indications show that the team at Sign was level-headed and serious about the problem of UFOs. It is reasonable to suppose, then, that *other* prominent figures also took the Chiles-Whitted sighting seriously—and by extension the entire UFO phenomenon. If so, then Vandenberg's conclusion would have been exactly what Keyhoe said it was: a means to keep the low-level investigation at Project Sign from straying into highly classified territory. In such a situation, Vandenberg would certainly not want his staffers to know very much.

While the Estimate of the Situation was being prepared, Gen. Charles P. Cabell, head of the USAF Directorate of Intelligence, ordered Air Force Intelligence Headquarters to prepare its own analysis of the UFO situation. This document, completed in December, was prepared jointly with the Office of Naval Intelligence, and titled "Analysis of Flying Object Incidents in the United States." Some have referred to it as the "Ghost of the Estimate," as a kind of watered-down version of the Estimate, but the two documents are independent. Indeed, as the Analysis was prepared by USAF Intelligence, which superseded the authority of ATIC, the Analysis also superseded the Estimate.[10]

Meanwhile, still in the immediate aftermath of the Eastern Air Lines UFO sighting, President Truman began receiving formal UFO briefings.

TRUMAN, LANDRY, AND UFOS

Col. Robert B. Landry was President Harry S. Truman's air force aide, serving as liaison with the air force for administrative and policy functions. Landry had previously been the executive officer to Air Force Chief of Staff Gen. Carl Spaatz and took the position of air force aide in early February 1948. He remained Truman's aide for the next five years and later earned a general's rank.

The following is an excerpt from an oral history interview conducted in 1974.[11] Speaking of 1948, Landry stated:

> I was called one afternoon to come to the Oval Office—the president wanted to see me. We talked about UFO reports and what might be the meaning for all these rather way-out reports of sightings, and the subject in general. The president said he hadn't given much serious thought to all these reports; but at the same time, he said, if there was any evidence of a strategic threat to the national security, the collection and evaluation of UFO data by Central Intelligence warranted more intense study and attention at the highest government level.

I was directed to report quarterly to the president after consulting with Central Intelligence people, as to whether or not any UFO incidents received by them could be considered as having any strategic threatening implications at all. The report was to be made orally by me unless it was considered by intelligence to be so serious or alarming as to warrant a more detailed report in writing. During the four and one-half years in office there, all reports were made orally. Nothing of substance considered credible or threatening to the country was ever received from intelligence.

Landry downplayed Truman's interest in all this, but several things stand out.

1. Landry gave Truman quarterly briefings for four and a half years, through the end of Truman's presidency, adding up to possibly eighteen briefings. All this, even though Truman supposedly thought little of UFOs.
2. Landry was Truman's liaison with the CIA regarding UFO reports, providing independent confirmation of Hillenkoetter's remark to Keyhoe that the CIA was interested in UFO reports from very early on.
3. Landry's reports were oral, which he interpreted as therefore *not* significant. But such a claim does not follow logically, and in fact the reverse is more plausible. As CIA Director Richard Helms once put the matter, "the first rule in keeping secrets is nothing on paper."

LATE 1948: KEY DEVELOPMENTS

UFO sightings dropped off somewhat within America, but American military personnel still reported them everywhere. On October 1, 1948, an Air National Guard F-51 pilot in Fargo, North Dakota, named Thomas Gorman had a dogfight with a small, flat, circular UFO. While flying, Gorman saw a light about eight inches in diameter displaying incredible movements. He repeatedly gave chase, each time outmaneuvered by the object. It eventually departed upward at high speed. Gorman said he "had the distinct impression that its maneuvers were controlled by thought or reason." Others witnessed this bizarre encounter. The light was seen near the aircraft by control tower operators and people from other locations at all angles. All gave consistent descriptions of what they saw. The air force, nevertheless, said that Gorman and the other witnesses had seen a lighted balloon. UFO researcher Jerome Clark agreed, calling this case greatly overrated. Others disagreed. Jacques Vallee put the matter this way: "twenty-minute ball lightning would be more surprising to the physicists than flying saucers piloted by vegetable men." James McDonald years later reinvestigated the sighting, concluding that it was indeed valid, and something extraordinary.[12]

Two weeks later, on October 16, came a remarkable UFO sighting in

Cache, Japan. This was an encounter of an F-61 Black Widow aircraft with an indeterminate number of UFOs. While on night patrol, the pilot and his crew picked up an object on radar at about 200 mph. As he closed to intercept, the object speeded up to 1,200 mph, then slowed down again. Six times the crew tried to close on the UFO; each time, the object accelerated out of reach. On one pass the crew saw the object's silhouette, which looked "like a rifle bullet" twenty to thirty feet long. Intelligence reports indicated the UFO carried radar warning equipment, because it "seemed cognizant of the whereabouts of the F-61 at all times." The sighting certainly impressed itself upon the pilot, who stated that "in my opinion, we were shown a new type of aircraft by some agency unknown to us."[13]

More radar sightings occurred in early November at Goose Bay, Labrador, and Japan. During the night of November 18, near Andrews AFB in Maryland, a strange chase took place by a USAF Reserve pilot in pursuit of an oval-shaped UFO that appeared as something like a ball of light (reminiscent of the Gorman case).[14] Then, on November 23, the first documented simultaneous visual and radar sighting of an unidentified flying object took place at Fursten-Felbruck AFB near Munich. An object was detected circling rapidly at twenty-seven thousand feet. An F-80 pilot sent to intercept described it as bright red. While he was moving to intercept, the object abruptly climbed to fifty thousand feet—at 900 mph, far beyond the capability of any known aircraft. A second F-80 pilot verified the report. According to the air force intelligence officers investigating the encounter, the object was not a balloon, and there were no reported aircraft in the area. The object, in fact, was "nothing we know of." To the investigator, there remained a slim possibility that the object was some kind of experimental aircraft, except for the problem that such craft were "not in Germany, can [not] climb twenty-three thousand feet in a matter of minutes, [nor] travel 900 miles per hour." The sighting was never officially solved.[15]

THE GREEN FIREBALLS

At 9:27 P.M. on December 5, 1948, an air force C-47 pilot at eighteen thousand feet near Albuquerque observed a huge green fireball arch upward, then level off to horizontal trajectory. Seven minutes later, a Pioneer Airlines pilot saw a large orange object approach in a flat trajectory, become green, then dodge to the side and fall away toward the ground. Thus began the mystery of the green fireballs, which the U.S. defense establishment in the Southwest studied intensely.

According to Ruppelt, "everyone, including the intelligence officers at Kirtland AFB, Air Defense Command people, Dr. La Paz, and some of the most distinguished scientists at Los Alamos had seen at least one." That is, all the people Kaplan had spoken to the previous April following the White Sands sighting. No one could figure it out. From December 1948 through April 1949, at least thirty-nine reports of green fireballs were sent to Air Material Command. Afterwards, they were seen sporadically in the area for years.

La Paz saw his first green fireball on December 12, 1948. He tracked the object's path and decided it was distinctly possible that it had flown over Los Alamos. Even more startling, however, was that the object maintained a horizontal path at the extremely low altitude (for a meteorite) of eight to ten miles. Moreover, it moved too slowly to be a meteor, and was completely silent. In a confidential memo dated December 20, 1948, La Paz argued that it was no meteor or fireball; if so, it was certainly no type he had ever studied. He later told Ruppelt that he did not believe it was a natural phenomenon.

By December 20, the interest in fireballs inspired the creation of an informal group called the Los Alamos Astrophysical Association. Its members, all scientists and engineers with security clearances, gained permission to examine several of Project Sign's classified reports on the green fireballs. They agreed with La Paz that the objects were not meteors. Some wondered whether the objects were missiles being fired into the Earth's atmosphere. But if so, how was such a thing possible, and who would do it? Naturally, the question allowed for no satisfactory answer.[16]

Top Secret Documents

By the end of 1948, Project Sign had received several hundred UFO reports, of which 167 had been saved as "good." Of these, about three dozen were classified as "unknown." Ironically, as UFO reports became better and more numerous, the encouragement to study them waned. Elsewhere, however, people were thinking about the UFO problem. On December 10, 1948, air intelligence completed its top-secret, nineteen-page "Analysis of Flying Object Incidents in the U.S." The document did not suggest that UFOs might be extraterrestrial. But it did state that the objects seen were real and baffling:

> The frequency of reported sightings, the similarity in many of the characteristics attributed to the observed objects, and the quality of observers considered as a whole support the contention that some type of flying object has been observed. . . . The origin of the devices is not ascertainable.

The paper made no attempt to explain individual reports or offer a definitive conclusion on flying saucers. It did, however, rest on the assumption that the Soviets were a reasonably likely source for UFOs, as indicated in this statement:

Assuming that the objects might eventually be identified as foreign or foreign-sponsored devices, the possible reason for their appearance over the U.S. requires consideration. Several possible explanations appear noteworthy, viz: (1) to negate U.S. confidence in the atom bomb as the most advanced and decisive weapon in warfare; (2) to perform photographic reconnaissance missions; (3) to test U.S. air defenses; (4) to conduct familiarization flights over U.S. territory.

This document remained classified until 1985. While its conclusion may be less incendiary than those claimed for the Estimate of the Situation, the report shows continued concern about UFOs, continued speculation about the possibility of their Soviet origins, and a continued lack of evidence to support such a belief.[17]

The matter of extraterrestrial origins, on the other hand, was studiously avoided. If one accepts the existence of the Estimate of the Situation, and the account from Ruppelt and others about how the air force leadership responded to it, then the tenor of the analysis is readily understandable: an ET explanation was off-limits, and analysts naturally considered the remaining possibilities. However, even if the estimate were merely a figment of Ruppelt's imagination, the conclusions of the analysis leave us with the distinct impression of the ET hypothesis as the elephant in the dining room that no one would acknowledge.

On December 16, 1948, General Putt changed the name of Project Sign to Project Grudge; the official switch occurred in February 1949. It signified a more serious debunking and dismissal of UFOs. Grudge's methods were twofold: explain every UFO report, then tell the public how it had solved all sightings. The change was so pronounced that Ruppelt even wondered whether there was a hidden reason. "Was it actually an attempt to go underground—to make the project more secretive?" On the basis of what the record reveals, and especially in light of the recent Analysis, the answer is yes.[18]

1949: General Developments

In 1949, crashed disc stories circulated within the military. A Los Angeles UFO researcher, Max Miller, later wrote about a story he heard in 1949 concerning a flying saucer crash somewhere in the Southwest. The saucer had supposedly been retrieved and brought to an unnamed air force base; several tourists nearby even took photos. Miller's source for the story was an unnamed army sergeant. Later that year, *Variety* columnist Frank Scully reported that the U.S. government had recovered spaceships that had crashed somewhere in the southwestern desert. This article served as the basis for Scully's book published in 1950, *Behind the Flying Saucers.*

Another rumor making the rounds in 1949 was the military's determination to capture a flying saucer. U.S. Air Force Capt. Edward Stone later told Donald Keyhoe that the air force was ordered to "get" a flying saucer "by any possible means." Keyhoe tried to substantiate the story and claimed that an intelligence major named Jere Boggs admitted to him that it was true. Today, these stories remain only old rumors. Yet, it is noteworthy that they were circulating through the military as early as 1949.[19]

The CIA's Office of Scientific Intelligence continued to maintain an interest in UFOs at this time, according to a 1952 CIA memorandum (Good 1988, 330). An interesting sidelight to CIA activities of 1949, which indirectly concerns UFOs, featured the country of Albania. That year, the CIA took over the ambitious British effort to build a sizable resistance movement there. Frank Wisner organized and manned the operation. His first choice was a young man named Robert Low. Low became infamous twenty years later for his manipulation and sabotage of the University of Colorado project to investigate UFOs, known as the Condon Committee. But can we be sure this was the same Robert Low working for the CIA in Albania? In his study of the Condon Committee, David Saunders mentioned in passing that Low had been a combat intelligence officer aboard a destroyer during the war, was honorably discharged in 1946, and earned a master's degree from Columbia University in 1948. The least we can say is that everything seems to fit. The Albanian project, incidentally, failed miserably. One contributing factor was the inclusion of another person on the team: British double-agent Kim Philby.[20]

The U.S. intelligence community conducted other interesting operations in 1949. Paperclip was running smoothly by now. Widespread, illegal spraying of U.S. cities with bacteria and pathogens began this year, courtesy of the U.S. Army, in order to test biological weapons. This program continued for twenty years.[21]

Things were not as they appeared in the land of the free.

DIVERGING OPINIONS

The U.S. military and intelligence communities were clearly not as one regarding UFOs. The pattern continued to emerge: Air Material Command and ATIC stonewalled on UFOs to their colleagues.

On January 13, 1949, a U.S. Army Intelligence memo to the Pentagon expressed great concern over the green fireballs. The memo discussed the possibility of Soviet mischief, but considered it more likely that "the United States may be carrying on some top secret experiments. . . . It is felt that these incidents are of such great importance, especially as they are occurring in the vicinity of sensitive installations, that a scientific board be sent to this locality. . . ."[22]

On January 30, hundreds of New Mexico residents saw a spectacular green fireball. Kirtland AFB immediately notified Washington and organized an investigation. La Paz managed a rough triangulation of the object, and estimated its speed at between 25,000 and 50,000 mph. This should have caused an "ear-shattering" sonic boom. Instead, the object was totally silent. The sighting gave La Paz more ammunition: he subsequently told Air Force Office of Special Investigations Agent Paul Ryan that the objects were "surely artificial." Of course, that begs the question: to whom did they belong?[23]

On January 31, the FBI issued a memo on UFOs, titled "Protection of Vital Installations." The classified document was sent to Hoover, the Army's G-2, the Office of Naval Intelligence, the Office of Special Investigations, and mentioned a meeting among these groups concerning UFOs. The key statement of the document:

> Army intelligence has recently said that "the matter of 'Unidentified Aircraft' or 'Unidentified Aerial Phenomena,' otherwise known as 'Flying Discs,' 'Flying Saucers,' and 'Balls of Fire,' is considered top secret by intelligence officers of both the army and the air forces."[24]

On February 16, 1949, a secret conference was held at the Los Alamos Scientific Laboratory to discuss green fireballs and flying saucers in general. La Paz was there, as was Edward Teller, the inventor of the fuse for the atomic bomb, and a number of military and scientific personnel. There were no representatives, however, from ATIC's Project Sign/Grudge—an accurate signifier of how irrelevant ATIC's project really was. Even then, the air force's investigation of flying saucers was not the only game in town, nor, it is clear, the most serious. A few matters about the conference are known. La Paz told attendees of Kaplan's assurance that the green fireballs could not be explained by any secret training exercises. Teller thought the objects might not be solid, but perhaps some kind of electro-optic phenomenon. The panel recommended that the government or military set up a series of stations to photograph and analyze the fireballs. AFOSI in fact sent this recommendation to AMC, which did nothing.[25]

That month, Project Sign issued a final report on UFOs. Of the 237 UFO cases it contained, forty-eight (or 20 percent) were unexplained, not including an additional 13 percent where the "lack of evidence preclude[d] an explanation." Many of the explanations themselves were, in Hynek's words, "force-fits." Despite the huge unexplained rate, the report concluded that there was too little evidence to prove or disprove an objective existence of flying saucers. It recommended closing the project when the air force determined the sightings did not represent a security threat to the nation. The report conceded that UFOs could *not* yet be dismissed as a security threat, and it rejected the likelihood that UFOs were Soviet. What, then, was the source of the threat? Implied, but not stated, was that the threat would have to be coming from *somewhere.*[26]

Opinions in the classified world diverged on UFOs. A March 15 CIA memo on UFOs from the Office of Scientific Investigation (OSI) dismissed the idea of UFOs as foreign aircraft, and suggested the possibility that they were misidentifications of other phenomena. On March 25, an FBI memo sent to a large number of offices and officials stated the opposite conclusion, that they were "believed to be man-made missiles rather than natural phenomenon." The memo also stated that the Soviets had been developing an "unknown type of flying disc" since 1945, although this statement has never been substantiated.[27] On March 31, another CIA memorandum on Project Sign and UFOs stated the belief that UFOs "will turn out another 'sea serpent.' However, since there is even a remote possibility that they may be interplanetary or foreign aircraft, it is necessary to investigate each sighting."[28] On April 19, the Air Force Office of Special Investigations at Kirtland AFB sent a list of fireball reports to Air Force Headquarters. The cover letter noted:

> The common characteristics of most of the incidents are: (a) green color, sometimes described as greenish white, bright green, yellow green, or blue green; (b) horizontal path, sometimes with minor variations; (c) speed less than that of a meteor but more than any other type of known aircraft; (d) no sound associated with observation; (e) no persistent trail or dust cloud; (f) period of visibility from one to five seconds.[29]

Although AFOSI wanted to continue investigating the fireballs, it received no cooperation from Air Material Command.

A key UFO sighting of the spring occurred during the launch of a top-secret Skyhook balloon on the morning of April 24, about fifty miles from White Sands. Several well-qualified observers, such as scientists, engineers, and officers, saw a UFO visually and measured its movement with a 25-power theodolite.

Interestingly, one of the observers was Charles B. Moore, whose name appeared in the air force's explanation of the Roswell incident of 1947. Moore launched the balloon at 10:20 A.M. and observed it through a theodolite with an assistant. Accompanying him were five others, including navy men and balloon personnel from General Mills. At 10:30, someone saw a whitish-silver, elliptical object in another part of the sky, and everyone turned to observe and track it with the theodolite, where it filled the scope. The object was "plainly visible." The men ruled out the possibility of another balloon, having just checked the direction of the wind. They computed the altitude of the object when they initially saw it at fifty-six miles and its initial speed at seven miles *per second*, or over 25,000 miles per hour (although its estimated speed for the duration of the sighting was 18,000 mph). They judged the object's size to be forty feet wide by one hundred feet long, but it moved too fast for anyone to identify surface details. The object moved along its major axis and covered the entire sky in about one minute. While in view, the object rapidly dropped its angle of elevation, then shot upward out of sight. It made no sound. The case was reported in detail in *True* a year later (March 1950).

The air force failed to follow up in a way that inspired the confidence of the observers, who ended up "disgusted" with the lack of a thorough investigation into the matter. But the CIA seems to have been interested in the case. A report in its files stated that the object

> was not a balloon and was some distance away . . . the flight would have probably gone over the White Sands Proving Ground, Holloman AFB, and Los Alamos. . . . Information is desired if this was some new or experimental aircraft or for any explanation whatsoever.[30]

THE AIR FORCE DEBUNKS

On April 27, 1949, the air force released to the public its final report of Project Sign, still known publicly as Project Saucer. Although the data and conclusions were a weak fit, journalists did not read the actual data, but instead took their cue from the report's conclusions and the air force's public statement. On the heels of this came Sydney Shallett's dismissive "What You Can Believe About Flying Saucers" in the April 30 edition of the *Saturday Evening Post*. Air force intelligence had helped Shallett to prepare the article, which was widely interpreted to be official policy. Indeed, according to *True* magazine editor Ken Purdy, Shallett "had Forrestal's backing." In all essentials, Purdy was right. Since November 1948, the air force had known, with some alarm, about Shallett's project. An intelligence memo stated the position that "publicity of this nature is undesirable but, if such articles are written, they will be less harmful to the national interest if a degree of guidance in their preparation is exercised by the Directorate of Intelligence." A memorandum was also drawn up for Secretary of Defense James Forrestal but, according to UFO researcher Jan Aldrich, was probably never sent. Small wonder, as Forrestal was then having problems of his own. Still, the tenor of the letter spelled out the air force attitude well enough:

> It appears that articles of this nature would be less harmful to national interests if the Department of the Air Force were authorised to assist the Press in the preparation of such articles as they insist upon writing. It is recommended that the Department of the Air Force be authorised to assist the Press, upon request, in preparing such articles as they insist upon writing.

In effect, the air force was saying, if you *insist* upon writing about UFOs, allow us to guide you. It personally took care of Shallett's visit, with predictable results.[31]

On May 9, Purdy asked Donald Keyhoe to investigate the flying saucer mystery for *True*, and warned him to "watch out for fake tips" at the Pentagon. At this point, Keyhoe thought that UFOs would probably turn out to be either American or Soviet missiles, and did not seriously entertain the idea of extraterrestrials.[32] His opinion changed after speaking with several of his old friends who were now prominent within the navy, including Adm. Delmar Fahrney, a leader in the navy's guided missile program, and Adm. Calvin Bolster, who later became the director of the Office of Naval Research (ONR). In 1949, Bolster was in charge of the special design section of the Bureau of Aeronautics. He told Keyhoe:

> Don, I swear it's nothing the U.S. is doing. I'm in on all the special weapons programs and I'm sure I would know. Our big cosmic-ray research balloons may have caused a few "saucer" reports, but they don't explain all the sightings— especially those by experienced service and airline pilots. I honestly don't know the answer.

Fahrney told Keyhoe that "we're years from anything like the saucers' performance. And if we ever do match them, nobody'd be crazy enough to test the things near cities or along airways."[33]

In early May 1949, while the air force debunked, the 4th U.S. Army approached AFOSI in San Antonio to offer assistance in investigating the green fireballs. The army actually insisted on participating, even after the initial response was no. On May 5, the 4th Army arranged a meeting with personnel from AFOSI, ONI, Army Counterintelligence Corps (CIC), the FBI, and the Armed Forces Special Weapons Project (AFSWP). The meeting took place at Camp Hood, and was the first of a planned series of weekly meetings to discuss the fireballs. At that meeting, army and navy representatives agreed that they remained unexplained and were a legitimate source of "grave concern." AFSWP people believed the fireballs to be natural phenomena; AFOSI and FBI gave no opinion. The 4th Army pressed for a formal observation system, and in fact had just created one secretly.[34]

The attitude taken publicly by the air force about UFOs continued to be the opposite of the private attitudes prevalent in every other service. Following Shallett's article, and amid the near-complete inactivity of Project Grudge, UFO sightings suddenly jumped sharply. Air Force Headquarters claimed that the recent publicity was to blame and issued a press release saying that UFOs were nothing but mass hysteria and misidentification of natural phenomena.[35]

THE DEATH OF JAMES FORRESTAL

The decline and death of James Forrestal remains an unresolved problem of history. That Forrestal suffered from a spectacular mental breakdown through 1948 and 1949 is undisputed. The reasons are less clear, but with possible relevance to this study.

Throughout 1948, Forrestal locked horns with Air Force Secretary Stuart Symington over defense spending. Truman demanded an impossibly balanced budget, and Forrestal's job was to keep the services in line. He could not do this and, to some degree, would not. The result was the erosion of Truman's confidence. It may not have mattered to Forrestal: like most of the country, he assumed Truman's political career was over and that by the end of the year a Republican, probably Thomas Dewey, would be in the White House.

But Forrestal, not Truman, was the doomed man. His relationship with Symington went from bad to worse. For reasons still unclear, Symington "embarked upon a kind of personal guerrilla warfare" against the Secretary of Defense. Throughout the fall and winter of 1948, Forrestal's mental health, physical condition, and authority as Secretary of Defense deteriorated. When Truman shocked the world in November by winning the presidential election, Forrestal had still not obtained a budget consensus from the Joint Chiefs. Friends commented on his growing paranoia. He was convinced that "foreign-looking men" were following him and that Symington was spying on him. Forrestal's belief eventually came to the attention of Truman and Secret Service Chief U. E. Baughman, who decided that Forrestal was suffering from "a total psychotic breakdown."

On January 11, 1949, Truman informed Forrestal that Louis Johnson would soon be replacing him as Secretary of Defense. By now, Symington and Attorney General Tom Clark were feeding stories to journalist Drew Pearson, in particular that Forrestal complained of "being followed by Jews or Zionist agents." Forrestal accused Clark of having the FBI shadow him, which Clark denied, but which could well have been true. Forrestal finally left office in a formal ceremony on March 28, his last public appearance.

What followed after the ceremony remains mysterious. "There is something I would like to talk to you about," Symington told Forrestal, and accompanied him privately during the ride back to the Pentagon. What Symington said is not known, but Forrestal emerged from the ride deeply upset, even traumatized, upon arrival at his office. Friends of Forrestal implied that Symington said something that "shattered Forrestal's last remaining defenses." When someone entered Forrestal's office several hours later, the former Secretary of Defense did not notice. Instead, he sat rigidly at his desk, staring at the bare wall, incoherent, repeating the sentence, "you are a loyal fellow," for several hours.

Forrestal was taken home, but within a day the air force flew him to Hobe Sound, Florida, home of Bob Lovett (a future Secretary of Defense). Forrestal's first words were "Bob, they're after me." He met with Dr. William Menninger, of the Menninger Foundation, and a consultant to the surgeon general of the army. Capt. George N. Raines, chief psychologist at the U.S.

Naval Hospital at Bethesda, soon arrived. It is not exactly clear what transpired during Forrestal's brief stay in Florida. One story from Pearson was that Forrestal had several hysterical episodes and made at least one suicide attempt, certain that the Communists were planning an imminent invasion. Menninger, however, explicitly denied that Forrestal had attempted suicide while in Florida. Forrestal did tell him that on the day before Menninger's arrival, he had "placed a belt around his neck with the intention of hanging himself, but the belt broke." Menninger, however, saw no marks on Forrestal's neck or body. Nor did anyone find broken belts of any kind. Menninger considered it all a nightmare.

On April 2, 1949, "for security reasons," Forrestal's coterie flew him to Bethesda. During the trip from the air field to the hospital, Forrestal made several attempts to leave the moving vehicle and was forcibly restrained. He talked of suicide, of being a bad Catholic, and several times of those "who are trying to get me." He was admitted to Bethesda under care of Raines, who diagnosed Forrestal's illness as involutional melancholia, a depressive condition sometimes seen in people reaching middle age, often who saw their life as a failure. Upon arrival at Bethesda, Forrestal declared that he did not expect to leave the place alive. In a highly unusual decision for a possibly suicidal patient, Forrestal's doctor was instructed by "the people downtown" (e.g., national security) to place him in the VIP sixteenth-floor suite. Meanwhile, Forrestal's personal diaries, consisting of fifteen loose-leaf binders totaling three thousand pages, were removed from his former office and brought to the White House, where they remained for the next year. The White House later claimed that Forrestal had requested Truman to take custody of the diaries. Such a claim, frankly, is preposterous. Throughout 1948, Forrestal had become increasingly alienated from Truman. Prior to the election, he had even met privately with leading Republicans to help insure his future with the Dewey administration. Truman then abruptly fired him and replaced him with a man not even remotely qualified for the job. Forrestal's diaries contained very sensitive information that Truman's people wanted to know about. Presumably they had ample time to review them during the seven weeks of Forrestal's hospitalization.

During Forrestal's first week in Bethesda, he received a treatment called narcosis, essentially sedatives and tranquilizers. Throughout Forrestal's time at the hospital, access to him was severely restricted. His wife (with whom he was not close), his two sons, Sidney Souers, Louis Johnson, Truman, and Congressman Lyndon Johnson each visited him once. Menninger visited twice. However, Forrestal was not permitted to see the several people he repeatedly called for: his brother, a friend, and two priests. Henry Forrestal, for example, had repeatedly tried to see his brother but was refused until he threatened to tell the newspapers and sue the hospital. He then visited his brother four times. Henry told Raines and the hospital's commandant, Capt. B. W. Hogan, that James wanted to talk with a close friend, Monsignor Maurice Sheehy. Hogan acknowledged that the patient had requested this several times but said he still would not allow it. Indeed, Sheehy had tried *seven times* to see Forrestal, each time told his timing was "not opportune." Sheehan, a former navy chaplain, argued several times with Raines and received the impression that Raines was acting under orders. Another priest, Father Paul McNally of Georgetown University, was also barred from seeing Forrestal, as was at least one other friend of the former Secretary.

By mid-May, observers and visitors agreed that Forrestal was improving. Henry said that his brother was "acting and talking as sanely and intelligently as any man I've ever known." On May 14, 1949, Raines decided that he would leave Washington in four days to attend a meeting of the American Psychiatric Association. After their last meeting on the morning of the eighteenth, Raines wrote that Forrestal was "somewhat better than on the corresponding day of the preceding week." Forrestal continued in good spirits throughout all of the twentieth and twenty-first. He showed no signs of depression, was well dressed, shaved, and in good appetite.

The official account of Forrestal's death runs as follows. During the night of May 21–22, Forrestal was awake at 1:45 A.M., copying a chorus from Sophocles's *Ajax* from a book of world literature. A navy corpsman guarding Forrestal's room checked in, as was his job every fifteen minutes. Forrestal told the corpsman that he did not want a sedative, as he intended to stay up late and read. (A variation of this story appeared in the *New York Times*, which reported that Forrestal had been asleep at 1:30, then awake at 1:45.) The corpsman reported Forrestal's refusal to the psychiatrist—Raines's assistant—sleeping next door. They returned five minutes later to an empty room. The assistant later claimed that Forrestal had sent the corpsman out on a "brief errand." During this time, Forrestal walked to the diet kitchen across the hall, tied one end of his bathrobe cord to the radiator, the other end around his neck, removed a flimsy screen, and jumped from the sixteenth floor. The cord came untied, and he fell to his death after hitting part of the building on the way down.

Forrestal's most recent biographers discounted the possibility of murder, calling the Secretary's death "a series of chance events." Yet, the discrepancies in the official suicide story were never clearly resolved, and several people close to Forrestal did not believe it. An early biographer of Forrestal, writing in the 1960s, noted that "even now . . . certain details have not been made public," and that some believed Forrestal's death to be "very much desired by individuals and groups who, in 1949, held great power in the United States." Others went further and maintained that Forrestal was murdered. Henry Forrestal, for one, believed strongly that "they" murdered his brother—they being either Communists or Jews within the government. (Forrestal's geopolitics gave him a pro-Arab disposition.) Indeed, Henry later said that the more he thought about his brother being shut up at Bethesda and denied the right to see Father Sheehy, the more it bothered him. He decided he was going to take his brother to the country to complete his recovery, and made train reservations to return to Washington on May 22. He also reserved a room at the Mayflower Hotel for that day, then phoned the hospital to announce that he would arrive on May 22 to take custody of his brother.

Father Sheehy had reason to suspect murder. When he arrived at Bethesda Naval Hospital after learning of Forrestal's death, an experienced-looking hospital corpsman approached him through the crowd. In a low, tense voice he said, "Father, you know Mr. Forrestal didn't kill himself, don't you?" Before Sheehy could respond or ask his name, others in the crowd pressed close, and the man quickly departed.

There are several odd elements concerning Forrestal's final moments. First, the corpsman guarding Forrestal was a new man, a young man named Robert Wayne Harrison, Jr., someone Forrestal had never seen before. The regular guard during the midnight shift was absent without leave and, the story goes, had gotten drunk the night before. Harrison was the only person to have had direct contact with Forrestal in the moments before his death, and it was on his word only that the official account rested.

Also, Forrestal never finished writing the chorus from Sophocles, and in fact stopped in the middle of a word. Quite possibly, Forrestal had not even written the fragment that evening, especially if he had been asleep at 1:30 A.M. How reasonable is it to suppose that, sometime between 1:30 A.M. and 1:45 A.M., he woke up, got out some writing material, located a gloomy poem within a huge anthology, copied out seventeen lines, put on his robe, crossed the hall to the diet kitchen, where he tightly wrapped and knotted his bathrobe cord around his neck and presumably tied the loose end to the radiator under the window; then climbed up on the window sill and jumped.

There is also an odd juxtaposition of a tightly knotted bathrobe cord around Forrestal's neck and the assumption that he tied the other end so loosely to a radiator that it immediately came untied and allowed him to fall to his death. This radiator was a rather improbable gallows: it was about two feet long, the top was six inches below the sill, and it was attached to the wall with its base a good fifteen inches above the floor. But there was no evidence that the bathrobe cord had ever been tied to the small radiator in the first place. If the cord had snapped under Forrestal's weight, one end would have been found still fastened to the radiator. The cord did not break, however, and there was not a mark on the radiator to indicate it had ever been tied there. Moreover, if Forrestal wanted to hang himself, why choose a tiny window by anchoring himself to a radiator when he much more easily could have done the job from a door or sturdy fixture, such as the shower curtain rod in his own bathroom? On the other hand, if Forrestal wanted to go out the window, why bother with a cord? Why not simply jump, a far easier proposition?

In sum, we do not know that the cord was ever tied to the radiator, but we do know is it was tied *tightly* to Forrestal's neck.

Later inspection found heavy scuff marks outside the window sill and cement work. Proponents of the suicide theory claim these were made by Forrestal's feet while he was hanging by the neck from the radiator, and perhaps that he belatedly changed his mind and tried to climb back in. But the scuff marks could just as easily have been made by his struggle with someone pushing him out the window.

There are many other suspicious elements to this story, such as the decision to place Forrestal on the sixteenth floor, which was exactly opposite what medical opinion desired (the bottom floor of a nearby annex had been the first choice of his caretakers), but was pressed by unnamed individuals in Washington. Also, the official investigation of Forrestal's death was as much of a sham as that of President Kennedy would be fourteen years later. The hospital labeled his death a suicide before any investigation; the county coroner hurried over to confirm the hospital statements. In cases where there is even a slight possibility of murder, it is normal for a coroner to delay signing a death certificate until a thorough investigation, an autopsy, and an inquest have been made. This did not happen. Since the death occurred on a U.S. naval reservation, local police did not investigate. Instead, the head of the naval board of inquiry immediately announced he was "absolutely certain" that Forrestal's death "could be nothing else than suicide."[36]

Why discuss the death of James Forrestal in a book about UFOs? Given the definite possibility that he was murdered, the UFO connection becomes intriguing. In the first place, Forrestal's position within the defense community made him *de facto* a key player in the formulation of UFO policy. The problem was of great importance to people high up the national security food chain: we can infer that Forrestal, too, had an interest, even though the official records and biographers of Forrestal are silent about UFOs.

Forrestal's concern about being followed by "foreign-looking men" is a common description of the legendary-to-the-point-of-cliché Men in Black. He never stated clearly just who he believed to be following him, at least not consistently. Others assumed that he was talking about Communists, Jews, and Washington insiders, but they could only assume. Then there is the disconcerting relationship with Air Force Secretary Symington. True, Symington considered Forrestal to be an enemy. But why, in the moment of Forrestal's departure from politics, amid a spectacular psychological collapse, did Symington take it upon himself to have a secret conversation with Forrestal that left him utterly incoherent? This goes beyond mere conventional political maneuvering: what did Symington say—or do—to Forrestal?

If for the sake of argument we speculate that Forrestal was murdered, we must ask why. What could have prompted someone in the national security apparatus to plan the death of the former Secretary of Defense? The budget issue? Hardly; that was settled by then. One proponent of the murder theory blamed Communists within the U.S. government, or perhaps even the KGB. The reason, it was claimed, had to do with Forrestal's diaries and plans for a book after his release from the hospital. Forrestal certainly was an inveterate anti–Communist and might have been perceived as problematic for agents of the Soviets. It is also true that the Soviets were no strangers to the art of staged suicides. But neither were the Americans, a fact unremarked by proponents of the "communist murder" thesis.

UFOs, on the other hand, constitute the great hole of contemporary history. We know, at the very least, that this was a topic of great concern to those at the top of American national security policy, despite the near-complete absence of public references to it. An explanation centering on the UFO phenomenon accounts better than most for the complete unhinging of a successful and brilliant individual, and more importantly, the need to silence someone who could no longer be trusted. Did Forrestal learn a truth about UFOs that contributed to his breakdown?

Perhaps Forrestal's psychological state was such that he *did* commit suicide. The facts of his death do not point toward this conclusion, but we do not have definitive knowledge. But consider the case of American journalist George Polk. A year before, Polk had been investigating corruption in the Greek military regime, elements of which then murdered him. The Communists were promptly blamed, while America's intelligence and media communities knowingly went along with the charade. Or, just a few years later, in 1953, when American biological weapons expert Frank Olsen "fell" from the tenth floor of the Statler Hotel in New York City, after he had a *very* bad LSD trip, courtesy of the CIA, and had become a security risk. Hiding unpleasant realities from the public was nothing new.

SUMMER AND FALL 1949

The U.S. military recorded several intriguing UFO encounters during the late spring of 1949, most of which Project Grudge wrote off brazenly as conventional objects. On May 21, the last day of Forrestal's life, an F-82 fighter took off from Moses Lake AFB, near Hanford, Washington, to intercept a flying disc seen visually and by radar over restricted airspace at twenty thousand feet. Before the F-82 became airborne, the disc veered south at a speed greater than a jet fighter. The pilot took off in pursuit, instructed to "intercept it in hopes that it might be a disc." But the object was long gone.[37]

The key UFO sighting of the season was once again at White Sands, during navy-conducted upper-atmosphere missile tests. On June 10, 1949, observers saw two round white UFOs suddenly enter their field of vision and maneuver around a missile traveling at over 1,300 mph. The objects paced the missile on either side, then one object passed through the missile's exhaust and joined the other. The now-unified object accelerated upward and left the missile behind. According to Navy Capt. R. B. McLaughlin, five separate observation posts saw the incident. McLaughlin later reported the sighting, adding that "many times I have seen flying discs following and overtaking missiles in flight at the experimental base at White Sands. . . ."[38]

In August 1949, a mere six months after Project Grudge commenced, it issued its classified final report, firmly debunking flying saucers. No evidence, it argued, showed the objects to be the product of a foreign government with a superior technology, or were of any danger to American security:

> All evidence and analysis indicates that reports of unidentified flying objects are the result of: (1) misinterpretation of various conventional objects; (2) a mild form of mass-hysteria and war nerves; (3) individuals who fabricate such reports to perpetuate a hoax or to seek publicity; (4) psychopathological persons.

Thus, UFO witnesses were either ignorant (unable to identify conventional objects), hysterical with "war nerves," liars and hoaxers, or crazy. "[F]urther study along present lines," the report added, "would only confirm the findings presented herein." Considering such a categorical conclusion, fifty-five of the Project's 244 cases were unidentified, or 23 percent.

The report suggested downscaling the investigation and study of UFO reports "to reflect the contemplated change of policy," while at the same time keeping a heavy lid over them. In a key foreshadowing of the Robertson Panel more than three years later, the memo recommended that press releases should be created to "aid in dispelling public apprehension."

Allen Hynek helped to write the reports of Projects Sign and Grudge but later criticized them. He complained about "the lackadaisical and irresponsible manner in which many of the UFO reports were treated," and contended that "[o]ver the years, the Pentagon played loosely with statistics to support their position that *all* UFOs are misidentifications of natural phenomena—or outright hoaxes. Often statistical information was not fairly presented." In the case of the Grudge Report, this complaint surely hits home. Throughout the entire history of air force public reporting of UFOs, less than 2 percent of UFO sightings turned out to be hoaxes or "psychological." And yet the air force emphasized precisely that element of reports.[39]

One remarkable thing about the Grudge Report is how opposite its tone was from the "Analysis of Flying Object Incidents in the U.S.," which, after all, had been finalized only the previous December. That report had recognized the reality of UFOs, assumed the sighted objects were craft of some sort, and gave strong consideration that the Soviets were behind it. What had happened in a mere eight months to overthrow this assessment? The phenomenon had not gone away. If anything, it had become more serious, and a wider group within the classified world was now concerned. Nor had the Grudge team suddenly solved the UFO phenomenon. This was 1949, the height of the cold war. American defense analysts were continuing to harden their policy toward the Soviets, which by the spring of 1950 would culminate in NSC-68, an alarmist statement that in effect warned Truman that the United States was losing the cold war. Within such a context of unexplained airspace violations, of agitation and bewilderment expressed by nearly every sector of the defense establishment, during the very month that the Soviet Union exploded its first nuclear device, what is one to make of this cavalier disregard of unexplained objects in American skies known as the Grudge Report? With everything known about the nature of the UFO problem in 1949 and the over-all context of the cold war, one must conclude that the Grudge Report flies in the face of defense logic. It does, however, comply entirely with the needs of the defense community to manage the UFO problem from a public relations standpoint. The Grudge Report had no scientific value, but was of supreme value as a management tool. In the twenty-first century, along with various statements about UFOs by the air force, CIA, NSA, NASA, and other organizations, it continues to retain this value as part of the official explanatory structure, as a way to manage the intractable problem of UFOs.

So much for the famed Grudge Report. By the late summer of 1949, AMC stated that the green fireball phenomena would no longer be included in its UFO reports. Does this mean that the fireballs were officially discounted as unidentified flying objects? Not exactly. AMC simply handed the fireball problem to the air force's Cambridge Research Laboratory, which established what became known as Project Twinkle. The plan was to triangulate and photograph the fireballs through three cinetheodolite stations. Dr. Lincoln La Paz directed the effort. By mid-September of 1949, Hoyt Vandenberg ordered the new AMC commander, Lt. Gen. Benjamin Chidlaw, to have his Boston labs evaluate the New Mexico and Texas sightings, and to consider the creation of an instrument network.[40]

Meanwhile, the Los Alamos meetings continued. On October 14, 1949, sixteen representatives from the U.S. 4th Army, Armed Forces Special Weapons Project, FBI, AEC, Geophysical Research Division of Air Material Command, and the Air Force Office of Special Investigations met to discuss the green fireballs. In the words of an AFOSI confidential memo, ". . . the continued occurrence of unexplained phenomena of this nature in the vicinity of sensitive installations is cause for concern." The debate was not *whether* the phenomenon was real, but whether it was natural or artificial. UFO researcher Jerome Clark later pointed out that if the fireballs were all natural phenomena, why would they be localized in New Mexico, and why so recently? The meeting attendees probably wondered the same thing.[41]

Sometime during the fall of 1949 there occurred a UFO sighting over "a key atomic base," possibly in New Mexico, involving a high-ranking air force officer and the tracking by radar of five apparently metallic UFOs. The objects flew over the base "at tremendous speed and great height." Radar tracked them at up to one hundred thousand feet, moving three hundred miles in less than four minutes (about 4,500 mph). The incident is one of many missing from the archived Blue Book files but was reported in a 1952 *Life* magazine article. According to UFO researcher Richard Hall, there is "no doubt about its authenticity," even though the case eludes complete documentation.[42]

"THE FLYING SAUCERS ARE REAL!"

In late December 1949, Donald Keyhoe's article "The Flying Saucers are Real" appeared in *True* Magazine. Keyhoe argued that the higher-ups in the military, primarily the air force, knew that flying saucers were real, were of *alien* origin, and were covering up the information from the public in order to avoid panic. The edition was *True*'s best-selling ever, and the air force found itself buried under letters, telegrams, and phone calls demanding information about the flying saucers.

The air force responded by releasing the six-hundred-page Grudge Report (completed the previous August) on December 27, 1949, and announced the project's termination. It strongly implied that it would no longer investigate reports of unidentified flying objects, and repeated the thesis that UFO reports were "the result of: (1) misinterpretation of various conventional objects; (2) a mild form of mass hysteria; or (3) hoaxes."[43]

Press coverage was either sympathetic or apathetic, but in any case uncritical. The media failed to pick up on the significance of a 23 percent unexplained ratio. Instead, it acted as a nearly single entity in accepting the air force's "final word" on the subject, that there was nothing to the UFO phenomenon. The Grudge Report therefore received minimal publicity. History repeated itself twenty years later, when the deeply flawed Colorado University study of UFOs encountered a similarly compliant media that read introductions instead of data.

UFO SECRECY AND PUBLICITY IN EARLY 1950

On the night of January 22–23, 1950, near the Bering Sea at Kodiak, Alaska, navy patrol pilot Lieutenant Smith made a routine security flight. At 2:40 A.M., he obtained a radar reading of an object twenty miles north, which quickly vanished. Eight minutes later, he picked up either the same or a different object. He radioed Kodiak to learn that no known aircraft were in the area. The Kodiak radar officer then reported that *he* was receiving interference, the likes of which he had never experienced.

At about 3 A.M., the USS *Tillamock* was south of Kodiak when one of the men on deck saw "a very fast-moving red glow light, which appeared to be of exhaust nature." The object came from the southeast, moved clockwise in a large circle around Kodiak, and returned to the southeast. Another officer came out to look, saw it in view for thirty seconds, and described it as like "a large ball of orange fire." No sound came from the source of the light.

At 4:40 A.M., Lieutenant Smith, still on airborne patrol and experiencing no radar problems, now picked up another blip on his radar—so fast that it left a trail on his screen. Smith called his crew, who immediately saw the object close a five mile gap in ten seconds, an apparent speed of 1,800 mph. He tried to pursue the object, but it was too maneuverable. Witnesses described two orange lights that rotated around a common center. At some point the object made a sharp turn and headed directly toward Smith's plane. He "considered this to be a highly threatening gesture" and turned off his lights. The UFO flew by and disappeared.

At least thirty-six copies of the navy's detailed report were sent to various security agencies, including the CIA, FBI, air force intelligence, and the Department of State. None of these copies were ever released or published, although a truncated FBI copy surfaced in the 1970s as the result of a Freedom of Information Act request. The document's explanation: "the objects must be regarded as phenomena . . . the exact nature of which could not be determined."[44]

And yet publicly, the air force had stopped investigating UFOs! Ruppelt claimed that UFO investigations at this time rated "minimum effort." The old Project Grudge files, he said, had been "chucked into an old storage case," and many reports were missing when he sifted through them a few years later. What, then, of the Kodiak case? We do not know the military's response to this, but Ruppelt noted that early in 1950, the director of air force intelligence (one of the recipients of the Kodiak report) sent a letter to ATIC indicating that he had never issued any order to end Project Grudge. ATIC replied weakly that it had not actually disbanded Grudge but merely transferred its project functions and no longer considered it a special project. It is possible that the Kodiak incident sparked this exchange.[45]

Throughout the early part of 1950, bizarre accounts of alien crashes and bodies persisted. *Time*'s January 9 issue reported rumors about crashed saucers and small humanoid bodies in New Mexico. A January 16 air force intelligence memo to headquarters reported that stories of crashed saucers in the Southwest were making the rounds in Denver, and were reported in a Kansas City newspaper. The bodies were said to be three feet tall, and the recovered metals defied analysis.[46]

In March, J. Edgar Hoover himself wrote a memo: "Just what are the facts re 'flying saucers'? A short memo as to whether or not it is true or just what air force, etc., think of them." The air force replied with the standard "misidentifications" and "weather balloons" routine. We do not know what Hoover's response was.[47] On March 18, the air force publicly denied that UFOs were secret missiles or space-exploration devices.[48]

More controversial is a March 22, 1950, memo addressed to Hoover by FBI Agent Guy Hottel of the Washington Field Office. It was titled "Flying Saucers—Information Concerning." According to the memo:

> An investigator for the air forces stated that three so-called flying saucers had been recovered in New Mexico. They were described as being circular in shape with raised centers, approximately fifty feet in diameter. Each one was occupied by three bodies of human shape but only three feet tall, dressed in metallic cloth of very fine texture. . . .[49]

UFOs continued to vex American pilots. One January night on the Seattle–Anchorage route, an air freighter was paced for five minutes by an unidentified flying object. The pilots decided to close on the object, which then zoomed away. The airline head was later questioned by intelligence officers for four hours. In his words: "From their questions, I could tell they had a good idea of what the saucers are. One officer admitted they did, but he wouldn't say any more."[50] Near Davis-Monthan AFB on February 1, 1950, a bomber pilot chased a UFO which left a smoke trail. The head of the University of Arizona Department of Astronomy was certain the object was no meteor or other natural phenomenon. At Key West, Florida, on February 22, navy pilots and others saw two glowing UFOs, confirmed by radar, above the Boca Chica Naval Air Station. A plane was sent up to investigate, but was "hopelessly outdistanced." Radar men tracked the objects as they momentarily hovered at an extreme altitude. After a few seconds, the objects rapidly sped away.[51]

Meanwhile, the interest in flying saucers that had been raised by Keyhoe's article continued into the spring. In March of 1950, *True* published, "How Scientists Tracked Flying Saucers," by Cmdr. R. B. McLaughlin, which described the events at White Sands from the previous year. The navy cleared his story, even though it directly contradicted every air force press release on the subject. But the competition between the navy and the air force was intense at this time, and may well have affected the decision to print the article. The air force offered no direct comment, except "behind nearly every report tracked down stands a crackpot, a religious crank, a publicity hound, or a malicious practical joker."[52]

SPRING 1950: AN OUTBREAK OF UFOs

Despite air force statements, the UFOs kept coming. During the early spring of 1950, they made a number of startling appearances over American and international skies. Apparently their operators had not read the Grudge Report.

An extraordinary encounter took place on March 8, 1950, once again right over ATIC in Dayton. In mid-morning, TWA pilot Capt. W. H. Kerr reported to the Civil Aeronautics Administration (CAA) that he and two other TWA pilots saw a UFO hovering at a high altitude. The pilots were unaware that CAA had received about twenty other reports describing a UFO in the area. ATIC control tower operators saw the object, and their radar had an unidentified target in the same position. Something was up there.

Wright-Patterson AFB sent four F-51 fighters to intercept. Two of the pilots saw the object, which appeared round and, in the words of one of them, "huge and metallic." It appeared to be hiding in a cloud formation, which prevented the pilots from closing on it. They eventually turned back. The master sergeant who tracked the object on radar stated, "The target was a good, solid return . . . caused by a good, solid target." Witnesses reported that the UFO climbed vertically out of sight at high speed.

A report was sent to the Civil Aeronautics Authority in Washington, then turned over to air force intelligence. ATIC's official answer was that the UFO had been the planet Venus. The radar return, they said, was caused by ice-laden clouds. The pilots and radar men vehemently disagreed.[53]

A variety of military encounters occurred in rapid succession. One was at Selfridge AFB in Michigan, where a lone UFO caused multiple radar sightings and was tracked at up to 1,500 mph. Another occurred March 16 at the naval air station in Dallas, when a chief petty officer saw a disc-shaped UFO approach a B-36 from below, hover for a moment, then speed away. The air station commander confirmed the sighting.[54]

All spring, commercial airline personnel reported UFOs in droves to the air force. These typically involved objects of disc or circular design, combined with exceptional maneuverability and speed. In at least one case, an airport watch supervisor saw an unidentified light split into two lights which revolved around each other, similar to the Kodiak case. Yet another sighting at Los Alamos occurred on April 17, 1950, when more than fifteen people reported seeing a UFO for twenty minutes at two thousand feet on the eastern horizon. One observer, a scientist from the University of California, watched one of the three objects through a telescope and said the object looked flat, metallic, roughly circular, and about nine feet in diameter. The object moved "faster than any known conventional aircraft." It apparently put on quite a show.[55]

Up to this point, there had been a few photographs taken of UFOs, some of them of reasonably good quality. But the two pictures taken on May 11, 1950, surpassed in quality and credibility anything up to that point, as well as most photos since. These were the photographs taken in McMinnville, Oregon, by Mr. and Mrs. Paul Trent, a farming couple who saw a classic flying saucer over their land early one evening. They took two clear shots of it. Fortunately, between pictures, as the object was moving away, the couple also changed their position, therefore allowing a detailed photographic analysis of the object. The Trents assumed they had seen some type of exotic military aircraft. They did not develop the film in their camera until they used it up, and showed the photos only to a few friends. Eventually it reached the cover of *Life*, but even then the Trents never showed any desire to make money from the photos.

In 1968, the Condon Report said of the photos:

> This is one of the few UFO cases in which all factors investigated, geometric, psychological, and physical, appear to be consistent with the assertion that an extraordinary flying object, silvery, metallic, disc-shaped, tens of meters in diameter, and evidently artificial, flew within the sight of two witnesses.

In the weeks after their sighting, the Trents were visited by representatives of the air force and FBI and were asked many questions. An air force agent demanded and received the pictures and negatives from Bill Powell, who had persuaded the Trents to loan them to him. Although Powell repeatedly requested the photos and negatives back, the air force never returned them.

Over the years, skeptics made several attempts to prove the photos were a hoax. This was the only viable method of debunking them, as the image cannot in any sense be interpreted as something other than a "flying saucer." Several computer enhancement tests, however, proved conclusively that the object was *not* a model suspended on a string—the only seemingly possible hoax method. The Trents themselves have been universally judged to be low-key, honest individuals. As late as 1990, they stood by their story, and the photographs remain a major piece of UFO evidence.[56]

KEEPING THE LID DOWN

The sightings of the spring of 1950 were the most significant wave since 1947. Ironically, they occurred on the heels of the "final" word by the air force on the subject of flying saucers. So far as the public was concerned, the matter was supposed to be dead, and had appeared to be manageable. But by the middle of 1950, it did not necessarily appear so.

The outbreak of war in Korea on June 23 monopolized American attention and provided the impetus for quadrupling the U.S. military budget.

Meanwhile, concern persisted for keeping the lid over UFOs. A July 6 air force memorandum expressed strong interest to acquire motion pictures of a UFO taken by a civilian, but not in a way to arouse suspicion of air force interest.[57] Another memorandum dated July 19, from the chief of the Intelligence Technical Analysis Division, stated that too much time was being spent in investigating flying saucer reports. "Excessive contacts can only serve to keep our interest in these matters a subject of discussion by more people than we would like."[58]

The air force was not the only service investigating UFOs. Navy pilots reported many. On June 24, a cigar-shaped UFO paced a United Airlines plane for twenty minutes about one hundred miles northeast of Los Angeles. The object was seen by the plane's crew, as well as the crews of another commercial airliner and a navy transport plane. The navy pilot saw the UFO for three minutes. He described it as dark gray and giving the appearance of a faint, shimmering, heat radiation at the tail end. He estimated the object's altitude at between fifty thousand and one hundred thousand feet, and moving at 1,000 to 1,500 mph. The object changed direction while he had it in view. The crews of the three planes discussed the matter with two CAA ground stations. Another navy sighting occurred July 11. Two navy aircraft crews near Osceola, Arkansas, saw a domed, disc-shaped object pass before them; the sighting was confirmed by airborne radar. The object first appeared to be a round ball ahead and to the left of their plane. It crossed their flight path and looked like "a shiny, shallow bowl turned upside down." Around this time, Keyhoe's friend Adm. Delmar Fahrney told him privately, "There have been too many convincing reports, and if the flying saucers do exist they must be interplanetary. Certainly neither we nor the Russians have anything remotely like them."[59]

The U.S. Army was also interested in UFOs. A July 30 memorandum from Maj. U. G. Carlan stated that objects from this date were being seen over the Hanford Atomic Energy Commission Plant. Air force fighter squadrons and the FBI were alerted to the matter. AEC stated that "the investigation is continuing, and complete details will be forwarded later."[60]

The FBI and CIA continued their interest. An August memo received by FBI Headquarters was titled, "Summary of Aerial Phenomena in New Mexico." The memo discussed the ongoing green fireball phenomena and noted that OSI was concerned with the continued appearance of unexplained phenomena in the vicinity of sensitive installations in New Mexico. The memo reiterated that Lincoln La Paz did not believe the objects to be meteors.[61]

Meanwhile, the CIA was collecting reports about UFOs overseas. An August 4 report described a sighting from a ship in the north Atlantic en route from Nova Scotia to an eastern U.S. port. The object was fifty to one hundred feet above the water, initially moving at about 25 mph, appeared to be about ten feet in diameter, of a shiny aluminum color, and cylindrical-shaped. It made no noise and wobbled slightly, disappeared over the horizon, then reappeared. The ship's captain was among the three witnesses and observed the object at about a mile away through binoculars for ninety seconds. He described it as "the like of which I have never seen before." Shortly after the men sighted the object, it rapidly accelerated and traveled away at a "tremendous rate of speed." One of the other witnesses described the sighting as "one of the most frightening experiences I have ever had." The CIA report concluded that

> it is quite evident to the intelligence officers who interviewed these men that they had certainly seen some very unusual object which they could not identify but was just as certainly not any conventional type of aircraft.[62]

THE MONTANA FILM

The year 1950 was not only the year of a first-rate photograph of a UFO (actually two, by the Trents), but of a startling sighting caught on 16 mm movie camera film. The man operating the camera was Nicholas "Nick" Mariana, general manager of a local baseball team in Great Falls, Montana. The exact date of the sighting is unclear, the main candidate being August 5, although several researchers lean toward the fifteenth. While inspecting a baseball field prior to a game, Mariana saw two odd, bright lights. He retrieved his movie camera and began to film the objects, which were now moving. He captured them passing behind a water tower, which provided a frame of reference for measuring distance, size, altitude, azimuth, and approximate speed.

Excited by what he had captured on film, Mariana sent it out immediately for development. He showed the film to various civic groups during September and October, and met with an air force officer in October, who took it for analysis. Upon returning his film, the air force said that two jet interceptors had been in the area when the film was taken and might have been responsible for the sighting. Mariana disagreed, as he (and his secretary, who was with him during the filming) claimed to see the jets in another part of the sky.

In 1952, officers at Wright-Patterson AFB asked Mariana if they could review his film again, and he sent it to them. The navy also appears to have reviewed it. Once again, air force records showed that two F-94 fighters had landed at the local air force base at the time of the alleged UFO sighting. Several problems emerged, however. First, analysis showed that Mariana had been mistaken in his claimed time of observation, judging by the particular reflections given off by the objects. Second, Mariana still claimed to have seen the air force jets in another part of the sky. Third, a photogrammetric analysis by Dr. Robert Baker of Douglas Aircraft concluded that the air force explanation—that the images were reflections off jet aircraft—was "quite strained."

Identifying the sighting as "possible aircraft," the air force once again returned the film to Mariana. This time, Mariana claimed that the film was missing the thirty-five best frames, which had shown the objects more clearly as disc-shaped. The air force responded that it had removed a single, damaged, frame and had said so in a letter to Mariana. Mariana claimed that the air force had sent him a letter that would prove his accusation, but he never produced it.

One final problem associated with the date of the film. The air force considered both August 5 and 15 as the two possibilities. Later examination showed that the Great Falls baseball team had no home games between August 9 and 18, which would appear to eliminate August 15 as a candidate. If this is so, then the air force's "possible aircraft" explanation is no longer tenable, as records did not show any aircraft on the fifth in the correct location at the time of the filming. (Of course, Mariana claimed to see those jets.) Seemingly supporting Mariana's claim is the statement of Edward Ruppelt, who also reinvestigated this case. Ruppelt determined to his satisfaction that the two jets were nowhere near where the UFOs had been.

All studies of the Montana film agree that it was not faked, that the objects appeared to be disc-shaped. The Condon committee analysis of the film in the 1960s said that the evidence eliminated the possibility of the objects being birds, balloons, mirages, or meteors, and considered it unlikely, although not impossible, that the objects were jets.[63]

SCULLY, SARBACHER, SMITH, AND KEYHOE

In early September, the first book on UFOs was published, Frank Scully's *Behind the Flying Saucers*. It is best known for its tale of dead humanoid aliens and captured flying saucers in the American Southwest, beginning in 1948. Almost universally, the book was panned. His main source for this information was an oil prospector named Silas Newton and a mysterious "Dr. Gee," later identified as Leo GeBauer, a con man with a long arrest record. In 1952, *True* commissioned J. P. Cahn to check Scully's story, which Cahn exposed as a hoax in his article "The Flying Saucers and the Mysterious Little Men." The story, wrote Cahn, was a ploy to gain the attention of potential investors in a bogus oil detection scheme allegedly linked to ET technology. UFO researcher Jerome Clark called Scully "naive" and wrote that "there seems no doubt that Scully was a victim, not a perpetrator, of the hoax." Most UFO researchers agree with this assessment.[64]

Not all, however. Jim and Coral Lorenzen analyzed claims of occupant sightings more thoroughly than any other researchers during the early years.

In 1975, they wrote that Scully was either telling the truth or was "a prophet." Small humanoids generally answering his description had been seen a number of times, they said. But the approval of the Lorenzens never overcame the effect of Cahn's article.[65]

Scully may have been duped. Nevertheless, his book received serious attention from some people in the Pentagon. This should not be surprising, as secret UFO-related conversations had been taking place all summer long among government, military, and intelligence people. On September 15, Canadian government official and engineer Wilbert Smith came to the U.S. with several colleagues and met in the office of Robert Sarbacher, a physicist with the U.S. Defense Department Research and Development Board. During this meeting, Smith and Sarbacher discussed Scully's book and UFO secrecy in general. Sarbacher told Smith that "the facts reported in [Scully's] book are substantially correct." To Smith's question as to whether saucers exist, Sarbacher replied, "Yes, they exist," and "we have not been able to duplicate their performance." He also told Smith that the UFO subject was "classified two points higher even than the H-bomb. In fact, it is the most highly classified subject in the U.S. government at the present time." As for the reason for the classification, Sarbacher replied, "You may ask, but I can't tell you."

Both men confirmed the reality of this conversation. A handwritten transcript of the conversation was found among Smith's papers after he died. Sarbacher confirmed its truth in 1983, a few years before his own death. Sarbacher also confirmed that debris recovered from an alien vessel was "extremely light and very tough" and described the debris in a manner consistent with descriptions of the Roswell wreckage.[66]

Smith found Scully's theory of UFO magnetic propulsion to be of interest, as it coincided with his own thoughts on the matter. He was also interested in Keyhoe's thoughts on UFOs (Keyhoe himself was about to publish his first UFO book). While in the U.S., he met Keyhoe for the first time, discussed UFO questions, and began a long friendship. Smith mentioned the Canadian government's plans for "Project Magnet," which was designed to track UFOs, but does not appear to have told Keyhoe of the conversation with Sarbacher. Regarding UFOs, Smith said the Canadians have

> weighed three possibilities. One, they're interplanetary. Second, they're a United States secret device. Third, they're Russian. The last two don't stand up. From the weight of evidence I believe the saucers come from outer space. And I think their appearance is what suddenly increased your government's interest in space travel and an artificial satellite. Judging from our own operations, I'm sure your government also is vitally concerned with learning the secret of propulsion.[67]

After Smith's return to Canada, his government quietly pushed forward with Project Magnet. On November 21, 1950, Smith wrote a Top Secret memo mentioning flying saucers:

I made discreet enquiries through the Canadian embassy staff in Washington, who were able to obtain for me the following information: (a) the matter is the most highly classified subject in the United States government, rating higher even than the H-bomb; (b) flying saucers exist; (c) their modus operandi is unknown, but concentrated effort is being made by a small group headed by Dr. Vannevar Bush; (d) the entire matter is considered by the United States authorities to be of tremendous significance.[68]

If Smith knew what he was writing about, and he appears to have, then here is yet more evidence of the sham nature of the moribund Project Grudge.

ANOTHER CRASH?

Military encounters with UFOs continued at a brisk rate for the remainder of the year. Beginning on October 12, a substantial wave of UFO sightings began again over restricted airspace in Oak Ridge, Tennessee. For the next three weeks, no fewer than sixteen UFO incidents there were recorded in an FBI memo and continued into late December.[69]

The FBI wrote another UFO memo (author unknown) on December 3, 1950, advising army intelligence in Richmond, Virginia, "very confidentially" that they have been put "on immediate high alert for any data whatsoever concerning flying saucers." It stated, "CIC (Counter Intelligence Corps) advises data strictly confidential and should not be disseminated."[70]

It is possible that a UFO crashed near Laredo or Del Rio, Texas, on December 6, 1950, although less is known about it than the event at Roswell. Col. Robert Willingham signed an affidavit in 1977 stating that while F-94s were being tested at Dyess AFB, radar caught a UFO on a high-speed intercept course with the planes. Some of the personnel saw the object shortly afterward, which Willingham claimed was not a missile. The object "played around a bit" and even made ninety-degree turns at high speed. North American Air Defense (NORAD) tracked it, and the object was said to have crashed near the Mexican border. Willingham said that he and a copilot took a light aircraft to the site but were immediately escorted away. On his way back, he saw what looked like part of the crash field and picked up a small piece of metal, possibly debris, from the ground. Willingham claimed that, like the Roswell debris, this metal "just wouldn't melt." He took it to a Marine Corps metallurgy lab in Hagerstown, Maryland, for analysis, never saw the metal again, and was even told that the man he asked for had never worked at the lab, nor did anyone there know anything about it. He claimed he was later told never to discuss the matter.[71]

One noteworthy feature of Willingham's affidavit is the year he gave it: 1977, a full year before Stanton Friedman spoke with Maj. Jesse Marcel, and well before the development of the Roswell lore.

1950 TO 1951

Thanks largely to Keyhoe, and despite all efforts by the air force and even the White House, UFOs became an important media issue for the first time in three years. The year 1950 was also a year of significant sightings by many trained airline personnel. It featured one of the best-ever photographs taken of a UFO, and the most striking motion footage to date. It was a year of continued, and seemingly unharassed, violations by UFOs over restricted military airspace, including Air Force Headquarters and several key scientific sites. During the summer, intelligence personnel in the air force, navy, and army, as well as FBI and CIA staffers, were involved to some extent in the investigation of UFOs, while at the same time diligently hiding this fact from the public. Throughout the year, rumors of crashed discs and dead aliens pervaded the air force, reached the FBI, and even spilled over into the media. It was a year of several high-level conversations confirming interest and secrecy about UFOs, of various plans by the American and Canadian governments to track UFOs, and may have featured a crash and recovery of one.

A measure of control over the UFO problem slipped away from the air force during 1950. Other branches of the military and government showed greater behind-the-scenes interest, and the public showed nascent signs of independent thinking on the subject. Still, the problem appeared manageable, at least from a public relations point of view. The beliefs of people like Keyhoe and Scully were still a small minority, and during these years after the Second World War and the peak of the cold war, most Americans held an almost worshipful attitude toward their military. But even a reverential and compliant public could only go along with the program as long as the UFOs themselves—whatever *they* were—remained in the background, as they had more or less done in 1948 and 1949. If 1951 proved to be as active as 1950 had been, things could be difficult for those managing the problem.

Fortunately for those people, 1951 was a less active year for UFOs. During the first half of the year, activity was modest, and it seemed possible that the air force had buried the flying saucer. During April, May, and June, for example, AMC received a mere seventeen UFO reports. But the problem did not exactly go to sleep. Several UFO encounters were spectacular, and not all of them official. On June 1, 1951, one of these occurred directly over Wright-Patterson AFB in Dayton, Ohio. An official at the base saw a disc make a turn too sharply for any known aircraft. He described it as a "clearly defined outline similar to a stubby cigar" and moving "faster than an airplane, slower than a meteor." Years later, when he reported the sighting to NICAP, he requested confidentiality because of his position.[72] Another interesting encounter took place on July 9, 1951, over Dearing, Georgia. While flying an F-51, Air Force Lt. George Kinmon saw a white, disc-shaped object "completely round and spinning in a clockwise direction" making a head-on pass at his aircraft. The air force intelligence report noted that the object was

> described as flat on top and bottom and appearing from a front view to have round edges and slightly beveled. . . . No vapor trails or exhaust or visible means of propulsion. Described as traveling at tremendous speed. . . . Pilot considered by associates to be highly reliable, of mature judgment and a creditable observer.[73]

Less than a week later, on July 14, near White Sands, two radar operators picked up a fast-moving UFO. One tracker watching a B-29 through binoculars saw a large UFO near the bomber. Simultaneously, another observer with a movie camera shot two hundred feet of film of the object, which supposedly showed a round, bright spot. Unfortunately, the film disappeared and has not been seen since.[74]

Project Grudge could hardly be expected to investigate even this minimal activity: by the summer of 1951, it had a single person serving as investigator of flying saucer reports.[75]

THE LUBBOCK LIGHTS

The air force containment of the UFO problem depended first and foremost upon the cooperation of the UFOs themselves. As the pace of good sightings increased during the latter half of 1951, the air force had to decide whether it needed to manage the problem differently. The problem started with the Lubbock Lights.

On August 25, 1951, three college professors relaxing in a backyard in Lubbock, Texas, saw a formation of about twenty to thirty soft, glowing, bluish-green lights silently pass over them. They saw a similar group of lights a few hours later. The lights seemed to move "exactly" together. During the next two months, they saw at least ten more. Other people also noticed the odd lights. On the evening of the thirtieth, a young man named Carl Hart took five photographs of them in his backyard. The lights were visible only a few seconds each time Hart saw them, but they appeared to be at a high altitude. Ruppelt, who was later sent to investigate the incident, said of them, "In each photograph, the individual lights in the formation shifted position according to a definite pattern." The photo labs at ATIC studying Hart's photos commented:

> [T]he two rows of spots behaved differently. One row shows only slight variation from a precise "V" formation throughout, whereas the other row appears to pass from above the first row, through it to a position below.

The objects in the photographs were never identified, and no evidence ever emerged to suggest that Hart's photographs were hoaxes.

Dr. Donald Menzel of Harvard tried to discredit the Lubbock Lights incident in *Look* and *Time* magazines and in his book *Flying Saucers,* with the theory that the professors were merely looking at refracted city lights. ATIC eventually labeled the Lubbock Lights sighting as light reflecting from birds (plover), though the idea of birds reflecting blue-green light fails to convince many people. Also, the photographs of the lights show a symmetrical and rigid formation, quite unlike a formation of plover.

While the Lubbock Lights bewildered the people of Texas, a low-flying V-shaped object appeared over Sandia AFB, a key atomic base in New Mexico. The object looked larger than a B-26, was silvery in color, had six or eight lights grouped in pairs, and flew at 400 mph. Like the lights in Lubbock, it was silent, but in this case reflected the city lights as it flew over. Ruppelt wondered whether the two seemingly distinct objects could be the same.[76]

As intriguing as the sightings themselves was Ruppelt's description of who studied the reports. He noted that access to the information regarding the Lubbock Lights was restricted to two groups: (1) ATIC's UFO investigative body and (2) another, unnamed group of people who, "due to their associations with the government, had complete access to our files." These people

were scientists—rocket experts, nuclear physicists, and intelligence experts. They had banded together to study our UFO reports because they were convinced that some of the UFOs that were being reported were interplanetary spaceships, and the Lubbock series was one of these reports.[77]

Ruppelt could not have stated the matter any clearer. He described an extragovernmental group with preponderant influence within the government (how else could they have complete access to ATIC's UFO files?) who believed that UFOs were extraterrestrial. Whatever the truth about the MJ-12 documents, Ruppelt described perfectly a group fitting the description of MJ-12. Their evident goal was to manage the UFO problem, and they appeared to supersede the authority of ATIC.

THE REAL CONTROLLERS?

At Fort Monmouth, New Jersey, on the morning of September 10, a student radar operator, giving a demonstration for top military officials, caught an object "going faster than a jet." His audience was incredulous. Twenty-five minutes later, however, a pilot and major aboard a T-33 jet trainer out of Dover AFB in Maryland saw a "dull, silver, disclike object" far below them. They obtained a radar fix on the object, which was traveling as fast as 900 mph. As the pilot descended rapidly to get a better view, the object hovered, then sped off and vanished out toward the sea.

A few hours later, Fort Monmouth Army Signal Center received an "almost frantic call" from headquarters to pick up a target high and to the north in the same area where the earlier UFO had been spotted. Another unidentified object was on the screen, traveling very slowly at the incredible altitude of eighteen miles. Visually, the object was discernible as a silver speck. The next morning, two radar sets picked up a target that performed nearly vertical climbs and dives, leveled off for a while, then performed more acrobatics.

The next day, on September 12, 1951, a three-foot-long teletype arrived at Wright-Patterson AFB from Fort Monmouth, a copy of which went to Washington, D.C. Almost immediately, ATIC's new chief, Col. Frank Dunn, received a phone call from the office of the director of air force intelligence, Maj. Gen. Charles Cabell. Cabell wanted somebody from ATIC to get down to New Jersey and find out what was going on. Dunn sent Lt. Jerry Cummings (head of what remained of Project Grudge) and Lt. Col. N. R. Rosengarten. A few days later, the two officers briefed Cabell at a meeting that included his entire staff "and a special representative from Republic Aircraft Corporation." Ruppelt's words on this matter once again hint toward the existence of some kind of MJ-12 group:

> The man from Republic supposedly represented a group of top U.S. industrialists and scientists who thought that there should be a lot more sensible answers coming from the air force regarding the UFOs. The man was at the meeting at the personal request of a general officer.

According to Ruppelt,

> every word of the two-hour meeting was recorded on a wire recorder. The recording was so hot that it was later destroyed, but not before I heard it several times. I can't tell everything that was said but, to be conservative, it didn't exactly follow the tone of the official air force releases.

Cabell supposedly learned at this meeting that Grudge had effectively been dead for some time. He demanded to know "who in hell has been giving me these reports that every decent flying saucer report is being investigated?" He ordered the men to get moving and report to him when a new project was ready to go.[78]

As a result, Ruppelt was placed in charge of the "new" Project Grudge. He soon appointed Hynek (already an air force consultant in astronomy) as chief scientific consultant. But Grudge continued to lack funds to do serious investigating. Just how important could the new and improved Project Grudge have been to a national security establishment that had undertaken the Manhattan Project, won the Second World War, and was fighting communism in Korea, when it even lacked a routine way of getting fresh UFO reports? UFOs were violating restricted and sensitive American airspace with complete impunity practically every month, and the air force continued to dole out the fiction that Grudge's pathetic operation was the vehicle for meeting that threat.

There was an undeniable discrepancy between the public and real policy regarding UFO reporting. The official and public version had all reports going to ATIC; the real policy was that each branch of military reported UFOs, but many of those reports never made it to ATIC. JANAP 146(B), authorized in August 1949, made it clear that all important reports went elsewhere: to Air Defense Command, the Secretary of Defense, the CIA, and "other appropriate agencies." Could one such "agency" be the group of "scientists and industrialists" described by Ruppelt? Since they had unlimited access to ATIC files, it is at least plausible that they had comparable access to navy and army files, and possibly CIA or FBI files. Whoever comprised this nebulous and powerful group, they are the best candidates for being managers of the "real" investigation, of which ATIC's contribution was merely a share.

Why, then, did Cabell get so angry over the dilapidated state of what *he had to know* was a fiction of an organization? As director of air force intelligence, Cabell knew that the UFO problem was being monitored at levels higher than ATIC, as indicated by the presence of the "man from Republic" in his office. The most probable scenario is that from the summer of 1948 onward—that is, following Vandenberg's rejection of the Estimate of the Situation—the main policy was to keep Project Sign/Grudge in the dark. Most likely, the main contours of the UFO problem were evident enough to those at the top that it seemed counterproductive to continue stirring the pot at the lower levels, when the result would not be new information about UFOs but simply heightened interest by those who did not need to know. This would be especially important regarding Grudge, since it was publicly known to be the military's UFO investigative body, and as such, was the key to the Pentagon's public relations on the subject. The last thing desirable would be to have your most visible office actually *believe* in UFOs. The best way to avoid this would be to strangle the flow of good information going into ATIC, as much as could reasonably be done.

Cabell had never entirely agreed with Grudge policy. For several years, he had wanted to augment its reporting capabilities, although his efforts met with failure. Perhaps he thought that the last two months presented him with the chance to drive home his point that better UFO reporting was needed, that the new wave of activity warranted a new approach. Maybe *not* everything was known about the UFOs.

ATTEMPTED INTERCEPTS AND NEAR MISSES

While Ruppelt busied himself reactivating Project Grudge, the UFO party continued. On September 23 at March AFB near Long Beach, California, two F-86 jets tried to intercept an object in controlled orbit at around fifty-five thousand feet, but they ran low on fuel and had to land. Two more F-86s were scrambled, with the same results. Three of the pilots reported seeing a "silver airplane with highly swept-back wings," although one of them said the UFO looked round and silver. Regardless, in 1951 the U.S. had no plane that could fly higher than the F-86.[79] Encounters continued during October and November. In Korea, fourteen American ships tracked an object on radar as it circled the fleet, then departed at over 1,000 mph.[80]

Amid this renewed surge of sightings, the new Project Grudge was officially established on October 27. Before reporting directly to General Cabell on his method of operation, Ruppelt decided to try out his ideas on some "well-known scientists and engineers" who regularly visited ATIC. He learned that "UFOs were being freely and seriously discussed in scientific circles." On or around December 11, Ruppelt traveled with ATIC Chief Frank Dunn to the Pentagon. Maj. Gen. John A. Samford had replaced Cabell as air force director of intelligence but seemed "familiar with the general aspects of the problem." Samford's aide, Gen. W. M. Garland, told the two that ATIC had the sole authorization to carry out UFO investigations for the entire U.S. military—a statement that Garland in no way could have meant to be true. He also told Ruppelt and Dunn unequivocally that the United States had no secret aircraft, or other device, which was being reported as a UFO. The three discussed security problems posed by UFOs at vital U.S. installations.[81]

SUMMARY

For three years the UFO problem was managed by the American military and intelligence community with only limited interference from its citizenry. True, by 1951 that interference was greater than it had been in 1948, but thanks largely to an acquiescent media, it still posed little of a problem. The UFOs themselves were more intractable. While many in the military honestly believed them to be nonsense, many others—usually expressing their opinions discreetly—did not. A large number of UFO sightings lent credence to their existence as real objects, and the American military seemed helpless to prevent them from doing as they pleased, such as violating sensitive airspace and appearing over areas where multiple witnesses could see them.

This period also provided scattered evidence that a select group of men from scientific, military, and intelligence circles supervised or monitored the activities at ATIC. It is not known whether this group answered to the president or another individual. It does seem clear, however, that they took the UFO problem more seriously than official pronouncements at ATIC indicated. Less apparent is whether they had any plan for dealing with it.

Chapter 4

Crisis and Containment: 1952 and 1953

The object possessed a superior speed, superior climbing ability, and was able to turn equally well as the F-94.
—Air force intelligence report on UFO interception from May 23, 1952

. . . indicates an actual appearance of "unidentified flying objects."
—Field intelligence officer description of a multiple-witness sighting of UFOs over Walker AFB (formerly Roswell AAF), observed through a theodolite, July 1952

The Air Force has had teams of experts investigating all reports for several years, since the end of World War II, and they have never found anything to substantiate the existence of such things as flying saucers.
—General of the Air Force Hoyt Vandenberg, to the press, July 1952

Absolute power has no necessity to lie, it may be silent—while responsible governments obliged to speak not only disguise the truth, but lie with effrontery.
—Napoleon Bonaparte

OVERVIEW OF THE YEAR

In the history of the UFO, 1952 rivals 1947 as The Great Year. In the United States, the number of good sightings reached a still-unmatched peak. Even ATIC's new and improved Project Grudge (renamed Blue Book in early spring), with an enlarged staff of about a dozen people, could not keep up with the reports. By the middle of the year, the situation was in crisis. First of all, the public debate about UFOs threatened to go completely beyond the control of the Pentagon, where it had firmly resided for five years. Second, the sheer number of unidentified objects, including over the White House for two consecutive weekends, posed a substantial threat of unknown dimensions.

As a result, national security measures were taken to push UFOs deeper under cover. Not only was the air force involved in this, but so was the CIA. The policy met with some resistance behind closed doors, but by early 1953 it was clear that secrecy prevailed. The measures undertaken in 1952 created a policy that remained relatively unchanged for more than ten years—until the nationwide UFO wave of the mid-1960s.

BASE SIGHTINGS

The crescendo of UFO sightings that began in August 1951 continued onward. On the very first day of the new year, an object circled and maneuvered for eight minutes over a Royal Canadian Air Force Base at North Bay. It appeared to be very large and traveled at supersonic speed. On January 20 at Fairchild AFB near Spokane, two intelligence specialists saw a large, bluish-white, spherical object approaching, which they later determined to be moving at 1,400 mph. The next day, a U.S. Navy pilot chased a white dome-shaped object over Mitchell AFB on Long Island; the UFO simply accelerated and pulled away. The case stumped Ruppelt.[1]

On the following evening, a UFO once again violated restricted airspace. At a northern Alaska outpost on January 22, 1952, radar captured an object traveling 1,500 mph at twenty-three thousand feet. When an F-94 was sent to intercept, the target slowed down, stopped, reversed course, and headed directly for the radar station. It came to within thirty miles of the station, then disappeared from the screen. The F-94 headed back to refuel, and a second F-94 was scrambled. This pilot obtained a strong and distinct radar return. At first, the object was almost stationary, but then it dived suddenly, at which point ground radar picked it up again. A third F-94 was scrambled, also obtained the object on radar, and closed to within two hundred yards. At this point, the pilot pulled away for fear of collision, as the UFO was nearly immobile in the air. Since none of the pilots obtained a visual of the object, the air force concluded that the radar returns were weather-related, although the people involved in the incident strongly disputed this.[2]

In Korea on January 29, a bright, disc-shaped orange object, also described as a "huge ball of fire," paced two B-29s on the same night, eighty miles from each other in the towns of Wonsan and Sunchon. This incident received some media attention in mid-February, and added to the growing interest in Washington.

GRUDGE BECOMES BLUE BOOK

Under Ruppelt's leadership, Project Grudge became respectable. In early February, Ruppelt met with the commander of Air Defense Command, Gen. Benjamin Chidlaw, who issued a directive to all units explaining procedures in UFO situations. This began a period of cooperation between Project Grudge and ADC. The 4602nd AISS was also activated under ADC's command. Originally intended to obtain air combat intelligence, by mid-1953 the unit actually supplanted the staff at Dayton in the UFO arena.[3]

For now, however, Grudge was busy. After his meeting with Chidlaw, Ruppelt met with two Royal Canadian air force officers who brought their own UFO reports and wanted to know how Grudge operated. By March 1952, Project Grudge went from being a mere project within a group to a separate organization under the title Aerial Phenomena Group. By the end of the month, its name became Blue Book.[4]

On April 3, the air force announced that it had *not* stopped investigating and evaluating UFO reports, as it had previously stated. This may have been news to the public, but was common knowledge to those following the matter. On April 5, the secretary of the air force signed Air Force Letter 200-5, which stated that UFOs were not a joke, that Blue Book was making a serious study of them, and directed intelligence officers on every air force base throughout the world to report UFOs immediately to ATIC and all major air force commands, then to send a more detailed report later to ATIC (with copies to the air force director of intelligence). AFR 200-5 enabled Blue Book staff to communicate directly with any air force base or unit without going through the normal chain of command. AFR 200-5 noted that "reports should not be classified higher than 'Restricted' unless inclusion of data required . . . mandates a higher classification."[5]

On the heels of the announcement came an air force-sponsored article in *Life* titled, "Have We Visitors from Space?" *Life*'s answer: Maybe. The article came close to advocating the extraterrestrial hypothesis (ETH), and gave it more serious consideration than any other major publication hitherto. Although the *New York Times* criticized the article, its main source was clearly the air force itself. Ruppelt knew that "very high-ranking" Pentagon officers, "so high that their personal opinion was almost policy," had unofficially inspired the article, and that one of these men had given his opinions to reporter Robert Ginna. Why was the air force (or elements within) giving apparent support to the ETH?[6]

Perhaps because UFOs were everywhere that spring, with many sightings by the military. Just before the press conference, a remarkable incident had taken place, on March 29, near Misawa, Japan. The day was bright and clear, and an air force pilot was flying a T-6 target plane on a practice intercept mission for two F-84s. The first F-84 overtook him at six thousand feet when the T-6 pilot noticed a small, shiny disc-shaped object *gaining on the interceptor.* The UFO curved toward the F-84, rapidly decelerated, then flipped on edge in a ninety-degree bank. It flew between the two aircraft, pulled away, flipped again, passed the F-84, crossed in front, and accelerated out of sight in a near vertical climb. Both pilots noticed the object, which came to within thirty to fifty feet of the T-6; the pilot estimated it to be a mere eight inches in diameter. Although he saw no exhaust, he reported a ripple around its edge.[7]

In April, Blue Book received ninety-nine reports, a busy month. Many were baffling, such as this incident from San Jose, California, on April 25, when two formerly skeptical scientists saw "a small metallic-appearing disc rotating and wobbling on its axis." Years later, James McDonald interviewed the two men, who said they saw

> overhead a large, black circular object joined by two similar objects that dropped out of an overcast. The small disc accelerated upwards and one of the larger black objects, perhaps one hundred feet in diameter, took off after it on a seemingly converging course; both then vanished in the overcast.

One of the two remaining black objects then took off to the north. The scientists concluded that they had seen something extraterrestrial, using "some propulsion method not in the physics books." Despite the quality of their sighting, they told only a few colleagues, for fear of ridicule.[8]

Many sighting reports never made it to Dayton. Keyhoe's navy connections gave him one involving the Secretary of the Navy, Dan Kimball, and Adm. Arthur Radford during April 1952. While flying to Hawaii, Kimball saw two disc-shaped objects moving at about 1,500 mph. The UFOs circled his plane twice, then headed to another navy plane, which was carrying Radford, fifty miles east. The objects circled Radford's plane and zoomed up out of sight. Upon landing, Kimball sent a report of the encounter to the air force. But despite repeated inquiries, he received no information on his case. Instead, he learned the air force was aggressively demanding all copies of UFO reports from navy and Marine Corps witnesses, even before preliminary navy investigations had been made. Kimball therefore decided to initiate naval intelligence reports on UFOs—independent from Blue Book. He told the Office of Naval Research to start a special investigation "to be kept separate from the air force project." Keyhoe received this information from his old friend Adm. Calvin Bolster, chief of ONR, as well as from Kimball himself. According to them, the air force squawked at the news of a formal, independent navy body to investigate UFOs, and ONR eventually stopped its official investigation. Kimball never made his own sighting public, although mentioning it to Keyhoe amounted to the same thing.[9]

THE MERRY MONTH OF MAY 1952

Blue Book received seventy-nine UFO reports in May. Press coverage of UFOs was on the rise, an interest which was surpassed, in Ruppelt's words, "only by the interest of the Pentagon." He was in a good position to know. Throughout the spring and summer, he gave an average of one briefing in Washington, D.C., every two weeks, "and there was always a full house."[10]

The first day of the month set the tone, involving a classic case near Davis-Montham AFB, later investigated by Dr. James McDonald, in which an air intelligence officer, a B-36 crew, and an airman witnessed two shiny, round objects overtake their plane. The objects slowed down to match the plane's speed and remained in formation with them for about twenty seconds. At that point, they made a very sharp no-radius turn away from the B-36, flew away a bit, then one of the objects stopped and hovered. Both objects were silent. The Blue Book team dismissed the case as "aircraft." On the same day at George AFB in California, five independent witnesses saw a group of five day-light discs. The objects appeared to be very maneuverable, and seemed almost to collide, then break away. Blue Book labeled this as unidentified.[11]

Ruppelt also mentioned a remarkable UFO sighting in May by "one of the top people" in the CIA while he gave a lawn party at his home near Alexandria, Virginia. A silent object performed a nearly vertical climb, then dove straight down, leveled off, and zoomed away. "A number of notable personages" in attendance also saw it. They made some phone calls that night, and "the mention of their names on a telephone got quick results." The news reached General Samford, who phoned ATIC chief Dunn. Dunn in turn told Ruppelt to get to Washington on the double. Ruppelt quickly arrived to interview the host and learn what he could, but the object remained unknown.[12]

On May 8, Air Force Secretary Thomas Finletter and his staff received a secret one-hour briefing on UFOs from Ruppelt and Lt. Col. R. J. Taylor, covering the five-year ATIC investigation. Not much is known about the meeting. According to Ruppelt, Finletter listened intently and asked several questions about specific sightings when the briefing was finished. His only other comment was, "You're doing a fine job, Captain. It must be interesting. Thank you." An interesting sidelight to the matter: Finletter's special assistant, Joseph Bryan III. In a letter to Ruppelt in 1956, Bryan wrote that while he served under Finletter, he had tried "to have him prepare a statement for release when communication was established with a saucer." According to Bryan, Finletter declined to do so. Bryan, supposedly a mere special assistant, was a CIA man who had directed the agency's psychological warfare unit. (This was completely unknown until the 1970s but is well known now. The letter to Ruppelt was only published in 2000.) In 1960, Bryan joined the board of directors of NICAP, then the world's major civilian UFO organization.[13]

The latter part of May had its share of intriguing UFO sightings and lame explanations. Consider the following event from Chorwon, Korea, on the last day of the month. Several U.S. soldiers saw a bright UFO that looked like a falling star, except that it stopped falling and began to climb again. It then moved northeast at about 150 mph, reversed course twice, then climbed at a forty-five-degree angle and faded from sight. One guard reported a pulsating sound from the object. An air intelligence information report stated that an F-94 attempted to intercept this object. The pilot described it as round, of unknown size, "brilliant white," and leaving no exhaust. It undertook clearly evasive maneuvers and pulled away from the F-94 at thirty thousand feet. According to the intelligence report, "the object possessed a superior speed, superior climbing ability, and was able to turn equally as well as the F-94" Blue Book's evaluation: "balloon with flare."[14]

The Pace Quickens

May had been a busy month for Blue Book; the pace doubled in June. That month, Ruppelt's staff received 149 sighting reports. He later described the month as "one big swirl of UFO reports." The air force, he believed, was taking the UFO problem seriously, partly because of the good reports coming from Korea. By now, Ruppelt had four officers, two airmen, and two civilians on his permanent staff. In addition, a number of scientists, including Hynek, were working in a significant capacity for the team. In the Pentagon, Maj. Dewey Fournet was a full-time Blue Book liaison. In terms of staffing and prestige within the air force, Blue Book was at its peak. It appeared that, through the Blue Book office at ATIC, the air force was serious about studying the UFO problem. Even so, the Blue Book staff was overwhelmed with reports.[15]

Amid the crush of sightings, discussion and activity about UFOs increased, within official circles and beyond. On June 4, Air Force Secretary Finletter publicized his recent UFO briefing, noting that the evidence remained inconclusive but warranted investigation. A few days later, Donald Menzel wrote in *Time* that most UFO sightings were light reflections caused by ice crystals in clouds, refraction, or temperature inversion. His theory soon became the official—and wrong—air force explanation for the Washington, D.C., sightings of July. Later that month, with air force help, *Look* printed "Hunt for the Flying Saucer." It featured the declaration by Gen. Hoyt Vandenberg that "we cannot afford to be complacent" about UFOs. According to

Keyhoe, the article upset the Pentagon "silence group." Of course, if that were true, what group was Vandenberg in?[16]

The most serious discussions occurred behind closed doors. In the middle of June, Ruppelt briefed General Samford and his staff. Two navy captains from the Office of Naval Intelligence and (in Ruppelt's words) "some people I can't name" also attended. The meeting was tense and contentious. One of Samford's staff members, a colonel, argued that Blue Book's investigation was biased against the interplanetary thesis. After this statement, "you could almost hear the colonel add, 'O.K., so now I've said it.'" This started an emotional debate with nothing accomplished. Blue Book was directed simply to "take further steps to obtain positive identification" of UFOs.[17]

The military encounters continued. On June 18, 1952, a UFO paced a B-25 in California for thirty minutes. On the nineteenth, at Goose Bay Air Base in Labrador, members of the ground crew saw a strange, red-lighted object approach the field, climb steeply, then disappear; radar crews also tracked the object. On the twenty-first, just before 11 P.M., an unidentified object trespassed, once again, the restricted airspace at the AEC's Oak Ridge facility in Tennessee. The craft was observed visually, tracked on radar, and pursued by the pilot of an F-47 on combat patrol. During the ensuing aerial dogfight, the UFO evidently attempted to ram the F-47 several times before leaving the area.[18]

THE JULY CRISIS

From Ruppelt's perspective, the split in opinions about what to do about UFOs widened every day. One group was "dead serious about the situation." They wanted (1) a policy of starting from the assumption that UFOs were interplanetary, and (2) a clampdown on the release of information. According to Ruppelt, this group thought that the security classification of the project should go up to Top Secret. He wrote that their enthusiasm "took a firm hold in the Pentagon" and many other agencies throughout the government. By the end of the month, events forced a public confrontation and a behind-the-scenes decision on the matter of UFOs. Small wonder, since ATIC received a whopping 536 reports that month, with unknowns running at 40 percent.[19]

One of the key UFO sightings of the month, and indeed of the modern era, took place in Tremonton, Utah, on July 2. Delbert C. Newhouse was a warrant officer and veteran naval aviation photographer who owned a 16mm Bell & Howell movie camera. While out driving with his family, he noticed unusual objects in the sky and got out of the vehicle with his camera, which had a telephoto lens. The objects were originally at close range, "large, disc-shaped, and brightly lighted," and "shaped like two saucers, one inverted on top of the other." By the time he had the camera ready, they were directly overhead but had receded quite a bit from their original position. He shot about seventy-five seconds' worth of color film that captured what seemed to be twelve to fourteen shiny points of light maneuvering at high speed. He claimed steadfastly that he held his camera steady.

The film went to ATIC and Blue Book. Ruppelt told Fournet in Washington about it, and Fournet arranged for the original film to be shown to a group of high-ranking intelligence officers. It then arrived at the air force's photo reconnaissance laboratory at Wright-Patterson AFB. A few weeks later, this lab told Ruppelt that "we don't know what they are, but they aren't airplanes or balloons, and we don't think they are birds." The complete air force investigation of the Utah film lasted for months. Although the analysts tried to identify the objects as something conventional, they were unable to do so, except to suggest "possible birds."

The navy soon asked for the Utah film. Specialists at the U.S. Navy photographic laboratory in Anacosta, Maryland, spent two months and nearly one thousand man-hours studying it frame by frame. They determined that if the objects were as much as five miles distant, they would have been moving at around 3,780 mph; if only one mile distant, then 472 mph. They ruled out natural phenomena and concluded that the objects were not reflecting sunlight, but instead were internally lighted spheres. Moreover, the lab concluded that "changes in the light's intensity, among other things, eliminates the possibility that the images were aircraft or birds." The objects, they said, were intelligently controlled vehicles of some kind—"unknown objects under intelligent control." This clearly implied, but did not explicitly state (who would?) a nonhuman, extraterrestrial answer. Newhouse's film became a featured piece of UFO evidence for the CIA-sponsored Robertson Panel of January 1953.[20]

But Newhouse's sighting was merely one of many that month. On July 5, two Florida pilots reported seeing a flying saucer hover above the AEC's Hanford atomic plant in Richlands, Washington. Like the plant at Oak Ridge, the Hanford plant was a sensitive AEC nuclear installation that had been the scene of repeated UFO airspace violations. The UFO was said to be round and flat; it gained speed, reversed course, then quickly disappeared. The next day, the Dayton *Daily News* ran the headline, "Flyers Report Saucers Near Atomic Plant." The press contacted ATIC for comment, but received no reply. Ruppelt called them the next day to say that all he knew about the sighting was what he had read in the papers. No surprise, since Ruppelt and Blue Book were out of the loop. Shortly after these calls, ATIC instructed Blue Book officers to "stall" off the press "with a no-comment answer." The plant was again visited by UFOs on the twelfth, this time two yellow globes with a fiery appearance; air force investigators confirmed the sighting.[21]

At 3 A.M. on the thirteenth, during an evening of excellent visibility, a

National Airlines pilot about sixty miles southwest of Washington, D.C., radioed CAA that a blue-white light was approaching him. It came to within two miles of his plane, then paced him off his left wing. Willing to try anything, the pilot turned on all of his lights, and the UFO took off "up and away like a star" at an estimated speed of 1,000 mph.[22]

ATIC received an "extremely accurate" report describing a UFO from the evening of the fourteenth by two Pan Am pilots near Langley AFB, Virginia. They witnessed a formation of six illuminated disc-like objects, appearing to be about one hundred feet in diameter, making incredible maneuvers at unbelievable speeds. One of the objects made a sharp turn below the airliner and was joined by two more discs. The objects accelerated away at a speed calculated by the pilots to be two hundred miles per minute (12,000 mph).[23]

The sheer quantity of good reports, preceded by a steady buildup throughout the spring, gave the military more than just something to think about. Ruppelt described rumors that in mid-July, the air force was braced for an invasion by flying saucers. "Had these rumormongers been at ATIC in mid-July they would have thought the invasion was already in full swing."[24]

Around this time, Ruppelt talked for two hours about the buildup of UFO reports along the east coast of the United States with "a scientist, from an agency that I can't name." The scientist said to Ruppelt that they were "sitting right on top of a big keg full of loaded flying saucers." He predicted that "within the next few days, they're going to blow up and you're going to have the granddaddy of all UFO sightings. The sightings will occur in Washington or New York, probably Washington." What was this man's agency? How did he obtain this information? Did his remarks mean that UFOs were part of some secret military organization? Or that he knew the alien agenda? Or that he was a lucky guesser? Ruppelt did not answer these questions, nor has anyone else.[25]

THE WASHINGTON, D.C. SIGHTINGS

Washington, D.C. had already been the scene of UFO activity. But what happened for the next two weekends went far beyond anything up to that point. The Washington sightings were among the most compelling and dramatic UFO sightings in modern American history, and remain—despite any official pretense to the contrary—unsolved.[26]

At 11:40 P.M. on July 19, radar at Washington National Airport picked up a formation of seven objects near Andrews AFB, moving along at a leisurely pace of 100 to 130 mph. Before long, two of the targets suddenly accelerated and vanished off the scope within seconds. One of them apparently reached 7,000 mph. This got the attention of several controllers, especially when they learned that a second radar at the airport, as well as the radar at Andrews AFB, also picked up the objects. For six hours, between eight and ten UFOs were tracked on radar.

The senior air traffic controller for the CAA, Harry G. Barnes, "knew immediately that a very strange situation existed." In his opinion:

> . . . [The] movements were completely radical compared to those of ordinary aircraft. They followed no set course [and] were not in any formation, and we only seemed to be able to track them for about three miles at a time. . . . [F]or six hours . . . there were at least ten unidentifiable objects moving above Washington. They were not ordinary aircraft. . . . I can safely deduce that they performed gyrations which no known aircraft could perform.

Several times, at least two of the radar stations displayed the same targets simultaneously. But the phenomenon was not restricted to radar tracking. Several Capitol Airlines pilots saw the objects visually as orange lights in the same area that radar indicated they should be. Just where were they? Over the White House and Capitol!

A radar-visual sighting of eight to ten UFOs over such highly restricted airspace is certainly cause to send a few jet interceptors, and this is exactly what happened. But by the time the interceptors arrived, shortly before dawn, it was too late. The objects were gone.

The sighting made headlines the next day. And yet, according to Ruppelt, "nobody bothered to tell air force intelligence about the sighting." At least nobody bothered to tell ATIC, which by now was receiving about thirty UFO reports per day. When Ruppelt arrived in Washington to investigate, he learned that President Truman was personally interested in the affair and wanted a full investigation. Good news for Ruppelt, except that all the while he was in Washington, Ruppelt could not obtain a military vehicle, and had to use a bus. Who, then, did Truman want to do this full investigation? Clearly not Blue Book.

In the week that followed, sightings continued at an intense pace throughout the country. Several occurred over military bases. According to the Washington, D.C., *Daily News*, the Defense Department ordered jets to shoot down UFOs which refused to land when ordered to do so. Meanwhile, senior air force officers urged Intelligence to hold a press conference to relieve public tension.

Dozens of new reports reached Blue Book every day. Near Boston on July 23, a bluish-green object easily evaded a pursuing F-94 that tracked it on radar. On the same day in Culver City, California, several aircraft-plant workers saw an elliptical-shaped object through binoculars. The object stopped and hovered, and they saw two smaller discs emerge from it, circle, rejoin the "mother" ship, then vanish at tremendous speed. [27] On July 24, two air force colonels flying a B-25 over the Sierra Nevada saw three "bright silver, delta wing craft with no tails and no pilot's canopies." They estimated its speed at 1,000 mph, and believed it came to within four hundred to eight hundred yards of their plane.[28]

But, somehow, flying over the nation's Capitol was *different*, and on July 26, the UFOs returned there. At 8:15 P.M., the pilot and stewardess of a National Airlines flight saw several objects resembling the glow of a cigarette high above them. The lights moved slowly, perhaps at 100 mph. Before long, Washington National Airport and Andrews AFB were tracking a dozen UFOs throughout most of the sky, all traveling between 90 and 100 mph. Andrews alerted Newcastle AFB shortly after 9 P.M. Finally, by midnight, two F-94s were scrambled to intercept. Meanwhile, the press had been dismissed from the air traffic control tower on the grounds that the procedures used to intercept were classified. Ruppelt called this reason absurd; rather,

> not a few people in the radar room were positive that this night would be the big night in UFO history—the night when a pilot would close in on and get a good look at a UFO—and they didn't want the press to be in on it.

The objects had been tracked continuously for nearly two hours—an important point, as this appeared to rule out atmospheric phenomena. But as the F-94s approached, they disappeared from the radarscopes. Visibility was excellent, but the pilots saw nothing. As the pilots returned to their base, the targets returned to the area.

Near Newport News, Virginia, reports were reaching Langley AFB about odd, rotating lights that gave off alternating colors. Tower operators saw these lights. Another F-94 was scrambled, obtained a radar lock, and the target sped away.

Back at Washington National, the objects reappeared shortly before dawn, and two more F-94s were scrambled. The pilots obtained radar locks and moved toward the targets. Again, the objects sped away. Eventually, one appeared to stay put, and an F-94 moved to intercept. The target then disappeared.

Dewey Fournet was in the Washington National tower throughout the night. He said that everyone in the radar room believed the targets were "very probably caused by solid metallic objects." One of the F-94 pilots, William Patterson, commented, "I saw several bright lights. I was at my maximum speed, but even then I had no closing speed." An air force intelligence report, classified until 1985, stated that the entire radar crew was emphatic that the returns were solid, and not temperature inversions or other atmospheric phenomena. Years later, Dewey Fournet and Al Chop restated this belief.

Everyone, even the anti-UFO *New York Times*, reported air force efforts to intercept objects over Washington. At 10 A.M. on the morning of the twenty-seventh, President Harry Truman told his air force liaison, Robert B. Landry, to find out what was going on. Landry called ATIC in Dayton, where he reached Ruppelt. Ruppelt told Landry that weather might have caused the radar targets, but there was no proof. He later learned that Truman was listening to the conversation.[29] Across the ocean, British Prime Minister Winston Churchill wrote to his Secretary of State for Air: "What does all this stuff about flying saucers amount to? What can it mean? What is the truth?"[30]

On July 28, Blue Book received the astonishing total of fifty UFO reports in a single day. UFO inquiries were jamming the Pentagon's telephone circuits. Even skeptical air force generals and CIA officials conceded there was a problem, if only because the Soviet Union might take advantage of the situation through some kind of psychological warfare or even by launching an attack.[31]

There is an uncorroborated claim that the air force shot down a UFO during the July crisis. The source is Canadian government official and UFO researcher Wilbert Smith. In an interview conducted almost ten years later, Smith claimed to have shown his friend, U.S. Navy Rear Admiral H. B. Knowles, "a piece which had been shot from a small flying saucer near Washinton in July [1952]." Smith told the interviewers:

> I showed it to the admiral. It was a piece of metal about twice the size of your thumb which had been loaned to me for a very short time by your air force. . . . As a general thing they differ only in that they are much harder than our materials. [It was] in reality a matrix of magnesium orthosilicate. The matrix had great numbers—thousands—of 15-micron spheres scattered through it.

When asked if he returned the piece to the air force, Smith replied, "Not the air force. Much higher than that." Was it the CIA? Smith chuckled and said, "I'm sorry, gentlemen, but I don't care to go beyond that point. I can say to you that it went into the hands of a highly classified group. You will have to solve that problem, their identity, for yourselves."[32]

THE PRESS CONFERENCE

In Washington, D.C., at 4 P.M. on July 29, 1952, the air force held its largest and longest press conference since the end of WWII. Maj. Gen. John Samford, Director of Air Force Intelligence, led the press conference. He was accompanied by Gen. Roger Ramey, the man who five years earlier had ended speculation about the Roswell crash. Relying on Donald Menzel's theory of temperature inversion, Samford explained the recent UFO sightings over Washington as caused by "weather phenomena." The atmospheric condition caused the radar beams to bend and pick up objects on the ground.

Samford was no scientist, and would not answer many questions. His assistant, Capt. Roy James, a radar specialist from ATIC, provided more technical explanations. James actually knew little of the incidents and had arrived in Washington only that morning. Attending but silent were three men who had been in the Air Route Traffic Control radar room at Washington National Airport during the affair: Maj. Dewey J. Fournet, Jr., public relations officer Albert Chop, and Lieutenant Holcomb, a navy electronics expert assigned to the air force. These three rejected the temperature inversion explanation.

Despite the inversion theory, Samford acknowledged that

> there have remained a percentage of this total [of all UFO reports received by the air force], about 20 percent of the reports, that have come from credible observers of relatively incredible things. We keep on being concerned about them. . . . Our present course of action is to continue on this problem with the best of our ability, giving it the attention that we feel it very definitely warrants. We will give it adequate attention, but not frantic attention.

Few realized how weak the air force explanation was, and most newspapers accepted the temperature inversion theory without reservation. According to Ruppelt "somehow out of this chaotic situation came exactly the result that was intended—the press got off our backs."[33]

Was the temperature inversion explanation valid, or not? Fifteen years later, Condon Committee member Gordon Thayer concurred with it. He believed the visual sightings were caused by meteors and scintillating stars. Atmospheric physicist James McDonald disagreed and argued that Thayer's data did not support that conclusion. Michael Wertheimer, a psychologist with the Condon Committee, later interviewed many of the radar operators. Nearly all disagreed with the temperature inversion explanation. They maintained that experienced operators had no trouble identifying such inversions. Ironically, years later, an official air force scientific report discredited the "temperature inversion" explanation, but this received no publicity.[34]

Apparently there were no complaints with Samford's handling of the job. A few years later, he became head of the National Security Agency.

SIGHTINGS CONTINUE

Public debunking of UFOs did not affect sightings themselves, which continued at a torrid pace. On July 29, the day of Samford's briefing, ATIC received more remarkable UFO reports. One described a sighting over Los Alamos, which included several pilots and a guard who saw a fast, metallic-looking UFO with yellow lights. At some point, it hovered over the base, made a 360-degree turn behind the fighters trying to intercept it, and streaked away. In Albuquerque, an air force reserve colonel saw an ellipse-shaped light moving rapidly. Nearby, an unidentified sighting occurred at Walker (formerly Roswell) AFB, involving a base weather officer and three other weather observers, who saw several flying discs through a theodolite. The object moved much faster than any conventional aircraft. The field intelligence officer wrote "indicates an actual appearance of 'unidentified flying objects.'" Another ATIC report from that day described a sighting at an aircraft and warning station in Michigan in which a UFO was tracked on radar at over 600 mph. Several F-94s pursued the object; one pilot obtained a radar lock while seeing a bright flashing light in that location. In Miami, movie film was taken of a high-speed UFO, submitted to the air force, and never released.[35]

These, and many other sightings, all occurred on the day of Samford's briefing. None of them received any press.

And so it went into August. On August 1, 1952, an Air Defense Command radar station outside of Yaak, Montana, picked up a UFO. It was daytime, and the station crew saw a "dark, cigar-shaped object" right where the radar indicated. On the same day, a UFO was seen near Wright-Patterson AFB, in Bellefontaine, Ohio. This was another radar-visual case, in which people on the ground saw an object that was also being tracked on radar. Two F-86s moved to intercept. As they reached thirty thousand feet, the pilots saw a bright, round, glowing object maneuvering above them. They took several feet of film using a gun camera, but the object quickly accelerated and disappeared.[36]

An ATIC report from August 3 described a sighting near Hamilton AFB in California. Two huge silvery discs, observed visually and tracked on radar, circled the base at 4:15 P.M. After F-86s were dispatched to intercept, six more discs appeared, took up a diamond formation, and quickly accelerated out of sight. Two days later, at Haneda AFB in Japan, a UFO was observed visually and tracked on radar. The object was seen as a bright light that hovered over the base, then swiftly accelerated away at 400 mph. As it did so, it appeared to divide into three units.[37]

On August 20 at Congeree AFB in South Carolina, Air Defense Command radar tracked a UFO at 4,000 mph. On the twenty-second, air force jets chased a pulsating yellow light over Elgin, Illinois. On the twenty-fourth, an air force pilot in an F-84 saw two round, disc-shaped, silvery objects over Hermanas, New Mexico, and then again at El Paso, Texas. The objects displayed extreme maneuverability and acceleration.[38]

THE CIA ACTS

The public explanation is always one thing. What the explainers actually believe is another. Ruppelt wrote that "several groups in Washington were following the UFO situation very closely," and available documents from a variety of agencies support this claim.[39]

The research and development board noted in a classified memo that the air force had made "very little progress in learning what the phenomena or objects are and what causes them."[40] Air Defense Command, trying to keep current with all UFO reports, maintained records on the ATIC evaluation while undertaking its own preliminary evaluation, separate from Blue Book.[41] An FBI memorandum from July 29 discussed a classified briefing about UFOs by Cmdr. Randall Boyd of the Air Intelligence Estimates Division. According to the memo, the air force had "failed to arrive at any satisfactory conclusion" regarding UFOs. He noted that reports were being received from all parts of the United States as well as distant parts of the world. Boyd stated that, while it was possible there could be some as yet unknown natural phenomenon causing these UFO sightings, he considered the extraterrestrial explanation as possible. He suggested that, "the objects sighted may possibly be from another planet . . . [but] that at the present time there is nothing to substantiate this theory but the possibility is not being overlooked." He stated that "air intelligence is fairly certain that these objects are not ships or missiles from another nation in this world."[42]

Boyd also confirmed that the air force was indeed sending jet interceptors after UFOs, but each time a pilot approached such an object, it invariably faded from view.

Boyd's remarks were significant. In the first place, one would think that even stating the extraterrestrial thesis as a *possibility* before a group of intelligence officers would take some strong beliefs. Boyd also confirmed that air intelligence had essentially ruled out foreign (e.g., Soviet) technology as an explanation for UFOs. Just a few years prior, several American generals had considered the likelihood that the Soviets were behind all this. They had no doubt that real, technological objects were being seen, and looked into the possibility of Soviet manufacture. Rather quickly, that path appeared to reach a dead end, and Boyd's statement confirmed this. Note that Boyd, although conceding the possibility of natural phenomena as the explanation for UFOs, stated that there was as yet *no known* natural explanation.

Thus, after more than five years of UFOs, the Americans offered no known natural explanation, the Soviets were ruled out, and the ET hypothesis was being seriously discussed.

We must remember that in the highly compartmentalized world of intelligence, various solutions might be considered, based on the available knowledge. Several possibilities present themselves. (1) Boyd had complete access to all relevant information, and was in effect speaking on behalf of the highest official position, which would mean that UFOs continued to present a real mystery to those running America's military, and possibly indicated an alien presence; and (2) Boyd did not have all the available answers, but, as a man several rungs removed from the top levels of power, he struggled to formulate his conclusions based on his best-available data.

If the first possibility were true, it would mean that the U.S. military failed for more than five years to arrive even at a working assumption about a potential threat of a technological and intelligent source (during some of the cold war's darkest days). This would certainly be an alarming prospect, but also unlikely, unless natural phenomena, after all, were the explanation. Such a natural phenomenon, however, would somehow have to look like metallic craft.

The second scenario, that Boyd did not have all the answers, appears far more plausible. This leaves very few follow-up options. One is that an alien presence had been known in secret for some time; another is that some secret American technology was causing the UFO phenomenon. A naturalistic explanation does not fit here. In the first place, the most difficult UFO cases do not admit of a naturalistic solution. More to the point: there would be no reason to hide such an explanation from one's own military (whereas there would be very good reasons in the case of secret American technology or an alien presence).

In other words, by 1952, the historical documentation, as well as the logic of the situation, pointed to one of two possibilities. UFOs were either American, or they were alien. They were not Soviet, nor natural. Within the military and intelligence community, many understood this. Boyd, in his presentation, did not examine the possibility that UFOs were a domestic project. But could they have been? Certainly, the door is open, but there are major problems with this explanation. First, there is no documentation linking UFOs to American technology. Second, there is no evidence in the history of technology. That is, the *known* American technology from the 1940s through at least the 1960s does not suggest UFO reports.[43] Third, the behavior of UFOs, including airspace violations and repeated attempts at intercept, does not suggest a domestic project. Nor does the history of American warfare.

American military personnel who had to confront this issue were placed into an exceedingly difficult position, one in which they could almost never speak candidly. The obvious possibilities—alien or American origin—were usually ignored or talked around, while other explanations, e.g., natural phenomena, were not allowed to die.

At the CIA, the most important discussions about UFOs were taking place. Indeed, the agency had been monitoring a separate wave of UFOs all summer long in Europe and Africa. Algeria, Morocco, and Spain, in particular, were the scene of many low-flying, agile, fast, and oval-shaped objects, often seen by many people. In many cases, the objects made "impossible" no-radius turns, and were silent.[44] One CIA report even cited an alleged encounter between short humanoid aliens and a German man and his eleven-year-old daughter. While in a wooded area, the two got close to a landed craft that looked like a "huge frying pan . . . [with] two rolls of holes along the periphery . . . on top of this metal object was a black conical tower about three meters high." Short beings were nearby, examining the ground; they wore silvery suits, and one had a flashing box. When the beings realized they were being watched, they entered the craft and left at high speed. One of the most fascinating of the CIA reports concerned two "flying saucers" over uranium mines in the Belgian Congo. This was seen by many ground witnesses and reported in extreme detail. The objects glided in "elegant curves," changed position several times, hovered, moved in a unique zigzag pattern, and made a "penetrating hissing and buzzing sound." A fighter plane was sent to intercept, and the pilot came to within about three hundred feet of the objects. He described them as saucer shaped, about fifty feet in diameter. "The inner core remained absolutely still, and a knob coming out from the center and several small openings could plainly be seen. The outer rim was completely veiled in fire and must have had an enormous speed of rotation. . . . Changes in elevation from eight hundred to one thousand meters could be accomplished in a few seconds." Both objects left in a straight line at more than 1,000 mph. The officer was regarded as "a dependable officer and a zealous flyer."[45]

In the case of this last incident, it is ludicrous to ascribe the sighting to some as yet misunderstood natural phenomenon. It seems clear that the objects seen in the Belgian Congo were craft of some sort. But the CIA report studiously avoided discussing any implications of the incident.

While the air force press conference may have bought some time as far as the public was concerned, elements within the CIA believed that much more needed to be done, not necessarily from the vantage point of *solving* the UFO riddle, but from the more pragmatic position of managing the flow and release of data. On July 29, Ralph L. Clark, acting assistant director for the CIA's Office of Scientific Intelligence, sent a memorandum to the Deputy Director of Intelligence indicating that, despite the air force explanation, the agency would be looking into matters a little more thoroughly:

> Although this office has maintained a continuing review of such reported sightings during the past three years, a special study group has been formed to review this subject to date. O/CI will participate in this study with O/SI, and a report should be ready about 15 August.[46]

Clark's memorandum is also noteworthy for stating that the CIA "has maintained a continuing review of such reported sightings during the past three years," that is, since 1949.

On August 1, an informal CIA memo was sent by Edward Tauss, acting chief of Weapons and Equipment Division at the Office of Scientific Intelligence, to the deputy assistant director of OSI. Tauss listed the four main possible explanations: secret American technology (which was "denied at the highest level"), secret Soviet technology (which he said was not rational and supported by no evidence), alien technology (which had "no shred of evidence"), and misinterpretation of natural, "as yet little understood," phenomena. Tauss believed the last was true, although he acknowledged that "interplanetary aspects and alien origin [were] not being thoroughly excluded from consideration." The main thing, however, was to keep all this under control. He recommended that the CIA continue surveillance of UFO sightings, "in coordination with proper authorities of primary operational concern at ATIC." He strongly urged that

> no indication of CIA interest or concern reach the press or public, in view of their probable alarmist tendencies to accept such interest as "confirmatory" of the soundness of "unpublished facts" in the hands of the U.S. government.

The CIA initiated a series of informal discussions about UFOs with other agencies. One of the matters under review was the "clogged channel" problem. CIA Director of Scientific Intelligence H. Marshall Chadwell chaired these meetings and visited Wright-Patterson AFB on August 8 for a "thorough and comprehensive" briefing about UFOs from Blue Book officers. He was accompanied by CIA official Frederick Durant and power scientist H. P. Robertson.[47]

On August 14, a newly established CIA special study group from the Office of Scientific Intelligence gave a briefing which referred to an "official query from the White House" regarding UFOs. Once again, secrecy was of great importance:

> In view of the wide interest within the agency . . . it must be mentioned that outside knowledge of agency interest in flying saucers carries the risk of making the problem even more serious in the public mind than it already is, which we and the air force agree must be avoided.

The briefing offered an analytical description of UFOs dating to the ghost rocket phenomenon. It grouped radar and visual sightings into various categories, described the sightings as "objects" ranging in size from two to three feet across, to the common one-hundred-foot diameter object, to some as wide as one thousand feet. It described three general levels of speed: hovering, moderate, and "stupendous." It also noted that "evasion upon approach is common." The report ruled out the possibility of Soviet secret weapons and mentioned "sightings of UFOs reported at Los Alamos and Oak Ridge, at a time when the background radiation count had risen inexplicably." In this case, wrote the report's author, "we run out of even 'blue yonder' explanations that might be tenable, and we are still left with numbers of incredible reports from credible observers." Despite these many admissions, the report stated there was "no shred of evidence" to support the view that UFOs were caused by extraterrestrials. There was no bother, however, to explain just *what* could be behind these reports. Once again, we are in the presence of an elephant in the dining room, never to be discussed.

The CIA/OSI study group prepared a six-page document of its findings on August 19, 1952. The agency was puzzled that the Russian press had not mentioned a single report on UFOs, not even a satirical one. They perceived a danger that the Soviets might infiltrate American UFO groups:

Air force is aware of this and has investigated a number of the civilian groups that have sprung up. . . . AF is watching this organization [Civilian Saucer Group] because of its power to touch off mass hysteria and panic.

More serious was the danger that the Soviets could launch a nuclear attack during a UFO wave, when Americans might not distinguish Soviet missiles from UFOs. In the words of the August 19 CIA report, "we will run the increasing risk of false alerts and the even greater danger of tabbing the real as false."[48]

Was this the sum total of CIA interest in UFOs? Was there any indication that the CIA was interested in understanding the nature of UFOs themselves? Was there any concern that the country appeared to be under siege by UFOs? It would certainly be surprising if there were none. Certainly there was common recognition within the agency that *other* people and groups were leaning toward an extraterrestrial explanation. Moreover, even as OSI was studying the problem, many CIA-authored UFO reports were coming in from overseas. There is some tangible evidence, as we shall soon see, that ranking CIA officials were genuinely interested in the UFOs themselves. Nevertheless, whatever OSI's opinion on the actual nature of UFOs, it supported the air force's efforts to keep the matter as far removed from the public as possible.

At this time, astronomer Allen Hynek conducted a covert poll for the air force. In early August, he questioned forty-four professional American astronomers regarding UFOs. His results were somewhat surprising: five of them (11 percent) had actually seen a UFO! Seven were indifferent to the subject, more expressed at least some interest, while a few were *very* interested. Those interested, however, were fearful of publicity.[49]

Some intelligence agency, most likely CIA, appears to have surveilled civilian UFO groups at this time. In 1952, the Aerial Phenomena Research Organization (APRO) was founded in Sturgeon Bay, Wisconsin, by Coral Lorenzen. It soon became one of America's most influential and respected UFO organizations. Months before the first appearance of the organization's periodical, the *APRO Bulletin*, a man claiming an intelligence background became an active supporter and attempted to lead the organization into "metaphysical areas of research." Coral Lorenzen said she "gently parried" these attempts. She later discovered light embossing on a letter she received from him, and used a soft pencil to discern what looked like an intelligence report about her. During the summer of 1952, two suspicious men posing as painting contractors called on her and engaged her in conversation. The men did not seem interested in selling any services. After they left, they parked their car where they had a clear view of the back of her home. These two men also visited APRO's treasurer and secretary the same day, but apparently not any other homes in the neighborhood.[50]

It is worth mentioning that by 1952, 74 percent of the CIA's money (and

60 percent of personnel) went toward covert operations. Action, not analysis, had become the CIA hallmark. Contrary to the 1947 National Security Act, which stipulated that the CIA's activities be confined outside the United States, the agency had already infiltrated and financed many U.S. labor, business, church, university, student, and cultural groups, usually channeling the money through various foundations. In 1952, it began opening the mail through a new program known as HT Lingual, which targeted correspondence between U.S. citizens and communist nations. For twenty-one years, with FBI help, the program photographed two million envelopes and opened 215,000 letters. No one, not even the president, was exempt. By 1952, also, the CIA was using unwitting subjects to test the effects of LSD.[51]

A NATO Encounter

UFO reports slowed down somewhat in September, but there seems to have been a miniwave of sightings in the southeastern U.S. One that received much publicity was the "Flatwoods Monster" case in West Virginia on September 12, 1952. Fireball reports had come from several cities, including Baltimore, before one appeared to "land" at the small town of Flatwoods. Seven people, mostly children, trekked to the sight and claimed to see an enormous creature, over ten feet tall, with glowing eyes and an overpowering stench. The county sheriff, initially skeptical, encountered the odor at the site and noticed a circular area of flattened grass. Many visitors came by, including UFO researchers Ivan Sanderson and Gray Barker, as well as members of the air force. Sanderson interviewed quite a few people from the area and concluded that "a flight of intelligently controlled objects flew over West Virginia." The air force concluded that people had seen a meteor, the glowing eyes of an owl, and had just gotten hysterical. The Flatwoods case is certainly odd, but even skeptics ruled out a hoax.[52]

Not far from Flatwoods, an interesting report came from Camp Drum, near Fairfax, Virginia, on September 22. For thirty minutes, several soldiers watched an orange-red UFO circling and hovering over their camp, while they heard a distinct hum from the craft.[53] But the most significant series of UFO sightings that month took place during NATO naval exercises in the North Sea near Britain, known as Operation Mainbrace. At least four sightings occurred. At 10:52 A.M. on September 19, 1952, a silver and spherical UFO appeared above Topcliffe Airfield in North Yorkshire. Several ground crew members and civilians saw the object. An RAF Meteor jet was scrambled, and the pilot got close enough to describe the object as rotating around its vertical axis and wobbling slightly. The UFO moved in a zigzag fashion and then flew off. The British Air Ministry set up an investigation into the report.

The next day during Mainbrace exercises, a silvery disc, similar to the object seen the day before, was observed following a Meteor jet, then descended with a pendulum motion. Once again, there was no shortage of competent observers, who noticed the object flying "extremely fast behind the naval fleet." An American photographer aboard the U.S. aircraft carrier *Franklin Roosevelt* took three photos. The object was determined not to be a balloon, but no photos were ever released.

The Mainbrace "wave" continued the next day, when six RAF jets over the North Sea saw a spherical object heading towards them. They tracked it, lost it, and found it as it appeared directly behind them. One Meteor pilot tried to intercept the object, but it easily outpaced him. UFO researcher Jenny Randles pointed out that this was precisely the behavior displayed by the objects seen over the Capitol in Washington, D.C. The last Mainbrace sighting occurred three days later, on September 24, when a Meteor fighter came close to a silvery spherical UFO revolving around its axis. The object flew away before the pilot got too close.

Ruppelt followed the Mainbrace sightings and learned from an RAF exchange intelligence officer in the Pentagon that the reports "caused the RAF to officially recognize the UFO." Of course, *official* differs from *public*, and the British government has been as silent on UFOs as the American.[54]

During the Mainbrace sightings, UFOs continued to be seen throughout Europe and North Africa. On September 21, Morocco was flooded with reports throughout the country. On the twenty-sixth, ATIC reported strange green lights approaching the Azores, observed by U.S. Air Force personnel. On the twenty-ninth, a large cigar-shaped craft was seen over Denmark, flying with several smaller disclike objects, and was reported throughout the country.[55]

CHADWELL AND UFOS

On September 24, 1952, the final day of the Mainbrace UFO sightings, H. Marshall Chadwell wrote a letter to CIA Director Walter Bedell Smith, stating that since 1947 unexplained sightings were running at 20 percent, and that for 1952 they were at 28 percent. Chadwell wrote:

I consider this problem to be of such importance that it should be brought to the attention of the National Security Council in order that a community-wide coordinated effort toward its solution may be initiated.[56]

Chadwell played the familiar themes of mass hysteria and the potential for Soviet mischief. Parts of the letter showed concern about the UFOs themselves and the need to identify them. His memo did not indicate any interest in the possibility that UFOs represented alien intelligence. Rather, the CIA consultants he spoke with

> stated that these solutions would probably be found on the margins or just beyond the frontiers of our present knowledge in the fields of atmospheric, ionospheric, and extraterrestrial phenomena, with the added possibility that the present dispersal of nuclear waste products might also be a factor.

By extraterrestrial, Chadwell did not mean alien life-forms, but any phenomena originating from space. Overall, he strongly suggested the conclusions later arrived at by the Robertson Panel: to keep the profile of UFOs as low as possible while the real investigation and activity could continue. At all cost, mass hysteria and panic must be avoided.

Ruppelt, meanwhile, continued to give standing-room-only lectures on UFOs for military and scientific groups. Interest in this subject remained high. Around the time of Chadwell's letter, Ruppelt briefed General Chidlaw and his staff at Air Defense Command on the past few months of UFO activity. One of the attendees was Maj. Verne Sadowski, the ADC Intelligence's liaison officer with Project Blue Book. During an informal exchange, Ruppelt encountered a great deal of skepticism, not regarding UFOs, but of Project Blue Book's honesty in analyzing UFOs. Sadowski said that no one "can understand why Intelligence is so hesitant to accept the fact that something we just don't know about is flying around in our skies, unless you are trying to cover up something big."[57]

During the fall, the Navy delivered its evaluation of the Tremonton, Utah, film to the air force. The navy's conclusion: "Unknown objects under intelligent control." As if this were not bad enough, the navy study had an impressive amount of technical support. Clearly, the air force efforts to dismiss UFOs had not yet succeeded. Navy Secretary Dan Kimball appeared to be moving toward acknowledging UFOs. However, on November 5, 1952, Dwight D. Eisenhower was elected to the presidency of the United States, which meant that Kimball and many others would soon be out of a job.[58] November 18 is the alleged date of the MJ-12 briefing papers that Roscoe Hillenkoetter, late of the CIA, was to have presented to Ike. As discussed earlier, the documents may have been faked, although they are not as easily dismissed as some writers on the subject would have it. But even if the national security state was not preparing Eisenhower for UFOs, it *was* preparing the UFO problem for the Eisenhower administration.

The most significant event of late 1952 was the creation of the National Security Agency. On October 24, 1952, President Truman signed National Security Council Directive 6, a seven-page document that eliminated the first attempt at uniting all military signal intelligence (SIGINT) operations, and now replaced it with the NSA. Directive 6 remains classified to this day. The U.S. *Government Manual* says only, "The National Security Agency performs highly specialized technical and coordinating functions relating to the national security." It would be many years before Americans learned about the sprawling apparatus that lay behind that bland phrase. No public law defined or limited its powers. According to *Blank Check* author Tim Weiner, the only known mention of the agency in the public laws of the United States is a 1959 statute: "Nothing in this act or any other law . . . shall be construed to require the disclosure of the organization or any function of the National Security Agency."[59]

The NSA describes its main function as planning, coordinating, directing, and performing foreign signals intelligence (SIGINT) and information security (INFOSEC) functions. That is, to safeguard all American national security electronic and signals communication, and to intercept all foreign communications. It is widely acknowledged to possess the world's leading cryptologic (e.g., code making and breaking) capability. Therefore, it was only logical that the newly created organization also inherited responsibility for Operation Shamrock. Only three NSA staff members—the director (DIRNSA), the deputy director (D/DIRNSA), and one lower-level manager—knew the full extent of the project. It is unclear whether Harry Truman knew about Shamrock when he signed the order creating the NSA.

The NSA immediately became involved in UFO reports. Proof of 239 UFO documents was recovered from NSA through FOIA requests, and 160 of those originated from within NSA itself.[60] This is surely a tiny proportion of actual NSA-UFO documents, but obtaining anything at all from NSA is no easy task. As authors Barry Greenwood and Lawrence Fawcett pointed out:

> The NSA shreds forty tons of documents per day in its operations, but 239 UFO documents are saved. Why? Certainly not for reference to NSA interception techniques and personnel. These are easily available to NSA personnel elsewhere within the agency. It is evident that these are saved for the UFO subject matter. Simple narrative accounts of UFO incidents will not be released by NSA under any circumstances despite our efforts to purge the documentation of any reference to NSA operations. Why?[61]

NSA's collection of UFO reports began no later than 1953, that is, right away. This is further evidence of the serious nature of the UFO phenomenon.

THE WAVE SUBSIDES—A BIT

While the CIA and ATIC worked toward a "final solution" to the UFO problem, the UFOs themselves were seen just about everywhere. The pace had slowed down from the summer, but by no means were unidentified flying objects absent from the skies of America, or for that matter, other nations. Press coverage of flying saucers was negligible, so this was a nonissue as far as the public was concerned. Still, many unsettling sightings continued to occur over restricted military areas, and jets continued to pursue unknown objects. Noteworthy events included a September 30 sighting of two discs at Edwards AFB in California, an October 11 domed disc sighting at Newport News, Virginia, an October 13 sighting of a round or elliptical object in Oshima, Japan, by an air force pilot and engineer, and an October 29 report from Hempstead, Long Island, involving a sighting by the pilots of two F-94s. The report included a statement by one of the pilots:

> Based on my experience in fighter tactics, it is my opinion that the object was controlled by something having visual contact with us. The power and acceleration were beyond the capability of any known U.S. aircraft.

On November 16, 1952, hundreds of people near Landrum, South Carolina, saw a large disc-shaped object, also seen by an air traffic controller through binoculars. On December 4, 1952, an F-51 pilot had a near collision with a blue-lighted UFO moving with "extreme" speed, maneuverability, and rate of climb. Intelligence officers questioned the pilot for two hours.[62]

Another near collision occurred two days later near the Gulf of Mexico between a B-29 and an incredibly fast UFO at eighteen thousand feet, observed visually and on radar. Before converging with an enormous "mother ship," the object appeared to travel at 5,000 mph. The large object then departed at 9,000 mph. Although the speeds appeared simply unbelievable, the radar operators checked and rechecked, and were confident their results were accurate. When the National Security Council learned that this information had reached Keyhoe, "there was immediate consternation." Apparently, the air force told Ruppelt to "find out how Keyhoe got those reports!" Ruppelt then told a surprised colonel that Keyhoe had already been cleared for them.[63]

The CIA continued to report an intense wave of UFO sightings in Algeria, France, Equatorial Africa, and elsewhere for the remainder of the year.[64] ATIC received reports from abroad, too, including defense radar trackings of two UFOs over the Panama Canal Zone during the night of November 25-26, 1952. Later on the twenty-sixth, an F-94 chased a disc-shaped UFO near Goose Bay AFB in Labrador. Two crews at the base tracked a similar object again on December 15. A detailed UFO report came from American air force personnel in Japan from December 29, 1952. This case included ground and airborne radar, as well as visual confirmation involving the officers and crews of three aircraft regarding the UFO's position, movements, and speed.[65]

On January 6, 1953, UFOs were reported from Dallas and Duncanville, Texas, by weather bureau and CAA personnel. Another Japan sighting occurred on January 9, including radar tracking and an interception attempt by an F-94. On the same day, B-29 pilots saw bluish-white, rapidly moving UFO lights in formation over Santa Ana, Texas.[66]

THE AIR FORCE GETS READY

Thus, despite the drop-off of UFO reports, the air force remained motivated to do something about the UFO problem through the rest of 1952. Of great importance was the work being coordinated by Air Force Maj. Dewey Fournet, who was leading a study based on the "top fifty" UFO reports to analyze the objects' reported motions in an attempt to determine whether they were intelligently controlled. The project had originated from the summer following discussions among Ruppelt, Fournet, and two of Fournet's superiors, Col. Weldon Smith and Col. W. A. Adams. The project was active throughout the late summer and autumn. By now, Fournet's group concluded that the movements of UFOs *did* show intelligent control and indicated they were probably extraterrestrial. Fournet was excited by his progress, and he planned a special, surprise press conference that would show the Tremonton, Utah, film, the navy analysis, and other strong UFO reports. He planned to conclude that alien spacecraft were observing the Earth.[67]

Ruppelt followed the project and said the report "was hot because it wasn't official and the reason it wasn't official was because it was too hot." The report circulated through high command levels of intelligence and was read with much interest. In Ruppelt's cautious phrasing, its conclusions were accepted by people "just a notch below General Samford." Yet no one was willing to stick his neck out and officially send it to the top. The CIA wanted to see the report, and Frederick Durant asked Fournet to present his findings to the CIA. The FBI referred to Fournet's project in an October 27 memo:

> Air intelligence still feels flying saucers are optical illusions or atmospherical phenomena, but some military officials are seriously considering the possibility of interplanetary ships.[68]

Events at Blue Book and ATIC were reaching a climax. By December, Blue Book was down to thirty UFO reports per month, but unknowns were still running at 20 percent. Nevertheless, Ruppelt at this time asked for a transfer out of Blue Book, agreeing to stay until the end of February. His book gave no reason for this request, and mentioned it only in passing. At the very least, his request seems odd. Although not yet thirty, Ruppelt had managed an air force project that had risen to prominence within a year, and which enabled him to travel around the country and give high-level briefings to senior Pentagon officials on a subject that fascinated millions of people. By all indications, he was respected for his work. Why, then, would he request a transfer out? And why withhold the reason? There are no certain answers, but perhaps Ruppelt had gotten some indication of the nature of the upcoming CIA-sponsored Robertson Panel. Or maybe he began to realize that the Blue Book operation was not what the air force said it was—the military's primary

UFO investigative unit. Whatever the reason, it appears that Ruppelt had an idea of what was shortly to come to ATIC.[69]

THE CIA GETS READY

On November 21, 1952, an air force review panel met at ATIC for three days and recommended that a "higher court" be formed to review the case of the UFO. They tentatively scheduled this to take place in late December or early January.[70] On December 2, 1952, H. Marshall Chadwell prepared another secret memo for CIA Director Walter Bedell Smith. The controversial memo stated:

> At this time, the reports of incidents convince us that there is something going on that must have immediate attention. . . . Sightings of unexplained objects at great altitudes and traveling at high speeds in the vicinity of major U.S. defense installations are of such nature that they are not attributable to natural phenomena or known types of aerial vehicles.[71]

The fact that Chadwell could write such a statement shows that there *were* high-level people within the CIA who thought the UFO problem was relevant for more than its effect on the cold war. Chadwell clearly was concerned about the UFOs *themselves*, although he studiously avoided arriving at a conclusion on the matter. A National Security Council memo was attached to this, stating that the UFO problem had "implications for our national security." It directed the CIA to "formulate, and carry out a program . . . to solve the problem of instant, positive identification of unidentified flying objects."[72]

Two days after Chadwell's memo, the Intelligence Advisory Committee gave the go-ahead for the panel. It recommended that the director of Central Intelligence "enlist the services of selected scientists to review and appraise the available evidence in the light of pertinent scientific theories." Chadwell was the driving force and wanted H. P. Robertson to lead the panel. Robertson accepted it "against his will," then brought in the other four members.[73]

A week later, on December 12, another meeting was held at ATIC, attended by representatives from CIA, ATIC, and the Battelle Memorial Institute from Columbus, Ohio. For some time, a group at Battelle had been studying the UFO problem, in Hynek's words, in "very great secrecy." When members of this group learned of the impending CIA-sponsored study, they sent an urgent letter, classified Secret, to the CIA via the Blue Book office. They wanted the upcoming scientific panel postponed until they finished their own study. In January 1953, H. C. Cross, a senior staff member at Battelle, wrote a letter to Miles Coll at Wright-Patterson AFB, with attention to

Captain Ruppelt. Cross, realizing it was futile to delay the impending panel until Battelle could complete its study, argued that "agreement between Project Stork (Battelle) and ATIC should be reached as to what can and what cannot be discussed" at the meeting. He also suggested a "controlled experiment" be undertaken by the air force in order to obtain better physical data. This would consist of "observation posts with complete visual skywatch, with radar and photographic coverage, plus all other instruments necessary or helpful in obtaining positive and reliable data on everything in the air over the area." Cross actually suggested that the Air Force release "many different types of aerial activity . . . secretly and purposefully," presumably in order to generate spurious UFO reports. There is no evidence that any such program occurred. However, while Battelle failed to delay the timing of the Robertson Panel, it did eventually release its own report, named Blue Book Special Report Number 14, which developed an interesting history of its own.[74]

THE ROBERTSON PANEL

In 1952, concern about UFOs had peaked within the United States military, the intelligence community, and, as far as we can tell, the presidency itself. Chadwell's December memo, written four months after the public debunking of UFOs, showed extreme bewilderment about the nature of UFOs, as well as concern over what exotic things were over American skies. The navy and air force both had a strong contingent, possibly a majority, that believed UFOs were extraterrestrial. The FBI continued to report on UFO developments to Hoover. Most importantly, American jets continued their efforts to intercept unidentified craft over their airspace, craft that seemed to be posing greater dangers to American personnel than they had before. Every indication was that the American government was taking this problem very seriously, and that the problem itself continued in a state of crisis.

Moreover, since the summer of 1952, it had been fairly clear that Dwight Eisenhower would win the presidential election against Democratic opponent Adlai Stevenson. Truman's staff knew the Republicans gleefully awaited a major housecleaning after November. Administration changes, especially party changes, always bring their share of difficult adjustments. Even within the CIA, a Republican victory would likely mean changes for DCI Walter Bedell Smith. But what about adjustments for a UFO control group? Ever since UFOs had been a recognized problem, Truman had been president. With that prospect ending, surely those managing the problem wanted to keep it away from the wrong people. Mere changes in the presidency and controlling party could not be permitted to affect the handling of this all-important problem.

At the same time, something else was happening: a nascent "UFO Party" was forming, within the military (e.g., Fournet and a few higher-ups) and in the civilian sector (e.g., Keyhoe, Frank Edwards, and the civilian groups). Of course, this had been a problem for some time. Now, in the aftermath of the Great Wave, and facing the prospect of the uncertainties inherent in a new administration, this "UFO Party" most assuredly needed to be silenced and discredited, posthaste. Otherwise, they might make even bigger waves (and generate bigger leaks) within the new administration.

The last months of the Truman presidency give reasonable grounds to assert that leading men in the administration had two basic goals: one for the immediate period, and one for the long term. The immediate goal was to silence and discredit the UFO party. The long-term goal was to ensure that no major mistakes would occur by the new people about to take charge. Hence the significance of the Robertson Panel, which officially convened from Wednesday, January 14, to Sunday, January 18, 1953. This was the last matter of any consequence in Truman's eight years in the White House. Eisenhower was sworn in as president two days later, on Tuesday, January 20.

Seen in this perspective, the panel's significance is not that it merely served to "debunk" UFOs—something all researchers have acknowledged. Rather, *it was a final insurance policy to steer the UFO issue away from the wrong people*, to keep it from being investigated by too many individuals and departments in the Eisenhower presidency. The Robertson Panel was the Truman administration's final bit of housecleaning.

Obviously, this was no job for the National Science Foundation. It is a matter of some importance that the organization entrusted with organizing the panel was the same organization involved in mind-control experiments, disinformation, foreign coups (Iran in 1953, Guatemala in 1954), media manipulation, the secret collection of UFO reports, and surveillance against American UFO researchers. (Indeed, just days before the panel convened, the CIA had been caught tapping the phone of the new president of Costa Rica, and continued for some time to wage a disinformation campaign against him.) If the job was not to get to the bottom of a scientific question, but rather to control a multiheaded hydra, then the CIA was the ideal choice.

Thus the setting for the Robertson Panel, held in secrecy and denied until 1958.

ROBERTSON PANEL: AGENDA

The initial meeting convened at 9:30 A.M. on Wednesday, January 14. Its panel members included Dr. H. P. Robertson, Dr. Luis Alvarez, Dr. Thornton Page, and Dr. Samuel A. Goudsmit. CIA members Philip G. Strong, Lt. Col. Frederick C. E. Oder, David B. Stevenson, and Frederick Durant also attended. A fifth panel member, Dr. Lloyd V. Berkner, was absent until Friday afternoon, when the panel was almost over.

The Wednesday meeting reviewed the CIA interest in the matter, including the OSI study from August (authored by Strong, Eng, and Durant), the ATIC November 21 meeting, the December 4 IAC decision, the visit to ATIC by Chadwell, Durant, and Robertson, and CIA concern over "potential dangers to national security indirectly related to these sightings." The group also saw the Tremonton and Montana films that morning.

In the afternoon, Ruppelt, Hynek, and Fournet were present, as were Capt. Harry Smith and Dr. Stephen Possony. Navy analysts Harry Woo and Robert Neasham of the USN Photo Interpretation Laboratory in Anacosta presented their analysis of both films, which "evoked considerable discussion." This segment lasted two hours. Ruppelt then spoke for forty minutes on Blue Book's methods of handling UFO reports. The meeting adjourned at 5:15 P.M.

The group met again on Thursday. In addition to panel members and CIA personnel, Ruppelt and Hynek attended. Ruppelt spoke some more about Blue Book; Hynek described the work in progress at Battelle. The CIA also showed a motion picture film of seagulls, a clear hint at the conclusions they were seeking to reach. (Why would the CIA obtain motion pictures of seagulls flying, anyway?) Lieutenant Colonel Oder gave a forty-minute presentation on Project Twinkle. That afternoon, General Garland attended and stated his desire to: (1) increase the use of thoroughly briefed air force intelligence officers to investigate UFO reports, (2) "declassify as many of the reports as possible," and (3) enlarge Blue Book.

Excepting Garland, everyone met again on Friday morning. Hynek and Fournet each spoke at some length. Fournet gave no indication of his press release plan, but was confident in his material and assumed the panel would accept his evidence and agree on the need to prepare the country.[75] His description of individual cases evoked "considerable discussion." After Berkner finally arrived that afternoon, Robertson reviewed the panel's work and offered "tentative" conclusions. Moreover, "it was agreed" that Robertson would draft the panel report (which had primarily been done in advance by Durant). On Saturday morning, the final day the group met, Robertson presented a "rough draft" of the panel report. Strangely, Berkner had previously reviewed and approved this draft. So did Robertson and Berkner burn the midnight oil on Friday night? Unlikely. Especially since by 11 A.M. CIA Director Walter Bedell Smith was shown the draft, as was Air Force Director of Intelligence General Samford, both of whom were favorable to it. Fast work, indeed. The day was spent primarily in reworking the draft (presumably, *some* of the report had to reflect the week's work).

ROBERTSON PANEL: CONCLUSIONS

The panel report noted "the lack of sound data in the great majority of cases, and concluded that most sightings could be reasonably explained if more data were available." Trying to solve every sighting, however, "would be a great waste of effort." The panel concluded that UFOs presented no evidence of a direct threat to national security, despite Chadwell's memo from the previous month which stated otherwise. Toward this end the report indicated that both Robertson and Alvarez had been involved in investigating foo fighters during the Second World War [!] and had found them unexplained but harmless.

While the panel members seemed uninterested in UFOs themselves, they were quite concerned about the public dimension of the UFO problem. It is questionable why a group of scientists would express an opinion on a matter of national security, something wholly outside its collective expertise. At least, it would be if these men were functioning as scientists. They decided it was "possibly dangerous in having the military service foster public concern in 'nocturnal meandering lights.'" Therefore, it recommended an "educational or training program" targeted to the public to eliminate "the popular feeling that every sighting, no matter how poor the data, must be explained in detail." The educational program aimed toward "training and debunking":

> The debunking aim would result in reduction in public interest in "flying saucers" which today evokes a strong psychological reaction. This education could be accomplished by mass media such as television, motion pictures, and popular articles.

And the problem of gaining influence over the mass media? A foregone conclusion. The panel members were not short on their knowledge of people and channels within the media. Despite Hynek's claim in later years that he was "negatively impressed" by the attitude taken by the panel leaders, he "suggested that the amateur astronomers in the U.S. might be a potential source of enthusiastic talent 'to spread the gospel,'" that is, of debunking UFOs.

The Robertson Panel report gives more evidence that, even in this early period, Blue Book did not receive all UFO reports. The report's text indicated over 1,900 UFO reports for 1952, although Blue Book only reported 1,503 for the year. Where were the other reports filed?

The Panel also noted the existence of such loose cannons as Civilian Flying Saucer Investigators (started in 1951) and APRO, and believed the organizations needed to be watched—which, of course, they were. "The apparent irresponsibility and the possible use of such groups for subversive purposes should be kept in mind." Hynek said that APRO was not discussed during the week, other than as a passing reference. Thus, the Lorenzens came to believe, logically enough, that the idea was not the product of the panel, but of the CIA itself.[76]

THE ROBERTSON PANEL: ANALYSIS

Many of the assumptions in the panel's report were alarmingly uninformed. Thornton Page, for example, considered the extraterrestrial hypothesis "quite preposterous," as it was unlikely that intelligent life was elsewhere in the solar system, and that UFOs should confine themselves to "any one continent." Could Page really not have known about the global nature of UFOs? If so, one can only conclude that actual science was absent from this scientific study.

The panel also rejected Fournet's UFO reports as "raw" and "unevaluated," although it provided no example as to what would *not* constitute a raw report (presumably one that offered a mundane explanation for a UFO). The Montana film was said to portray aircraft. Hundreds of verified UFO reports were ignored. Panel members rejected the navy's detailed analysis of the Tremonton film and ascribed the sighting to the "high reflectivity of seagulls in bright sunlight." The navy's mistaken conclusion, argued the panel, was probably due to the "apparent lack of guidance" with UFO reports and explanations. Ruppelt later pointed out that nobody bothered to obtain witness testimony from Delbert Newhouse himself, the man who shot the Tremonton film. Ruppelt himself only did so later and was much impressed. According to Ruppelt, Newhouse "didn't think the UFOs were disc-shaped; he knew that they were."

The panel's conclusions were preordained. Hynek said he discerned the panel's debunking mood right from the beginning. Fournet suspected right away that the actual author of the conclusions was not Robertson but Durant, and that he wrote them late on Friday. Work by UFO researcher and historian Michael Swords pushes the date further back: "Fournet did not know that the report, in draft form, existed before Friday and possibly before the panel was even convened on Wednesday."

Many have questioned whether the CIA could manipulate a group of scientists to reach their desired conclusion. Kevin Randle, for example, doubted that "someone in the government [would be] confident enough in his own abilities to micromanage the data [and] influence the conclusions. . . ." But micromanaging data is not necessary when the right people are selected. The members of the Robertson Panel were power scientists, strongly connected with the military and national security state. They were certainly no detached, impartial jury, withholding a decision until an objective review of the evidence. Quite the contrary.

Of later writers about the Robertson Panel, only Ruppelt was misled. He believed the panel accepted Garland's recommendation that Blue Book be expanded. He also misinterpreted the panel's education and debunking recommendation, thinking it meant that "the American public should be told every detail of every phase of the UFO investigation." Others hit closer to home. Keyhoe believed the panel was a CIA program to bury the UFO. Hynek—years later—stated he was "negatively impressed." The Lorenzens understandably came down hard against the panel. Even one of the panel members, Dr. Thornton Page, said in 1980 that the panel "tended to ignore the five percent or ten percent [sic] of UFO reports that are highly reliable and have not as yet been explained." Many years later, Page made the matter crystal clear:

> H. P. Robertson told us in the first private (no outsiders) session that our job was to reduce public concern, and show that UFO reports could be explained by conventional reasoning.[77]

Authors Barry Greenwood and Lawrence Fawcett called the panel not so much a "scientific" panel as a "propaganda" panel. In their words:

> Labeling a twelve-hour roundtable discussion of UFOs a "scientific study" is ludicrous, especially considering the fact that, in at least one instance, one thousand man-hours was spent on one case . . . by navy analysts, and the conclusion was unknown.

Point well taken. It seems odd, does it not, that following such a grave crisis of well-documented UFO sightings from 1952, the best the scientific-military-intelligence establishment could come up with was . . . the Robertson Panel? A study of the problem that was, from a scientific perspective, utterly inadequate and inept? On the face of it, it makes no sense at all.[78]

After all these years, the Robertson Panel still leaves a bad taste. In part, this is because Nobel-caliber scientists were involved in such scientifically shallow and deficient work. Berkner showed up just in time to put his name on the final document. The rest sat around for a few hours—precious time away from busy calendars—to listen to a few presentations, probably feeling bored with a subject they all believed was nonsense long before they arrived. Would the CIA really entrust policy-making authority to a group which, prestigious though it certainly was, was unable to render an informed decision on the subject? Here we arrive at the core meaning of the Robertson Panel: a group that, by its very prestige, was able to sanction a policy already decided upon. Within the classified as well as the public world, it is always a good idea to cover your vulnerable areas. What better way than with a panel composed of Nobel-caliber scientists needed to help defuse the UFO problem, certainly not to figure it out. This is the point that the people at Battelle missed. What the CIA and air force wanted was not an actual *study* of the problem—they had enough of those already. What was needed, and fast, was adequate justification for a policy decision.

The policies that followed as the result of the Robertson Panel, what we may with justice call the true crackdown against UFO publicity, were not the result of the Robertson Panel's decisions. They were the result of the same policy that created the panel itself, and which since the summer of 1952, had determined that UFOs were finally and truly going to go to sleep, as far as the public was concerned.

ROBERTSON PANEL: AFTERMATH

On January 20, 1953, Dwight Eisenhower was inaugurated as the thirty-fourth U.S. President. On that day, Robertson wrote a letter to his good friend Chadwell, stating "perhaps that'll take care of the Forteans for a while." (This referred to followers of Charles Fort (1874–1932), author and early collector of UFO reports.) Robertson also mentioned a scheduled meeting with the "NSA group" on Thursday, February 5. Robertson, clearly, was well plugged in with both the CIA *and* the NSA, the mere existence of which was unknown to the American public and its elected representatives.[79]

The Battelle Report, incidentally, remained secret until the air force deemed it useful to publish in October 1955. Its conclusion, essentially identical to that of the Robertson Panel, was that it was "highly improbable" that any UFO reports indicated technological developments "outside the range of present-day scientific knowledge." An interesting difference with the Robertson Panel was that the Battelle study actually had data. Unfortunately for the report, the data contradicted the conclusion by conceding a UFO "unknown" rate of 22 percent for the period 1947–1952 (434 unknowns of a total of 2,199 reports analyzed). No wonder the people at Battelle had been unhappy with their data back in December 1952. None of this mattered, however, as the negative spin of the 1955 air force press release predetermined the media response. For added insurance, the air force released a paltry one hundred copies of the report, so that no one really got a chance to read it anyway. Hynek later called the Battelle Report a "shamefully biased interpretation of statistics to support a preconceived notion."[80]

On January 24, Ruppelt was off to Ent AFB in Colorado Springs to give a one-hour briefing for the 4602nd. Something interesting must have occurred, as in February, Benjamin Chidlaw (commander of continental air defenses at Ent AFB) told future UFO researcher Robert Gardner that he had "stacks of reports about flying saucers. We take them seriously when you consider we have lost many men and planes trying to intercept them." On March 5, 1953, General Burgess (commander of Ent AFB) sent a memo to Air Defense Command and the director of intelligence at Ent AFB. Titled "Utilization of 4602nd AISS Personnel in Project Blue Book Field Investigations," the memo suggested that field teams of 4602nd personnel interview UFO witnesses. ADC approved the plan a few weeks later.[81]

Ruppelt was in Washington on January 29, when the press learned about the Tremonton, Utah, film. In addition to Fournet, there were several others, such as Al Chop of the DoD Office of Public Information and Colonel Teabert of AFOIN-2, who believed that the movies should be released in accordance with the promise made the previous summer that no UFO information would be withheld. Ruppelt was still under the idea that the Robertson Panel had recommended full disclosure about UFOs. Hence, he agreed to release the Tremonton film for the newsmen. Ruppelt saw no danger in explaining the film as seagulls, or so he implied in his book. By February 9, Al Chop had written the press release and had shown it to Colonel Smith. They decided to release the air force and navy analyses; otherwise, they thought, the press might suspect a cover-up of "hot" material. They seem to have assumed that the air force analysis (possible aircraft) would outweigh the navy report ("self-luminous or light sources"). They recommended that the movie be released with air force statement that although positive identification had not yet been made, it was confident that with more analysis it would be.[82]

Once the press release was ready, it moved on to General Garland of ATIC, who approved it. It then went to the Pentagon, which, in Ruppelt's words, "screamed 'No!'" Suddenly, there would be no movie for the press and no press release whatsoever. Ruppelt was ordered into silence. Chop said to Keyhoe:

They [e.g., the CIA] killed the whole program. We've been ordered to work up a national debunking campaign, planting articles in magazines and arranging broadcasts to make UFO reports sound like poppycock.

Ruppelt told Keyhoe:

We're ordered to hide sightings when possible, but if a strong report does get out we have to publish a fast explanation—make up something to kill the report in a hurry, and also ridicule the witness, especially if we can't figure out a plausible answer. We even have to discredit our own pilots. It's a raw deal, but we can't buck the CIA. The whole thing makes me sick—I'm thinking of putting in for inactive.

Fournet, already inactive, was ordered not to reveal his UFO conclusion. His secret report was bottled up at Air Force Headquarters as an "unfinished document," although it was quite finished.[83]

It is impossible to know how straightforward this group was, whether they were genuinely, albeit mistakenly, trying to implement the recommendations of the Robertson Panel, as Ruppelt implied, or were doing everything possible to get the word out before the clampdown would take effect. Keyhoe's opinion—always dramatically expressed—still seems the most plausible. He called this group the "censor fighters" who fought "a last battle to reveal the Utah film." Certainly, all the main players were soon out of the picture. Fournet was gone, Chop soon resigned in disgust, and Ruppelt was gone soon after. Before long, only Hynek remained of the Blue Book team. As a civilian scientist, he was less of a threat inside the project, and was willing to keep quiet. According to Hynek, "Blue Book was now under direct orders to debunk."[84]

At the end of February, Ruppelt left Blue Book for a seven-month assignment in Denver, replaced by Lt. Bob Olsson, whose staff consisted of one airman. Olsson later told Ruppelt that his five months as head of Blue Book "was like being president of Antarctica on a nonexpedition year."[85]

By March, prominent people in defense were privately urging Keyhoe "to tell the Utah film story."

Keyhoe continued to be a magnet for military personnel. Already, rumors reached him that the CIA was "slamming the lid down on the saucer stuff." One source told him:

> The air force gave some of their top men a secret briefing. The CIA people advised them to put out a new report, debunking the saucers the way they did in '49—tell the public the project was ended, and then carry it on underground. It'd probably be top secret.

Keyhoe responded, "They'd never get away with it, not with all they've let out now." But the fight was already over.[86]

SUMMARY

The year 1952 had brought about the most severe UFO crisis yet. The problem threatened to overwhelm the military in every way: by causing a mass panic, by clogging military communications, by presenting the Soviet Union with an opportunity to make mischief or worse, by causing dissension among the various services and within the ranks, by the air force's continued inability to stop UFOs from trespassing over restricted airspace, and by the sheer number of objects in the sky that seemed capable and ready to overwhelm the nation.

In such a situation, not everything could be solved. One fixes what one can. If the objects themselves remained beyond control, then at least *some* things could be managed. The Robertson Panel—never intended as a scientific study of UFOs—gave the sanction to remove the problem not only from the general population, but from the vast majority of military personnel. Why involve the military needlessly when it was incapable of acting and could not provide any new information on this obviously intractable problem? The matter of control became more urgent than usual, not only because of the new wave of UFO activity, but because the uncertainties of a new administration, however conservative and reliable it might be in some respects, demanded extra insurance of secrecy. From 1953 onward, the small control group that managed the UFO problem held the reins ever tighter, if such a thing were possible. For a few years, this policy of extreme secrecy met with more success than failure.

Chapter 5

Shutting the Lid: 1953 to 1956

I have discussed this matter with the affected agencies of the government, and they are of the opinion that it is not wise to publicize this
matter at this time.

—Sen. Richard Russell (D-Georgia), head of the Senate Armed
Services Committee, in a 1/17/56 letter to journalist
Tom Towers regarding his sighting of a UFO
during a recent trip to the Soviet Union.

I know of no country in which there is so little independence of mind
and real freedom of discussion as in America.

—Alexis de Tocqueville, *Democracy in America*.

BELOW THE SURFACE

From the perspective of later generations, the 1950s were an idyllic
period in American history. Prosperity increased and even became slightly less
top-heavy. America reigned unchallenged as leader of the free world, and
compared to the following decade, the social order was remarkably stable.
Below the surface of America's "consensus culture," however, the image of a
nation striving for truth, justice, and the American way was contradicted by
events that remained submerged, often for decades.

With an official budget exceeding $100 million by 1953, the CIA was an
important part of America's subterranean history. DCI Allen Dulles had more
resources and money than Hitler's Abwehr, the KGB, or Britain's secret intelligence service, and none of it was accountable to Congress.[1] One burgeoning

area within the agency was its mind control program, renamed MK-Ultra in April 1953, and led by Sidney Gottlieb. MK-Ultra was deeply secret and recruited ethically challenged scientists to modify the behavior of people through covert chemical or biological means. The program is best known for its use of LSD, but it tried many other ways to harness the human mind, much of which was so sensitive that documentation remains scarce. Very soon, Ewen Cameron would be working for MK-Ultra. In 1953, Cameron was elected president of the American Psychiatric Association and eventually became the first president of the World Psychiatric Association. One of his goals was to treat schizophrenics by inducing complete amnesia, then to guide the patient to recall only "normal" (or selected) behaviors. He had limited success, then inflated his claims. His grisly experiments, conducted off American soil, included some that were terminal. He was a modern-day Dr. Frankenstein.[2]

Meanwhile, the U.S. Army secretly sprayed American cities with biological agents. From April through June, the army targeted St. Louis, as it had done previously with Minneapolis. This time, however, it tested only the black ghetto sections, and arranged for local police surveillance "to minimize the possibility of loss of equipment." The burdens of slumming it paid dividends in secrecy. The army reported "much less public interest and curiosity" during this field test than in Minneapolis.[3]

Meanwhile, it seemed that the UFOs all flew away, at least compared with the year before. They didn't, of course, and actually appeared more frequently than in many prior years, with the exception of 1952. Study of them continued, as well. In April, Canadian Wilbert Smith wrote to Keyhoe that Project Magnet's report was "well along in the draft stages" and had concluded "the saucers are *probably* [original emphasis] alien vehicles, since there is no other explanation which fits the facts." Smith doubted that his government would accept his recommendation to study the physics and technology of UFOs. He completed the classified report in August, writing, "We are forced to the conclusion that the vehicles are probably extraterrestrial. In spite of our prejudices to the contrary." To his superiors at the Department of Transportation, Smith suggested setting up an electronic station to maintain a twenty-four-hour watch for UFOs, in order to learn anything possible about their technology. To Smith's surprise, his request was approved, and a small station was set up in a DOT-owned hut at Shirley's Bay, near Ottawa. Smith's project received some press in November, but it appears that the participants worked on their own time, and that for the year of its operation, only one incident of note (on August 9, 1954) took place. On that date, the gravimeter at Shirley's Bay indicated a greater deflection in the gravitational field than a passing aircraft or other conventional object would have caused. Smith was there at the time and rushed outside to see, but heavy clouds obstructed his view. The station was closed soon after, although this apparently had been planned some time earlier.[4]

One controversial incident involved a British airliner that crashed six minutes after takeoff from Calcutta on May 2. No one survived, and wreckage was scattered over a wide area. An investigator from the British Ministry of Civil Aviation announced that the plane had "collided with a fairly heavy body." Witnesses saw no other planes when the airliner "seemed to stop short in midair." UFO rumors persisted about the crash for over a year. On June 1, 1954, an official of the British Ministry of Civil Aviation told the London *Daily Mail* that any UFO connection to the crash was "utter balderdash."[5]

On May 21, a UFO may have crashed near Kingman, Arizona. The account derives from Arthur G. Stancil, (known previously under the pseudonym Fritz Werner), an engineer affiliated with the Atomic Energy Commission and the air force who claimed to have worked on a retrieval of a crashed alien disc. Stancil claimed he was taken with other specialists in blacked-out buses to a desert site where he saw a thirty-foot-wide saucer embedded in the sand. He claimed to see a humanoid figure, apparently dead, three to four feet tall inside a guarded tent. Stancil produced diaries indicating he was on a special mission at the time. Researcher Leonard Stringfield also spoke with a naval intelligence officer who told him of alien bodies at Wright-Patterson AFB, allegedly from Kingman. To this day, many UFO researchers believe that a UFO may indeed have crashed at Kingman, but follow-up efforts have produced nothing definitive.[6]

Global sightings continued. The CIA reported an incident from May 18, 1953, in Iran, in which a very bright, large, and fast-moving object was seen for twenty minutes over oil areas in Khuzistan. On May 23, South African radar tracked a UFO near the Cape moving at 1,000 mph. On the twenty-sixth, according to CIA files, a UFO followed a man driving from Capetown to Uppington. On July 13, a CIA officer clipped the full text of an article in the Stockholm daily newspaper, *The Morgon-Tidningen* with the headline, "Danish Authorities Take a Serious View of the Problem of Flying Saucers."[7]

WHO WAS INVESTIGATING?

Gen. Charles Cabell became deputy director of the CIA on April 23, 1953. Cabell, it will be recalled, preceded Samford as Air Force Director of Intelligence, and had demanded better UFO reporting following the Fort Monmouth sighting of September 1951. Thus, the number two man at CIA was someone not only well versed in UFOs but personally interested in the subject.

Meanwhile, Blue Book was disabled as a UFO investigative body, and the 4602nd AISS slowly acquired more responsibility. By July, the 4602nd had taken over nearly all of Blue Book's UFO field investigations.[8] It appears that, rather than going through a single, unified military protocol, UFOs were being reported through various military channels to the offices deemed most appropriate. Observe how these three important UFO sightings of the summer were handled.

First came an astounding report that described yet another violation of restricted airspace over the Oak Ridge nuclear facility. This one occurred on July 19, 1953. Witnesses saw a black object moving out of a high white cloud for about five minutes. At times, the object appeared to be cigar-shaped, at other times round. According to the report:

> This object was extremely black in color, having an appearance of a deep black metal exterior with a fine gloss. It did not leave a vapor trail or were there any lights of shine noticed. No sound was heard. The object flew east at a tremendous speed for what appeared to be approximately three miles, where it stopped. The object was then joined by two more of these same objects. A formation similar to a spread "V" was formed, and the objects at a tremendous speed flew in an eastward direction.

This report was made by the Atomic Energy Commission, and addressed to the adjutant general in Washington, D.C.[9]

Another UFO report was from Perrin AFB on July 26. The top read "Emergency," and the text made clear why:

> Ground observed seven unidentified flying objects, with one bright red light, on each object hovering at estimated altitudes from five to eight thousand feet. Visually observed from Perrin tower and citizens of Denison and Sherman, Texas. No lateral movement was observed. Formation was in groups of three with one trailing and then coming together to form the letter zebra. Formation then circled while gaining altitude and faded from sight one at a time. No air-to-air contact made. No radar contact made by Perrin radar. Visual contact was maintained from 2139C to 2155C. Visibility unlimited with clear sky condition.

This sixteen-minute sighting of seven UFOs in formation was classified as a "Vital Intelligence Sighting" and sent to Air Defense Command, the U.S. Secretary of Defense, and the CIA.[10]

The third major sighting of the summer occurred on the night of August 12 or 13, near Rapid City, South Dakota. This time, Blue Book *was* involved, although probably not solely so. At around 8 P.M., Ground Observer Corps, or GOC, saw an unidentified object. Soon after, radar at Ellsworth AFB tracked a "well-defined, solid, and bright" object. The base scrambled an F-84, and the pilot saw the UFO. Many witnesses then saw the object accelerate and climb. The F-84 pursued, but reached no closer than three miles. Now low on fuel, the F-84 returned—followed by the UFO. Immediately, another F-84 was airborne. Before long, the pilot received strong radar returns of an object right in front of him. Although the pilot was a combat veteran, fear prevailed, and he broke off the chase. The UFO went off the scope, traveling northeast toward Bismarck, North Dakota, about two hundred miles away.

Reports soon came from Bismarck of a fast-moving, bright bluish object, identical to what had just been encountered in Rapid City. It hovered near an air filter center in Bismarck, seen by many witnesses. After performing various maneuvers, it disappeared after midnight. Before it left, three other UFOs appeared and were seen at ten thousand feet for three hours. The air force had no planes in Bismarck to pursue the objects.

Ruppelt personally investigated this case and called it "the best" in the air force files. Hynek also investigated, but did not say whether he worked with Ruppelt. In his report he wrote that "the entire incident . . . has too much of an Alice-in-Wonderland flavor for comfort." Vallee called the encounter "one of the most remarkable events in the history of American sightings." The official file of the incident is several hundred pages long, with interviews and accounts from many military personnel. Yet, Blue Book later removed the case from its list of unknowns.[11]

The air force sought to clarify UFO reporting procedures with the issuance of AFR 200-2 on August 26, 1953, which superseded AF 200-5 from the previous year. The order tightened UFO reporting and investigating procedures and further restricted the release of UFO information. It directed that all confirmed UFO reports be rushed electronically to air force intelligence. When possible, all tangible evidence would go to ATIC at Dayton.

The order also confined UFO investigations to three groups: air force intelligence at the Pentagon, the 4602nd AISS, and ATIC. However, it stipulated that ATIC would only receive UFO reports after they passed through the 4602nd. AFR 200-2 thus formally stripped Blue Book of its investigative function, leaving it little more than a public relations front. Freelance investigators were definitely off-limits: even top-ranking air force officers were warned not to probe beyond the first stage of investigating a UFO, which essentially meant securing preliminary UFO reports for the three groups based on clearly specified questions to be asked of witnesses. Sightings were to be discussed only with "authorized personnel."

The order further provided that only hoaxes, practical jokes, and erroneous UFO reports could be given to the press. All radar-scope photographs of UFOs were now classified, and public release of unexplained sightings was forbidden.[12]

AFR 200-2, a clear implementation of the Robertson Panel recommendations, signified a rapid drop-off in reported sightings by air force personnel. Henceforth, Blue Book cases constituted a distinct minority of compelling UFO sightings. That reality contrasted starkly with Blue Book's public image as *the* UFO investigative office. Some good sightings still reached Blue Book, but fewer escaped as "unidentified" than in previous years. For three consecutive nights, for example, from July 29 to August 1, a disc-shaped UFO descended over Sequoia-Kings National Park in California. On the final night, a squadron of air force fighters tried to force it to land, but the craft easily outmaneuvered the jets and soared away.[13] Then, on August 6, at least seventy-five lighted objects appeared between 5 P.M. and midnight near the Naval Air Station at Pearl Harbor. The objects were seen visually and tracked on radar (both ground and air); some hovered, others moved swiftly. Finally, in Moscow, Idaho, on August 9, several GOC personnel reported a large glowing disc, and three F-86 fighters tried to close on the object. The disc dived toward the three aircraft before speeding away. None of these cases were Blue Book unknowns.[14]

The few sightings Blue Book now classified as unknown were usually less dramatic and more innocuous than the others. This tendency became more pronounced as the years passed, so that most of the unknowns were of the vague "lights in the night sky" variety. One of the few unknowns for the second half of 1953, and among the more interesting, occurred on August 20, near Castle AFB in California. The crew of a TB-29 bomber/trainer plane saw a greyish oval object shortly after 9 P.M. The object made four passes at the airplane, then dived vertically as if it were two objects.[15] Only a handful of officially unsolved cases remained for 1953, none of which were especially memorable, despite several involving military personnel.[16]

Of greater interest were the reports that went elsewhere. These came to light in various ways, through people like Keyhoe, internal documents released through FOIA, foreign news stories, and so on. A GOC report from San Rafael, California, dated August 28, 1953, is one such case. This report was forwarded to the Joint Chiefs of Staff, the CIA, and the newly formed National Security Agency. It does not appear to have gone through ATIC. The report described:

Fourteen cigar-shaped objects without wings with . . . lights on them in loose v formation. About the size of a bi-motor . . . acft. No sound or means of propulsion observed. One object appeared to be leading the formation at an estimated speed of 200 mph. . . . Objects were first observed heading west . . . through breaks in the clouds. Then objects appeared to turn and head north disappearing behind clouds . . . observer appeared to be reliable and has been an observer on duty with GOC for sev years during WWII and during postwar years.[17]

The U.S. appears to have been interested in a UFO encounter from Port Moresby, New Guinea, on August 31, 1953. (Vallee gives the date August 23.)[18] The deputy director of the Civilian Aviation Department in New Guinea took ninety-four frames of motion picture film that showed a disc-shaped object come out of a peculiar cloud, make a ninety-degree turn, and climb steeply. The former Minister for Air described the man who took the film as a "reliable, credible person." The *Australian Flying Saucer Review* claimed the film was studied by the Royal Australian air force intelligence and the U.S. Air Force. Little surprise that aviation experts of 1953 would want to know how to duplicate *that* fear.[19]

Near London, England, on November 11, a huge, white, metallic and "completely circular" UFO was tracked on radar and observed visually through a telescope by the 256th Heavy Anti-Aircraft Regiment. Radar picked up a circular object that remained stationary for a long time, then slowly moved off until it passed beyond tracking range. An RAF pilot and his navigator in a Vampire fighter at twenty thousand feet saw the object far above them, which seemed like a bright star. Suddenly, it "buzzed" them, passing over them at tremendous speed. The pilots were questioned for ninety minutes after landing. The object was observed for another twenty-five minutes by four aircraft technicians, which they described as "quite definitely not a balloon." The RAF pilots described their sighting on British television two days later. On the twenty-fourth, the British parliament discussed this incident and others, and the Ministry of Defense said that two experimental meteorological balloons had been observed, a comment that received much laughter. One MP called the incident "all ballooney."[20]

Probably the most bizarre and controversial UFO case of the year was the November 23 incident over Soo Locks, Michigan. Keyhoe and Frank Edwards were the main people involved in ferreting this out. What appears to have happened is that an Air Defense Command Ground Control Intercept controller was alerted to the presence of an unidentified and unscheduled target on his radar scope at Soo Locks. An F-89, piloted by twenty-six-year-old Felix Montcla and co-piloted by Lt. R. R. Wilson, was scrambled to intercept the object. The radar station had the F-89 and the UFO on the scope as the two blips merged into one. For a moment the single blip remained on the scope, then disappeared. No trace of wreckage or the missing men was ever found. The story was carried briefly on AP, but Keyhoe and Edwards faced continual stonewalling by military brass.

The Pentagon's official explanation was that the unknown radar blip turned out to be a Canadian C-47. The F-89, far from colliding with it, never got closer than several miles from the aircraft. Montcla's plane then crashed for unknown reasons, but he may have suffered from vertigo and lost control of his plane. The explanation was weak—no records indicated that he was flying on instruments, and no transcript of his conversations with traffic controllers was ever released. Furthermore, the Canadian government repeatedly denied any connection of its aircraft to the incident.

A few years later, a script for a production of the Soo Locks case was developed—and cleared—at Lackland AFB in Texas, promoting a strongly pro-UFO perspective. The script died a quick death, before which it was sent to Keyhoe and Richard Hall. Both believed the script was the creation of UFO enthusiasts acting on their own, not at the direction of Air Force Headquarters. Years later, Hall continued to think of the entire incident as "extremely odd."[21]

A few noteworthy sightings occurred in December, all outside of Blue

Book's purview. On the seventh, army personnel saw an unidentified object above Fort Meade, Maryland, future site of the NSA. On the ninth, the CIA reported an incident from France in which multiple witnesses saw a high, motionless, luminous object suddenly change position and shape, then disappear. On December 17, the Swedish Defense High Command ordered a full-scale investigation into sightings of a wingless circular object which had flown rapidly over southern Sweden.[22]

On the final day of the year, U.S. Marines at Quantico Marine Base, Virginia, claimed to see a flying saucer land for a few minutes near their base, then take off. The object was said to be round and emitted red pulsating lights. On four previous nights, near the same base, UFOs were seen maneuvering in the air, one at tree-top height. They seemed to be under intelligent control.[23]

In addition to the above, there always seemed to be rumors about events that no one recorded. One incident, undated and unconfirmed, is alleged to have occurred during the summer at Ernest Harmon AFB, near Stevensville, Newfoundland. Base radar picked up an unknown blip, and two F-94 jets pursued. One pilot saw an object visually, picked it up on radar, and climbed steeply in pursuit. According to one witness, "The next thing I know was the jet going straight down in a dive. It crashed into a mountain."[24]

KEYHOE'S ACTIVITIES

Donald Keyhoe had an eventful fall of 1953. He learned of AFR 200-2 in September, then he met with Adm. Arthur W. Radford, Chairman of the JCS, for an article on national defense. Years before, Keyhoe and Radford had trained together, and Keyhoe had served under him in Washington during the war. During this meeting, UFOs were not mentioned, although it will be recalled that Radford had his own UFO sighting in 1952. In October, Keyhoe's *Flying Saucers from Outer Space* came out, eventually becoming one of the most widely read books of the decade. His message: aliens are here, observing our world; the military knows this and, in a well-meaning but mistaken notion, is hiding this information from the public, mainly to avoid panic. Keyhoe argued that the public would be able to handle the news, if it were delivered in a calm and straightforward manner. Moreover, the public—at least the *American* public—had a right to know. Then and later, Keyhoe's conspiracy thesis came under attack.[25]

Probably the most stunning aspect of Keyhoe's book was that he had been able to get clearance through Ruppelt and Chop for fifty-one classified UFO reports and included these in his book. The air force stated that Keyhoe "misrepresented" the official analysis of these reports. Keyhoe took this personally and doggedly worked to clear himself of the charge. On October 1, he sent a telegram to Air Force Secretary Talbott and General Sory Smith, with copies to the press wire services. He said that the air force "publicly implied" that he had misrepresented their UFO position. "If this is true," he wrote, "then as a Marine Corps officer I should be subjected to disciplinary action." The air force provided "no comment" on the telegram. This would not be the last of the affair, however.[26]

Keyhoe's book sold very well, but reaction from major media was generally negative, although it was not universally condemned as Scully's book had been in 1950. The review in *Library Journal*, for example, stated that he was either "very right or very wrong." Keyhoe's most significant critic in the media was Jonathan N. Leonard, the science editor for the *New York Times*. Leonard reviewed Keyhoe's book in November, ignored its main strength— the clearance for over fifty UFO classified reports—and attacked it as teeming with "unidentifiable authorities and anonymous sources."[27]

ALBERT BENDER AND "THE MEN IN BLACK"

Although this incident is not the first alleged case of the infamous "Men in Black," it is the first "classic" case and the first to receive any attention. It concerns a young man named Albert K. Bender, who had an interest in UFOs. In the fall of 1952, a letter of Bender's was printed in Ray Palmer's *Other Worlds* magazine, announcing the formation of a new organization, the International Flying Saucer Bureau (IFSB), which welcomed new members. West Virginia resident Gray Barker soon offered his help and told Bender what he knew of the Flatwoods case, which, along with others like Ivan Sanderson, he had investigated. In January 1953, Bender asked Barker to head IFSB's new "Department of Investigation."

In September 1953, Bender told Barker that three men in black suits, members of the U.S. government, had threatened him into abandoning his research. Barker was surprised, as the organization now had representatives in much of the country and abroad. In early October, Barker and other members interviewed Bender at his home. To their many questions, Bender said simply, "I can't answer that." In the final issue of IFSB's *Space Review*, Bender wrote that he knew the solution to the flying saucer mystery but that a "higher source" ordered him not to publish it. The IFSB closed down.

Some UFO researchers concluded that Bender had been pressured out of business by government agents. Others, such as Coral Lorenzen, wrote in the *APRO Bulletin* that perhaps the IFSB was secretly backed by a pulp magazine publisher (Palmer?) who suddenly withdrew his funds. Bender then cooked up a fantastic story in order to get out from underneath. Barker, in turn, called this scenario "fantastic."[28]

Albert Bender dropped out of the UFO scene after this. Ten years later, he wrote a book that told a different story. In the late summer of 1953, wrote Bender, he *was* visited by three men. But these were not government agents; rather, they were aliens. They gave him an unusual piece of metal, similar to a coin, to help him communicate with them. He soon contacted the three beings again and was transported to a large room, perhaps a flying saucer. A being told him telepathically that their race would be here only briefly, in order to take "a valuable chemical from your seas." He told Bender they had infiltrated "numerous places about your planet." The being had initially appeared human to Bender but later showed its true hideous appearance. It warned Bender against "continued experimentation with radioactive material," which

will undoubtedly have effects upon future generations. This could even lead to loss of reproductive capabilities, which could eventually leave your planet devoid of human life. These things are ahead of you and you must face them and solve these problems if you can. To us, your progress is of academic interest, but little more.

Bender soon found himself alone, lying on his bed. He was met with disbelief from a friend on the IFSB executive committee, and realized that he could not tell his story. He decided to tell the committee "part of the truth": (1) that certain individuals had warned him against further investigation of UFOs; (2) they had impressive credentials; (3) they had revealed the secret of the saucers; (4) the saucer mystery was approaching a solution. After this fantastic statement, Albert Bender once again dropped out of sight, this time for good.[29]

Perhaps Coral Lorenzen was right all along. Still, it is true that from late 1953 through early 1955, several UFO enthusiasts in Australia, Canada, and New Zealand left the field amid rumors they were silenced by MIBs.[30]

SILENCING THE UFO

Whatever it was that silenced Albert Bender—aliens, government agents, lack of funds, or his own dementia—certain groups worked toward silencing the UFO problem. During the latter part of 1953, as the 4602nd AISS assumed greater responsibility for investigating UFO reports, the Pentagon and intelligence community continued to monitor the situation for leaks and to take additional measures to tighten the secrecy. Very little appeared to be as it seemed outwardly. For example, Harvard astronomer and professional

UFO debunker Donald Menzel was in close touch with air force intelligence regarding UFOs. On October 16, Menzel wrote to Air Force Director of Intelligence Gen. John Samford that he was

> planning to be in Washington on government business . . . October 22 and 23 [1953] . . . From various reports I judge that some of my explanations of flying saucers have been misinterpreted or misunderstood. . . . I should be delighted to meet with as many members of ATIC as find it convenient to come.[31]

On October 22, Menzel met at the Pentagon with representatives of the Air Force Headquarters and ATIC. The details of his meeting are not known. Of course, Keyhoe would undoubtedly have loved to know that Menzel was secretly corresponding with Samford and meeting with air force intelligence.

Two months later, the Air Force Headquarters representative from the meeting with Menzel wrote to the ADC deputy for intelligence regarding the new responsibilities of ADC. It was understood that the 4602nd would do the "leg work" of UFO investigations and provide ATIC with its findings. The letter also clearly stated how to handle truly unidentified sightings:

> . . . As you realize, there is a 10 to 20 percent area of unexplained objects in this program . . . we would like to offer you guidance in the publicity angle as it pertains to your activity . . . if they can verify the object as a balloon, aircraft, helicopter, etc., go ahead and inform interested parties. However, for those times where the object is *not explainable*, it would be well to advise your people to say something on this order, "The information on this sighting will be analyzed by the Air Technical Intelligence Center at Dayton, Ohio," and leave it go at that. If your people get into analyzing the 10 to 20 percent area to the public, every news media across the country will pick up the story.[32]

This was a basic restatement of AFR 200-2, which ordered that no UFO information of value reach the public.

As if AFR 200-2 were not stringent enough, the Joint Chiefs of Staff reissued JANAP 146 (Joint-Army-Navy-Air-Publication) in December 1953. This made any public release of a UFO report a crime under the Espionage Act, punishable by a one- to ten-year prison term or a $10,000 fine. It differed from AFR 200-2 primarily in that it applied to anyone who knew of its existence, including all branches of the military, and even commercial airline pilots. According to historian David Jacobs, "this action effectively stopped the flow of information to the public." Keyhoe, as usual, was on the ball, and learned of JANAP 146 almost immediately. That month, President Eisenhower issued an Executive Order (10501) abolishing the classification of "Restricted." Keyhoe considered this a "stunning blow" to the silence group, as both JANAP 146 and AFR 200-2 were Restricted defense documents. But UFO secrecy was unaffected, as meaningful sightings were simply classified at higher levels.[33]

On December 4, General Burgess chaired a conference with 4602nd officers and stated that the 4602nd was the agency responsible to ATIC for investigating UFOs. Captain Cybulski then left for Wright-Patterson AFB to coordinate activities more closely with ATIC. He reported that the project astronomer (Hynek) was "ready to quit." The astronomer said:

> [P]ut yourself in my position. I am being ridiculed by members of my profession for chasing those imaginary objects. . . . I have not been able to get support from the air force. It seems they all think this is a hot subject, and they want to drop it. . . . No one wants to be quoted.

Cybulski himself took a hard line against the extraterrestrial hypothesis and stated that "in all but a few cases a satisfactory solution has been reached and the air force feels that adequate, thorough investigative procedures can solve the small percentage of unsolved sightings. This is where we come into the picture."[34]

Blue Book now had scarcely the ability to handle *any* report it received, since its staff consisted of two people. No wonder Cybulski said that AISS would "exhaust all efforts to identify a sighting before turning it over to ATIC." As a result, the AISS maintained a complete file on all UFO sightings. Reports would be unclassified, "unless data included necessitates a higher classification," or if "and this I rather doubt . . . it happens to be the real thing." Despite Cybulski's skepticism, he stated that reports would include such items as maneuvers and intercept attempts. This begs the obvious question: maneuvers *by what*, intercept attempts *of what*?[35]

LSD, MIND CONTROL, AND THE DEATH OF FRANK OLSEN

By this time, methods of assassination and neutralization had become quite sophisticated among the world's leading intelligence organizations. It is believed, for example, that the Soviets were delving into the biological effects of microwaves as early as 1953.[36] Americans were working hard to develop biological and chemical weapons for use against large populations and individual targets. One specialist and casualty in this quest was Frank Olsen, a leading scientist at the army's Chemical Corps, Special Operations Division (SOD) at Fort Detrick, Maryland. The CIA had been working with Olsen for some time, as SOD provided the agency with an array of deadly chemicals and microbes that were undetectable upon a detailed autopsy. SOD also made various "operational systems" to infect foes with diseases such as anthrax. Only a very few CIA officials knew that the agency was paying SOD $200,000 per year for these services, a relationship that continued at least until 1969, by which time SOD had stockpiled a veritable mountain of bacteriological agents.

Olsen had been duped into meeting with MK-Ultra director Gottlieb and other CIA officials for a meeting at a secluded cabin on November 19, 1953. That evening, Gottlieb spiked Olsen's alcoholic drink with LSD. This sort of thing had been going on at the agency all year, but principally among CIA staffers. Usually, the trip would last a little while, the unwitting subject would recover, and notes would be taken on the experience. All good fun. Frank Olsen, however, had a *very bad trip*. Days later, he still wasn't right. He was depressed, incoherent, and uncommunicative to friends or family. His CIA handlers took him to a "doctor" in New York City, who prescribed him more alcohol. Olsen then plunged to his death from the tenth floor of the Statler Hotel. According to the CIA man assigned to him, Olsen simply rushed out of his bed and crashed through the window. Of course, there were no other witnesses, and Olsen *was* a security risk. Twenty years later, Olsen's family finally learned the truth, such as it was revealed, and received $750,000 from Congress in compensation. Throughout, the CIA's main concern was to maintain plausible deniability.[37]

In this context, it is useful to recall that the son of American activist Paul Robeson claimed the FBI slipped his father hallucinogenic drugs during the 1950s in order to neutralize him. Many people dismissed these claims as paranoid, but it is true that for three decades the bureau harassed Robeson and spread false rumors about him. The case of Frank Olsen makes the claims of Robeson's son a bit more plausible, whether the actual culprit was the bureau or the agency.[38]

The most serious work was done in great secrecy. On February 19, 1954, the CIA's Morris Allen conducted the ultimate hypnosis experiment: the creation of a "Manchurian Candidate," or programmed assassin. Allen first hypnotized a secretary to remain sleeping until he—and only he—commanded her to awaken. Next, he hypnotized another secretary to try to awaken the first, and if she could not, to become so enraged as to kill her. He left an unloaded gun nearby. Not only did the second woman "shoot" the sleeping woman, but she could not recall the incident and denied shooting anyone. As significant as this milestone was, researcher John Marks pointed out that most of the CIA's work on hypnosis is unavailable, but that terminal experiments involving hypnosis and torture could easily have been conducted on behalf of the CIA by friendly police in countries such as Taiwan or Paraguay. Marks tried, but failed, to obtain more information about this.[39]

A Brief Outbreak of Truth

In 1953, an issue of *American Magazine* featured a one-page article on Coral Lorenzen, bringing worldwide publicity for APRO and enabling its membership to climb. (She soon met with Hynek, who appeared "not deeply engrossed" and "certainly skeptical" of the reality of UFOs.) Stories about Coral Lorenzen were small potatoes, however. By the end of 1953, news services had virtually ceased to carry UFO reports. The few that did were strictly local affairs. Even the Soviet Union provided some help in American censorship efforts. On December 7, 1953, Radio Moscow stated that "flying saucers are figments of the imaginations of western war mongers designed to make taxpayers swallow heavier military budgets."[40]

On December 8, the CIA reported that UFO sightings had fallen dramatically from the previous year—no doubt, it argued, due to its policies. The report acknowledged that there were still UFO cases "of possible scientific intelligence value," but emphasized pursuing these carefully. Otherwise, "a fanatical saucer believer" might notice an interest and accuse the government of a cover-up.[41]

There remained a few voices in the United States fighting UFO censorship. Keyhoe's was probably the most significant, but close behind was that of his friend, Mutual Radio broadcaster Frank Edwards. Before Art Bell, there was Frank Edwards, who was one of the key disseminators of UFO information during the early 1950s. In a 1953 nationwide poll of radio-TV editors by the trade paper *Radio Daily*, Edwards was named among the top three news broadcasters in the nation, along with Edward R. Murrow and Lowell Thomas. His audience was estimated at 13 million people every night. On January 13, 1954, Edwards alleged on his show that the wreckage of a flying saucer was being stored at a "west coast military field." Journalist Richard Reilly of the *Washington Times-Herald* was another "fanatical saucer believer." In three articles that began on December 26, 1953, Reilly questioned the air force's professed openness about UFOs, as it had become nearly impossible, he wrote, to obtain UFO reports.[42]

Shortly after Reilly's article came the scoop (1/4/54) that U.S. Marines at Quantico had seen UFOs for several consecutive nights. The *Washington Daily News* even reported that it "ran into what seems a deliberate attempt to cover up certain facets of the investigation." At this time, the *Cleveland Press*, a Scripps-Howard paper, was asking authorities at ATIC for permission to see the Tremonton, Utah, film. The Pentagon dragged its feet but finally agreed to let a journalist see it at Dayton. By the time the reporter was ready to make the trip, ATIC told him that their only copy had just burned up. No worry, said ATIC, as there was a master copy at the Pentagon. When the reporter spoke with an air force spokesman at the Pentagon, he was told, "we have no copy here, but we believe there is one at Dayton." The reporter gave up. The *Press* ran a January 6 headline, "Brass Curtain Hides Flying Saucers."[43]

Isolated segments of the media continued to work this theme. On February 11, 1954, several Scripps-Howard papers charged that the air force knew what flying saucers were and was hiding the truth for fear of panic. Papers also reported that Eisenhower's executive order abolishing the "Restricted" classification was deceptive, as

> many military had upgraded documents to "Confidential" or "Secret." Some security officers had created a new grade—"for official use only." By this device, even declassified information could not be released to the newspapers.[44]

On February 13, Jim G. Lucas of Scripps-Howard reported that representatives of major airlines were planning to meet in Los Angeles with intelligence officers of the Military Air Transport Service. The purpose was to speed up UFO reporting procedures. Lucas wrote that airline pilots were reporting large numbers of UFOs during their flights and were now being asked "not to discuss their sightings publicly or give them to newspapers." Lucas had accurate information. On February 17, 1954, officers of the Military Transport Intelligence met with officials of the Airline Pilots Union at the Roosevelt Hotel in Hollywood. The goal of the meeting was to implement JANAP 146, specifically to arrange for pilots to radio UFO reports to the nearest airport and make no public statements about them. Violations brought prison terms of up to ten years and/or a fine of $10,000.[45]

Scripps-Howard papers followed up on February 23 to report that "the nation's 8,500 commercial airline pilots have been seeing a lot of unusual objects while flying at night, here and overseas." It confirmed that plans for a detailed reporting system were agreed upon to enable the air force to investigate UFOs quickly. Each airline had an "internal security specialist" to meet with the air force.[46]

Meanwhile, on February 13, 1954, astronomer (and discoverer of Pluto) Clyde Tombaugh gave a talk to the Astronomy Society at Las Cruces, New Mexico. To the surprise of many, he predicted an increase in UFO sightings and told the audience to keep their eyes open and be ready to report any sighting quickly and precisely. Two days later, on February 15, 1954, journalist Dorothy Kilgallen wrote: "Flying saucers are regarded as of such vital importance that they will be the subject of a special hush-hush meeting of world military heads next summer."[47]

Also during February 1954, a new civilian UFO organization sprang into existence: the Civilian Saucer Intelligence of New York (CSI). Its members included Ted Bloecher, Alexander Mebane, Isabel Davis, and others. They soon helped prepare the books of French UFO research Aimé Michel for the American public.[48]

These direct attacks against UFO secrecy ultimately made it more difficult to obtain information from the Pentagon. Public information officers now refused all requests to see UFO reports, including even those previously released, and reporters seeking information were banned from Wright-Patterson AFB. The British government seems to have been working in concert: on January 25, 1954, the British Air Ministry and the British War Office ordered soldiers and airmen to tell the public nothing of UFOs.[49]

In addition to clamming up, the Pentagon also initiated its own media offensive. This included an article planted by the air force in *American Aviation Daily* on February 21, that debunked UFOs and "definitely" attributed the latest wave of sightings to Keyhoe's latest book, *Flying Saucers from Outer Space*.[50] After the appearance of Keyhoe's new book, a Yale professor named Thomas B. Eickhoff asked the air force if it had actually cleared the intelligence reports Keyhoe listed in his book. The answer: No—Keyhoe had *not* used cleared ATIC sightings. Early in March, Eickhoff informed Keyhoe of this fact. He quoted the air force letter:

> [T]he publication to which you have referred was not submitted to the air force for authentication prior to publication. There is no official recognition and the air force does not choose to comment upon it.[51]

Keyhoe never needed much provocation for a crusade; he now set out to gather his proof. Ruppelt had just left the air force, succeeded at Blue Book by Capt. Charles Hardin and a total staff of two. Wasting no time, Keyhoe met with Ruppelt at the Hollywood Roosevelt Hotel on April 4. They shared UFO accounts, and Ruppelt mentioned an upcoming UFO article he helped to write for *True* (his conclusion: if flying saucers were real, they were interplanetary). Ruppelt agreed to write a letter supporting the claim that Keyhoe had used genuine ATIC sightings for his book. His letter, dated a week later, also stated: (1) The request to clear classified UFO reports for Keyhoe came from air force intelligence and the Office of Public Information; Ruppelt's superiors at ATIC then declassified them. (2) Keyhoe had correctly quoted the ATIC material. (3) The analysis of the Utah film was classified, and the press release Ruppelt had prepared at Dayton had not been made public. (4) A letter by Albert Chop to Henry Holt and Company which attacked "the silence group" was honest and correct in all respects. (5) Except in a very few cases, ATIC rejected Donald Menzel's theory that UFOs were sun dogs, halos, light refractions, etc. It appeared Ruppelt had chosen his side of the battle.[52]

The stew over Keyhoe's book continued until November, when General Samford decided to end the mess. He summoned Col. John O'Mara from Dayton and directed him to clear up any misunderstanding about Keyhoe's use of air force data. O'Mara was directed to write to Eickhoff and explain that he had misunderstood the air force, that Keyhoe's latest book *did* contain officially released air force reports—which it did, of course.[53]

Meanwhile, another independent UFO organization came into existence. In March 1954, Leonard Stringfield formed Civilian Saucer Research, Interplanetary Flying Objects (CRIFO) out of Cincinnati. Within months, Stringfield gained national recognition after Frank Edwards plugged him on the radio. Stringfield was swamped with requests for his newsletter—six thousand in one week—and interviewed with newspapers and radio stations coast to coast.[54] Stringfield soon met with UFO contactees and became suspicious. Some of them, he believed, were "official plants".[55] Stringfield may have been on to something. Covert ops never ceased in the national security state. Later that spring, for example, Hoover's FBI gained authority to engage in unrestricted microphone surveillance, including any illegal trespasses along the way. This neatly circumvented a Supreme Court decision that bugging was unconstitutional. David Wise called the order "virtual carte blanche to break and enter, installing bugs and wiretaps." All this had long been going on; now it was just easier. The order remained fully in effect until 1965, when FBI bugs became subject to the Attorney General's approval. Even then, however, Hoover still did as he pleased.[56]

UFO SIGHTINGS OF EARLY 1954

The outbreak of UFO news occurred, in part, because UFOs themselves appeared in significant numbers once again. Not all of the reports were verified. Wilkins is the source of several Australian sightings from early 1954, including two from Alice Springs. The area is near America's NSA facility at Pine Gap, one of the largest and most secretive information-gathering stations in the world. America's involvement in the area began in the mid-1960s, and the area has been heavy with UFO rumors for years.[57] The CIA continued to monitor flying saucer reports worldwide, especially in France, where UFO sightings were recorded on January 4, January 7, and January 9. One involved a sighting over an airfield, another described extreme maneuverability, and another was seen by multiple witnesses in several locations. On the eighteenth, the CIA noted a UFO sighting over three towns in Algeria. CIA files also noted a March 1 sighting of a UFO over a beach at Montevideo by multiple witnesses; the object appeared to be a metallic disc emitting yellowish reflections and was stationary for two minutes at a high altitude.

Four days later, a much-discussed and certainly authentic photograph of a disc-shaped UFO was taken over Rouen, France, by a French fighter pilot. Close analysis showed it to be nearly identical to the object photographed by the Trents in McMinnville, Oregon, back in 1950. Unfortunately, no CIA records have surfaced regarding this photograph, even though the agency was clearly following French UFO sightings at this time. Incidentally, two Blue Book unknowns occurred in French Morocco during March. At 8 P.M. on March 5, the same day as the Rouen photograph, crews of USAF KC-97 aerial tanker planes over Nouasseur, French Morocco, saw an object or light make several passes at their aircraft. Another unidentified object flew nearby. On March 12, again at Nouasseur, an air force lieutenant flying an F-86 chased an object at more than 530 mph for thirty seconds, but was unable to catch it. The object appeared to be the size of a fighter plane but had neither tanks nor trails. The CIA recorded more UFO sightings in France through April.[58]

The United States had a few interesting reports. At 11 P.M. on February 4, 1954, a UFO sighting occurred over Carswell AFB in Texas. About fifteen miles from the base, ground control radar detected the object. The "mystery aircraft" then passed over the Carswell tower at a little over three thousand feet, where personnel saw it through binoculars. The object was like nothing they had ever seen: long fuselage, elliptical wings, some kind of stabilizer, and no visible means of propulsion. The object had a bright light on its nose and tail, two yellowish lights on the bottom of the fuselage, with possible lights on each wing tip. No one heard a sound. The report was sent directly to the Joint Chiefs of Staff, the CIA, the NSA, and other leading intelligence groups. This showed again how little even the official new system of UFO reporting meant with sightings that mattered.[59]

The South and West were the main areas of American UFO activity in early 1954. On March 8, a pilot at Laredo AFB in Texas reported a glowing red round object moving at tremendous speed, then vanishing. On March 24, a Marine Corps jet pilot in Florida saw a round object streak downward, stop, then speed away after he pursued it. Then, on March 29, a CIRVIS report described an "unidentified object glowing bright green" seen in Wyoming by a United Airlines pilot, and confirmed by another airliner. Recipients of the report included the CIA and DIRNSA.[60]

Leaks, rumors, and odd news items continued to appear. In April, Wilkins heard of an alleged visit by Dwight Eisenhower to Edwards AFB in California, where Ike saw alien bodies and debris. This was said to have occurred from February 17 to 20, 1954. The public explanation was that Eisenhower saw a dentist named Purcell. The story lay dormant for decades, until William Moore (of MJ-12 fame) interviewed the dentist's widow. While vague about Eisenhower's dental treatment, she provided explicit detail about a presidential reception they attended during that time. Moore found no evidence at the Eisenhower Library that Eisenhower was treated by a dentist at that time. He also found no thank-you messages, although Eisenhower tended to be scrupulous in such matters. On the other hand, Eisenhower's secretary did mention the event in a diary.[61]

Few UFO stories received any media attention, although several interesting cases took place. Late on April 14, a United Airlines plane over Long Beach, California, narrowly missed a collision with an unknown object that came "out of nowhere" at five thousand feet. The captain turned the wheel hard and brought the plane up so fast passengers were thrown to the floor, and a stewardess and one passenger sustained broken legs and ankles. On April 22 at San Nicholas Island in California, American servicemen saw a gray cigar-shaped object descend. Smoke rose where it landed, but a search yielded no results. On the twenty-third, two Pan Am airliners, about two hundred miles apart, each sighted a UFO between Puerto Rico and New York. The object pulsated an orange-greenish light and streaked past both planes. On the twenty-ninth, three members of the Second Army Radio Station at Fort Meade, Maryland, saw an unidentified round, brilliant, blinking object, three or four times the size of a large star, moving across the sky in a straight path. As it arrived above Fort Meade, it disappeared by shooting straight up. Eastern Air Defense Command and army intelligence were notified of this sighting.[62]

At midnight on May 1 came a terrific explosion from Logan City, Utah. Several people saw a brilliant object, like a glowing ball, plunge rapidly in the sky just before the explosion. A man driving on the highway was terrified to see a "dazzling red half-globe come out of the ground, ahead of his auto, and to the left." Less than ten seconds later, according to the man, a violent blast shook his vehicle and apparently threw open doors over 250 square miles. Other eyewitnesses also claimed to see a flash at ground level. Researchers the next morning found a crater sixteen feet wide and six feet deep. La Paz was on the scene, heading the investigation and assisted by Utah state geologists. On the assumption that the object was a meteor, his crew drilled to a depth of twenty-five feet, but found no meteoric debris. The crater also seemed too small for the shock wave recorded. A Geiger counter reading showed no unusual radiation, and an artesian well appeared in the crater.

La Paz was mystified. "If it's a meteorite," he told reporters, "it must have been a whopper." Excavation at the site continued for five days. La Paz then issued the following statement:

> In the region from Clarkston to Paradise, numerous persons saw or heard the explosive phenomenon at midnight on May 1. The testimony thus obtained, and material evidence recovered as a result of subsurface investigation, has disclosed that the crater was not produced by a conventional meteorite fall. For these reasons, operations have been discontinued.

La Paz did not say what could have caused the explosion, and was silent on what he found. Keyhoe checked his Washington sources, but came up empty.[63]

WASHINGTON SIGHTINGS, REVISITED

Shortly after midnight on May 6, Washington, D.C. radar once again tracked UFOs, causing an Air Defense alert. Each time Air Defense fighters approached, the UFOs vanished. Then, on May 13—a week later—two major

UFO sightings occurred in the city. The first involved multiple radar and visual tracking of an object that appeared to be 250 feet in diameter and fifteen miles above the city, or eighty thousand feet. In another year, the U-2 aircraft would be operational and capable of such altitudes. In 1954, however, no aircraft could reach that height. Moreover, the object moved in a way impossible for any aircraft, from point to point in a rectangular pattern at about 200 mph. After three hours of being tracked by several governmental radar installations, the object disappeared. At the same time, two police officers at the Washington National Airport saw two large, glowing, oval objects approach the airport and maneuver over that part of the city. Military Air Transport confirmed its presence, and the object was seen for over an hour. An air force spokesman in the Pentagon even told reporters it was an "Unidentified Flying Object."

Frank Edwards carried both UFO stories that evening on Mutual Network Radio. Only the second of the reports made it to the press—a single edition of the *Washington Post*. In Edwards's words: "The lid was on." Not surprising, judging by what had happened in Washington, D.C., less than two years earlier.[64]

Gen. Nathan Twining, by now the air force's Chief of Staff, made the news after speaking at an Armed Forces Day dinner at Amarillo AFB on May 14, 1954. Twining said "the air force has the best brains in the country working on the flying saucer problem." Twining gave while he took away. He claimed 90 percent of reports were "pure imagination," but 10 percent could not be explained. (By now, it was commonplace for officials to concede a 10 percent unexplained rate, although the number had been running at 20 percent for years.) The author of the then-still-secret 1947 memo claimed "no facts" had shown that there was anything to substantiate flying saucers, although "some very reliable persons have reported flying objects that can't be identified." Keyhoe reached Twining's press officer about this but was told Twining was "talking off the cuff."[65]

In an event that was presumably not pure imagination, four veteran National Guard pilots engaged in "high-altitude tag" over Dallas with sixteen UFOs before being outmaneuvered and outdistanced. This was reported in the May 25 *Dallas Herald*, but nowhere else. Another nonimagined event occurred on May 24 and included a photograph of a UFO from an RB-29 aircraft that left Wright Field. The photo was overexposed. On May 31, an AP story described a glowing disc seen by a pilot, an air traffic controller, police, and residents from Spokane to Portland. The next day, a TWA pilot saw a large, bright disc-like object as his plane approached Boston; eight airport personnel also saw it.[66]

A RUCKUS AT WRIGHT-PAT

On June 2, the air force reported eighty-seven UFO sightings for the first four months of the year, a rather low total. Shortly afterward, however, Col. John O'Mara, deputy commander of intelligence at ATIC, told Stringfield something a little different: that the air force was receiving an average of seven hundred sighting reports per week! Soon, Frank Edwards announced the news to the whole country. Stringfield was becoming quite a nuisance. Then, on June 9, Col. Frank Milani, Director of Civil Defense in Baltimore, publicly attacked air force UFO secrecy. The air force denied any UFO secrecy or censorship and restated its 1954 UFO statistics. Back in Dayton, however, O'Mara said over one thousand scientists were working on the UFO problem. The air force PIO denied O'Mara said this. Finally, Blue Book chief Capt. Charles Hardin told the press:

Colonel O'Mara's words were misinterpreted. What he meant to say was that if all the sightings were reported to the air force, they would total about seven hundred per week.[67]

A rather weak correction, and not enough to stop UFO news. On June 12, Baltimore GOC members spotted a UFO shortly before midnight. Soon after, Ground Observer Corps (GOC) radar in Delaware tracked a very large object that stopped and hovered near the Capitol. Jets located it, but could not climb high enough. Two days later, a large UFO returned to the Washington-Baltimore area. Again, Air Defense Command scrambled jets, and again the jets could not reach the object.[68]

SUMMER 1954—ONCE AGAIN, MATTERS GET OUT OF CONTROL

To make sense of the past, historians must do more than record events. The sheer quantity of data forces us to select carefully and to shape an interpretation that makes the most sense. The process is never neat, it always involves errors in judgment that can only be seen at a distance, and it must always undergo revision. The summer of 1954 illustrates these problems. A typical history of UFOs focuses on the events of 1947, early air force interest, the periods of Sign and Grudge, the Great Wave of 1952, and the Robertson Panel. Then, it would seem, not much happened until the 1960s. Certainly this is a reasonable conclusion from reviewing the Blue Book files—the typical approach. From over two hundred Blue Book unknowns in 1952, there were only thirty-two in 1953, forty-six in 1954, and a mere twenty in 1955.

There *was* a drop in UFO activity during these years and, to an extent, the rest of the 1950s. Yet, the drop-off was less significant than official data indicate. As we have seen, Blue Book became a marginal operation after 1953. All these years later, we still do not know the true number of UFO reports that were made by U.S. government agencies during the 1950s, nor any other era. Sometimes a researcher's doggedness pays off, and a new report surfaces. How many elude us? All we can say with confidence is that many UFO reports were not part of an official, public system, and undoubtedly there are many we will never see.

As we have seen many times by now, Blue Book did not receive many of the best UFO reports. Despite so-called CIA disbelief in UFOs, the agency monitored them worldwide. A June 18, 1954, report from French Equatorial Africa described a luminous globe suddenly stop, rise, drop, stop, gyrate, and shake. Some noise previously heard stopped. The center appeared dark, but rays of light emanated out. After fifteen minutes of observation, the object shot away.[69]

That the CIA's reports escaped Blue Book is understandable, due to the agency's worldwide scope. But many cases within the United States continued to remain outside of Blue Book. Consider a dramatic UFO chase that took place on June 23, 1954, was obtained by Keyhoe, and confirmed by an air traffic controller before the military forced him into silence. Just after 8 P.M., Lt. Harry L. Roe, Jr., was flying an F-51 Mustang fighter from Columbus to Dayton, Ohio. He saw a "brilliant white light" race down and pace him. Roe swerved left, then right, then slowed down suddenly. Each time, the light stayed with him. As he approached Dayton, he radioed the CAA tower at Vandalia Airport and asked the traffic controller, George Barnes, if he could see it. The light was too bright for either man to see the actual object, but both saw it pace Roe's aircraft precisely, no matter what maneuver Roe attempted. Finally, the UFO passed the F-51 and vanished toward the southeast.

Barnes's report quickly reached Intelligence at Wright-Patterson, and Roe was told not to discuss his encounter. However, enough people already knew the story, and it leaked to AP. Barnes confirmed the report when he assumed the air force had released it, and Roe admitted it as well, adding that he had been silenced by the air force.[70]

Just as this story was making news, another startling event occurred over an Atomic Energy Commission plant in eastern Idaho. After midnight on June 26, witnesses saw "a blinding glow, like an enormous floodlight," overhead. The source remained motionless for a few seconds, illuminating the ground for several miles around. Then, rising at a tremendous speed, the light vanished. This story received coverage in the local newspaper and eventually reached AP. Later the same day, Air Defense radar picked up a UFO over Ohio. A commercial aircraft, including the plane's sixty passengers, saw the object near Columbus. The story made the papers about a week later. But like the Roe story, it was absent from the Blue Book files.[71]

On the twenty-ninth occurred a sighting that did make it to Blue Book and also received a good deal of media attention. It involved a BOAC (now British Airways) commercial airliner flying from New York to London. Former RAF pilot James Howard was in command, Lee Boyd was the first officer, Capt. H. McDonnell the navigator. The plane was crossing Goose Bay, Labrador, in the early evening when Howard saw a large cigar shape and six smaller black ovals about five miles away. The six smaller objects followed the "mother ship" upward into a thin layer of cloud. Howard's crew saw the same thing and found no reasonable answer. The objects appeared to be following and tracking the airliner, and the crew informed Goose Bay of their "escort." As they sent their message, the six mini UFOs entered the larger craft, and the object shot away. Goose Bay had the object on radar and sent a jet. When the BOAC landed at Labrador to refuel, Canadian and American intelligence officers hustled Howard and Boyd off for a debriefing, causing the takeoff to be delayed. McDonnell said that USAF personnel took the flight logs without authorization. After reaching London, Howard and Boyd were called into the Air Ministry, which then explained to the press that the crew and passengers had seen a solar eclipse. An eclipse did occur, but not until 7 A.M. the next morning, about twelve hours after the sighting. Some months later, McDonnell met up with Howard and asked what had happened at the Air Ministry. Howard's response: "Sorry, I can't say. You know the score."

Years later, Condon investigator Gordon Thayer maintained the sighting was a mirage. He admitted there were problems with his explanation and added this "natural phenomenon" was "so rare that it apparently has never been reported before or since." He made this statement without irony. James McDonald countered: "No meteorological-optical phenomenon . . . could reasonably account for the reported phenomenon." Thayer's review of the case was a perfect example of the sterile analysis that occurs when "official culture" collides with the world of the UFO. No attempt was made to confront the social context of the problem, in this case, the pressure placed on the British pilots. The essence of the living fact, as Tolstoy once wrote, was left aside, and the argument was constructed in such a way as to "shut out the possibility of that essence being discovered."[72]

The BOAC case made clear that the American military could silence not only its own military and commercial pilots but also British commercial pilots. Even now, however, reports continued to leak out. On June 30, a UFO was observed visually and tracked on radar at Brookley AFB in Mobile, Alabama. The next day, a tragedy occurred near Utica, New York. Griffis AFB radar had tracked a UFO; soon an F-94 was in pursuit and, sure enough, the pilot saw a disc-shaped object. As he closed, a furnace-like heat filled his cockpit, forcing him and his radar man to eject. The plane crashed into the town of

Walesville, killing four people and injuring five others. The pilot told reporters about the strange heat, but quickly recanted this position under air force pressure. The story was now that engine trouble caused the disaster.[73]

Two sightings of green UFOs took place on July 3. Near Albuquerque, nine green spheres were seen visually and tracked on radar. On the same day, the captain, officers, and 463 passengers on a Dutch ocean liner saw a single "greenish-colored, saucer-shaped object about half the size of a full moon" as it sped across the sky and disappeared into high clouds. On July 8, a British astronomer in Lancashire saw a silvery object with fifteen to twenty smaller satellite objects. More UFO news came from the Washington-Baltimore-Wilmington area. On July 9, the Wilmington *Morning News* ran the headline, "100 Flying Objects Spotted Here." The article reported over one hundred UFO sightings by GOC personnel, including forty during the first five months of 1954. All reports, it stated, were studied by the air force.[74]

Early in August, Ruppelt wrote a scathing attack on Blue Book's current methods of analysis in a letter to Keyhoe. He described an officer in the Air Force Directorate of Intelligence as "taking the old ostrich approach to keeping his head in the sand, thinking they [UFOs] will go away. He is wrong." The air force claimed they had gotten unknowns down to 10 percent, wrote Ruppelt

> but from what I saw this is just due to a more skeptical attitude. The reports are just as good as the ones we got, and their analysis procedures are a hell of a lot worse.[75]

One wonders what the attitude must have been of the CIA personnel who handled the agency's UFO reports. On July 25, the CIA reported a twenty-minute sighting of six UFOs, almost immobile, in southern Rhodesia (now Zimbabwe) by a policeman and others. On August 4 came another CIA report from The Hague, Netherlands. In this instance, ten firemen and their chief saw two UFOs between 11 P.M. and midnight. It was a clear night, and the object was at a high altitude. It displayed "incredible speed, [and] at times remained motionless for as long as thirty seconds." It appeared as a light-colored, flat oval, and in the opinion of the observers could not have been aircraft or balloons.[76]

Another UFO incident came from the Netherlands a few days later. Dutch newspapers reported that on August 7, Capt. Jan P. Bos of the SS *Groote Beer* saw a strange, flat, "moonlike" object rise out of the ocean, eighty or ninety miles east of Cape Cod. Through binoculars, he saw clearly illuminated ports on the rim. The object then moved at a "fantastic" speed. On August 6, people in Santa Fe, New Mexico, saw another fireball for fifteen minutes, a brilliant white ball in the sky that left a luminous trail. It apparently shot up and away. Lincoln La Paz said it was not a meteorite.[77]

Frank Edwards had announced UFO reports all year on his nationwide radio program. On August 11, 1954, his primary sponsor, the American Federation of Labor, fired him. According to AFL President George Meany, he failed to differentiate between news and his opinion. According to Edwards, Meany said, "because he talked too much about flying saucers." Edwards said he had broadcast only seventeen "brief" UFO reports in all of 1954. Soon after, the Pentagon offered Edwards a job at $18,500, on the condition he be sworn to secrecy over the things he encountered. Edwards declined. His departure from national broadcasting was a serious blow to the cause of antisecrecy.[78]

AFR 200-2 DECLASSIFIED

On July 23, probably under air force pressure, the navy issued a new UFO directive which ordered immediate reporting of UFOs, using the code word "Flyobrpt." Reports were to be phoned or teletyped to the following destinations: Director of Air Force Intelligence, ATIC, Commanding Officer of Air Defense Command, Commanding Officer of Eastern Air Defense Command, Director of Naval Intelligence, Commanding Officer of the Eastern Sea Frontier, and the Commandant of the Potomac River Naval Command. The directive cited JANAP 146, AFR 200-2, and two previous navy orders, OPNAV 3820 and Directive 3820.2 by the Commander of the Eastern Sea Frontier. It was intended to plug the leaks that were coming from navy and marine personnel. Although the directive was unpublicized, it was also unclassified. It thus threatened disclosure of AFR 200-2, which *was* still classified. As a result, the air force began work on a new version of AFR 200-2, one without the "restricted" label.[79]

Then, on the heels of the Edwards firing, Air Force Chief of Staff Nathan Twining declassified AFR 200-2 on August 12. Pentagon rumors had the navy forcing Twining's hand. The public, to the extent that it cared, could now learn that Air Defense Command—not Blue Book—was responsible for UFO field investigations, and that Blue Book did not even get all the reports. Moreover, the air force admitted to legitimate interest in UFOs, which were "any airborne object which by performance, aerodynamic characteristics, or unusual features, does not conform to any presently known aircraft or missile type, or which cannot be positively identified as a familiar object." The document stated that

> interest in unidentified flying objects is twofold: first as a possible threat to the security of the United States and its forces, and second, to determine the technical aspects involved.

Just what were the "technical aspects involved"? The public would never know, as the air force would release information only about objects that were "positively identified as a familiar object." Anything truly unconventional would not be discussed with the public.[80]

The day AFR 200-2 was declassified, an incredible CIRVIS report describing a UFO was sent to the DIRNSA. It was headed "Emergency," from the flight service center at Maxwell AFB, Alabama, to the Commander of Air Defense Command at Ent AFB, Colorado Springs. The report described the entry into airspace of a "strange stationary object variable in brilliance" which moved rapidly, then returned to its original position. The base sent a helicopter to investigate; "definitely not a star," said the pilot. The object began receiving a great deal of attention. A number of people watched it from the tower, and Columbus CAA radioed in that they had it in sight. The object soon became dimmer, showed a slight red glow, and disappeared. According to the report:

> pilot of helicopter wished to stress fact that object was of a saucer-like nature, was stationary at 2000 ft. And would be glad to be called upon to verify any statements and act as witness.[81]

Although sightings trailed off by the end of summer, on August 28, a formation of fifteen UFOs approached Oklahoma City, tracked on radar. Jets were sent to intercept them, and the objects quickly vanished out of sight. Hundreds of city residents watched the chase. Tinker Field officers nevertheless refused to admit the sighting.[82]

THE HUMANOID SIGHTINGS

What follows constitutes one of the most bizarre and baffling UFO events ever. Between September and December 1954, a heavy concentration of UFO reports—at times dozens per day—came from France, Italy, Britain, Germany, North Africa, the Middle East, and South America. People were seeing more than objects in the sky: they claimed to see landings of UFOs and short humanoid beings. In France, the first area of intense activity, UFO researchers Raymond Veillith and Aimé Michel did the brunt of rounding up newspaper accounts and interviewing witnesses. Without their work, this wave might well have been forgotten by the public. It is noteworthy that the Lorenzens had collected a few humanoid sighting reports from South America during 1953 and early 1954, which closely match the events of this autumn.[83]

Press coverage was mostly local, and many witnesses did not know that a UFO wave was taking place. Most of them described beings between three and four feet tall, some of which were human-looking, others "almost" human-looking, others wore "diving suits," others were hairy, gray, or even shorter than two feet. None of the sightings included descriptions of what are now called "Grays," the small, thin creatures with big, dark eyes, made famous from the cover of Whitley Strieber's *Communion*. (The first definite description of such entities did not occur until the Hill abduction of 1961, although a few possible descriptions occurred during the mid-1950s.)

The response to all this was uneven. Several governments followed events carefully and even created special sections for gathering and studying UFO reports. Some American UFO organizations, such as CSI and APRO, were also impressed. Others, such as NICAP (formed in 1956) dismissed the reports as too closely resembling "crackpot" cases. Scientists ridiculed the events. "Such fantastic stories," one French scientist said, "could only come from deranged minds," to which Michel responded, "what would these people have said if I had published *all the data!*"[84] The CIA, despite collecting many European UFO reports from this period, has offered none pertaining to humanoid beings.

France had been the scene of steady UFO activity throughout 1954. Multiple-witness sightings occurred in France and Tunisia in late August and early September. CIA files recorded a UFO encounter from the French town of Aisne, near the Belgian border on September 7. At 3 A.M., a husband, wife, and her father were driving when they saw a luminous red-orange disc stop across the road about one thousand feet up. The object rose and took off at high speed.[85]

The first sighting of a UFO occupant in France occurred three days later, not far from the previous sighting. On September 10, near the Belgian border in Valenciennes, Marius Dewilde, a thirty-four-year-old metal worker, was reading at home at 10:30 P.M. His wife and children were in bed. His dog barked, and Dewilde took a flashlight outside in time to see his dog whining and crawling on its belly. He heard hurried footsteps to his right. His dog barked again. Shining his flashlight, he saw two creatures just beyond his fence, walking in single file toward a dark mass at the railway tracks. The creatures were about three and one-half feet tall with very wide shoulders, short legs, and helmets covering what seemed to be enormous heads. Dewilde could not make out any arms.

Recovering from his initial shock, he ran to cut them off and got to within six feet of them. At that point, a powerful orange light came from a square opening in the dark mass, blinding him. Dewilde felt paralyzed; his legs would not move. He saw the creatures continue toward the tracks, the dark object rise and hover, and a door close. The object rose to about one hundred feet, turned east, and disappeared.

After recovering use of his legs, Dewilde woke his wife and a neighbor, and told the police, who thought he was crazy. Dewilde would not be put off. He spoke to the police commissioner, who was impressed by his determination and sent investigators to the area, which included local police and the French air police from Paris. They found five places on three wooden railroad ties with identical impressions, each about one and one-half inches square.

The marks were fresh and deep. Engineers later calculated the weight needed to produce these cuts to have been about thirty tons. The Dewilde case received some international press notice. Naturally, the local police had no explanation and were shut out of the air police investigation.[86]

Throughout France, UFO activity was heavy. A few days after the Dewilde case, on September 14, a daytime UFO sighting occurred before "hundreds of witnesses," about 250 miles southwest of Paris. Another sighting on the nineteenth involved a flat, gray, circular object which slowed, stopped, hovered motionless for thirty seconds, swayed, and took off.[87]

Then, on the afternoon of September 26, in the town of Valence, a woman also claimed to see a humanoid being while she was gathering mushrooms in the woods. Her dog barked, and she saw a short being wearing a translucent helmet and suit; she saw large eyes looking at her through the helmet. The being approached her, moving awkwardly; she screamed and ran. When she turned around, she saw a large circular and flattened metallic object rise from behind the trees and depart rapidly, gaining altitude all the time. Other people, including her husband, were nearby, and they soon arrived to see a circular area about ten feet in diameter. Inside the circle, shrubs and bushes were crushed; tree branches were broken as if from above. Some of the people claimed to hear a whistling sound when the craft departed, and the police were struck by her state of nervous shock.[88]

Yet another humanoid encounter took place two nights later in the town of Bouzais. A man had noticed that someone had stolen grapes from his vineyard and decided to stay up late and catch the thief. At about 10:30 P.M., he saw a luminous object descend and three figures emerge. He was then paralyzed and lost consciousness. There was no sign of anything when he regained consciousness. On the thirtieth, eight construction workers near Marcilly-sur-Vienne saw a disc-shaped object on the ground, and a small helmeted being standing nearby.[89]

THE "INVASION" OF FRANCE: OCTOBER 1954

By the end of September, about 250 people throughout France had recently claimed to have seen flying saucers and humanoids.[90] October was just as surreal, and even busier. Keyhoe was probably right when he believed hysteria to be behind some of them. Still, it is not so easy to dismiss all of these supposed encounters with aliens. Here is a brief synopsis of some of the more remarkable accounts from the first half of that month.

October 1.

In the town of Bry, a man and his dog were paralyzed as a bright white object dove toward them and climbed again. Later that evening in Bergerac, a fireman returning home saw a light in the sky similar to a shooting star. Later, he saw an intense light in his yard and rushed out to see a disc rise from the ground with a whistling sound. It became luminous and flew off. A neighbor also saw the object and estimated it to be ten feet wide.[91]

October 2.

At 8 P.M., in Croix d'Epine, a man on his motor scooter saw a bright, oval object land off the road fifty feet from him. He saw short, dark shapes "like potato bags" moving around the object, which was the size of a small bus. It quickly took off, changing from orange to blue, then grayish-blue. The man fainted while telling his story. Two people in nearby villages independently reported seeing the object.[92]

October 3.

At dawn in Bressuire, a fifty-five-year-old stockyard employee was going to work when he saw a small being wearing a diving suit standing near a circular craft about ten feet in diameter. The object swiftly took off. Shortly after noon, a man saw a circular craft between the towns of Montmoreau and Villebois-Lavalette. It seemed to be gliding on or near the ground, had luminous spots, and became illuminated when it took off. The man found flattened and scorched grass over an area twenty-five feet across. At around 7:30 P.M., a crowd at a fair in Chereng saw a fast luminous object in the sky suddenly stop, give off sparks, and descend to ground level. As people ran to the spot, the object took off again.[93]

October 4.

At 8 P.M., in Poncey, Madame Yvette Fourneret saw a luminous orange object, about ten feet wide, land in a meadow on her farm. She ran to tell two men, who arrived with rifles, but found no object. Instead, they saw a strange, "quadrilateral" hole from which soil appeared to be sucked up. Unlike what could be expected from an ordinary excavation, the roots were not damaged. The French air force and local police investigated and learned that other citizens of Poncey reported seeing a luminous object rise and take off at this time.[94]

October 5.

At 6:30 A.M., near Le Mans, some Renault employees were going to work when they saw a luminous object on the ground near the road. They felt "pricklings and a sort of paralysis." The object then emitted a burst of green light and flew away very low over the fields. At 3:45 P.M., near Beaumont, several people saw a bright object coming toward them. When it was about five hundred feet away, they felt a strange sensation and became paralyzed. The object left a smell similar to nitrobenzene. Two reports that day also emerged of hairy dwarfish beings; in both cases the creatures took off in crafts that swiftly departed.[95]

October 6.

At 9:30 P.M. in La Fere, near military barracks, French soldiers saw a "torpedo-shaped" object on the ground a little less than a quarter mile away. As one soldier approached it, he became paralyzed.[96]

October 7.

A landing or near-landing case of a UFO shaped like a "giant artillery shell" with portholes near Isles-sur-Suippes.[97]

October 9.

A man on a bicycle in Lavoix saw a figure in a diving suit with very bright eyes aiming a double beam of light at him, which paralyzed him. The being then walked into the forest. In Carcassone, a man saw a metallic sphere in the road. The top half of the object was transparent, and he saw two human-shaped figures standing inside. The craft soon left at high speed.[98]

October 10.

The second landing observed by Marius Dewilde, this time with his four-year-old son. Dewilde saw a disc about twenty feet wide and three to four feet high, landing again on the railroad tracks. He saw seven small men emerge and heard an unknown language. The craft vanished without noise or smoke and left traces larger than the first. Dewilde initially refused to report the case. Also that afternoon, a math professor in Saint-Germain-de-Livet saw a silvery, spinning disc about twenty-five feet in diameter silently rise from a short distance off the road. The object dived from an altitude of about half a mile, then swiftly flew off.[99]

October 11.

Two men driving at 4:30 A.M. in the town of Sassier felt an electric shock as their headlights died. About 150 feet away, they saw a thick cylindrical craft in a pasture and three dwarfs nearby. A small red light paralyzed them until the craft left. A third witness saw a lighted object fly over the nearby woods. In the early evening near Taupignac, three men left their car to watch a bright red sphere in the sky. It was about a tenth of a mile away and appeared to be a domed, roundish machine, hovering at thirty feet, now giving off a yellow light. It was silent and motionless but then moved horizontally for a short distance and landed behind a wooded area. Two of the men went closer and saw four short beings working on their craft. The men came to within fifty feet when they were blinded by a burst of blue, then orange, then red light. The beings rushed inside and the object took off vertically at "fantastic" speed.[100]

October 13.

At about 7:30 P.M., three men near Toulouse, one an ex-pilot, described the same small being with a large head and eyes, wearing a bright suit "like glass." The being was near a reddish, glowing craft about fifteen feet wide.

One man approached to within sixty or seventy feet and was paralyzed. The object took off, throwing him to the ground.[101]

October 14.

A farmer in Meral saw an orange spherical object land. As he approached, he saw it was a dome-shaped disc with a flat bottom. For ten minutes, it gave a blinding light for two hundred yards around. The color then changed to red, and the object took off at a great speed. The man's clothes were covered with a white, sticky residue, which soon disappeared.[102]

October 16.

Dr. Henri Robert in his village of Baillolet saw four objects flying at one thousand feet, each above the other. One floated down like a leaf, landing about 350 feet in front of his car. The doctor felt an electric shock while his engine and headlights died. Paralyzed, he saw a four-foot figure moving in the light of the object, then everything went dark. Some time later, his car was normal and he saw the object take off. He then reported this to the police. That day in Cier-de-Riviere, a young man returning with a mare from the fields noticed the animal become restless. He saw a small gray object, perhaps five feet wide, rise and hover above them. The mare then rose ten feet in the air, forcing him to release the bridle. After the animal fell, it could not move for about ten minutes and stumbled about for some time after. By then, the object was long gone. The man himself felt nothing.[103]

GLOBAL SIGHTINGS

Something odd was happening in France. But strange activity was going on everywhere. A hovering disc was photographed in Nelson, New Zealand, on September 9. The CIA noted a seven-second, multiple-witness sighting in Helsinki on September 14 of an intensely bright circular object that left a trail of reddish smoke. On the fifteenth, in Bihar, India, a disc-shaped UFO set off a panic, as it descended to five hundred feet and hovered over an American AEC mine. Eight hundred people fled to their homes. After apparent close-range observation, the craft swiftly ascended vertically. On September 17, thousands of people in Rome, Italy, watched a disc-like object that was tracked by Italian air force radar. On the eighteenth, green fireballs made another appearance in the American Southwest (Colorado, New Mexico, and Texas), and were again investigated by Lincoln La Paz. The next day, in the French West Africa town of Danane, officials saw an oval UFO with a dome and searchlights. Apparently there was activity of UFOs in Eastern Europe. On October 1, Romanian newspapers blamed the U.S. for launching a drive to induce a "flying saucer psychosis" in their country. In Yugoslavia, an especially dense wave of UFO sightings occurred between October 15 and 25. In the words of two investigators, flying saucers were seen "all over that country." Thousands of witnesses near Belgrade, Sarajevo, and Lubljana described low-flying discs as well as large cigar-shaped objects at high altitudes. All this activity hardly reached the press in the land of Tito; the little that did was ridiculed.[104]

Worldwide, UFO sightings occurred briskly through October. Many were reported in the Middle East and North Africa. On October 5, hundreds of people in Mehalla-el Kobra, Egypt, saw a "spindle-like" object for twenty minutes. In Behnay, Egypt, cylinders in the sky emitted a thick smoke. One exploded, and the debris killed and burned two cows. A military officer photographed a "rotating saucer" that gave off smoke near the Suez Canal and sent it to the Egyptian army public relations office and the Helouan Observatory. Adm. Youssef Hammad, director of ports and lighthouses, alerted pilots and astronomers to watch for UFOs over Cairo.[105]

Late on October 9, a German man in Beirut, Lebanon, saw a strange object land, then ascend vertically with a spinning motion. On the tenth, in Alexandria, Egypt, observatories saw a red and green cylindrical flying object. In Teheran, at 2:30 A.M. on October 12, a man on the second floor of his house saw a luminous, white object hover about fifty feet from his window. Lights shone from various parts of the craft, and the witness clearly saw a small figure inside the craft, dressed in black, and wearing a mask with a hose. The man screamed and woke his neighbors, and the object shot straight up, emitted sparks, and vanished. Later that day in Morocco, a French engineer saw a small being in silver clothing enter an object which quickly took off.[106]

Another Iranian sighting occurred on the fourteenth, in Shamsabad. A man leaving his house in the early morning saw a bright object almost twenty feet long. A "short young man" was standing nearby on a circular piece of metal, laughing at the man's frightened expression. Evidently the craft departed at incredible speed. A UFO was seen in Kenya on October 14, by a lieutenant colonel of the British army and his wife. The two saw a light green object moving at tremendous speed. A humanoid sighting took place in Tripoli, Libya, on October 23. At around 3 A.M., a farmer saw a flying object descend to ground level about 150 feet away, making a sound like that of a compressor. It appeared to be an oval machine with six wheels and complex machinery. The top half was transparent and filled with bright white light. Six human-looking men were aboard wearing protective masks and yellowish coveralls. The witness touched part of the craft and felt a strong electric shock. One of the occupants motioned for him to stay away. For the next twenty minutes, the witness was able to watch the six men, apparently busy with instruments. According to Vallee,[107] reliable investigations were made of this encounter. The following day, another humanoid sighting occurred in Algeria, in the town of Ain-el-Turck.[108]

In Europe, some high-quality UFO sightings occurred not only in France, but Britain, Italy, Sweden, Germany, Austria, Holland, Czechoslovakia, Yugoslavia, and elsewhere. Several governments took action on the UFO problem. On October 1, the Swedish Defense Ministry ordered a new secret inquiry into UFOs. The next day, the French Air Ministry ordered an official investigation. On the seventh, the Italian Air Ministry ordered day and night vigilance at detection posts by "saucer spotters." On October 10, the Royal Belgian observatory at Liege opened a file on UFOs and asked for public reports of sightings.[109]

The concern was for good reason. It seemed like the United States from the summer of 1952, with a twist. The traditional sightings by military pilots continued, such as an October 4 incident in which a "saturn-shaped" UFO buzzed an RAF Meteor jet. But increasingly, people with no apparent reason to lie were claiming to have seen, for lack of a better word, *aliens*. A man named Willi Hoge, from Munster, Germany, had one such experience on the evening of October 9. Returning from work, he saw a blue light and thought an airplane had made an emergency landing. As he approached, he saw four small beings with short legs, very large chests, and oversized heads. They wore some sort of coveralls and were working on a cigar-shaped craft about 250 feet off the road. Another landing and humanoid report came from Castelibranco, Portugal, on October 13. In this case, the beings were seen picking flowers, twigs, and shrubs, "as if gathering data."[110]

Another startling encounter with a UFO by an RAF pilot came on October 14, 1954. A pilot flying a Meteor jet over Southend at sixteen thousand feet saw two circular objects streak between two other Meteor planes high above him. Turning to look through his windscreen, he saw a similar object coming towards him. In his words, "it was silvery in color, had a bun-shaped top, a flange like two saucers in the middle and a bun underneath, and could not have been far off because it overlapped my windscreen!" The object passed around him at "tremendous speed."[111]

The next day, an English woman in Southend named Pat Hennessey claimed to see a UFO landing. With much common sense, she ran away. When she turned around to look again, it had vanished without a sound. On October 21, a woman from Ranton, Great Britain, and her two children saw a disc-shaped metallic object hovering above their house. Like the case from Teheran, they also claimed to see occupants through "transparent" panels—in this case, two men with white skin, hair to their shoulders, very high foreheads, transparent helmets, and turquoise-blue clothing that resembled ski suits. The craft hovered at a tilted angle while the two beings looked at the scene "sternly, not in an unkind fashion, but almost sadly, compassionately."[112]

November and December 1954:
World Sightings Continue

By mid-October, the main area of humanoid sightings shifted from France to Italy; by November it was in South America. Many of the Italian cases involved the theft of plants or small farm animals, reports of witness paralysis, and alleged guttural or unintelligible sounds coming from the short aliens. Several of them also received investigations by law enforcement officials.

One case from the night of October 20, near the town of Como, involved thirty-seven-year-old Renzo Pugina. He had just parked his car when he saw, standing near a tree, a four-foot being wearing a "scaly" luminous suit. The being paralyzed Pugina with a beam from an instrument. It didn't work fully: Pugina made a motion when clenching his fist that seemed to free him. He then rushed at the being, who fled to a craft and took off. An oily spot was found at the site. Pugina, known locally as a trustworthy person, arrived home in shock and went to bed with a high fever. Italian police investigated the sighting. The next night, in Melito, Italy, a man walking in a field heard a rustling noise and saw a strange craft land. As he got closer, he saw a being wearing a diving suit coming out of the craft, which emitted rays of light that flooded the countryside (claims of intensely bright light have appeared in many military reports of UFOs, including those from the United States). The witness was paralyzed. A dog barking in the distance may have prompted the being to re-enter the craft and depart.[113]

A multiple-witness sighting of a landed craft and humanoid occupants occurred in Milan on October 28. The story has several dubious elements, but on the same night, U.S. Ambassador to Italy, Clare Booth Luce, saw a UFO over Rome. Meanwhile, across the Adriatic Sea, the Yugoslav government ordered its own secret inquiry into UFOs on October 27.[114]

Another typically strange Italian case occurred on November 14 in the northern town of Isola. A farmer saw a cigar-shaped craft land nearby and hid to watch it. Three very short creatures emerged, dressed in metallic diving suits. They became interested in his caged rabbits, a step that caused the man to reach for his rifle. When he tried to shoot, however, the rifle not only failed to work but became so heavy that he dropped it. The beings took his rabbits, entered their craft and departed silently, leaving a bright trail. Interviewers considered the man to be reliable.[115]

Across the Atlantic Ocean, reports coming from South America were equally strange. To be sure, there was no shortage of traditional UFO reports. On October 24, for five hours in the afternoon, Brazilian air force officers and men, as well as airline personnel and civilians, saw a formation of apparently mechanical devices moving at tremendous speeds over Porto Alegre AFB. According to a local press release, the phenomenon was reported immediately to the air ministry in Rio De Janeiro with a request for investigation. The base command stated that "it was impossible to calculate the altitude or velocity at which the objects moved, but the speed was greater than any of which the base has knowledge. Their general shape was circular, silver-colored, and shimmering." A startling incident involving a Brazilian airliner occurred on November 21. The plane was bound for Rio de Janeiro flying at eight thousand feet when it encountered a formation of nineteen glowing UFOs, each more than one hundred feet in diameter. Thirteen passengers stampeded the plane, including one screaming woman who ran into the pilot's compartment. The objects flew by at a tremendous speed, and the story made the Brazilian press. The next evening, in Santa Maria, Brazil, a radio operator at a local air base saw a dark object about one hundred feet in diameter hovering at treetop height. Accompanied by four other people, he watched it for several hours. It glowed at times and occasionally came close to the ground.[116]

However, people in Brazil also claimed to be seeing aliens. In Pontal on the night of November 4, a man fishing in the Pardo River saw a wobbling craft descend and land. It looked like two washbowls placed together and was perhaps twenty feet in diameter. Too terrified to move, he saw three small men, dressed in white and wearing tight-fitting skull caps, exit the craft. They gathered vegetables and water, then flew away. In Curitiba, at 3:30 A.M. on November 13, a witness saw a disc-shaped object on the railroad tracks, and three dwarfs nearby wearing tight-fitting suits. The object took off when the man approached.[117]

By late November, strange sightings had come to Venezuela. An incredible tale came from Caracas on November 28. At 2 A.M., two truck drivers claimed to see a luminous spherical object hovering six feet off the ground, blocking their way. They stopped the truck and one of them investigated. He saw a hairy, three-foot-tall being with claws and glowing eyes, who knocked him about fifteen feet. The man drew a knife and struck the creature, but it glanced off as though he had hit steel. Another creature shone a light which blinded the man, and his assailant entered the craft while two other beings, carrying various samples, also got in. The craft then swiftly took off. The man was hospitalized for a deep scratch on his side, and both men received sedatives. Authorities who investigated considered them reliable.[118]

Three bizarre events were reported in Venezuela on December 10, all of which involved close-up sightings of landed or low-hovering UFOs, encounters with small beings (most of them covered with hair), two of which involved physical encounters and attempted kidnappings which left bruises on the witnesses.[119] On December 16, three young men driving in the suburbs of San Carlos pulled over so that one of them could relieve himself. The man screamed; his friends found him unconscious and saw a small hairy creature enter a shiny disc hovering off the ground, then take off with a deafening buzzing sound. The man was taken to a hospital in a state of shock, and all three were interviewed by authorities.[120]

Back in Europe, close encounters were reported in Belgium, Spain, Germany, and France (including another "paralysis" case in late December); but aside from Italy, the wave of alien sightings declined after mid-November, and more so in December. In November, the Hungarian government announced that UFOs did not exist, since all flying saucer reports came from bourgeois countries. On December 15, a Royal Australian Navy pilot was paced by two UFOs. The incident was confirmed on radar and kept out of the press for several months.[121]

Around this time, Melbourne University scientist Harry Turner wrote a report on flying saucers for the Royal Australian Air Force, which remained classified until 1982. Turner stated:

> The evidence presented by the reports held by [the Australian air force] tend to support the . . . conclusion . . . that certain strange aircraft have been observed to behave in a manner suggestive of extraterrestrial origin.

It would be interesting to see the reports that Turner analyzed. The RAAF, however, seems to have dismissed his report. A key reason was that Turner included references to Keyhoe's book, *Flying Saucers from Outer Space*. According to Australian UFO researcher Bill Chalker,[122] the Australian Director of Air Force Intelligence inquired of the Americans about Keyhoe. The Australians were told that Keyhoe's books deceptively conveyed the impression that they were based on official documents (they didn't, the Pentagon implied), made "improper use of information," and that "a dim view" was taken officially of Keyhoe and his works. Thus, Turner's findings and recommendations (which included greater official interest) were dropped.[123]

AMERICA DEBUNKS

While bedlam swept through Europe and South America, the U.S. Air Force released a statement through the *Chicago Tribune Press* on October 9 under the headline: "Finds Saucers Exist Solely in Imagination." The article stated:

> The air force said today that after seven years of exhaustive investigation by its Air Technical Intelligence Center at Dayton, Ohio, it has failed to uncover any proof that flying saucers exist except in the imagination of observers. . . .[124]

UFOs were not prominent in America at the time. Why, then, would the air force issue such a statement? Keyhoe pointed to the crazy stories from

France and elsewhere which, while "obviously inspired by excitement or hysteria," nevertheless had sown "the seeds of panic" in most of the world.

That may be, but the American military continued to encounter UFOs and express varying levels of concern about them. The 4602nd AISS noted in a September 1954 memo that it was receiving about fifteen reports per week, a bit busier than its average pace of one per day during the latter half of 1954. From mid-August through the end of the year, the 4602nd received 112 raw reports and conducted twenty-five field investigations. Thirty-five cases (31 percent) were unsolved and went on to ATIC/Blue Book, which recorded twenty-two unsolved cases for that period. In November, members of the 4602nd met with Blue Book representatives Capt. Charles Hardin and Allen Hynek, who were to release the "rule of thumb" criteria to evaluate UFOs. Hynek was better qualified than Hardin to do this, and probably helped the 4602nd to compile its own detailed UFO Guide, which it was then doing.[125]

In September, Air Defense Command in Columbus, Ohio, asked Leonard Stringfield if he would help screen GOC reports from southwestern Ohio. It wanted the local Ground Observer Corps to forward UFO reports to him, which he would evaluate and the best of which he would pass to ADC. ADC asked only that Stringfield not ask any questions; he agreed. He later learned that air force jets were scrambled several times on the basis of his reports. Once again, the evidence is that ADC, not ATIC, was doing the serious work on UFOs. Stringfield served for two years in this capacity and gathered that the air force private and public activities regarding UFOs were very different.[126]

On October 14, Keyhoe learned of a "Crashed Object" program at the 4602nd AISS, which someone within the unit had leaked to his friend Lou Corbin. According to the informant, the program was known as the "investigation of unidentified crashed objects." Corbin told Keyhoe that he "got the impression they'd recovered some kind of 'objects'—probably something dropped from a saucer." Corbin also related a recent encounter he had had with an air force captain who had just returned from Alaska. When Corbin asked why the air force was so secretive about flying saucers, the captain angrily blurted out, "What good would it do you if you did know the truth?"[127]

In the wake of the global rush of up-close-and-personal UFO sightings, one obvious question was, how much did the U.S. authorities know about it? Certainly, Keyhoe had known of it, and even Blue Book contained a report from that period describing a UFO occupant. The incident occurred in the Azores Islands on September 21, 1954. An airport guard reported a ten-foot-wide metallic blue object with a clear glass or plastic nose. It made a humming sound, hovered, and landed vertically about fifty feet from the witness. A normal-sized blond man emerged from the object, spoke in an unknown language, and patted the witness on the shoulder. The strange man returned to the craft, attached a harness, pressed a button, and ascended vertically. The total encounter lasted three minutes. This incident was listed in the Blue Book files not as a hoax, but as an *unknown*! Other Blue Book unknowns in late 1954 occurred in the Philippines, Japan, Iceland, Greenland, Morocco, and South Africa—in addition to a rash of quality sightings within the American Midwest. These facts, combined with the knowledge that America had close military relationships with most of the countries experiencing UFO sightings, give us strong reason to believe that American authorities had a very good, if not total, awareness of what was going on.

One thing we know for certain: no one can ascribe these UFO encounters to America's secret U-2 spy plane—a favorite recourse from the CIA's official historian, Gerald Haines. On December 1, 1954, the CIA's Richard Bissell, in conjunction with the Pentagon, initiated the development of the U-2. It would not fly until August 1955.[128]

At a press conference on December 16, President Eisenhower was asked about flying saucers and the recent attention they had been getting from European governments. Eisenhower repeated the air force statement that such things existed "only in the imaginations of the viewers." When asked whether he believed they were extraterrestrial, Eisenhower gave a good example of circumlocution. The last time he talked on this subject, he said, an air force official whom he trusted had told him that, as far as he knew, it was "inaccurate" to believe that the objects were coming from another planet. The air force supported Eisenhower by stating there was "no evidence that we are being observed by machines from outer space, or by a foreign power."[129]

It is unclear whether Eisenhower actually believed what he said. Immediately after the press conference, he asked the air force for a full briefing on the latest UFO developments. Air Force Secretary Harold Talbott admitted as much in a talk at the National Press Club.[130]

By the end of 1954, two things were all too clear. First, UFO sightings and landings were worldwide, and completely beyond the ability of the United States to affect. If one accepts the witness reports, several types of aliens appeared to be examining the world's life-forms—including human life—and conducting some sort of global survey. These aliens did not always care whether humans observed them but they did not want people pestering them, and showed no desire to interact or "make their presence known" to humans in any official way.

Second, the American government, in conjunction with several other nations, seemed to have succeeded in discrediting UFOs. Edwards lost his job in mid-1954, effectively silencing the last national voice in the media that opposed UFO secrecy. In the aftermath of such an intense global wave of UFO sightings, the public dimension of the problem still remained under control. Now, throughout the country, belief in UFOs became truly a marginal affair, something only crackpots took seriously. This was a great success for policymakers who, since 1952, had deemed it essential to end public speculation on this matter once and for all.

Throughout 1955, 1956, and most of 1957, UFOs faded from public view. Some excellent-quality reports came out during this period, but they punctuated long periods of apparent inactivity and general media silence.

INTELLIGENCE OVERSIGHT? NAH

Two commissions studied the American intelligence community in 1955. The first of these was the (Second) Hoover Commission, charged with recommending ways "to promote economy, efficiency, and improved service" in the executive branch of the federal government. Headed by former President Herbert Hoover, it gave its final report to Congress on June 29, 1955. Gen. Mark Clark headed the commission's task force on intelligence—he noted the CIA's lack of accountability and recommended establishing an intelligence oversight committee.[131]

Not surprisingly, this flopped at Langley and the White House. Eisenhower immediately commissioned another study headed by Gen. James Doolittle, which focused on clandestine and covert operations. Doolittle submitted his report on September 30, 1955. Declassified in 1976, it laid out America's prevailing cold war consensus:

> There are no rules in such a game. . . . We must develop effective espionage and counterespionage services and must learn to subvert, sabotage and destroy our enemies by more clever, more sophisticated, and more effective methods than those used against us.[132]

Doolittle's report negated the Hoover Commission recommendations on intelligence oversight. Instead, the National Security Council established a new committee, known as the 5412 Committee, to approve important covert operations. Eisenhower's first representative on it was Gordon Gray, who changed its working name to the Special Group. Henceforth, all proposals passed through the Special Group on their way to the desk of Richard Helms, the CIA's Director of Plans, and the man responsible for clandestine and covert operations.[133]

Protected from oversight, CIA and army behavioral experiments accelerated. During 1955, an MK-Ultra experiment took place in which an army "volunteer" was sealed in a sensory deprivation box for forty consecutive hours. In panic and terror, he kicked his way out, and wept uncontrollably for a day. This resulted in a change of policy: the box was strengthened. Around this time, Dr. Maitland Baldwin told Morris Allen of MK-Ultra that he could do *terminal* experiments in sensory deprivation, as long as the CIA provided the cover and the subjects. This was too grisly even for the CIA at this point, and it was shot down as morally reprehensible. In time, however, the CIA had complete access to Ewen Cameron, who gladly used his own patients for precisely this purpose. Cameron actually left one woman in sensory deprivation for thirty-five days, irreversibly scrambling her mind. The foundation for Cameron's work was laid in 1955 by the incorporation of the Society for the Investigation of Human Ecology, a CIA-funded group that secretly supported mind control research.[134]

In March 1955, the CIA obtained quantities of *Hemophilus pertussis*, the whooping-cough bacteria, from Fort Detrick. It then field tested it along Florida's gulf coast. According to Florida state medical records, the incidence of whooping cough in Florida tripled that year (339 cases and one death in 1954; 1080 cases and twelve deaths in 1955). Unfortunately, the CIA's role remained unknown until 1979.[135]

In 1955, the air force began promoting its influential myth about a bomber gap. The Soviet Union, intent on world domination at any cost, was supposed to have five hundred bombers with which to blow the U.S. into the next millennium. Three years later, after Sputnik, the air force invented a missile gap. These were sheer fabrications, created, in the words of one historian, as "scare tactics to distort information to further its weapons buildup." By 1961, CIA photo interpretation experts, using data derived from U-2 overflights, learned that the Russians had in fact only *four* missiles capable of launching a first-strike attack on the U.S.[136]

BLUE BOOK COOKS ITS BOOKS

Disinformation also prevailed in the world of UFOs. A January 7, 1955, Air Force Information Services Letter ordered silence over UFOs. Air force public relations officers began issuing UFO fact sheets containing a few (occasionally mathematically impossible) statistics and reaffirmations that the small percentage of undetermined unknowns were harmless. The ATIC UFOB Guide was ready by mid-January and sent to the 4602nd AISS. It contained guidelines for follow-up investigations and examples for identifying UFOs. Despite the new guide, a month later (February 15), ATIC sent a memo to 4602nd officer Major Cybulski. The high number of unknowns recorded by the 4602nd was unacceptable. Instead:

> . . . it is necessary that both the 4602nd AISS and the ATIC strive to reach as many case solutions as possible, thereby reducing the percentage of unknowns to a bare minimum.[137]

The message: solve as many cases as possible before sending them to

ATIC. These solutions did not need to be strictly scientific. That is because most UFOB cases, according to the memo, "when sufficient information is contained, will fit *to some extent* [emphasis added] one of the hypotheses contained in the Guide and, therefore, may be considered as solved." The memo encouraged the 4602nd to use such terms as "possible," "probable," and "definite" in identifying UFOs. The implication was clear: ATIC would then conflate them all as identified. In all subsequent air force press releases and Blue Book statistics, "probable" and "possible" subcategories disappeared.[138]

A month later, the air force revised the UFOB Guide again, ordering investigators to use "common sense" in identifying UFOs. This ruled out the possibility that the witness saw anything truly extraordinary. The policy worked: unknowns for 1955 became a mere 5.9 percent and remained low for years. Interestingly, the AISS Squadron Guide of March 15 mentioned that ATIC was dissatisfied over not receiving UFO reports quickly, or even at all in a number of cases.[139]

What was Blue Book in 1955? It was an organization that (1) claimed to be the sole repository of military UFO reports, but was not; (2) was under orders to use any means necessary to identify UFOs as conventional objects, regardless of how strained the explanation became; (3) intentionally misled the public with meaningless and even fictitious statistics; and (4) had a barely breathing investigative capability. The conclusion is self-evident: Blue Book was the mask worn by the air force for public viewing. Its UFO reports and evaluations—intellectually dishonest in the extreme—can therefore have no scientific value whatsoever. The fact that the U.S. military and other official sources continue to use them tells us more about the organizations than it does about UFOs.

Much of the foregoing also applies to the 4602nd, which was determined to keep all UFO explanations conventional, no matter how strained. In late May 1955, at the Fifth AISS Commanders' Conference, on the subject of UFOs, it was stated that the "general public [was] not qualified to evaluate material propounded in science fiction." Such "absurd and fantastic theories" as spacemen were "given credence solely on the basis of ignorance." An investigator had to be careful in evaluating UFO reports, depending on what the witness believed about the sighting:

> Abnormal predisposition to attach belief to the more fanciful aspects of UFOBs, e.g. "Flying Saucers" would tend to negate the source's reliability as a factual observer.

Thus, never believe anyone who believed in the extraterrestrial hypothesis. The approach had limited effect on reducing the percentage of unidentifieds. By June 30, the 4602nd AISS reported that of its 194 preliminary UFO reports for 1955, it had made twenty-three field investigations and had twenty-five unsolved reports—an unknown rate of 13 percent. Going back to August 12, 1954, and removing cases of insufficient evidence, the percentage of unknowns was lower: twenty-three unknowns from 306 reports, or about 7.5 percent. In reality, however, none of these numbers mean very much; they reflect little more than the creativity, and at times audacity, of the explainers at ADC and ATIC.[140]

VOICES IN THE DARK AGES

The period of the mid- to late-1950s may with some justice be viewed as the Dark Ages of the UFO. Effectively marginalized from the mainstream, the little publicity it received was almost all negative. The Soviet Union once again debunked UFOs, declaring on April 30, 1955, that they did not exist.[141]

In 1955, Thomas Eickhoff (who had recently corresponded with Keyhoe and the air force) tried to force the U.S. government into suing UFO contactee George Adamski for an act of fraud involving the U.S. mail system. The pretext: Adamski claimed to be in contact with beings from Venus and was using the U.S. postal service to help sell his books. Eickhoff's efforts reached Allen Dulles, whose attorney advised that the government did have a case against Adamski. The problem was that Adamski would himself be able to "prevent anyone from testifying in court concerning this book because maximum security exists concerning the subject of UFOs." The phrase is worth repeating: *maximum security*. Dulles' lawyer said the government "would be left high and dry and would be open for countersuit." They dropped the case.[142]

Somewhat beleaguered, UFO researchers continued to plug away. In January 1955, the first edition of the British publication *Flying Saucer Review* appeared under the editorship of former RAF pilot and aviation journalist Derek Dempster. Editorship soon passed to the honorable Brinsley le Poer Trench (later the Earl of Clancarty), and in 1959 to Waveney Girvan.

Several well-known people made waves regarding UFOs. During the summer of 1954, the British Air Marshal Lord Dowding, the leader of the Battle of Britain, stated his belief in June that UFOs were interplanetary. During early 1955, the legendary American inventor William P. Lear (1902–1978) also made his opinions public. Although remembered primarily as inventor of the Lear Jet, Lear had also invented a car radio that was responsible for launching Motorola. RCA had purchased one of his radio amplifiers for use in their entire product line. During the Second World War, his corporations filled more than $100 million in defense orders. He was a 1949 recipient of the prestigious Collier Award given annually for the greatest achievement in aeronautics or astronautics in America. During the 1960s, Lear designed the eight-track player as well as navigational aids for aircraft. In 1981 he was posthumously inducted into the International Aeronautics Hall of Fame.

On February 2, 1955, Lear gave a press conference in Bogota, Columbia, stating his belief that "flying saucers come from outer space and are piloted by beings of superior intelligence." He gave four main reasons:

(1) Numerous manifestations over a long period of time. (2) Many observations come simultaneously, and from reliable observers. (3) There are great possibilities linked with the theory of gravitational fields. (4) There are now serious efforts in progress to prove the existence of antigravitational forces and to convert atomic energy directly to electricity.

Lear's prominence ensured wide press coverage. On February 10, back in Grand Rapids, Michigan, Lear told reporters that he had seen a flying saucer two months earlier, while flying near Palm Springs, California. He also disclosed that "an American aviation company" was conducting gravitational-field research.

Lear himself certainly got the antigravity bug. A *New York Herald-Tribune* article from November 1955 quoted him as believing it was possible to create "artificial electro-gravitational fields whose huge polarity can be controlled to cancel out gravity." According to the article, Lear for several months had been "going over new developments and theories relating to gravity with his chief scientists and engineers."[143]

Shortly after the *Herald-Tribune* article, the *Miami Herald* gave a rare glimpse of the state of 1950s gravity research in a three-part series. Work was under way at many of America's elite universities and laboratories: the Institute for Advanced Studies at Princeton, New Jersey; Princeton University; the University of Indiana's School of Advanced Mathematical Studies; the Purdue University Research Foundation; the Massachusetts Institute of Technology; and the University of North Carolina. The last had the approval of Dr. Gordon Gray, then-president of the university (and alleged member of MJ-12). Most of America's major aircraft firms were also either directly involved or "actively interested" in gravity. Among those mentioned in the article were Martin, Convair, Bell Aircraft, United Aircraft, Lear, Clarke Electronics, and Sperry-Rand Corp.

The article stressed that antigravity research was no rarefied theoretical endeavor. Many of the scientists believed its implications were farther reaching than atomic energy, perhaps providing mankind a nearly unlimited source of power. Space ships based upon electromagnetic principles that created their own gravitational field "would be a reality," able to accelerate to many thousands of miles per hour within seconds, and make sudden turns without subjecting their passengers to the g-forces caused by gravity's pull. Several theoretical studies had been made of round or saucer-shaped vehicles "for travel into outer space." Lest the connection was lost, a cartoon image of a flying saucer accompanied the article.

Most research, noted the article, had come from unnamed private funds and corporations. Although leaders of the military had been periodically briefed on the progress, their attitude was described as "call us when you get some hardware that works." No tangible breakthroughs were known to have taken place, and many of the scientists refused to predict when any might occur. However, the head of the advanced design division of Martin Aircraft, George Trimble, declared, "I know that if Washington decides it will be vital to our national survival . . . we'd find the answer rapidly."[144]

One of the pioneers in gravitational theory, and a man whose career also intersected with the UFO, was Thomas Townsend Brown. Born in 1905, he studied physics at Caltech and Denison University. In 1930, he joined the navy and conducted advanced research in electromagnetism, radiation, field physics, spectroscopy, gravitation, and more. After joining the reserves, he worked for Glenn L. Martin, then returned to active service in 1939. With the rank of lieutenant commander, he was assigned to the National Defense Research Committee (NDRC) and later its successor, the Office of Scientific Research, headed by Vannevar Bush. For several years, Brown also served under Adm. Arthur Radford. In 1944, following an illness and discharge from military service, he worked as a radar consultant for the advanced design section of Lockheed-Vega Aircraft Corporation in California.

Since the 1930s, Brown had also worked on his own to create a localized gravitational field and invented a machine called a "Gravitator." In 1952 and 1953, he devised a series of experiments involving disc-shaped objects tethered by a wire to an electrically charged pole. Essentially, Brown concentrated extreme electrostatic charges along the leading edge of a disc to create propulsion. His discs achieved speeds of eleven miles per hour and higher, but Brown believed that he could ultimately produce an aircraft capable of Mach 3, well beyond the fastest aircraft speeds of the day. Despite the success of his experiments in many respects, Brown did not create an independent gravitational field. One researcher maintained that it was more convenient to think of Brown's result as "electrostatic propulsion which has its own niche in aviation," something which deserved follow-up in its own right.[145] Indeed, while neither the Pentagon nor the world of science expressed interest in Brown's theories, one of his follow-up experiments was allegedly classified. (However, I have been unable to confirm this.)

In 1955, Brown went to England and France, hoping for better sponsorship. In France, under the auspices of the La Société National de Construction Aeronautique Sud Ouest (SNCASO), he flew his discs in a high vacuum with excellent results. Despite his French colleagues' initial excitement, the plans for supporting his work fell through. He returned to America.[146]

Not surprisingly, Brown was interested in the phenomenon of flying saucers and believed that an extraterrestrial intelligence was probably responsible for them. Before long, he would delve into that topic more systematically.

Meanwhile, around the time of the Lear publicity, Keyhoe received a letter from Hermann Oberth in response to an inquiry. Oberth was even more prominent than William Lear in the history of aviation and aeronautics. He is generally considered to be the most brilliant and visionary of the three pioneers of modern rocketry (along with American Robert Goddard and Russian Konstantin Tsiolkovsky). In 1922, Oberth's doctoral thesis on rocketry was rejected. A year later, he earned worldwide acclaim when he published it as *Die Rakete zu den Planetenraumen* (The Rocket into Planetary Space), followed by a longer version in 1929. Oberth argued that it was feasible for rockets to be "built so powerfully that they could be capable of carrying a man aloft," even above the Earth's atmosphere. This book provided much of the mathematical foundation for space travel. During the 1930s, Oberth took on the young Wernher von Braun as an assistant in his rocketry research, and during the war assisted von Braun on the V-2 rocket. During the early 1950s, Oberth designed anti-aircraft missiles for the Italian navy. Around 1953 or 1954, according to Frank Edwards, the West German government hired him to head a commission studying UFOs. As a result of this study, Oberth had made a statement, during the summer of 1954, that UFOs were "conceived and directed by intelligent beings of a very high order. They probably do not originate in our solar system, perhaps not even in our galaxy." Like William Lear, Townsend Brown, and Wilbert Smith, Oberth decided that UFOs were "propelled by distorting the gravitational field, converting gravity into useable energy."[147]

In a letter to Keyhoe, Oberth explained his electromagnetic propulsion theory which he believed was the true explanation for UFO propulsion. With the ability to create their own gravitational fields, UFOs would be able to do all the things witnesses had attributed to them: hover motionless above the earth, accelerate at tremendous speed, and make violent turns that would cause ordinary aircraft to disintegrate. Within the year, Keyhoe published these thoughts in his next book.[148]

Oberth's views did not hinder him from being hired in July 1955, under a Paperclip contract, to work for the army in Huntsville, Alabama, where he joined much of the old Peenemünde crew. It is hard to say just what Oberth did at Huntsville. According to the definitive study of the origins of space travel by Frederick I. Ordway III and Mitchell R. Sharpe (1979), Oberth worked on "a number of complex projects" dealing with "advanced space studies," mostly classified secret. He prepared several analyses of the stability of satellite orbits, and seems to have done some work on designing a prototype of a lunar module. Oberth's own book, *Man into Space*, written in 1957 during his Huntsville years, reads like a layout of the Apollo program and beyond, with discussions of satellite rockets, "the spaceman's equipment," designs for space stations, a "moon car," and other interesting topics. He remained in the U.S. until 1959. Writers and biographers of Oberth politely ignore his unfortunate interest in flying saucers. A 1962 biography gave passing mention of his beliefs on the subject. None of the dozens of biographies and *homages* to him on the World Wide Web today mention it, either.[149]

UFO-related news continued to seep out in 1955. *The Los Angeles Examiner* ran a piece by Dorothy Kilgallen on May 22, in which she reported from London that British scientists and airmen had examined the wreckage of a "mysterious flying ship." These investigators were convinced that UFOs were not optical illusions or Soviet inventions, but extraterrestrial. Kilgallen wrote that her source was "a British official of cabinet rank who prefers to remain unidentified." Still, the informant told her:

> We believe on the basis of our inquiries thus far, that the saucers were staffed by small men—probably under four feet tall. . . . It's frightening but there is no denying the flying saucers come from another planet.

Kilgallen's account was soon reprinted in several journals and books, including the New York *Journal American*, *Flying Saucer Review*, Morris Jessup's *UFO Casebook* of 1956, and other books through the years.[150]

Jerome Clark emphasized that Kilgallen's statement has never been substantiated. It depends on one's perspective of the problem. In May or June, one of Harold Wilkins' legion of informers wrote to him on UFOs and the British government. According to Wilkins' seemingly well-placed source:

> I can get no British naval or air officer to pass any comment on *ufos*. . . . One thing I can tell you: every time I mention the phenomenon, or speak of *ufos* to one particular naval officer-friend of mine, I come against a wall of silence. He turns the subject aside, and won't say a word. I am sure the subject of *ufos* is definitely taboo in naval and air circles.

Wilkins himself wrote of "a conspiracy of silence" at this time among the press and world governments.[151]

Frank Edwards, out of a job at Mutual Broadcasting, tried to keep busy. On June 13, 1955, he traveled with a TV film producer to the navy department and asked for some unclassified navy pictures of rockets. This appeared to be no problem until the navy learned that Edwards intended to show them on television during a panel discussion on UFOs. Suddenly, the Navy informed Edwards it would not cooperate on any publicity connected with flying saucers.[152]

Keyhoe remained the most visible and dangerous opponent of UFO secrecy. In the latter half of 1955, his third book on the subject, *The Flying Saucer Conspiracy*, appeared. Keyhoe maintained his knack for writing about all the things the military was trying to keep low-key. From over three hundred sources, he presented accurate descriptions of the UFO cover-up by analyzing such documents as JANAP 146 and AFR 200-2, the air force's attempts to discredit him, as well as many well-researched and vividly described UFO encounters. As in the past, critical reviews were mixed. Jonathon Leonard of the *New York Times* called it a "repetitious and unconvincing attack on the major's great enemy: the air force 'silence group.'" *Library Journal*, on the other hand, conceded that Keyhoe's conclusions were "less fantastic than those of other writers in this field, and it must be admitted that the book makes fascinating reading."[153]

His book directly resulted in the publication of the Battelle Report, also known as Blue Book Special Report #14. The air force had declassified it in May, then waited until a press conference on October 25, 1955, to release it to the general public. The report dismissed UFOs as a significant scientific or national security problem and claimed that all but a few UFOs were explainable. Air Force Secretary Donald Quarles added that (1) no one had reason to believe flying saucers have flown over the U.S.; (2) the three percent unknowns for 1954 would be identifiable if more data were available; and (3) the air force had recently tested a new circular vertical takeoff jet, built by the AV Roe company in Canada, known as the AVRO disc. Quarles said this would probably cause UFO sightings in the future (it did not, as it was soon scrapped). He also stated that the report found "no evidence of the existence of the popularly termed 'flying saucers.'" Quarles implied that the fictitious three percent unknown figure for 1954 applied for the 1947–1952 period—which it did not.

Like so many official reports before and since, the Battelle Report's conclusions did not match its data. The report's unexplained rate was 20 percent, which rose to 22 percent when removing cases lacking sufficient data. It also indicated that the better rated the witness, the better quality the sighting. Ruppelt's opinion of the report was succinct: "worthless." In his view, Blue Book had been founded not to solve the overall UFO problem, but to learn of new technological developments. "This is not a good study." The major media, however, such as the *New York Times*, accepted Quarles without reservation and lauded the report as the final word on UFOs.[154]

1955 SIGHTINGS: MORE HUMANOIDS

The lid may have been down, but UFOs continued to appear worldwide. Many of the reports are unofficial in that they are not Blue Book reports, some were not military related, and some—not investigated thoroughly—remain just stories. On January 1, 1955, a formation of five UFOs was seen over Lima, Peru, by many witnesses. The objects hovered over the city and gave off an intense silvery light. In San Sebastian, Spain, on January 5, a red circular object about ten feet wide was seen to land and take off again. On January 14, an unknown object hit the wing of a B-47 jet bomber in California; the plane landed safely. On February 2, a veteran airline pilot and copilot in Venezuela had a clear view of a UFO with lights and portholes. Their receiver went dead, and the object sped away. More green fireballs were observed over Texas on February 14.[155]

A humanoid sighting is said to have occurred during the spring of 1955 in Loveland, Ohio. A businessman saw three short beings by the side of the road at 4 A.M., believed he lost consciousness, and found himself driving to the police station without remembering what had taken place. This odd incident was investigated by researchers Ted Bloecher and Leonard Stringfield. On July 3, near Stockton, Georgia, a woman was driving when she saw four beings near the road that looked similar to later descriptions of Grays. She said they were small, with thin arms, pointed chins, no visible mouths, and "bug eyes." Two were turned away from her, while one was bent over with something like a stick in its hand; and the fourth one faced her with its right arm raised. In Bradford, England, on August 16, a man and his teenaged son claimed to see a four-foot-tall being in skin-tight black clothes. On its chest was a silver disc perforated with holes, and it seemed to walk by jumping. The witnesses were too amazed to follow it.[156]

The best-known humanoid sighting of the year occurred near Hopkinsville, Kentucky, by the Sutton family on the night of August 21–22. A man in his yard saw a "spaceship" in a nearby field and ran inside to tell the others. Within minutes, several creatures were roaming the area. They were about three feet high with a roundish head, elephantine ears, a slit-like mouth extending from ear to ear, no visible neck, long arms ending in clawed hands, and wore glowing silver clothing. Their eyes were huge and wide-set. When running, the beings dropped to all fours. When one of them approached the house, a man fired his shotgun through the screen door, scoring a direct hit. The creature was knocked over, but got back up and scuttled off. Another man walked out the door, and one of the creatures reached for his head. According to the family, this kind of activity continued for the greater part of the night, and included heavy gunfire at times. At one point, one of the entities was knocked down from the roof by a bullet and "floated down." Running out of ammunition, the Suttons mustered enough courage to scramble into their car and head for the police station. They brought back the deputy sheriff, who saw a fast-moving lighted object in the sky, but nothing else unusual.

Not surprisingly, the story received nationwide ridicule, and many assumed it was a hoax. Still, later researchers found the family credible, and many were inclined to believe the story. Even the chief of police agreed that "something scared those people—something beyond reason—nothing ordinary." Strange as it may seem, the Hopkinsville incident to this day has its defenders among UFO researchers.[157]

MILITARY UFO ENCOUNTERS AND THE U-2

On June 4, 1955, an RB-47 aircraft of the Air Force Special Security Service (the air arm of the NSA) tracked an unknown aircraft visually and by radar for nine minutes near Melville Sound, in the Canadian Northwest Territories. The crew chief described what he saw as "glistening silver metallic." The crew obtained gun camera film, but of poor quality. Three days later, another RB-47 en route to Eielson AFB, Alaska, registered electronic contact southeast of Bank's Island at thirty-five hundred yards. The plane's radar was jammed, apparently by the UFO. This was a matter of serious concern, since the purpose of the RB-47 was quick penetration of Soviet airspace to trigger radar alerts and thereby determine operating frequencies.[158]

On July 12, a memorandum from Todos M. Odarenko, the CIA/OSI Chief of the Physics and Electronics Division, cited a radar-visual UFO report from Pepperell AFB, Newfoundland. According to the memo, the pilot maintained visual contact with the UFO and noted "direction changes [which] correlated exactly with those painted on scope by controller." The object was "observed by radar, at least, for forty-nine minutes," a rather long time. Odarenko sent the memo to the CIA's acting assistant director for scientific intelligence. "It is reasonable to believe," he wrote, "that more information will become available on this when complete report . . . is issued."[159]

On August 6, 1955, the U-2 spy plane took its maiden flight, which occurred over the remote, and newly developed, region known as Area 51 in Nevada. In the debate over which organization was more powerful, the air force or the CIA, it is noteworthy here that the U-2 program was CIA all the way, despite the strong wishes of Air Force General and SAC Commander Curtis LeMay. Instead, the air force had to provide the muscle and equipment to serve on the agency's latest and greatest black project.[160]

On August 23, 1955, a military UFO encounter took place over Cincinnati, Ohio. Personnel at the GOC tower in Hamilton County noticed three white spheres between Columbus and Cincinnati. Tracking the objects on radar, they notified Strategic Air Command at Lockbourne AFB, which scrambled jets to investigate. The UFO soon approached the tower and hovered in pendulum-like motions directly above it. The interceptors then swooped in and gave chase, but the craft disappeared at "incredible speed." Meanwhile, UFO reports were coming in from throughout the region to Leonard Stringfield's filter center in Cincinnati. The Greater Cincinnati Airport also tracked unidentified blips on radar. To his surprise, Stringfield obtained clearance to write about the sightings in his newsletter. A mistake or a big change in policy, he thought. But when he tried to get the story to the press, "the Cincinnati newspapers weren't interested." A spokesman at Wright-Patterson not only denied the incident to a newspaper, but claimed to know nothing of Stringfield's relationship with Air Defense Command. Stringfield was bewildered.[161]

Stringfield remained in touch with the air force during the late summer and into the autumn. One air force officer on active duty broke the law and told Stringfield privately, "What bothers me is what's happening to our aircraft." He then described a crash of a U.S. jet while it chased a UFO in Iceland. "We couldn't explain the crash." Officially, the men died during a routine training mission. The officer gave Stringfield the impression that this kind of event was not unusual.[162]

Other interesting UFO sightings occurred sporadically during the summer of 1955. One was a multiple-witness sighting of a long silvery object emerging from the water in Santa Maria, California. Another involved a brilliant round object with a long trail approaching National Airport in Washington, D.C. The object stopped, oscillated, and moved off at high speed. The airport ceiling lights went out when it approached, and turned on when it left. Other close-range sightings were reported in America and England.[163]

SENATOR RICHARD RUSSELL SEES A UFO

One of the key UFO sightings of the year involved U.S. Senator Richard Russell (D-Georgia), head of the Senate Armed Services Committee, during a trip to the Soviet Union on October 4, 1955. Russell was on a Soviet train from Kiev and passing through the Transcaucasus region. He was accompanied by Armed Services Committee consultant Ruben Efron and Lt. Col. E. U. Hathaway. Shortly after 7 P.M., Russell looked out his window to see a disc-shaped object slowly ascending vertically. Its outer surface revolved slowly to the right, and a spark or flame emanated from the bottom. It reached an altitude of about six thousand feet, then headed north at a very fast speed. Russell rushed over to tell his two companions. Hathaway looked quickly enough to see the UFO; Efron missed it. To everyone's astonishment, a second disc then appeared about two minutes later and performed exactly the same maneuver as the first. This time all three men saw it. A distraught Soviet trainman then closed the curtains of the car, and directed the three not to look outside.

The report went past Blue Book to much higher levels, and someone leaked it to the *Los Angeles Examiner* in late 1955 or early 1956. Aviation reporter Tom Towers tried to get the details from Russell, but received no response. After Towers tried again, Russell replied on January 17, 1956:

> I have discussed this matter with the affected agencies of the government, and they are of the opinion that it is not wise to publicize this matter at this time.

The matter was classified Top Secret until 1959 and remained Secret until 1985 when Stanton Friedman was able to get it declassified following a FOIA request. Interview notes about the sighting stated:

> [T]here were two lights toward the inside of the disc, which remained stationary as the outer surface went around. . . . The lights sat near the top of the disc. If a line representing the diameter of the disc were divided into three segments, the lights would have been located at the two points of division between the middle segment and the two outside segments. . . . The aircraft was circular. The aircraft was round, resembled a flying saucer.

There can be no doubt that Sen. Richard Russell saw something extraordinary. Let us assume that, just as he described, he *did* see a flying saucer. Could it have been what it appeared to be, a Soviet flying saucer? If so, it would mean that human beings have had flying saucer technology for a long time. It would be a secret as amazing as that of aliens themselves. But of course, the leap to such a revolutionary method of aerodynamics and propulsion seems impossible. Contrast the image of a WWII-styled propeller-driven aircraft with a multi-Mach, silent, exceptionally maneuverable disc-shaped craft. The issue had been raised back in 1947 and 1948 at Wright-Patterson AFB: could the Soviets, Germans, Americans, or anyone else, have created the kind of breakthrough in aerodynamics that UFOs appeared to represent? The answer at that time was *no*. If, therefore, the Soviets (and presumably the Americans) did achieve such a breakthrough, all has been silent in the public domain, as well as on the field of battle.

Russell did see a craft. If it was not of human design, then the only alternative is that it was of alien design, and that both the Soviet and American governments knew this.

This much is certain: the Soviet government was deeply secretive about UFOs in its territory, and the American government—at the height of the cold war—cooperated in this secrecy.[164]

Although the Russell sighting remained well submerged within the media, a *New York Times* article from October 8, 1955, printed a cryptic remark from General Douglas MacArthur that world nations would have to unite against enemies from outer space. He refused any further explanation. Two days later, the air force released a statement from Fort Worth, Texas, to explain that any flashing lights seen for the next two months across the U.S. would be wind-driven experimental plastic balloons that might travel as fast as 110 mph.[165]

Presumably, it was not an experimental balloon or U-2 spy plane that hit a B-47 near Lovington, New Mexico, in October. According to the sole survivor, something solid definitely hit the plane. No other planes were in the area. One witness claimed a "ball of fire" appeared near the plane just before the crash. Several weeks later, another such incident occurred in Texas.[166]

On November 20, two shiny, elliptical UFOs, "like two dirigibles," traveled over the restricted area at Oak Ridge. On December 11, navy jets engaged in a dogfight with a round, reddish UFO near Jacksonville, Florida. The object had been reported by the crews of two airliners, as well as by people on the ground. Two navy jets were in the area on a night practice mission and were directed to the area by the Jacksonville Naval Air Station. The jets located the object and attempted to close in on it. At that moment, the object shot up to thirty thousand feet, then dived back, circling and buzzing the jets. All the while, Naval Air Station officers and tower controllers watched on radar. In this case, as with so many others, it is reasonable to ask: if this UFO was an experimental, classified American project, what might account for this type of behavior—to say nothing of the performance of the object itself?[167]

GOVERNMENT OUT OF CONTROL

By the mid-1950s, more signs emerged that the executive office, even headed by a war hero, was losing control of its military. Throughout the year, President Eisenhower and Air Force Chief of Staff Nathan Twining tried to get some kind of information from Curtis LeMay at SAC as to what his actual strategic bombing plan was. In October 1955, LeMay finally briefed the Joint Chiefs of Staff. The shocked attending members learned that LeMay's plan called for the instantaneous destruction of 645 military targets, 118 cities, and 60 million people in the Soviet Union. LeMay had not drawn up his plan as defensive, in accordance with the official U.S. policy of massive retaliation. A firm believer in first strike, LeMay said, "I'm going to knock the shit out of them before they get off the ground."[168]

For other branches of the national security state, it was business as usual. In August 1956, the FBI began running Cointelpro (counter-intelligence program). These various programs were deployed against American dissidents and their organizations; the first one targeted the American Communist Party. Typical Cointelpro methods were anonymous or fictitious letters, false defamatory or threatening information, forged signatures, and other methods of disinformation to disrupt an organization. The FBI blackmailed insiders to spread false rumors or promote factionalism. It created bogus organizations to attack or disrupt a bona fide group, and instigated hostile actions through third parties such as employers, elected officials, and the media. It enabled the FBI to investigate any political organization on the pretext of checking for Communists, including the NAACP, women's rights groups, and gay rights groups. Cointelpro and related programs prompted nearly 330,000 FBI investigations and created a Security Index of over 200,000 dangerous Americans to be detained in the event of war.

The FBI programs were also noteworthy in that documents relating to them were marked "Do Not File." This meant they were withheld from the FBI filing system, offering no clues that they even existed. (The cover was blown after activists broke into an FBI office in Media, Pennsylvania, in 1971.) The relevance for UFO-related information is obvious, but to spell it out: regarding matters connected with "national security," there appears to be a wealth of information that does not exist officially. Thus, a request to find such documents through a Freedom of Information Act request would be in vain. Add to this the likelihood that perhaps the most sensitive information regarding UFOs may not even exist in document form ("the first rule in keeping secrets is nothing on paper," Richard Helms), and one can appreciate the difficulty that an honest UFO researcher has in ferreting out the truth.[169]

SILENCING POLICIES OF 1956

Throughout 1956, UFOs all but disappeared from the news. The air force kept matters low-key, answering queries with a fact sheet referring people to Special Report 14. Unknowns for the year were officially listed at 0.4 percent. According to the air force, the much higher percentages of prior years were simply "from inadequate data and poor reporting." Ironically, from this point onward, no one within ATIC seriously questioned the air force's investigative or analytical methods. This included J. Allen Hynek. It must be remembered that the air force still denied the existence of Twining's 1947 letter, the 1948 Estimate of the Situation, Dewey Fournet's 1952 study of UFO maneuverability, and the existence of the Robertson Panel.[170]

One sharp note of discord against the harmony of Blue Book's efforts to debunk UFOs came from Capt. Edward Ruppelt. In January 1956, his *Report on Unidentified Flying Objects* was published. It possessed an alarming candor for its day and contradicted much of the current air force position. The Estimate of the Situation *did* exist, wrote Ruppelt, because he had personally seen it. He also confirmed the existence of Fournet's study and provided the basic contours of the Robertson Panel. What truly characterized the book was its clarity and detail, a potent combination. Ruppelt, Chop, and Fournet also assisted in the production of Clarence Greene's semidocumentary motion picture, *UFOs*, released in May 1956. The group was able to obtain copies of the Montana and Utah films. The air force carefully monitored the film's reception and readied itself to counter the film's impact. It seemed that Ruppelt could become a formidable obstacle against the official position on UFOs. In the end, he did not. By 1959, he printed a second edition of his book that essentially debunked his first, and was dead a year later.

Meanwhile, Jonathan Leonard of the *New York Times* sought to discredit

Ruppelt's book. In the same article that reviewed Keyhoe's *Flying Saucer Conspiracy*, Leonard described Ruppelt's work as "cultist," and "the longest and dullest of the current crop of saucer books." This was not merely grossly unfair, it was exactly the opposite of the truth.[171]

Recent books notwithstanding, UFO secrecy generally prevailed. Ruppelt himself had said nothing about the CIA's ongoing interest in UFOs. On January 9, 1956, the CIA's Applied Science Division (ASD), within OSI, took on the job of holding UFO reports. One month later, a CIA memo titled "Responsibility for Unidentified Flying Objects" indicated that ASD would retain UFO reports that might provide information on foreign weapons research and development. All other reports were to go to the fundamental sciences area for review of information on foreign science developments. Researchers Fawcett and Greenwood remarked that "this group could have been a clearinghouse for genuinely mysterious reports of UFOs which contained much detail but could not be linked to a foreign government." The memo went on to state that ASD was trying hard to avoid collecting trivial UFO reports and recommended destroying unimportant reports.[172]

UFO secrecy was the norm everywhere. On February 18, Leonard Stringfield received a letter from the British Lord Dowding that stated, "I am sorry that I cannot tell you anything about the British official attitude to UFOs. I don't think there is one." On March 16, 1956, Stringfield received a letter from Gen. John Samford, still director of air force intelligence, ending Stringfield's affiliation with Air Defense Command. In April, Capt. George T. Gregory, a hard-line UFO debunker, succeeded Charles Hardin as director of Project Blue Book. A typical statement of the period came from Air Force General Joe Kelly in a letter to Sen. Harry Byrd on May 1, 1956: "There is a total lack of evidence that they [UFOs] are interplanetary vehicles."[173]

UFOs During a Period of Silence

Just what was the UFO evidence for 1956? The year offered about the same quality of reports as in previous years, but less quantity. One noteworthy case was the "washtub" incident off Pusan, Korea, on January 15. Townspeople saw an object about fifty yards offshore "about the size of a large washtub and emitting a blue-gray glow." The sighting lasted for about ninety minutes, the object glowing all the time, until it "apparently sank into the sea." Meanwhile, the Korean military police arrived and alerted U.S. military police. An American M.P. saw the object floating in the water for almost an hour. He described the glow as similar to flames from burning alcohol or benzene.[174]

Very few UFOs were reported during the early months of 1956. The spring brought more of interest. First came the Ryan Case of April 8. American Airlines Captain Raymond E. Ryan was en route from New York to Buffalo by way of Albany, Syracuse, and Rochester. At 10:20 P.M., near Schenectady, Ryan and his First Officer William Neff saw a peculiar and very bright glow to his right, far too bright, they agreed, to be another plane. Ryan decided to veer away somewhat from the light, just to be safe. Instantly the object performed a ninety-degree turn and shot ahead of them. Ryan estimated the speed at 900 mph. The object then paced the airliner, remaining slightly ahead. Ryan radioed Griffis AFB near Rome, New York. The base confirmed that they tracked the object, too, and scrambled two jets. By now, the plane's passengers saw the strange light and were uneasy.

What followed was most unusual: Griffis ordered the pilots to change course and follow the UFO. Civil aeronautic regulations did not allow for military control of an airliner, but Ryan obeyed nonetheless. He turned his plane away from Syracuse toward the object, which was heading northwest. Flying in the black of night miles off course, Ryan waited for the jets. As the object led him to the edge of Lake Ontario, it began to accelerate. Ryan wisely decided to turn back toward Syracuse. As he approached the city, the CAA operators told him they had no word on the jets, but that Albany and Watertown CAA operators had also sighted the UFO. Normally, Ryan and his crew would not have been permitted to reveal their UFO chase, but since he filed no CIRVIS report, no restrictions applied. Thus, when the plane landed in Buffalo, Ryan and Neff spoke with a *Buffalo Evening News* reporter who had been tipped off. The story ran on April 10, stating that the military had directed the American Airlines flight to follow a UFO.

Although no one else picked up the story, Keyhoe was onto it quickly. He tried to get an air force comment. No luck. Ryan failed to return Keyhoe's messages, and the CAA was silent. The incident faded away for a year, until Keyhoe obtained a copy of the CAA report with a statement from Ryan in which he admitted to seeing an object but "did not deviate" from his course "at any time." Keyhoe's conclusion: Ryan had been forced to lie. After more CAA stonewalling, he contacted the *Buffalo Evening News*, which backed the original story "one hundred percent." Keyhoe threatened to take the matter to the Senate: perhaps elected representatives would question why the CAA allowed airliners to chase UFOs. After more digging, Keyhoe received a flight log from the air force, but this also stated Ryan did not deviate from his prescribed course. In Keyhoe's thinking, "if the Ryan interview was true, there was only one answer. The Convair's flight log had been deliberately falsified."

But was it? The answer would have remained unknown had Keyhoe not then received a taped recording of an interview with Ryan and Neff from April 16, 1956, a week after the encounter, on the show *Meet the Millers*. On the tape, Ryan and Neff were crystal clear about the events. Griffis AFB, they said:

asked us our next point of landing and to identify the aircraft. I told them Syracuse and identified the flight number. Then they told us: "Abandon that next landing temporarily. Maintain your course and altitude. We're sending two jets to intercept the object."

Of the UFO, Ryan said, "This was absolutely real. I'm convinced there was something fantastic up there." The ensuing detail given by the two pilots left no doubt. Keyhoe believed that "if the Ryan story were played up, the air force could be accused of deliberately exposing the Convair passengers and crew" to danger. Keyhoe later tried to use the incident as a wedge to open congressional investigations on UFOs, but ultimately the case fizzled out.[175]

Reports continued to trickle out showing ongoing navy interest in the matter of UFOs. A June 26, 1956, article from the *News Tribune* from Fullerton, California, reported that the navy ordered its pilots to engage UFOs in combat if the objects appeared hostile. The navy refused to discuss the matter with journalists, however.[176]

UFO sightings picked up slightly during the summer. On July 19, in Hutchinson, Kansas, a naval air station tracked "a moving unidentified object" on radar. The state police observed it visually as a teardrop-shaped light source. The object moved horizontally and vertically over much of the sky. A humanoid sighting was reported from Panorama City, California, on July 20, by three independent witnesses who claimed to see ordinary-looking humans with long blond hair and tight green suits. The beings were near a large ball-shaped object. Two days later, Air Force Major Mervin Stenvers was flying at sixteen thousand feet over Pixley, California. Before he was silenced by the military, he told reporters that his C-131-D was suddenly staggered and knocked to the right by a terrific blow of some sort. He radioed that his plane had been "struck by a flying saucer," and made an emergency landing at the Bakersfield Airport.[177]

On August 13, 1956, one of the best-documented encounters between the military and UFOs took place at the NATO bases of Bentwaters and Lakenheath in England. At 9:30 P.M., radar personnel at Bentwaters picked up an object moving toward them at the astonishing speed of between 4,000 and 9,000 mph. It moved in a straight line to a position about fifteen miles northwest of Bentwaters. Within a few minutes, about a dozen normal targets were spotted eight miles southwest of Bentwaters, moving northeast at about 100 mph. In front of the targets were three objects in a triangular formation, about one thousand feet apart. Something odd then occurred: all the targets appeared to converge into one extremely large target, which then remained stationary for almost fifteen minutes. It resumed moving to the northeast, then stopped for a few minutes, then resumed, and was lost to radar. The entire sighting up to this point took twenty-five minutes.

Five minutes later, another solid target appeared, flying at 4,000 mph, or more, and vanished when it moved out of range. At 10:55 P.M., another target was picked up thirty miles to the east, traveling west at 2,000 to 4,000 mph. It passed directly overhead and was seen visually by both air and ground observers. Bentwaters notified Lakenheath AFB of what was going on, and Lakenheath personnel saw a luminous object stop, then zoom off to the east. Apparently, two white lights were seen joining from different directions, which were tracked on two radar screens at Lakenheath.

At midnight, Lakenheath notified the RAF station at Neatishead, Norfolk, that a strange object was buzzing the base. A Venom night fighter, with four highly technically trained personnel, was scrambled. All four soon found the object on radar and saw it as a bright white light, which then disappeared. The crew found the target north of Cambridge; the navigator said it was the "clearest target I have ever seen on radar." The object, however, was behind the plane, and stayed there for some time, despite climbs, dives, and circling. Ground radar operators said the object was glued right behind the Venom fighter. After ten minutes, the fighter headed back. The UFO followed briefly, then stopped and hovered. Another Venom was scrambled but experienced equipment malfunctions and aborted its mission. The object was tracked on two radars leaving the area at 600 mph.

The encounter was classified until 1969, when it was analyzed in the University of Colorado UFO Project, also known as the Condon Committee. It was listed as unknown and indeed as one of the most compelling of all cases. Physicist Gordon David Thayer, who studied the incident for the project, called it "the most puzzling and unusual" of radar/visual cases. He suggested that "the apparently rational, intelligent behavior of the UFO suggests a mechanical device of unknown origin as the most probable explanation of this sighting."[178]

SUMMARY

The year 1953 had started with the Robertson Panel and a defeated faction that opposed secrecy about UFOs. The memory of unidentified objects over the Capitol was still fresh. Three years later not a single group within the U.S. military or intelligence apparatus dared to challenge a policy that became progressively more restrictive over divulging UFO information. Fresh outbursts of dissent did come from outside. Keyhoe continued to be a nuisance, Edward Ruppelt took his stand, and other big names occasionally supported the idea of UFOs as extraterrestrial. Yet, there can be no mistaking this period as repressive regarding UFOs.

The policy of repression was partly responsible for the relatively low number of well-documented sightings during 1955 and 1956. In several cases, civilian and military pilots were muzzled after initially talking, and in the case of Capt. Raymond Ryan, CAA logs may have been falsified. It may well be, however, that actual UFO activity did decline during those years, and it is unlikely that UFO awareness would have emerged on the strength of things seen during those two years. In the context, however, of the years of sightings that had preceded them, some of these remained quite compelling.

Through it all, the national security apparatus retained the initiative on managing UFO information. Project Blue Book became inconsequential, while Air Defense Command received many of the key UFO reports. The CIA also retained an interest in UFO reports, both domestically and worldwide, and certainly not because of the U-2 program. Citizen groups, meanwhile, were a peripheral and ineffective lot. But in late 1956, a civilian group that was led by a core of Annapolis boys made a play to challenge the air force on UFOs. What the leaders of this new group, the National Investigations Committee on Aerial Phenomena (NICAP), did not realize, however, was that the CIA was already on board.

Chapter 6

The Fight to End Secrecy: 1956 to 1962

I'm positive they don't [exist]. . . . There's not even a glimmer of hope for the UFO.

—Edward Ruppelt, from his revised book, 1960

The air force cannot do any more under the circumstances. It has been a difficult assignment for them, and I believe we should not continue to criticize their investigations. I am resigning as a member of the NICAP board of governors.

—Roscoe Hillenkoetter, in a letter to
Donald Keyhoe, February 1962

THE BIRTH OF NICAP

The air force's monopoly on UFO information could not last forever. Although other civilian UFO groups had emerged in the 1950s, none challenged the authority of the air force to have the final word. NICAP did. Founded on August 29, 1956, by Townsend Brown in Washington, D.C., it soon developed into an organization dedicated to ending UFO secrecy.

Brown's leadership was brief. As mentioned previously, he had been conducting experiments in electromagnetism and gravity. In 1956, he joined an informal flying saucer discussion group and immediately envisioned a larger organization to collect, analyze, and disperse information about UFO reports, and also to promote his own research. He soon appointed an acting treasurer, acquired a secretary, and obtained office space. When NICAP's corporate charter was approved on October 24, 1956, Brown appeared ready for business. However, NICAP quickly ran into financial trouble. At a meeting in January 1957, Brown and NICAP member Donald Keyhoe argued openly about Brown's leadership, and Brown resigned from the organization. Keyhoe became the new director.

From the outset, NICAP was packed with navy men. Brown and Keyhoe both had strong navy connections and both recruited board members. As a result, NICAP started its existence with three admirals on its board of governors: Rear Adm. Delmar Fahrney, known in the navy as the "father of the guided missile;" Vice Adm. Roscoe Hillenkoetter, better known for having been the first director of the CIA; and WWII submarine commander Rear Adm. H. B. Knowles. Other early governing members were Dr. Earl Douglass, Maj. Dewey Fournet, J. B. Hartranft, Col. Robert B. Emerson, Frank Edwards, Prof. Charles A. Maney, Rev. Albert Baller, Dr. Marcus Bach, and Rev. Leon C. Le Van. Soon after, NICAP added such people as Leonard Stringfield, who served as public relations director until 1972, and Delbert Newhouse, of Utah film fame. This board of governors remained remarkably stable for most of the organization's existence.

Keyhoe, however, was the driving force. Unlike Brown, he was no scientist; his interests were far more political. Under Keyhoe, NICAP continued to define itself as a collection center of UFO reports, just as Brown had wanted. But the scientific impetus that Brown had given NICAP was now replaced by the force of Keyhoe's personality, and the organization took on a new mission: to end UFO secrecy once and for all.

An interesting twist to the history of NICAP was that it was not merely the home of many former navy men. Unknown to other members, a number of "ex-CIA" people were also involved in the formation of NICAP. Count Nicolas de Rochefort, a Russian immigrant and scriptwriter for the Voice of America, was NICAP's first vice-chairman. He was also a member of the CIA's psychological warfare staff. Bernard J. Carvalho, connected to the Fairway Corporation, one of the CIA's dummy companies, was another early member; he later chaired NICAP's membership committee.

Links to the agency continued over the years. Rochefort's boss at CIA was Col. Joseph Bryan, who joined the NICAP Board in 1960. A bit later, former CIA briefing officer Karl Pflock joined, chairing NICAP's Washington, D.C., subcommittee in the 1960s. Over the years, Pflock denied that the CIA ever asked him for information on either UFOs or NICAP. During NICAP's decline in the late 1960s and early 1970s, more individuals associated with the CIA became involved in the organization. Several of these were central in replacing Keyhoe as director, just as he began to focus on the CIA instead of the air force as the source of the UFO cover-up.

Could it be, as Pflock maintained, that the CIA had no real interest in NICAP, that the participation of these people with longtime agency connections was just a coincidence, based solely on their personal interests? Piercing endless walls of denial can be fruitless, with the heap of evidence never leading to proof. Yet the guidelines of the Robertson Panel, still secret in 1956, emphasized the need to monitor civilian UFO organizations. Could the most formidable of these really escape CIA notice? As early as 1957, CIA agents coerced NICAP advisor Ralph Mayher to give them a movie film depicting a UFO, which they later returned with the best frames cut out. NICAP clearly elicited interest from the CIA.[1]

CIA infiltration aside, it is not surprising navy men predominated within NICAP, although other military personnel also provided input. In retrospect, this seems logical. By the late 1950s, the navy was the only military branch without a UFO secrecy directive, insofar as Keyhoe could determine. Proud navy personnel resented the heavy-handed manner typical of air force investigators. When the board of governors met to decide NICAP's fate after Townsend Brown's resignation, much discussion centered on how to confront the air force. Army Colonel and physicist Robert Emerson wanted to avoid a fight. Fahrney agreed, but added, "I'm sure many of them don't like the [secrecy] policy." This is not to say that NICAP had no support from air force officers; quite a few who dissented from air force policy provided what help they could. But the navy had developed a history of dissenting from the air force's management of the UFO problem. Very likely, this was part of the navy's larger struggle for self-assertion during the still-newly unified military of the 1950s. (The famous "Revolt of the Admirals" of the late 1940s was a fresh memory—when the navy outspokenly pressed for a supercarrier with nuclear capability, challenging the air force's claim to have sole possession of The Bomb.)

NICAP's inception came at a time of unquestioned air force dominance over the issue of UFOs. An air force fact sheet of the time claimed a mere 3 percent unexplained ratio, and Blue Book briefings were public relations exercises. Other services participated in clamping down on UFO information. On January 31, 1957, U.S. Army Order number 30-13, "Sightings of Unconventional Aircraft," stipulated that personnel involved in sightings would "not discuss or disseminate such information to persons or agencies other than their superior officer(s) and other personnel authorized by the Acting Chief of Staff, G-2, this headquarters." The situation appeared to be fairly well in hand, and the presence of NICAP threatened to disrupt it.[2]

It happened on January 16, when Admiral Fahrney (who had become chairman of the organization after Brown's resignation) gave a press conference to announce the group's formation. "Reliable reports," he said, "indicate there are objects coming into our atmosphere at very high speeds and controlled by thinking intelligences." Many citizens, he continued, had stopped reporting UFOs to the air force because of frustration over the policy. Press coverage was good, and NICAP quickly developed a network comprised of hundreds of people throughout the U.S.[3]

Privately, military personnel may have been interested in working in some capacity with NICAP. In late March 1957, Stringfield told Keyhoe that he was working secretly with the Columbus, Ohio, Air Filter Center at the request (and expense) of the air force. Stringfield said the officers were "dead serious" about getting UFO reports and wanted sightings "relayed immediately—even if it's 3 A.M." Stringfield believed the air force would "give a lot to get NICAP's reports," if Keyhoe would do it privately. Keyhoe rejected the idea, but NICAP did offer the air force its cooperation in investigating and solving the UFO riddle. The problem was that NICAP's eight-point plan was a genuine attempt to get to the bottom of the UFO question, something the Air Force clearly was not interested in doing—at least not in conjunction with NICAP.[4]

Publicly, the Pentagon quickly moved to discredit NICAP. In early April, the air force launched a press attack against NICAP and UFOs. Brig. Gen. Arno Leuhman, director of air force information, told the press that flying saucers were a dead issue:

Our Intelligence checks out everything. The funny reflections you see at night, the lights from the rear end of jets, the meteorological balloons, everything including the hoaxes. There's no valid evidence that there are flying saucers.

An unnamed air force spokesman at that time also ridiculed NICAP as an "upstart organization" and insisted that the air force had explained all but 3 percent of sightings. The same month, however—on April 8, 1957—Maj. Gen. Joe Kelly, air force director of legislative liaison, answered a question from Representative (later Senator) Lee Metcalf of Montana. Kelly denied that the air force muzzled pilots or concealed UFO reports. "Answers are provided on any unidentified flying objects," wrote Kelly, "which have attracted national attention." Surprisingly, Kelly admitted that air force interceptors still pursued unidentified flying objects "as a matter of security to this country and to determine the technical aspects involved." He quickly added that flying objects had so far "imposed no threat" to U.S. security.[5]

Not surprisingly, many of NICAP's early reports came from the navy, some directly through Fahrney. One example (of which an identical report was given independently in 1958 to NICAP advisor Lou Corbin), concerns an incident that took place in 1953. According to the report, a squadron of carrier-based Navy AD-3s had been practicing offshore combat maneuvers. As Keyhoe described it, when the planes reformed:

an enormous rocket-shaped machine swooped down over them. Swiftly decelerating to their speed, it leveled off a thousand feet above the squadron . . . the pilots spread out . . . and climbed at full throttle toward the giant spaceship. The huge craft turned sharply . . . and with a tremedous burst of power it shot into the sky, vanishing in seconds.

Three air force intelligence officers were flown to the carrier, and an air force colonel grilled the navy men. Without consulting the carrier captain, he warned them "to forget what you saw today! You're not to discuss it with anyone—not even among yourselves!" However, since no navy order backed up the air force colonel, the report leaked to Fahrney.[6]

In May, NICAP nearly printed a phony UFO crash story that was said to take place in the Everglades, based on an account it received by AP wire. The crash story struck Keyhoe as too sensational to be credible, and he checked directly with AP, which acknowledged that, while the wires looked genuine, the story was "definitely fake." The company traced the story to an AP employee who had been "a former Signal Corps engineer" familiar with teletype systems. The employee admitted to faking the stories, refused to give any motive, and stubbornly denied involvement of anyone else. This was pretty strong stuff when Keyhoe published the account in 1960. But neither Keyhoe nor anyone else knew at that time that Shamrock—an operation run by the NSA, formerly by the Signal Corps—was intercepting electronic transmissions on a daily basis throughout the U.S. and abroad. Evidently, Shamrock was also spreading disinformation relating to UFOs.[7]

The preceding incident becomes more interesting when we note that in November 1956, Air Force Director of Intelligence John Samford succeeded Julian Canine as DIRNSA. Like Cabell, Samford was a general who assumed an even more prominent role in the world of intelligence after spending time on the UFO problem. While Cabell was the number two man at the CIA, Samford now became the number one man at the NSA, America's most secretive intelligence agency. Samford was only one of three people who knew all the details of Shamrock. Is it simply a coincidence that NICAP was nearly discredited by a phony AP story, planted by a "former" Signal Corps member, just months after Samford took charge of the NSA? Hard proof of the NSA's involvement will surely never surface, but considering NSA activities and capabilities from 1957, a little AP disinformation would have been child's play.[8]

CREATING ZOMBIE ROOMS

UFOs, of course, were by no means the only secret of the U.S. government. By 1957, the CIA's MK-Ultra program had moved six drugs into active use. In February, Sid Gottlieb organized field trials of psilocybin (the active ingredient of hallucinogenic—"magic"—mushrooms) for injection into nine black inmates at the Addiction Center in Lexington, Kentucky. At the end of February, Dulles approved Ewen Cameron's application for mind-control experiments to be administered at McGill University in Montreal, funded through the Society for the Investigation of Human Ecology, a CIA cutout organization. Cameron, the most prestigious psychiatrist in North America at the time, coined the terms "depatterning" and "psychic driving" to describe what he did to people. He was also a leading proponent of "psychic surgery," that is, lobotomies. Cameron immediately began serious work on sensory deprivation and created a "sleep room." This was a dimly lit dormitory of about twenty beds where patients were drugged, given electroshock, and lobotomized. The nurses aptly called it "The Zombie Room." The importance of keeping this grisly work off American soil was self-evident, hence its location in Canada. The Canadian government, as far as anyone can determine, was unaware of these activities. At the same time, U.S. Army Intelligence, in conjunction with the Army Chemical Corps and the CIA, began using drugs such as LSD and PCP on *their* subjects (something Cameron was doing as well) at the Medical Research Laboratories at Edgewood Arsenal. The focus of their testing was on unwitting test reactions.[9]

At around this time, the Soviets made a noteworthy medical breakthrough, in this case better assassination techniques. The new method involved a small metal canister that contained a firing device which would spray poisons in the form of the vapor. Once inhaled, the vapor quickly caused death by contracting the blood vessels, as in a cardiac arrest. After death, the blood vessels quickly relaxed so that an unsuspecting pathologist would conclude the victim had died of an ordinary heart attack.[10]

WORLDWIDE MILITARY AIRCRAFT ENCOUNTERS

During late 1956, UFOs were tracked on military radar stations around the world. In August and September, Danish radar tracked several moving at 1,800 mph. On October 26, two American jet fighters collided above the sea near Okinawa as they tried to identify several unknown objects detected by radar. Japanese fishermen rescued one pilot; the other one died.[11]

An air force cat-and-mouse game with a UFO took place sometime in late 1956 at Castle AFB in California. Control tower personnel spotted a luminous elliptical object, and two interceptors closed in. The object eluded them by using cloud cover, but the pilots saw it at various angles and as close as a few hundred yards. It appeared to be a flattened circular shape. Ground radar tracked the object, and the pilots obtained weak returns before the object accelerated away. Several officers arrived from another base to debrief the pilots and appeared very knowledgeable of UFOs. They sought "confirmation, not information," and told the pilots not to discuss the sighting at all, not even with each other. Citizens who had seen the episode were told that the pilots had been chasing ducks or geese. UFO researcher Richard Hall, who reported this incident, added that he personally knew of many instances in which military witnesses were debriefed by officers who displayed detailed knowledge of UFOs.[12]

On November 21, at the port of Kobe, Japan, a customs official and a maritime safety station officer heard an explosion as they walked along the pier. They saw something resembling fireworks on the bay and two balls of fire, whirling and then submerging.[13] In "the Far East" in December, two USAF jet pilots obtained strong radar returns from an object twenty miles away, "at least as large as a B-29 four engine bomber." Flying at 750 mph, one of the pilots got to within eight miles of the signal and saw it as a round object, about three hundred feet in diameter, exactly where radar showed it to be. Suddenly, strong interference jammed his radar. Using anti-jam procedures, he reestablished a lock-on and continued to close. The UFO then accelerated so quickly that his radar could not read it accurately, though he estimated its speed at 2,000 mph. This report, dated February 1957, went all the way up the chain of the U.S. Far East Air Force Command, and was leaked to NICAP by "a member of air force intelligence." While it was not officially classified, it remained unknown to the public for about a year. When the United Press ran the story on October 1, 1957, the air force press desk issued "no comment."[14]

Air force jets were also scrambled at least once during a multi-day UFO sighting near Pierre, South Dakota, from November 24 to 25, and possibly longer. At one point during this series of sightings, state police chased the object. On December 13, 1956, a Swedish ship radioed harbor control at La Guaira, Venezuela, that a bright, cone-shaped object had fallen vertically into the sea off the Venezuelan coast. It gave off "strange glares," and when it hit the water, the crewmates heard an explosion, and the sea became brilliantly colored. After the colors subsided, a boiling motion continued to disturb the sea. On January 21, 1957, shortly before the army UFO secrecy order, army intelligence reported a sighting of a "large shiny metal ball" and other objects over APO Army base. On March 23, 1957, another object plunged into a Venezuelan body of water, Lake Maracaibo.[15]

A number of civilian pilots reported UFOs in the coming months. On March 8, 1957, a pilot flying near Baudette, Minnesota, saw a luminous circular object flying against the wind. It was about twenty feet in diameter and flew so low that it appeared to suck up the snow. The next day, at 3:30 A.M., a pilot flying a DC-6 off Florida saw a bright UFO coming toward his plane; he estimated it to be "at least the size of a DC-3." His evasive action threw some passengers from their seats, injuring a few, and ambulances met the plane. Other pilots also reported the object. Miami Air Traffic Control sent a "Flash" to the Civil Aeronautics Board which described the near collision:

> Pilot took evasive action, object appeared to have a brilliant greenish-white center with an outer ring which reflected the glow from the center. . . . Above description fits what seven other flights saw. . . . Miami reports no missile activity. . . . Original reports of jet activity discounted.

The story received some press coverage, and the CAB, required by federal law to investigate, began a thorough check. Without waiting for a CAB opinion, however, the air force quickly explained the object as a shooting star. Although the CAB listed the case as unsolved, it mattered little, as most press accounts mentioned only the air force debunking.[16]

In Long Beach, California, on March 23, 1957, large numbers—perhaps thousands—of people, including three Ventura County deputy sheriffs, saw four strange flying objects. They appeared to be large, round, and flashing a brilliant red light. CAA radar tracked them, and by midnight, air force personnel at Oxnard AFB also saw them. When an F-89 was sent to pursue, the objects climbed and swiftly maneuvered away. Because there was no CIRVIS report, the incident did not fall under JANAP restrictions, and news about it quickly leaked out. The tower operator said the first object

> was moving much faster than anything I'd ever seen. About forty miles away, it came to an abrupt stop and reversed course, all within a period of about three seconds.

Each object was tracked moving thirty miles in thirty seconds, or 3,600 mph. Keyhoe and NICAP tried to get the Oxnard report, and were referred to the 4602nd Intelligence Squadron, which in turn told Keyhoe that only Air Force Headquarters could release it. Although NICAP had the tower operator's report, he was no longer inclined to jeopardize his career by talking.[17]

Another radar tracking of a UFO occurred on April 4 in Wigtownshire, Scotland, when three radar posts tracked an object which moved across the sky at sixty thousand feet, dived to fourteen thousand feet, circled around, and sped away. On April 19, members of the *Kitsukawa Maru*, a Japanese fishing boat, saw two metallic silvery objects descend into the sea. They estimated the size to be about thirty feet long, with no wings of any kind. As the objects hit the water, they created "a violent disturbance."[18]

Sightings of landed UFOs with humanoid occupants were reported in Argentina, Pennsylvania, and France in May 1957. The sightings did not differ in essentials from those of the great wave of 1954. The French sighting of May 10, for example, involved a man who was riding a bicycle on the Miraumont-Beaucourt road in France. At 10:45 P.M., he saw a bright light and four human-shaped silhouettes less than five feet tall. He ran off the road and found a path to the home of some friends. He arrived in a panic, and four others returned with him. They all saw a luminous object, pulsing red and white, and three silhouettes with huge heads. The people watched for twenty minutes, during which time they were joined by another person. Finally, a car approached, and the lights went out; after it passed, a light appeared just above the road. It rose rapidly and silently at a forty-five-degree angle and was gone.[19]

NICAP AND THE U.S. SENATE

In July 1957, NICAP learned that the U.S. Senate Subcommittee on Investigations was considering hearings on UFOs and wanted NICAP's assistance. Keyhoe contacted several board members for advice; Hillenkoetter suggested withholding the best cases, at least initially. "Just give them a good, strong sample of the evidence. There's nothing wrong in reserving something for the hearings." Keyhoe decided to ask Ruppelt to join NICAP's board of directors. Ruppelt was now an engineer with Northrop Aircraft, a major air force contractor, and—some NICAP members feared—under pressure to keep quiet. Nevertheless, Keyhoe caught up with Ruppelt at a rehearsal for the *I've Got a Secret* television program, which featured an episode about UFOs. Ruppelt said NICAP was doing a fine job, and Keyhoe mentioned the rumors about air force pressure. "It's not true," Ruppelt said. "Would I be here if it was?" On the show, he stated that 20 percent of sightings were unsolved while he was on Blue Book. Afterwards, Keyhoe invited Ruppelt to join NICAP's board. He added, "We won't load you with work, Ed. We mainly want your advice and your help in our fight against the censorship." Ruppelt agreed, and considered it "an honor." Keyhoe stressed the workload for a reason: Ruppelt had recently had a heart attack. Ruppelt wasn't obese, and was only thirty-four at the time. Three years later, he would be dead of a second heart attack. Did Ruppelt have a pre-existing medical condition that put him at risk? It would be helpful to learn the reasons for these multiple heart attacks at such a young age, but no researchers have offered any idea.[20]

In mid-July, Keyhoe met with the Senate Chief Investigator Healey regarding air force secrecy about UFOs. Keyhoe spoke strongly about the cover-up and the "silence group." He showed Healey the Grudge Report, released by the air force in December 1949. Keyhoe appears to have persuaded Healey that most of the answers to the report's 244 cases were "sheer speculation" or "deliberately fitted." He also presented Gen. Joe Kelly's letter to Lee Metcalf, indicating genuine air force interest in UFOs and conceding that pursuits of UFOs continued. There is no question that some senators took UFOs seriously. Arizona Senator Barry Goldwater wrote to one of his constituents on August 31, 1957, that "I, frankly, feel there is a great deal to this."[21]

During the summer of 1957, the Air Defense Command disbanded the 4602nd and reassigned UFO investigating duties to the 1006th Air Intelligence Service Squadron (AISS). (Clark has the 4602nd disbanding a year sooner.) Soon after, the air force reduced funds for the 1006th, impairing its investigative ability. Meanwhile, the army reimposed a UFO secrecy order in August, after NICAP protests had prompted its removal the previous spring.[22]

SUMMER 1957: CRASHES, NEAR COLLISIONS, OPENING FIRE, AND SILENCE

As NICAP confronted the air force over UFO secrecy, sightings and encounters occurred worldwide. One of the classic radar-visual UFO cases took place on July 17, 1957. A six-man crew, including three electronic warfare officers, was flying a USAF RB-47, equipped with state-of-the-art electronic intelligence gear. The crew obtained a strange radar signal over Mississippi, at first thought to be an anomaly. Soon, however, they saw an intense blue light moving toward them very fast. Before they could take evasive action, the object streaked by in front of them. For many hours, the crew continued to see the object while obtaining multiple air and ground radar signals (including ground radar from an air force unit in Duncanville, Texas). The object's maneuverability was extraordinary: at one point it stopped suddenly and the RB-47 flew past it; at another point it easily pulled away when the RB-47 accelerated to 550 mph; at yet another point it blinked out visually and on radar simultaneously, then reappeared a little later. All instruments were functioning perfectly, and the experienced crew was extremely uneasy about their escort. After accompanying the crew for eight hundred miles, the UFO disappeared over Oklahoma City. Air Defense Command intelligence and Blue Book investigated the encounter, although no printed account appeared before the Condon report of 1968. Condon Committee investigator Gordon David Thayer declared the case unexplained, and later described the official air force explanation ("airliner") as "literally ridiculous."[23]

On the same day as the RB-47 incident, an airliner one hundred miles east of El Paso nearly collided with a UFO "at least the size of a B-47." Two passengers were injured and hospitalized; no known aircraft was near.[24]

On July 24, it appears, Soviet anti-aircraft batteries on the Kouril Islands opened fire on UFOs. According to a Reuters news dispatch:

> Last night, the batteries of the Kouril Islands have opened fire on UFOs. Japanese authorities have reported that the whole of the Soviet artillery was in action and that powerful searchlights were searching the sky. The guns have fired again in the morning.

The U.S. Air Force stated that no American craft flew near Soviet coasts. Radio Moscow quoted the U.S. communiqué and stated that the objects fired upon were luminous, flew very fast, and none had been hit. Although the encounter may well have happened as indicated, we must recall that the KGB spent immense sums on disinformation, that no information left the Soviet Union without state sanction; also that the Americans could easily have been lying about not violating Soviet airspace—U-2s did this all the time. Still, *Americans* pursued UFOs, and at times attempted to down them, so why not the Soviets?[25]

More sightings occurred in Brazil. On August 14, near Joinville, Brazil, a Varig airlines pilot saw a domed disc which affected the aircraft engines. Humanoid reports continued, including a July 25 incident by a professor at the Catholic Faculty of Law in Sao Sebastiao, and a September sighting of a domed disc and three normal-sized humanoid occupants who collected samples. Then, on September 10, 1957 (approximate date), according to an anonymous letter sent to a Brazilian journalist, there occurred another "crash" incident. Near Sao Paulo, in the town of Ubatuba, several people saw a disc dive down and explode, showering the area with flaming fragments. The anonymous correspondent mailed some small samples, which were soon analyzed by associates of Brazilian APRO member Dr. Olavo T. Fontes. The tests showed the fragments to be of apparently pure magnesium. The Condon Committee later rejected the fragments as not pure and determined that they "could have been produced by earthly technology known prior to 1957." No one explained where the fragments could have come from, however.[26]

During the final phase of a U.S. Air Force training flight on September 19–20, 1957, an amazing UFO encounter occurred, reminiscent of the RB-47 case from two months earlier. Many of the details of this encounter are unavailable, as the incident never made it to the Blue Book files. While in flight, a B-25 crew practiced locating ground radar and turned on their ECM (electronic counter measure) equipment. They were surprised to learn that it was being jammed, first on one frequency, then another. Just then, a glowing white UFO was seen from the cockpit and played "tag" with the aircraft for several hundred miles. Ground radar picked up the B-25 and UFO separately, with visual maneuvers matching what was seen on radar—both of the plane and on the ground. Upon landing, the entire crew was questioned by Air Defense Command intelligence personnel, who confiscated all ECM equipment and in-flight wire recordings. The story only surfaced ten years later, when the University of Colorado, under contract to investigate the UFO phenomenon, stumbled across it during a meeting with air force personnel. One of the attendees happened to be the plane's pilot (now a colonel); project investigators checked with the copilot and radar operator, who confirmed the story.[27]

SPUTNIK AND A BIZARRE GLOBAL WAVE

Mankind formally entered the space age on October 4, 1957, when the Soviet Union launched *Sputnik*, the first man-made satellite. Scientifically and historically speaking, this was an achievement of the first magnitude, and caused a great commotion worldwide. In the United States, a better word would be panic.

Sputnik also kicked off the first major UFO wave since 1954. Faced with an unexpected barrage of UFO reports, the air force dismissed them as confusion, misidentification, and even hysteria caused by *Sputnik*. But although the wave began in October, it did not reach the United States until November. Most Americans did not know that this wave of sightings was global.

The first incident of the wave is perhaps the most remarkable of all. It involved a series of incidents involving Antonio Villas-Boas, a twenty-three-year-old farmer living near Sao Paulo, Brazil, and culminated in the first unmistakable alien abduction report. On the night of October 5, in the bedroom he shared with his brother, Boas saw that a bright light from an unknown source had lit their room. He saw a silvery glow in the yard, but no object. The light moved and passed over the house. On October 14, Boas was plowing the field at night with his brother. Between 9:30 and 10 P.M, the two saw a light as large as a "cartwheel," about three hundred feet above the ground. It shined an extremely bright, pale red light over the field, so bright that it hurt their eyes. Then, suddenly, the light moved "with enormous speed" to the opposite end of the field and stopped. Apparently not in a state of terror, Boas followed it, but the light returned to its original position. Boas said this maneuver happened at least twenty times. Then, the light simply disappeared "as if it had been turned off."

Boas plowed the field alone the following night—one might wonder why. At 1 A.M., he noticed a red object in the sky approaching him slowly. Then it moved very rapidly directly over his position, and hovered at about 150 feet. It gave off blinding light, and Boas was terrified. After a few minutes, the object dived forward to a position about forty feet in front of his tractor, and he discerned a large object with three metal legs, and something on the top that rotated rapidly. His tractor had been running all the while, but now the engine died when he tried to drive. Boas ran. After a few steps, his arm was caught by a small being in strange clothes. Boas gave the being a strong push and continued to run, but was captured and dragged into the craft by three others.

Boas later gave an exceptionally detailed description—about eight thousand words—of the inside of the craft and its occupants, who wore tight, white clothing with a light on their belt, white shoes with no heels, large gloves, and opaque helmets with a slit at the level of the eyes. Boas claimed he was stripped naked and subjected to a medical examination in which one of the beings "spread a liquid all over my skin." He was led to another room where the beings took some blood from his chin, then left him alone briefly. He noticed an unpleasant odor, "as if a thick smoke was stifling me," and he vomited in a corner of the room. After what seemed like an eternity, an alien female entered the room, entirely naked. She was beautiful, considering that she was an alien: blond hair that was "nearly white" and parted in the center, large, slanted blue eyes, a well-formed straight nose, small but ordinary ears, high cheekbones, and a pointed chin. Boas described her body as "much more beautiful than any I have ever seen." Her height was short, but not extremely so, perhaps four-and-a-half feet. Like the others, the alien woman spoke with unintelligible, "guttural" sounds. She seemed amused by Boas's look of amazement. She embraced Boas and made no mistake as to her intention. Boas became "uncontrollably" excited and wondered whether the liquid that had been spread on his body contributed to this. The two had a normal sexual encounter, considering the circumstances, and the woman "reacted as any other woman would." Of course, considering that the woman was an alien, a few cultural discrepancies presented themselves. Boas said that "some of the growls that came from her at certain times nearly spoiled everything, as they gave me the disagreeable impression of lying with an animal." She also never kissed him, but instead bit him softly on the chin. When Boas attempted a second act, the woman became uninterested and soon left. He felt used, like "a good stallion to improve their stock." Just before she left, said Boas, she turned to him, pointed to her belly, then pointed to the southward sky.

He soon received his clothes and dressed, and returned to the room where three crew members sat in swivel chairs, communicating among themselves. Boas later described the furnishings and equipment in detail. One of the beings led him out of the craft, and Boas watched the door close and legs retract. The craft rose slowly to about one hundred feet, hovered, and became brighter. It created an increasingly loud buzzing sound, and the top began to rotate at a terrific speed. The craft then took off "like a bullet." As Boas said, "these people really knew their business." By now, it was about 5:30 A.M., and Boas had been aboard for over four hours.

At first, Boas told only his mother, but soon wrote to a magazine that had published articles on flying saucers. From there the story reached Dr. Olavo Fontes, APRO's man in Brazil, who persuaded Boas to visit him, expecting to trip him up. Instead, Fontes found Boas poised, "perfectly normal," with no signs of emotional instability or mystical tendencies, and "extremely intelligent." Under questioning, Boas revealed embarrassment over the sexual experience, which he had not mentioned in his letter to the journalist. Boas also held a "down to earth" view of the aliens themselves:

> [He] did not think that the crew were angels, supermen, or demons. He believed them to be human beings such as we are, only coming from other countries on some other planet. He declared that because one of the crew . . . pointed to himself, then to the earth, then to some place in the heavens . . . .

Boas gave descriptions of such detail, and presented his encounter with such levelheadedness and plausibility, that Fontes wrote a detailed report to the Lorenzens. Initially, they tried to explain the encounter as sexual fantasy but never quite convinced themselves. Finally, in 1962, they published a truncated version of the experience, and then fully in 1965. Boas eventually became a lawyer and made no public appearance until 1978. Then, as before, his sincerity seemed beyond argument.[28]

More Brazilian encounters were reported throughout October and November, describing sightings of humanoids and landed craft, in one case a reported healing of a girl near death from cancer by two short beings dressed in white.[29] On the night of November 3-4, the day that the Soviets launched *Sputnik II*, carrying a dog named Laika, another Brazilian Varig plane encountered a UFO, just as one had on the preceding August 14. This time, Capt. Jean V. de Beyssac and his copilot saw an object zooming in toward their plane at 1:30 A.M. It caused several of the plane's systems to burn out, forcing them to head back.[30]

On the next night, a truly remarkable incident occurred, involving Brazilian army personnel at Fort Itaipu. A circular, orange-glowing object about one hundred feet in diameter descended silently. With no visible beam, it gave off intense heat at two sentries, and other soldiers saw it quickly ascend out of sight. The burned soldiers were isolated and hospitalized for weeks with first- and second-degree burns over more than 10 percent of their bodies. The fort was placed under martial law, discussion of the encounter was prohibited, and a top secret report was prepared. The Brazilians contacted the American embassy for help in the investigation, and within days, U.S. Army officers appeared in the company of Brazilian air force personnel. They questioned the two victims and other witnesses. Amazingly, Olavo Fontes learned of the incident and investigated before the month ended. Initially, he found only the two soldiers but within two years had located other witnesses who corroborated the original story in all details.[31]

Brazil was not the only country claiming a great deal of UFO activity. A close-up sighting of a UFO craft was reported in France on October 31. Several reports came from Korea and South Africa early in November, including a November 1 description of an attempted intercept by a South African air force jet pilot who climbed to forty-five thousand feet, but was still unable to reach what appeared to be a hovering machine.[32]

In late October or early November—the exact date is unknown—a UFO sighting took place in the Australian outback country of Maralinga, not far from Alice Springs. In the late afternoon, following three recent nuclear detonations, a British RAF team was preparing to return to the U.K. when, according to Derek Murray (later a Home Office photographer), a man rushed in to report a UFO. Others laughed but went outside to see an object with a flat base and dome on top, of silvery blue metal. Because they had an extremely clear view, they also discerned several squarish portholes across the center. The object tilted at forty-five degrees and hovered. "It was perched there like a king on his high throne looking down on his subjects . . . it was a magnificent sight." The sighting lasted for fifteen minutes, until the object shot up out of sight without a sound. The RAF men were astonished. British researcher Jenny Randles wrote:

Murray could, of course, be telling lies, but there is absolutely no reason to suppose so. He says, "I swear to you as a practicing Christian this was no dream, no illusion, no fairy story—but a solid craft of metallic construction."[33]

On the eighth, four Australian government astronomers at Mount Stromlo Observatory saw a UFO too slow to be a meteor, and neither Sputnik 1 nor 2. The assistant director, Dr. A. R. Hogg, thought the unknown object could have been circling the Earth like an artificial satellite. The same day, in Edinburgh, Scotland, fourteen people reported to the police that a disc-shaped object followed their truck, dived toward it, came within sixty feet of them, then left toward the sea, leaving a double vapor trail. On November 22, in Gesten, Denmark, a shop owner saw a pyramid-shaped, luminous, transparent object fly rapidly across the road. Although it was over a tenth of a mile distant, he claimed to see two figures who looked like human beings sitting behind one another aboard the craft.[34]

NOVEMBER 1957: A RASH OF AMERICAN SIGHTINGS

On October 31, 1957, Donald Keyhoe met with Healey again, who informed him that the air force had made "a strong attempt to disprove your claims." Meanwhile, the UFO wave hit the United States, concentrating mainly in the South and Southwest, especially Texas. An interesting feature of this rash of sightings was the widespread reports of electromagnetic (EM) effects on automobiles. For two weeks in particular, newspapers reported many UFO cases that affected car ignitions, radios, and lights. Less well known is that various sightings of aliens or humanoids occurred through December.[35]

At 3:30 A.M. on November 2, just west of the town of Canadian, Texas, military and civilian witnesses reported a red and white submarine-shaped object at ground level, two or three times as long as a car and about ten feet high. A figure and possibly a white flag were near it; when a car stopped nearby, the object flashed a light, and the headlights failed.[36]

The best-known sighting of the wave, however, occurred on the night of November 2, in Levelland, Texas. Pedro Saucedo and passenger Joe Salav were driving a truck along Highway 116 toward Levelland. An immense, glowing object swept down over their truck and landed on the highway. Their engine died, and they heard faint clanking or hammering, as well as what sounded like unintelligible voices. The object itself was quite large: about two hundred feet long and dirigible-shaped. After three minutes on the ground, it rose swiftly and noiselessly, glowing brilliant red, and flew away. Levelland was buzzing with UFO reports all night. Sheriff Weir Clem and his deputy, Pat McCulloch, reported the Saucedo-Salav incident to the air force and believed

that they saw the same or a similar object a short time later as they investigated another UFO report, their fourth that night. Other reports from
Levelland also described a low-flying object, over two hundred feet long,
equipped with a bright light, and which interfered with car engines. In some
cases, people claimed the object landed on the road.[37]

Later that night, in White Sands, New Mexico, two men on army patrol
in a jeep saw a bright, controlled object about 150 feet above the ground near
the site of the first atomic bomb explosion. The object descended to ground
level after about three minutes and landed a few miles away at the northern
end of the testing grounds.[38]

After Levelland, the deluge. In Elmwood Park, Illinois, at 3:15 A.M. on
November 4, two police officers and a third man were looking for the cause
of a headlight failure. At that moment, a luminous object descended about two
hundred feet from them. The car headlights functioned properly again, and
they drove toward the object but had to stop at a cemetery wall. They turned
off all lights and watched the object for two more minutes. In Alamogordo,
New Mexico, later that day, White Sands engineer James Stokes watched an
elliptical UFO swoop over the mountains as his car stalled. Stokes told
reporters the object "was at least five hundred feet long. As it passed over, I felt
a wave of heat." He estimated its speed at between 1,500 and 2,500 mph.
Because of Stokes's training and his position, the story circulated widely.[39]

The wave continued on the fifth. In addition to the many sightings
reported by civilians, one involved the U.S. Coast Guard cutter *Sebago*. The
ship was in the Gulf of Mexico when it tracked an object on radar reaching
1,000 mph at one point and which stopped in midair. Four crew members saw
the object visually as a bright, glowing, circular craft. Before the Pentagon
expressed awareness of the incident, the story made the press.[40]

Sightings were even stranger the next day, and a few included claims of
seeing human-looking occupants of UFO craft. Late that night in Montville,
Ohio, a twenty-eight-year-old plasterer named Olden Moore was driving
home when he saw an object that looked like a bright meteor split into two
pieces, one of which went straight up. The other became larger while its color
changed from bright white to blue-green. It hovered about two hundred feet
above a field and landed with a soft whirring sound, perhaps five hundred feet
away. Moore watched cautiously for fifteen minutes, then approached. What
he saw was unforgettable. The object was shaped like "a covered dish" and
fairly large: about fifty feet in diameter, fifteen feet high, with a cone on top
about ten feet high. It pulsated slowly, and a haze surrounded it. Moore
reported his flying saucer sighting to the sheriff the next morning, and a civil
defense director investigated the site. He found high levels of radioactivity,
two perfectly formed deep holes six inches in diameter, and unusual foot-
prints that "came from nowhere and went nowhere." In the investigator's
opinion, "a foreign object landed in that field."

The Moore sighting was of exceptionally high quality, and the air force noticed it. After his encounter, Moore disappeared for a few days. When he returned, he refused to say where he had been, but eventually told his wife and friends that the air force had taken him to Washington, D.C. Much later, to a private UFO investigator, Moore stated that on November 10, the sheriff, deputy, and an air force officer appeared at his house and asked to take him to Youngstown, Ohio, for an interview with the military. Moore agreed, and the group first took him to the field where he saw the UFO, an unsettling experience for him. He then went by helicopter to Youngstown. A week later, an air force car with two officers returned; this time Moore was flown to Washington, D.C., for extended questioning (the flight stopped at Wright-Patterson AFB to exchange an officer). Moore was under constant observation while in Washington, and several groups of people interrogated him. They showed him slides and still photos of UFOs, and even presented a UFO movie film taken from inside a military aircraft. Moore was told the objects must be extraterrestrial, and signed a document swearing him to secrecy. He never tried to make his story public. His interviewer, C. W. Fitch, got to know him well as an honest man involved in his church.[41]

On the morning of November 9, an Eastern Air Lines captain saw a large UFO hovering over Lafayette Airport in Louisiana. In his words, "the Air Defense Command in Baton Rouge was on the phone, waiting for our report, when we landed there." During the evening of November 10 in Hammond, Indiana, hundreds of people saw a rocket-shaped machine race overhead. The police followed it, and the captain said a loud beeping sound blocked the radio reception; residents also reported radio and television failure as the UFO passed by. On the eleventh, airline passengers near Los Angeles saw an elliptical UFO below their plane.[42]

Another intriguing UFO event of this wave occurred on November 13, when an object exploded over the State Hospital at Crownsville, Maryland. Burned pieces of metal fell on hospital grounds, were checked for radiation, and confiscated by army intelligence officers from Fort Meade. The materials were said to be relayed to Air Research and Development in Baltimore, where an ARD colonel told NICAP member Lou Corbin he had no idea what the metal was. From there, at least some of the material was flown to ATIC, although ATIC's deputy director denied ever hearing about it. Fort Meade was the site of the NSA's headquarters.[43]

Despite the density of sightings and nature of the reports, the Blue Book investigation consisted of one man from the 1006th who took two trips to question witnesses (ignoring the majority of them), stated incorrectly that lightning had been in the area at the time, and blamed it all on weather. On November 14, the air force explained the Levelland case as ball lightning, the Stoke report as a hoax inspired by the Levelland case, and the *Sebago* case as caused by confused radar men who mistook ordinary plane blips for a UFO.

Menzel supported the air force conclusions and added that the wave of sightings was "tied in with the sensitization of people to the Sputniks." The Levelland case was a mirage, he said, and the stalled car merely the result of a nervous foot on the accelerator. An FBI report from November 12 also adhered to the Sputnik theory, noting the "great increase in the number of flying saucers and other UFOs" reported by people across the country.[44]

The air force also issued another fact sheet titled "Air Force's 10-Year Study of Unidentified Flying Objects." This denied the existence of flying saucers, emphasized the absence of a threat to U.S. security, and claimed an unidentified rate of 2 to 3 percent.

Not everyone lined up to agree with these conclusions. A journalist friend of Keyhoe read the air force list of explanations of UFOs. When he came to "large Canadian geese flying low over a city at night, with street lights reflecting from their bodies," he asked, "Don, how dumb do they think people are?" "You should see the full list," Keyhoe answered.[45]

Edward Ruppelt entered the picture, taking issue with Donald Menzel's conclusions about Levelland. A mirage, he said, was not the answer. "There is sufficient evidence of flying saucer existence to warrant further investigation," he told reporters. Moreover, Ruppelt said, Blue Book had received several electrical interference reports when he was chief. He urged the air force to "stop playing mum." Lincoln La Paz also reversed his judgment of the Levelland and Stokes sightings, which he initially said were caused by fireballs. In the midst of the wave, he stated his belief that they were not fireballs or celestial phenomena.[46]

The press reported general perceptions not in accord with the air force line. A November 7, 1957, article from the *Times* of El Paso noted:

> Some of the nation's top scientists are "pretty shook up" about the mysterious flying objects sighted in New Mexico and West Texas skies this week, said Charles Capen (a scientist at White Sands). "This is something that hasn't happened before."[47]

Keyhoe, meanwhile, wanted to dispute the air force conclusions openly. He knew, for example, that the crew of the *Sebago* had not merely tracked a UFO on radar, but had seen it visually—something not mentioned in the air force summary of the incident. But even though Keyhoe had lined up three *Sebago* witnesses for public statements, each one withdrew his permission to use his name in the Senate investigation. One witness, a pilot, told Keyhoe, "I'm sorry, but I've got a family and my job to think about."[48]

UFO sightings dropped off after mid-November. A reported landing occurred on December 8 in Woodward, Oklahoma, when a UFO allegedly took complete control of a car with three passengers. The driver, an employee of an aircraft company, said the object caused his heater, windshield wipers, and radio to fail, and the engine just stopped. Above the car, a disc-shaped object, about fifty feet in diameter with portholes around the edge, emitted hot air and a high-pitched sound. As it rose, the car started by itself. In a sequence reminiscent of the Olden Moore case, the man spent four hours with two Kirtland AFB officers who told him of similar observations; but the case was never reported to Blue Book. On December 12, a radar-visual sighting of a multicolored UFO occurred in Tokyo, causing jets to be scrambled. On the eighteenth, Dr. Luis Corrales, of Caracas, Venezuela, made a time exposure on a photographic film to record the passage of *Sputnik II*. He succeeded and photographed a second trail alongside it, then veering away, then returning to pace it. Detailed analysis disproved double exposure, scratches, internal reflections, or other debunking explanations.[49]

One last report of note surfaced in 1957. Like the Villas-Boas case, it is one of the few abduction reports in the pre-Hill era. It also seemed to describe a type of being—the so-called Grays—that became common in later years. The story is sketchy in the extreme and was reported on December 11, 1957, at least five years after it supposedly took place. A man serving in the U.S. Army in Austria claimed to have been paralyzed by a humanoid being, taken inside a UFO, and flown (he believed) to another planet. He saw other humans who did not acknowledge his presence. He was then returned to his base. This report received no thorough investigation, and there was no mention of the man's name.[50]

The wave did not make a dent in the Blue Book record. Despite the amazing activity that had occurred, Blue Book acknowledged a mere fourteen unidentified sightings for all of 1957, less than 2 percent of the 1,006 reports it received. In truth, for the past two years, AISS had completely taken over ATIC's job of analyzing UFO reports. Moreover, by the end of the year, the wave was all but forgotten by the public.[51]

THE AIR FORCE PARRIES NICAP

Although records are never complete, it appears that from 1958 to 1963, American UFO sightings waned significantly. Air force fact sheets became less frequent, and simply restated the position of November 1957. Not everyone took the air force seriously. On January 16, 1958, a writer for *Life* magazine stated that "during the ensuing year there will be authenticated sightings of roughly two hundred Unidentified Flying Objects, of which the Pentagon will be able to disprove 210."[52]

NICAP membership grew. By 1958, it reached five thousand, although the organization was always strapped for cash. Meanwhile, elements within the U.S. Senate pondered the UFO question. In January 1958, the Senate Subcommittee on Government Operations (headed by Sen. John McClellan) asked to meet with representatives from the secretary of the Air Force Office of Legislative Action (SAFLA) to discuss the possibility of holding open hearings of the air force UFO program. The air force feared "uncontrolled publicity," but agreed to go along. Very soon, however, Richard Horner, the air force assistant secretary for research and development, persuaded the subcommittee chief counsel, Donald O'Donnell, that hearings were "not in the best interest of the air force," nor necessary for national security. Blue Book, said Horner, had the situation well in hand. Horner also told Sen. Barry Goldwater that month that allegations about the air force withholding information about UFOs were "entirely in error." People who reported UFOs, stated Horner, simply wanted confidentiality, and the air force respected that.[53]

KEYHOE CENSORED ON TELEVISION

On January 22, 1958, Donald Keyhoe appeared on the popular CBS television show *Armstrong Circle Theater* for a program titled "UFO—Enigma of the Skies." He had been invited as a guest in December, along with Kenneth Arnold, C. S. Chiles, Edward Ruppelt, Donald Menzel, and an air force representative, Col. Spencer Whedon from ATIC. Keyhoe wondered why the air force would subject itself to a barrage of questions so soon after the November sightings. He learned the reason from CBS representative Irve Tunick: the entire event was to be scripted and preapproved by the station, in conjunction with the air force itself. Would the Tremonton, Utah, film be shown? asked Keyhoe. No, said Tunick, the air force explained it as seagulls. "You told me," said Keyhoe, "this wasn't a censored program." "It's not," replied Tunick, "but we can't buck them on those pictures."

Keyhoe's notes juxtaposed key UFO cases with implausible air force claims and added statements from William Lear and Hermann Oberth. His main thrust, however, struck at the heart of UFO secrecy: he planned to refer openly to four key documents and events still officially denied. These were the 1947 ATIC (Twining) letter, the 1948 Estimate of the Situation, the 1952 air force intelligence analysis of UFO maneuvers (led by Dewey Fournet), and the Robertson Panel of January 1953. Keyhoe submitted his script, expecting "minor editing." Instead, CBS edited out his key points, with the explanation that the script was too long. After Keyhoe threatened to bolt from the program, CBS appeared to give in and said he could tighten the script himself, then phone in the changes.

When Keyhoe arrived at the studio for rehearsals, he saw that all his efforts were wasted: his changes had not been made, and his statements about hidden documents were still absent. He angrily told the show's producer, Robert Costello, that "the air force *is* censoring this program!" "No," said

Costello, "but they deny there ever were any such conclusions. If we let you say it, they'll stand up and deny it." "Let them," said Keyhoe. But Costello's answer remained no. Keyhoe then tried a different tactic: he now wanted to use the cases that the air force had officially cleared for him in 1952. This made Tunick unhappy. "Even if the cases were cleared," Tunick said, "the air force will try to refute them now. We'd never get a final script." Keyhoe by now was thoroughly exasperated. He was down to six items CBS agreed to: statements by Goldwater, Oberth, and Lear, plus three UFO cases not involving the U.S. Air Force. One was a 1954 U.S. Marine Corps sighting, another involved the RAF, and the third was a November 1954 Brazilian airliner case. Now, even these sightings became a problem. Whereas Tunick had earlier agreed to use them, he now shook his head. It was "too much to cover." Keyhoe prodded and got the real reason from Tunick: "the Armstrong Company won't stand for an open battle with the air force."

Kenneth Arnold was on the set and overheard the exchange. "It's a raw deal," he told Keyhoe. "I'm having trouble too; they won't let me make any changes." Two days later, Arnold pulled out of the program and advised Keyhoe to do the same. "The way it's rigged," he said, "the air force will make you look like a fool." By then, Ruppelt and Chiles had also backed out of the program—in Chiles's case, specifically due to pressure from his employer, Eastern Air Lines. In Ruppelt's case, no reason was offered. With all these vacancies opening up, Keyhoe tried to get Hillenkoetter on the show, but the show's management said no.

During the show itself, Colonel Whedon denied air force censorship over UFOs and gave the standard explanations. Keyhoe then presented his piece— "a skeleton of a story," as he put it later, forcing himself to read the lines of the teleprompter. Suddenly, on the air nationwide, his frustration vented. He stated, "And now, I'm going to reveal something that has never been disclosed before." That was the end of Keyhoe's announcement. Without his knowledge, the main microphone switch was turned off. Keyhoe continued:

> For the last six months, we have been working with a congressional committee investigating official secrecy about UFOs. If all the evidence we have given this committee is made public in open hearings, it will absolutely prove that the UFOs are real machines under intelligent control.

A more distant microphone did transmit this statement, but television listeners could hear Keyhoe only by turning up their volume controls. Most did not. Minutes after Keyhoe was cut off, Air Force Assistant Secretary Richard Horner stated on television that

> there has been a mistaken belief that the air force has been hiding from the public information concerning unidentified flying objects. Nothing could be further from the truth. And I do not qualify this in any way. . . . There is no evidence at hand that objects popularly known as "flying saucers" actually exist.

After so crudely silencing the air force's most determined opponent, Horner's statement carried little weight for many viewers. Callers swamped CBS, asking why Keyhoe's sound had been cut.

Although he was in an excellent position to exploit the situation, Keyhoe inexplicably declined to do so. He briefly considered giving the deleted paragraph to the media, and of discussing the air force pressure on the program. He "reluctantly gave up the idea," he said, because it would put the network producers on the spot. They were also "victims of official pressure." Within days of the program, CBS admitted to air force censorship. In response to a complaint by a member of NICAP, the CBS director of editing, Herbert A. Carlborg, stated:

> This program had been carefully cleared for security reasons. Therefore, it was the responsibility of this network to insure performance in accordance with pre-determined security standards. . . . As a consequence, public interest was served by the action taken in deleting the audio on Major Keyhoe's speech at a point where he apparently was about to deviate.

It was a sign of the times that even APRO criticized Keyhoe for deviating from the script. Yet, the *Armstrong Theater* program had raised a question that could not be erased: if there was nothing secret about UFOs, why did the program have to be cleared for security, and why was Keyhoe's audio cut?[54]

In the aftermath of the program, more official statements were released that conceded UFO secrecy. On January 23, 1958, Capt. G. H. Oldenburgh, information services officer at Langley AFB in Virginia, wrote that "the public dissemination of data on Unidentified Flying Objects . . . is contrary to air force policy and regulations."[55] A few days later (1/28/58), Congressman William H. Ayres (R-Ohio) admitted to a NICAP member that

> Congressional investigations have been held and are still being held on the problem of unidentified flying objects and the problem is one in which there is quite a bit of interest. . . . Since most of the material presented to the committees is classified, the hearings are never printed. When conclusions are reached, they will be released if possible.[56]

Within the military, interest in UFOs remained high. Earlier in January, Lackland AFB in San Antonio had asked for Keyhoe's permission to use his 1955 book, *The Flying Saucer Conspiracy,* to develop a script for closed-circuit broadcast throughout the base. Keyhoe was surprised and gave his assent.[57]

THE SENATE STOPS ITS INVESTIGATION

Shortly after the *Armstrong Theater* program, the air force revised AFR 200-2 and re-created the system of air base commanders conducting initial investigations of UFO sightings in their areas. It also continued ATIC's formal UFO responsibility for analysis and evaluation and stated that "air force activities must reduce the percentage of unidentifieds to the minimum."[58]

At the same time, Keyhoe phoned Senate Subcommittee Chief Investigator Healey, whom he told that the *Armstrong Circle Theater* really *had* been censored, and cutting Keyhoe's audio was not just an accident. Healey acknowledged that several congressmen were inquiring about the UFO investigation. When they met a few days later, Healey told Keyhoe the air force was now claiming the *Armstrong Theater* program "proved there are no such things as flying saucers." Keyhoe then gave Healey the facts of the Ryan case of 1956, which strongly pointed to tampering with the CAA and CAB reports. By air force order, said Keyhoe, pilots Ryan and Neff did follow a UFO, regardless of what the official documents said. Healey remained incredulous until Keyhoe told him he had the tape to prove it—he had recently obtained the highly incriminating tape of Ryan and Neff from *Meet the Millers*. Keyhoe knew full well that a complete transcript of the Ryan-Neff interview would be a convincing document. He felt confident about his chances for the moment and offered to get a transcript to Healey and McClellan.[59]

A month later (3/8/58), Keyhoe appeared on a Mike Wallace television interview. Without Keyhoe's knowledge, the air force gave Wallace key information which Wallace announced on the show. "The air force told us," said Wallace, "the [Senate] subcommittee members have already talked with them and they show no interest in any hearings." That was news to Keyhoe. It must be false, he said. It was true, however. While Keyhoe was angry, Hillenkoetter was philosophical: "What counts is that NICAP is still operating. Losing one battle isn't fatal." A few days later, two letters from the McClellan committee to NICAP members confirmed that it did "not intend to investigate the United States Air Force."[60]

What had happened? It appears that air force pressure succeeded when arguments failed. By late March, NICAP began a new campaign to open another government UFO investigation. This time it approached the Department of Justice, the National Security Council, the CIA, and the U.S. Army. Not surprisingly, it received rebuffs and denials.[61]

NICAP was stalled, but still trying. The organization obtained a formal statement in May 1958 from Dewey Fournet that confirmed (1) the 1948 Estimate of the Situation and (2) his own 1952 intelligence analysis of UFOs, which argued that they exhibited signs of intelligent control. Since the air force had been denying the existence of both of these documents, this was helpful to NICAP's arsenal. Keyhoe learned that spring from a source that Gen. Nathan Twining, still chairman of the JCS, was concerned about UFOs, and about what to tell the public.[62]

There was reason to believe this was true. On April 9, 1958, the air force finally released parts of the Robertson Panel report, undoubtedly due in part to the pressure that Keyhoe's television appearance had created. Why not seek an interview with Twining, thought Keyhoe. He wrote a letter to Twining and received an answer in May from Executive Officer Col. John Sherrill. Sorry, no interview, but Sherrill wrote cryptically:

> No effective means have been developed for the establishment of communication by radio or otherwise with unknown aerial objects. The technical obstacles involved in such an endeavor, I am sure, are quite obvious to you.

Keyhoe's letter to Twining reverberated in the Pentagon. In June, an air force officer met secretly with Keyhoe. The officer gave him three UFO reports, then warned him that the air force was going to ask him "for certain UFO information. Think it over carefully before you decide." NICAP could be in trouble, the officer warned, and NICAP "must have something that has upset the Pentagon." Two days later, an air force request did arrive. Keyhoe's recent letter to Twining had indicated NICAP had files indicating intelligent maneuver by UFOs, and the air force wanted these cases. Keyhoe wondered, the air force already had *many* good cases. Why desire NICAP's hidden cases? In light of NICAP's recent tangle with the air force, there only seemed one reasonable answer: in order to disprove the cases and silence the witnesses. NICAP refused the air force request.[63]

In June 1958, Richard Hall joined NICAP as an associate editor. Hall had been in the air force and, since that time, "had accumulated a large file of verified UFO evidence." He impressed Keyhoe with connections to serious UFO investigators and soon established a prominent place for himself in NICAP, eventually as NICAP's acting director in the 1960s.[64]

The Lackland AFB request reached an interesting point in late spring of 1958. On May 16, the base's chief of education planning, Maj. Warren Akin, publicly suggested that UFOs were spacecraft. Then, in June, Keyhoe finally received word from the base. They had prepared a seventeen-page script based on a very straightforward interpretation of his book and conclusions. It even included the 1953 Kinross case, which involved the loss of an F-89 over Michigan in pursuit of a UFO, and a comment that rehearsals at the base were to begin immediately. The script itself stated that "the most logical explanation is that the saucers are interplanetary. This is the *only* answer which meets all the known criteria." Elsewhere, it stated:

> Acting in the best interests of the public of the United States of America, the federal government in conjunction with the U.S. Air Force has carefully concealed

information which was thought to be of danger because of the impending possibility of hysteria and panic which could result in an economic collapse and dissipation of our social structure.

Once again, Keyhoe was astonished. Why do this? he wondered. Baffled but interested, he approved the script, then did not hear another word from the base for six months, when the script was shot down without explanation.[65]

Ruppelt Is Turned

In June 1958, Ohio Representative John E. Henderson, after reading Edward Ruppelt's *Report on Unidentified Flying Objects*, sent a list of UFO questions to the air force. Blue Book responded with a special, comprehensive briefing for Henderson and other interested congressmen. Afterwards, the congressmen expressed confidence in the air force UFO program and agreed that publicity would be "unwise . . . particularly in an open or closed formal congressional hearing."[66]

Ruppelt, however, proved to be a problem to the air force no longer. Already, on May 6, 1958, he had written to NICAP member George Stockey of his strong *support* for Blue Book:

. . . I have visited Project Blue Book since 1953 and am now convinced that the reports of UFOs are nothing more than reports of balloons, aircraft, astronomical phenomena, etc. I don't believe they are anything from outer space.

How could Ruppelt have performed such a swift and complete about-face? Stockey offered his own opinion in a letter he wrote to Keyhoe in early June. Ruppelt, wrote Stockey, "works for an aircraft corporation which has got contracts with the air force. While they might not order him to reverse his opinion, obviously they could make their desires known." Or, in fact, they *might* have ordered him to reverse his opinion. Keyhoe concluded sadly that Ruppelt had buckled to air force pressure. Seen in relation to the strong air force pressure on several fronts of the UFO problem during 1958, Keyhoe's conclusion seems correct. Ruppelt's public statements during the November 1957 wave had been straightforward and completely contradictory to the air force position. He had unquestionably become a serious problem for the air force. The only conclusion can be that sometime near the airing of the *Armstrong Theater* program in late January 1958 someone had gotten to Ruppelt.

Researcher Jerome Clark called this interpretation possible but argued that "in absence of evidence to this effect, it can only be speculative explanation." He suggested an alternate scenario, offered by Ruppelt's widow, that Ruppelt's exposure to southern California contactees helped to sour him on the UFO phenomenon. Yet, while direct evidence for air force pressure is lacking, it remains the most probable reason. Could crazy contactees really have soured Ruppelt within the two months between November 1957 and January 1958, when he backed out of the television program?[67]

1958: AMERICA BECOMES A UFO-FREE ZONE

Perhaps the subheading overstates the case somewhat, but by 1958, the United States was generating very few UFO reports. Matters were different elsewhere, where more people reported UFOs at close range, as well as the occasional UFO being. Australia provided several such reports. On January 13, in Farm Hill, a frightened young man claimed that a dome-shaped craft followed him for about three miles, a mere thirty feet above the ground, and perhaps 150 feet away. It then flew silently by, interfering with his radio. On February 2, in New South Wales, Australia, witnesses reported an elliptical UFO with two "porthole-like" markings.[68]

For most of 1958, however, South America was where the UFO action was, especially Brazil. For years, this region had seen its share of bizarre UFO activity. Now, on January 16, 1958, one of the best-documented UFO sightings took place at Brazil's Trindade Isle. While aboard the International Geophysical Year naval survey ship *Almirante Saldanha*, many people saw a gray, metallic, and solid-looking object, partially enveloped in a green haze. A ring ran through its midsection, making it resemble the planet Saturn. A professional photographer took three photographs, which the Brazilian navy ministry subjected to careful analysis before pronouncing the negatives and photos genuine. Under the order of Brazil's president, Juszelino Kubitschek, they were released to the press with a statement that the photographed object was not a meteorological object, balloon, or a U.S. guided missile. A Brazilian naval source later told Olavo Fontes that the day before the sighting, the ship's radar had tracked an unknown object at 2:30 A.M. Many years later, the photographer stated that just before the object appeared, the ship lost electrical power.

This incident received a great deal of attention in Brazil, and that nation's House of Representatives demanded an investigation from its navy. The navy complied and delivered a top secret report of its investigation to the Congress. That document in turn leaked in late 1964 to Coral Lorenzen. The report's author concluded that

the existence of personal reports and photographic evidence, of certain value considering the circumstance involved [absence of evidence of tampering, the presence of other witnesses], permit the admission that there are indications of the existence of unidentified aerial objects.

Compelling evidence notwithstanding, Menzel and the U.S. Air Force each supplied a debunking explanation.[69]

Trindade Isle was the best known, but by no means only, UFO report that year from South America. Most of these were reported by private citizens throughout the continent, many were at close range by multiple witnesses (including law enforcement), several involved automotive electrical disturbances and intense heat, a few included sightings of humanoid beings, and one involved an object with portholes hovering over the sea for more than an hour. On May 5, in San Carlos, Uruguay, a veteran pilot reported "intense heat and electromagnetic effect" from a disc-shaped UFO that hovered over his plane near the Curbelo Naval Base. On July 22, 1958, a major blackout occurred in Salta, Argentina, while a large UFO was observed.[70]

In Brazil, the banks of the Peropava River in Iguape (near the Sao Paulo Province), became the location of a UFO sighting on the afternoon of October 31, 1958. Twelve people heard a loud roar overhead, accompanied by metallic clanking sounds. A shiny disc, about fifteen feet in diameter and four feet thick at the center, approached the river erratically. The people watched the craft crash into the trunk of a palm tree, gouging out a notch. It hovered briefly over the river, then plunged in. The river was fifteen feet deep at the point of entry, and very muddy. A loud hissing noise followed, and bubbles surged up. Police and investigators interviewed witnesses and, for two weeks, searched in vain for the craft.[71]

Elsewhere in the world, UFO activity was considerably less intense. On January 26, 1958, in Shimada City, Japan, several chemical workers saw a very bright object land, and claimed that beings fell from the sky without parachutes. They wore strange suits and spoke an unknown language. In Korea on March 8, American air force radar tracked a slowly descending UFO. On April 11, a Danish fighter pilot near Jutland saw a UFO formation. The objects accelerated away when he tried to close. The pilot's commanding officer then broadcast an appeal to Danish citizens to report any strange flying object they saw. On August 3, a large section of Rome, Italy, was blacked out while a luminous and large UFO maneuvered overhead. In Switzerland on August 16, about a dozen people were out on Lake Leman in perfect weather when they saw a bright light descending. They stopped their boat as the object hovered fifty feet over them. It looked like a classic flying saucer: about thirty-five feet in diameter, an upper half with a cabin and windows, and an outer spinning portion. The craft was silent and created a current in the water as it approached. After several "leaps," it flew off at an amazing speed.[72]

An incident somewhere in the Soviet Union was said to have occurred on November 17, at 10 P.M. A bright object, with an apparent diameter greater than that of the full moon, was observed for two minutes descending from a high altitude, hovering at tree height, then landing. CIA files record a UFO incident along the Soviet-Indian border that took place on December 6, 1958.

According to the files, an "artificial object having a continuous brightness of magnitude" was seen through a telescope traveling north to south. Although the observer originally thought the object was *Sputnik III*, "subsequent observations proved [this to be] negative." The report requested an evaluation by the Air Force Office of Special Investigations. Regarding the report's distribution, it noted "Field dissemination: none."[73]

Meanwhile, in America, all was quiet, and Blue Book files listed only ten officially unidentified sightings for all of 1958. Although some of this probably reflected an actual drop-off in UFO activity, the greatly increased censorship also contributed. One NICAP report described an encounter during the summer at an unnamed air force base in the southwestern United States, in which two maneuvering UFOs evaded jet interceptors. At Offutt AFB in Omaha, Nebraska, on September 8, an air force major and other officers saw a rocket-like UFO accompanied by satellite objects.[74] The CIA also maintained an interest and genuine puzzlement over UFOs. On October 1, 1958, an unknown author of a CIA memo wrote of a civilian who had managed repeatedly to photograph "geometrically shaped flying objects as they passed between his telescope and this moon." These photos were "remarkably clear and certainly indicated a phenomenon for which he had no ready explanation." The writer requested advice on "how we might get our hands on these materials to examine them firsthand and to make a more complete analysis of them."[75]

Perhaps the most interesting event in America from 1958 occurred on October 26 in Lock Raven, near Baltimore. Two men saw a large, disc-shaped object, about one hundred feet wide, hanging between 100 and 150 feet off the top of a bridge over a lake. They drove to investigate and reached to within seventy-five feet of the object. At that point, the car's electrical system died, and one of the men felt a burning sensation. The object rose vertically and quickly disappeared. Investigators uncovered corroborating testimony from several other witnesses, and Blue Book announced it as unexplained. Another interesting case took place on the afternoon of November 3, in Minot, North Dakota, when a master sergeant and medic named William Butler saw a bright green object shaped like a dime. He also saw a smaller, silver object. The first object exploded, whereupon the second object rapidly moved toward the location of the first one. The entire sighting lasted one minute; it remained unexplained by Blue Book.[76]

THE MCCORMACK COMMITTEE FIASCO AND AFTERMATH

Although UFOs were scarce in 1958, NICAP continued to make waves. During the summer, after Congress had adjourned, Keyhoe learned from a congressman that NICAP was "in a big fight—big league." The congressman warned Keyhoe: "Don't let up for a second. Keep boring in with facts, facts, more facts, and you'll break this open." Keyhoe never got the chance to do so. In August, Congressman John McCormack's House Subcommittee on Atmospheric Phenomena (part of the House Select Committee on Astronautics and Space Exploration) requested a briefing on UFOs. McCormack wanted an extended hearing in closed secret session, unrecorded, with all witness names held in confidence. Even this level of secrecy was insufficient for the air force. Instead, Blue Book Captain Gregory persuaded the subcommittee to allow the air force to give a briefing, while allowing outside people like Menzel, Ruppelt, and Keyhoe to offer their opinions. NICAP as a whole should be ignored, he emphasized. The subcommittee took the recommendation, and the main witnesses turned out to be official air force policymakers such as Gregory and Tacker. The subcommittee commended Gregory for his presentation on Blue Book's "improved" methods. Of the outsiders invited, only Keyhoe opposed the official air force line, and his effect seems to have been nil.[77]

The McCormack committee was Captain Gregory's final service toward debunking and defusing the UFO problem. In October 1958, Maj. Robert Friend succeeded him as Blue Book chief. Friend was a trained physicist and less hostile to UFO reports than Gregory. Although he improved Blue Book's filing methods, and supported changing Blue Book policies toward greater acceptance of UFO reports, he received little outside support. About this time, an air force fact sheet stated that recent refinements in its investigative procedures had reduced unsolved sightings to 1.8 percent. The refinement came mainly from lumping "probable" and even "possible" cases into "identified." The fact sheet also mentioned the Robertson Panel for the first time publicly, although it passed over the Panel's recommendation regarding UFO debunking.[78]

During the fall of 1958, air force intelligence officers ordered a staff study to reevaluate its UFO program and public relations. The staff labeled Keyhoe a "political adventurist" and stated—incorrectly—that Ruppelt was affiliated with NICAP. The two represented "a formidable team from which plenty of trouble can be expected." This had been true a year earlier, when Ruppelt still opposed the air force line, but it was certainly true no longer. In any case, the staff decided that the air force lacked credibility regarding UFOs, needed to respond more quickly to reports, and needed to become more sophisticated in its UFO investigations. ATIC tentatively approved the plan, but the air force dropped it. The study's recommendations, which were simultaneous with air force claims of *greater* sophistication regarding UFO investigations, show perfectly that the air force deliberately lied to Congress regarding UFOs, and that Congress allowed itself to be duped with frightening ease.[79]

FIGHTING A LOSING BATTLE

The failure of Congress to do anything productive about ending UFO secrecy did not reflect the wishes of citizens who were directly affected by it. On December 22, 1958, came the report that 450 airline pilots had signed a petition—alas, futile—protesting the official policy of debunking UFO sightings. This was an extraordinary and unheard-of development. One pilot described the policy as "a lesson in lying, intrigue, and the 'Big Brother' attitude carried to the ultimate extreme." Of the signatories, over fifty had personally reported UFO sightings (!) but had been told by the air force they were mistaken. Even so, the air force still warned them that they faced up to ten years in prison under JANAP 146 if they revealed details of their sightings to the media.[80]

The ability of the air force and its allies to disable the movement against UFO secrecy was most impressive. It was certainly not above playing dirty pool: back in 1957 *someone*—most probably the NSA—was behind the attempt to feed NICAP false information in order to discredit it. During 1958, the air force exerted heavy-handed, but effective, control over television to censor Keyhoe, was deft and deceptive in managing the press and Congress, and—in the case of Ruppelt—seems to have disabled a key individual who threatened its position on UFOs. Not a bad year.

The trend continued in 1959. In retrospect, it is astonishing that Keyhoe entertained the idea of besting his nemesis, "The Silence Group." He was going up against an organization that was into much more than he could dream of. The horrific experiments conducted by the army and CIA at Edgewood Arsenal and McGill University, unchecked by any responsible authority, only got worse. By 1959, LSD was a sideshow compared with another chemical: quinunclidinyl benzilate, or BZ. Incredibly, this drug possessed effects far more profound than LSD and which lasted for three days, although effects lasting as long as six days occurred at times. Between 1959 and 1975, an estimated 2,800 U.S. soldiers were given BZ at Edgewood Arsenal. About this time, Jose Delgado invented a device he called the stimoceiver. This was a miniature depth electrode able to receive and transmit electronic signals over FM radio waves. By stimulating a correctly positioned stimoceiver, an outside operator could wield a surprising degree of control over the subject responses.[81]

Writing of such developments in a book about UFOs is no mere exercise in paranoia. Such tools of mind control, developed and used by the American national security state, show what these official branches of the American government were capable of. We must assume that inventions such as Delgado's were not merely drawing room experiments done for reasons of pure science. Inventions such as these had to be field tested. Against whom? Probably, as we have seen elsewhere, against hapless prisoners, minorities, and unsuspecting patriotic soldiers. It is maddening but true that the full dimension of this history will never be revealed. We shall never know whether an important or prominent person *really* died from an ordinary heart attack at just the wrong time. We can never know if someone lost their mind because of the inscrutable workings of their brain chemistry, or because the CIA made them lose it. Because America's official culture pretends that such realities do not exist, even stating these as possibilities places one into the crackpot paranoia category of public discourse. But the fact is that from the 1950s onward, and with increasing effectiveness with each passing year, America's national security groups developed effective, and wholly secret, means of disabling individuals as well as large groups.

All this is a separate issue from whether or not such techniques were ever used against people in the UFO field. Surely, however, if the government deemed it fit to experiment upon patriotic and trusting soldiers, may one at least assume they would have had fewer qualms about using such means against irritating pests within the UFO arena? We must realize, of course, that in matters such as this, "proof" will never, ever arise. One is left only with suspicion.

By 1959, President Eisenhower himself had many suspicions over the motives and activities of this sprawling national security apparatus. In February, he expressed his reservations about American nuclear strategy to Gordon Gray, his national security assistant and alleged MJ-12 member. If we blow up the Soviet Union, said Ike, "there just might be nothing left of the Northern Hemisphere." Eisenhower's qualms aside, he did little or nothing to stop the train, which received a strong push on January 1, 1959, when Fidel Castro led his triumphant procession into Havana. Just hours before, American-backed dictator Fulgencio Batista had fled into exile with $300 million in cash, mainly bribes from Havana's Mafia-run gambling casinos. Castro soon made himself America's Public Enemy No. 1 by expropriating about $1 billion in American assets, possibly the single most popular act in Cuban history, but the one which earned him decades of assassination attempts by the CIA. With a communist amid America's longtime realm of control, there was no way on earth Eisenhower could consider slowing down America's national security locomotive.[82]

Back to the matter of UFOs. The recent air force successes had prompted its hope of cleansing itself once and for all of this issue and eliminating the UFO from public consideration. One noteworthy civilian UFO organization, Civilian Saucer Intelligence of New York, folded in 1959. In February 1959, the air force held several policy meetings to review the UFO situation and ATIC's overall approach. Hynek brought together several ATIC and Blue Book staffers in a series of meetings. They agreed to phase out the phrase "unidentified flying objects" and to reevaluate their older cases "in light of greater scientific knowledge." Of course, this simply meant retroactively debunking previously unexplained sightings. The group met at various intervals during the year and trailed off in 1960.[83]

SOME THOUGHTS ON J. ALLEN HYNEK[84]

Considering Hynek's later reputation as the "Galileo" of UFO research, his complicity in publicly debunking UFOs for years cannot be ignored. Hynek's own justification is well known: in order to retain access to official UFO reports, he could not afford to risk an open confrontation with the air force. Hynek made these claims as a matter of self-defense, years after the fact in the 1970s, after he had been criticized by nearly everyone in the UFO field as an air force lackey. That this was Hynek's reputation in the 1950s and 1960s seems all but forgotten today.

Jacques Vallee worked very closely with Hynek for years during the 1960s and eventually concluded that "the air force kept Hynek around only as long as he was silent." This is certainly true. The question is, *why* did Hynek keep silent? Was it because he was an unassertive type of person—that is, because of a feature of his personality? Nearly all UFO researchers who have written about Hynek say, in effect, yes, for all of his scientific virtues, he was not a fighter—an unfortunate but all too human weakness.

A detached analysis of the historical record does not justify this conclusion.

Generally speaking, Hynek *was* a genial man who did not seek out open confrontations. This, in fact, was one of the important traits that made him valuable to national security interests. In the first place, Hynek was much more than a mere civilian scientist who "helped out" the air force. From 1942 to 1946, Hynek took a leave of absence from Ohio State University to work at the Johns Hopkins University in Silver Springs, Maryland. While there, he was in charge of document security for the highly classified project sponsored by the navy to develop a radio proximity fuse. Along with radar and the atomic bomb, this is often considered one of the three great scientific developments of the war. The device was a radio-operated fuse designed to screw into the nose of a shell and timed to explode at any desired distance from target.[85]

Many scientists, of course, performed work for the defense establishment during World War Two. But Hynek's project was of considerable importance, and it does not appear that his main contribution was scientific: after all, he was an astrophysicist. Rather, one of his main efforts was in a security-related area.

Vallee kept a diary during the period that he worked with Hynek. It was published in 1992 as *Forbidden Science*, long after Hynek was dead and enshrined as the "father of scientific ufology." When read with care, Vallee's observations make it clear that there was much more to J. Allen Hynek than initially met the eye. And yet, the UFO research community has continued to ignore the implications, and even the plain facts, that Vallee related.

For example, rumors had abounded through the 1960s that Blue Book was a public relations facade, and that there was a "secret study" of UFOs going on. Vallee, too, had his suspicions and broached this subject with Hynek every so often. Hynek inevitably rejected such opinions without reservation. Blue Book, Hynek maintained, was the real thing, albeit a project that was being done incompetently. Vallee was never quite convinced. He noticed Hynek's cagey attitude about UFOs, that he seemed to know much more than he usually let on about the subject, that he often appeared to be more interested in self-promotion than actual study of the problem, and that his personal records were in a state of near disaster. Then Vallee found the infamous "Pentacle Memorandum" in Hynek's office. This was a highly classified document from January 1953, proving the existence of a separate study group of UFOs, and urging that the Robertson Panel be delayed until *they* had come to their own conclusions. Very strong stuff. In the mid-1960s, there was still no inkling among the wider public that there was any such study as this. Understandably, Vallee agonized before broaching this topic.

On another occasion, a colleague of Vallee and Hynek showed Vallee "some very interesting photographs taken from an airplane." Here is the relevant passage:

> "Do you know who took these? Allen did! But he hasn't recorded the place, the date or the time. . . . " It turns out Allen was aboard an airliner when he suddenly noticed a white object at his altitude, seemingly flying at the same speed as the plane. He made sure it wasn't a reflection and he convinced himself it must be some faraway cloud with an unusual shape. He pulled out his camera "to see how fast he could snap pictures." In all, he took two pairs of stereoscopic photographs and gave it no more thought.

The photographs themselves appeared in a book authored by Hynek and Vallee in 1975, *The Edge of Reality*. They may or may not be of a flying saucer, but they are certainly not clouds. The importance of stereoscopic photographs cannot be overemphasized. Such a camera is of outstanding evidentiary value. Hynek, in effect, had captured a possible Holy Grail on film. But what happened? Vallee continued:

> Fred only learned about this a few weeks later. But then Hynek had lost the negatives and one shot from every pair was missing. . . . Naturally the loss of the negatives makes it impossible to determine whether it was really a cloud or not. Fred is indignant: "Sometimes I have the feeling Allen doesn't want to know," he says.

Hynek, who had headed document security for the proximity fuse project, "lost" one (and only one) negative from such a set as this. One might well wonder, to whom did he actually pass this material?

During another conversation, Hynek mentioned to Vallee that the air force had sent him a new contract draft. He did not know whether or not he should sign it and gave it to Vallee to read. Vallee wrote:

> The contract, I was surprised to read, was not really with the air force but with the Dodge Corporation, a subsidiary of McGraw-Hill. "What's McGraw-Hill doing in the middle of all this?" I asked, without trying to hide my bafflement. "Is that some sort of cutout?" "Oh, they are just contractors to the Foreign Technology Division," Hynek replied. "By working through companies like McGraw-Hill, which is a textbook publisher, it's easier for them to hire professors and scholars to conduct some intelligence activities, keeping up with Soviet technology, for example. Many academics would be nervous saying they were working for the Foreign Technology Division." The contract clearly puts Hynek under the administrative supervision of a man named Sweeney, who is not a scientist. And it clearly specifies Hynek's task as *evaluating* [original emphasis] the sightings of unknown objects to determine if they represent a danger for the security of the United States.

Hynek's substantial air force money was passed to him through a third party. Thus, Hynek's relationship with "security" continued right through the 1960s. We also learn from Vallee that Hynek, despite his monthly trips to Wright-Patterson AFB, almost never saw Blue Book chief Hector Quintanilla, but was received personally by the commander, who usually took him to lunch at the officers' club. When Vallee asked Hynek what they talked about, Hynek replied, "innocently," the weather and foreign cuisine.

The preceding passage raises other unanswered questions, such as how many other academics were receiving cutout money to hide their intelligence value. Hynek's remarks implied that he knew a lot about this topic, but unfortunately the conversation appeared to stop dead at that point. One might also wonder, who was Sweeney? And, since Hynek was being funded through one cutout organization, why not two (not at all an unusual intelligence practice)? That is, was the air force itself a cutout for another organization? This is currently an unanswerable question, but well worth asking in light of the clear evidence that the CIA was a major—perhaps *the* major—player behind the scenes in the UFO mystery.

Another interesting and generally ignored fact about Hynek was the close relationship he had with Donald Menzel. The astronomical community has always been small, and of course it is not surprising that, aside from the issue of UFOs, the two men would know each other well. But this relationship was more than a simple professional acquaintance. From 1955 to 1960, for instance, Hynek was associate director of the Smithsonian Institution's Astrophysics Observatory in Cambridge, Massachusetts, and headed its optical satellite tracking program. During this period he also lectured at Harvard University. Menzel, meanwhile, had been a full professor at Harvard since 1938 and was the most prestigious astrophysicist in North America. For all intents and purposes, Menzel *was* Harvard's astronomy department. While Hynek was in town, Menzel was full director of the Harvard observatory, and (as Vallee noted in passing) was *Hynek's mentor*. On one occasion, Hynek declined to write a foreword for Menzel's book. One assumes, then, that Menzel asked in the first place.[86]

When considering the public opposition the two occasionally had (such as their participation in a scientific debate on UFOs in late 1952), this closeness seems out of place. But the public view is often the misleading view. Menzel, of course, was not merely one of the world's leading astronomers. He was a man tightly connected to the upper levels of the American national security community and personally close to Vannevar Bush. During the war, Menzel chaired the Radio Propagation Committee of the Joint and Combined Chiefs of Staff and the Section of Mathematical and Physical Research of U.S. Naval Communications. He was a top-level cryptologist who had a long-standing association with the National Security Agency, possessed a Navy Top Secret Ultra security clearance, consulted for thirty companies on classified projects, and worked for the CIA. Through the entire 1950s, Menzel was still a serving intelligence officer.

Revelations such as these are especially important when one considers how sanitized Hynek's treatment continues to be at the hands of most writers in the UFO field. Indeed, even Menzel is sanitized. Jerome Clark, for instance, claimed that Menzel's secret government work "does not significantly differentiate him from many other elite scientists of his generation."[87] There is some truth in this statement, but the larger picture is missed. What matters is that the surface and undercurrent move in different directions. In the 1950s, as today, UFOs were a topic of great secrecy. They were *important*. In this context, the classified lives of men like Hynek and Menzel matter a very great deal. These were men strongly connected with the topic of UFOs, who by their outward appearance were at antipodes. Yet, below the surface, many commonalities existed.

Hynek's defenders have remained at the surface, claiming that his position on UFOs evolved over the years from skeptic to believer. Such a simple transition is unlikely. For years, Hynek had access to classified air force UFO reports. Many of those reports were unusual and unconventional—as Hynek himself stated years after the fact—and the air force official explanations for many of these were clearly absurd. Yet, for year after year, he did nothing. Even followers in good faith might ask, what took him so long?

Hynek's remarks and insights, provided years later, remain of value to the UFO researcher. But the careful reader must remain mindful of Hynek's history in this subject. It is a history that, depending upon which character flaw was his correct one, leads any serious researcher into a stance of wariness regarding J. Allen Hynek.

1959 UNFOLDS

While Hynek played along with the air force's UFO program, others spoke out more openly about UFOs. On January 1, 1959, Wernher von Braun, the greatest scientist in aerospace history, made this statement in reference to the deflection of the U.S. *Juno 2* rocket from its orbit:

> We find ourselves faced by powers which are far stronger than we had hitherto assumed, and whose base is at present unknown to us. More I cannot say at present. We are now engaged in entering into closer contact with those powers, and in six or nine months' time it may be possible to speak with more precision on the matter.

Von Braun said this while he was in Germany during the holiday season. He never followed up on it, and no further information is available on it. A one-time slip up?[88]

The year 1959 provided some interesting moments in the history of the UFO. An incredible story came from none other than Blue Book chief Robert Friend. In a 1974 interview, Friend related an account that he claimed occurred in 1959, concerning a Maine woman who was in "contact" with UFOs. The Canadian government learned of this and sent Wilbert Smith to investigate. The U.S. Navy also sent two officers, and eventually the CIA invited her to Langley. After she demonstrated her trance technique, one of the CIA officers apparently made contact. When others in the room asked for proof, the officer replied "look out the window." To everyone's astonishment, a UFO was plainly visible and was also being tracked by radar at Washington National Airport. Friend said the CIA briefed him on this incident, and he claimed to have sat in on an uneventful trance session. Blue Book never analyzed the development, while the CIA took punitive action against the officer and transferred all relevant people elsewhere.[89]

On January 11, Wilbert Smith spoke about UFOs in Ottawa before the Illuminating Engineering Society, Canadian Regional Conference. "Various items of 'hardware' are known to exist," he stated to the audience, "but are usually clapped into security and are not available to the general public."[90]

NICAP, still reeling from the failures of 1958, struggled to find direction. Early in 1959, Keyhoe received a lead from Delmar Fahrney, now out of NICAP but still helpful, on a hidden report regarding Navy Commander George Benten and a UFO encounter from 1956. That spring, he met with Hillenkoetter at the New York Yacht Club to discuss NICAP strategy. The secrecy was tighter than ever, Keyhoe told the admiral correctly, and Air Force Public Information Officer Lawrence Tacker even sent NICAP a "sharp letter" telling them to stop writing members of the air force and to confine all questions to his office. (NICAP ignored this request.) Meanwhile, the air force continued to fight strenuously against NICAP's efforts for congressional hearings on UFOs. Keyhoe also told Hillenkoetter that three scientists had privately reported UFO sightings to a particular congressman. Hillenkoetter said, "we'll have to do something to speed things up."[91]

THE KILLIAN CASE AND OTHER NOTEWORTHIES

At 8:20 P.M. on February 24, 1959, another commercial airliner had an unusual encounter with a UFO. Veteran pilot Capt. Peter W. Killian was flying an American Airlines plane in excellent visibility over Bradford, Pennsylvania, at 8,500 feet and 350 mph. Killian noticed three bright lights south of his plane, in a precise line. As first he assumed it was Orion, until he realized these were not stars, and he could see Orion higher up in the sky. As Killian pondered this, one of the objects abruptly left the formation and approached the plane, slowed down before Killian took evasive action, then rejoined the other two. Although unable to discern a distinctive shape, he believed the object to be huge—at least three times the size of his plane.

Killian alerted his copilot, John Dee, to the objects. Then, in a most unusual decision, he opened the plane's intercom to make a "calm announcement" about the objects. He reasoned that warning the passengers now would be better than risking a full-blown panic. After Killian personally calmed one jittery passenger who was brought to the cockpit, one of the UFOs again approached the plane and then rejoined the others. Killian put out a radio call to other pilots. Moments later, an American Airlines captain flying north of Erie stated, "We've been watching the formation for ten minutes." After this, another American Airlines pilot, near Toledo, also called in to report the sighting. It was soon learned that three United Airlines crews also saw the formation. Before landing in Detroit, Killian reported the sighting to the airport there, intending to keep the story quiet. One of his passengers, however, was an aviation expert who spoke to the Detroit press about the sighting. After the story broke, Killian received permission from American Airlines to discuss the sighting, and the story was carried across the country.

Without bothering to investigate or even review the evidence, the air force entered the picture three days later, stating that Killian saw Orion through broken clouds. On the following day, an air force spokesman described some UFO observers as people "who can't remember anything when they sober up next day." Killian fired back strongly. The clouds, he said, were 3,500 feet *below* the plane. Also, he and the other witnesses saw Orion and the objects at the same time, repeatedly. Keyhoe asked Killian if he would tell this to a congressional committee. "I certainly would!" Killian replied. Meanwhile, American Airlines appeared to be backing Killian and reprinted the account in its magazine.

The air force's vapid Orion explanation caused a loss of credibility. Therefore, on March 20, air force spokesman Lawrence Tacker officially retracted it. Instead of Orion, he said, the pilots had seen the wholly ordinary spectacle of B-47 bombers refueling in flight from a KC-97 tanker. The press ran this without comment or critique, and ridicule about "little green men" began to reach Killian. He did not take the comment lying down. "I don't care what the air force says," the New York media quoted him. He knew exactly what B-47s looked like during refueling, he said. He knew the KC-97 tanker and how many lights it had. He stated again that the objects "were at least three times the size of any tanker or bomber we have. They could travel at 2,000 mph. And they were *not* conventional aircraft." It was unusual for an airline pilot to continue so brazenly to defy the air force. Ryan and Neff, only three years prior, had kept their mouths shut following an even more spectacular incident. But the arrogance of the air force had forced Killian to defend himself.

Killian's defiant stance gave Keyhoe hope that a congressional investigation might come out of all this. As was too often the case, however, Keyhoe was overly optimistic. NICAP member Lou Corbin told him that Maryland Congressman Sam Friedel was "all set to hop on this Killian business." Keyhoe began to plan for Killian to meet with Friedel and even to get Senator Barry Goldwater involved for a "red-hot press conference." As planned, Corbin did meet with Friedel. Then, on March 27, Keyhoe learned from Killian's wife that he had been silenced by the air force. According to Mrs. Killian, he was under strict orders not to "meet or talk with anyone about what he saw." It so happened that Friedel had agreed to allow Killian to testify as part of a new congressional UFO investigation, but that Killian would have to make the first move; Friedel would not subpoena him. When Killian told a U.S. Senator that he would not risk losing his job by volunteering to testify, the issue became dead at once. Neither Senate nor House was willing to fight the air force. Soon after, the air force released this statement by Killian: "Having never seen night refueling of jets by a tanker, I suppose that could be what we saw." Keyhoe was appalled but helpless.[92]

Several intriguing UFO encounters were occurring overseas early in the year. Several of these were monitored by the CIA, such as an encounter from January 20 in Stigsjoe, Sweden. A craft twenty to twenty-five feet in diameter, surrounded by a glowing ring, approached a group of people at Lake Laangsjoen and was observed for three minutes. UFOs were seen in Britain, too. In January, a landing and paralysis incident was reported in Stratford-upon-Avon.[93] On February 26, four witnesses at London Airport, including a traffic control officer, saw a UFO through binoculars. An RAF description reported: "Bright yellow light varying in intensity, about two hundred feet above the ground. Stayed in one position for about twenty minutes, then climbed away at great speed." Vallee reported an incident that occurred in

March in which Polish soldiers at the coast near Kolobreg noticed the sea becoming agitated. To their astonishment, a triangular object, each side about twelve feet long, emerged from the water. The object initially circled over the barracks, then zipped away. The CIA noted a UFO sighting involving a procession of bright bodies over Bergen, Norway, that took place on March 12. The next day several Australian witnesses had a ten-minute sighting of a dome-shaped object at a field a quarter mile away. It looked like a huge circus tent with flashing lights. As they approached, the object hovered, then took off at tremendous speed. Investigators from the Woomera Rocket range questioned one of the witnesses. At Australia's Port Elliot on March 31, a man was driving home in the afternoon when he saw a glowing, reddish object with a row of portholes. The object was resting on the ground, was about twenty feet wide. The man drove around a wooded area in time to see it take off. The area was tested for radioactivity, and none found.[94]

America rounded out the early spring with a few odd and ominous sightings of its own. On February 28, Army Private Gerry Irwin stopped his car in Cedar City, Iowa, to investigate what he thought was a crashing plane. He was later found unconscious and treated at an army hospital. He suffered from some amnesia, continued to have fainting spells, and returned more than once to the site in a trancelike state. Soon, Irwin deserted and seemingly disappeared.

On April 1, a radio emergency call came from a C-118 plane with four men aboard ("we've hit something—or something hit us") about an hour after take-off from McChord Field AFB in Tacoma, Washington. Thirty minutes later, the plane crashed into the side of a mountain, leaving no survivors. Although the military sealed off the site, APRO found witnesses who had seen the plane in its final moments. All described two orange or yellowish objects closing in on the plane.[95]

THE STRANGE CASE OF MORRIS JESSUP

Morris K. Jessup wrote several popular books about UFOs. He was the first to use the term "UFO" in a book and was one of the earliest ancient astronaut theorists. In 1955, he published *The Case for the UFO*. Shortly after its publication, a paperback edition of the book was sent anonymously to the chief of the Office of Naval Research in Washington, D.C., filled with handwritten annotations that appeared to reflect a detailed knowledge of UFOs. There were three distinct personalities in the annotations, and it appeared that the book had been passed from person to person, in the form of an extended conversation. Later that year, the Office of Naval Research republished the book—with the annotations. Several hundred copies were then printed by the Varo Corporation in Garland, Texas.

The people at ONR seem to have been impressed by the mysterious annotations. The introduction to the Varo edition stated that the notations implied an "intimate knowledge of UFOs, their means of motion, their origin, background, history, and habits of beings occupying UFOs. . . ." The notes referred to the building of undersea cities and of various types of ships used for transportation. The ONR introduction stated that terms such as mothership, home-ship, dead-ship, great ark, great bombardment, great return, great war, little-men, force-fields, deep freezes, undersea building, measure markers, scout ships, magnetic and gravity fields, sheets of diamond, cosmic rays, force cutters, undersea explorers, inlay work, clear-talk, telepathing, burning, "coat," nodes, vortices, magnetic "net," and many others are used quite naturally by these men.

The navy introduction concluded that the remarks and explanations of the unknown commentators "may be worth consideration."

By early 1956, Jessup received two anonymous, strange letters postmarked from Gainesville, Texas, about sixty miles north of Garland. The author of the letters appeared to be one of the annotators of the book. The letters described something later known as the Philadelphia Experiment. According to the author (who wrote the letter in a bizarre English with copious and cryptic allusions to men of science such as Albert Einstein, Bertrand Russell, and Michael Faraday), the U.S. Navy conducted an experiment involving Einstein's unified field theory in October 1943. In the words of the author (all emphasis in original):

> The "result" was complete invisibility of a ship, Destroyer type, *and all* of its crew, While at Sea. (Oct. 1943) The Field Was effective in an oblate spheroidal shape, extending one Hundred yards (More or Less, due to Lunar position & Latitude) *out* from each beam of the ship. Any Person Within that sphere became vague in form BUT He too observed those Persons aboard *that* ship as though they too were of the same state, yet were walking upon nothing. Any person without that sphere could see Nothing save the clearly *Defined shape of the Ships Hull in the Water* PROVIDING of course, that that person was just close enough to see yet, just barely outside of that field. Why tell you now? Very Simple; If You choose to go Mad, then you would reveal this information. Half of the officers & the crew of that Ship are at Present, Mad as Hatters.

The author added that the ship, after disappearing from the Philadelphia dock, appeared "within minutes" in the Norfolk-Newport News-Portsmouth area of Virginia, and that the experiments were discontinued. The second letter expressed a desire for more work to be done in field theory in order to continue developing "the form of transport that the navy accidentally stumbled upon (to their embarrassment) when their [experimental ship] took off & popped up a minute or so later" in the Chesapeake Bay. According to his good friend Ivan Sanderson, these letters mystified Jessup, but did leave him feeling that there was too much in them to ignore wholly.

Several years later, in October 1958, Jessup met with Sanderson in New York, seeming depressed. He gave Sanderson a Varo edition of his book and asked him to store it safely "in case anything should happen to me." In mid-April of 1959, Jessup wrote a depressed letter to a friend, which Sanderson later read and characterized as "a straight suicide note." On April 20, Jessup was found near death in his car near his home in Coral Gables, Florida, an apparent suicide. A hose was attached to his exhaust pipe and ran into his vehicle through a small crack in a window. He died later that night.

Jessup's death never escaped rumors of murder. The main theory was that Jessup knew too much about the Philadelphia Experiment. Gray Barker made this the theme of his book, *The Strange Case of Dr. M. K. Jessup*, and others followed suit, arguing that the suicide was a frame-up. The author of the Varo notes is now generally believed to be a man named Carl Allen (alias Carlos Allende), after he essentially confessed as much to the Lorenzens in 1969, then recanted. Allende's own parents later described him as a "master leg puller," and his brother called him a "drifter." If this is meant to discredit the notes, it fails to address that the ONR analysis concluded there were three authors. Sanderson, as usual, put it well: If the authors were nothing but crackpots, "where did they dredge up all these facts or allegations . . . requir[ing] many years of research to unearth?" In any case, subsequent research into the Philadelphia Experiment long ago reached a dead end. Barring a radical development, the story will remain a legend attached to a disreputable individual.[96]

THE REVEREND GILL SIGHTING AND ACTIVITY IN THE OCEAN

As the reader should discern by now, UFOs have a long history of being seen in and around large bodies of water, a fact generally unremarked upon by most researchers. (The great exception, of course, is Ivan Sanderson.) Upon reflection, it is easy to see why there should be a large share of UFO activity at sea, and why most people, landlubbers that we are, tend to ignore it. The world's surface is, after all, 70 percent water, and little of it is known below a few hundred feet, even today. Time and again, however, we come across encounters with strange objects at sea. In June 1959, the Argentine navy trapped a large silver object in the harbor at Buenos Aires. It was "shaped like a huge fish," with a tail similar to the vertical stabilizer on a B-17. Divers obtained a good look at it but could not identify it as a submarine; moreover, the object seemed too maneuverable and fast to be a sub.[97]

In late June occurred yet another "classic" sighting, out in the remote region of Papua, New Guinea. Actually, it was a series of encounters over

June 26 and 27, 1959, and involved multiple, close-up sightings of a hovering UFO craft, with much mutual waving and seemingly goodwill exchanged. The main witness was the Rev. William Booth Gill, a respected man on the island, known by all as scrupulously honest and decent. On the evening of the twenty-sixth, Gill, accompanied by thirty-eight witnesses, saw a shining object at around 6:45 P.M., hovering in the air at about three hundred or four hundred feet. The object was circular and had legs under it, and a bright blue light shone from the craft upwards into the sky. Everyone also saw four figures on what appeared to be a deck.

The visitors returned the next night at about 6 P.M. Father Gill quickly arrived on the scene, along with many others. Again, they saw four figures on top of the ship, and this time saw two smaller craft nearby. In Father Gill's detailed account of the incident (an eleven-page, single-spaced report signed by over twenty-five witnesses):

> [T]wo of the figures seemed to be doing something near the center of the deck. They were occasionally bending over and raising their arms as though adjusting or setting up something (not visible). One figure seemed to be standing, looking down at us.

At this point, Father Gill waved to the figures. To everyone's surprise, the figures waved back. A teacher among the witnesses then raised both of her arms and waved, and two of the figures did the same. The mutual waving went on for some time. When it became dark, Father Gill used a flashlight to make a series of movements toward the craft, and the craft eventually made several wavering motions back and forth.

The Rev. Norman E. G. Cruttwell (not present) who investigated the event wrote that

> the facts of this sighting and the waving by the men and the responses to the [flashlight] signals are fully corroborated by . . . many of the other witnesses in personal interview with myself.

Cruttwell also reported that between June 26 and 28, there were several UFO sightings at nearby Giva, Baniara, and Sideia. Allen Hynek also interviewed Gill some fifteen years later and found him to be completely credible.

Donald Menzel and Philip Klass wrote debunking pieces on the sighting. Menzel did not impugn Gill's integrity, but theorized that the whole thing was an optical illusion of the planet Venus caused by Gill's bad eyesight. The malleable natives merely wanted to impress "their Great White Leader" who had a "god-like" status with them. True to form, Klass did impugn Gill's character. He claimed that the reverend invented or imagined the encounter in order to please Cruttwell. Considering the incredible nature of the claims, it is interesting that these were the most damaging arguments skeptics could come up with.[98]

The expanses of the Pacific Ocean continued to be the scene of UFO activity that summer. On July 11, 1959, about nine hundred miles northeast of Hawaii, a Pan Am Airways crew saw a strange craft with satellite objects make sharp turns. For a time, the crew feared the possibility of a collision, although the air force privately told interested congressmen that the crew only saw a meteor. Just two days later, a farm woman in Blenheim, New Zealand, saw a domed disc descend and hover. She said it was about thirty-five feet in diameter, had two intense, green lights and two rows of jets around the rim, and gave off orange flames. She also claimed to see two men in metallic suits inside a clear dome. The craft took off rapidly with a high-pitched sound, giving off heat. The next day, July 14, a group of hunters on Australia's Prince of Wales Island saw a red object land on the island. Other hunters claimed to see a similar object nearby.[99]

GETTING UP-CLOSE AND PERSONAL

The nature of UFO sightings changed from the 1940s to the late 1950s. Reports in the 1950s continued, as in the previous decade, to describe impossible objects seen in the sky. Increasingly, however, they also included vivid descriptions of craft at close range, encounters with the beings operating them, and physical effects. The phenomenon had always been global but somewhat dominated by American sightings from 1947 to 1954. After 1954, however, quality reports came in large numbers from around the world, often overshadowing the American reports.

In 1959, the trend continued and provided some remarkable alleged encounters, in particular during the late summer. On August 9, in Sombrero, Tierra del Fuego, a petroleum engineer and two other witnesses stopped their car when they ran out of gas; they then saw a large, bright light descending like a pendulum, making a swishing sound. One of the men aimed a rifle at it, but the object zoomed away. In Brion, Spain, on August 12, a farmer saw an object land in a pasture, take off vertically, and fly away. On the thirteenth, in Freeport, Texas, a bright, low-flying object passed over a car, whose engine stalled, and landed in a wooded area. Six people in two separate groups saw the object and called the police, although the dense underbrush prevented an investigation. On August 17, a low-flying UFO appeared to cause a power interruption in Minas Gerais, Brazil. Late morning on August 25, in Werdehl-Eveking, Germany, a man approached a bright object in a forest but fainted when he got too close. As he regained consciousness, it took off silently and vertically. It was round, had a tripod landing gear, two rows of bright openings, and was about one hundred feet in diameter. On September 7, in Wallingford, Kentucky, a postal worker saw a bluish, disc-shaped object at ground level; it flew away horizontally, leaving a stained ring on the ground.[100]

Meanwhile, the air force once again reassigned UFO investigative duties. In July 1959, the 1127th Field Activities Group stationed at Fort Belvoir, Virginia, replaced the 1006th AISS as the main field investigative unit. According to Jacobs, the group made few investigations. In September, AFR-200-2 went through another revision, which again emphasized that "unidentifieds" must be reduced to a minimum—something which had been the policy for quite some time.[101]

REDMOND, OREGON: SIX JETS ATTEMPT AN INTERCEPT

The extraordinary UFO encounter at Redmond, Oregon, of September 24, 1959, discussed at length in this book's introduction, contained all the ingredients that make the UFO story so compelling: (1) a multiple-witness, visual sighting of an object that defied conventional explanation; (2) clear tracking on multiple radars; (3) a serious and daring attempt by the air force to intercept the object, in this case with six F-102 jets; (4) strong indications that the military forcibly silenced the personnel involved; (5) continued stonewalling and deception on the part of the air force to explain the incident away, ending with the classic of all debunking solutions: the planet Venus; (6) the work of civilian UFO organizations—in this case, NICAP—to obtain documentation (FAA logs) that disproved the air force claims; (7) the loss of air force credibility to everyone involved in the incident; and (8) the mixed nature of success in covering up the incident—not enough to prevent it from reaching the attention of outside snoops who could then write about it, but enough to keep it from becoming a problem in the media or Congress.[102]

Fundamentally, the encounter provided more evidence that the military took UFOs very seriously and was doing everything possible to stifle all information about them—in short, that the government was hiding something big about UFOs.

Four days after the Redmond incident, on September 28, ATIC issued a report reassessing its UFO role. It recommended that the UFO program be transferred to an air force division with better scientific capabilities, which could then implement an active public relations campaign with the goal of "the eventual elimination of the program as a special project." This did not mean that the air force would stop receiving UFO reports, but would merely eliminate Project Blue Book and the public dimension of the problem. ATIC's problem now became to convince any other area of the air force to take the program, and none were foolhardy enough to agree.[103]

By October, NICAP was again gathering congressional support for a renewed investigation of the air force's censorship over UFOs. Several former air force officers and NCOs provided statements for NICAP. Among them was Lt. Col. Richard T. Headrick, a radar bombing expert who devised key missions during the Second World War:

> Saucers exist (I saw two). They were intelligently flown or operated (evasive tactics, formation flight, hovering). They were mechanisms, not United States weapons, nor Russian. I presume they are extraterrestrial.

Another, Air Force Sgt. James H. Sawyer, stated:

> Many airmen asked for more UFO information; I received strict orders there would be no discussion. I am convinced the unexplained UFOs are guided by advanced, intelligent beings. I believe the censorship is a grave error.

A third, Sgt. Oliver Dean, was also a NICAP member. In 1958, two officers at Kirtland AFB grilled him about his personal UFO investigations. He told NICAP, "I was warned, 'If you continue this, Sergeant Dean, be careful; it can get you into serious trouble.'"

In addition to testimonies such as these, Keyhoe and NICAP collected a number of tentative statements by senators and congressmen favoring UFO hearings, provided such hearings not jeopardize national security. NICAP's leaders also hoped that the Killian case might be a useful instrument in their hands. Ultimately, however, October was just not the right time to push ahead. It was too late in the session to gather enough momentum. Keyhoe learned from one congressman that "you don't have enough support yet to ram it through. Get everything in shape for next year and keep on lining up with more backing."[104]

RUPPELT REVISES HIS BOOK, THEN DIES

Throughout the spring of 1959, Keyhoe and NICAP encountered rumors that Ruppelt, under great pressure, would be revising the conclusion of his 1956 book, *The Report on Unidentified Flying Objects*. The more extreme of these reported that Ruppelt was being forced "to make a right about-face" on UFOs, and to ridicule the phenomenon. In May, Ruppelt phoned Keyhoe from California to inform him that he was bringing his book "up to date" and wanted NICAP's latest information. When Keyhoe asked him how he was getting his latest UFO cases, Ruppelt answered that the air force was giving him full cooperation. Discerning Keyhoe's growing unease, he added that he was still "middle of the road" on the issue. When Keyhoe asked Ruppelt about his debunking-oriented letter from the spring of 1958, Ruppelt—according to Keyhoe—changed the subject and ended the call.

The telephone conversation made Keyhoe uneasy, and he decided to write an open letter to Ruppelt for NICAP's June issue of the *UFO Investigator*. The letter, which listed many of Ruppelt's past statements on UFOs, urged him not to let the air force trick him into falling into an untenable position that, in the end, would only damage his credibility. All was for naught. In December 1959, Frank Edwards obtained an advance copy of Ruppelt's book. He called Keyhoe immediately about it. Ruppelt, said Edwards

> rewrote the last three chapters. It's absolutely incredible. Now he sneers at people he formerly labeled expert witnesses. He plays up the wildest contact stories—completely backs the air force policy line. . . . The writing doesn't even sound like him. And he takes sarcastic cracks at serious investigators, especially NICAP and you.[105]

This was not quite accurate. Ruppelt had not changed anything from his original book. What he had done was *add* three new chapters, each of which debunked the UFO phenomenon as explainable in conventional terms and ridiculous to take seriously. There was no "middle of the road" here, although he did try to maintain the pretense of objectivity by listing some interesting UFO sightings from the mid- and late 1950s. After that, it was all downhill. The new chapters offered a striking contrast to the detached and evenhanded account that characterized Ruppelt's first edition.

After taking several cracks at "saucer fans," Ruppelt directed snide remarks toward Keyhoe and NICAP. While the air force was conducting itself responsibly and scientifically toward UFOs, wrote Ruppelt, "Keyhoe and his hungry NICAPions . . . wanted blood, and that blood had to taste like spaceships or they wouldn't be happy." Such a tone seemed truly incredible, but here was Ruppelt insulting an organization he nearly joined less than two years earlier. NICAP, far from being a detached organization interested in solving the UFO problem, merely "bombarded" busy congressmen and senators who had important work to do but were "polite enough to listen." Ruppelt even smeared Keyhoe personally, repeating supposed rumors that he was accused of "minor social crimes" ("But personally I doubt this," he explained). There was no air force secrecy over UFOs, emphasized Ruppelt. Instead, the air force wanted to keep the nuts at NICAP from rummaging through their files—which surely would result in "proof" that UFOs really were visitors from space.

Ruppelt emphasized the extremely high percentage of solved UFO cases. Directly contradicting statements he had made not long before in private, Ruppelt now repeated the standard air force line:

> [M]ore manpower, better techniques, and just plain old experience has allowed the air force to continually lower the percentage of "unknowns" from twenty percent while I was in charge of Project Blue Book, to less than one percent today.

Ruppelt also spilled much ink on George Adamski and the Contactee movement, essentially lumping them together with serious UFO groups and throwing more discredit upon UFO researchers. He then offered his definitive conclusion that UFOs simply don't exist. Ruppelt was "positive" about this. "There's not even a glimmer of hope for the UFO," he wrote.

Ruppelt easily explained many supposedly unidentified sightings. He debunked the ability of so-called experienced observers and used a number of authorities, including Hynek, to support his position. The Levelland sightings, which at the time prompted him to contradict the air force in public, now turned out to be exactly what the air force claimed all along: St. Elmo's fire. Disregarding the McMinnville, Rouen, or Trindade photos, Ruppelt stated there was no shred of photographic evidence for UFOs "other than meaningless blobs of light." The Lubbock Lights provided the coup de grace, as Ruppelt now explained them as "night-flying moths reflecting the bluishgreen light of a nearby row of mercury vapor street lights." He concluded in resigned fashion that, because of the fanaticism of saucer fans, the world was "stuck with our space age myth—the UFO."[106]

Ruppelt's book shocked the UFO researchers who knew him. Was it really possible that he had changed his mind on the subject in an unforced, honest way? Matters are complicated greatly by the fact that Ruppelt was dead less than a year later, of a second heart attack, while living in Long Beach, California, at the age of thirty-seven. As with Morris Jessup, rumors of suspicious death circulated. We might add, for good reason. First, it must be stated that Ruppelt's conversion to the air force point of view shows all the signs of undue pressure. He worked for Northrop, a major defense contractor, and was therefore subject to pressure from both his current and past employer. Rumors of such pressure had been circulating for years; certainly not proof, but then again, who was starting the rumors? Observe the following scenario:

(1) Ruppelt actively working against UFO secrecy from 1954 through the end of 1957, by which time he had made himself a positive nuisance to the air force, and was considering membership in NICAP; (2) a period in early 1958 when he removed himself from the *Armstrong Theater* program on UFOs, amid rumors of general air force pressure on other participants; (3) strongly debunking statements in private by mid-1958; (4) burned bridges with former colleagues by 1959; (5) death a year later.

Jerome Clark thought little of this sequence. "Ever since [Ruppelt's death]," he wrote, "rumors have circulated that he was forced to recant his earlier more-or-less pro-UFO sympathies. But no evidence to this effect has ever surfaced." With that statement, all is dismissed. Ruppelt's widow, continued Clark, told interviewers that the reasons for this change had nothing to do with pressure. Rather, her husband's continuing association with Blue Book personnel, plus exposure to the Contactee movement in southern California "soured him." And Ruppelt's widow is supposed to be a detached witness for what reason? We are to believe that his "exposure" to the Contactees prompted him publicly to insult Keyhoe, a man whom Ruppelt knew despised Contactees? Ruppelt, who had written such a detached and mature work three years prior, now wrote this sophomoric diatribe because he "soured"? The key lies in Ruppelt's "continuing association" with Blue Book and air force personnel. No doubt, that was a crucial factor, but certainly not the kind implied by Clark. In the context of Ruppelt's recent stance toward the air force on UFOs, his rapid and total conversion, and his death at such a young age, matters *ought* to look suspicious, particularly in the light of the capabilities that existed within the American national security apparatus by this time. Whether he actually was killed, or whether he died from the stress brought on by what he had gone through (the belief of Edwards and Keyhoe), there seems little reason to doubt that Ruppelt was coerced.[107]

1960: SERIOUS BUSINESS

On December 24, 1959, the inspector general of the air force issued the following warning regarding UFOs to every air base commander in the continental U.S.:

> Unidentified flying objects—sometimes treated lightly by the press and referred to as "flying saucers"—must be rapidly and accurately identified as serious USAF business in the ZI [Interior Zone]. . . . Technical and defense considerations will continue to exist in this area.

It also noted that UFO investigators sent out from air bases "should be equipped with binoculars, camera, Geiger counter, magnifying glass, and a source for containers in which to store samples." Samples of what? Once again, it appeared that air force policy on UFOs was inconsistent. Actually, it was not. The air force leadership, we know, *always* considered UFOs of great importance; it was for that reason that it had gone out of its way for years to ridicule the phenomenon in public. The problem had always been, how to track UFOs without it seeming to be important. This included deciding how most air force and military personnel were to deal with the matter. Generally, it was considered best to keep them away from such matters, and ridicule worked well for this. But some response to the problem was needed, and the ridicule policy had caused reporting to become lax. Hence, the "serious business" memo.[108]

The year 1960 brought no shortage of serious business in other realms of secrecy. That year, the National Reconnaissance Office (NRO) was formed. Essentially, the NRO is America's spy satellite department, a Pentagon-CIA-NSA central office that determines surveillance targets. Its existence was not revealed publicly until 1973, and even into the 1990s its name could not be mentioned in Congress or in any unclassified government document. Already in 1960, optics capabilities had become quite advanced. An optics expert that year wrote that it soon should be possible to develop satellite cameras capable of "resolving two objects three inches apart from 125 miles up."[109]

Also in 1960, CIA Director of Plans Richard Bissell asked MK-Ultra Director Sidney Gottlieb to undertake research on assassination techniques. Gottlieb's support of people like Ewen Cameron already placed him in the Mengele class of mad scientists. He was glad to oblige Bissell, and had already developed a perfume that could be sprinkled on pillows and sheets which, upon inhalation, was instantly lethal.[110] Speaking of Cameron, by early 1960 he was taking his sensory deprivation experiments to their ultimate conclusion: the irreversible scrambling of the human mind. Cameron was happy to take CIA money, courtesy of Gottlieb, but he had no need of "expendables" from the agency—he simply used his own patients. Researcher John Marks wrote:

> It cannot be said how many, if any, other agency brainwashing projects reached the extremes of Cameron's work. Details are scarce. In what ways the CIA applied work like Cameron's is not known.[111]

Probably the most significant new CIA project of 1960 was its secret war in Laos, which continued until 1973. This covert operation raised a thirty-thousand-man army, consisting mainly of Meo tribesmen, to fight the communist Pathet Lao. Air America, a CIA airline, provided air support.[112]

Project Paperclip showed that extremely secret programs could continue in the U.S. for well over ten years without a significant leak. Throughout the 1960s, Paperclip (along with National Interest, a similar program), sponsored the arrival of at least 267 more people into America. Another project, known as 63, brought an unknown number of others. These recruits worked everywhere. Among the government-related organizations were NASA, Edgewood Arsenal, Wright-Patterson AFB, Fort Monmouth AFB, and the Naval Ordnance Testing Station in China Lake, California. Private corporations included Pennsylvania State University, MIT, Bell Laboratories, RCA, CBS Laboratories, Martin Marietta, Convair, and Mobil Oil.[113]

In April 1960, worried over the Frankenstein nature of America's military state, President Eisenhower asked the dying Foster Dulles, "How are we going to scale our programs down?" If we did not, suggested Ike, "in the long run, there is nothing but war—if we give up all hope of a peaceful solution."[114]

1960: MONITORING THE UFOS

On the UFO front, the secret state never ceased in its efforts to monitor, and probably undermine, the civilian organizations. In early 1960, Keyhoe published yet another UFO book, *Flying Saucers: Top Secret*. As

always, Keyhoe's narrative style—fast, impetuous, and full of snappy dia-
logue—did not lend credibility to conservative readers. Yet, this made four
books in ten years on the subject, and a careful reading of them provided a
huge cache of information to the serious UFO researcher. No doubt some of
those careful readers were in the air force, CIA, ONR, NSA, and elsewhere.
Despite his busy pace throughout the 1950s, this book would be Keyhoe's last
for another thirteen years. He was now in his sixties, and his NICAP duties
undoubtedly took much of his time. Still, it was obvious that Keyhoe needed
watching. Perhaps coincidentally, in 1960 Col. Joseph J. Bryan III joined
NICAP's board of directors. It would not be known until 1977 that Bryan had
founded and led the CIA's psychological warfare staff. Prior to this, he had
vehemently denied any connection to the agency. Although he made a number of strong pro-UFO statements throughout his history with NICAP, he later
became strongly suspected in helping to facilitate the eventual demise of the
organization, and certainly of Keyhoe's role in it.

APRO, although much less dangerous than NICAP, had become a substantial organization in its own right. By 1960, it had a good investigative
network, both within the U.S. and abroad, including South America, New
Zealand, Australia, and several European countries. Led by Coral and Jim
Lorenzen, APRO differed considerably from NICAP in its indifference to the
drive for congressional hearings and disbelief in an air force cover-up. UFO
organizations, the Lorenzens believed, ought to be conducting investigations,
and NICAP's obsession with a cover-up was a supreme waste of effort.
Despite this entrenched attitude, APRO was also monitored. In 1960, the
Lorenzens moved from Alamogordo, New Mexico, to Tucson, Arizona. On
their third day in Tucson an "exterminator" visited them, offering to inspect
their premises for free. This unusually well-dressed exterminator, with very
polished shoes, failed to mention the name of his company. Although the
Lorenzens were renting, he did not ask for the name of the landlord and did
not seem interested in his profession. He was, however, very interested in
conversing with Coral Lorenzen at length over their reason for moving,
where Jim Lorenzen was employed, and UFOs.[115]

Meanwhile, ATIC sought in vain to transfer the UFO problem to such
places as the Pentagon Information Office, SAFOI, NASA, the Smithsonian
Institution, and the Brookings Institution. Maj. Lawrence Tacker remained
the air force's main public representative on UFOs, and he seemed to become
more sour each year. In 1960, Tacker released a book, *Flying Saucers and the
U.S. Air Force*, a straight promotion of the air force line. He toured the country, appeared on radio and television, and took shots at Keyhoe and NICAP.[116]

Tacker was never anything more than an air force front man, paid and
ordered to be a mouthpiece. The people within the air force generally knew
better than to believe his statements, and certainly this applied to Blue Book
staff. According to Richard Hall, a former Blue Book chief (Robert Friend?)

told him that during the late 1950s and early 1960s time-gun camera films of UFOs were being "routinely" obtained during jet interceptor chases and sent to the CIA's National Photographic Interpretation Center (NPIC) for analysis. The individual also stated that "none of the . . . analysis data in these cases has been released, nor has the existence of these films ever been acknowledged." Although no one said anything about the role of the newly formed NRO, may we at least acknowledge that it was ideally suited for contributing in this area?[117]

On February 27, 1960, Roscoe Hillenkoetter released to the media copies of the air force directive of the previous December about "serious business." He also made a public statement on UFOs, quoted the following day in the Sunday *New York Times*:

> It is time for the truth to be brought out in open congressional hearings. . . . Behind the scenes, high-ranking air force officers are soberly concerned about UFOs. But through official secrecy and ridicule, many citizens are led to believe the unknown flying objects are nonsense. . . . [T]o hide the facts, the air force has silenced its personnel through the issuance of a regulation.

The air force admitted that it had issued the order; it added that the copy was merely part of a seven-page regulation which had been issued to update similar past orders, and that it made no substantive change in policy.[118]

UFO sightings dribbled along in 1960. Rumors of huge mystery satellites had existed for many years. Now, on February 11, 1960, another such story broke out. Papers in Britain reported a U.S. Defense Department announcement that an unidentified object orbiting Earth had been discovered by a navy-operated space surveillance unit and was under constant observation. *Flying Saucer Review* covered this in several issues. The object was said to be about fifteen tons, orbiting the poles, and had thus far preserved total radio silence. The Pentagon said the object "may have been of Soviet origin," a statement that brought a skeptical reply from a Soviet astronomer, who maintained that all Soviet satellites were fired into orbits of sixty-five degrees to the equator, well clear of the poles. In late August of that year the satellite was seen for several days and photographed by Grumman Aircraft Corporation.[119]

The mystery satellite also figured into a CIA file dated March 17, 1960, which described a March 6 sighting and photograph of two UFOs over Norrtalje, Sweden. A man had gone out that morning "to photograph the unidentified satellite, *1960 Alpha*." Just before the satellite became visible, he saw two objects moving slowly, "not entirely unlike that of the satellites he had seen before. Suddenly, however, the direction of movement changed, and the objects turned such that they were going back in the same direction they came from."[120]

Thus, despite year after year of blanket denials issued by the American military and government regarding the validity of UFOs, the CIA continued to gather reports from around the globe. Who determined this agency policy? And why were UFOs deemed of interest to the CIA? Could these really be evidence of interest in possible Soviet technology?

PROJECT OZMA GETS A SIGNAL

By the late autumn of 1959, Frank Edwards, still receiving UFO information from many sources, was able to confirm a tip he had originally gotten back in April: that a "giant telescope" was under construction at Green Bank, West Virginia, by the National Science Foundation, with the purpose of searching for intelligible signals from outer space. The NSF promptly denied this, but the story was true. The project, soon known as Project Ozma, was directed by Dr. Otto Struve, who was assisted by Dr. Frank Drake, a protégé of Lloyd Berkner.

Word on Project Ozma leaked sufficiently that by early 1960, Struve announced that Ozma was an attempt to establish communication with intelligent extraterrestrial civilizations. Then, at 4 A.M. on April 8, 1960, Project Ozma's radio telescope at Green Bank, West Virginia, focused on the star Tau Ceti and received a powerful signal. In Drake's words, the signal "knock[ed] the needle off the dials" for five minutes. It seemed amazingly quick to receive an intelligent signal from outer space, yet it appeared to be so. Then, two weeks later, after repositioning the telescope, the signal reappeared. This gave strong support to the idea that the signal had been terrestrial, most likely from a nearby and extremely powerful transmitter. The Naval Research Laboratory later revealed that its staff had been listening to these same signals for the past six months. It is curious that they were unable to determine the source. The best guess is that the NSA ran the transmitter, as it happens to have a major facility at Green Bank. Drake himself later said that he "never really knew what we made contact with that first day."

What we do know is that by 1961, Project Ozma was washed up, and Struve reversed his earlier statements on the project's importance. "Come back in a hundred years," he told reporters. Actually, however, the project did not die, as Struve implied; it simply moved to Arecibo, Puerto Rico.[121]

THE U-2 AFFAIR: A PEEK DOWN THE RABBIT HOLE

On May 1, 1960, CIA pilot Francis Gary Powers was shot down in a U-2 over the Soviet Union. This was the first time in five years of overflights that anything like this had occurred. Quite serious, indeed, and no announcement appeared while both governments were determining just what to do. On May 5, Soviet Premier Nikita Khrushchev announced that the plane had been shot down. He made no mention of Powers. The U.S. State Department confidently replied that the plane was not a spy plane; rather, it was a NASA weather plane that had drifted over the border from Turkey when its pilot had oxygen trouble. Sorry about the confusion. State was able to lie so confidently because it knew Powers had been instructed, in case of trouble, to eject from the plane and blow it up with a remote-control device. They did not know that Powers had not activated the mechanism. After letting this story sit for two days, Khrushchev triumphantly revealed that he had both pilot and plane. Whoops. The State Department now admitted to the spy flight (what else could it do?) but maintained that it had not been authorized in Washington. This was weak, and everyone knew it. Therefore, on May 9, Eisenhower reversed the State Department position, took full responsibility for the U-2 flight, and issued a statement that was widely interpreted to mean that the flights over Soviet territory would continue. Khrushchev, indignant, stormed out of a much-heralded summit conference.[122]

Khrushchev played the U-2 affair exceedingly well, but none of this changed American policy. Here is a snapshot of mid-1960. In May, the CIA sponsored the covert arrival of the first Cubans in Guatemala and soon built a secret airstrip. The U.S. Ambassador was generally aware of the operation, but stayed clear since it was black. Meanwhile, the CIA was deeply involved in the elections of the former Belgian Congo, newly independent. The Congo had the misfortune to be the site of some of the world's richest mineral deposits, including high-grade uranium. It was therefore a universal target of domination, a game won by the Americans. In June, the CIA began providing arms to the anti-Trujillo underground in the Dominican Republic. In July, it made a payment to arrange for an "accident" to Raul Castro, Fidel's brother. In August, the agency's Office of Medical Services poisoned cigars destined for Fidel. Meanwhile, J. Edgar Hoover assiduously recorded JFK's reckless womanizing at the Democratic convention, and may have fed this information to his friend Lyndon Johnson to use for blackmail purposes against Kennedy, perhaps even to influence JFK's choice of a running mate.[123]

MID-1960: NICAP PRESSES CONGRESS ONCE AGAIN

While 1960 was a busy year for the covert world, UFO reports were scarce. Not only within the United States, but worldwide, flying saucers seemed to disappear. The few interesting sightings cannot obscure the fact that, by now, the fight to end UFO secrecy had become more engaging than the sightings themselves. Nevertheless, a few incidents are worth mentioning from this period.

On May 14, 1960, a six-state area in Brazil experienced an unusual number of UFO sightings. One of these included a sighting of small, pale, human-like beings standing near two landed discs near Paracura, Ceara State (northeast Brazil). The beings beckoned to the witness, named Raimondo dos Santos, who fled. He claimed they wore blue uniforms and white helmets. Later, with others, he found marks in the sand where the crafts had rested. The previous day at 7 P.M., over one hundred people had seen a dark-gray, circular craft, sixty-five feet in diameter with a powerful light, maneuvering and hovering.[124]

Within a few days of July 1, 1960, according to Wilbert Smith from an interview in late 1961, the "Canadian Research Group" handling UFOs recovered "one mass of very strange metal." There were about three thousand pounds of it, said Smith, and the Canadians did "a tremendous amount of detective work on this metal."[125]

Between August 13 and 18, a miniwave of UFO sightings took place in California, mostly in the north, and included several police witnesses.[126]

On September 3, the London *Daily Telegraph* reported on the mysterious object recently appearing over New York—five times since August 23. A tracking camera at the Grumman Aircraft plant on Long Island had apparently photographed the object, which was believed to be three times faster than the satellite *Echo I*, and traveled from east to west, rather than the west-to-east path followed by artificial satellites.[127]

On October 3, announced a Canadian Broadcasting Corporation newscast, six "flying saucers" and a "mother ship" were reported from the Australian island state of Tasmania. A Church of England minister claimed to see the craft but had been reluctant to report them. He finally did report the matter when other people in the area claimed to see the objects.[128]

On the evening of December 9, 1960, in Carignan, France, three witnesses saw a glowing object in a park, about twelve feet in diameter, with vague shadows inside. A circle of yellowed grass was found at the site after it took off.[129]

The lack of current UFO reports weakened NICAP's hand in its bid for open UFO hearings. During the first half of 1960, Keyhoe spoke at length with Congressman John McCormack, urging him to consider holding another congressional investigation. According to Keyhoe, McCormack believed that UFOs were "real" and not familiar objects or delusions. In June, NICAP sent a confidential report to members of Congress outlining its accumulated UFO evidence. In early July, members of the Senate Preparedness Committee, and the House Science and Astronautics Committee, requested an air force briefing on the UFO program. The CIA also asked to attend. The air force gave a major briefing on July 15 before a number of people: Congressmen Richard Smart (Armed Services Committee), Spencer Bereford (House Science and Astronautics Committee), Richard Hines, and Frank Hammit, and two men from the CIA (Richard Payne, technical advisor, and John Warner, assistant for legislative liaison to Allen Dulles). Air force representatives included Tacker, Friend, Hynek, and three generals. This meeting was somewhat antagonistic, especially because of Smart, who charged the air force with withholding information and said he expected to be informed of all significant sightings. Still, the air force succeeded in preventing open hearings and avoiding significant changes.[130]

Again, the air force knew that NICAP had provided most of the initiative behind the anti-secrecy rumblings in Congress and was none too pleased. On July 26, Tacker stated that there was "absolutely no truth in the charge that the air force or any other governmental agency [was] withholding information on the subject of UFOs from the general public."[131]

But of course, such a statement could not possibly be true, no matter how one chose to interpret the meaning of UFOs. By July 1960, the United States had eleven small satellites in orbit, and the Soviet Union had sent a single large satellite. All of these objects were following predictable paths. According to *Newsweek*, however, tracking gear seemed to show something else in orbit. Certainly, an American satellite program would be interested in this development but would not want to publicize such a thing. Within this context, the U.S. launched its first truly successful spy satellite on August 10, 1960. This was *Discoverer*, which had a camera so powerful that its photos could resolve images as small as three feet. (This turned out to be an embarrassment for the air force, which had been hammering its missile gap agenda, now irrefutably proven wrong.) Days later, on August 15, the secretary of the air force wrote a memo titled "Air Force Keeping Watchful Eye on Aerospace." It stated:

> The air force maintains a continuous surveillance of the atmosphere for unidentified flying objects. . . . There is a relationship between the air force's interest in space surveillance and its continuous surveillance of the atmosphere near Earth for unidentified flying objects—UFOs.

It would be difficult to state the matter any clearer, and yet the message, once again, eluded the larger public.[132]

Matters dragged on through the fall and winter with no change. In November, the air force informed Congressman Smart it had "not yet" implemented his requests for improvements to Blue Book. On December 5, 1960, Keyhoe debated Tacker on NBC's *Today* show. Tacker said he wrote his book, *Flying Saucers and the U.S. Air Force*, because he "felt the air force was being set upon by Major Keyhoe, NICAP, and other UFO hobby groups who believe in spaceships as an act of pure faith." Keyhoe brought out his guns, and host David Garroway seemed to side with Keyhoe. The exchange generated many phone calls and letters to NBC, most of which were critical of Tacker and the air force.[133]

The last item of significance to UFOs from 1960 was the famous Brookings Institution report, released on December 14, which gave credence to the concept of extraterrestrial life. Titled "Proposed Study on the Implications of Peaceful Space Activities for Human Affairs," the one-hundred-page report was prepared on behalf of NASA to discuss the implications of the space program. Because of NASA's status as a government agency, the report was sent to the Senate Committee on Science and Astronautics, chaired by Overton Brooks, for approval. The report discussed much of interest to UFO researchers, such as the possibility of finding alien artifacts on Earth and elsewhere in the solar system. Contact with aliens, argued the report, could be dangerous. Not only would it be traumatic to religious fundamentalists and scientific circles, but indeed might result in social "disintegration." It suggested that if evidence of extraterrestrial life were uncovered, withholding such knowledge from the public might be a good idea. Of course, it might not matter. In relation to UFOs, the report stated:

> It is possible that if the intelligence of these creatures were sufficiently superior to ours, they might choose to have little if any contact with us.[134]

THE SECRET STATE IN 1960 AND 1961

By late 1960, Eisenhower was on his way out, Kennedy in. From a review of what declassified information exists, it appears that America's national security state went through significant expansion during this period, and, no doubt emboldened by years of secrecy and success, its activities became ever more brazen. More exotic methods of controlling the human mind emerged, such as the innovation by Defense Intelligence Agency (DIA) biophysicist Alan Frey, who announced in 1961 that human beings were capable of hearing microwave broadcasts. More traditional methods of disposing of enemies remained the rule, however. In September 1960, Sid Gottlieb of MK-Ultra prepared a lethal biological agent intended for Patrice Lumumba, then in the protective custody of the United Nations. His concoction never reached Lumumba, but on January 17, 1961, Lumumba was "shot trying to escape" by the troops of CIA-backed Joseph Mobutu.[135]

By October 1960, as Castro's poisoned cigars were ready, the CIA decided that a force of perhaps one hundred Cubans would make a landing in Cuba in late autumn. This was planned to be a major, well-trained guerrilla group within Cuba and a rallying point for other guerrilla groups. In November, the CIA began airdropping supplies into Cuba. President-elect Kennedy was soon briefed on the Cuban operation (11/17/60) by Dulles and Bissell at Palm Beach and gave the go-ahead.[136]

Eisenhower, still president, finally learned of SAC's war plan in late November, called the Single Integrated Operational Plan, or SIOP. The plan distressed him: ten nations would be totally obliterated, and 500 million people would die. By this time, the United States had roughly twenty-three thousand nuclear warheads in its arsenal, and Eisenhower probably realized that he had lost command over America's nuclear arsenal.

Dwight Eisenhower delivered his farewell address on January 17, 1961. It became famous for introducing the phrase "military-industrial complex." His key statement:

> We annually spend more on military security than the net income of all United States corporations. This conjunction of an immense military establishment and a large arms industry is new in the American experience. The total influence—economic, political, even spiritual—is felt in every city, every statehouse, every office of the federal government. . . . In the councils of government, we must guard against the acquisition of unwarranted influence, whether sought or unsought, by the military-industrial complex. The potential for the disastrous rise of misplaced power exists and will persist.

Famous last words, but they could not undo the damage of eight years of alternately encouraging and acquiescing in the growth of that complex.[137]

The CIA's Cuban operation was the main subterranean event of 1961. Eisenhower broke off relations with Cuba on January 3. Sketchy reports in *The Nation*, the *New York Times*, and the *Miami Herald* described the Guatemalan base but failed to break into the mainstream. By February, the CIA-fostered guerrilla movement within Cuba had collapsed. In early April, the State Department accused Castro's regime of offering "a clear and present danger" to the Americas, and Kennedy soon felt compelled to announce that no U.S. forces would invade Cuba. Within days, however, American-supplied B-26s tried to destroy the Cuban air force, but only alerted the Cubans. Still, the CIA told the Cuban pilots in Guatemala that Castro's planes had been destroyed. When Kennedy gave his final go-ahead, the plan had no chance to succeed. Why do it, then? Bissell may have thought events would force Kennedy to commit American troops. If so, he was mistaken.[138]

The invasion took place at Cuba's Bay of Pigs on Monday morning, April 17, 1961, as State Department and White House spokesmen denied all knowledge. Six of the eleven B-26s were lost, and the exile brigade withered quickly on the Cuban beaches. The next evening, Bissell desperately asked Kennedy to authorize the use of navy jets. Kennedy, knowing that plausible deniability was at the breaking point, first said no, then relented to allow unmarked navy jets to support the B-26s for one hour, purely defensively. The navy fliers arrived at the wrong time; no one remembered their time zone was one hour off. The operation ended in disaster.[139]

Kennedy was determined that CIA heads would roll, and they did, just in time for the opening of the new Langley headquarters. On September 27, Allen Dulles resigned as DCI; Rockefeller associate John A. McCone replaced him. Bissell soon left clandestine services, replaced by Richard Helms. Charles Cabell, who played a small but crucial role in the invasion's failure, was also gone. But despite new faces, little changed. If anything, the debacle heightened Kennedy's burning desire to get Castro the hell out of Cuba. The result was Operation Mongoose, a "full court press" against Cuba that included coup attempts, contamination of exports, and counterfeiting, often with Mafia assistance. Ironically, the Soviet Union also tried to remove Fidel, who was not especially servile in the early years. Castro's security forces disabled a KGB-organized plot against him in the fall of 1961.[140]

The last key event of 1961 was the birth of the Defense Intelligence Agency on October 1, 1961. The DIA was mandated to coordinate all military intelligence and became an instant competitor to the CIA. Interservice rivalries, however, impeded its effectiveness. Before long, the DIA was an unwieldy organization "rutted with independent intelligence fiefdoms and esoteric study groups."[141]

UFOS IN 1961

The trend of scant UFO sightings continued in 1961. Some were interesting for the attention they received; others simply in their own right. During the test-firing of a Polaris missile at Cape Canaveral, Florida, on January 10, "an unidentifiable object," much larger than the missile itself, tracked it, and got so close that radar momentarily locked on to it, according to official logs. The incident made it to the NICAP files and was reported in the January 1965 issue of *True* magazine.[142]

On January 22, at Eglin AFB in Florida, a metallic-looking and elliptical UFO approached from over the Gulf, made a U-turn, and sped back. A civilian apparently photographed it on 8 mm movie film. From February 5 to 7, several UFO reports came from Maine describing strange lights in the sky. Some of these blinked and moved up and down. Local press wrote, "The military had us just about convinced that no such objects existed. The only trouble was that many people—good, reliable observers—continued to see these things." In Antarctica on March 16, a meteorologist saw an odd, multi-colored, fireball-like object.[143]

On April 18, just six days after Yury Gagarin became the first person to orbit the Earth, and while the Bay of Pigs invasion was disintegrating, a strange UFO encounter allegedly took place at Eagle River, Wisconsin. At 11 A.M., Joe Simonton claimed to hear a whining sound and then saw a craft, thirty feet in diameter and twelve feet high, resting on his property. A man about five feet tall appeared from the craft; he wore a black, turtleneck pullover with a white band at the belt and black trousers with a vertical white band along the side. Inside the craft, Simonton discerned two more figures;

he said all three resembled "Italians." The strange man held up a metallic jug, which Simonton took and filled with water. He noticed one man frying on a flameless grill and motioned for some food. He received three ordinary pancakes or cookies, about three inches in diameter, perforated with small holes. Soon after, the craft departed. The air force investigated the case and even analyzed the pancakes, finding them to be entirely ordinary, except for the lack of any salt. The case was inconclusive: nothing ever pointed to a hoax, but little evidence supported anything more.[144]

The rest of 1961 provided few, albeit intriguing, reports. On April 29, 1961, near Newport, Rhode Island, a man on the beach saw a spherical object bobbing on the waves two hundred yards out. It then rose about sixty feet and took off in a straight line out to sea at an estimated 100 mph. Another water-related incident occurred in Savona, Italy, early on June 3. Four people in a boat were shaken by growing waves; at some distance, they saw the sea swell up, and a cone-shaped object emerge. It hovered briefly over the water, showed a glowing underside, then left at high speed.[145]

In Exeter, England, on June 19, a flying object was reported to have hovered for over an hour above an airport. The object appeared on radar and was observed "for some time." It appeared to be large, highly reflective, and about fifty thousand feet high. Officials were baffled.[146]

A month later, on July 17 at 2 A.M. in Las Vegas, Nevada, two people traveling on U.S. Highway 91 saw a low-flying object in the rearview mirror that overtook their car, bringing a rush of cold air. The object stopped, circled the vehicle, then flew off behind the mountains, where the witnesses believed it might have landed. Vallee said the ensuing military investigation was "exceptionally complete," yet no one found evidence of a landing.[147]

Another low-flying UFO was seen by car passengers sometime around August 25, 1961, in Toulouse, France. Five people claimed to see a luminous, yellow sphere, about twenty-five feet in diameter, flying about thirty-five feet above the road. The object ascended rapidly when the car reached town.[148]

On September 18, Fourth Officer G. Gendall of the vessel *Queensland Star*, in the Indian Ocean, reported seeing a white-colored UFO through a cloud formation. It vanished into the clouds, reappeared, then descended into the sea. The surrounding water then grew bright, and white particles fell into the sea for some time.[149]

1961: ANOTHER ROUND WITH CONGRESS

By early 1961, the air force gave Blue Book slightly more money and staff, which appeased Congressman Smart, but which affected neither operations nor public statements. An air force release from January 19, 1961, stated the old news that ". . . no physical or material evidence, not even a minute fragment of a so-called 'flying saucer' or spaceship has ever been found." The Soviet Union issued similar statements. On January 9, 1961, *Pravda* denounced Soviet citizens who reported UFOs as "either feebleminded or delicate liars."[150]

In March, Maj. Lawrence Tacker used his strongest language to date on UFOs. Claims for UFOs were either "absolutely erroneous," "a hoax," "sensational theories," or the work of "amateur hobby groups." NICAP's evidence was "drivel," its claims "ridiculous," and it made "senseless accusations." In April, the air force reassigned Tacker to Europe. He had been associated with the UFO project for three years and had written a book on the subject, but his UFO career was now abruptly over.[151]

Despite official statements, some prominent people remained interested in UFOs. In March 1961, House Majority Leader McCormack privately told Donald Keyhoe he had urged a UFO investigation by the Science and Astronautics Committee. Pressure was rising in Congress against UFO secrecy. In May, Congress announced a new UFO investigation to be headed by Congressman Joseph Karth of Minnesota. Among other things, the plan called for a statement by Hillenkoetter. NICAP also released a joint statement by twenty-one American scientists which demanded an open investigation of UFOs without secrecy, the need for the air force to improve its manner of investigation, and disclosure of all facts on major UFO sightings. By June, Congress had received many requests for an investigation of UFOs.[152]

Before matters could reach a breakthrough, however, they fizzled out. The air force wasted no time to kill the investigation and briefed key congressional committees in private between July 11 and 15, 1961. Once again, that was the end of the matter. Keyhoe seemed undaunted and continued to push for open hearings, full disclosure of UFO secrecy, and a government body authorized to release UFO data to the public. He thought it was still possible to make something happen during 1961, but began to consider early 1962 as more realistic.[153]

Soon enough, the air force Office of Legislative Liaison learned of Keyhoe's new plans and directed its efforts toward heading them off. On August 4, 1961, Rep. Thomas W. Downing sent a letter to NICAP, advising them that "an investigation of the UFO phenomenon [was] being contemplated by the Science and Astronautics Committee." He believed that Congressman Joseph Karth might serve as chairman of the three-man subcommittee. Meanwhile, Sen. Overton Brooks met privately with Hillenkoetter and Keyhoe. According to Keyhoe, Brooks asked them to bring a "cross section of [NICAP's] strongest and best-documented evidence, also proof of official censorship." Brooks set a UFO congressional conference for August 24.

But the Blue Book staff was also at work. In mid-August, Friend briefed Congressman Richard Hines on Blue Book's operation, which favorably impressed him, and "enlightened" him about Keyhoe's intentions. Accompanying Friend on this mission was J. Allen Hynek, who continued to provide valuable service to his benefactor, the air force, while helping to undermine NICAP. Hines immediately wrote back to Friend, informing him that Brooks had decided not to pursue UFO hearings after all. That would be putting it mildly. Overton Brooks suddenly became ill and died. Brooks's successor was Congressman George P. Miller of California, who stated that he would not order UFO hearings.[154]

Once again, Roscoe Hillenkoetter placed himself on the public record for ending UFO secrecy. On August 22, 1961, he signed a NICAP letter to Congress urging immediate congressional action on the matter. It must have impressed a few members of Congress that a former director of the CIA should continually take such a stand on this matter:

> Acting with the majority of the NICAP Board of Governors, I urge immediate congressional action to reduce the dangers from secrecy about unidentified flying objects. . . . Two dangers are steadily increasing:

1. The risk of accidental war, from mistaking UFO formations for a Soviet surprise attack.
2. The danger that the Soviet government may, in a critical moment, *falsely* claim the UFOs as secret Russian weapons against which our defenses are helpless.

Shortly after this (8/28), Karth sent a harsh letter to Keyhoe, attacking him for a "headline-seeking" desire to grandstand in a direct confrontation with the air force. "I am not a captive of the air force," wrote Karth. Keyhoe apparently smoothed matters over, and on September 19, Karth wrote to Keyhoe that, "now that we better understand each other," perhaps they could proceed with a new hearing early in 1962, "providing that the new chairman authorizes hearings." But Miller, the new chairman, had no such intention. Another year was passing, and still no congressional hearings on UFOs. NICAP was chasing its tail.[155]

THE HILL ABDUCTION CASE

The case of Antonio Villas-Boas aside, the modern alien abduction era can be said to have started on September 19, 1961, near Portsmouth, New Hampshire. A couple driving at night lost over two hours without realizing it after seeing a UFO at close range. Under hypnosis much later, they gave detailed and similar accounts, which in turn correspond closely to many abduction claims starting in the 1970s.[156]

Barney and Betty Hill were socially aware and politically active citizens. Barney, thirty-nine, was the legal redress chairman of the Portsmouth NAACP, a member of the state advisory board of the United States Civil Rights Commission, and on the board of the Rockingham County Poverty Program. He also served three years in the army during World War II, and had received several awards for his community work. Betty, forty-one, was a state social worker known for her work with the poor; she also assisted the NAACP and was the United Nations envoy for her Unitarian-Universalist Church.

On the night of September 19, 1961, the Hills were driving home with their dog, Delsey, from a vacation. At 10:05 P.M., they left a diner in Colebrook, New Hampshire, and drove south along U.S. Route 3. Barney predicted they would get home by around 2:30 A.M., or 3 A.M. "at the latest."

Shortly after leaving Colebrook, they were puzzled by an object with an "unpredictable movement." Barney, a strict rationalist who was indifferent to UFOs, first thought it was a satellite, then a star. Betty discounted both explanations as ridiculous, especially after the object erratically changed its course. Then it must be a commercial plane, said Barney. Betty was unpersuaded. Through binoculars, she saw the object's silhouette against the moon. She later said it "appeared to be flashing thin pencils of different colored lights, rotating around an object which at that time appeared cigar-shaped."

Barney continued to maintain the object had to be a plane, even after it changed its speed several times. He did admit, however, that it seemed to be tracking them and "playing games." They drove on to Cannon Mountain at about five miles per hour while Delsey whined and cowered. The object then descended to a few hundred feet. As it did so, it became clear to them that it was huge—a "structured craft of enormous dimension." Betty noticed a double row of windows. Both were terrified.

Barney stopped the car in the middle of the highway and got out, motor still running. The object had swung toward them and hovered "not more than two treetops away." It was tilted and looked like a large, glowing pancake. It then swung in a silent arc directly across the road. Barney walked across a field toward the craft, possibly to within a hundred feet of it. Betty screamed after him, but he did not hear her. Now he, too, saw a double row of windows, and at least six figures inside. They seemed to be wearing uniforms and stared directly at him. Barney recalled thinking that one of them appeared to be the leader, but his memory became blurred at this point. He remembered running back to the car, screaming and hysterical. Back in the car and driving again, the two heard a strange electronic beeping sound, which seemed to vibrate the car. They felt an odd tingling sensation, and a drowsiness overcame them.

After some time had passed, the beeping sound repeated itself, their consciousness returned, the car was moving, and Barney was still driving. They were now near Ashland, thirty-five miles south of where the first beeping sound had occurred. Finally, at 5 A.M., they arrived home, "a little later than expected," Barney noted.

Immediately and inexplicably, Barney felt an urge to examine his abdomen and became aware of an unexplained soreness on the back of his neck. Nor could he explain why the tops of his shoes were so badly scuffed. He later commented, "I didn't know why at the time, but I felt unclean." The sighting still baffled him, but he continued to contend it was a known aircraft, in spite of its total silence and other unconventional features.

Although both agreed to tell no one about their encounter, Betty called her sister, Janet, who had seen a UFO in 1957. Janet repeated the story to a physicist neighbor, who suggested that an ordinary compass might show evidence of radiation. Janet passed that on to Betty, who took a compass to her car. Barney opposed dwelling on the event, but he and Betty noticed a dozen or more shiny circles scattered on the surface of their trunk, all perfectly circular and the size of a silver dollar. The circles were highly magnetic.

Janet also described the incident to a former local police chief, who suggested the Hills notify Pease AFB in Portsmouth. Betty was afraid she had been exposed to radioactivity, and called. She gave only the bare details to the officer on the phone (not mentioning, for example, the double row of windows or the shiny spots on the car). Barney also spoke to the officer, who informed him the call was being monitored. Whereas Betty had felt the officer was "cynical and uncommunicative," Barney thought he was "intensely interested." The base called back the next day for more details, but received little more from the Hills. That appears to be the sum total of the Blue Book investigation into the Hill case. Two years later, on September 27, 1963, its final report cited "insufficient evidence" to make a determination, although the author of the report stated the object "was in all probability Jupiter," and that "no evidence was presented to indicate that the object was due to other than natural causes."

For now, however, intrigued by their encounter, the Hills decided to draw the object from memory while in separate rooms; the drawings were remarkably similar. Betty decided to learn more about UFOs and found Keyhoe's *The Flying Saucer Conspiracy* in the local library. On September 26, 1961, she wrote to Keyhoe, describing their experience (mentioning the windows and figures) and requesting more information. Then, beginning around September 29, and continuing for five consecutive nights, Betty Hill began having a series of awesome and vivid dreams. These were far more intense than anything she had ever experienced and even dominated her waking life. They involved encountering a strange roadblock on a lonely road and being approached by a group of men, all dressed alike. As they reached the car, she became unconscious, then awakened to find herself and Barney aboard a strange craft, being given a complete medical examination by "intelligent, humanoid beings." Barney was taken down a corridor, and both were assured that no harm would come to them, and that they would forget everything that happened.

On October 4 and 5, 1961, two more individuals, C. D. Jackson and Robert Hohman, entered the story. Jackson (presumably not the C. D. Jackson with extensive intelligence and journalistic connections) was a "senior engineer" for a company that no one would specify, but which was "one of the world's most notable corporations in the electronic industry." Hohman worked for the same company as a staff scientific writer on engineering and science. The two were in Washington for the Twelfth International Astronautical Congress, as part of their "regular routine." They were "deeply involved" in work on the space program and were in the process of preparing a paper on Nikola Tesla, David Todd, and Marconi to suggest that these men were monitoring interplanetary communications between 1899 and 1924—possibly from Tau Ceti. Incredible as this sounds, both Keyhoe and journalist John Fuller attested to it. (Jackson and Hohman are odd and shadowy figures in this episode, but recall William Lear's earlier comments regarding secret research in the aerospace industry on antigravity propulsion methods—clearly related to UFOs.) Jackson and Hohman were also members of NICAP and arranged for lunch with Keyhoe to gain relevant UFO data for their research. When Hohman said that UFO reports seemed to be dropping in frequency, Keyhoe showed them Betty Hill's letter, which he had just received. The two were impressed.

On October 19, NICAP secretary Richard Hall wrote to Walter Webb, a lecturer at the Hayden Planetarium in Boston and NICAP scientific advisor. Would Webb investigate the Hill case? Initially reluctant, he met with the Hills on October 21, confident he would find holes in their story. Instead, he interviewed them for eight hours. In his words, he was

> so amazed, so impressed by both the Hills and their account that we skipped lunch and went right through the afternoon and early evening. During that time, I cross-examined them together, separately, together, requestioned them again and again. I tried to make them slip up somewhere, and I couldn't. Theirs was an ironclad story. They seemed to me to be a sincere, honest couple driving home from vacation late at night on a lonely road, when suddenly something completely unknown and undefinable descended on them. Something entirely foreign or alien to their existence.

If anything, Webb felt the Hills underplayed the dramatic aspects of their encounter. The three were so caught up in the account that the Hills forgot to show Webb the spots on the car, although they mentioned them. Barney, meanwhile, was still running up against a "curtain," beyond which he could go no further. Webb's report to NICAP on October 26 gave great detail on the interview and concluded that the two were telling the truth. As far as Webb was concerned, the incident occurred just as they claimed.

On November 5, Hohman wrote to the Hills, mentioning his and Jackson's interest in their encounter, and asked to meet them. He and Jackson, wrote Hohman, had a "close familiarity with most of the unclassified (military) literature" on UFOs. The two mystery investigators met with the Hills on November 25, 1961. Also visiting the Hills that day was Maj. James McDonald, a recently retired air force intelligence officer and a close friend who had already discussed the case "many times" with them. The five discussed the encounter for nearly twelve hours, during which Hohman and Jackson asked several obscure and technical questions. One of them asked, "What took you so long to get home?" When Betty and Barney realized that they could not account for over two hours, they were "flabbergasted." McDonald suggested they undergo hypnosis, but no one could suggest anyone specific.

The holiday season came and went, and in February 1962, the Hills—due to Betty's initiative and Barney's acquiescence—began a series of pilgrimages to the scene of their encounter, which continued for several months. By March, she was looking for a psychiatrist who used hypnotism. On March 25, 1962, the two met with a doctor who ruled out simultaneous hallucination. That spring, Barney developed a series of warts in an almost geometrically perfect circular ring in his groin. Feeling exhausted and a general malaise, he began to see a psychiatrist. Throughout his entire period of treatment, more than a year, Barney never associated his problems with the UFO incident. Meanwhile, he and Betty put aside the idea of hypnosis.

In September 1963, the Hills were invited by their church to a discussion about their UFO experience, which was taped by one of the attendees, a journalist. Another of the attendees was Capt. Ben Swett of Pease AFB, known locally for his study of hypnosis. The positive reception their story received encouraged the Hills, and Barney mentioned the subject during his next session. His doctor recommended Dr. Benjamin Simon, a well-known Boston psychiatrist and neurologist with much experience in hypnosis. Simon had also worked on an extensive scale as chief of neuropsychiatry and executive officer at Mason General Hospital, the army's chief psychiatric center in World War Two.

The Hills' sessions with Simon lasted from January 4 to June 6, 1964. Throughout, they underwent separate sessions, and for most of the period they did not remember their experiences following the sessions. These sessions were intense, especially for Barney. Under hypnosis, he remembered driving off Route 3, instructed against his will by a "mind voice" to drive deep into the woods. He saw six men standing in the road, wearing dark clothing, with a bright orange glow behind them. Three men approached his car and told him to stay calm and to close his eyes. Barney said, "I felt like [their] eyes had pushed into my eyes." The men led Barney and Betty out of their car, and Barney felt his shoes dragging on the ground. They went up a ramp and inside a craft. He saw three men in an "operating room," and he lay down on a table. His shoes were removed and a cup was placed over his groin; he later believed his semen was extracted at this time. Someone scraped his left arm, examined his ears and throat. A cylindrical device was inserted up his rectum, and someone counted his vertebrae.

Betty's story under hypnosis closely matched her dreams from over two years earlier, except that in her sessions the aliens had no hair and smaller noses. A "doctor" on board took scrapings from her skin, cut off a sample of her hair, studied her mouth, throat, ears, and hands, and took clippings from her fingernails. She was asked to lie down on an examination table, and the doctor pulled a machine over. One of the procedures involved a "pregnancy test" with a needle, four to six inches long, which was inserted into her navel. Later, she had time to speak with the leader, who seemed to communicate in English, but which Betty later believed was through telepathy. She asked if she could bring something back that would prove her experience to others. The leader agreed, and she picked up a large book with strange symbols. She was forced to give it up, however, when the other crew members objected. She also asked the leader where he was from. He went to a wall and pulled down a strange map of space, with stars of various sizes. Many stars were connected by broken or solid lines, all curved. The lines, said the leader, represented expeditions, but he lost interest in explaining once he realized Betty knew little astronomy. He told her she would forget all about this encounter; she was determined to remember.

Barney's and Betty's accounts were extremely consistent with each other. Both described the men as about five feet tall, with gray skin, oddly shaped heads with broad foreheads. They had large eyes and spoke to each other with a humming sound. The descriptions differed in certain details, mostly related to the appearance of the crews. (Betty said they all wore caps, Barney only recalled the leader wearing one—although his conscious recollection to Webb was that all the crew wore caps.)

Simon discounted the possibility of alien abduction. He simply did not believe in UFOs, and, according to Webb, declined to read any relevant literature on the subject. Thus, he tried to persuade the Hills that Betty's initial dreams had inspired Barney's account, which was simply a fantasy. The Hills were unconvinced. Barney pointed out the many unique aspects of his account; indeed, he said, he wished the whole thing *had* been a hallucination.

The Hill story became public in 1965, after their taped conversation from several years earlier was released. In 1966, journalist John Fuller wrote *The Interrupted Journey*, cementing their place in UFO lore. The response from UFO researchers was mixed. Despite Webb's strong endorsement, NICAP accepted only that the Hills saw occupants and considered the abduction to be "highly questionable." Jerome Clark pointed out that, while all debunkers of this case took their cue from Simon, no one mentioned that Simon was both hostile and ignorant regarding UFOs. Nor could Simon's theory explain why Barney felt trauma immediately after the experience, before Betty even had her dreams, or account for the various pieces of physical evidence. Debunkers Klass and Sheaffer even went so far as to endorse the air force's Jupiter explanation, losing all credibility in the process, as far as this case was concerned.

The main problem in accepting the Hill case was its novelty: stories of alien abduction were unknown in 1961. Even among UFO researchers, accustomed to dealing with the unconventional, this seemed just a little too far-out. But the Hills were obviously not hoaxing, nor did they seem crazy. During the 1970s, as the abduction phenomenon became more widely claimed, discussed, and acknowledged, the case of Betty and Barney Hill seemed increasingly plausible. Indeed, if one concedes the existence of UFOs as the product of a nonhuman intelligence, and the possibility of occupants in at least some of the craft, then it is hard to accept anything other than the obvious: that Barney and Betty Hill were abducted by aliens.

Following the experience of Barney and Betty Hill, people continued to see UFOs at close range. One of the most compelling sightings occurred on October 2. This was a classic sighting of a daylight disc that took place in Salt Lake City, Utah, by Waldo J. Harris, a private pilot and real estate broker. Harris was about to take off from the runway at Utah Central Airport when he saw a bright spot in the sky. He continued to see the spot after he was airborne, assuming it was some aircraft reflecting the sun. He became curious when he realized the spot was not moving, and he moved toward it. As he did so, he could see that the object had no wings or tail and "seemed to be hovering with a little rocking motion." He could now see it was a disc-shaped object, between thirty-five and fifty feet in diameter and perhaps five or ten feet thick. It looked like "sandblasted aluminum," showed no windows, openings, or landing gear. At about two miles distant from the object, it rose suddenly about one thousand feet above him, affording a clear view of the underside, which seemed exactly like the top side. He continued to approach the object, when it departed abruptly and was gone in about two or three seconds. Harris said, "I can keep our fastest jets in sight for several minutes, so you can see that this object was moving rather rapidly." He later described the speed as in the thousands of miles per hour. Others at the airport also saw the disc, including airport controller Jay Galbraith, who saw it for fifteen continuous minutes; at least six others in Salt Lake City also saw it. One airport witness, Virgil S. Redmond, had just landed when he saw the object; he watched it with others, sharing field glasses. "Whatever it was seemed to be rocking while hovering almost stationary just south of the field. At times, as it turned, it looked like a zeppelin," he said. The air force investigated this case; a check with the U.S. Weather Bureau confirmed there was no cloud cover, with visibility at forty miles. No balloons were in the area. No air traffic was in the area that could account for the sighting.

A week after the sighting, the official Blue Book report stated "all logical leads have been exhausted in an effort to identify the object." Yet the Pentagon overruled Blue Book on October 11, when unnamed officers told reporters that Harris had seen the planet Venus, or possibly a research balloon. Harris shot back that they were "really off the beam." The object he saw "was saucer-shaped, had a gray color, and moved under intelligent control. I got within three miles of it, and that is a lot closer than Venus is. I have seen a lot of balloons, too, and this was no balloon." It became obvious that the Venus explanation was impossible, and the air force dropped it. Eventually, it dropped the balloon explanation as well. The eventual explanation was "sun dog," also known as a mock sun and parhelia. Menzel endorsed it, despite the fact that sun dogs do not move, and that several witnesses clearly saw the object move. No one bothered to tell Harris of the official explanation until atmospheric physicist James MacDonald asked him in 1966 if he knew what a sun dog was. (Harris did.) Both agreed that the official explanation was impossible.[157]

MOVING TO 1962

In the fall of 1961, NICAP obtained a photocopy of an air force intelligence sketch of a flying saucer. This came from a restricted manual for intelligence officers titled AFM 200-3. Somebody in the military had forgotten to reclassify it as Confidential when the Restricted classification was canceled.[158] More information slipped out from unmanageable sources. In November 1961, Wilbert Smith was speaking at length in an interview with two Ohio UFO researchers, C. W. Fitch and George Popovitch. He reiterated that he had handled "quite a bit" of UFO hardware and some "very strange metal," which had been recovered around July 1, 1960. He said:

We are speculating that what we have is a portion of a very large device which came into this solar system . . . we don't know when . . . but it had been in space a long time before it came to Earth; we can tell by the micrometeorites embedded in the surface. But we don't know whether it was a few years ago—or a few hundred years ago.

Smith also said that he had shown his friend and fellow NICAP board member Adm. H. B. Knowles a piece which had been shot from a small flying saucer near Washington during the July 1952 flap, and which had been loaned to him briefly by the U.S. Air Force. Smith emphasized that it was not the American air force but "a small group very high up in the government" who determined UFO policy.[159]

Air force intelligence decided to select personnel for two secret projects in November 1961: Moon Dust and Blue Fly. A classified memo about Moon Dust stated:

Moon Dust: As a specialized aspect of its overall material exploitation program, Headquarters USAF has established Project Moon Dust to locate, recover, and deliver descended foreign space vehicles. . . . Blue Fly: Operation Blue Fly has been established to facilitate expeditious delivery to FTD [the Air Force's Foreign Technology Division based at Wright Field in Ohio] of Moon Dust or other items of great technical intelligence interest.

These . . . peacetime projects all involve a potential for employment of qualified field intelligence personnel on a quick reaction basis to recover or perform field exploitation of unidentified flying objects. . . .

Journalist Howard Blum called this a UFO SWAT team. What these teams actually did, however, remains largely speculation. Other than this document, information on either project is scarce. The argument can be made that these two projects were related to terrestrial satellites. Still, the inclusion of the phrase "unidentified flying objects" appears to make the connection with unconventional craft explicit.[160]

HILLENKOETTER RESIGNS FROM NICAP

By early 1962, according to Keyhoe, the CIA struck at NICAP in order to block a threatened showdown which might have ended the UFO cover-up. This is entirely plausible. Although NICAP had lost battle after battle, it continued to fight doggedly on. In February, a plan was germinating among congressmen to end UFO secrecy using a statement by Roscoe Hillenkoetter, by far NICAP's most prestigious member. Keyhoe was involved in these machinations and met with "a congressman who had strongly supported Karth" to discuss the strategy of bringing the UFO matter to the congressional floor. This congressman confirmed to Keyhoe that Hillenkoetter would be a key person involved. Keyhoe therefore planned to see Hillenkoetter directly at his residence in New York. The telephone did not seem like a good idea.

Before leaving, Keyhoe decided to check into a UFO report he received from a lead by Delmar Fahrney. The story concerned a navy pilot named George Brent. While flying a navy transport plane near Newfoundland, Brent and his crew got a close-up view of a "huge flying disc with a glow around the rim." They believed it to be "well over" three hundred feet in diameter and at least thirty feet thick at the center. They saw a reflecting surface, apparently smooth metal. After a rapid approach and near collision, the crew saw the object for another ten seconds before it zoomed away. Air force intelligence officers interrogated Brent and the entire crew; he was later shown secret photos of UFOs, one of which portrayed a disc like the one he saw. Brent was also interviewed at Wright-Patterson AFB, although no one there would answer any of his questions. This account was undated but occurred (according to one of Keyhoe's sources) "some time back."

Seeing more ammunition for a congressional investigation, Keyhoe sought to get more detail on this case. He contacted a former navy man—using the pseudonym of Jack Morton—and asked Morton to find out where Brent was currently stationed. Morton believed the navy had flagged Brent's file, which meant that personnel would refuse requests for information and report any queries. Despite this, for some reason, Morton thought he could get the information for Keyhoe. Several days passed with no word from Morton. Keyhoe finally reached him after repeated calls to his house. "That navy call," said Morton, "raised hell." Less than an hour after his inquiry, he said, two CIA agents were at his door and gave him "the third degree." They demanded to know who wanted Brent's address and why. Morton ended up telling the CIA agents everything about the congressional plan, including Hillenkoetter's role. "For heaven's sake," Morton told Keyhoe, "don't try to call or see me again."

Keyhoe did not get the chance to see Hillenkoetter. Immediately after the incident with Morton, Keyhoe received a letter from Hillenkoetter which announced his resignation from NICAP and stated that he decided not to proceed with any UFO investigation or announcement. The air force, said Hillenkoetter, was doing all it could. Keyhoe knew Hillenkoetter, his former Annapolis classmate, well. Hillenkoetter had been "absolutely convinced" that the UFO cover-up should be exposed. "The only answer," decided Keyhoe, "was persuasion at a very high level." It is hard to credit any other interpretation. The only question is why would Hillenkoetter be pressured, and what means were used. The more benign interpretations are that Hillenkoetter's statements were of "considerable embarrassment" to the CIA. In the context of clear indications of pressure on Ruppelt, it appears that embarrassment was only the beginning of the problem. As far as the manner used, we can only say that it seems unlikely that Hillenkoetter would have backed down following a mere request.[161]

SUMMARY

For five years, despite some hopeful moments, NICAP had tried and failed to deliver the goods. In 1962, a congressional hearing on UFOs was as far away as ever. Keyhoe, who early on had predicted a NICAP membership of 100,000, could not seem to get it much past 5,000, and the organization was in financial straits from the beginning. On the other side, the air force, CIA, NSA, and other intelligence organizations involved in UFOs had enormous reserves of money, secrecy, and power. NICAP had given it a good effort but was out of its depth and sinking slowly but surely.

UFOs themselves continued to appear in the late 1950s and early 1960s, but with much less frequency than in previous years. Clearly, this helped the secrecy, but was also to some extent the result of secrecy. We simply do not know how many sightings were recorded through unofficial channels. That said, the period was a quiet one but saw steady numbers of up-close sightings and the development of something new: claims by credible individuals to have been abducted by aliens. In the early 1960s, almost no one took these seriously, but the phenomenon had begun nonetheless.

Also, the handling of this problem appears to have gone deeper underground. There are many indications of various "unofficial" dealings with the UFO problem, well beyond the authority of ATIC and Blue Book. The NSA and CIA certainly fit in here, but so do air force programs like Moon Dust.

Finally, there appears little doubt that *some* organization was pressuring individuals into silence and worse regarding UFOs. Ruppelt and Hillenkoetter are undeniable examples of this, and we must remember that agencies such as the CIA operated with almost total impunity during this period, carrying out grandiose and at times horrific schemes against undesirable individuals whenever it suited their needs. The UFO cover-up restricted more than the flow of information; it targeted people, as well.

Chapter 7

Open Confrontation: 1962 to 1966

After talking with both officers involved in the sighting, there is no doubt in my mind that they definitely saw some unusual object or phenomenon.

—Air force investigating officer, reporting a Blue Book unidentified, September 1965

I think there may be substance in some of these reports and because I believe the American people are entitled to a more thorough explanation than has been given them by the air force to date.

—Congressman Gerald R. Ford, March 1966

When the enemy starts to collapse, you must pursue him without letting the chance go. If you fail to take advantage of your enemy's collapse, they may recover.

—Miyamoto Musashi

OVERVIEW

The 1960s was a decade of confrontation. The war in Vietnam opened a permanent cultural chasm and estrangement among Americans. Civil rights, black power, feminism, gay rights, and the generation gap distinguished the era. It was a decade of assassinations: the Kennedy brothers, Malcolm X, and Martin Luther King, Jr., to name the most prominent. Riots became widespread, many of them inflicting permanent damage on the cities where they occurred: Watts never recovered from 1965, and it would be a long time until

Chicago again hosted a national political convention. Intellectuals challenged old assumptions about America's place in the world, and revolution was in the air. That this revolution ultimately failed did not make it any less dramatic for those who lived through it. For a while during the sixties, everything was up for grabs.

The struggle to end UFO secrecy partook of the general upheaval. But here, as in most matters, the decade started quietly. Sightings of unidentified craft were at a low ebb and received little publicity. The air force's heavy-handed management of the problem was messy at times, but effective enough. Undesirable leaks and statements continued to occur, but only within a context of official dismissal and ridicule which impeded forward motion. In near total media isolation, NICAP's struggle for congressional hearings met with failure year after year. Hillenkoetter's departure from the scene went unremarked. Keyhoe was no longer writing books and seemed to be slowing down. NICAP did publish a remarkable collection of its UFO evidence, which it sent to members of Congress, but even this work achieved only a modest distribution. To the public, the UFO question appeared to be settled, with the air force getting the final word.

Then, almost all at once, everything changed. By the end of 1964, UFOs began appearing in large numbers and continued on a steady rise through 1966. The intensity of the wave equaled the Great Wave of 1952, and surpassed it in duration. By now, Blue Book had long ceased investigating most reports first-hand; only rarely did it send a man to the scene of a reported sighting. Instead, the Blue Book goal was *explaining away*, so that of the thousands of UFO reports from the mid-1960s, only a handful remained officially unidentified, and most of those were fairly innocuous.

The actions of Blue Book had become too transparent, however. By 1966, the impossible had happened: UFOs were a matter of public concern, and members of Congress had even brought the matter to the floor. Suddenly, NICAP's goal of open UFO hearings, independent of air force control, seemed attainable. Then, in October 1966, the air force announced that it had awarded a contract to the University of Colorado to conduct a scientific study of UFOs. It would be independent and serious and led by a physicist of world renown. For the moment, all sides of the UFO debate were satisfied that someone was *finally* doing something about this. It was an ephemeral satisfaction, and a grave illusion.

THE LAS VEGAS UFO CRASH

On April 18, 1962, an unidentified, red, glowing object was seen moving west very rapidly over Oneida, New York. Was it a meteor? If so, it was quite unusual. In the first place, it was tracked on radar, which, while possible, is exceedingly rare. Second, as it passed across the country, Air Defense Command alerted all bases along its path, and at least two air force bases—Luke AFB near Phoenix and Nellis AFB in Nevada—sent jet interceptors after it. Why pursue a meteor? Finally, the entire sighting—from New York to Nevada—lasted thirty-two minutes. This gives an average speed of 4,500 mph, well below the slowest speed ever recorded for a meteor.[1]

When the object passed over Nephi, Utah, people on the ground heard jets following it. The object then *landed* at Eureka, Utah. Several witnesses saw it as a "glowing, orange oval which emitted a low, whirring sound." When it landed, it disrupted the electrical service from a nearby power station. It then rose, maneuvered, and headed toward Nevada. It was seen at Reno, then turned south and was spotted somewhat east of Las Vegas, when it went off the radar screens. Many witnesses saw it as a "tremendous flaming sword." By now, it had been seen by thousands of people. It exploded near Mesquite, Nevada, at which time it was being pursued by armed jet interceptors from Nellis AFB.

The *Las Vegas Sun* reported the incident in its April 19 edition under the headline, "Brilliant Red Explosion Flares in Las Vegas Sky." The article broached the UFO topic and mentioned the air force alert in several states. The Clark County sheriff's office was swamped with calls, investigated the incident, but found nothing of consequence. On May 8, 1962, the air force sent Blue Book chief Robert Friend and J. Allen Hynek to investigate. Their results were quite unsatisfactory. The two did not go to Nevada, but confined themselves to central Utah. Despite their knowledge that jets had pursued the object, they concluded it was a bolide, an especially fiery meteor.

Blue Book ultimately listed the sighting as two separate incidents, in a manner so slippery and misleading that intentional deception seems likely. First, it listed an April 18 multiple radar sighting at Nellis AFB, which it initially labeled as unidentified, then changed to "Insufficient Data for a Scientific Analysis." The report noted that the object's speed varied, that it was initially observed at ground level, then disappeared at ten thousand feet. It stated "no visual," despite the many people in Las Vegas who telephoned the sheriff's office. The "second" incident, investigated by Hynek and Friend in Utah, was listed as a bolide, and said to occur on April *nineteenth*. Except that this was uniquely logged in Zulu, or Greenwich Mean Time, which added seven hours and thus gave the wrong date! In reality, the Utah and Nevada sightings occurred within minutes of each other (around 8:15 P.M. Mountain Time or 7:15 P.M. Pacific Time). Even so, the official file on the Utah incident conceded that the power in Eureka was knocked out and that fighters had been scrambled from Nellis AFB.

On September 21, 1962, Maj. C. R. Hart of the air force Public Information Office responded to a letter from a New York State resident about the

UFO. Air force records, he said, listed the April 18 Nevada sighting as "insufficient data" but stated that the object's movement suggested a "U-2 or high balloon." He also stated that it was "not intercepted or fired upon." All of the claims and suggestions in this letter were entirely wrong. A U-2 is fast, but not Mach 7 fast, and the idea of a balloon causing the sighting was absurd. Moreover, the juxtaposition of a U-2 and balloon as alternate explanations was nonsensical: their respective movements and speeds were totally distinct.

For the next few years, only Frank Edwards mentioned this incident, and he confined himself to the *Sun* article. Much later, Kevin Randle dug deeper, interviewed many witnesses, and reviewed the Blue Book files, where he discovered the time discrepancy. Randle also communicated with an anonymous man who claimed to be an officer at Nellis AFB at the time of the crash. He and thirty others, claimed the man, were driven into the desert early the next morning to retrieve the crash debris. They were loaded into a bus with blacked-out windows, but one window was not entirely covered, and the man claimed to have seen a damaged saucer-shaped craft.

Although no independent source has confirmed the story, we may at least acknowledge that an object able to scramble jet interceptors from two air bases, and apparently crashed, would warrant a top-level military retrieval. This much is clear: a UFO did crash or explode near Las Vegas on the evening of April 18, 1962, and the air force hid the event from the public and in its official records. Precisely *what* crashed remains unknown, but the pursuit of the object by U.S. jets appears to preclude natural phenomenon or American experimental aircraft as the explanation.

UFOs in America: 1962

In February 1962, the month that Hillenkoetter was pressured to quit NICAP and drop out of the UFO business, the air force issued the last of its old-style fact sheets. For the next three years, it released occasional public relations packages dealing with UFO reports, typically reevaluating ("solving") earlier cases. For all of 1962, Blue Book recorded only fourteen unidentified sightings, but the category of unknown became so diluted as to be meaningless and so broadened that it included many vague and incomplete cases. Several of these occurred in the eastern U.S., through the spring and summer, of round, oval, triangular, diamond-shaped, and even rectangular objects, usually red in color, performing intricate maneuvers. Meanwhile, the air force tried hard throughout the year to ditch its program to places such as NASA and the National Science Foundation, with no success.[2]

As noted, the Las Vegas crash was not among the unknowns, although it was by far the most spectacular UFO event of the year. Other good-quality sightings were ignored or mishandled by Blue Book, two of which involved American X-15 aircraft. The first occurred on April 30 during Joe Walker's record-breaking fifty-mile-high flight. Although Walker saw no object, his instrumentation photographed five or six "cylindrical or discoid-shaped" objects. On May 11, 1962, at the Second National Conference on the Peaceful Uses of Space Research in Seattle, Washington, Walker showed slides of the objects and said this had been the second time they were photographed. According to the Paris paper, *Le Matin*, he also admitted that one of his appointed tasks was to detect UFOs. Both NICAP and the publication *Flying Saucer Review* tried, but failed, to obtain prints of the slides. NASA told *FSR* that the objects were actually ice flaking off the aircraft, as "ice forms on the aircraft after it is filled with liquid oxygen." No still photos were available, said NASA.[3]

The ice explanation seems weak, if only because another X-15 pilot saw a strange object in space at the top of his climb on July 17, 1962. Maj. Robert White was about fifty-eight miles high when he saw a grayish object "about thirty to forty feet away." According to *Time* magazine, White reportedly exclaimed during the flight, "There *are* things out there. There absolutely is!" Presumably he did not mean ice crystals.[4]

By July, the lack of UFO publicity, combined with an economic recession, contributed to an open rift between APRO and NICAP. In an *APRO Bulletin* editorial, Coral Lorenzen wrote that NICAP was little more than a lobbying group; if forced to choose, members should retain their APRO membership, since it was a truly research-oriented organization that refrained from pointless attacks against the air force.[5]

NICAP, of course, could not change what it was, and besides, it had a valuable role to play. In the August issue of the *NICAP Bulletin*, the organization reported that an air force spokesman at the Pentagon, Maj. C. R. Hart, revealed that UFO investigations and evaluations involved "hundreds" of air force intelligence officers, as well as

> the best scientific brains available in the laboratories of all government agencies, also scientific investigators in commercial laboratories, whenever needed.[6]

Indeed, only the month before, the Air Force re-released AF 200-2, covering seven pages of instruction in tightly spaced eight-point type. It described UFOs as

> any aerial phenomena, airborne objects, or objects which are unknown or appear out of the ordinary to the observer because of performance, aerodynamic characteristics, or unusual features.

It also restated the threefold air force interest in UFOs: first as a possible security threat, next to determine the "technical or scientific characteristics" involved, finally to explain or identify all sightings. All air base commanders were to "conduct all investigative action necessary" before submitting an initial report. Air Force Intelligence and Air Defense Command had "a direct and immediate interest" in UFO reports within the country. Base commanders could only release information to the public "after positive identification of the sighting" as a familiar or known object. Discussion with unauthorized persons remained prohibited.[7]

Many of those persons were members of Congress. On October 29, 1962, Department of Defense Assistant Secretary Arthur Sylvester admitted that, when necessary, the government *did* withhold UFO data from the public. He cited air force regulation 11-7, which stated that sometimes information requested by Congress might not be furnished "even in confidence."[8]

The air force received more UFO reports during the second half of 1962. In mid- to late-September, northeastern New Jersey experienced a flurry of sightings. Something strange occurred near the Oradell reservoir on September 15, when witnesses claimed to see two bright discs descend toward the reservoir, one of which was heard touching the water. Someone called the police, but the object soon departed. ATIC investigated, but neither this nor any New Jersey sighting was classified as unknown. Most official unknowns were less interesting, such as the sighting in Tampa, Florida, on November 17, by a former Marine Corps captain who saw three star-like objects approach horizontally and hover for about fifteen minutes.[9]

On November 15, Carl Sagan presented a remarkable paper to the American Rocket Society, arguing that not only was space travel possible, but that other civilizations "must today be plying the spaces between the stars." Indirectly critiquing the Ozma/Arecibo program, he stated that radio was not always the best way to establish contact with others. What would be, then? Apparently, direct, physical contact. Sagan assumed that if there were about a million worlds in the galaxy capable of such feats, they might visit one another once in every thousand years. Thus, he said, scouts may have visited the Earth a total of ten thousand times over the full span of Earth's history. Sagan quickly added that there were no reliable reports of such visitation, but urged scholars to study ancient myths and legends for clues. It was "not out of the question," said Sagan, that relics of such visits could yet be found. There might even be a hidden base, perhaps on the far side of the moon. Indeed, a remote location could very well be used for protection against weather and elements, and to avoid meddling with Earth's inhabitants. Throughout his public life, Sagan came down hard against UFO reports, eventually describing belief in UFOs as pseudoscience. Yet, what an amazing speech! Especially considering that Sagan was no mere independent academic, but rather an advisor to the U.S. military at the time on such matters as extraterrestrial life.[10]

On December 27, 1962, Wilbert B. Smith died. He had contributed to the cause of ending UFO secrecy and developed some interesting, if unprovable, ideas about aliens, essentially in line with the interpretation offered by many of the so-called contactees. Smith had long asserted privately that he had established a telepathic communication with the aliens. He did not publicize this or attempt to profit by this belief, but believed it sincerely. A speech he delivered in Ottawa on March 31, 1958, contains a fair sampling of his thoughts. Although alien science, he said, might be "forever beyond our comprehension," the aliens were our "blood brothers." Despite their interest in us, they remained aloof because of a basic law that "grants each and every individual independence and freedom of choice. . . . No one has the right to interfere in the affairs of others. . . ."[11] For believers in the UFO phenomenon, this was among the most hopeful of philosophies.

WHO RAN THE CIA?

The U.S. presidency was not the only office that could be out of the decision-making loop in the netherworld of the secret state. By late 1962, a full year into John McCone's tenure as DCI, he remained unaware of the MK-Ultra program, or of the agency's connection to the Mafia. Richard Helms, who did know about such things, simply neglected to tell him. This is yet another lesson in trying to understand the nature of the UFO cover-up, a slippery entity if there ever was one. What did McCone know about UFOs? We don't know.[12]

On February 11, 1963, the CIA established a domestic operations division for its clandestine services, conducted within the U.S. against "foreign targets." David Wise noted that this was actually one of at least half a dozen CIA operations operating domestically in the U.S. In reality, no one can really determine what was going on at the CIA. For example, MK-Ultra was supposedly terminated in 1963. More accurately, this refers to the program's official name only. True, Cameron's work was terminated following the Kennedy assassination. But during 1964 and 1965, Sid Gottlieb authorized over a dozen subprojects related to Cameron's work under a new acronym, MK-Search. Many of those investigations dealt with ways to destabilize human personalities.[13]

The NSA's Operation Shamrock benefited from new technology during 1963. This was RCA Global's development of computerized magnetic tape, which revolutionized communications and intelligence gathering. Instead of poring through messages for days, analysts now searched for key words and phrases relating to a particular subject. The NSA soon had many customers for this service: the FBI, CIA, Secret Service, and others who asked for "watch lists" of names and organizations.

UFOS IN THE WORLD: 1962

Project Blue Book may have ignored UFO reports in the rest of the world, but the CIA did not, nor did APRO and NICAP. Globally, UFO sightings in 1962 were of two basic categories: South American and non-South American. Within South America, Argentina by far had the most intense activity, which claimed the attention of that nation's military and the CIA.

The wave started in May, when dozens of UFOs were seen in Argentina, at least four by Argentine navy pilots. On May 12, in Argentina's La Pampa province, two men claimed to see a humming, illuminated, landed object off the road at around 4 A.M. It rose, crossed low over the road, ascended with a flame, and, to their astonishment, divided into two sections that flew away separately. The object left a huge circle about three hundred feet in diameter; grass was burned within it, and insects were "carbonized." The Puerto Belgrano Naval Base analyzed the site. About twenty-four hours later, dozens of people in the Argentine towns of Uncativo, Cordoba, Carranza, and the Los Molinos Dam saw a bright, elongated object with a bright trail. A fog soon filled a wooded section near Uncativo, and people saw an object on the ground. Little else is available about the incident. CIA files recorded a "most extraordinary" sighting over Bahia Blanca, south of Buenos Aires, witnessed by many people on May 21. A strange luminous object hung as though suspended for several minutes, then quickly disappeared. A photographer took two pictures, showing the object to appear as a "luminous oval." A FOIA request by CAUS failed to obtain the photo. On or near May 22 or May 24, in the town of Winifreda in the La Pampa province, a woman was hospitalized after she and her husband claimed to see an object land and two large "robot-like creatures" emerge. According to the Lorenzens, Argentine air force officials found a circle of scorched grass.[14]

Argentines reported UFOs through the summer of 1962. An amazing near-landing was reported at the Camba Punta airport on August 2, 1962. A round object rapidly approached the airport and circled overhead. The airport's director, Luis Harvey, ordered a landing strip to be cleared after he and his staff saw it. It descended and hovered extremely low above the runway for three or four minutes. The object spun while giving off flashes of blue, green, and orange light. It took off quickly when excited witnesses ran out to get a closer look.[15]

Activity spread to Brazil during the late summer, including a bizarre, ominous incident on the evening of August 17, in the town of Duas Pontes. A diamond prospector named Rivalino da Silva, a man ignorant of UFOs, told several people that he saw two short beings digging a hole near his house. They ran away when he approached, and an object took off from behind the bushes. No one believed him. Two nights later, Rivalino's son, Raimundo, woke to the sound of steps, saw odd shadows, and heard voices saying "this one looks like Rivalino," and that they would kill him. The next night, Raimundo reportedly saw two spherical objects hovering near his house, humming and emitting a flame. Rivalino warned Raimundo to stay back, and he approached. The two objects merged, spread a yellow mist, and gave an "acrid smell." According to the story, Rivalino was never seen again, local police investigated, and several frightened people left the area.[16]

On December 21 in Angel Falls, Venezuela, a bright, teardrop-shaped light rose from the jungle floor, apparently filmed from an aircraft. On the same day, another Argentine airport incident was reported, this time at the Buenos Aires Ezeiza International Airport, shortly after 2 A.M. The airport's two control tower operators, Horado Alora and Mario Pezzuto, saw a large, fiery disc on or low over the runway. The crews of two aircraft also saw the object. It soon rose to about thirty feet off the ground and flew away to the northeast. During these few minutes, an incoming flight held a holding pattern over the airport.[17]

Elsewhere, there were fewer UFO sightings, but several which recalled the 1954 European wave. In the Australian town of Norwood, a woman was driving with her three children on the evening of October 28, 1962, when they all saw an illuminated oval object land near the road. She stopped the car and watched the object for forty minutes, claiming to see a man wearing a helmet and gas mask near the craft. On the morning of February 15, 1963, in the Australian town of Willow Grove, a man saw an object approach and stop over his farmhouse at an altitude of about fifty feet. It was about twenty-five feet in diameter and about ten feet tall. The object was blue, made a swishing sound, and the underside spun counterclockwise. It hovered for about five seconds, then took off amazingly fast. The man had a strong headache for the rest of the day. Landings and humanoid sightings were reported in Italy in December 1962 and January 1963, including one case of witness paralysis. Meanwhile, on December 12, in Amagasaki City, Japan, five students saw, and independently sketched, a Saturn-shaped UFO.[18]

THE UFO SCENE IN 1963

In January 1963, Robert Friend left as Blue Book's director. He had tried, and failed, to disband it. His replacement, Maj. Hector Quintanilla, held to a simple policy: make no changes whatsoever. No changes meant no improvement, as the April 1963 issue of the *Yale Scientific Magazine* commented:

Based upon unreliable and unscientific surmises as data, the air force develops elaborate statistical findings which seem impressive to the uninitiated public, unschooled in the fallacies of the statistical method. One must conclude that the highly publicized periodic air force pronouncements based upon unsound statistics serve merely to misrepresent the true character of UFO phenomena.

Despite the new leadership at Blue Book, 1963 was essentially a repeat of 1962. Once again, it recorded a mere fourteen official unknowns (this time, five outside the United States). Once again, the unknowns were an unimpressive lot: mostly oddly maneuvering lights. Once again, most of the good UFO reports were going elsewhere.[19]

NICAP recorded more interesting and difficult sightings, including two from June 26, 1963. First, at 1 P.M. in Rockland, Massachusetts, a number of people heard a loud roar and saw a silhouette of a Saturn-shaped UFO; a white light on top and orange light on bottom were visible. The object hovered, then moved away horizontally. The same day in Pine Crest, California, a technician and many others saw three glowing, greenish objects with halos move westerly. They were approached by a similar object from the west; the fourth object stopped and hovered while the others approached, split formation, and continued west. It then continued east.[20]

Once again, South America was the source of many UFO reports. An especially dense wave of sightings occurred there in October. Several times in Argentina, humanoids or figures were seen, and sightings included gunfire, witness burns, and local panics. Two interesting naval sightings occurred in November 1963. The first involved an Argentine navy transport vessel, *Punta Medanos*, which suffered interference from the presence of a large UFO that followed it at a distance of one mile on November 12. Equipment returned to normal after the craft left. The second involved the Scottish vessel *Thrift* on the night of November 21–22, in the North Sea. Four members, including the captain, saw a "flashing red light" pass within a mile of port side, about fifteen to twenty feet above sea level. It made no sound, then disappeared at a distance of three miles. The vessel went out to search for it and twice obtained a radar fix, both of which disappeared a quarter mile distant. They never found a trace of the object, but the captain said "something definitely fell into the water."[21]

The most interesting UFO incident of 1963 occurred in Britain, where throughout the mid-1960s landings and crop circles were increasingly common. In many of these cases, reeds and grass were found in a clockwise swirl. On July 15, in the English town of Charlton, Wiltshire, a farmer named Roy Blanchard discovered a strange crater in his potato field, about eight feet wide and four inches deep. A hole at the center was three feet deep and less than a foot in diameter. All vegetation inside the circle was burned, leaving only the bare earth, and there were four "slots" in the ground around it, each about four feet long and a foot wide. A small piece of metal was recovered from the hole. British astronomer Patrick Moore stated that a "shrimp-sized meteorite" caused the crater. A military investigation, however, showed no burn or scratch marks, nor any trace of an explosion. Just prior to the appearance of this crater, several UFO reports had come from the neighborhood. Moreover, a number of "craters" also appeared in other areas in England and Scotland, some quite large. The series of events gained much coverage in *Flying Saucer Review*, and the journal of the British UFO Association (BUFOA). Soon after, on August 1, a former RAF pilot and current flying instructor in Garston, Hertfordshire, England, saw a triangular UFO which hovered for a long period of time, then climbed out of sight. An air traffic controller four miles away also saw it.[22]

But Britain was over there. Across the Atlantic, congressional interest in UFOs was extremely low. On July 18, 1963, Georgia Congressman Carl Vinson made the last congressional inquiry into UFOs for the next three years.[23]

ASSASSINATION AND SECRET DOINGS: 1963 AND 1964

In Dallas, on November 22, 1963, John F. Kennedy was assassinated. Working from the premise that one contentious conspiracy theory is quite sufficient for one book, we will restrict ourselves to a few remarks regarding the official investigation.

FBI Director J. Edgar Hoover had a hatred of all things Kennedy. He had known about, and used, JFK's womanizing to his advantage. He detested his direct superior, Attorney General Robert Kennedy. In August 1962, when Marilyn Monroe died, Hoover had information connecting RFK to Monroe's residence that day; he used this information to his advantage, too. In June 1963, when JFK met with Martin Luther King, Jr., at the White House, Kennedy actually took King outside, where there were no FBI bugs, to warn him about Hoover's surveillance.

After the assassination, Hoover's office filtered nearly all information going to the Warren Commission. Caught in the net, among much else, were connections to the world of organized crime, which the assassination suggested at myriad points. Hoover may have had connections to that world and may even have been blackmailed by it.[24] He also filtered out ties to the FBI itself. Within mere hours of the assassination, Hoover stated definitively that Lee Harvey Oswald had acted alone. He denied that either Oswald or Oswald's own assassin, Jack Ruby, had ever been FBI informants. Yet, it later surfaced that Ruby had, in addition to his links to the Mafia, no fewer than nine contacts with the FBI and was listed in FBI files as potential criminal informant. If Hoover misled the Warren Commission about Ruby, what about Oswald? Oswald was well-known to the CIA long before the assassination, a fact unknown to the Warren Commission.

By this time, the U.S. intelligence community was spending an estimated

$4 billion annually via federal channels; this was distinct from money generated through private ventures, of which there are no financial records, but which was probably considerable. Even Truman commented on the growing secret state. On December 22, 1963, the *Washington Post* quoted him as "disturbed by the way in which the CIA has been diverted from its original assignment." It had "become a government all of its own and all secret. They don't have to account to anybody."[25]

These were true words. Year after year, the CIA seemed to outdo itself. Its activities in Southeast Asia have already been discussed. During 1964, the CIA also fixed the Chilean elections to defeat Marxist candidate Salvador Allende. Richard Helms, chief of clandestine operations, coordinated the action. Incredibly, more than half of all money spent on this election came from the CIA. In addition, CIA was flying Cuban exile pilots—Bay of Pigs veterans—in B-26 bombers over the Congo, under the cover of a dummy company. Their mission was now to suppress a revolt against the Central Congolese government of Joseph Mobutu, who had wasted no time in his quest for personal enrichment at the expense of his people.[26]

Clearly, American intelligence agencies were not alone in committing dastardly subterranean deeds, and the foregoing is not intended to make it appear so. Not only the CIA and KGB, but intelligence agencies around the world regularly commit acts that are denied officially, and which would have serious repercussions if known. Rather, it is important to be mindful that organizations like the CIA were not immune to such activities. One should beware of fighting monsters, for there is danger in becoming one. By the 1960s, lying and deception, whether for the perceived greater good or not, had long been a hallmark of the American national security state in all areas within its realm of interest, including UFOs.

UFOs in 1964: The Pace Quickens

The year 1964 began with few UFO sightings. By the year's end, however, UFOs had shown themselves with greater frequency than in many previous years. The year also produced several intriguing statements and rumors. An issue of *Astronomical Journal* mentioned Soviet studies that called attention to possible extraterrestrial space signals. More intriguing were rumors that Jacques Vallee claimed to be hearing from "quasi-official sources" in Paris during 1964. One was that the British military was carefully monitoring the UFO situation and pooling its information with the Soviets! Another was that U.S. law enforcement agencies had compiled exhaustive studies of the American cases, "a rumor," wrote Vallee, "that appears at least partially true."[27]

NICAP published its seminal *The UFO Evidence* that year, and sent it to every member of Congress. Edited by Richard Hall, the book impressively documented and categorized a massive number of UFO sightings, with a heavy emphasis on military encounters. It also provided useful information on the development of air force policies, NICAP's efforts on behalf of a congressional investigation, and a generous sample of quotes from public figures. If meant to stir congressional interest in UFOs, however, the book was a disappointment. Donald Menzel published another book as well, essentially rehashing his material from 1953. Menzel supported Blue Book, attributed most sightings to mirages and optical effects, and blamed sighting waves on overexcited imaginations and the media.

Two interesting U.K. cases occurred in December 1963. One involved two RAF airmen witnessing a dome-shaped object appearing to land; the other, an apparent landing of a craft that left flattened grass over a circular area. Otherwise, little was reported until April 1964. On April 8, during the first orbital launching of a Gemini spacecraft, reports came that while the craft was in its first orbit, it was accompanied by four unknown, seemingly controlled objects. After one complete orbit, the objects broke away and went off into space. This incident, reported in *True* magazine, led to an inquiry by members of Congress and a formal denial by NASA. Yes, said NASA, there *were* other objects on radar, but these were related to the separation of the capsule and booster rocket.[28]

CLOSE-UP SIGHTING IN SOCORRO

On April 24, 1964, one of the classic UFO-alien sightings occurred at Socorro, New Mexico. At 5:45 P.M., Police Sergeant Lonnie Zamora was pursuing a speeding vehicle when he heard a roar from outside the car. He saw a "flame in the sky" and thought a nearby dynamite shack had exploded. He abandoned his pursuit and drove partially up the hill, over which the flame had passed. He walked the final part and at the top saw a shiny object about 150 to 200 yards away. At first, Zamora thought a car had overturned, and he moved forward to help out. He also saw what appeared to be two children in white coveralls. Then he noticed the object was resting on four legs and that the "children" were examining or repairing the craft. They did not notice him at first; when they did, they hurried back into the object.

Zamora moved quickly back to his car, either out of fear, or in order to drive closer, or perhaps both. Just then, the object began to roar, a flame appeared on its underside, and it ascended slowly. Zamora now discerned it was oval in shape and very smooth. Although he saw no windows or doors, he did notice an insignia with red lettering of some type. He ran after the object as it continued to rise in the air and accelerate toward the southwest. By the time it disappeared, the flame was gone, and the craft was silent, leaving no trail.

Zamora was so shocked by what he saw that he asked to see a priest before releasing his report to the authorities. Quite simply, he believed he saw an alien craft. Everyone came down to look into this one. Within two hours, army intelligence from White Sands Proving Grounds was there, along with an FBI agent. Hynek arrived the next day. Air force intelligence also investigated, as did Kirtland AFB and Blue Book Sergeant James Moody. The CIA had a file and probably investigators as well. Among civilians, NICAP and APRO were there, and also, a bit later, debunker Philip Klass. (During APRO's investigation of Socorro, Blue Book's Sergeant Moody told the Lorenzens, "you get lots of cases that we don't.") Everyone but Klass thought the case was among the most legitimate and compelling of all UFO encounters.

There were several reasons for such an assessment. For a week after the event, Zamora was subjected to an almost continuous barrage of interviews by the many investigators on the scene. He impressed everyone with his honesty, his genuine puzzlement and even shock, and his extremely detailed report. No one questioned his integrity or ability to discern what he claimed to have seen. Other reasons were the deep landing marks left by the legs of the craft, as well as a charred area where it had taken off. These traces forced Hynek into writing about this as a "real, physical event."

Much of the scrutiny Zamora received centered over his description of the beings he saw, and of the strange insignia he saw on the side of the craft. He later refused to discuss these elements of the story because, he said, he was asked to keep quiet about "some things" he had seen.

In a 1966 classified article for *Studies in Intelligence*, Blue Book chief Hector Quintanilla, while not endorsing the extraterrestrial hypothesis, wrote:

> There is no doubt that Lonnie Zamora saw an object which left quite an impression on him. There is no question about his reliability. . . . He is puzzled by what he saw and frankly, so are we. This is the best-documented case on record, and still we have been unable, in spite of a thorough investigation, to find the vehicle or other stimulus that scared Zamora to the point of panic.

Publicly, Quintanilla debunked and even ridiculed the story. Philip Klass came into town years later and decided the whole thing was a tourism-related hoax. No one took Klass seriously, and no evidence for a hoax ever emerged. Hynek later wrote that the case strongly affected him. It also forced NICAP to reconsider its position on occupant sightings. Henceforth, occupant reports were viewed as credible, even in this conservative bastion of UFO believers.

Lonnie Zamora's sighting of aliens in Socorro is generally considered among the most compelling and interesting UFO encounters ever. Certainly, it was a fascinating close-range sighting, backed by strong physical evidence and personal testimony. Zamora's experience, however, was not unique. Such sightings were reported with great frequency over the years in South America and were a major event in Europe in 1954. Many of those encounters were equally well substantiated. What made the event at Socorro special was merely that it took place in America. The focus of American researchers on the event as the "classic" alien sighting has more to do with native provincialism than anything else.

The final chapter to the Socorro story occurred during the summer. On July 31, 1964, Ray Stanford and Richard Hall visited NASA's Goddard Space Flight Center at Greenbelt, Maryland, in order to have the lab there analyze metals on a rock from the landing site. Dr. Henry Frankel, head of NASA's Spacecraft Systems Branch, directed the analysis and agreed to Stanford's request that only half the rock's metal be scraped off. Frankel declared that some of the particles looked like they had been in a molten state when they got onto the rock.

When the rock was returned to Stanford, it had been scraped clean. "There was nothing, not a speck of the metal left," said Stanford. On August 5, he phoned Frankel, who told him that

> the particles are comprised of a material that could not occur naturally. . . . This definitely strengthens the case that might be made for an extraterrestrial origin of the Socorro object.

Frankel instructed Stanford to phone again in a week, after he had time to analyze the metal further. On August 12, Stanford phoned Frankel's office but could only reach Frankel's secretary, who said he was unavailable. Stanford called again the next day—no luck. He called yet again on the seventeenth, and was told by Frankel's secretary that "Dr. Frankel is unprepared, at this time, to discuss the information you are calling about." Stanford tried to reach Frankel again on the eighteenth and nineteenth, both times without success. Amid failure, he had the virtue of persistence.

On August 20, 1964, Stanford received a phone call from Thomas P. Sciacca, Jr., of NASA's Spacecraft Systems Branch. "I have been appointed to call you," said Sciacca,

> and report the official conclusion of the Socorro sample analysis. Dr. Frankel is no longer involved with the matter, so in response to your repeated inquiries, I want to tell you the results of the analysis. Everything you were told earlier by Dr. Frankel was a mistake. The sample was determined to be silica, SiO_2.

By now, these games had become monotonously depressing. How could one hope to obtain confirmation of any sort within such a setting, against such forces?[29]

SOCORRO AFTERMATH: A YEAR OF UFOS

Depending on one's choice of sources, 1964 was either a very active year for UFOs or business as usual. UFO reports to NICAP and APRO shot way up. Blue Book, on the other hand, tallied only twenty official unidentifieds (including the Socorro incident) for the year. Then again, it received about five hundred reports and had long since mastered the art of fake explanations. Most of Blue Book's unexplained cases continued to be of the lights in the night sky type. Without a doubt, however, the Socorro case heralded a new spate of UFO sightings in the U.S. and sparked new media coverage. A large number of landing, electromagnetic (EM), and occupant cases were reported throughout the summer and fall, several quite vivid in detail, and at least one describing high-pitched voices. The air force investigated several of these cases.[30]

Just two days after the Socorro sighting, and about two hundred miles north, Orlando Gallegos near La Madera, New Mexico, saw a metallic, oval-shaped object on the ground about two hundred feet away. He saw blue flames circle the bottom of the machine, which was silent and about the length of a telephone pole. The local police captain, Martin Vigil, reported scorch marks and four imprints at the site. Another New Mexico sighting occurred on April 28, near the town of Anthony. According to many witnesses, including police officer Paul Arteche, a reddish, round object hovered at a low level, then took off swiftly toward the west.[31]

On April 30, 1964, according to APRO, the pilot of a B-57 bomber from Holloman AFB, Alamogordo, radioed to his control tower that he was watching an "egg-shaped, white" UFO with markings that matched the one at Socorro. As he continued to observe the UFO, it landed on the base. Both Lorenzens claimed that they got this story from a very reliable source. Others, too, had heard the story, including a ham radio operator who claimed to have monitored the exchange between the pilot and control tower. A journalist called Holloman about it and received a denial. But Jim and Coral Lorenzen were adamant that they had three "entirely independent, unconnected sources of information" for this story. Shortly after the incident was said to have occurred, an airman walked into an Alamogordo clothing store and blurted out an incredible story of a UFO being parked in a hangar at Holloman AFB, under heavy guard. A day or two later, he returned to the store to insist he had made a mistake. There was no such thing as an alien spacecraft at Holloman, he said. An incredible story; can it be believed? The story *was* circulating, and the Lorenzens never wavered in their claim to have gotten it from several inside sources. It should be remembered, too, that for years, they were exceedingly cautious in assessing U.S. military involvement in UFOs.[32]

UFO sightings increased through May, especially in the western U.S. Several multiple-witness sightings that month occurred in the small town of Rio Vista, California. On May 5, in Comstock, Minnesota, a farmer saw an oval object rise from a field and fly into the clouds. It left a depression and imprints. A boy in Hubbard, Oregon, reported a silvery object, about ten feet long, resting on four legs in a wheat field on May 18. It made a beeping noise, rose about twenty feet, then ascended vertically. Flattened wheat was found at the site.[33]

Two incidents at White Sands Proving Ground occurred in the latter part of May 1964, neither case going to Blue Book. On May 22, a UFO was tracked on radar; a week later, on the twenty-ninth, two objects "moving leisurely across the range" were tracked on radar. This time, witnesses saw them visually as football-shaped.[34]

Blue Book unknowns, meanwhile, were more of a joke than anything else. Consider these two from May 26. The first, from Cambridge, Massachusetts, took place at 7:43 P.M. by an RAF pilot and ex-Smithsonian satellite tracker, who saw a thin, white object fly straight and level for about four seconds. The other took place in Pleasantview, Pennsylvania, at 11 P.M., when a man saw a yellow-orange light in a field, then chased it down the road for two miles. Such unknown cases were surely nothing to get excited about. Perhaps the entire point.

THE DAM BREAKS

Despite a number of well-documented UFO sightings, NICAP remained stalled in its efforts to break the secrecy throughout 1964. On the other side of the fence, the air force was also stymied in its efforts to unload the Blue Book program. Allen Hynek was showing signs that he was no longer a certain air force ally. Moreover, Gen. Curtis LeMay's autobiographical *Mission with LeMay* appeared in 1965, in which LeMay stated that he was "asked about flying saucers all the time." Unable to quote classified information, he gave "the straightest answers" he could. Contrary to what the public perceived, wrote LeMay, the air force was not deliberately trying to debunk UFOs. In fact:

> There is no question about it. These were things which we could not tie in with any natural phenomena known to our investigators. . . . There were some cases we could not explain. Never could.[35]

Such developments were generally ignored by the public, of which less than 20 percent believed in UFOs, according to various polls and private estimates by both the air force and NICAP. The air force reinforced such negative public perceptions on January 25, 1965, with the statement that only 2 percent of the UFO cases of the past five years had not been solved.[36]

The dam broke in 1965. The UFO activity of 1964 was a whisper compared with the following year. Along with the dramatic increase in sightings, there was an explosion of UFO-related literature, including the first significant discussions of the abduction phenomenon.

Incredibly, air force official statistics provide fewer unidentifieds for 1965 (sixteen) than for the previous year, although the number of reports received nearly doubled, to about nine hundred. But the Blue Book numbers were a small fraction of the total story. Flying saucers were being reported in great numbers around the world. Indeed, one of the early interesting reports of the year came from Waihoke, New Zealand, where a ring on the ground at the location of a UFO sighting remained visible for four years. The site contained a high concentration of an unidentified whitish material which resolved into fibers during an oil immersion test. Philip Klass said the material was from the urine of sheep feeding from some circular device; Vallee, who had the results of the tests, said the material was "vegetal in nature."[37]

On January 5, 1965, a large flying disc was seen over the NASA station at Wallops Island, Virginia. The station's satellite tracking chief calculated its speed at 6,000 mph. On the same day, the navy disclosed that two UFOs had been tracked on radar at the Naval Air Test Center in Maryland. One had made a sharp turn at 4,800 mph. The air force, which was working hard to debunk as many reports as quickly as possible, decided to do *something*. Therefore, Blue Book chief Hector Quintanilla went to Richmond for a debunking tour. Not a single UFO report was genuine, he told reporters.[38]

In Washington, D.C., at 4:20 P.M. on January 11, twelve Army communications specialists in the Munitions Building at 19th Street and Constitution Avenue., N.W., saw twelve to fifteen white, oval-shaped objects moving across the sky between twelve thousand to fifteen thousand feet. These objects were also tracked on radar, and two delta-wing jets were soon in pursuit but were easily outmaneuvered. The incident was reported in the *Washington Star* on January 13. The Pentagon had a ready response to the incident: the army personnel had seen nothing at all. Just in time, as the soldiers had been scheduled for an interview by a local television station. At the scene of the interview, a representative from the Pentagon prevented both military and civilian witnesses from speaking.[39]

Just past midnight on January 12, came a much-reported incident from a farm near Curtis, Washington, not far from Blaine AFB. A family reported seeing a glowing, circular, domed craft land in a snowy field. The object soon left, but melted the snow in a thirty-foot circle, and even scorched the earth. Air force authorities told the family not to discuss the incident, and the ground itself was plowed under. Additional confirmation of the incident came from Blaine itself, where, just before the landing, radar had tracked a thirty-foot object which had buzzed the car of Department of Justice officer Inspector Robert E. Kerringer while he was driving to the base. The man saw the object and even got out of his car and watched it hover for a minute or two before flying off. He described it as a "huge shining thing [which] swooped down, right over the car," then shot upward. As he reached for his radio microphone, the object climbed faster than any jet, into the clouds and out of sight. Kerringer was also told by Blaine officials to keep quiet about the incident. Later on the same day, an Oregon woman and her two sons reported seeing a triangular UFO coming slowly out of the southeast and "suddenly plunge into the seas" some miles offshore at Tillamook Head. It left two trails of fire behind.[40]

Following this, a wave of reports came from Virginia. At midnight on January 14, in Norfolk, Virginia, a man saw a bright, circular object rise from the ground. On January 19, 1965, in Brands Flat, a man cutting wood saw two hovering, saucer-shaped objects, one hundred feet and twenty feet in diameter. The smaller one landed and was so highly polished that the man said, "I would bet on a clear day you could not see it at five thousand feet." A door opened, and three human-looking pilots emerged, except that their skin was reddish-orange, they had "staring eyes," and one of them had an unusually long finger on his left hand. They spoke incomprehensibly and reentered the object. When the door closed, its outline became invisible. On the morning of January 23 in Williamsburg, a driver experienced engine failure at the intersection of U.S. Highway 60 and State Route 14. At the side of the road, he saw a huge metallic, light bulb-shaped object, perhaps seventy-five feet high, hovering very low over the ground. Something, presumably its engine, was making a noise, and it had a reddish and blue light on either side. It took off rapidly toward the west.[41]

Two days later in Williamsburg, a "top-shaped" metallic object descended rapidly from the sky, causing engine failure in the car of a real estate executive. It hovered low above the ground about half a minute, then shot up at tremendous speed. The Virginia State Police took the report. A few miles away on the same night, an object matching the same description descended near another businessman, whose car stalled as the object landed. On January 27, near Hampton, Virginia, two NASA engineers, one a former air force pilot, saw a UFO descend with flashing lights. One of them told NICAP that the object zigzagged to a brief landing, then rapidly climbed out of sight.[42]

THE WAVE OF 1965

On January 19, 1965, NICAP's acting director, Richard Hall, met with a CIA agent and obtained a direct telephone line to that agent's office. A CIA memorandum dated January 25 discussed the meeting at which time various samples and reports on UFO sightings procured from NICAP were given to [blank] for transmittal to OSI. The information was desired by OSI to assist them in the preparation of a paper for [blank] on UFOs.

Later, Hall wrote that he used this line only one time, "to report some high-quality UFO sightings" to the CIA. That would appear to be in addition to the meeting described in the CIA memo. Hall was the subject of a CIA security clearance, without his consent or knowledge, he wrote. He obtained several previously known documents after an appeal through FOIA, but the CIA refused to release the security clearance paper trail.

Barry Greenwood and Lawrence Fawcett wrote that the memo showed "an inordinate amount of interest in [NICAP], considering that the CIA's function is foreign intelligence." Exactly right, but it should be no surprise, given the longtime CIA interest in UFOs. A more pertinent question might be, what was the relationship between Hall and the CIA? Hall recently stated "emphatically" that "there was no CIA (or any other intelligence agency) influence on NICAP" while he was at the center of NICAP affairs during the mid- and late 1960s.[43]

Again, it must be stressed that the CIA's secret collection of UFO reports mirrored the activity of America's many intelligence agencies in all facets of society. In March 1965, for example, FBI offices were asked to compile lists of reliable reporters who could be called on for Cointelpro work. Hoover was meanwhile busy gathering data on antiwar groups as well as members of Congress. That summer, U.S. Army intelligence agents began to infiltrate and spy on a wide range of political groups involving about one thousand investigators and three hundred officers collecting questionable political utterances.[44]

UFO developments of 1965 were substantial enough to become a major public interest. On the night of January 29, the mayor of Monterey, California, and his family saw a bright light performing acrobatics in the sky. The light hovered, shot straight up, then faded and dropped down to hover some more. Finally, it dropped toward the water and disappeared. A local pilot also saw the event, and the Coast Guard investigated but offered no explanation.[45]

On the other side of Monterey Bay that night, radio technician Sid Padrick claimed to have encountered UFO occupants. At about 2 A.M., while taking a late stroll before going to bed, Padrick claimed he heard a loud humming noise and saw a machine shaped like "two thick saucers inverted." An entity told him not to be afraid and welcomed him aboard. "You may call me Zeeno," the being said to him. For what it's worth, Xeno is the Greek word for stranger, something Padrick did not know. The being asked Padrick if he wanted to pay his respects to the supreme deity, and Padrick reported having a deep spiritual experience. Perhaps surprisingly, officers from nearby Hamilton AFB interviewed Padrick for three hours. According to Padrick, "they wanted my account of it, word for word." He said there were certain details which they asked him not to talk about publicly, but he talked anyway. Reporters found that Padrick was backed up by everyone who knew him; he was not a nut, nor a religious fanatic, nor interested in UFOs.[46]

The UFO wave of 1965 was not merely nationwide, but a global affair. On the night of February 3, 1965, in South Brighton, New Zealand, flattened grass was found after a man saw a UFO, about twenty-five feet in diameter, rise to an altitude of about sixty feet, then depart. On February 11, an air force officer and flight crew, en route from Anchorage to Japan, obtained a radar-visual sighting of three huge objects that paced their F-169 freighter aircraft over the Pacific Ocean. The objects were red and glowing and, after thirty minutes, ascended swiftly at over 1,500 mph. The pilot later remarked that he had often seen UFOs on the Alaskan run. A sighting of three short humanoids emerging from a craft was reported in Chalac, Argentina, by about fifty people on February 21.[47]

On the night of March 14–15, 1965, James W. Flynn, a forty-five-year-old rancher and dog trainer who was hunting in the Florida Everglades, claimed to have gotten a close-up view of a UFO. The object descended after midnight, and Flynn investigated. He saw an enormous cone-shaped machine silently hovering a few feet over the ground and watched it for about forty minutes. Flynn estimated it was about seventy-five feet in diameter and twenty-five to thirty feet high and had four rows of ports or windows. He could see yellow light coming through the windows, and heard an engine-like sound. Evidently feeling lucky, he approached the craft with a raised hand. He got to within about six feet when a narrow beam of light struck him in the forehead and knocked him unconscious for close to twenty-four hours. The story was incredible, but Flynn spent five days in a Fort Myers hospital with a large bruise on his head, burns, and damage to deep muscle tissue. He had lost vision in the right eye and saw poorly with the left. Everyone, it seemed, vouched for his character. Evidence also existed at the landing site, where the ground showed definite scorch marks in a large circular area, and the *tops* of trees were burned by something.[48]

A major UFO sighting occurred on May 24 at Eton Range in Australia, forty-two miles from the city of Mackay. A round glowing object either landed or hovered just above the ground for about thirty minutes, where it was seen by three guests of the Retreat Hotel: Jim Tilse, Eric Judin, and John Burgess. One had been a WWII pilot, one was a veteran airline pilot, and the other was an engineer. According to Tilse, the commercial pilot:

> It was about three hundred yards from the hotel where we were staying. It had a bank of spotlights, twenty or thirty of them, along a circular platform. It was solid, metallic-looking, thirty feet or more in diameter.

The craft made a buzzing sound, illuminated trees as it settled, and was supported by a large tripod-type landing gear. When it rose to three hundred feet, it accelerated swiftly toward the northwest, leaving no exhaust or trail. These men had all been skeptics regarding UFOs, but no longer. Tilse went back the next day to photograph a circular impression on the ground at the site; its inside diameter was twenty feet and confirmed by local police as a perfect circle. A police investigation also found damaged trees and other landing traces. The regional director of civil aviation accepted the incident report as genuine, and Australian authorities interrogated the men at length.[49]

UFOs were being seen in both hemispheres, north and south. On June 4, they were also seen in space. Astronauts James McDivitt and Edward White were orbiting the Earth during the Gemini 4 mission. While the mission passed over Hawaii, and as White was sleeping, McDivitt saw a "weird object" with some sort of "projections" on it "like arms." He photographed the object with a movie camera. Soon after, both men saw two similar objects over the Caribbean. McDivitt later had this to say about what he saw:

> I noticed an object out the front window of the spacecraft. It appeared to be cylindrical in shape with a high fineness ratio. From one end protruded a long, cylindrical pole with the approximate fineness of a pencil. I had no idea what the size was or what the distance to the object was. I do not feel that there was anything strange or exotic about this particular object. Rather, only that I could not identify it.

After McDivitt turned the film over to NASA, the photographs disappeared. James Oberg, a flight controller at the Johnson Space Center who later became well known as a UFO skeptic, stated that McDivitt's eyes were affected by an accidental urine spill inside the capsule and were half-blinded by the sun's glare. These two facts, said Oberg, prevented him from recognizing the *Titan II* second stage. At least two images of McDivitt's film are available today on the Internet, although they do not show very much.[50]

The remote region of Antarctica also became the scene of significant UFO activity. On June 19, members of the Chilean military saw a large, lens-shaped flying object maneuvering on an erratic path at the Chilean station in the Antarctic. Not much more is known. On July 2, the English base in Antarctica at Hallet reported sighting an unidentified flying object for eight to ten minutes. Then, on July 3, Argentina reported an extraordinary encounter over *its* base in Antarctica. According to Argentina's secretary of the navy, with corroboration from the Chilean military, this is what happened: At 7:40 P.M. on Deception Island, a large, lens-shaped flying object, looking like a classic flying saucer, moved on a zigzag trajectory, maneuvering over the base. It then hovered motionless for about fifteen minutes. It interfered with radio communications, and its speed and maneuverability were beyond the capabilities of any man-made device. In addition, magnetic tapes registered the object, which caused strong interference with variometers used to measure the Earth's magnetic field. Thirteen members of the Argentine garrison and three Chilean sub-officers saw the object with high-powered binoculars. The crew took ten color photographs through a theodolite. Everyone at the base believed strongly that this was no terrestrial aircraft.

British scientific personnel learned of the report, and the incident was reported in one American newspaper, the July 7, 1965, issue of the *Baltimore Sun*. It also appeared in *La Razon* in Buenos Aires on July 6 and the *Manitoba Standard* on July 9. The American media otherwise ignored the event. To this day, no photographs, scientific data, or witness reports have been made public. Richard Hall attempted and failed to obtain reports through embassies in Washington, D.C. It is not known whether Hall informed the CIA of this sighting at the time, though we can assume the agency had other means of discovery.[51]

THE WAVE OF 1965: JULY

Over at Dayton, Blue Book either ignored or explained away the amazing UFO encounters of the year. The Antarctic encounter left no resonance in the States. Instead, Blue Book continued its insipid reporting of supposed "unknowns," of which there were a mere two during the month of July, of 135 reports received.[52]

As was the norm by now, most of the interesting events never made it to Dayton. On July 1, for example, an extraordinary sighting occurred in Valensole, France, by forty-one-year-old lavender farmer Maurice Masse. Masse heard a strange noise early in the morning and saw an oval object one hundred feet away in his field. Thinking it to be a prototype of some sort, he approached to within twenty feet of it to find that it was about fifteen feet long with a round cockpit. Supporting the structure were six legs and a central pivot about the size of a small car. Masse then saw two beings, completely hairless and very white, less than four feet tall, with extremely large heads, normal hands, and practically no mouth. They wore gray-green one-piece suits, small containers on their belts, and no headgear or gloves.

The beings appeared surprised when Masse came near and stopped their examination of a plant. One of them pointed a small tube at Masse, which paralyzed him while they looked at him with human expression in their eyes and made gurgling noises to each other. Masse remained conscious and unafraid and believed the beings were making fun of him. They entered their craft through a sliding door, and the object soon hovered, then ascended, then vanished at about sixty yards. Although it made a whistling sound as it departed, Masse was not certain if it vanished because of its incredible speed, or simply *vanished*. He remained paralyzed for another twenty minutes after the encounter and felt uncharacteristically drowsy for weeks. Masse was a former Resistance fighter, a successful farmer, and regarded as "absolutely trustworthy" by the police who investigated the incident. The object left holes in the ground which were examined by many people, including police.[53]

Less than a week later, an extraordinary encounter took place at sea. On the night of July 6, while passing near Portugal, a lookout on the Norwegian ship *T.T. Jawesta* reported a bright, blue object that appeared to emerge from the sea, then rapidly travel northward toward the ship. He alerted the captain, first officer, and others, all of whom watched the silent object issue "tongues of flame" and make sudden turns at tremendous speed. Through binoculars, it appeared to be cigar-shaped with a row of lighted portholes. It reached an altitude of about one thousand feet and left a bluish trail. The sighting lasted a little more than half a minute. In a report to the Geophysical Institute in Bergen, Norway, the chief mate stated "with complete certainty that it was no question of an aircraft of conventional type, or rocket, or meteor, or ball lightning."[54]

On July 14, an object descended near an Australian space station (perhaps Pine Gap?), interfering with its tracking of *Mariner IV*. It was also observed by control tower operators at Canberra International Airport. On the sixteenth, a similar sighting was reported from near Buenos Aires.[55]

Throughout late July, August, and September, citizens of Chile, Argentina, and Peru reported close-up sightings of UFO craft, landings (several of which left impressions in the ground), and small, human-shaped UFO occupants. In September 1965, the Argentine navy reported the occurrence of fifteen incidents since late 1963 in which UFOs had tracked its vessels and interfered with its equipment.[56]

In the U.S., too, the air force was swamped with reports. Keyhoe wrote that by midsummer of 1965, the "debunking system had almost broken down." Not exactly, since labored explanations continued to fly out of Dayton as rapidly as the UFOs themselves. But it was true that people were becoming less and less persuaded by the honesty of the air force effort to explain the UFO problem. By July, belief in UFOs had risen to 33 percent, up from 20 percent at the beginning of the year, and editorials were appearing in newspapers criticizing UFO secrecy and debunking policies. Hynek also called for a more systematic study of UFOs in a July 1965 letter to the air force. "I feel it is my responsibility to point out," he wrote, "that enough puzzling sightings have been reported by intelligent and often technically competent people to warrant closer attention than Project Blue Book can possibly encompass at the present time."[57]

THE WAVE OF 1965: AUGUST

The pace of American UFO sightings increased during August, when the Blue Book team received 262 reports, surpassing most of the months (except July) during the 1952 crisis. Now, however, Blue Book's explanatory methods were such that *everything* had to be explained, except a few token inoffensive sightings, and even these were exceedingly few—four, to be precise, or a mere 1.5 percent of reports for the month.

An intense barrage of UFO activity appeared in the Midwest from July 31 to August 2, 1965, witnessed by thousands of people across nine states, including astronomers, state police, and journalists. What they appeared to be seeing were UFO formations.

Shortly after 9 P.M. on August 1, police squadrons in Oklahoma reported seeing diamond-shaped formations of UFOs for more than half an hour. These moved northerly and changed colors from red to white to blue-green. In Oklahoma City, a police dispatcher said headquarters had received over thirty-five calls between 8 and 10 P.M., with most estimates indicating objects at between fifteen thousand and twenty thousand feet. A police officer in Wynnewood, Oklahoma, reported a forty-five-minute UFO sighting, which was reportedly captured on radar by Tinker and Carswell Air Force Bases. The Weather Bureau at Wichita said it tracked objects south and west of Wellington that first appeared on radar at about twenty-two thousand feet, then descended to four thousand feet. Observers described the objects as red, which "exploded in a shower of sparks and at other times floated like a leaf." Even the *New York Times* reported the sightings.

That night was just the warm-up, however. On the night of August 2–3, 1965, tens of thousands of people from South Dakota to the Mexican border watched formations of brightly colored lights speeding through the skies, occasionally stopping for a few seconds. The sightings at times were awe-inspiring, changing formation, speed, color, and size. According to state police reports, many of the objects were tracked on civil and military radars. In the Minneapolis area, fifty police and sheriff squad cars radioed and reported UFOs between 12:20 A.M. and 2:20 A.M. Several objects were photographed. A fourteen-year-old boy in Tulsa took a picture with a cheap camera which, under enlargement, seemed to indicate a disc-shaped UFO which was divided by two bands into three segments. The picture was published in newspapers and studied by photo experts who pronounced it genuine. Another photo was taken near Sherman, Texas, of an object that had been tracked by Carswell AFB radar in Fort Worth.

A few reports were of objects near or on the ground. Two deputy sheriffs in Justin, Texas, saw a very bright object land while they were on a patrol near Wagle Mountain Lake. The police investigated but found nothing. In

Oklahoma City, five children claimed to see a bright, round object descend close to the ground.

In Dayton, the air force dismissed the sightings as nothing more than four stars in the constellation Orion and denied that any air bases had picked up objects on radar. The problem with that explanation, as people quickly realized, was that Orion was not visible in the Northern Hemisphere at this time of year. It was an embarrassing gaffe, even by Blue Book's typically low standards of explanation. Wright-Patterson then ascribed the sightings to the planet Jupiter and other stars.

Not surprisingly, this met with widespread disbelief. An air force weather observer in Oklahoma City said:

> I have repeatedly seen unusual objects in the sky, and they are no mirage. One of them looked like it had a flat top and flat bottom, and it was not a true sphere. There seemed to be two rings around it, and the rings were part of the main body.

The *Seattle Times* wrote: "Do you ever get the feeling that . . . the air force makes its denials six months in advance?"[58]

During the morning following this extraordinary night of sightings, another encounter occurred which, if not a hoax, was even more amazing. On August 3, 1965, Los Angeles County Highway Accident Investigator Rex Heflin took four clear Polaroid photographs of a hat-shaped UFO near a lonely stretch of road near Santa Ana, California. The object was silent, said Heflin, and a beam of white light seemed to rotate underneath the object. He tried to communicate with his supervisor, but the radio went dead while the object was present, a fact corroborated by Heflin's supervisor. Back at his office, he put the pictures in his desk drawer. A few days later, one of Heflin's coworkers sent the pictures to UPI, where photo analysts concluded them to be genuine. Shortly after Heflin received them back a few weeks later, he was approached by a man claiming to be from North American Air Defense Command G-2 (NORAD), who demanded the prints. Unfortunately, Heflin gave them to the man, and the mysterious caller and photos were never seen again. The air force and NORAD both denied having the photos or any involvement with the matter. Copies of the photos existed, however, and were widely published. Heflin told reporters he was willing to take a lie detector test to prove his pictures were authentic. A number of UFO writers concurred with the air force assessment that the event was a hoax, but (1) the fact that the photos were Polaroids, (2) many particulars of the photos themselves seem hard to hoax (such as evidence of an air current creating dust directly below the object), and (3) the perspectives from which Heflin took the pictures do not easily lend credence to the hoax scenario, and no one ever indicated how Heflin could have done it.

Two years later, on October 11, 1967, Heflin was visited by a strange group of men in air force uniforms. Suspicious, he obtained their names and other information. His visitors, in turn, asked him about the photos and such things as the Bermuda Triangle. He saw their car parked in the street; inside was a figure in the back seat and a violet glow, which looked like instrument dials. Heflin believed he was being photographed or recorded. Meanwhile, his FM radio made several loud blips. Others investigated this, but no one ever learned who the men were, except evident imposters.[59]

Landings and close encounters were being reported in North and South America throughout August 1965. That month, the air force inquired further into the possibility of submitting UFO files to the Academy of Sciences, or some similar body. Before long, events reached a crescendo that enabled the air force to realize its dream of unloading the UFO problem.[60]

THE INCIDENT AT EXETER

UFO activity continued at a gallop's pace in September. On September 3, 1965, another monumental case occurred, this time in the small town of Exeter, New Hampshire. At 2:24 A.M., eighteen-year-old Norman Muscarello, just a few weeks away from joining the navy, arrived at the Exeter police station in a state of near shock. He had been hitchhiking on Route 51 from Amesbury, Massachusetts, to his home in Exeter about twelve miles away. Since there was little traffic at that hour, he walked most of the way. At 2 A.M., he said, he reached Kensington by an open field between two houses and saw an object coming out of the sky directly toward him. It was as big as or bigger than a house, he said, between eighty and ninety feet in diameter, with brilliant, pulsating red lights around an apparent rim. It wobbled and floated toward him without a sound. Muscarello dived in terror into a shallow shoulder off the road, and the object backed off slowly, hovering over the roof of one of the houses. As it backed off some more, Muscarello ran to the house and pounded on the door, screaming. No answer. A car drove by, and Mucarello ran out into the road and convinced the couple to drive him to the police station. Muscarello was so adamant that the desk officer agreed to send someone back with him.

Just then, patrolman Eugene Bertrand, an air force veteran who had fought in Korea, arrived at the station, reporting that about an hour ago near Route 101, he had come across a car parked on the bypass with a woman at the wheel, who was trying to regain her composure. She claimed that a huge, silent, airborne object had been trailing her car. It was only a few feet away, with brilliant flashing red lights. Then, according to the woman, the object took off at tremendous speed toward the stars. Bertrand thought she was a kook and calmed her down but did nothing else. Now, hearing Muscarello's story, the two left for the scene of Muscarello's encounter.

They arrived at the field on Route 150 at around 3 A.M. No wind and perfect visibility. At first, the two saw nothing. Before long, however, horses and dogs on the farm became restless. The two then saw a slowly rising object approaching them—silent, brilliant, and roundish. It wobbled toward them "like a leaf fluttering from a tree." Red light bathed the area. Bertrand radioed to the station, "My god, I see the damn thing myself!"

The object hovered near the police car about three hundred feet away, one hundred feet in the air, silently rocking back and forth. It was too bright to make out any definite shape, but the two clearly saw pulsating red lights that dimmed from left to right then right to left in a 5–4–3–2–1, then 1–2–3–4–5 pattern. Each cycle took about two seconds. The object hovered for several minutes, and all was silent but for the horses and dogs. Then, according to Bertrand, it "darted," turned sharply, slowed down, and began to move away. As this happened, another patrolman, David Hunt, pulled up. He, too, saw the pulsating lights, heard the animals, and saw the object moving and rocking. Bertrand returned to the station "all shook up," in the opinion of the desk chief. He later said that at one time the lights came so close, he fell on the ground and started to draw his gun. He also stated that the lights of the object were always in a line and at a sixty-degree angle, and that when the object moved, the lower lights were always forward of the others.

After daylight, the police station called Pease AFB to reconfirm the incident. By 1 P.M., two air force officers arrived to interview the three witnesses at length. Although they appeared "interested and serious," they made little comment and returned to their base.

Journalist John Fuller investigated this case during the next month. He quickly learned that the incident was not an isolated one in the area. The local population was in a buzz about UFOs, and a huge gap existed between media coverage and local perceptions. Newspapers near Boston and Exeter ascribed the sightings to a "flying billboard" owned by the Sky-Lite Aerial Advertising Agency of Boston. Raymond Fowler told Fuller that his NICAP subcommittee routinely checked with Sky-Lite regarding possible UFO misidentifications and learned that no Sky-Lite flights were flown between August 21 and September 10. Moreover, the company rarely flew down near Exeter, and the plane's lights in no way matched the description of lights of the Exeter incident.

On the other side were the witnesses. One woman said to Fuller:

> We've often seen them come along these lines [referring to power lines]. And right here by the poles one of these crafts came right down over my car, dropped down four or five feet off the ground. You could see a metal surface and the orange-red and white lights on it. Right there by that tree there.

He learned that many of the sightings in the area were occurring near electric power lines. Few could make out much beyond the very bright lights, though at least one person, using binoculars, said it was the shape of a football.

When an official report reached the Pentagon later in September about the incident in Exeter, an officer in army intelligence was said to turn to a colleague and remark: "I hope it's one of ours."[61]

The Pentagon gave its official determination of the spate of sightings on October 27, with a press release that gave two basic explanations. Some stemmed from a high-altitude Strategic Air Command exercise out of Westover, Massachusetts. The Exeter sighting was caused by weather inversion, a layer of cold air trapped between warm layers, which caused the appearance of stars and planets to dance and twinkle. "We believe," said the Pentagon's spokesman, "what the people saw that night was stars and planets in unusual formations."

Many people considered this explanation to be a joke. Police officer Bertrand said:

> [I]f they want to turn out ridiculous statements like that, that's their business. I know what I saw; they don't. . . . I know for sure it had nothing to do with the weather. I know for sure this was a craft, and it was not any plane in existence. I know for sure it was not more than a hundred feet off the ground.[62]

Bertrand took the debunking as a personal insult and complained to the air force. In late November, Quintanilla sent an undated and unpostmarked letter to Bertrand and Hunt, which explained the Exeter sighting as a high-altitude military exercise that occurred between midnight and 2 A.M. (giving the date of September 2, 1965). He stated the case was still in the process of final evaluation. Bertrand and Hunt wrote back on November 2, unequivocal about what they saw, and asked for a letter to clear their names. They received no response and wrote again on December 28. Finally, on February 9, 1966, the Pentagon wrote to Bertrand and Hunt that the Exeter sighting *was* unidentified, but that air force experience in these matters proved "almost conclusively" that UFOs were all either man-made, natural phenomena, or caused by celestial bodies or meteors.[63]

Philip Klass and Robert Sheaffer both tried to debunk this case. In fact, it marked Klass's entry (a year later) into the field of UFO research, as he attempted to explain the case as ball lightning. No scientist took his theory seriously. Sheaffer claimed that the witnesses saw the planet Jupiter.[64]

In terms of drama and quality of the UFO sighting, the incident at Exeter could not easily be topped. Yet, the following night—still September 3, 1965, at 11 P.M.—in Brazoria County, Texas, near the town of Damon, another extraordinary encounter occurred. Two area sheriffs saw a huge object from their car, over two hundred feet long and about fifty feet high. It had a bright, violet light at one end and a pale-blue light at the other. They stopped to watch it and saw the craft fly to within one hundred feet of them, casting a huge shadow when it passed by the moon. They felt a wave of heat and drove away in fear. They decided to return to the site but turned back around when they saw the object still there. One of the men had been bitten by an animal before the sighting, and his left index finger was swollen and bleeding. After exposure to the light from the object, however, the pain was gone, and the wound healed quickly. Both officers were badly shaken by the incident. Later that evening, two men found one of the officers at a restaurant and described the object in detail, adding he should keep future encounters to himself. The incident was, however, reported to NICAP.

Hector Quintanilla initially explained the Damon sighting as a star or planet. But the local air force investigating officer reported:

> After talking with both officers involved in the sighting, there is no doubt in my mind that they definitely saw some unusual object or phenomenon. . . . Both officers appeared to be intelligent, mature, level-headed persons capable of sound judgment and reasoning.

This forced Quintanilla to reverse his original debunking explanation and label the sighting unidentified.[65]

On September 23, in the Mexican city of Cuernavaca, a major blackout coincided with the appearance of a glowing, disc-shaped UFO hovering low over the city. Witnesses included the governor, Emilie Riva Palacie, the city's mayor, and a military zone chief.[66]

AIR FORCE CRISIS OF CREDIBILITY

In the past, the Blue Book policy of debunking all UFO sightings helped to submerge the problem. Now it only worsened matters. By early September, as a result of the recent sightings, many newspapers demanded better air force investigations of UFOs. An editorial in the *Ft. Worth Star-Telegram* stated:

> They can stop kidding us now about there being no such thing as "flying saucers." Too many people of obviously sound mind saw and reported independently from too many separate localities. Their descriptions of what they saw are too similar to one another and too unlike any familiar object. It is becoming clear to many that the air force explanations succeed only in making the air force look ridiculous.[67]

On September 28, the air force responded to Hynek's suggestion for a more serious UFO investigation and recommended more support for Blue Book. It called for

> a working scientific panel composed of both physical and social scientists [to] be organized to review Project Blue Book—its resources, methods, and findings—to advise the AF as to any improvements that should be made in the program to carry out the AF's assigned responsibility.[68]

That day, Maj. Gen. E. B. LeBailly, Air Force Director of Information, issued a memorandum stating that the inquiry into UFOs was important enough that all agencies and commands should support it. Rather than attempt to shop Blue Book's program elsewhere, the memorandum said that Blue Book should stay right where it was, at Wright-Patterson AFB. While hostility did not seem to be a factor in considering the unknowns, wrote LeBailly, they could not be ignored because of the excellent qualifications of many observers. Moreover, in an important admission, he stated that only an extremely small percentage of accounts actually made their way to Blue Book. Thus, he recommended that a new committee of both physical and social scientists, including Hynek, be convened to review the air force approach and policy with respect to UFOs offering a fresh perspective and recommendations.[69]

Meanwhile, the UFO controversy continued to stew through the autumn. On October 5, the *Oklahoma City Journal* printed an enlargement of the August 3 UFO photo from the Tulsa youth, which other papers reprinted for the next month or so. That day, astronaut James McDivitt spoke to the media about UFOs: "They are there without a doubt, but what they are is anybody's guess." Later that month, John Fuller published his article on the Exeter encounter in the *Saturday Review*, greatly stimulating public interest in UFOs. Before publication, Fuller wrote to his editors that

reliable, but off-the-record information from the Pease AFB in Portsmouth indicates frequent radar blips and fighters are *constantly* scrambled to pursue these objects. This information is not official, but it comes from a reliable source.

Fuller's bosses in New York were impressed by his report. Around this time, Fuller met with Richard Hall of NICAP. Hall said there was no pressure being put on NICAP by the air force or government and said that reports of close-range UFOs had been building up over the last year.[70]

Such reports continued to pour in. By late October, around the time of the Pentagon press release explaining the Exeter sighting, Fuller learned from an air force pilot that pilots had been ordered to shoot at any UFO they came across in order to bring it down. The UFOs, however, appeared to be "invulnerable" and were able to outmaneuver any air force aircraft. Fuller's informant personally disagreed with this policy, as he saw no gain in alienating the unidentified craft.

Fuller also obtained a report from a military radar operator who told him that a UFO came directly toward an unnamed base, was seen visually and clocked on the radar scope. For a moment, it appeared that the object would actually land at the base. Instead, the officer of the day watched it hover through a telescope, then suddenly accelerate to over 800 mph, while it was simultaneously clocked on the radar scope. Fuller also learned that "constant" radar reports were being made at the Portsmouth Naval Base. In one instance, an object hovered over a water tower at the base before taking off incredibly fast, also seen visually and on radar. By this time, at Pease AFB, at least fifteen pilots were no longer skeptical about UFOs. Other air force officers told Fuller they were "shocked and dismayed" by the Pentagon report on Exeter. They all believed that the report severely damaged the air force. Fuller theorized that the air force impotence against UFOs might be the underlying reason for the stonewalling.[71]

In early November, the air force Scientific Advisory Board met in Dallas to discuss the UFO question and the idea of an independent study of the problem. Within a year, this led to the announcement of the air force decision to commission a study of UFOs by the University of Colorado, otherwise known as the Condon Committee. The meeting in November 1965 was later offered by Jacques Vallee as "near proof" that the air force's policy regarding UFOs was more of a bungling than a conspiratorial nature. This is a frail reed upon which to base such an argument. Could it be possible that after almost twenty years of investigation, the air force was *still* trying to determine what UFOs were?[72]

BLACKOUT SEASON

Over the years, blackouts linked to UFO sightings had been reported in cities throughout the world. None, however, matched the massive blackout that affected 35 million people throughout the northeastern United States on November 9, 1965. Nearly 800,000 people were detained in elevators, subway cars, and commuter trains. The entire power grid for the region, supposedly invulnerable, failed. In addition, several local companies independent of the main power grid also failed, and short-wave and VLF transmissions and reception were jammed with static.

The blackout began in the Syracuse area at 5:15 P.M. At precisely that moment, there was a UFO sighting in the area. Pilot Weldon Ross was approaching Syracuse when he and his student pilot saw a huge red ball "of brilliant intensity" appearing over the power lines at the Syracuse substation. Ross estimated it to be about one hundred feet in diameter and determined that the fireball was where the New York Power Authority's two 345,000-volt power lines at the Clay substation passed over the New York Central's tracks between Oneida Lake and Hancock Field. At least three other people corroborated this sighting. One of them was Robert C. Walsh, who was the Syracuse area deputy commissioner for the Federal Aviation Agency. Walsh reported that he saw the same phenomenon just a few miles south of Hancock Field.

At 5:25 P.M., a teacher in Holliston, Massachusetts, saw through binoculars an intense white object in the sky moving slowly toward the horizon; a man from the same town reported an identical object. At the same time in

New York City, two witnesses declared separately that they saw unusual objects in the sky. "It was different from anything I had ever seen," said one.

So, did UFOs cause the blackout? The possibility received widespread discussion during the aftermath but was never offered as a serious explanation to the public. President Lyndon Johnson ordered an investigation to determine the cause. Early on, it was announced that a line break near Niagara Falls had done it. A quick check, however, ruled this theory out. Next, the announcement pointed toward a remote-controlled substation at the power authority's transmission lines at Clay, New York, about ten miles north of Syracuse. This did not stand up to scrutiny, either. The Niagara Mohawk men who looked into it found the substation in fine condition, with no sign of any failure or damage. The final, and official, conclusion was that backup relay #Q-29 at the Sir Adam Beck generator station in Queenstown, Ontario, was the source of the failure. Even so, this relay went right back into operation, and the line it protected was completely undamaged.

On the other hand, circumstantial evidence existed to show that some sort of electromagnetic condition existed that caused the blackout. The fact that stations outside the main power grid were affected suggested this. In addition, after the episode, Con Edison quietly installed expensive magnetic shielding devices around key equipment. Bell Telephone Company also switched from overhead lines to more expensive, heavily shielded cables buried under the ground. Beyond the somewhat suggestive UFO connections, however, hard evidence is lacking.[73]

The great northeastern blackout was the most publicized of a series of major blackouts during late 1965. On November 16, a series of power blackouts hit Britain, affecting dozens of sections of London. On November 26, NICAP learned of unexplained power failures in St. Paul, Minnesota, coming at the same time as UFO sightings in the area. From December 2 to December 5, 1965, a series of major blackouts began in Mexico, western New Mexico, and Texas, including an El Paso blackout affecting 700,000 people. Other areas affected included Alamogordo, Las Cruces, and Juarez, Mexico. A month later, on December 26, the entire city of Buenos Aires, and towns as far as fifty miles away, were also blacked out, with many trapped in subways and other enclosed places. On the same date, four major cities in south and central Finland were hit with blackouts. In all cases, the cause was said to be a single insulator.[74]

THE KECKSBURG CRASH

Less conspicuous than the Roswell crash of 1947, the event at Kecksburg, Pennsylvania, on the evening of December 9, 1965, has caused its own share of rancor among UFO researchers. Officially listed as a meteorite in the Blue Book files, the object that crashed may have been several things—but certainly it was not a meteorite.

That night, a brightly glowing object streaked eastward across Canada, Michigan, and Ohio before striking ground at 4:47 P.M., near the small town of Kecksburg. Thousands of people saw the object, which left an intense vapor trail that was visible for more than twenty minutes and was filmed by several people. Debris fell in many places. Many people, including pilots, who saw it thought it was an aircraft on fire. Pilots recorded shock waves from it.

At around 6:30 P.M., Frances Kelp phoned a local radio station, WHJB, in Greensburg, where she spoke with John Murphy, the news director. An object or fireball, she said, had crashed into the woods near her home. Her two sons had gotten to within a half mile of the impact until she called them back; all three saw smoke rising above the trees and a bright object off to one side, which Kelp described as looking like a "four-pointed star." State police and firefighters were on the scene quickly. Murphy was also there, interviewed Kelp and her sons in person, and saw the state police fire marshal walk into the woods with a Geiger counter, accompanied by a state investigator. These two men, Carl Metz and Paul Shipco, returned about fifteen minutes later. Murphy asked them if they found anything. "I'm not sure," said Metz. Murphy kept trying to pry something out, when Metz said, "you'd better get your information from the army."

Murphy drove out to the state police Troop A barracks in Greensburg. When he arrived, he said, there were "not only members of the United States Army there, but I also saw two men in air force uniforms, one of them wearing lieutenant's bars." Murphy found Captain Dussia of the Pennsylvania State Police who told him that after a thorough search, they were convinced "there [was] nothing whatsoever in the woods." Murphy overheard Metz talking about going back in and asked Metz if he could go in, too. Sure, said Metz, if it was okay with the captain. Dussia said, "of course." Just then, a state trooper came back in from the woods, talking about a pulsating blue light he saw in there. According to Murphy, the military was very interested in seeing this.

Back at the crash site, Murphy tried to enter the woods with Metz but was firmly told by Metz he could not enter. Evidently, somewhere on the road between Greensburg and Kecksburg, Metz had received new instructions. Before long, all entrances into the woods were cordoned off. Before this occurred, several firefighters had gotten inside. One of them, Jim Romansky, was interviewed years later by Stan Gordon, a researcher who had done extensive investigation into the incident. Romansky reached the stream bed where the object first touched down. It had cut a furrow into the bed and came to rest nearby. It was acorn-shaped, said Romansky, between nine and twelve feet in diameter, and had a gold band around the bottom with writing on it. It had no wings, motors, or fuselage. The writing looked like "ancient Egyptian hieroglyphics," more precisely with characters of broken and straight lines, dots, rectangles, and circles. The metal was dented, but Romansky saw no rivets, seams, or welds.

Gordon found another witness, named Bill Bulebush, who had gotten nearly as close as had Romansky. He, too, described the object as acorn-shaped, with a gold band along the bottom, about twelve feet long and six feet in diameter. He could see bright blue sparks coming from it, but heard no sound.

Another man, Bill Weaver, was much farther from the object, but claimed to see it glowing. He saw four men dressed in "moon suits" carrying a large white box into the woods on a stretcher. Soon after, a man in a business suit ordered him from the area and threatened to take his car if he did not move it. Romansky also spoke of men in business suits that he thought were military. He said they began to order the firefighters out of the area.

The media covered the story almost exclusively as a fireball. Dr. William P. Bidelman, an astronomer at the University of Michigan, for example, stated, "It was undoubtedly a fireball." Other astronomers chimed in with the same opinion, although none of them had seen the object. The air force said the object was not an aircraft, missile, or space debris. Thus, it seemed to be a meteorite. Adding to the evidence is the only known photograph of the object as it passed through the sky, which appeared in the February 1966 issue of *Sky and Telescope*, and showed a "train" (ionized air) often associated with a fireball.

In March 1966, Ivan Sanderson began to research the event and eventually sent a report to NICAP. He spoke with officers from many police desks, journalists, and witnesses. From these discussions and the available data, he calculated the object's speed at just over 1,000 mph, far too slow for a meteor. Kevin Randle, who later investigated the crash at length, said Sanderson's calculation may have been based on faulty assumptions. Even so, acknowledged Randle, if Sanderson's calculations were off by a factor of ten, the object would still have been flying slower than the slowest speed ever recorded for a meteor, which is 27,000 mph. After investigating this at great length, Sanderson also determined something else of interest: the object appeared to change direction, turning southward at around Cleveland. Subsequent investigations, however, could not confirm this.

Blue Book and the military had its explanation: meteor. Blue Book files, however, refer to a "three-man team" that had been dispatched to investigate and pick up an object that started a fire in the woods. Kevin Randle argued that this team was certainly part of Project Moon Dust. UFO skeptic James Oberg, writing in *Omni*, suggested that the crashed object was a Soviet *Kosmos 96* satellite, which he believed would have warranted the activation of Moon Dust. Could this be true? Researcher Stan Gordon said that U.S. Space

Command showed that *Kosmos 96* most likely crashed in Canada at 3:18 A.M., about thirteen hours before the Kecksburg crash.

About all we know with certainty is that within two hours of the crash, the military sealed off the site, but not before witnesses got close enough to see a crashed object in the woods. Publicly, officials were claiming that nothing at all had crashed and nothing had been found. But other witnesses claimed to see a flatbed truck with a tarp covering leave the area at high speed. A final note: John Murphy's then-wife stated some time after that Murphy "was convinced" the object was no meteor, and in fact that he had reached the crash area with a camera. The military confiscated his film and audiotape. She also believed that the military pressured him into silence.

In 1990, a person came forward claiming to be part of the military team sent in to retrieve the object. He claimed that he received orders to "shoot anyone who got too close" and that the object was transported to Wright-Patterson AFB. Another individual who worked at Wright-Patterson claimed that a strange object was shipped there on December 16, 1965. Before being escorted away, he claimed to see it and described it nearly identically to other witness descriptions.

Both the meteorite and the Soviet satellite explanation appear to be most unlikely explanations for the Kecksburg crash, and no researchers believe it was an American satellite. Was it an alien object? The possibility is real, and the case remains open.[75]

1966: A YEAR OF ESCALATIONS

The United States was heading toward a boil in 1966, and the escalating war in Vietnam dominated the news. Still, the status quo held. The Freedom of Information Act passed Congress that year, but it remained toothless until 1974. The CIA and the White House, meanwhile, defeated a Senate movement for an intelligence oversight committee. In March, Lyndon Johnson requested that the FBI develop dossiers on legislators and prominent citizens opposed to the Vietnam War. From June 6 to June 10, the army conducted biological warfare tests in the New York City subway system. Trillions of *bacillus subtilis variant niger* germs were released into the subway system during peak travel hours.[76]

In July 1966, with Richard Helms in place as the new director of central intelligence, MK-Search went into overdrive, reactivating abandoned projects. One of these was *Spellbinder*, an operation managed by Gottlieb. Its goal was to create a "sleeper killer," someone who could be turned loose after receiving a key word planted in his mind under hypnosis. According to Gordon Thomas, the project was a failure.[77]

Despite growing civil unrest everywhere, the American media contributed its share toward maintaining a rigid status quo, almost obsequious in its compliance to the national security community. Sen. William Fulbright commented about this on August 13, 1966, during Senate hearings on government and media. It was very interesting, said Fulbright,

> that so many of our prominent newspapers have become almost agents or adjuncts of the government; that they do not contest or even raise questions about government policy.[78]

Despite the dominance of news from Vietnam, UFO matters managed to break through for significant media coverage in 1966. The crescendo of qualified sightings was simply overwhelming. After working in practical solitude for years, Keyhoe and NICAP board members now found themselves sought for interviews and television appearances. By midyear, it was apparent that Americans were giving much more credence to the subject of flying saucers.[79]

Frank Edwards published his own successful UFO book during the year, *Flying Saucers: Serious Business*. The book beat the Keyhoe drum of cover-up and relayed many interesting UFO reports. Others criticized it, with some justice, for careless reporting and factual errors. Coral Lorenzen went so far as to consider it "catastrophic to researchers who deal with facts." This was going a little bit too far. It is true that Edwards graduated from the Donald E. Keyhoe School of Purple Prose and, more seriously, reported many stories without bothering to check them. Yet, Lorenzen's motivations derived at least in part from her feud with NICAP, of which Edwards was a longtime, high-profile member. In the 1960s as in later decades, UFO research was ridden with infighting and rivalries. Edwards's book, flawed though it was, remained undeniably valuable in many respects and contained much that was useful to contemporary and later researchers. His errors of fact certainly did not distinguish him from most other UFO writers of the period. Only a year before, Jacques Vallee's study of UFOs, *Anatomy of a Phenomenon*, had appeared in print and received widespread acclaim, and yet it, too, contained various mistakes. Even Coral Lorenzen, admittedly more scrupulous in such matters than most, was not immune to errors.[80]

On February, 3, 1966, the air force convened an ad hoc committee to review Project Blue Book. Chaired by Dr. Brian O'Brien, it included Carl Sagan, Jesse Orlansky, Launor Carter, Willis A. Ware, and Richard Porter. Also attending was Lt. Col. Harold A. Steiner, assistant secretary to the United States Air Force Scientific Advisory Board. The group, which met for one day, received a briefing from Quintanilla, reviewed the Robertson Panel report of 1953, and studied a few UFO reports.

At the end of this one-day analysis, the committee endorsed Blue Book, despite its knowledge that most of the ten-thousand-plus sightings had been investigated by a ghost of a staff. The committee concluded that UFOs did not represent extraterrestrial technology and that they did not pose a threat to U.S. security. Still, it recommended that Blue Book be strengthened to provide a better scientific investigation for a certain number of cases that appeared to be worthy of study. Its primary conclusion—actually a bit of a jolt to the air force—was that

> perhaps one hundred sightings a year might be subjected to this close study, and that possibly an average of ten man-days be required per sighting so studied. The information provided by such a program might bring to light new facts of scientific value.

The committee also recommended that the UFO problem be handed over to a few selected universities and the full reports of such work be "printed in full and be available on request." Moreover, Blue Book's data, which was then classified, should be widely circulated among members of Congress and other public officials. There can be no question that the O'Brien Committee's recommendations sat poorly with those seeking to keep the UFO problem buried. Ask Blue Book to subject one hundred sightings per year to *ten mandays* of study each? One can imagine the reaction at ATIC. All of the committee's proposals were disregarded.[81]

During the same month, a UFO panel discussion called Open Mind took place, which included John Fuller, Donald Menzel, Allen Hynek, Leo Sprinkle, and Frank Salisbury. Its moderator was Dr. Eric Goldman, on leave from Princeton to act as academic advisor to LBJ. Included in the discussion was the Exeter incident. Menzel called the police officers "hysterical subjects," although he could not even recall their names, and clearly knew nothing about the case. Fuller, who investigated the case thoroughly, was amazed at such a display.[82]

MICHIGAN SWAMP GAS

Not all the interesting sightings were in America. On January 19, 1966, an important crop circle event occurred in the town of Tully, North Queensland, Australia. George Pedley, aged twenty-seven, was driving his tractor at 9 A.M., when he heard a high-pitched sound and saw a gray-blue object rise from a swampy lagoon, then depart. According to Pedley, "It was all over in a few seconds; it moved at terrific speed." At the site was an area of flattened swamp grass, swirled in a clockwise direction, with a diameter of about thirty feet. Pedley soon brought others to the site, and before long, many investigators had come to see and verify the claim. One of the investigating bodies was the Royal Australian air force intelligence. Investigators actually found a variety of circles in the area, ranging in size from eight to thirty feet in diameter.

Within each circle, however, plant roots were pulled completely out of the soil, as if the ground had been subjected to an intense rotary force. There were rumors that blamed the Soviets for the landing, but investigators learned that dozens of people in the area had seen strange saucer-like craft, many before Pedley's sighting. It didn't seem to be the Soviets.[83]

February was a quiet month. Not so, March. On the fourteenth at 3:50 A.M., two deputy sheriffs in Dexter, Michigan, saw several disc-shaped objects maneuvering above the town. Three other police agencies had already reported similar sightings. Selfridge AFB confirmed tracking objects on radar at extreme speeds and maneuverability. However, the incident received no publicity. At midnight on March 17, in Milan, Michigan, another law enforcement officer saw a UFO. This time, a policeman saw what he thought was a plane about to crash, although its silence puzzled him. When he tried contacting headquarters, his transmitter malfunctioned. The object did not crash. Instead, it approached the patrol car to within about seventy-five feet, followed him for about half a mile, then flew off. It appeared to be about fifty feet in diameter, with lights spinning at the periphery.[84]

Something was going on in Michigan. At about 8 P.M. on March 20, near Dexter, Michigan, Frank Mannor and his son, Ronald, saw a luminous object hovering over a swamp. It was brown, cone-shaped, and had bluish lights that turned red. At once, the object lit up with a yellowish glow and flew away rapidly, making a whistling sound. That night, several lights were reported moving around in a swamp area. More strange lights were reported the next evening, near Hillsdale, Michigan. Civil defense director William Van Horn, and a group of students, saw a pattern of lights on the ground, the source of which appeared to maneuver for about two hours.[85]

Although the sightings of the past two nights had not been the most compelling of the recent Michigan sightings, they received national attention. To calm everyone down, and to stem the flood of calls to the Pentagon, the air force sent Hynek to Michigan to investigate. Hynek was pleased, as he had wanted to investigate the events there but the air force had not been interested until now. What happened next was disaster. Hynek arrived in Michigan and almost immediately gave a press conference. Unable to explain the UFO reports, he called for a thorough investigation but focused on the ground lights, suggesting they could have been marsh gas caused by decaying vegetable matter in the swampy areas. In other words, swamp gas.

Clearly, this was a greatly premature statement, and the press ridiculed Hynek and the air force. To those who had followed Hynek's longtime support of the air force position, it was a moment of poetic justice. Hynek, however, later said he had intended to conduct a serious investigation and did not learn until after his arrival in Michigan that this was not to be the case. Instead, the air force merely wanted a public relations ploy to defuse the situation. Hynek's job, said the air force, was to hold a press conference immediately and *explain*. This may be true; certainly Blue Book was not in the habit of pursuing UFO investigations energetically. Perhaps Hynek bungled it because the air force rushed him. Even so, Quintanilla offered a contradictory view later that year while in Colorado. According to him, Hynek was convinced he had solved the Michigan sightings ("This is it!"), and as a result, received permission to give the press conference.

Whether it was Hynek or the air force who pushed, the air force never looked so incompetent and duplicitous on the matter of UFOs as it did at that moment. Hynek's press conference all but destroyed Project Blue Book's image.[86]

While much of the media handed Hynek his head, many of the larger organizations and publications continued to debunk flying saucers. *Life* and *Newsweek* still supported Hynek and the air force, for example. *Life* quoted Quintanilla as "certain that no evidence [has] turned up to date that has even hinted at spacecraft of unearthly origin." Nothing was known of Quintanilla's classified article regarding the Socorro incident. Instead, his remarks for public consumption were:

> We are spending millions to develop our own rocket boosters to get our spacecraft to the moon and beyond. Imagine what a great help it would be to get our hands on a ship from another planet and examine its power plant.[87]

Shortly afterward, in May, CBS tried to calm the situation with a special program narrated by Walter Cronkite, which took a straightforward, debunking approach to UFOs. It focused heavily on fringe elements, such as the contactees, and remarks by Sagan about "flying saucer cultists." Menzel, Harold Brown, and even the exiled Lawrence Tacker were also featured, each claiming that no UFOs had ever been detected on radar screens, nor photographed, nor seen by satellite tracking stations. For "balance," Keyhoe and Hynek were included, but the tenor of the show was clearly to discredit their position.[88]

Meanwhile, Congress had finally decided to act, after its own fashion. On March 25, 1966, Michigan Congressman and House Minority Leader Gerald Ford demanded a formal congressional investigation on UFOs, supported by other congressmen. A few days later, Ford wrote to Armed Services Committee Chairman L. Mendel Rivers to the effect that he was dissatisfied with government actions regarding UFOs:

> I think there may be substance in some of these reports and because I believe the American people are entitled to a more thorough explanation than has been given them by the air force to date. . . . I think we owe it to the people to establish the credibility regarding UFOs and to produce the greatest possible enlightenment on this subject.[89]

Thus, on April 5, 1966, for the first time ever, Congress held an open hearing on UFOs, chaired by L. Mendel Rivers. Like the O'Brien Committee, it met for one day only and was an exclusive gathering. Only three people, Air Force Secretary Harold Brown, Quintanilla, and Hynek, were invited to testify. NICAP, pushing ten years for this moment, was *not* invited, but did submit material for the record. The results were predictable. Hynek, licking his wounds, said that UFOs deserved the scientific community's attention and called for a civilian panel of scientists to examine the program. Brown said there was no evidence to support the claim that UFOs were spaceships. Afterward, he reportedly directed the air force to accept the O'Brien Committee's recommendations and to arrange for a scientific team to investigate and review the over six hundred officially unidentified sightings. That was the end of congressional action.[90]

All this attention from Congress and the media affected public opinion. In the aftermath of the swamp gas fiasco, a Gallup poll revealed that 46 percent of Americans believed UFOs to be real. Moreover, 5 percent thought they had seen one personally: a figure that projected to 9 million people. Keyhoe saw this as a serious concern for the air force. Possibly, but it is still hard to credit public opinion as an important determinant of UFO policy.[91]

Throughout the spring, UFO sightings continued at a rapid pace. On the morning of March 23, just as the UFO controversy heated up in Congress, an electronics instructor named William "Eddy" Laxson was driving through Temple, Oklahoma, on his way to work at Sheppard AFB in Wichita Falls, Texas. At 5:05 A.M., he saw an object blocking the road. It was shaped like an airplane fuselage, about eighty feet long, had a bubble-shaped dome on top, rested on legs, and had bright lights. Laxson saw a door and a short stairway on the side and a man in coveralls appearing to examine the craft. He even saw an identification number on the craft: TL 4768. When he approached, the man went back inside, and the object took off, making a sound similar to that of a high-speed drill. Laxson was familiar with all conventional military aircraft but could not recognize this one. Researcher Jerome Clark called this case "one of the most impressive of all." Presumably, the existence of an ID number on the vehicle implies that it was a classified or experimental project. Unfortunately, no subsequent evidence ever arose to support this conclusion.[92]

Additional landing cases were reported in Lexisburg, Indiana, Mansfield, Ohio, and Vicksburg, Michigan on March 30 and 31. In two cases, an unidentified object followed or flew past an automobile; the other involved a sighting of a short humanoid inside a landed craft. On April 1 near Tangier, Oklahoma, a man who was driving at night reached a hilltop and saw a green object flying north rapidly, giving off a high-pitched noise and intense heat. His car engine died. Two close-range sightings of UFO craft by civilians in New York State occurred on April 5, and another one that night took place in Tennessee.[93]

THE PORTAGE COUNTY SIGHTINGS

On April 17, an amazing UFO sighting, high-speed police chase, and possible air force jet interception took place in Portage County, Ohio, and across the Pennsylvania border. The case involved at least eight police officers and several civilians, incredible air force stonewalling and investigative incompetence, and several ruined careers.

At 5 A.M. on the seventeenth, four miles east of Randolph, Ohio, and shortly after returning from an accident scene, Portage County Deputy Sheriff Dale F. Spaur, traveling with Wilbur Neff (an auxiliary deputy whose main occupation was airport mechanic), saw a rusty car parked on the highway's shoulder. Spaur got out to inspect the vehicle, while Neff stood by in front of the patrol car. As Spaur glanced over his right shoulder, he saw a moving light through the trees at the top of a hill to the west, headed in his direction. Spaur was intrigued, since only fifteen minutes earlier, he and Neff had overheard radio traffic between Portage and Summit counties about a report of a large, bright object. It had gotten some laughs, but now Spaur realized that he was looking at the probable source of the report. At 5 A.M., it was still dark, but Spaur and Neff both described this object as extremely bright, enough to cause Spaur's eyes to water. It passed over the road, then hovered fifty to one hundred feet in the air. Spaur and Neff raced back to their car, and Spaur contacted the sheriff's office, which told him to wait there until a car with a camera arrived.

Spaur did not wait very long: the object ascended vertically to three hundred or four hundred feet, getting brighter all the while, and emitted a humming noise. It then hovered some more. Spaur drove toward it, and he and Neff could now see it was perhaps forty feet in diameter and about twenty feet thick, a perfect oval shape. Soon, the object began to ascend and move away. Spaur followed it down Route 224 and was urged over the radio to shoot at the object, which he refused to do. Very quickly, he was driving at 100 mph. The object was so bright that Spaur hardly needed his headlights to drive. As the object reached Mahoning County, the pursuit was being broadcast over police radios in three counties. At this point the police car with the camera misunderstood the directions and got lost.

At Canfield, Ohio, Spaur and Neff continued to chase the object. They noticed the object become more clearly visible as the sun continued to rise, or perhaps they were just becoming accustomed to the object. Either way, they now discerned a metallic appearance, domelike top, and a long antenna protruding from the rear-center of the object. The object seemed to slow down for them when they had to slow down. As the officers neared East Palestine, Ohio, Patrolman H. Wayne Huston, who had been following the chase on his radio, also saw the object. Huston watched it go overhead and said "it was brighter than the sun when it came up." He followed Spaur and Neff, at times reaching 100 mph.

Just before 5:30 A.M.—nearly thirty minutes into the chase—in Salem, Ohio, two police officers near the border with Pennsylvania, who had been listening to the chase on the radio, saw the object. They described it as "a bright ball," much larger than a jet, of unvarying brightness in the distance. They also saw three jets following it. Columbiana County Sheriff's Deputy Dave Brothers followed the commotion on the radio and also saw three airplanes. An AP report later stated that Air Force Reserve pilots out of Youngstown attempted to follow the object, but that its speed, "estimated at one hundred miles an hour," was too slow for them.

At the same time in Conway, Pennsylvania, local police officer Frank Panzarella saw the object. In his words to Blue Book, it was "the shape of a half of [a] football, was very bright, and about twenty-five to thirty-five feet in diameter." The two Ohio police cars raced into Conway at 5:30 A.M. They had traveled about fifty miles in a half hour, and now received instructions to abandon the chase. For most of the past thirty minutes, the object had maintained a fairly consistent altitude of one thousand feet. But now, it rapidly ascended to about 3,500 feet, then hovered. Panzarella saw this and called the Rochester, Pennsylvania, police operator, John Beighey, asking him to contact the Greater Pittsburgh International Airport. Panzarella saw an airliner pass beneath the object, then saw what looked like jet trails. He heard a voice on his radio announcing that a jet interception was in progress. The object finally shot high into the air and disappeared.

The event seemed to be over. In thirty minutes, many police officers and civilians had seen the UFO, and the two police cars from Ohio now began their drive home. Just then, however, Panzarella received a call from Beighey that the air force office in Pittsburgh wanted to hear from the witnesses immediately. Beighey also said that during his call, he heard someone at the airport say the object was "on the screen," implying a radar return. Within minutes, Panzarella caught up with Spaur, Neff, and Huston; just before he stepped out of his car, he heard a fading voice on the radio say, "Hey, Frank, I saw two jets. . . ." The voice was that of Patrolman Henry Kwaitanowski. He had seen two jets, which looked like commercial airliners, flying behind a shiny, football-shaped object, which appeared to be about the same size and at about the same altitude.

The three Ohio police officers went to the Rochester police station, and Spaur phoned the air force at Pittsburgh. Speaking to "some colonel," he said the officer tried to convince him he had seen something conventional. The officer did not speak to the other two policemen.

The case gained national attention immediately. The air force began its investigation the next day, which consisted of a few phone calls to local media and checks for weather balloons (none were found). In any case, the wind near ground level was negligible that day and could not have accounted for the movement ascribed to the object. The air force personnel in Youngstown and Pittsburgh denied that anything had been out of the ordinary, or that anything had turned up on radar. Quintanilla phoned Spaur, asking him to "tell me about this mirage you saw." Spaur later said, "Hell, I talked longer with that colonel Sunday morning, and *he* didn't ask much." Quintanilla called Spaur briefly a few days later to confirm that he had seen the object for more than a few minutes (!).

On April 22, Blue Book announced the solution to the Portage County sighting: the officers had first seen an *Echo* satellite; after it had moved out of sight, Spaur had mistaken the planet Venus for the same object. When Quintanilla phoned Spaur's superior, Portage County Sheriff Ross Dustman, to give him this explanation, Dustman actually laughed out loud.

Another investigation was being conducted, however, by William B. Weitzel, a professor of philosophy and field investigator for NICAP. Unlike the air force, Weitzel actually spoke to the principal police witnesses. He considered the Blue Book explanation to be absurd and before long wrote a four-page letter to Congressman William Stanton, whose district included Portage County. Shortly afterwards, a Portage County judge who knew each of the three Ohio officers involved also wrote to Stanton, calling the air force explanation "ridiculous." Stanton was soon in communication with the air force commanding general. Then, after getting no reply for two weeks, he spoke with Air Force Chief of the Community Relations Division Lt. Col. John Spaulding, who promised to send an investigator to the site.

Quintanilla phoned Spaur again on May 9, obviously under pressure. He would be there the next day to interview him, he said. Spaur asked Weitzel to record the interview, and Weitzel brought *his* crew: two reporters and space-scientist/UFO researcher David Webb. In addition, Sheriff Dustman was present. Quintanilla, none too happy about the crowd, asked Weitzel and Webb to leave the room, and the reporters soon left as well. It didn't matter: the meeting was ugly. Quintanilla failed to persuade Spaur of the air force explanation, and the exchange, which was recorded, became heated at times. When Weitzel returned to the room, he and Quintanilla had their own exchange over the *Echo*/Venus explanation, which Weitzel said contradicted the mass of witness testimony, most of which Quintanilla never knew about.

Congressman Stanton continued to apply pressure on the case and complained to Secretary of Defense Robert McNamara about Blue Book's treatment of his constituents. Weitzel wrote to Quintanilla on May 17 with another critique of the Blue Book explanation. Even Hynek urged Blue Book to change the case to unknown. Still, in the words of Jerome Clark, Blue Book "withstood the onslaught." The official explanation remained *Echo*/Venus.

The incident ruined the career and marriage of Dale Spaur, who was apparently traumatized by the incident itself and then the subject of relentless ridicule. Immediately after the event, he seemed to change. His wife "never saw him more frightened before." He inexplicably became violent with her, and she filed assault-and-battery charges, then for divorce. Six months later, he had lost forty pounds, turned in his badge, and was working as a painter while living in a small motel room.

Huston also resigned from the force within a few months and became a bus driver in Seattle. He had been a seven-year veteran. "Sure, I quit because of that thing," he said. "People laughed at me. And there was pressure. You couldn't put your finger on it, but the pressure was there. The city officials didn't like police officers chasing flying saucers." Wilbur Neff wasn't a full-time police officer, but he, too, was affected. His wife said, "I hope I never see him like he was after the chase. He was real white, almost in a state of shock."[94]

The Portage County UFO sightings were among the most compelling of 1966, but there were other UFO sightings in the area at the time. On the night of April 18 in Battle Creek, Michigan, a gray, oval object, about eighty feet in diameter and fifteen feet high, was seen from a distance of about eighty feet by a forty-two-year-old witness driving a car. The driver claimed to see windows and three rows of lights. The next night, in Peabody, Massachusetts, a man saw what he thought was a crashing plane, then realized the object was oval, with multicolored lights. The object flew low over him, circled, came down with pendulum motion, and appeared to land on Route 114. Shortly afterwards, two men driving along that route saw a beam sweep the road. They stopped and saw a disc-like object with multicolored lights matching the description of the first report. On April 25, Florida Governor Haydon Burns and a group of newsmen had a close sighting of a UFO while on the governor's Convair during a campaign tour. The craft paced the plane, then climbed away. Several journalists aboard the plane also saw the object and gave the story wide publicity.[95]

James McDonald, an Outstanding Nuisance

During the spring of 1966, James McDonald, atmospheric physicist from the University of Arizona, entered the UFO picture. In March, he had written to Tom Malone, chairman of the National Academy of Sciences Committee on the Atmospheric Sciences, urging that a small panel be set up by some scientific body, which would avoid publicity but gain access to Blue Book and related files. McDonald also wrote to Congressman Morris Udall about the idea and urged Udall to pass the letter on in confidence to Gerald Ford, who was then making waves over the Michigan sightings. Naturally, McDonald hoped to participate on such a panel. The idea never materialized, but

McDonald soon received a small stipend from the Office of Naval Research to examine Blue Book material at Wright-Patterson AFB. The reason given: perhaps certain kinds of clouds could account for some of the radar trackings of UFOs.

On June 6, 1966, McDonald, at Wright-Patterson AFB, discovered an unedited copy of the Robertson Panel report. Seeing what surely appeared to be hard evidence that the CIA was directing a cover-up, McDonald was extremely disturbed. Two days later, he was at the office of J. Allen Hynek. Pounding his fist on Hynek's desk at one point, McDonald said Hynek should have spoken out about the cover-up of UFO information. Vallee was present and described McDonald as a man "afraid of nothing." This was true, a quality that eventually led to McDonald's downfall. But for now, the air force saw McDonald as a man they needed to fireproof. Hynek wrote that the Blue Book staff considered McDonald as an "outstanding nuisance." Certainly they gave him no assistance in his research: on June 30, he requested that Wright-Patterson photocopy the Robertson Panel report for him. This was denied. On July 20, McDonald learned that the report was "reclassified" by the CIA.[96]

During the summer of 1966, McDonald met with the Lorenzens at their home and repeated his complaint that Hynek should have spoken out long before. The Lorenzens were unimpressed. McDonald's complaints about "alleged censorship" did not persuade them, and he appeared to be "totally oblivious to the psychological aspects involved," whatever that meant. Besides, McDonald had not done much himself. Like Hynek, he had been collecting data for years, "but waited until others had paved the way before publicly stating his own opinions."[97]

Hynek, still reeling from the awful publicity he received in March, and further affected by McDonald's demonstration in his own office, wrote a letter that summer to *Science* magazine, which publicly contradicted the air force position of the recent Armed Services Committee hearing. He stated that the air force *did* have unexplained radar reports and photographs of UFOs. He called for an end to witness ridicule and, in a direct slap at Blue Book, stated that a scientific program had never been undertaken regarding UFOs. One should be initiated, he wrote, as soon as possible.[98]

The air force had reached a dead end in its public handling of the UFO problem. During the summer of 1966, Vallee heard rumors in Europe through "informal channels" that the air force was looking for an excuse to unload UFOs. The problem was "to find a university that was willing to write a negative report after a cursory examination of the facts." In fact, wrote Vallee, this rumor was taken seriously enough in Paris to prevent the creation of a French UFO investigative committee, where pressure was also rising for something of the sort.[99]

Meanwhile, UFO sightings continued at a fast rate, including a close-range sighting by a Michigan police officer on June 13 and an investigation by Selfridge AFB. On June 23, Apollo Space Project Engineer Julian Sandoval and other witnesses reported seeing a UFO about three hundred feet long near Albuquerque. It left at an amazing speed, they said, swiftly reaching over 3,000 mph. Through the summer, more close-range sightings were reported throughout the United States.[100]

AN AUTUMN BARRAGE

The autumn of 1966 may not have equaled the spring in number or quality of UFO sightings, but it still reminded people why all the action was stirring within the air force and elsewhere. On August 20, just before 5 P.M. in Donnybrook, North Dakota, a border patrolman saw a bright, shiny disc on its edge, about thirty feet in diameter, floating down the side of a hill, wobbling from side to side low over the ground. It reached the bottom, then climbed to about one hundred feet and moved across to a small reservoir. The patrolman then saw a dome on top. It hovered briefly and seemed ready to land but tilted back and zoomed into the clouds. Hynek personally interviewed the officer and believed him to be "above reproach."[101]

Another sighting occurred in North Dakota on August 24, this time involving Minot AFB. At 10 P.M., an airman reported on base radio that a multicolored light was visible very high in the sky. A team went to the location, confirmed the original unknown, then saw a second, white object pass in front of clouds. The base radar tracked the object, which was as high as 100,000 feet (almost twenty miles). The object rose and descended several times; each time it descended, an air force officer in charge of a missile crew found his radio transmission interrupted by static, even though he was sixty feet below the ground. The object eventually descended to ground level ten to fifteen miles south of the area. The air force sent a strike team to check. Apparently, they saw the object either on the ground or hovering very low. According to the official report:

> When the team was about ten miles from the landing site, static disrupted radio contact with them. Five to eight minutes later, the glow diminished, and the UFO took off. Another UFO was visually sighted and confirmed by radar. The one that was first sighted passed beneath the second. Radar also confirmed this. The first made for altitude toward the north, and the second seemed to disappear with the glow of red.

The incident lasted nearly four hours and was confirmed by three different missile sites but failed to reach the press.[102]

On September 13, 1966, an eleven-year-old in Stirum, North Dakota, saw a disc-shaped object land near a farm. It had a tripod landing gear, two red lights, two white lights, one green light, and a transparent dome. It left so quickly that it appeared to vanish. Two investigators, including an air force lieutenant colonel, went to the site and discovered three round impressions in the ground several inches deep, very compact. In Summerside, Canada, on September 21, eight members of the Royal Canadian air force saw a bright object that flew down rapidly, stopped abruptly, remained at ground level for twenty minutes, then ascended vertically.[103]

In the New York area, a number of UFO reports in October centered around Lake Wanaque, a large reservoir in northeastern New Jersey and the main feeder for the Jersey City water supply. In a story picked up by the wire services, tens of thousands of people poured into the area night after night to see lighted objects over the water. The military also arrived, as the reservoir was strategically important. The mysterious lights were not seen over the reservoir per se, but over the small mountain range or range of large hills on the west side of the lake. One resident said such sightings had been in that area for half a century.[104]

SLOUCHING TOWARDS COLORADO

Throughout the spring of 1966, the air force had sought a university willing to undertake a formal study of UFOs. In August, consideration centered on the University of Colorado, featuring the world-renowned physicist Dr. Edward U. Condon. The announcement would not be made for several months yet, but the team at Colorado was already working to decide how best to handle—or disable—the subject. On August 9, a memorandum was written by the person who quickly became, behind Condon, the number two man of the project. Although he was no scientist, Robert Low was a senior administrator of the university and a former intelligence officer who appears to have performed some serious work for the CIA in Albania twenty years earlier. On this day, Low wrote a memorandum addressed to Thurston E. Manning, the university's vice president and Dean of Faculties, and Dr. E. James Archer, Dean of the Graduate School. Low's memorandum laid out the strategy for handling the UFO problem. "The trick would be," wrote Low,

> to describe the project so that, to the public, it would appear a totally objective study, but to the scientific community would present the image of a group of nonbelievers trying their best to be objective but having an almost zero expectation of finding a saucer. . . .

The memorandum blew up a year later, after project members found it and leaked it. Ironically, Archer claimed never to have seen the memo until journalist R. Roger Harkins brought it to his attention in November 1967. In Harkins's judgment, Archer was genuinely shocked when he read it, even though it had been filed in his office. Harkins asked Archer if he thought the memo was deliberately *not* sent to him; Archer paused, then smiled. "No comment," he said.

For now, however, preparations seemed underway for a phony study that would placate the public as well as the skeptical, albeit unstudied, scientific community.[105]

On August 31, Col. Ivan C. Atkinson, deputy executive director of the air force Office of Scientific Research, formally approached the University of Colorado with the request to conduct a comprehensive examination of the UFO problem. This program was to be independent and beyond the authority of the air force. Of course, the CIA was another matter entirely. Moreover, just how independent could the Colorado study be, when it was wholly financed by air force money? For years, UFO researchers had argued that Congress should foot the bill for such an undertaking, an effort that the air force and its allies had thwarted every time. Part of the problem with a congressionally funded program, from the air force point of view, was the obvious loss of control, or at least influence, over the study's direction. Direct funding, with air force money, would mitigate such a problem, if for no other reason than that the air force itself would choose who would conduct the study. More than a decade earlier, when assembling NICAP's board of directors, Keyhoe also had understood the value of selecting the right people for the job.[106]

In August, however, the main UFO news was coming not from Colorado, but the *Washington Star*. On August 7, the *Star* carried an article on UFOs by Lt. Col. Charles Cooke, a retired air force officer and former intelligence officer in World War Two. After the war he became founder and editor of the *Air Intelligence Digest* and was later editor of *FEAF*, the Far East Air Force Intelligence Round-up. Cooke wrote that he had analyzed firsthand UFO encounters by air force pilots, which showed strong evidence supporting the extraterrestrial hypothesis. He strongly criticized Project Blue Book. Shortly after this, there was a renewed effort in Congress to break air force UFO censorship. Rep. Edward Hutchinson had already introduced a resolution, HR 866, for an investigation of Project Blue Book methods. Now, in the wake of Cooke's article, Hutchinson obtained new backing. By the middle of the month, an air force officer privately told Keyhoe that the CIA had gotten them into this mess, "and now they sit back out of sight while the air force catches all the hell."[107]

The other main piece of UFO-related news from August 1966, was the debut of debunker Philip Klass into the field. On August 22, he printed an article in *Aviation Week* explaining the UFO at Exeter from the year before as plasma discharges from high-voltage power lines. Klass received immediate attention, including a sympathetic *New York Times* article, which, in the words of journalist Howard Blum, made him "an instant authority" on UFOs. In early

October, Klass again discussed UFOs in *Aviation Week*. Even so, most serious researchers never took his plasma or ball lightning theory seriously. Unlike Klass, James McDonald *was* an atmospheric physicist and ripped Klass's plasma theory apart. ("Klass dismissed!") Klass soon left plasmas behind to move on to more traditional methods of debunkery: character assassination and ridicule. His first target was McDonald.[108]

SUMMARY

The year 1966 was a crucial turning point in the history of the UFO problem. For over two years, thousands of UFO reports had swamped America, many of them good quality and utterly baffling. As a result, UFO consciousness was as high as it had been in 1947 and 1952, and the belief in UFOs even higher. The debunking system, in place since the 1953 Robertson Panel and which explained away UFOs at all costs, had broken down completely. True, Project Blue Book continued to derive explanations for an awesome number of reports which, upon superficial review, seemed impressive. The problem was the loss of credibility: no one but the most trusting loyalist believed Blue Book any longer. The explanations coming from Dayton seemed, to many, absurd and even dishonest.

Blue Book's loss of credibility, however, did not mean the air force, or CIA, or whatever group in the caverns of American intelligence ran this thing, had lost control over the UFO problem. Project Blue Book, as a tool of the program, had become ineffective. What was needed, therefore, was a new tool. In obtaining one, the air force and its allies never lost the initiative and easily outmaneuvered Congress to control the destiny of the UFO problem within the public domain. The air force or the CIA—but not Congress—would choose the people who would, hopefully, end public speculation about UFOs.

Contrast the management of the problem by the military/intelligence community with the failure of NICAP to exploit its opportunity. For ten years, NICAP had pressed for congressional hearings on UFOs. Finally, amid the wave of 1966, Congress relented: a one-day hearing, to which NICAP was not even invited. Could the message have been any clearer? The UFO wave had given NICAP a rare opportunity which, had it occurred five years earlier, the organization might have been able to play more effectively. Now, however, NICAP lacked the leadership: Hillenkoetter and Fahrney were long gone, Keyhoe was getting old, and Hall, despite his abilities, was no Keyhoe. NICAP also lacked the money to launch an effective campaign for a real congressional investigation. Besides, NICAP never spoke for a unified "UFO community." APRO held views that diverged and at times opposed NICAP's, and neither organization was especially large, anyway. Undoubtedly, an ineffective organization is better than none at all. But opportunities pass quickly, and NICAP let this one slip away.

Finally, we may inquire about the attitude of the U.S. national security community to the UFOs themselves during this great wave. In 1947 and 1948, for instance, we see prominent generals and scientists studying the problem and seriously considering the extraterrestrial possibility; in 1952 we see the air force "bracing for an invasion"; what of 1966? The answer is hard to know with certainty. Internally, there appear to have been no major reevaluations of the UFO problem or policy. However, the air force moved efficiently toward dropping its great public burden: Project Blue Book. Not only had Blue Book damaged the overall credibility of the air force, but it probably hampered serious investigations to some degree, simply by stimulating public inquiry. It's hard to conduct a secret investigation that everyone knows about.

And the past few years had brought many UFO cases that demanded secret inquiry: two probable UFO crashes and military retrievals; a possible landing at Holloman AFB; definite landings near Minot AFB, Blaine AFB, and elsewhere; the sighting by a trustworthy police officer of a landed craft and its humanoid occupants; continued sightings by army, navy, and air force personnel; more attempted jet intercepts of UFO craft; the proliferation of crop circles in several countries; the continuation of UFO and humanoid sightings worldwide. These developments point to continued concern, or at least strong interest, by the national security state over unidentified flying objects, and the continuation in its belief that this was a matter that must never, ever, be allowed to escape its control.

Chapter 8

Winners and Losers: 1966 to 1969

My own present opinion, based on two years of careful study, is that UFOs are probably extraterrestrial devices engaged in something that might very tentatively be termed "surveillance."

—James McDonald, physicist,
before Congress in July 1968

If "they" discover you, it is an old but hardly invalid rule of thumb, "they" are your technological superiors.

—NSA analyst and author, 1968

[N]othing has come from the study of UFOs in the past twenty-one years that has added to scientific knowledge. Careful consideration of the record as it is available to us leads us to conclude that further extensive study of UFOs probably cannot be justified in the expectation that science will be advanced thereby.

—Edward U. Condon, Scientific Study
of Unidentified Flying Objects, 1969

COLORADO TO THE RESCUE

It was not merely the UFO activity itself, but the publicity around it, that had made the air force situation intolerable. Once it settled upon the University of Colorado for deliverance, it moved quickly. On September 19, AFR 200-2 was superseded by AFR 80-17, which stipulated that some data from UFO reports would not be sent to Colorado:

Every effort will be made to keep all UFO reports unclassified. However, if it is necessary to classify a report because of method of detection or other factors not related to the UFO, a separate report including all possible information will be sent to the University of Colorado.

Item #5 of Paragraph 12 also restated that all radar evidence of UFOs was automatically classified and could not be discussed or revealed to the public.[1]

On October 6, 1966, the Air Force Office of Scientific Research formally contracted with the University of Colorado at Boulder to conduct a "serious, objective, scientific, and independent investigation" of the UFO phenomenon. The study was to be directed by physicist Dr. Edward U. Condon, assisted by University of Colorado administrator Robert Low. The air force allocated $313,000 for the project, which was planned to run from November 15, 1966, to January 1968.

The decision appealed to all parties, including Hynek, Keyhoe, the Lorenzens, and McDonald. The relief was so strong that a body *other* than the air force would do an official study of UFOs, people assumed it had to be better than what the air force had inflicted upon the public.

The honeymoon was brief, however. Condon immediately demonstrated his dislike for the entire subject and his support for the air force position. On October 8, he was widely quoted as saying it was "highly improbable" UFOs existed. "The view that UFOs are hallucinatory will be a subject of our investigation," he said, "to discover what it is that makes people imagine they see things." The air force had done a good job, he told the *Denver Post.* "About 95 percent of the UFO reports are relatively easily identified," he said. "With more information, others could probably be explained . . . [which] indicates an appalling lack of public understanding." Low's remarks were similarly disparaging, but he acknowledged that "you don't say no to the air force."[2]

At the same time, James McDonald made the news. All year long, McDonald had been studying the old reports, interviewing hundreds of witnesses. For a scientist of world stature, as McDonald was, this was unprecedented. His analyses of older cases laid waste to the conclusions of Menzel, Klass, and the air force. For good reason, the air force feared James McDonald. So, after working diligently on the UFO problem for most of the year, McDonald went public on October 4, 1966. First to reporters in Tucson, and the next day at the University of Arizona Department of Meteorology colloquium, he gave his views on the reality of UFOs and the concealment of information. The faculty was wary; one of McDonald's friends called the decision "professionally risky."[3]

On October 7, McDonald spoke to reporters about the Robertson Panel report, which he had seen the previous June at Wright-Patterson AFB. The CIA had ordered the air force to debunk UFOs, he said. A few days later, he spoke at the American Meteorological Society meeting in Washington, D.C.

The speech was explosive:

> My study of past official air force investigations (Project Blue Book) leads me to describe them as completely superficial. They have, for at least the past dozen years, been carried out at a very low level of scientific competence. . . . Officially released "explanations" of important UFO sightings have often been almost absurdly erroneous. In only a few instances has there been any on-the-spot field investigation by Blue Book personnel, and much of that has been quite superficial. On the other hand, official press releases, statements to Congress, etc., have conveyed an impression that no significant scientific problem exists with respect to UFOs.

McDonald was rocking the boat with authority, saying things no one had said, at least not this well. Keyhoe had tried to convey this sort of thing, but there was only one James McDonald.[4]

Keyhoe remained in the mix, however. By mid-October, he was already distressed by what Condon and Low were saying, and decided to phone them. Both assured him they had been misquoted and asked for NICAP's support. Unpersuaded, Keyhoe nonetheless gave in. He expressed his reservations to Colorado University Project member (and NICAP member) David Saunders; with some effort, Saunders and Richard Hall convinced him that NICAP needed to support the project, at least for now.[5]

VISITS TO BOULDER

Condon shot from the hip again on November 5, 1966. The Colorado Project, he told the press, had "to take it on faith that the air force is not trying to deceive us." Referring to McDonald, he continued, "I know some people who believe the air force is misleading us, but I don't think so. Maybe they are. I don't care much." This was not an auspicious start to the project. By now, Condon was already using the phrase "damn UFO," to his colleagues. But Condon appeared to be a remote director of this project and was spending only half of his university time on it. More visible direction came from project coordinator Robert Low.[6]

Throughout November, the University of Colorado received a steady stream of visits from major UFO researchers. On November 11, Allen Hynek, accompanied by his protégé Jacques Vallee, visited the team at Boulder. Hynek gave a history of UFOs, describing them as the greatest mystery of the age, perhaps ever. Vallee discussed how UFOs might be studied scientifically. He brazenly (and presciently) predicted failure for the project: the duration of the study, he said, was too short and the current wave of sightings would probably not last very long. Hynek and Vallee both sensed that Low, not Condon, was "clearly the decision-maker." Privately, Hynek told project member physicist Roy Craig that the project *must* recommend that scientific investigations of UFO reports be continued.[7]

On the heels of the Hynek-Vallee visit, Blue Book chief Hector Quintanilla briefed the project on November 14. He generally restated Hynek's remarks, with none of the enthusiasm for the subject. He contradicted Hynek on one point: the account of the Michigan swamp gas incident, as noted earlier.[8]

On November 22, 1966, James McDonald informally visited several project members. He explained some radar complexities and mirage effects. He also told them that the time would come when they would find themselves "confronting astonishing evidence of mishandling of the UFO problems by your sponsoring agency," that is, the air force.[9]

Keyhoe arrived in Boulder with Richard Hall on November 28. They met Low first and showed him some strong NICAP reports. When Keyhoe brought out the 1959 Redmond, Oregon, case, however, Low dismissed it as too far back. "The witnesses wouldn't remember the details." Keyhoe was astonished: the case was only seven years old, and the witnesses were still available for interview. Moreover, Low, who knew nothing about UFOs, was posing as an expert. Keyhoe met privately with Condon and Saunders, during which time Condon did little more than quip about contactees. In their presentations to the project members, Keyhoe focused on the cover-up, while Hall argued that the best way to review the UFO evidence was not to isolate each case, but to assess their combined weight.

Later, Saunders told Keyhoe that most project members would work hard for a full investigation, "as much as the contract allows." Keyhoe failed to grasp the full flavor of this until he returned to Washington. Back home, he read this paragraph in the air force contract with the University of Colorado:

> Because of the continuance of Project Blue Book for the handling of all reports, it is our understanding that the university is under no obligation to investigate reported sightings other than those that the principal investigators [Condon and Low] select for study.

With Condon's and Low's attitudes already quite clear, this was bad news.[10]

Bad news continued when Low visited NICAP's headquarters soon after. After some prodding by Keyhoe, he admitted that Condon considered the early reports to be worthless. For Keyhoe, this was almost too much—nearly everything NICAP had was an "early" report. Before NICAP wasted any more time providing UFO reports to the Colorado Project, he said, he wanted to know from Condon about the recent 1965 cases NICAP had just provided. Otherwise, NICAP might pull out altogether. Low tried to assure Keyhoe of a fair investigation.[11]

On January 12, 1967, the air force advisory panel held a special briefing in Boulder. This time, Condon was deferential. He discussed project plans and asked for air force opinions on where the emphasis should be placed with respect to policy questions. Lt. Col. Robert Hippler, the chief liaison with the University of Colorado Project, replied, "You see, first of all, we (the air force) have not charged you, and you have not promised, to prove or disprove anything." Eventually, however, Hippler remarked that, "I don't think we want any recommendation from you unless you feel strongly about it." By January 16, Hippler's position evolved a bit more in a letter to Condon, stating that since no one knew of any extraterrestrial visitation, there was therefore "no visitation." Instead, Condon needed to consider the air force's cost of investigating UFOs and decide whether taxpayers ought to foot the bill on this wasteful project "for the next ten years."[12]

Despite such omens as these, others tried to keep faith in Condon. By the end of 1966, APRO had sent about 250 UFO reports to Boulder. Hynek, too, expressed hope in the project in a December 17, 1966, article in the *Saturday Evening Post*.[13]

THE PROJECT BEGINS

Throughout the later part of 1966, strange UFO reports continued, many of which were now headed for Boulder as well as ATIC. Several described UFO occupants, such as a November 2 incident in Parkersburg, West Virginia, and a November 17 case in Gaffney, South Carolina, in which two patrolmen saw a craft on the ground and a small man in a shiny suit who spoke perfect English. On the night of December 30, 1966, in Haynesville, Louisiana, a physics professor driving through a wooded area saw a bright, pulsing, orange and white glow, deep in the woods. The next day, he found traces of burns and called the air force and the University of Colorado.[14]

With the exception of David Saunders, however, project members showed little interest in UFOs. It is not surprising that the project started sluggishly. In November, Low took the project's first field trip—with Hynek—to Minot and Donnybrook, North Dakota, to investigate the August 1966 sighting. In December, project member Dr. William Scott, a psychologist, devised a questionnaire for UFO witnesses. He devoted only one page to fundamentals (size, shape, color, etc.) and about twenty pages to the psychological reaction of the observer. When Scott discovered that his perspective was not the project's main focus, he took his questionnaire and went home. Saunders began to wonder whether such a disparate academic group could work together as a team.

In December, Michael Wertheimer was in Washington investigating the 1952 sightings. Virtually every witness still disputed Gen. John Samford's public explanation. Wertheimer initially concluded the sightings could not be explained but soon wrote a paper discussing visual misperceptions, implying this as the explanation. It was a "logically indefensible jump," he said, from seeing something unexplainable to concluding that extraterrestrials were behind it.

On January 13, 1967, Low traveled with project member Jim Wadsworth to Joplin, Missouri. The trip stimulated much press interest and, according to contemporary reports, each man ran interference for the other the whole time.[15]

CONDON LOSING ALLIES

Condon continued to cause public relations mishaps. On January 25, 1967, he was in Corning, New York, making another speech. This time the *Elmira Star-Gazette* quoted him saying that he did not take UFOs seriously and that they were not the business of the air force:

> It is my inclination right now to recommend that the government get out of this business. My attitude right now is that there's nothing to it . . . but I'm not supposed to reach a conclusion for another year.

After this, Keyhoe told Saunders that NICAP was "through" with the Colorado Project. Saunders was astonished by Condon's remarks. It must be a mistake, he thought, and he checked with Condon the next day. No, said Condon, he had been accurately quoted: what is all this fuss about? Saunders convinced him to write a letter to Keyhoe to patch things up. Condon grudgingly sent off a weak note to the major.[16]

Within days, Keyhoe was back in Boulder for what he believed would be a final meeting with the Colorado team before NICAP withdrew its support. Condon alone seemed oblivious to the implications. NICAP's withdrawal of support, so early in the project, could be a serious blow to the entire effort. Other project members tried to convince Condon that the project needed NICAP. Condon was prevailed upon and threw Keyhoe a bone. The ignored NICAP reports, he said, would be examined as soon as possible. "I appreciate your cooperation and I hope NICAP will continue." Once again, Keyhoe accepted this for the time being, but Condon was angry at having to apologize.[17]

James McDonald also saw storm clouds. By late January 1967, he lobbied the president of the National Academy of Sciences, Frederick Seitz, with some relatively mild criticisms of the project and revived his idea for a UFO research panel. Seitz, however, was a former student of Condon's, and McDonald got nowhere.

By February 1967, according to Vallee, several project members had privately approached their scientific colleagues to learn their reactions to the recommendation that Blue Book be closed down. All this before any significant investigative work had even been done.[18] On the twentieth of that month, project members Condon, Low, Saunders, Price, and Rachford visited the CIA's National Photographic Interpretation Center (NPIC) to become familiar with the CIA's photographic analysis capabilities. The visit required a clearance level of Secret and established that no photographic work done for the project would be linked to the CIA. NPIC personnel would be available, according to a CIA document, to perform work "of a photogrammetric nature, such as attempting to measure objects imaged on photographs that may be part of Dr. Condon's analysis." No written comments or documentation from NPIC would be made public. Another CIA memo stated:

> Any work performed by NPIC to assist Dr. Condon in his investigation will not be identified as work accomplished by the CIA. Dr. Condon was advised by Mr. Lundahl to make no reference to CIA in regard to this work effort.

Obviously, it was essential to keep CIA involvement out of the realm of public knowledge, as McDonald and others were becoming vocal about the CIA's manipulation over the entire UFO controversy.[19]

Meanwhile, the University of Colorado Project's main opportunity to study UFO reports was slipping away. The first three months of 1967 continued to be an active period of American UFO reports, but practically no one at Boulder had the knowledge or resources to perform a serious investigation. Other than Low and the junior staff, nearly everyone lacked the basic equipment and tools, such as questionnaires, psychological tests, and even cameras or tape measures. "Most of the fish in this wave got away," said Saunders. Unfortunately, it was the only significant wave within the U.S. during the project's term. Vallee's prediction would prove true.[20]

In early March 1967, Robert Low wrote a position paper which expected that the project would fail to support the ETI theory, even after a diligent search and substantial record. Before sharing his paper with project members (which he did individually and confidentially), he shared them in talks and speeches with the Rand Corporation, Jet Propulsion Laboratory, and Boeing. Low was obsessed with "building the record," which appeared to mean creating a lengthy report that would persuade by its sheer bulk. Despite this ambition, the project's failure to move quickly had by now forced it to prepare a proposal to extend its contract.[21]

In March 1967, world-renowned physicist Dr. Paul Santorini revealed a long-hidden experience connected with UFOs. Santorini's credentials were surely impressive: he had helped to develop radar, fuses for the atomic bomb, and the *Nike* missile guidance system. Until 1964, he had directed the Experimental Physics Laboratory of the Polytechnic. Santorini stated that a "world blanket of secrecy" surrounded UFO reports and related his experience of twenty years prior, when strange objects flying over Greece had alarmed the government, which soon learned the objects were not Russian missiles. When Greek army commanders asked the U.S. Defense Department about the objects, he said, "they were quickly pressured into silence, (and) the army ordered the investigation discontinued." Santorini said he was later closely questioned by U.S. scientists from Washington. He offered one clear reason as to the secrecy: authorities were unwilling to admit the existence of a force against which we had "no possibility of defense." When asked about Santorini's statement, Condon brushed it off.[22]

Keyhoe continued to be unhappy. He met with Low once again during the spring and learned that of the thousand or so reports that NICAP had given to the project, "probably four or five," were to be spot-checked. So far, Low conceded, none of them had been. When, in March, Keyhoe met with his old friend Frank Edwards, Edwards recommended that NICAP withdraw its support. Although no longer nationally syndicated, Edwards still was on the radio and decided to blast the project over the airwaves. He began to work on an exposé and told Keyhoe that he was planning to speed it up.[23] Unfortunately, Frank Edwards died of a heart attack on June 23, 1967, at the age of fifty-eight. Amid the growing storm, APRO continued to support Condon. Members of the project visited APRO headquarters in March, and the Lorenzens gave leads on several classified cases which they had obtained with great effort. The project members tentatively agreed to try developing these leads, but in fact nothing happened with them. One of the main problems was that, despite the supposedly independent nature of the Colorado investigation, project members were directed by the Pentagon to rely primarily on current cases. Digging up old cases, they were told, was too expensive.[24]

SECRECY IN 1967

While the UFO was busily being solved, courtesy of the nation's tax money, the national security state spent much more money to solve other problems secretly. The escalation of the undeclared war in Vietnam pressed President Johnson and the entire intelligence community into new acts of illegality, partly to contain domestic discontent, partly to neutralize the Vietnamese enemy in new ways. According to Gordon Thomas, by 1967, many of the MK-Search projects were costing lots of money without producing results. In the spring of 1967, however, the CIA began to take Vietcong prisoners to a room where the men were strapped to tables and given electroshock. An unknown number of VC were subjected to the torture, and apparently all of them died as a result. The idea was to see whether the CIA could "depattern" the VC communist indoctrination.[25]

More gruesome activities lay in store for the Vietnamese. In May 1967, William Colby, head of the CIA's Far East Division of Clandestine Services, launched Project Phoenix. This was a comprehensive attack against the Vietcong infrastructure which soon turned into a straightforward assassination program of suspected Vietcong (or VC sympathizers), often as a bullet in the head while the victim slept. The CIA established a nationwide system of interrogation centers, about which little is known. According to Colby's testimony in 1971, Phoenix killed 20,587 suspected VC in two and a half years. The South Vietnamese government put the figure at 40,994.[26]

Not everything in Vietnam went according to CIA wishes. In late June 1967, a major debate emerged between the CIA, the chairman of the Board of National Estimates, and the Pentagon regarding the North Vietnamese Order of Battle—that is, the size of enemy forces. The gap was irreconcilable. Military numbers placed the number at 270,000, while the CIA's main analyst called this "ridiculously low"—more like 600,000, he said. By September, the military had compromised to 300,000. Just as it played with UFO statistics, so now did the military manipulate numbers and categories in this debate. When the CIA analyst proved the VC had more men in one category, the military reduced another category by a similar amount. On September 11, DCI Richard Helms ordered the CIA station in Saigon to accept the military's figure of 299,000. It soon went down to 248,000. Thus could the Pentagon prove that America was winning the war. Helms knew the numbers were phony, but he also knew what numbers President Johnson wanted. In January 1968, the Tet Offensive made the debate moot.[27]

Elsewhere for the CIA, it was business as usual. In Greece, a CIA-organized coup placed the military in power. In Bolivia, on October 8, 1967, the CIA-advised Bolivian rangers, in the presence of a CIA operator, tortured and murdered longtime irritant Ernesto "Che" Guevara.[28]

Aside from the dispute over the Order of Battle, Lyndon Johnson had other points of friction with the CIA during 1967. He shut down Operation Mongoose, for instance. Then there was the extended issue over CIA assassinations. In March, Johnson asked Richard Helms directly about the rumors of CIA assassination plans in conjunction with the Mafia. Helms said he would get on it. On April 24, the CIA's Inspector General presented to Helms a report on CIA assassination plots. Helms was *not* pleased. He often said, "the first rule in keeping secrets is nothing on paper." The document apparently was quite thorough and has never been published, although the Church Assassinations Committee used it a decade later. On May 10, Helms gave his answer to Johnson. What he said is not completely known, but he did inform the president about the CIA's longtime mail interception program "and some other things that were going on." Johnson essentially appears to have said, be careful and don't get caught.[29]

Throughout 1967, Johnson also pressured Helms to discover foreign connections behind the wave of student unrest. By August, this led to a partnership between the CIA and FBI for Operation Chaos, a large-scale domestic spying program. The program ran through 1973, amassing ten thousand files and computer indexes on over 300,000 individuals and over one hundred domestic groups. Some files were several volumes long. The NSA provided assistance through Shamrock, and the effort from the NSA's side was so significant that in 1969 the project there got its own name: Minaret. The NSA at this point had large files on at least seventy-five thousand Americans, including members of Congress and prominent businessmen. Aside from the obvious illegality of all this, the programs were unknown to the public for years. The program involved more than just surveillance, but direct action by *agents provocateurs*.[30]

Over at the FBI, the NSA attempted without success to persuade Hoover to expand his collection techniques. Decades of illegal programs were beginning to make the old director a bit nervous. Still, in August 1967, Hoover approved an intense and disruptive Cointel program against black nationalist groups in the U.S. In the fall, the NSA agreed to a request by army intelligence to monitor international telephone and cable traffic to support the army's civil disturbance responsibilities.[31]

UFOS IN EARLY 1967

Amid the controversy, social unrest, and secret dealings of 1967, one might forget that UFOs continued to present themselves around the world in large numbers. Although the investigators at Blue Book did very little, and the Colorado University Project was slow to start, NICAP and APRO were busy investigating reports. In 1967, NICAP's membership had risen to eleven thousand, while APRO's was at four thousand. Throughout the year, APRO collected many reports of UFO landings, near landings, and occupant sightings throughout the Western Hemisphere. The Lorenzens also printed the full version of the Villas-Boas incident in 1967, shortly after John Fuller had published the Betty and Barney Hill abduction story in *Look* magazine. James McDonald believed such stories would "set UFO research back ten years." But like it or not, abductions were part of the package, and the UFO phenomenon was becoming stranger and more complex than most people had realized. Abductions were simply the most sensational of the new dimensions of the problem. Crop circles were increasingly part of the story, and, before the year was out, animal mutilations.[32]

Several close-range sightings of landed UFO craft were reported in North and South America through the year. Many of these were detailed and presented by seemingly reliable people; multiple-witness sightings were not unusual, and several were South American military encounters.[33]

The U.S. military was too busy with its own UFO reports to worry much about sightings by civilians. An oblique reference to Project Moon Dust in connection to UFOs surfaced on January 18, when a U.S. Defense attaché in Rabat, Morocco, forwarded press clippings and added:

[T]he page one coverage afforded this sighting demonstrates a high level of inter-est in the subject of UFOs and presages further reporting which could be valuable in pursuit of Project Moon Dust.[34]

An air force memo from March 1, 1967, alluded to reports of visitations by Men in Black. "Information, not verifiable," said the memo,

has reached HQ USAF that persons claiming to represent the air force or other defense establishments have contacted citizens who have sighted unidentified fly-ing objects.

The memo ordered that all military personnel hearing of such incidents report them to their local OSI officers.[35]

But inquiries such as these were overshadowed by matters much more serious, involving airspace violations over bases near the northwestern U.S. border. On March 5, 1967, NORAD radar tracked a disc-shaped UFO over the Minuteman missile site at Minot AFB in North Dakota. Immediately, strike teams were scrambled to the area with orders to capture the object undamaged if it landed. Sure enough, at the site, they saw a metallic, disc-shaped UFO with bright flashing lights moving overhead. It stopped abruptly and hovered at five hundred feet, circled over the launch control facility, then ascended vertically and disappeared, just before NORAD ordered F-106s to intercept it. The incident reached Raymond Fowler and thence NICAP.[36]

Early in the morning on the sixteenth, at Malmstrom AFB in Montana, one of the most extraordinary events in the history of military-UFO encoun-ters took place. Under a clear and dark Montana sky, an airman with the Oscar Flight Launch Control Center (LCC) saw a starlike object zigzagging high above him. Soon, a larger and closer light also appeared and acted in similar fashion. He called his NCO, and the two men watched in awe as the lights streaked through the sky, maneuvering in impossible ways. The NCO phoned his commander, Robert Salas, who was below ground in the launch control center. Salas was dubious. "Great," he said. "You just keep watching them and let me know if they get any closer."

A few minutes later, the NCO called Salas again. As Salas later wrote, this time he was clearly frightened and shouted that a red, glowing UFO was hov-ering outside the front gate. "What do you want us to do?" asked the NCO. Salas told him to make sure the site was secure while he phoned the command post. "Sir," replied the NCO, "I have to go now, one of the guys just got injured."

Before Salas could ask about the injury, the NCO was off the line. The man, who was not seriously injured, was evacuated by helicopter to the base. Meanwhile, Salas woke his commander, Lt. Fred Meiwald. As he briefed Meiwald, an alarm rang through the small capsule, and both men saw a "No-Go" light turn on for one of the missiles. Within seconds, several more missiles went down in succession.

Twenty miles away, at the Echo-Flight launch facilities, the same scenario was taking place. First Lt. Walter Figel, the deputy crew commander of the Missile Combat Crew, was at his station when one of the Minuteman missiles went into "No-Go" status. He immediately called the missile site to determine the cause of the problem. Was it because of the scheduled missile maintenance, he asked the security guard? No, came the response, as the maintenance had not yet taken place. However, continued the guard, a UFO had been hovering over the site. Like Salas, Figel doubted the story. Before he had any time to reflect on this, however, ten more ICBMs in rapid succession reported a "No-Go" condition. Within seconds, the entire flight was down.

Strike teams were dispatched to two of the E-Flight launch facilities, where maintenance crews were already at work. Figel had not told the strike teams about the UFO report. Upon their arrival, however, the teams reported back to him that all of the maintenance and security personnel had been watching UFOs hover over each of the sites.

The missiles were down for the greater part of a day. The air force investigation included full-scale tests on-site, as well as laboratory tests at the Boeing Company's Seattle plant. No cause for the shutdown could be found. The Boeing engineering chief said, "there was no technical explanation that could explain the event."[37]

UFO reports continued to originate from that region, including several on March 24 from the Belt, Montana, region. One of these reports was of a UFO landing. Police and a Malmstrom AFB helicopter searched the area, but found nothing.[38]

Also during March 1967 (most likely) was the occurrence of the "Cuban jet incident," a story that years later fell into the hands of UFO researchers Stanton Friedman and Robert Todd, and was described at length by Fawcett and Greenwood, who labeled it "probably authentic." The story, in summation, is as follows: Cuban air defense radar controllers reported an unidentified craft approaching Cuba from the northwest, moving at 660 mph and traveling at thirty-three thousand feet. Two MIG-21s were scrambled to meet it and were guided to within three miles of the object. At that point, the flight leader radioed in that the object was a bright metallic sphere with no visible markings. He was unable to establish radio contact with the UFO, and Cuban air defense ordered the object to be destroyed. The flight leader reported that his radar was locked and missiles ready. Seconds later, a wingman screamed into the radio that the flight leader's jet had "disintegrated."

The UFO then quickly accelerated and climbed above ninety-eight thousand feet, heading toward South America. The U.S. 6947th Security Squadron, centered at Homestead AFB, was monitoring the incident all the while and, as AFSS units were under operational control of the NSA, sent a report to Fort Meade. NSA then ordered the 6947th to ship all tapes and pertinent data to the NSA and to list the Cuban aircraft loss in squadron files as due to "equipment malfunction." Friedman learned of the incident in 1978 through a security specialist stationed at Homestead AFB. After Todd learned of it shortly thereafter during the same year, he received an intimidating visit by the FBI at the behest of NSA.[39]

By April, just as the Colorado staff was ready for serious investigating, reports in America ebbed. Sightings of weird, close-range objects did continue, however. APRO, in particular, collected many reports of UFOs that hovered very low or landed in America and elsewhere. Some of these cases included multiple witnesses, EM effects, and ground traces.[40]

FALCON LAKE

The Colorado Project staff did not investigate many sightings that spring, either because the cases seemed too outlandish, or simply because the staff did not learn about them in time. The following report, however, did get an investigation, of sorts. On May 19, 1967, shortly after noon, Stefan Michalak, a fifty-two-year-old mechanic and quartz prospector, claimed to have seen two red, glowing objects flying at high speed while in the wilderness at Falcon Lake in Manitoba. They appeared to be disc-shaped as they became closer, and one of them abruptly stopped its descent to hover, then soon departed toward the west. Meanwhile, the other one landed. Michalak watched it from behind some bushes at a distance of about 160 feet. It was about thirty-five feet wide, ten feet thick, had a small dome on top that contained horizontal slits. As exotic as it looked, Michalak assumed it was an experimental American aircraft.

After thirty minutes of observation, a small door opened, showing a well-lit interior. Michalak then decided to approach it. At sixty feet distant, he heard voices which were somewhat muffled, in his words, "by the sounds of the motor and the rush of air that was continuously coming out from somewhere inside." Still, one of the voices was discernibly more high-pitched than the other. Michalak called out, "Okay, Yankee boys, having trouble? Come on out, and we'll see what we can do about it." The voices did not respond. Michalak, who was multilingual, tried other languages: Russian, German, Italian, French, and Ukranian. Still no response.

Michalak decided to peek inside the craft. In his words:

The inside was a maze of lights. Direct beams running in horizontal and diagonal paths and a series of flashing lights, it seemed to me, were working in a random fashion, with no particular order or sequence. I took note of the thickness of the walls of the craft. They were about twenty inches at the cross-section.

As soon as he moved his head back, three panels closed off the opening. When he touched the highly polished craft with his glove, its rubber coating melted.

Almost immediately, the object began to lift and angle off the ground so that the bottom of the craft faced Michalak. He saw what looked like an exhaust system which was in the form of a grid with a uniform pattern of small circular vents. A blast of hot gas erupted from the vents, hitting Michalak in the chest and knocking him back. Tearing off his burning shirt, he saw the object ascend, clear the treetops, and head off to the west. It left a fifteen-foot circle.

Michalak felt dizzy, and vomited for days afterward, and lost over twenty pounds in the coming weeks. He suffered minor burns to his face and more serious burns on his chest, a photograph of which showed a pattern matching his description of the exhaust grid. He experienced intense headaches, rashes, and swelling, especially in his hands, which "looked as if they had been inflated with air." He went to a hospital in Winnipeg, where the attending physician, an immigrant with limited English, attributed the marks to aircraft exhaust. Michalak was too tired to relate his experience to the doctor. On May 23, he saw a radiologist who found nothing wrong. A week later, he was tested for radiation at the Whiteshell Nuclear Research Establishment in Pinawa, Manitoba, with no unusual results. The grid pattern remained, however, with no explanation from doctors. After another trip to the hospital, he was told his swelling was caused by an allergy.

His symptoms continued into 1968, and Michalak, at his own expense, visited the Mayo Clinic in Rochester, Minnesota. He spent two weeks under study, with disappointing results. Doctors were able to describe his problems quite nicely but were unable to determine causes, nor provide a remedy. They found "no overt evidence of significant mental or emotional illness."

Meanwhile, researchers had been trying to investigate the landing site. These included the Canadian Aerial Phenomena Research Organization (CAPRO), the Royal Canadian air force, the Colorado Project, and numerous other groups. For a while, no one could find the site. Michalak, at first too sick to go with the parties, attended a helicopter search on June 2, 1967, and a ground search on June 25. Both failed to find the site.

The University of Colorado sent project investigator Roy Craig on June 4, 1967, but he was unable to find the site. He did, however, interview local individuals who might have been in a good position to have observed the object on May 19. This included a ranger, who noted that the forest was dry, and that a fire capable of burning a man would have started the forest burning. The watchmen in towers, who usually noticed smoke from campfires immediately, saw nothing unusual. Moreover, no watchtower personnel saw a metallic saucer. On the other hand, Craig found that those who knew Michalak considered him to be honest. Disgusted, Craig returned to Boulder.

Soon after, Michalak stated that during the search of the twenty-fifth, he had found the site he was originally looking for (as a quartz prospector) and had no intention of leading anyone else near the landing site until he had staked his claim. On June 30, Michalak found the landing site while searching with another person. They found an outline of the landed object, remains of his shirt, and the tape measure he had lost that day. Within a month, he had cooperated with the RCAF, who reached the site on July 28, and collected samples. The Canadian air force representative, Paul Bissky, also saw the outline, which he described as a "very evident circle." He wrote that it was

> an approximate fifteen-foot diameter circle on the rock surface where the moss and earth covering has been cleared to the rock surface by a force such as made by air at very high velocity.

The RCAF also found a high level of radiation in some samples from the site, which it deemed to be "a possible health hazard." Upon returning, they found a highly localized contamination at the site—right on the crown of the rock where Michalak alleged the landing occurred, and where the fifteen-foot-diameter circle was. No explanation ever emerged, other than by hoax, as to how this "smear" of radiation got onto the rock.

A year after the sighting, Michalak again visited the site with a friend and found pieces of radioactive material in a fissure of rock at the landing site. This had been missed, evidently, by a representative of Manitoba's Department of Mines and Natural Resources, who had visited the site several times. Some researchers believed the metals were planted. Craig wrote, "In view of the thoroughness of the earlier searches . . . it is improbable that the particles discovered a year later would have been missed." Several groups analyzed samples of the metal. Some tests confirmed the presence of Radium 226, which was also found in the soil samples from a year earlier; other tests were inconclusive. The Colorado Project simply noted the "inconsistencies and incongruities in the case" implying that the event was a hoax, a conclusion which has been disputed over the years.[41]

MCDONALD RIPS BLUE BOOK AND MENZEL

In a March 1, 1967, interview with the *Tucson Daily Citizen,* James McDonald stated, "I'd advise the public to view the Bluebook statistics as meaningless." Elaborating on this statement in another interview published on April 6, he explained:

As a result of several trips to Project Bluebook, I've had an opportunity to examine quite carefully and in detail the types of reports that are made by Bluebook personnel. In most cases, I have found that there's almost no correlation between so-called "evaluations or explanations" that are made by Bluebook and the facts of the case. . . . There are hundreds of good cases in the air force files that should have led to top-level scientific scrutiny of this problem, years ago, yet these cases have been swept under the rug in a most disturbing way by Project Bluebook investigators and their consultants.

And again:

I feel that the air force has misled us for twenty years. I equate almost all of that misrepresentation to incompetence and superficiality on the part of the air force investigators involved with Project Bluebook and its forerunners. Nobody there with any strong scientific competence is looking into the problem.

On April 22, 1967, McDonald assailed Donald Menzel before the American Society of Newspaper Editors. "When he comes to analyzing UFO reports," said McDonald,

he seems to calmly cast aside well-known scientific principles with almost abandon in an all-out effort to be sure that no UFO reports survives his attack.

"There is no sensible alternative," he argued, "to the utterly shocking hypothesis that UFOs are extraterrestrial probes. . . ." Menzel shot back that McDonald was a pseudoscientist with absurd views. A week later, McDonald told the press that he had learned from several "unquotable sources" that the air force had long been trying to unburden itself of the UFO problem and had tried twice to transfer its program to NASA.[42]

McDonald was vocal enough about UFOs that spring that he obtained assistance from United Nations Secretary General U Thant to lecture on the subject before the UN's Outer Space Affairs Group on June 7. By the end of the month, he was in Australia on a small ONR grant to perform research in cloud physics. Unfortunately for McDonald, he had announced his intention to do some UFO investigating and lecturing there, in a memo to Low. In short time, this innocuous statement would backfire on him with significant repercussions.[43]

THE COLORADO PROJECT IN MID-1967

By mid-1967, NICAP maintained what Keyhoe later called an "uneasy truce" with the Colorado Project. Actually, he had already decided to withhold any further cooperation: he was convinced that the air force was behind the project's effort to obtain NICAP files. As a result, he held back the remaining big cases, in spite of requests for more reports. Besides, Keyhoe felt that the project members had not looked seriously at the good reports NICAP had already provided. Part of the problem, it must be said, was Keyhoe's personality and authoritarian style of managing NICAP. Even the sympathetic Saunders conceded that the situation was tolerable for NICAP members "only because they are interested in the problem and the major is out of the office as much as he is in."[44]

On July 1, someone leaked information to the *Denver Post* that the project had requested an additional $280,000 to extend the project to September 30, 1968. The publicity noticeably upset Condon. The air force ultimately approved an additional $183,155, plus $29,750 to go toward a national opinion survey, bringing the final total to $525,905.[45]

Among themselves, project members were divided about UFOs. The situation recalls Project Sign in 1948. By midyear, several Colorado Project members, after reading reports and interviewing witnesses, believed the extraterrestrial hypothesis to be the most probable explanation of the difficult UFO cases. Moreover, as with Sign, the project's leadership was hostile to a pro-ET explanation of UFOs, a situation that would soon force a showdown.[46]

By July, driven by Low's insistence on "building the record," plans were underway to compile a case book of the project's best UFO cases. But this was no easy undertaking and would require a major effort by the whole staff. Richard Hall was therefore invited for two days of official consulting and narrowed the list to about one hundred cases of a good variety. A small group within the project then agreed to review those cases to decide which ones would receive more intensive analysis. From the beginning, the case book was behind schedule, despite its being Low's special project. First of all, Low himself was not reading any cases, although he continued to push the project all through the Summer of Love. By default, Saunders became the one responsible for selecting cases. By August, it was moving at a snail's pace—only twelve none-too-impressive cases were gathered—and clearly would not be ready by the hoped-for completion date of November 1967. The major problem, according to Saunders, was that the staff

found it difficult to adopt an attitude of judging a case by the *potential* that it displayed. Instead, we found ourselves discarding case after case because the evidence that might have made them airtight, and that might have been available if we really investigated, was not already handed to us on a silver platter.

After two meetings like this, Saunders was convinced the group was doing more harm than good. As a result, the project hired a University of Colorado law student to write the case book itself, based on the notes.[47]

It occurred to Saunders that although Blue Book was supposed to be sending its reports to Boulder, little was arriving, and most that did was of poor quality and late. Eventually, Saunders and project member Norm Levine traveled to Dayton to determine the problem. What they found disturbed them: thick cases in separate folders *adjacent to*, rather than *in*, the main folders. Other cases were stored in a classified safe, and it took some cajoling by Levine to get Blue Book's permission to look at them. The vast differences between Blue Book's and NICAP's reports also bothered Saunders. First of all, there was practically no overlap between the cases. Second, NICAP had much higher percentage of "good" UFO reports—where the object in question was not obviously a meteor or balloon. Another realization sank in: by now, the only witnesses reporting UFOs to the air force were either naive in the extreme or motivated by an overriding sense of duty.

Saunders was also finding problems with Blue Book Special Report Number 14 (the Battelle Report), released in 1955. Low had asked him to provide a statistical analysis of the report, since this was Saunders's area of expertise. The poor quality of statistical analysis within the report distressed him. He noticed how, "with remarkable regularity, whoever did these statistics combined the categories so as to minimize his chances of finding anything significant." To make matters worse, the original data, contained in IBM cards, had all been thrown away.[48]

Saunders later wrote that he sensed a lack of teamwork all summer among those with differing views on UFOs and an undercurrent of "mutual distrust and game playing." He began to wonder whether someone on the project was "acting in a double role" and was certain that others on the project also wondered about this. "The possibility that we were all being played as pawns in someone else's chess game," he wrote, "did not help morale, either." His thoughts drifted back to the summer of 1966, while the air force was wooing the University of Colorado for the contract. At that time, Saunders spoke with Low about the charges of Keyhoe, Edwards, and others that there was a UFO conspiracy on the part of the CIA. Saunders suggested that, if the university took the contract, the project should demand a written draft of its "need to know" from the highest possible level of government, either the president or the National Security Council. If the true story was foul-up, as opposed to cover-up, this affirmation should have been easy to obtain, argued Saunders, especially while the air force was still wooing them. "In fact," wrote Saunders, "this was my only suggestion about the proposal that was ignored." That is, it was not established that the Colorado Project had a need to know about all UFO cases. That fact by itself threw doubt over the legitimacy of the study.[49]

Of course neither Saunders nor anyone else surmised Low's position on the subject of UFOs and cover-ups back in 1966, when he wrote his infamous memorandum in which he stated that "the trick" to the project would be to describe it "so that, to the public, it would appear a totally objective study, but to the scientific community would present the image of a group of nonbelievers trying their best to be objective but having an almost zero expectation of finding a saucer." But in July 1967, like a body carelessly disposed of, Low's memorandum finally surfaced. That month, project member Roy Craig was searching through office files—at Low's suggestion, no less—for unrelated information and found the memo. Craig immediately recognized the seriousness of the problem. In his words, "my stomach caught in my throat." Norm Levine was sitting nearby. "See if this doesn't give you a funny feeling in the stomach," Craig said, handing him the memo. Levine, too, was distressed. Levine showed the memo to Saunders, who felt it "expressed concisely what we knew anyway based on Low's day-to-day behavior." Craig, who in his own book disagreed so fundamentally with Saunders about the Colorado Project, agreed with him that the memo's sentiments were consistent with Low's actions throughout the project and "clearly implied that we were involved in a whitewash noninvestigation, probably aimed at getting the air force off a public criticism hook."

The Low memorandum quickly made the rounds among project members, then went back into the file. Before the year was out, however, Saunders would also show it to Keyhoe, who in turn would tell McDonald about it—all without knowledge of Low or Condon (who did not even know the memo existed). By then, the problem would be beyond repair.[50]

APRO SUMMER CASES

Two cases that reached APRO during the summer of 1967 illustrate the up close nature of many UFO sightings at the time. One occurred at 4:20 A.M. on July 5, near Coventry, Connecticut, on Route 31, when a motorist saw what appeared to be an orange ball of light hanging from a tree. When police arrived, the area was deserted. APRO investigator Lawrence Fawcett notified the Colorado Project, which sent off two investigators. With Fawcett, they found a grassy area that had been compressed and swirled flat. No presence of radioactivity was established, and the photo taken by Fawcett came out completely blank. Several similar sites were found in the area at the time.[51]

Near Whitehouse, Ohio, at 11:30 P.M. on July 13, Robert Richardson was driving with a friend, Jerry Quay. As the car turned around a bend, the two saw a brilliant bluish source of light blocking the road. Richardson slammed on the brakes, closed his eyes, and felt an impact. The object, however, was gone, leaving both men shaken but unhurt. Local police dismissed the incident, but state police returned with them to the scene. All they found were Richardson's skid marks. The next day, Richardson found a lump of metal and noticed various dents and scratches on the hood of his car, and that some chrome on the bumper had been stripped off. On the fifteenth, he sent a telegram to the Lorenzens and gave his phone number.

At 11 P.M. on the following night, Richardson received a visit at his home from two friendly young men, who stayed about ten minutes to ask some questions but did not identify themselves (Richardson did not ask their names). He did check their car, however, a 1953 black Cadillac with license 8577-D. He later learned that the plate had not been issued. A week after this visit, Richardson received a classic Men-in-Black visit. Two men, different from the others, arrived at his door. They wore dark suits, had dark complexions, and were "foreign-looking." One had an accent of some sort but spoke fluent English. At first, Richardson thought these men were trying to convince him that he had not hit anything in the road. However, they soon demanded his two pieces of physical evidence. Sorry, said Richardson, but he had handed both pieces over to APRO for analysis. Is there any way he could get it back, the men asked. No, he replied. Just before leaving, one of them said, "If you want your wife to stay as pretty as she is, then you'd better get the metal back." He saw them drive away in a 1967 Dodge sedan but could not make out the license plate. What disturbed him, other than the threat, was that the metal had only been discussed on the phone twice: once between himself and Coral Lorenzen, and once between himself and APRO researcher Nils Paquette. Coral Lorenzen believed her phone call was monitored.

The case reached the Colorado University Project. In March 1968, Roy Craig conducted a test of the material, along with the fibrous metal taken from the front bumper of Richardson's car. The metal pieces were of iron and chromium, with traces of nickel and manganese. The fibrous metals on the bumper were 92 percent magnesium, not what one would expect to find on one's bumper, but nothing definitive, either.[52]

In 1967 there was yet another global wave of UFO activity. South America appears to have generated the most reports, most of which were collected by APRO. Sightings were so frequently characterized by multiple craft that the Lorenzens referred to it as the "fleet phenomenon." Several of these were seen by military personnel, such as a June 24 sighting of about ten silent, disc-shaped UFOs over Puerto Neuvo, Argentina. Venezuela and Brazil reported a great deal of UFO activity as the summer progressed, including many landings and sightings of small beings in silvery clothing.[53]

Many cases involved unknown craft in the sea. One of the more widely reported occurred about fifteen miles north of the Venezuelan town of Recife on the morning of August 4. Dr. Hugo Sierra Yepez, an engineer, was fishing on a beach when he felt a vibration and saw large bubbles in the water. A grayish-blue, metallic, flat disc, about twenty feet in diameter, emerged from the water. It briefly hovered just above the surface, dripping water, then rose slowly toward the east, ascended in a curve, and shot upward and away. Yepez discerned a "revolving section with triangular windows" on the craft. The entire sighting lasted less than one minute.[54]

Other remarkable water-related sightings were reported off the South

American coast. On July 20, 1967, an underwater "UFO" was reported by the *Naviero*, a ship with the Argentine Shipping Lines Company. The crew saw a shining, self-luminous object in the sea that paced the ship at an extremely close range—no more than fifty feet away starboard. It was cigar-shaped and estimated at 105 to 110 feet in length, emitted a powerful blue and white glow, was completely silent, and did not disturb the water. Was it a submarine, or perhaps a whale? The captain and chief officer decided no, it "could not possibly have been either of these things." They saw no sign of a periscope, railing, tower, superstructure, or other protruding part. After pacing the ship for fifteen minutes at 15 to 20 knots, the craft suddenly dived and passed beneath the ship and vanished into the depths "at great speed." Deep beneath the water, it continued to glow brightly. The captain told the Argentine press that he had never seen the like of it.[55]

About three weeks later, on August 8, just after dark, off the Venezuelan coast near Salina, a pastor noticed the water changing to various colors and becoming brighter. A glowing, orange, disc-shaped object then emerged from the sea and hovered at about 1,500 feet for several seconds. The pastor heard a buzzing sound and saw the object disappear quickly. Yet another water-related UFO case occurred in Venezuela on August 25. At 5 P.M. at Catia la Mar, Ruben Norato noticed a disturbance in the sea, then saw three large discs emerge and zoom out of sight.[56]

Reports such as these prompted the Lorenzens to see for themselves what was happening, and on August 11, they left for several destinations in South America. Upon arriving, they discovered, in their words,

> more than one government-sponsored agency engaged in an effort to solve the secret of UFO propulsion. Such endeavors, which proceed on the assumption that "flying saucers are real," could hardly have come into being without a certain amount of preliminary intelligence gathering.[57]

Throughout South America, hundreds of UFO sightings were reported, with many high strangeness cases. In late August and early September, several seemingly reliable witnesses, including a police officer, claimed to see short humanoid creatures who sought to take them to "their world." All individuals claimed to have successfully refused the offer. Meanwhile, landing and humanoid sightings were being reported worldwide, including the United States and especially the Soviet Union. Indeed, the Soviet Union experienced a major UFO wave during 1967, featuring many cases similar to those being reported in South America, although this fact went unknown for many years. It certainly throws cold water over the notion that these sightings are most easily explained by classified aircraft, an explanation that would be difficult to offer even without the Soviet dimension.[58]

PROBLEMS IN COLORADO

The South American wave was ignored by the American media and the Colorado Project. For the last ten days of August 1967, Robert Low was in Prague at the International Astronomical Union even though a bona fide project astronomer, Frank Roach, was there (Hynek also attended). What was Low doing in Europe? Certainly nothing relating to UFOs. He wasted an opportunity to visit Charles Bowen, the editor of *Flying Saucer Review*, and Aimé Michel (who received a visit from Bowen at that time). Instead, Low visited Loch Ness, because neither the Loch Ness monster nor UFOs existed, he explained privately. Upon his return to Boulder, Low gave an informal twenty-minute summary about his trip, including almost nothing about the conference itself.[59]

As the new academic year was about to begin, the project obtained a thirdhand report of a UFO sighting at Edwards AFB, said to have occurred on September 1. The route was certainly indirect: a civilian employee at the base saw the report, then mentioned it to a relative, who discussed it with a scientist voluntarily cooperating with the project. According to the story, six UFOs followed an X-15 while it landed. When project members called the base, they *"really* got the runaround." After two weeks of phone calls, they learned that no X-15 flew that day. No one, however, would deny a UFO sighting had taken place. Instead, base personnel sidestepped all pertinent questions and stated they had no such report in their files. The case went nowhere.[60]

The project also learned of a series of radar and visual reports from Lake Superior and Upper Michigan from September 6. At one point, more than twenty radar targets appeared and disappeared over the middle of the lake during a three-hour period, tracked at speeds of up to 2,000 mph (at times turning at right angles), and involving apparent separation and merging of distinct targets. Project members discovered from radar operators at Kincheloe AFB (who reported the incident to them) that radar operators at the other end of the lake, in Duluth, Minnesota, had gotten similar targets. The project sent John Ahrens and Norm Levine to investigate. While there, they checked into rumors of visual sightings over Sault Sainte Marie, although none of these correlated with the radar. When they reached Duluth, to their surprise, they drew a complete blank, with denials that anyone had obtained any such radar return. They returned home with a much weakened case. The Colorado Project's public status meant precious little when it came to important cases within the classified world.[61]

Shortly after Labor Day, Saunders suggested to Low that academic commitments might require a reorganization of project duties. Namely, that Low and principal investigator Roach each report directly to Condon. According to Saunders, Low "blew his stack." First of all, Roach had known Condon much longer than had Low; second, Roach was more sympathetic to Saunders's position. Low ultimately agreed to a change, but replaced Roach with Levine. Meanwhile, Edward U. Condon stirred up more controversy. A week before returning to campus, he gave an after-dinner talk about UFO crackpot cases to his former colleagues at the National Bureau of Standards in Washington, startling his audience with his cavalier attitude. When James McDonald briefed the project soon after on his Australian trip, he was dismayed that Condon asked no questions and dozed off three times.[62]

With leadership such as this coming from the project charged with conducting a scientific study of the UFO problem, and with the discovery of the Low memorandum now widely (and secretly) known among project members, it should be no surprise that discontent was the rule. On September 17, Franklin Roach submitted his resignation from the project, in order to pursue his academic interests. On the nineteenth, Saunders, Low, and Condon met for three hours to discuss Saunders's suggestions on improving the project's public image. Saunders argued that the public could already tell the project was headed toward a negative conclusion. Little came of the meeting, other than the speculation by Condon that *if* the project did find evidence to support the extraterrestrial hypothesis, he would either put the evidence in a briefcase and take it directly to the president, or else he would write a report to the air force and let them decide what to do with it. In either case, he would not disclose the fact publicly. Saunders interpreted this as a failure to honor the project's commitment to make a public report and to tell it like it was.[63]

On the following day, NICAP provisionally withdrew its support. Keyhoe had heard Condon's gaffe at the NBS, and told Saunders he had made this decision reluctantly and only under pressure from NICAP's Board. He hoped some means might be found to allow for a reversal of that decision and said he would not yet publicize the break. Keyhoe had other reasons to be angry. He had recently learned that Condon had not interviewed a single UFO witness, and had no intention of doing so. He also discovered—gasp!—that the only reason the Colorado Project wanted NICAP's support was for its own credibility. This was surely a difficult time for Keyhoe and NICAP. Just recently, for personal reasons, Richard Hall resigned from NICAP. Now, it looked as though relations with the Colorado Project might be irretrievably severed. But if all was not well at NICAP, neither was it in Boulder. Keyhoe may not have fully appreciated until his conversation with Saunders how wide the chasm was that separated the leaders from the led.

Saunders immediately told Low about NICAP's withdrawal of support. The news upset Low, who asked Saunders to patch things up. Saunders reluctantly said he would try. Meanwhile, on September 25, Low, Saunders, and Condon had another meeting, a brief one at Condon's home. Nothing new, nothing resolved. Saunders surely must have irritated Condon: this time, he pointed out that the problem with NICAP would not have arisen had Condon abided by his own rule of not speaking publicly about UFOs; it could also be resolved, he continued, by allowing other project members to do likewise. Condon said he understood the point but offered no change. In fact, two days later, the *Rocky Mountain News* published a commentary by Condon where he debunked UFOs and discounted NICAP's contribution to the Colorado Project. The article quoted Low in a similar vein. As a result, Low freely predicted Saunders's resignation from the project and told him privately that if he wanted to return to the administration, he needed to get on the team and work with him and Condon. The staff was understandably upset by the article.[64]

The lines of battle were drawn: it was Low and Condon against everyone else. Saunders probably expressed the majority view when he wrote:

> [W]e could no longer doubt that any prospect for successful completion of the UFO project depended on us and would have to circumvent the obstacles of our leadership as well as the complexities of the problem itself.

Indeed, the staff was close to an *en masse* resignation. On the night of September 27, 1967, project members held a meeting without Low and Condon to decide what, if anything, they would do. Norm Levine was the group's hardliner, pushing for mass resignation. Roy Craig, who expressed a "residual faith" in Condon, was the sole dissenter. Saunders essentially sided with Levine but still wanted to explore strategies that were not irreversible. Franklin Roach, his resignation already tendered, thought Condon was tired but ultimately reliable. Several members expressed the concern that Condon's final word on the subject would be so negative as to stifle further scientific research into UFOs for another twenty years, or even more. They decided, therefore, to prepare their own report, one "so compelling that Condon would be forced to accept it on its merits." Undoubtedly, a fond, trusting position.[65]

The following day, Condon met with all project members. He expressed some regret over his public remarks—not what he said in them, but that he made them at all. He retracted nothing and explained that the only misquote had been that he was disenchanted with the project. In fact, he said, he had never been enchanted in the first place. Members asked Condon the same question Saunders had recently asked: what would he do if the staff arrived at a pro-ET conclusion? This time, Condon was more diplomatic, albeit noncommittal. If they produced convincing evidence and could therewith convince him, he said, it would be the official project conclusion. The answer satisfied Roy Craig, and probably several others, but directly contradicted Condon's reply to Saunders and Low just a week before.[66]

Rocky times remained ahead. In early October, the Lorenzens visited the team at Boulder, and were unimpressed. The project's investigatory methods, they decided, were "sadly lacking" with "no standardized report form, no set method of investigations." Congress, too, continued to show signs of dissent. On

October 17, 1967, Congressman Louis Wyman submitted a congressional resolution for a full UFO investigation, without waiting for the Colorado report.[67]

AN ANIMAL MUTILATION

As if the UFO controversy were not contentious enough, it heated up further after September 9, 1967, with the first publicized animal mutilation case.
The victim was a horse named Lady (mistakenly called Snippy by the press),
who was found in the San Luis Valley of southern Colorado. Her body had
been stripped of flesh from the neck up, with the rest of her untouched. There
was no blood at the site. The cut around the neck was very smooth—perhaps
too smooth to have been made with a hunting knife. Her exposed skeleton
was so white and clean, that it looked as though she had lain in the sun for
days. But Lady had been alive and well only two nights before. Another odd
thing was that, according to her owner, who found her, Lady's tracks stopped
about one hundred feet southeast of her body, with no tracks of any kind
between her and where she was found.

When Lady's owner returned to the site the following day, the soil
beneath Lady was damp, and a medicine-like smell pervaded the area. Nearby
was a bush that was flattened to within ten inches of the ground. Near the
bush were fifteen circular marks pressed into the ground; close to that were
six additional indentations in a three-foot circular configuration—each was
two inches across and four inches deep. Lady's owner also found a piece of
horse flesh encased in skin. When she punctured it, she said, a sticky green
paste came out, burning her. Alamosa County sheriff, Ben Phillips, was less
impressed by the unusual elements at the scene and blamed the horse's death
on lightning.

John Henry Altshuler, M.D., was a doctor of pathology and hematology
at Ross Medical Center in Denver. He happened to be camping illegally in the
area at the time of Lady's death. During his extended camping sojourn, he
claimed, he saw three UFOs over the valley, and in fact had gone to the area
in the first place because it was a UFO hotspot. Before long, park rangers
apprehended him, but when they learned of his profession (medical hematol-
ogist), they brought him to see the horse.

Altshuler saw Lady ten to twelve days after her death. He conducted a
thorough examination, and concluded that she had been surgically worked on
with some type of burning instrument. "Most amazing," he said, "was the lack
of blood." He added:

> I have done hundreds of autopsies. You can't cut into a body without getting
> some blood. But there was no blood on the skin or on the ground. No blood any-
> where.

Upon looking at the inside of the horse's chest, he found no organs. "Whoever did the cutting," he continued, "took the horse's heart, lungs, and thyroid. The media sternum was completely empty—and dry. How do you get the heart out without blood? It was an incredible dissection of organs without any evidence of blood."

The case finally made the press when the *Pueblo Chieftain* reported it on October 7, replete with all UFO connections. Soon, everyone came out to investigate: the Colorado Project, Blue Book, NICAP, and APRO had their own people on the scene. All but APRO attributed Lady's death to conventional causes. Still, the theory connecting mutilations to UFOs retained its defenders, especially after the mid-1970s, when a wave of animal mutilations spread throughout the western U.S. Following APRO's lead, MUFON (Mutual UFO Network) gave credence to the UFO connection, and Linda Moulton Howe placed herself at the forefront of the issue with her film and book, *Strange Harvest*. But while the phenomenon did not become widespread for several years hence, there were still a significant number of animal mutilation reports that followed in the wake of Lady's death. In Alberta, Ontario, Manitoba, and western Colorado, animal mutilation reports were made through 1968.[68]

SHAG HARBOR

A most extraordinary UFO incident occurred off the coast of Shag Harbor in Nova Scotia in the fall of 1967. During late September, several area residents had noticed odd nocturnal lights. Then, during the night of October 4, two sightings of a bright orange light took place one hour and one hundred miles apart. In the second instance, two men saw an orange light first, which was joined by two more lights, forming a forty-five-degree angle. A few minutes later, other witnesses saw *four* lights moving in a horizontal line, flashing on and off in sequence. They positioned themselves at a forty-five-degree angle and descended, or glided, into the sea, about a half mile offshore.

For some time, a single white light bobbed on the water, and some people heard a hissing noise from the area. The light seemed to be carried out by the tide and disappeared before anyone could reach it, but witnesses also noticed a yellowish, bubbling froth about eighty feet wide. No one had ever seen anything like this before. A statement from the Royal Canadian navy said there were no missing aircraft or ships in the area, and in fact no planes operating in the area at the time.

The object appeared to go into the sea between the mainland and Cape Sable Island. On October 6, Canadian navy divers from the H.M.C.S. *Granby* began searching the waters and ocean bottom but found nothing, even after other divers joined in. The search ended on October 8. On the eleventh, several witnesses reported seeing perhaps the same lights. They hovered about three-quarters of a mile offshore, at about five hundred or six hundred feet altitude, then disappeared; they soon reappeared, positioned at a thirty-five-degree angle, and descended toward the horizon.

Norman Levine of the Colorado Project investigated the incident but did not explain it. During the 1990s, Canadian UFO researchers Chris Styles and Don Ledger conducted an exhaustive investigation, which included interviews with several of the divers and military personnel involved in the search. According to what they learned—all officially unconfirmed, of course—the searchers realized that the object had moved northeast, near a then-top-secret submarine detection station run jointly by Canada and the U.S. As a flotilla of ships positioned themselves over the submerged craft, a second underwater UFO joined the first and engaged in a repair operation. The members of the ships observed but did not interfere. Seven days later, a Soviet submarine appeared but was escorted away. Soon after, the two UFOs moved off toward the Gulf of Maine. Emerging from the water, they ascended rapidly and flew off.[69]

CLOAK AND DAGGER

As a result of James McDonald's public focus on the UFO cover-up, several key documents relating to UFOs and secrecy were released in late 1967. The two most important of these were (segments of) the Robertson Panel report and the Twining Letter of September 1947, which stated that UFOs were real, mechanical objects under apparently intelligent control. While McDonald could justly claim credit for release of the former, if correct procedures had been followed, it would have been declassified in January 1965. The public now learned that the Robertson Panel had known of 1,900 UFO reports to the Pentagon in 1952, not the 1501 as Lawrence Tacker and others had long reported. With the release of such documents, the rush began to counter their effectiveness for UFO researchers. Condon, for example, told the Lorenzens that the Robertson Report meant nothing since it was not based on any scientific study as such. That was true, of course, but also evaded some fundamental questions, to wit: (1) to what extent was the CIA running UFO policy; (2) why was it necessary to hide CIA interest in UFOs; (3) what *about* those four hundred missing UFO reports; (4) why wasn't the report released in 1965, according to federal regulations; (5) if the study "meant nothing," why did the CIA gather Nobel-caliber scientists and use their conclusions as the basis of policy?[70]

The Lorenzens visited Boulder on October 10. Aside from their aforementioned disappointment with the project, they also met with Boulder journalist Roger Harkins, who had been covering the Colorado Project from the beginning. The Lorenzens and Harkins were both curious about the possibility of CIA manipulation of the media and decided to see whether they could bait the hook. The Lorenzens gave Harkins a seven-point rationale for CIA interest in UFOs, mainly to see whether the AP would print it and whether the CIA would try to suppress it. The seven points, summarized, were:

1. The CIA was created to ensure that a surprise attack like Pearl Harbor would never happen again.

2. UFO reports exist.

3. The reports give patterns indicating that they are based on real occurrences.

4. If UFO reports are based on real occurrences, that is, actual physical objects invading U.S. airspace, this is a national security matter of prime importance—exactly what the CIA was designed to handle.

5. The existence of unidentified vehicles invading U.S. airspace must be interpreted as indicating the existence of a possible unknown enemy.

6. Intelligence procedures would require that all such information be withheld from the public until firm conclusions could be reached; premature disclosures might help the enemy.

7. Therefore, the CIA could not possibly avoid responsibility for the UFO mystery. In this perspective, the Robertson Panel was a device used by the CIA to establish a cover program (Blue Book) that would draw attention away from a covert program designed to meet the UFO challenge.

After dictating the story to the Denver AP Bureau, Harkins waited. And waited. Nothing happened. The story never surfaced.[71]

During the latter part of 1967, the Lorenzens were working on their newest book, soon to be published as *UFOs over the Americas*. They speculated on the possibility that the Colorado University Project was infiltrated in some way by the CIA:

> [I]f we are right in our theories concerning CIA involvement [in the Condon Committee], there is an agent on or near the committee quietly monitoring its activities and preparing to subvert the final report for intelligence purposes if it seems advisable.[72]

LEAKS FROM BOULDER

Two months after Keyhoe informed Saunders that NICAP had withdrawn its support of the Colorado Project, he continued to keep the door open. On November 14, 1967, he wrote separate letters to Condon and Low, asking if they would agree to investigate NICAP's UFO evidence. Their responses, both sent on December 1, were noncommittal but praised the assistance NICAP had provided. Low wrote: "Our working relationships have been excellent. . . . It would be a great pity if they were terminated."

Before Keyhoe received these responses, Saunders paid him a surprise visit on November 22. That day, Saunders allowed him to copy the Low memo and encouraged him to share it with NICAP's board of directors. "I wanted Keyhoe to know," Saunders wrote, "that I was under no illusions as to the one-sided nature of the Colorado University Study, because I felt that this might facilitate NICAP's continued support of our efforts to salvage something of it." Indeed, the internal conflict had only worsened after Condon's late September meeting with the project members. Keyhoe assured him he would not release the Low memorandum without Saunders's permission. Around this time, also, Boulder journalist Roger Harkins learned of the memo. The word was getting out.[73]

On December 12, project members Levine and Saunders, along with project secretary Mary Lou Armstrong, brought Hynek and McDonald face-to-face for the first time since their unpleasant meeting in June 1966. The hope was to get these two to bury their differences and work with them after the project ended. This would be an organization of scientists to promote UFO studies. After an initial clearing of the air, the meeting went fairly well. Hynek left, then McDonald raised the issue of the Low memorandum. This was an unwelcome surprise—how did McDonald know about it? The answer: Keyhoe. (Keyhoe acknowledged that he confidentially told McDonald of the memorandum, but maintained that he did so in January 1968.) Since the secret was out, the project members decided to give McDonald an actual copy.

Soon after the meeting, Levine approached Roy Craig, hoping to bring him on board for the new project. But Craig, a stalwart Condon loyalist, was a tough nut to crack. He considered the suggestion to be "mutiny." Besides, he said, Condon assured them that all findings and conclusions would be represented in the report, regardless of his personal conclusion. Certainly, Craig was not sympathetic to the extraterrestrial hypothesis, although he later conceded that in some instances, "people can be, and are, convicted of serious crimes by personal testimony of the type we had heard [regarding UFOs]." But Craig believed that something as extraordinary as flying saucers needed more than personal testimony.[74]

Leaks came from a variety of sources that December. Early in the month, Low leaked information to Philip Klass regarding McDonald's UFO-related activities in Australia. On December 16, Klass launched a letter-writing campaign to bureaucrats at the Office of Naval Research, asking who had been responsible for funding McDonald's UFO research in Australia. Moreover, asked Klass, who is funding his upcoming trip to Europe and USSR? The problem was that ONR officially authorized money to McDonald—known to everyone for his interest in UFOs—for atmospheric and cloud research. Of course, as we have seen, ONR had its own history of interest in UFOs. Indeed, ONR replied that it was satisfied with McDonald's work and had no objections to his UFO research. But Klass wanted to intimidate ONR into discontinuing future funding for McDonald. He succeeded because of his position with *Aviation Week*, where he could embarrass them. From here on, Klass made McDonald his pet project, attacking not only his arguments but his integrity, implying that he was a habitual liar.[75]

THE SCHIRMER ABDUCTION CASE

Early in the morning on December 3, 1967, a young police officer named Herb Schirmer of Ashland, Nebraska, had what appeared to be an extraordinary close encounter with alien entities. At 2:30 A.M. he noticed an object on the road with flickering lights. Believing it to be a truck, he flashed his high beams. To his surprise, the object took off. It was aluminum-colored and flashed a red-orange beam. His report read: "Saw a flying saucer at the junction of highways 6 and 63. Believe it or not." When he tried to sleep, a strong headache and buzzing noise prevented him from doing so. A red welt developed below his left ear.

Schirmer realized that he had twenty minutes of missing time from the experience. He was hypnotized by Wyoming psychologist R. Leo Sprinkle as part of the Colorado Project. During the session, he revealed that his radio and car engine died and a "white, blurred object" came out of the UFO and mentally communicated with him. He could not draw his revolver. He had somehow gotten information that the craft belonged to a sister ship; the occupants were based in our solar system but originated from another galaxy; they were here to prevent humans from destroying the Earth.

Colorado Project members dismissed Schirmer's account as delusional, although Sprinkle, the consultant who performed the hypnosis, believed otherwise. Schirmer, meanwhile, continued to experience uneasiness. Eventually, he underwent a second hypnosis, and revealed much more. He now described the object as metallic, football-shaped, and glowing. He heard a whooshing sound and saw legs under the craft. Although he wanted to leave, something in his mind prevented him. Then, beings came out of the craft, wearing coveralls with an image of a winged serpent. They shot a greenish gas toward the car and flashed a bright light at him. He then passed out. When he regained consciousness, one of the beings asked him, "Are you the watchman over this place?" They pointed to the power plant and asked, "Is this the only source of power you have?" They took Schirmer aboard, and he saw control panels and computer-like machines. They told him they came from a "nearby" galaxy, had bases in the U.S., that their craft was operated by electromagnetism, that they drew power from large water reservoirs, and that radar and ionization disrupted the functioning of their ships. They had been observing the Earth for a long time and would continue to contact more people. Schirmer said, to a certain extent, they wanted to puzzle people. They told him, "You will not speak wisely about this night. We will return to see you two more times."[76]

Compared with later abduction stories, Schirmer's was not especially unusual. At the time, however, this was not only outlandish, but almost unheard of, in a small class of cases like the Boas and Hill abductions. Small wonder the staff at Colorado could not swallow it.

Nor did Project Blue Book. But by now, of course, Blue Book was hardly much of an operation, anyway. In 1966 and 1967, despite 2,049 UFO cases logged by the group at Dayton, a mere fifty-one cases, or 2.5 percent, were acknowledged to be unidentified. The trend reached its apex in 1968, the final full year of Blue Book's existence, when it logged a total of *three* official unidentifieds. These numbers, it must again be stressed, were due not to investigative expertise, but policy. However, no one was paying attention any longer to what Blue Book was doing. All the attention had shifted over to Boulder. The relief felt by Quintanilla and his small staff must have been very great.

THE CRISIS

McDonald, armed with the Low memorandum, posed a distinct threat to the University of Colorado Project. For a year, he had professed his intention to help the project in any way possible. It was obvious, however, that he was disappointed with its leadership and direction. And the memorandum itself was dynamite. It was inevitable that he would raise the matter with Low. The only question was when.

On January 19, 1968, the two spoke by phone, and McDonald raised some of his concerns about the project. The conversation was unsatisfactory, and the two reached an impasse. McDonald decided to write a letter to Low. It ended up as a seven-page, single-spaced document, dated January 31, 1968. Masterful in every way, it was fully worthy of McDonald. He stated the importance not only of the UFO phenomenon, but in particular of the Colorado Project, which increasingly had attained an aura of being the final authority over the matter; nearly everyone, McDonald noted, was now saying, "Let's wait for Colorado." The UFO question itself would hinge for many years hence upon its conclusions. For such a major question to depend upon a single study was unusual, and, in this case, especially distressing.

The problem pivoted around Condon, wrote McDonald, and he cited five reasons: (1) Condon's repeated negative comments in the press; (2) Condon's "disturbing preoccupation" with the crackpot aspects of the UFO problem; (3) the evident conclusion that Condon himself was not personally examining the kinds of witnesses and cases that had made the UFO problem so compelling; (4) "the distinct impression" that the communication between Low and Condon on the one hand, and the bulk of investigators actually reviewing good case material, was "so weak as to seem almost nonexistent"; and (5) the failure of the project to investigate cases of "obfuscation," that is, cover-up cases.

Midway through the letter, McDonald mentioned Low's memorandum from August 1966. He had heard about this memo and, "since it was in the open files," had asked for a copy. McDonald then quoted the memorandum in full. "I am rather puzzled by the viewpoints expressed there," he wrote, "but I gather that they seem entirely straightforward to you, else this part of the record would, presumably, not be available for inspection in the open project files."

He continued on for several more pages, concluding:

> I'm not opposed to negative findings—on UFOs or other scientific questions; what bothers me is that it appears that these negative findings were being adumbrated as early as January 1966, and perhaps even earlier.

To make sure that Low could not possibly ignore the letter, McDonald sent a copy to the project's open files, in hopes that "the more open the discussion, the sooner I shall be straightened out on points where I am either in outright error or where I am making unreasonable arguments."

The letter arrived in Boulder on Monday, February 5, 1968. Low was out of town, and the staff read it first. He returned the next day but did not see the letter until 4 P.M., when Mary Lou Armstrong called it to his attention. As she later recounted, "Bob exploded." Whoever had given that memo to McDonald should be fired, said Low furiously. He phoned Condon, who reacted in like fashion.

Meetings in Condon's office dominated the rest of the week. Just before 11 A.M. on the morning of Wednesday, February 7, Low summoned Saunders to Condon's office. Did you know of the existence of the memo, Condon asked Saunders. Yes, said Saunders. Did McDonald know about it? Yes. How long did you know this? A couple of months. Why didn't you tell me? I didn't think it was necessary, since McDonald was a friend of the project.

Condon pointed his finger at Saunders. "For an act like that, you deserve to be ruined professionally!" Low asked Saunders why he was dissatisfied with his and Condon's way of running the project. "Haven't we let you do everything you wanted to do?" Saunders brought up several issues, including the failure to resolve their problems from September. When Condon asked Saunders if he gave the memo to McDonald, Saunders hedged significantly. No, he said—since it was not *he*, but the small group to which he was a part that did.

When Norm Levine arrived at 11:30, Low physically ushered Saunders out of the room. "We don't want you here anymore." Levine pointed to the chair Saunders had been sitting in and asked, "Is this the victim's chair?" From Levine, Condon finally learned it had been a group effort. He considered Levine's actions treacherous, he said, and told him not to discuss the meeting with other project members, nor to communicate with McDonald. Levine was "not prepared to do that," to which Condon replied, "I'm not sure what use you could be to the project anymore." "I guess that's it, then," said Levine, and he walked out.

Condon and Low summoned staff members, one by one, for the rest of the day. That evening, and the next day, they met with Thurston Manning, the school's vice president and Dean of Faculties, and Stuart Cook, chairman of the Psychology Department. On the eighth, Condon told Armstrong that Levine and Saunders were going to be fired. Low typed the letters himself, and Condon signed them.

On Friday morning, February 9, Condon called Roy Craig into his office. It was Craig's first visit there. As expected, Low was also present. Craig told Condon he knew of the memorandum "and was quite concerned about its implications until frank discussions with you relieved my qualms about those apparent implications." For this, and the fact that he had not been present when the memo was given to McDonald, Craig kept his job with the project. He left the meeting, however, "deeply concerned" about the project's viability.

That day, journalist Roger Harkins wrote about the events, including revelations about the Low memorandum. While interviewing Condon, Harkins became convinced that Condon "honestly didn't know anything about that memo until a couple of days ago." Off the record, Condon revealed to Harkins that, in contrast to his statement to the press, in which he announced Saunders and Levine had been discharged for incompetence, the real reason was "contumacy," that is, insubordination.

Not surprisingly, the credibility of the Colorado Project suffered in the aftermath of the firings. McDonald soon told the press about the "entirely inadequate job" by the Colorado Project, and the general media treatment angered Condon. Publicly, he told the press that McDonald was probably jealous, "another case of an Arizonan wanting some Colorado water." Privately, he phoned the president of the University of Arizona and charged that McDonald was "unethical" and had "stolen" the Low memorandum from committee files, that McDonald's act was "treacherous" and "disloyal."

On February 22, Mary Lou Armstrong, for some time secretary to both Condon and the project, told her boss that the staff had no confidence in Low as project coordinator, that he had no interest in UFO sightings or reports, and that "the entire working staff had arrived at a radically different conclusion about UFOs than Low had." Two days later, she resigned from her dual roles. Four days later, Condon suffered a mild heart attack. The day after that, project member Jim Wadsworth was arrested for possession of marijuana; he soon resigned from the project. February 1968 had not been a good month for the University of Colorado UFO Project.

An interesting commentary on the progress, or lack thereof, that the project had made: when John Fuller arrived on March 1 to prepare an article, he spoke with the project members, most of whom felt they learned more from him about UFOs than the reverse.[77]

AIRING THE DIRTY LAUNDRY

Fuller's article hit the newsstands on April 27, 1967. It was titled, "The Flying Saucer Fiasco: The Half-million Dollar Cover-up on Whether UFOs Really Exist." As Fuller put it:

A strange series of incidents in the University of Colorado Unidentified Flying Objects study has led to a near mutiny by several of the staff scientists, the dismissal of two Ph.D.'s on the staff, and the resignation of the project's administrative assistant.

In discomforting detail, Fuller described the Low memorandum, the firing of project scientists, and NICAP's complete break with the project. The latter was announced by Keyhoe himself:

After seventeen months, NICAP has broken with the University of Colorado UFO Project. We join *Look* and John G. Fuller in disclosing the facts as a public service. . . . NICAP will submit plans to the president and Congress for a new official investigation. . . . Meantime, to offset the Colorado failure, our investigations will be intensified.

The effect on public opinion was devastating. *Look*'s circulation, after all, was 8 million. Low spent the morning of Monday, April 29, doing damage control before the press, claiming to have been quoted out of context. He maintained that the word "trick" from the 1966 memorandum did not carry the meaning Fuller implied. For the rest of the morning, Low was in Condon's office, conferring with legal counsel. There could now be no question that Robert Low had to go for the project to retain any credibility.[78]

Condon protested to *Look*'s publisher that the article contained falsehoods and misrepresentations, but failed to specify them. *Look* stood by the article, and on April 30, the project was denounced in Congress by Rep. J. Edward Roush, a member of the House Science and Astronautics Committee. The *Look* story, said Roush, raised "grave doubts as to the scientific profundity and objectivity of the project." Roush wrote to Air Force Secretary Robert B. Seamans to ask for his comments "on this deplorable situation," and then to the comptroller general to investigate the use of public money for the project. The Colorado Project, Roush said, was rigged from the start.

Keyhoe followed up with a letter to President Lyndon Johnson (attaching the now-infamous memorandum) and urged a new, impartial investigation. He received a reply from the air force secretary's office: "[W]e expect Dr. Condon will fulfill the terms of the agreement." Through May and June, NICAP worked with Roush, assembling, in Keyhoe's words, its "most powerful evidence" in anticipation of a full-scale investigation.

Back at Boulder, Condon was concerned over the loss of so many people from the project. On May 15, the announcement was made that Low would be relieved of "90 percent" of his duties from the project, effective May 24, and would return to his previous job as special assistant to Thurston E. Manning. Moreover, although the project had received an extension to complete its work, the project members nevertheless were anxious to get on with their careers. Roy Craig was among these, but Condon pleaded with Craig not to leave the project on June 30, 1968, as planned. Ever the loyalist, Craig stayed on, if for no other reason than to assist the editor of the final report—who had yet to be selected!

In late May 1968, Condon finally hired science writer Daniel S. Gillmor to be the editor of the project's final report. Gillmor received editorial help from Dr. Joseph H. Rush, a physicist on loan to the project from the National Center for Atmospheric Research. Also assisting was associate editor Harriet Hunter and several specialists from the local lab of the Environmental Science Services Administration (including Gordon Thayer). Franklin E. Roach also returned to the project to work on astronaut sightings; Roach had been involved in briefing and debriefing astronauts on *Mercury* and *Gemini* flights from 1961 to 1966. Thus, by June 1, 1968, the date on which the Colorado study formally completed its investigative phase, a substantially new crew had come aboard from that which existed at the beginning of the year—just in time to write the final report.

Meanwhile, James McDonald continued to try, vainly, to persuade Frederick Seitz of his idea for a UFO research panel. McDonald asked Seitz to give him the names of the 11 scientists who were going to review the Colorado Project Report; he wanted to let them know of his own views and criticisms. Seitz refused.[79]

THE SYMPOSIUM

The efforts of NICAP and Congressman Roush bore fruit on July 29, 1968, when the House Science and Astronautics Committee began a "symposium" on

UFOs. Congressman George P. Miller, of California, was the chairman of the committee, but Roush, who was acting chairman, directed most of the proceedings. Some of the major figures in UFO research were invited to testify before Congress, including Hynek, McDonald, and Sagan. Others included Dr. James A. Harder, associate professor of civil engineering at the University of California at Berkeley; Dr. Robert L. Hall, head of the department of sociology at the University of Illinois at Chicago; and Dr. Robert M. L. Baker, Jr., of the Computer Sciences Corporation and the department of engineering at the University of California in Los Angeles. Baker, it will be recalled, had analyzed the Tremonton, Utah, film in 1955. Donald Menzel also attended, largely on the basis of his complaint that the symposium presented a wholly pro-UFO point of view. Although he did not testify, he submitted a paper, which the committee included in its records.

The symposium, while decidedly pro-UFO in orientation, was no free-for-all; it remained carefully managed. Menzel, for example, was not the only attendee unable to speak to the committee. Keyhoe, too, learned that, despite NICAP's role in securing the hearings, NICAP representatives could not testify or submit information. Chairman Miller also warned that no criticism of the air force's Project Blue Book, nor of the University of Colorado's UFO Project, would be permitted. Although several prepared statements critical of the air force made it into the official hearings record, they went unnoticed by the press.

It was James McDonald who made the greatest impression during the symposium. Providing thirty pages of verified UFO reports, his long statement included the following remarks:

> I have become convinced that the scientific community, not only in this country but throughout the world, has been casually ignoring as nonsense a matter of extraordinary scientific importance. . . .

> My own present opinion, based on two years of careful study, is that UFOs are probably extraterrestrial devices engaged in something that might very tentatively be termed "surveillance." . . .

> I believe no other problem within your jurisdiction is of comparable scientific and national importance. These are strong words, and I intend them to be. . . .

> I have interviewed several hundred witnesses in selected cases, and I am astonished at what I have found. I had no idea that the actual UFO situation is anything like what it appears to be. . . .

> I now regard the [extraterrestrial hypothesis] as the one mostly likely to prove correct.[80]

McDonald may have made an impression, but the symposium had no lasting impact. Aside from some grumbling about the University of Colorado Project, Congress did nothing.[81]

With the symposium fizzling out, and the Colorado University Project clearly headed toward a negative conclusion, NICAP's situation was dismal. The main problem was always a lack of funds, and by the summer of 1968, the situation was becoming desperate. In August, Keyhoe pleaded with members in NICAP's *UFO Investigator* that the organization was "on the brink of disaster," facing "an imminent shutdown." The response barely kept NICAP limping along.[82]

UFO HYPOTHESIS AND SURVIVAL QUESTIONS

The involvement of the National Security Agency in the tracking and analysis of UFOs has long been the subject of speculation. Indeed, several documents obtained through Freedom of Information Act requests have proven, despite NSA denials, strong interest in UFO reports. One document from the caverns of NSA that surfaced in 1984 as a result of a FOIA request is, while not an official NSA document *per se*, nevertheless a remarkable piece.[83]

In this brief essay, the author methodically considered the various "human survival implications" suggested by the major competing hypotheses that explained UFOs. He then analyzed each hypothesis.

The first hypothesis, that UFOs were hoaxes, seemed highly unlikely, the author wrote. Historically speaking, hoaxes have been characterized by infrequency of occurrence and a restricted geographic nature. If UFOs were hoaxes of a worldwide dimension, "then a human mental aberration of alarming proportions would have appeared to be developing," an alarming conclusion in itself.

The next hypothesis, that UFOs were hallucinations, also seemed unlikely. While people do hallucinate, group hallucinations are rare. Machines, too, can "hallucinate," in that radar can at times mistakenly "see" a temperature inversion. However, "a considerable number of instances exists in which there are groups of people and a radar or radars seeing the same thing at the same time. . . ." If, in spite of the evidence, UFOs did turn out to be hallucinations, then "such a growing impairment of the human capacity for rational judgment [should] be subjected to immediate and thorough scientific study."

The third hypothesis, that UFOs were natural phenomena, seemed unlikely due to the many instances of trained military observers seeing UFOs behaving like high-speed and high-performance aircraft, with an apparent solidity and craft-like shape. If the hypothesis turned out to be correct, we must question the ability of air warning systems to diagnose an attack situation. It was disturbing, the author noted, that "many responsible military officers have developed a mental 'blind spot' to objects which appear to have the characteristics of UFOs." The implication is that many officers see, but do not report, UFOs.

Are UFOs secret Earth projects? The mysterious author failed to speculate much on this fourth hypothesis, but agreed that it had some validity. All UFOs, he argued, should be scrutinized to ferret out such enemy or friendly projects. Otherwise, we risk the possibility of intimidation by a new secret weapon.

The fifth hypothesis, UFOs as extraterrestrial intelligence, was the one that most intrigued the author, and the one to which he gave his strongest endorsement. He cited such scientists as McDonald, Hynek, Vallee, and Seymore Hess, and argued that the 1952 Washington, D.C., sightings "strongly support this view." If the ET hypothesis is true, he wrote, the human survival questions are far-reaching. "If 'they' discover you, it is an old but hardly invalid rule of thumb, 'they' are your technological superiors." Human history surely demonstrates the dangers to weaker cultures when confronted by a technologically superior civilization: a loss of identity and absorption by the others. Citing the example of Japan, he noted that it is at least theoretically possible for a "weaker" society to survive such a confrontation, but he criticized the leisurely approach scientists had hitherto taken to the possibility that UFOs represented alien intelligence. "If you are walking along a forest path," he continued, "and someone yells 'rattler,'"

> your action would be immediate and defensive. You would not take time to speculate before you act. You would have to treat the alarm as if it were a real and immediate threat to your survival. Investigation would become an intensive emergency action to isolate the threat and to determine its precise nature. It would be geared to developing adequate defensive measures in a minimum amount of time.

It would seem, he concluded, that a little more of this survival attitude is called for in dealing with the UFO problem. Chimpanzees in captivity, for example, become confused, disoriented, and pattern their behavior after humans. Such a behavior, wrote the author, offers no survival value in the wild. "Do the captivity characteristics of modern civilization," he wondered, "cause a similar lessening of man's adaptive capability, of his health, of his ability to recognize reality, of his ability to survive?"

The NSA maintained that, while the document in question does exist, "it was never published, issued, acted upon, or responded to by NSA or any other government agency. Its author wrote it for personal reasons. As explained above, NSA has not been tasked to monitor or assess allegations of UFO activity worldwide."[84]

Despite not being an official NSA document, this remarkable paper, which places credence in the extraterrestrial hypothesis, makes it reasonable to assume that others within NSA, including those in leadership positions, could well have thought likewise.

"THE RAND DOCUMENT"

The NSA was not the only place in 1968 where internally distributed UFO papers supported the ET hypothesis. The RAND Corporation, one of the elite research institutions in the world since its founding in 1948, and a major player in the formulation of U.S. national security policy, also produced an interesting UFO paper that year. RAND emphasized that, while written by staffer George Kocher, it was not an official RAND document. Moreover, according to UFO researcher Jan Aldrich, it generated "little or no response."

It remains an interesting paper, in particular for its theory on the possible number of worlds inhabited by technologically superior civilizations (100 million in our galaxy alone, Kocher theorized), and the average distance between them (about ten light-years). Kocher noted the likelihood that UFOs have been with mankind for ages, looked at some compelling reports, and pointed out that it was "practically impossible" to estimate the number of worldwide sightings "because of the lack of suitable data collection means."

Kocher was certainly a believer in the extraterrestrial hypothesis, but his main goal was to point toward a suitable direction for future action. His answers made sense and were therefore entirely impractical: essentially to expand and improve on the models of NICAP and APRO. This would mean establishing a central report receiving agency, staffed by permanent and experienced UFO investigators of all disciplines. Such an agency would provide uninterrupted scientific analysis of UFOs and would be completely open and available to the public.

Although the paper was supposedly meant for internal distribution (at top it stated, "Do not quote or cite in external RAND publications or correspondence"), a copy of this paper nevertheless made it to the Wright-Patterson AFB and thence to the desk of Blue Book chief Hector Quintanilla. He wrote a "blazing letter" to RAND, which never responded. That appeared to be the end of the matter.[85]

UFOs IN 1968

The year 1968 turned out to be the last year of any significant UFO activity until late 1973, and most of it occurred outside the United States. We must remember, however, how difficult it is actually to measure UFO activity. By early 1968, for example, most UFO witnesses had stopped making public reports, thanks to air force ridicule. The result was that Blue Book went through the entire year with the incredible total of just three unidentified sightings.[86]

Throughout the world, many of the sighting reports were outlandish, and humanoid sightings were common. A February 1, 1968, sighting in the Azores by a watchman at the air station involved an oval, metallic craft and four beings. The witness fainted, and the case was said to be investigated by American military authorities.[87]

Once again, however, South America was the main area of reported activity. From May through July, many sightings of alien beings were reported by professional, low-key individuals. UFO researcher Gordon Creighton wrote at the time that "something very odd is again happening to many people in the southern part of South America." In May, five UFOs were seen diving into the ocean off the coast at Arrecife, Venezuela. On the night of June 4, at the southern tip of Chile, two veteran pilots of Argentine Air Lines, and several of their eighteen passengers, saw a shining, reddish cylinder flying high above them. The sighting lasted five minutes. After landing at the airport in Chile, they learned the object had been seen and photographed from there. On June 8, the senior pilot and copilot were interviewed in *La Razon,* a Buenos Aires newspaper, and were adamant that they had seen a UFO.[88] On the sixteenth of June, two high-ranking police officials of the Argentine town El Choro saw a round object with a vivid blue light. It landed, left a strong odor, and burned vegetation. Throughout the month, close-range sightings and ground traces were reported by a broad group of witnesses in Argentina, several of whom claimed to lose consciousness, and others who reported physical aftereffects from the encounter. Many of these cases were investigated by police.[89]

Some of the stories were hard to take. The *New York Times* made light of the reports on July 13, 1968, with an article titled, "UFOs Add Spice to Life of Latins." Despite the article's tone, it did quote an Argentine government official who said seriously, "I have no doubt that flying saucers have arrived here. I worry about what they are up to. I just can't understand why they have picked on Argentina."[90]

UFO reports worldwide dwindled after August. One of the last major sightings of 1968 occurred in France just before 4 A.M. on November 2. The witness was a prominent doctor (known as "Dr. X. Clark"), and veteran in the Algerian War, who heard his fourteen-month-old son crying during a thunderstorm. The doctor entered his son's room and saw two large, disc-shaped objects outside his house merge into one. The single object sent a beam of light in his direction, then vanished with a sort of explosion, leaving a cloud that slowly dissipated. Shortly after his sighting, the man's leg, which had been wounded during the war, healed. Unfortunately, he also soon began experiencing nightmares, pains in his abdomen, and a red pigmentation that appeared around his navel, forming a triangle. He went to a dermatologist but gave no information about the UFO sighting; the doctor could not explain it. The case was even reported to the French Academy of Sciences, again with no UFO connections.

Incredibly, the man's fourteen-month-old son, who was in the same room when the sighting occurred, also developed a red triangle. UFO researcher Jerome Clark called this incident one of the most fantastic UFO stories ever, with "physical evidence of an eerily compelling sort." The case was unusually well tracked and investigated, with a great deal of effort done by Aimé Michel.[91]

THE CONDON REPORT

During the fall of 1968, the Colorado Project was running down the home stretch. On September 13, Condon called together his new inner circle of project members—Craig, Gillmor, Franklin Roach, and Joseph Rush—to discuss what the project's recommendation should be. He wrote the recommendation segment of the report shortly thereafter.[92]

The Colorado University Project delivered its long-awaited report, titled *Scientific Study of Unidentified Flying Objects*, to the air force on October 31, 1968. The following is a synopsis of its contents.

The first two sections were written by Condon himself; these were the project conclusions and recommendations, and a summary of the study itself. His general conclusion was that

> nothing has come from the study of UFOs in the past twenty-one years that has added to scientific knowledge. Careful consideration of the record as it is available to us leads us to conclude that further extensive study of UFOs probably cannot be justified in the expectation that science will be advanced thereby.

As to what the government should do about UFO reports received from the public, Condon answered, nothing. It was a clear recommendation to shut down Project Blue Book.

Condon refuted the charge that the UFO subject had been shrouded in official secrecy and the subject of a cover-up. There was no such evidence, he stated. "What has been miscalled secrecy has been no more than an intelligent policy of delay in releasing data so that the public does not become confused by premature publication of incomplete studies of reports." Moreover, a UFO cover-up was unthinkable because no one could keep such a secret for so long, and "no useful purpose would be served." He refuted the claim that the CIA had installed one of its own agents within the project. Considering the probable history of Robert Low as a CIA covert operative in the 1940s, this denial takes on a surreal quality.

Condon's conclusions, while strongly negative about UFOs, left the door open for future research. "Any scientist with adequate training and credentials who does come up with a clearly defined, specific proposal for study," he wrote, "should be supported." Still, Condon himself doubted such a study could be done on those terms anytime soon. He expressed his approval of the air force and Donald Menzel and his disapproval of UFO "amateurists" and especially NICAP. The last, he wrote, tried more than once "to influence the course of our study."

Condon acknowledged limitations to the project. Only a few "old" cases could be studied, since most appeared to offer little "probative value" in that (1) there was usually nothing to analyze other than witness testimony, (2) such anecdotal records were usually misidentified sightings of ordinary objects, and (3) it made little sense to re-interview people who had already been interviewed thoroughly before. Of course, this meant ignoring most of the compelling cases of the past twenty-plus years. Instead, the project focused almost exclusively on reports that occurred during its term. This approach proved to be unsatisfactory in many key respects. First, resources were too limited to allow any but a few UFO reports to be investigated. Second, it was rare when an investigation occurred within a week of the sighting. Third, only rarely was sophisticated instrumentation used—the most typical piece of equipment being a tape recorder.

Many of the UFO investigations, Condon wrote, were a waste of time. He openly wondered why, if aliens were here, they did not simply announce themselves. The entire matter of alien visitation would be settled in a few minutes, he wrote,

> if a flying saucer were to land on the lawn of a hotel where a convention of the American Physical Society was in progress, and its occupants were to emerge and present a special paper to the assembled physicists, revealing where they came from and the technology of how their craft operates.

While conceding the likelihood of intelligent life elsewhere (ILE), he rejected the extraterrestrial hypothesis. The distance between stars, argued Condon, is simply too vast to allow for practical communication. *"We therefore conclude* [emphasis added]," he wrote, "that there is no relation between ILE at other solar systems and the UFO phenomenon as observed on Earth."

This is a key element of the report. One may wonder why, with such an opinion, would it be necessary to study any UFO reports with a view toward a possible ET explanation? Condon's answer was, no reason at all. More than any other reason, this probably explains why Condon himself never investigated any UFO reports for the project. Despite his statements about the need for scientific objectivity and clarity in the study of UFO reports, it is clear that Condon's own position of UFOs, while based upon contemporary scientific theory and knowledge, nevertheless was fundamentally antiempirical, and therefore antiscientific.

In passing, we may note that Condon also ruled out experimental, classified aircraft as the primary source of UFO reports, since he thought it unlikely that any nation would test its secret aircraft over different countries.

The report also included summaries of the project's various types of studies: field studies, photographic evidence, direct physical evidence, indirect physical evidence, optical and radar cases, and astronaut sightings. Roy Craig was the workhorse of the group, writing three of these reports: field studies, direct physical evidence, and indirect physical evidence. Each time, he concluded that the available evidence did not point toward extraterrestrial answers.

In the field study section, Craig conceded that some of the past cases suggested something extraordinary. A few, such as the Great Falls, Montana, case, appeared to show evidence of air force deception. Others, such as the RB-47 report, would, if accurate, represent an unusual and puzzling phenomenon, "which, in the absence of additional information, must be listed as unidentified." Moreover, while witness testimony could never be taken without reservation, some cases involved testimony which appeared to describe experiences explainable "only in terms of the presence of strange vehicles. These cases are puzzling," wrote Craig, "and conclusions regarding them depend entirely upon the weight one gives to the personal testimony as presented." He concluded, however, that early cases such as these took place too long ago to offer much hope of obtaining significant data about the objects sighted. Ultimately, Craig, like Condon, doubted the value of UFO field investigations. Even if an alien culture were visiting us, "such a report would be buried in hundreds or thousands of similar reports triggered by ordinary earthly phenomena."

Craig's section on direct physical evidence concerned reports dealing with crop circles, impressions in the ground, alleged pieces of UFOs, and the like. Unfortunately, there were no physical tests, he said, which could determine the origin of imprints at a landing site. Even when the impression was real and conceivably from a large saucer, "it was impossible to establish as factual the claims that the imprints actually were made by an extraordinary object or being." Heavily compacted soil allegedly caused by UFO "landing legs," for example, could theoretically be achieved with a sledge hammer. The main feature of this section was Craig's analysis of the Ubatuba fragment, which did not prove to have the unusual purity of magnesium as claimed and did not show a unique or unearthly composition. (APRO responded that this fragment was not the same kind of fragment that had been submitted earlier and which had been destroyed by air force tests.)

Indirect physical evidence included electrical or electromagnetic effects, such as the failure of a car engine or headlights, radio and television interference, local power failures, terrestrial magnetic disturbances, and so on. The Antarctic sightings of July 3, 1965, wrote Craig, did not cause abnormal magnetic fluctuations, and the visual observations were made by nine "untrained" people, according to a Chilean astronomer. In cases of automotive engine failure, the project looked toward magnetic disturbances as the most likely cause. Independent tests determined that magnetic fields could indeed stop an engine, but they would have to be very strong and would leave definite traces, even years after an event. Of the two cases in which such tests were conducted, the results did not indicate a sufficient intensity to have interfered with the car's functioning. Robert Low contributed a small piece to this section, focusing on the northeastern blackout of 1965. He cited the Federal Power Commission report on the incident, which explained the outage by an incorrectly set relay at the Sir Adam Beck generating station in Queensland, Ontario (Q29BD), which caused the circuit breaker to trip. A query with one expert indicated that he was aware of no mysterious power outages.

William K. Hartman wrote the project's report on photographic evidence. The cases broke down roughly into four equal categories: fabrications, misidentifications, poor image quality, and clear images which lacked sufficient data for analysis. Two cases, wrote Hartman, made it past all these obstacles: Great Falls, Montana, and McMinnville, Oregon. In the case of the McMinnville photos, Hartman wrote:

> This is one of the few UFO reports in which all factors investigated, geometric, psychological, and physical, appear to be consistent with the assertion that an extraordinary flying object, silvery, metallic, disk-shaped, tens of meters in diameter, and evidently artificial, flew within sight of two witnesses. It cannot be said that the evidence positively rules out a fabrication, although there are some physical factors such as the accuracy of certain photometric measures of the original negatives which argue against a fabrication.

Still, Hartman could not go all the way. "No matter how strange or intriguing," he wrote, "it is always possible to 'explain' the observations, either by hypothesizing some extraordinary circumstance or by alleging a hoax."

Gordon David Thayer reported on optical and radar cases. He discussed the prevalence of anomalous propagation (AP), typically false radar returns caused by atmospheric conditions. Thayer worked ingeniously to find natural explanations to some extraordinary sightings. In order to do this, he frequently disregarded witness testimony; even then, his explanations at times broke the boundaries of the plausible.

The BOAC sighting of June 1954 is an example. The British commercial pilots had clear visuals of what seemed to be several craft, and a fighter sent to intercept the objects obtained a radar fix. The fact that the commercial plane obtained no radar, wrote Thayer, was suggestive of a mirage. He conceded the problem with this explanation was that an extremely thin and sharp temperature inversion would have had to appear just above the aircraft. Thayer wrote that

> this unusual sighting should therefore be assigned to the category of some almost certainly natural phenomenon which is so rare that it apparently has never been reported before or since.

Another case, at Selfridge AFB in 1953, was also puzzling. A pilot and radar operator in an F-94 were sent to intercept unknown targets over Detroit. Both men saw "tiny specs in the sky, which appeared to look like a ragged formation of aircraft." As they approached at 500 mph, the pilot was surprised that he could not make out wings or tail. Ground radar had the F-94 and the objects as "good, strong targets." The pilot looked at his instruments momentarily—when he looked up, the objects were gone. Radar tracked the objects for another four minutes. Thayer conceded that "the only admissible hypothesis would seem to be that [the UFOs] became invisible as the fighter approached, but this does not account for the fact that they could not be picked up on airborne radar while the aircraft was searching the area." He therefore hypothesized "an inferior mirage," which "is another example of a natural phenomenon so rare that it is seldom observed. . . ." Such a mirage would require a drastic temperature change—on the order of ten to fifteen degrees Celsius within the space of one centimeter.

And so on. Thayer attributed the Washington 1952 sightings to weather-related anomalous propagation of radar signals, combined "most probably" with meteors and scintillating stars. The Rapid City-Bismarck sighting of 1953 was caused by a combination of (1) stars seen through an inversion layer, (2) at least one meteor, (3) AP echoes on radar, and (4) possible ghost echoes on ground radar and malfunction of an airborne radar gunsight. Thayer acknowledged that the commanding officer of the Rapid City detachment was doubtful of that last point.

Despite the many ways in which atmospheric phenomena can mislead the human and electronic eye, Thayer acknowledged a "small, but significant, residue of cases from the radar-visual files that have no plausible explanation as propagation phenomena and/or misinterpreted man-made objects." One was a Utica case from 1955, in which an object was seen by a pilot and copilot and described as "light gray, almost round, with a center line. . . . Beneath the line there were several (at least four) windows which emitted a bright blue-green light. It was not rotating, but went straight." Although the object was reported to be moving at above Mach 6, there was no sonic boom, a serious inconsistency, Thayer wrote. Still, he conceded that "it does appear that this sighting defies explanation by conventional means."

Thayer's most intriguing radar-visual case was the Lakenheath, U.K., incident of August 1956. This involved the tailing of an RAF fighter by an unidentified object. Thayer examined the possibility of atmospheric conditions, but to no avail. He commented that

> this is the most puzzling and unusual case in the radar-visual files. The apparently rational, intelligent behavior of the UFO suggests a mechanical device of unknown origin as the most probable explanation of this sighting.

But this was too radical a conclusion without some qualifier: in this case, "the inevitable fallibility of witnesses," which kept alive the possibility of a conventional explanation.

Despite, or because of, his dogged approach to arriving at conventional explanations, Thayer recommended several measures—all of which involved expending more resources—to improve UFO investigations. Thus, he parted ways with Condon and Craig as to whether UFOs warranted full-time study. Thayer appeared to be saying that they did.

Franklin Roach discussed astronaut sightings, mostly attributed to space debris seen under typically poor observational conditions. Still, three cases remained unexplained and "a challenge to the analyst." Two were from the *Gemini 4* mission of June 4, 1965, by James McDivitt; the third from the *Gemini 7* flight by Frank Borman, who saw what he referred to as a bogey flying in formation with the spacecraft.

The fifty-nine case studies constituted the heart of the book. Many of these reports showed impressive detective work to explain what initially appeared to be an extraordinary, and extraterrestrial, event. Others showed more signs of fanatical determination to debunk than investigative expertise. Within the fifty-nine cases studied, there were actually ninety UFO reports, of which thirty were not explained. Many of the explanations were on something of a sliding scale of probability, a reasonable way to do things, but not so easy to attribute hard quantitative results. Not all conclusions were clearly stated (as in Case 34, the Shag Harbor incident). Many were deemed to have insufficient data for analysis, or to have little probative value. One case did not belong in the study at all: the failure of a predicted UFO landing. Some of the unexplained cases nevertheless had the possibility of various conventional explanations proffered. Several explained cases were stretches that could only be attained by disregarding seemingly rational witness claims.

Looking at each of the fifty-nine case studies as a unit, however, the report produced sixteen cases in which the origin of the event could be considered unknown. Considering a total of fifty-eight cases (minus the nonevent), that produces an unexplained percentage of almost 28 percent. Of those sixteen cases, eight were what one might consider to be "good" cases, and two extraordinary. If *only* these two extraordinary cases (numbers two and forty-six) are included, one is still left with an unexplained rate of 3.4 percent. In other words, the Colorado Project produced results that were nearly identical with those of the air force, NICAP, and APRO, with the difference that it was charged with conducting its study at a more rigorous level. It is perhaps significant that of the most compelling cases presented in the study, all were of the period preceding the term of the project, that is, "classic cases."

The remainder of the report consisted of mostly padding: a historical study of UFOs, an essay (by Condon) dealing with the 1947–1968 period, a short paper on UFO studies by other governments, and a public opinion survey. Another 250 pages consisted of essays on various problems of "scientific context," such as perceptual problems, psychological aspects, optics, radar, sonic boom, atmospheric conditions, balloons, instrumentation, and statistical analysis. Several of these papers demonstrated perplexity regarding UFOs, such as one author comment that the reported absence of sonic booms from UFOs in supersonic flight "cannot be explained on the basis of current knowledge."

The Colorado University report, known more widely as the Condon Report, was massive. At over 950 pages in its soon-to-be published paperback form, it probably fulfilled Robert Low's desire to "build the record." Despite its intimidating length, however, the Condon Report suffered from several major failings. In the places where it counted most, the case studies, the report was skimpy. Why, a reader might ask, with eighteen months to investigate, did the project produce so few studies? True, many reports were conducted more thoroughly than Blue Book, NICAP, or APRO had done, but fifty-eight cases is still not much to go on. Of the 550 then-unexplained reports in the Blue Book files, the Colorado Project had considered only three. Also, many of the sightings investigated by the project were poor bets to begin with.

Probably the most striking discrepancy in the report, however, was between its contents and conclusions. Condon had concluded that science could gain nothing from studying UFOs. Yet, the report ended up with a near 30 percent unexplained rate, and a core of cases that came within a hair's breadth of being conclusive evidence for the reality of alien technology—cases which, under the most rigorous analysis, appeared to be the result of extraordinary craft in the skies.

Ironically, the Condon Report, which rejected so many cases as "lacking probative value," itself lacked value as a definitive statement of the UFO phenomenon. The fact that it showed *most* UFO sightings to be the result of natural or conventional causes was nothing new: everyone had known that for years. From the beginning, Condon and Low were clear in their belief that *all* UFO sightings could be explained conventionally. While Condon chose to ignore the unsettling data contained within the project's report, he could not hide the glaring reality: the Colorado Project failed to get the strikeout.

REVIEW AND RELEASE OF THE REPORT

Upon receiving the report, officers at Air Force Headquarters began a quick review. On November 15, the air force sent it to the National Academy of Sciences for review by an eleven-member panel, charged with an independent assessment of the scope, methodology, and findings of the project. With little delay, the NAS panel of scientists unanimously accepted Condon's conclusions and praised the project. The panel stated it was "unanimous in the opinion that this has been a very creditable effort to apply objectively the relevant techniques of science to the solution of the UFO problem." Keyhoe was not alone in believing that the scientists had either read only Condon's two opening sections, "or else they had deliberately ignored everything disproving his conclusions."[93]

In December 1968, before the Condon Report was released to the public, David Saunders published his own side of the story, *UFOs? Yes! Where the Condon Committee Went Wrong*. In addition to better timing, the book had other advantages over the official report. Coauthored by journalist Roger Harkins, it was better written. Second, it offered an insider's account of the workings of the committee, including the biases of Condon and Low, and the dissension that characterized the project. Rather than attempting to make a definitive argument in favor of the ET factor (to which Saunders was certainly sympathetic), the book's main argument was that Condon and Low never intended to consider a pro-ET solution to the UFO problem, that the project's conclusions were preordained. Moreover, in the unlikely event that the project arrived at such a determination, Condon would not have published such a fact. Instead, he would have taken it through classified channels.

The Condon Report was released to the public on January 9, 1969; the press had gotten a copy one day before, along with the glowing NAS review. With no time to conduct a careful review, the media read Condon's conclusions and recommendations, and little else. Critical press comment was minimal, and most of the media applauded the work. With justice, Keyhoe called this "steamroller tactics."[94]

On January 11, 1969, attempting to mitigate the disaster, Keyhoe, Saunders, and McDonald held a press conference and harshly criticized the report. Hynek also quickly denounced the report, speaking of its "trivial and irrelevant discussions, practically padding." But McDonald was the most forceful. He circulated critiques, communicated with other scholars, and sought to reinvestigate several of the project cases. He even battled to get access to the photocopied Blue Book material used by the project; Condon saw to it that these were destroyed. The tide had turned; in the public realm, UFOs were debunked.[95]

It also appeared that Blue Book's days were numbered. In early March 1969, SAFOI representative, Maj. David J. Shea, attended a meeting at the Pentagon in which "there was no doubt that Project Blue Book was finished."[96] Condon spoke publicly about the report for the first time in April. At a meeting of the American Philosophical Society, he seemed to state in seriousness that

> publishers who publish or teachers who teach any of the pseudosciences as established truth should, on being found guilty, be publicly horsewhipped and forever banned from further activity in these usually honorable professions.[97]

FROM JOHNSON TO NIXON

The most noteworthy feature of the American national security state during the late 1960s was its covert pervasiveness throughout American society. First, Hoover's FBI. In 1968, the bureau initiated a Cointel program against the Students for a Democratic Society (SDS). From 1969 to 1971, the Chicago police department routinely, and illegally, funneled intelligence to the FBI. Still, Hoover was falling behind. Both the NSA and CIA were increasingly unhappy with the FBI, which they wanted to be more aggressive. Hoover in his old age had not so much mellowed as become nervous and, with good cause, concerned about exposure.[98] The FBI also had made a fine shambles of the investigation of the assassinations of Martin Luther King and Robert F. Kennedy in 1968. (Ten years later, a congressional inquiry concluded there was a conspiracy to kill King. James Earl Ray, the man convicted for King's murder, claimed that the FBI pressured him to confess. The RFK investigation was similarly mishandled.)

Next to the bureau, the military intelligence services became the most important component of the domestic intelligence scene. Army intelligence had nearly unlimited funds, extensive manpower, specialized personnel, deep planning and training resources, and the most sophisticated communications and data processing capability. This ensured a unique versatility. The army's intelligence surveillance did not focus on tactical and reconnaissance data, but on political and ideological intelligence within the United States. These were wholly illegal.[99]

Then there was the CIA. By the late 1960s, there were more spies than diplomats in the State Department, or employees in the Department of Labor. The CIA was using the NRO's spy satellite apparatus to gather intelligence on domestic demonstrations. One of its domestic intelligence operations, known as Chaos, expanded steadily through 1968 and 1969, pacing the antiwar movement itself. When the Weather Underground, a radical splinter of the SDS, had an "acid test" to detect *agents provocateurs*, they had no idea that the CIA had been tripping on LSD throughout the 1950s, creating a special caste of "enlightened agents" for precisely these occasions.[100]

The agency continued its work on mind control. Following the work of Dr. Jose Delgado, a Yale psychologist, Dr. Robert Keefe, a neurosurgeon at Tulane University, conducted work in Electrical Stimulation of the Brain (ESB). This involves implanting electrodes into the brain and body, with the result that the subject's memory, impulses, and feelings could all be controlled. Moreover, ESB could evoke hallucinations, as well as fear and pleasure. "It could literally manipulate the human will, at will," said Keefe. In 1968, George Estabrooks, another spook scientist, spoke indiscreetly to a reporter for the *Providence Evening Bulletin*. "The key to creating an effective spy or assassin," said Estabrooks, "rests in creating a multiple personality with the aid of hyp-nosis," a procedure which he described as "child's play." Estabrooks even suggested that Lee Harvey Oswald and Jack Ruby "could very well have been performing through hypnosis." By early 1969, teams within the CIA were run-ning a number of bizarre experiments in mind control under the name Operation Often. In addition to the normal assortment of chemists, biologists, and conventional scientists, the operation employed psychics and experts in demonology.[101]

Over at the NSA, all one can say with certainty is that its budget dwarfed all others within the intelligence community. The FY 1969 budget for the NSA was estimated at upwards of $2 billion, a staggering amount of money at the time, supporting, among other things, a cryptologic community of ninety-five thousand personnel—five times larger than the CIA.

A basic feature of the pervasiveness of domestic spying was the general lack of civilian control. In the words of historian Frank Donner, "the civilian leadership of the Defense Department, the White House, and the attorney general's office, were left in the dark about the military intelligence colossus. But it is fair to conclude that they preferred it that way."[102]

By the time Richard Nixon entered the White House in 1969, nearly every American intelligence organization was involved in major violations of the law. Still, Nixon found this to be insufficient. He distrusted the CIA and was frustrated with Hoover's jealousy and timidity. Of course, Nixon gladly accepted the useful dirt offered by Hoover, under the code name "Inlet." By June 1969, Nixon ordered seven wiretaps to be placed on the phones of his staffers.[103]

Internationally, the American press remained silent while the rest of the world commented on the devastation of America's "secret" bombing of north-ern Laos, described in *Le Monde* as "a world without noise, for the surrounding villages had disappeared." It took nearly an entire year before the *New York Times* was willing to publish this fact, which it finally did (without editorial) in May 1969. By then, the U.S. was also bombing and defoliating Cambodia, an operation which remained covert until 1970. The official denials kept coming. On October 1, 1969, Air Force Secretary Robert Sea-mans visited the Plain of Jars in Laos and reported that he saw "no evidence of indiscriminate bombing."[104]

A final event of some interest. The year 1969 saw the publication of an interesting, little known book by Andrew Tully, with the hyperbolic title *The Super Spies*. The book is significant as an early report on the NSA, and even more so as its first chapter discussed the UFO controversy, albeit superficially. Tully stated that UFOs were products of secret military technology:

> Despite efforts by the military and the Central Intelligence Agency to debunk the flying saucer as a natural phenomenon, informed speculation has continued to maintain that it existed—as an intelligence device.

It was common knowledge, wrote Tully, that the American and Russian intelligence communities were launching unmanned aircraft electronically equipped to eavesdrop from the skies on each other's secrets. Within and outside government, "many of those who have given the flying saucer their scientific attention have concluded that they are mechanical creatures of the nation's most hush-hush espionage outfit, the code-breaking National Security Agency and its Soviet counterpart." Although these unmanned craft operated mostly in space, they occasionally lost control, "and thus are sighted by the Norman Muscarellos of Exeter, and, probably, by the Ivan Ivanoviches of Smolensk." That essentially ended the UFO segment of Tully's book, as shallow as it was brief.[105]

THE END OF PROJECT BLUE BOOK

On October 20, 1969, Brig. Gen. Carroll H. Bolender, the Air Force Deputy Director of Development, wrote a classified memo recommending the termination of Project Blue Book. As a result of the Condon Report recommendations and its endorsement from the scientific community, he stated, "we agree, that the continuation of Project Blue Book cannot be justified, either on the ground of national security or in the interest of science." Blue Book data, he argued, served neither the air force's environmental research program nor any intelligence function. Moreover, wrote Bolender,

> reports of unidentified flying objects which could affect national security are made in accordance with JANAP 146 or Air Force Manual 55-11, *and are not part of the Blue Book system* [emphasis added] (Atch 10). The air force experience therefore confirms the impression of the University of Colorado researchers "that the defense function could be performed within the framework established for intelligence and surveillance operations without the continuance of a special unit such as Project Blue Book."

An indisputable statement that UFOs affecting national security—the *important* sightings—were "not part of the Blue Book system." As if Bolender had not been clear enough, he restated his point: "Reports of UFOs which could affect national security would continue to be handled through the standard air force procedures designed for this purpose."

The implications are obvious. Blue Book served no useful purpose. It was "an administrative burden" and had not been taking serious UFO reports, anyway. What could it have been, other than a public relations facade? Unfortunately, Bolender said nothing else about other air force or military UFO activities. The very existence of military channels to investigate UFOs as part of national security, however, makes it self-evident that *someone* must have thought the phenomenon was a threat of some sort.[106]

The rest was a formality. On December 17, 1969, Air Force Secretary Robert Seamans, back from his jaunt to the Plain of Jars, announced the termination of Project Blue Book. On the basis of recommendations by Dr. Condon, Seamans stated, Blue Book could not be continued because it "cannot be justified either on the grounds of national security or in the interest of science." While Seamans did not go so far as to say that all UFO reports had been explained, he came very close:

> As a result of investigating UFO reports since 1948, the conclusions of Project Blue Book are: (1) No UFO reported, investigated, and evaluated by the air force has ever given any indication of being a threat to our national security; (2) there has been no evidence submitted or discovered by the air force that sightings categorized as "unidentified" represent technological developments or principles beyond the range of present-day scientific knowledge; and (3) there has been no evidence that sightings categorized as "unidentified" are of extraterrestrial vehicles.

Project Blue Book records were to be retired to the USAF Archives at Maxwell AFB in Alabama. In theory, adequate public access to the records would be provided by the Air Force Office of Information (SAFOI). In practice, it did not follow automatically that Blue Book files were freely open to the public. As late as the mid-1970s, the files, while not classified, were kept in a building that was. As Vallee remarked, "the interesting result [was] that one need[ed] a security clearance in order to see these 'unclassified' papers." (Incidentally, the files of the Condon Committee became similarly unavailable, apparently locked up by the University of Colorado, transferred to a private home, then burned.) Eventually, the Blue Book files, minus the witness names, were consigned to the Modern Military Branch, Military Archives Division, National Archives, Washington, D.C.[107]

Ironically, in October 1969, NICAP acquired a copy of a chapter on UFOs used by the USAF Academy which took the subject very seriously, and even said the problem warranted extensive scientific study. Among its references were two of Keyhoe's books, as well as NICAP's *The UFO Evidence*. Keyhoe and others were stunned. After the inevitable publicity, the air force shortened the chapter, removed all actual sighting descriptions, and more closely followed the party line.[108]

Thus, the air force ended its public involvement with UFOs. In the future, it continued to find UFO reports of interest, just as other military and intelligence services did, but with vastly improved privacy. Meanwhile, citizens wishing to report a UFO sighting now had no place in the government to go. Previous estimates by both Hynek and the Colorado University project indicated that less than 10 percent of people witnessing a UFO ever filed a report with any organization, be it Blue Book, NICAP, APRO, or elsewhere. Henceforth, that number plummeted even further.

THE END OF NICAP

The real demise of NICAP came on December 3, 1969, when the board of governors, meeting for the first time since 1960, demanded Donald Keyhoe's resignation. Keyhoe did so, under protest. He was seventy-two years old. Leading the effort was Col. Joseph Bryan, board chairman and former chief of the CIA psychological warfare staff. Bryan also dismissed NICAP stalwart and assistant director, Gordon Lore, Jr., replacing him with G. Stuart Nixon, who then became acting director. Although Bryan had initiated the meeting, and had written and distributed a memo calling Keyhoe inept, he later denied that he had anything to do with the ouster. However, UFO researcher Todd Zechel pointed out some history regarding Colonel Bryan. In late 1959, for example, Colonel Bryan, ostensibly an air force officer, approached Keyhoe, asking to see some of his "really hot cases." Keyhoe suspected an air force plot to infiltrate NICAP, and resisted. Soon, however, Bryan put Keyhoe at ease with several public comments regarding the interplanetary nature of UFOs and criticisms of government UFO secrecy. Before long, Bryan was a member of the NICAP board. Although he denied any association to the agency while on NICAP, he finally admitted to it in 1977. He had withheld this knowledge, Bryan said, because "it might embarrass CIA."

A new leadership took over at NICAP following Keyhoe's ouster. John L. Acuff, an outsider to NICAP and not a UFO researcher, was suddenly elected to serve on NICAP's board. In May 1970, he became the new director. For some time, Acuff had been executive director of the Washington-based Society of Photographic Scientists and Engineers (SPSE). SPSE had already cooperated with NICAP informally in the area of photographic analysis. It was later discovered that SPSE had significant intelligence connections: many members were photo analysts within the various intelligence components of the Department of Defense and CIA. The group had also been the target of KGB espionage.

Judged by Acuff's management of NICAP, he was either wholly inept or else he deliberately sought to sabotage the organization. Assisted by G. Stuart Nixon, he implemented a wholesale reorganization that ended the long-standing existence of NICAP affiliates throughout the country, groups that had vigorously promoted NICAP for years. He ended the UFO subcommittee system organized by Keyhoe, Hall, and Gordon Lore that existed at the state level. Regional members were told to operate independently from one another and were discouraged from communication and cooperation. Acuff declared all regional UFO data to be NICAP proprietary knowledge, which could not be disseminated without the approval of NICAP headquarters. Criticism of the government's UFO policy was no longer permitted, and NICAP turned into a mere "sighting collection center." The *UFO Investigator* became a four-page newsletter.

G. Stuart Nixon was also in regular communication with CIA agents. Zechel mentioned an undated CIA document, probably from 1970, written by an unnamed person within the agency, which indicated a familiarity with G. Stuart Nixon. NICAP daily activity logs from the late 1960s and early 1970s reflected that Nixon frequently met with CIA personnel such as Art Lundahl, director of NPIC; Fred Durant, author of the Robertson Panel report and a former CIA Office of Scientific Intelligence missile expert; and Dr. Charles Sheldon, a consultant to the agency later with the Library of Congress. Another person Nixon was meeting with frequently in 1968 was John L. Acuff. Oddly, none of the NICAP logs reflected any conversations between Nixon and Colonel Bryan, either by phone or in person, although almost every other daily occurrence was denoted in the logs. When questioned about this, Nixon refused comment.

Keyhoe supporters, meanwhile, were pressured to quit. Raymond Fowler, chairman of the NICAP Massachusetts Investigating Subcommittee, found his position eliminated soon after Acuff's appointment, and he became a regional investigator. Other subcommittee investigators lost their investigator status altogether. In 1971, Fowler's Massachusetts crew resigned *en masse* from NICAP, most joining MUFON which, as Fowler put it, "oddly enough, first appeared in the fortuitous year of 1969." The organization, formed as the Midwest (later Mutual) UFO Network, was founded by Walter Andrus, a Motorola executive and former APRO member. The Lorenzens were furious, but MUFON quickly became a successful organization, bringing in members from APRO as well as NICAP.

Acuff served as director until 1978. His successors, too, all had CIA connections, some tenuous, some strong. By then, serious management problems already caused the demise of NICAP. Even by 1973, its files were taken over by the newly formed Center for UFO Studies (CUFOS) in Evanston, Illinois. CUFOS was formed by J. Allen Hynek, late of the defunct Blue Book program. It is reasonable to assume that copies of anything of interest also found their way to Langley.[109]

THE END OF UFOS

The "definitive" explanation of UFOs coincided with a downturn of UFO reports. For the next two or three years, very little activity was reported worldwide. A bit in Australia and Brazil during 1969, some in Malaysia in 1970, and little anywhere in 1971.[110]

One of the better-known UFO sightings of 1969 was the Jimmy Carter sighting of January 6. Carter, along with ten residents of Leary, Georgia, was waiting for a Lions Club meeting to start when all noticed an unusually bright light at about thirty degrees elevation in the western sky between 7:15 and 7:30 P.M. Carter recalled later that it appeared slightly smaller than the apparent size of the moon. In his words, it "came close, moved away, came close, then moved away." He estimated its distance to be between three hundred and one thousand yards. The only analysis of the incident was offered by debunker Robert Sheaffer, who established the presence of Venus in that part of the sky. To which one answers: so? Carter himself later attributed the sighting to an "electrical occurrence of some sort."[111]

There were a few fairly well-researched UFO sightings that year which appeared to leave physical effects. Early in the day on June 17, 1969, in the Brazilian town of Ibiuna, several people saw a "brilliantly illuminated window" hovering above the ground. It appeared to be about thirty feet in diameter, ten feet high, and illuminated a small part of the ground. The sighting lasted for forty-five minutes, the object appearing to be stationary all the time. It then vanished. Later examination of the ground underneath showed a circle of flattened grass, twenty-five feet in diameter, swirled counterclockwise, with some small "secondary" swirls.[112]

On July 5, two children in the rural town of Anolaima, Colombia, saw a glowing object about three hundred yards away. It came to within sixty yards, when they ran over the hill to tell others. Thirteen people, including their father, returned to see the object. This man, Arcesio Bermudez, took a flashlight with him and returned in terror, claiming to have seen a small person and a craft that lit up and flew away. Within two days, Bermudez lost all appetite, his skin temperature dropped, blue spots appeared on his skin, and his stools became bloody. Within a week, two Bogota physicians, unaware of his UFO experience, concluded he had gastroenteritis. Within hours of his exam, Bermudez died. His doctor claimed he had previously been in good health.[113]

The following week, July 12, in Van Horn, Iowa, a mysterious circular patch of shriveled soybean crop was discovered. It was 425 feet wide and slightly elongated. Intense heat or radiation was attributed as the cause. During the fall, two women near Kansas City claimed to see a craft descend close to the ground, then to hear sounds of an animal being slaughtered as the object took off.[114]

On September 4, 1969, a forty-foot diameter circle was found in some scrubland in Hamilton, New Zealand. Within the circle, vegetation was dehydrated and radioactive; three deep depressions, about ten feet apart, formed a triangle in the circle's center. Vegetation remained healthy outside the circle. A horticultural consultant said it appeared some object had landed on that spot and had taken off, emitting a short-wave, high-frequency radiation that cooked the plants from the inside out. "I know of no earthbound source of energy," he concluded, "capable of creating a circle in this manner." Nuclear scientists brought in by the New Zealand government, however, attributed the cause to "root rot and blight."[115]

In the public realm, nothing was heard about these incidents. The UFO was a dead issue, solved by the University of Colorado. Blue Book, even before its official demise, had ceased to take reports. NICAP and APRO were both in disarray. In all likelihood, there were more sightings out there, more accounts to relate, but no one was talking, and no one listening. By the end of 1969, estimated Jacques Vallee, perhaps twenty thousand or so fairly clear and dated UFO reports existed in official and private files. There appeared little hope, however, that these scattered files would ever find their way to an organization that would seek to do anything with them.[116]

THE FINAL GASP

December 1969 surely was an important month in the history of UFOs. Blue Book ended, Keyhoe was fired, and the American Association for the Advancement of Science, impressed by Hynek's and McDonald's attacks on the Condon Report, held a symposium on UFOs at its annual meeting in Boston on December 26. Two of the main forces behind this were Carl Sagan and Thornton Page, former member of the 1953 Robertson Panel, and the chairman of the astronomy section of the AAAS. While neither man was a UFO "believer," Page at least felt more open-minded about the subject than in past years. Edward U. Condon, a former AAAS president, strenuously opposed the idea and received backing from several members. Condon went so far as to attempt to enlist the support of Vice President Spiro Agnew. The obvious likelihood was that the report would be criticized somehow. Actually, the AAAS board had approved this symposium for the previous year's meeting in Dallas, but postponed it, partly because of the opposition, partly because the Condon Report had yet to be published.

As he had been everywhere he went for the past few years, James McDonald was the most dominant and noteworthy force to reckon with and made the most lasting impression on the event. He knew this was a last-ditch effort to get UFOs on the scientific agenda. "I am enough of a realist," he said, "to sense that, unless this AAAS symposium succeeds in making the scientific community aware of the seriousness of the UFO problem, little response to any call for new investigation is likely to appear." Rising to the occasion, McDonald presented a brilliant paper. Titled "Science in Default: Twenty-two Years of Inadequate UFO Investigations," it is perhaps the most damning statement about UFO research ever made. Speaking before the convention at Boston's Sheraton Plaza Hotel, McDonald came down hard on everyone: Condon, Menzel, Hynek, and finally the scientific establishment itself. He said:

No scientifically adequate investigation of the UFO problem has been carried out during the entire twenty-two years that have now passed since the first extensive wave of sightings of unidentified aerial objects in the summer of 1947.... In my opinion, the UFO problem, far from being the nonsense problem that it has often been labeled by many scientists, constitutes a problem of extraordinary scientific interest. The grave difficulty with essentially all past UFO studies has been that they were either devoid of any substantial scientific content, or else have lost their way amidst the relatively large noise content that tends to obscure the real signal in the UFO reports.

He criticized mainstream scientists for complacency in not recognizing the "signal" from the "noise" in UFO reports and expressed dismay over the probable bleak future of UFO research in the aftermath of the Condon Report. McDonald also went after Project Blue Book and J. Allen Hynek:

The assurances that substantial scientific competence was involved in air force UFO investigations have, I submit, had seriously deleterious scientific effects.... My own extensive checks have revealed so slight a total amount of scientific competence in two decades of air force-supported investigations that I can only regard the repeated assertions of solid scientific study of the UFO problem as the single most serious obstacle that the air force has put in the way of progress towards elucidation of the matter.

Projects Sign, Grudge, and Blue Book had conducted "scientifically mean-ingless investigations." The UFO panels and studies commissioned by the air force had all brought "almost negligible scientific scrutiny into the picture." This was a direct hit at the Robertson Panel, and thus Thornton Page, who sat listening. The Condon Report was "quite inadequate," padded with fluff, but unable to hide the fact that it studied only "a tiny fraction" of the truly difficult UFO reports. Its level of argumentation, said McDonald, was "wholly unsatisfactory." He added:

Furthermore, of the roughly ninety cases that it specifically confronts, over thirty are conceded to be unexplained. With so large a fraction of unexplained cases... it is far from clear how Dr. Condon felt justified in concluding that the study indicated "that further extensive study of UFOs probably cannot be justified in the expectation that science will be advanced thereby."

Finally, the National Academy of Sciences came under McDonald's censure:

That a panel of the National Academy of Sciences could endorse this study is to me disturbing. I find no evidence that the academy panel did any independent checking of its own; and none of that eleven-man panel had any significant prior investigative experience in this area, to my knowledge.

There was no one else like James McDonald. He was a first-rate scientist, on a mission, afraid of nothing, able to say precisely what he meant. But McDonald by himself could not turn the situation around, and he knew it.

One suspects he was speaking to posterity. While his passion may have impressed, it failed to persuade. Sagan rejected the extraterrestrial hypothesis, much as Condon had, *a priori*. Others felt likewise. Menzel, who could not attend due to heart problems, submitted a paper describing UFOs as a modern myth. It is true that the majority of participants urged Air Force Secretary Seamans not to destroy Blue Book's files, but few would take on the imposing figure of Edward U. Condon, not to mention the entire mainstream scientific establishment. In fact, a few weeks later, Menzel wrote to Page that he favored impounding the files for ten years and keeping them off limits to the likes of Hynek and McDonald.[117]

SUMMARY

The UFO problem reached its climax and resolution between 1966 and 1969. What had begun as a situation where anything seemed possible, in which flying saucer reports deluged the globe, ended with the sound of a door slamming shut. The air force, at the nadir of its credibility on the UFO issue in 1966, rode tall with the sanction of official science in 1969. The University of Colorado study on UFOs was riddled with dissension and saddled with bad publicity; it produced a report that, for all its bulk, was remarkably skimpy where it mattered. Its conclusion did not coincide, even remotely, with its own data. But none of that mattered—a telling statement on the state of mainstream science, and a lesson in how to ride that capricious horse known as the public. It also surely helped that UFO reports dropped, as if off a table.

The air force and the CIA had finally gotten what they had wanted for so long. Whatever UFOs represented to them, they could work on the situation henceforth in relative isolation from the prying eyes of the public. For, contrary to what Bolender claimed, UFOs were much more than an administrative burden. They continued to represent, and be, a *real* burden. The mere publication of a weakly supported scientific refutation could hardly be expected to change the judgments of those within the intelligence community, whether they be anonymous authors within the NSA, the strike team members at Minot AFB who saw a hovering UFO over their launch facility, or famous scientists such as Paul Santorini. The explanations passed off to the public were not congruent with the situation the classified world continued to deal with.

Winners need losers, and by 1969 NICAP had lost in a big way. For all of Donald Keyhoe's faults, he had been NICAP's driving force, the major who led the charge. His ouster loosened the organization from its mooring, and it soon crashed into the rocks. It may be that there was little Keyhoe could have done to save NICAP had he continued at its helm. The future looked bleak from any vantage point. But, old man that he was, Keyhoe remained its best hope. Without him, instead of going down fighting, NICAP committed suicide—perhaps, with the CIA in mind, we should say, committed assisted suicide.

Did the public lose, as well? The answer depends on whether one believes truth to be of greater value than social stability. In 1968, Richard Nixon was elected president on a platform of law and order, amid a society with a disintegrating social consensus. Not everyone cared about truth at all cost; many just wanted to keep the machinery moving. At the front of the line, as it is in all places and all eras, was the national security apparatus, which saw the maintenance of stability and the status quo as its preeminent goal. Viewed from this perspective, at once paternalistic and self-serving, one might say the public interest was served. With the issue of UFOs at rest, the country, and perhaps the world, could move on to other pressing items.

There remains the small matter of truth, however. The problem with truth is that it ever remains the uninvited guest who crashes the party. Even in disgrace, truth is hard to get rid of. With the wrong conclusion coming from the Colorado University project—and it *was* the wrong conclusion—a new era of deception about UFOs had begun, one with the sanction of science. Inevitably, truth would pop up again—never without a challenge, of course, but there all the same. Within such a context, in the face of official denials about UFOs, truth could only erode the public's confidence in its leaders. It may be hard for later generations to appreciate the faith placed by those of an earlier time in their government, in their country. The death, long ago, of this faith testifies to the dangerous power of truth, not simply in relation to UFOs, of course, but to all activities of the national security state, *including UFOs*.

Chapter 9

The Problem Renewed: 1970 to 1973

To condemn a thing thus, dogmatically, as false and impossible, is to assume the distinction of knowing the bounds and limits of God's will and of the power of our mother Nature. . . . It is dangerous and presumptuous, besides the absurd temerity that it implies, to disdain what we do not comprehend.

—Michel de Montaigne, "Measuring the True and False"

NATIONAL SECURITY STATE TRIUMPHANT

UFOs were a dead issue in 1970. The national security apparatus, which had intersected with the phenomenon for thirty years, now pretended, and perhaps hoped, that UFOs really *were* a thing of the past. As for the present, the activities undertaken by the new administration of Richard Nixon would themselves be hard to believe, had they not been so thoroughly documented. In 1970, the American national security state was more expansive and invasive than at any previous point in the nation's history. Let us briefly assess the situation, before matters hit a snag in 1972.

The CIA

America's premier covert action agency was busy. From 1970 to 1973, urged by the White House, the agency tried to thwart Chile's Marxist presidential candidate—then president—Salvador Allende. Kissinger expressed the prevailing sentiment in June 1970: "I don't see why we have to let a country go Marxist just because its people are irresponsible." Nixon agreed. The CIA soon bugged the Chilean embassy and began planning a military coup.[1]

The CIA also controlled an army of thirty-six thousand men in Laos, which cost perhaps $300 million annually. Although Congress never authorized this activity, there was little to fear, considering the agency's classified budget and its many private sources of income.[2]

The HTLingual program remained aggressive. By the early 1970s, the New York City component examined over 2 million mail items per year, photographed over thirty thousand envelopes, and opened eight thousand to nine thousand letters. In 1971, CIA Director Richard Helms gave a rare public address, in which he insisted that the CIA did not surveil domestic targets. "The nation must to a degree take it on faith," he said, "that we who lead the CIA are honorable men, devoted to the nation's service."[3]

Meanwhile, CIA mind-control guru Sid Gottlieb had developed a strong interest in electronic stimulation of the brain (ESB), which he persuaded Helms to support. The idea was to program a human being to attack and kill upon command, to be done through the CIA's Operation Often.[4]

The NSA

By now, the NSA was examining over 150,000 telegrams per month, as part of Operation Shamrock. According to Victor Marchetti, it was still unable to break the high-grade cipher systems and codes of the USSR and China, although third-world nations and American allies provided easier targets.

The FBI

Hoover, increasingly paranoid about exposure of the enormity of FBI activities, severed all relations with the CIA in the spring of 1970, and soon thereafter with all other intelligence agencies. The consensus around Nixon was that Hoover had lost his guts and had to go. But Nixon was not the first president who had trouble firing J. Edgar Hoover.[5]

Nixon

One of Nixon's most persistent goals was the reorganization of the intelligence community, an immense undertaking. The most famous result of his efforts was the Huston Plan, named after Tom Huston, his point man on the project. At the June 1970 meeting in the Oval Office, all the main players attended: Haldeman, Ehrlichmann, Huston, and intelligence chiefs Hoover (FBI), Helms (CIA), Adm. Noel Gaylor (NSA), and Lt. Gen. Donald Bennett (DIA). Nixon made it clear he wanted a major effort against domestic dissidents. The group was chaired by Hoover and named the Inter Agency Committee on Intelligence (ICI). Even the formidable presence of the now-cautious Hoover, however, could not prevent its far-reaching recommendations: expanded mail openings, resumption of illegal entries and "black bag" jobs, electronic surveillance of Americans and foreigners within the U.S., an increase in the number of "campus sources," and expansion of the army's counterintelligence mission.

Nixon endorsed the plan in mid-July but would not sign it, nor would Haldeman and Ehrlichmann. Who, then, at the White House, put his name to this dramatic authorization? Why, Nixon's young staffer, Tom Huston. Hoover easily torpedoed the plan on July 23, when he announced that he would certainly go along, just as soon as he received written authorization from the president for all these break-ins and wiretaps. Thus, the plan to "institutionalize burglary as presidential policy" (the words are those of David Wise) failed. In practice, it made little difference, as these agencies were already engaging in many of the practices for which they sought approval. They did not cease simply because official sanction was not forthcoming. In some cases, they even expanded their activities.[6]

The first cracks in the facade appeared in 1971. With intelligence community break-ins widespread, Hoover ended the Cointelpro program in April, not due to any recognition of impropriety but to fear of exposure. The bureau continued to be aggressive against its Cointelpro targets but was less systematic. Hoover's fears proved well justified, for in May 1971, burglars broke into the FBI Field Office at Media, Pennsylvania, escaping with about a thousand documents and exposing the FBI's massive surveillance of blacks, students, radicals, and other mischievous groups. The word "Cointelpro" escaped into society.[7]

Then, on June 13, 1971, the *New York Times* began publishing a series of highly sensitive documents known as the Pentagon Papers. These were a classified history of the Vietnam War, leaked by Daniel Ellsberg, whom the White House immediately sought to smear and discredit. In September, a group of Cuban-Americans connected with the CIA, along with G. Gordon Liddy and E. Howard Hunt, broke into the office of Ellsberg's psychiatrist. These people were Richard Nixon's personal covert action squad, nicknamed the "plumbers group." In April 1972, it was almost certainly Nixon people who broke into the home of CBS White House correspondent Dan Rather.[8]

Also in April 1972, the residence of J. Edgar Hoover was broken into twice. According to Hoover biographer Anthony Summers, the second break-in allowed for the placement of a poison (thiophosphate) into Hoover's personal toilet articles. The chemical is a compound used in insecticides, highly toxic if taken orally, inhaled, or absorbed through the skin. It causes fatal heart seizure and is detectable only if an autopsy is performed within hours of death. J. Edgar Hoover died between 2 A.M. and 3 A.M. on May 2, 1971. He received no autopsy, and the cause was ascribed to cardiac arrest, although Hoover's doctor claimed he had been in good health. That morning, about twenty government agents methodically ransacked Hoover's residence, but Hoover's secretary destroyed countless files before anyone reached them. The official establishment lionized and glorified Hoover, and twenty-five thousand people flocked to the Capitol to pay homage to him. Nixon called him "a great force for good in our national life." Privately,

Nixon feared Hoover even in death. A year later, he spoke of the old Director as though he were still alive: "He's got files on everybody, goddamnit!"[9]

Shortly after Hoover's death, Nixon's plumbers group burglarized the Chilean embassy in Washington. Then, on June 17, 1972, they were caught while breaking into the Democratic National Committee in Washington's Watergate Office Building. Many believe Watergate was just the tip of the iceberg, since there had been at least a hundred similar types of break-ins, all apparently politically motivated, all unsolved, an unknown number of which were connected to Nixon. At any rate, Nixon's position seemed strong. It took some time before the FBI realized the break-in was not a CIA operation. Moreover, even after eyes turned toward the president, prosecutors appeared to be in his pocket.[10]

THINGS FALL APART

Nixon's several failed attempts to reorganize the intelligence community showed that he was no better than his predecessors at controlling this sprawling octopus. Dissatisfied with and mistrustful of Helms, Nixon fired him following his re-election to the presidency in November 1972. Helms now began two months of vigorous cleanup at the CIA, closing down such vulnerable programs as Operation Often. During his last days as DCI in January 1973, Helms ordered Gottlieb, also on his way out, to destroy all files relating to MK-Ultra, MK-Search, and related endeavors in mind control. Among other things, Helms was worried that the lawsuits of Ewen Cameron's former patients could blaze a trail straight to Langley. Inexplicably, Gottlieb failed to destroy about 130 incriminating boxes in the archives. Had he destroyed these, MK-Ultra might have remained unknown to this day. Meanwhile, the CIA was also working to prevent the publication of an expose by former agent Victor Marchetti. HTLingual and the NSA's Minaret programs also ended in 1973, the latter in order to prevent exposure during the Weathermen Trial.[11]

In February 1973, immediately after Helms left the CIA, he was questioned by the Senate Foreign Relations Committee, subject to approval for an ambassadorial post to Iran. (He was there, incidentally, during an amazing UFO sighting in Tehran in 1976.) Helms was questioned by none other than Sen. Stuart Symington, the former air force secretary and enemy of James Forrestal. Symington asked Helms whether the CIA had tried to overthrow the government of Chile. "No, sir," replied the ex-DCI, who also denied that the CIA had been involved in domestic intelligence activities. Seven months later, Salvador Allende died in a CIA-coordinated military coup.[12]

James Schlesinger, a CIA outsider, replaced Helms, then named William Colby as head of clandestine services. At Colby's urging, Schlesinger soon ordered CIA employees to report all suspected violations of the law, or of the CIA's charter, to the CIA's Inspector General. The result was a 693-page report called "Potential Flap Activities," known more commonly as The Family Jewels. It discussed Operation Chaos, bits of MK-Ultra (although nothing significant), illegal domestic wiretaps and bugging, and so on. As amazing as these revelations were, there is little doubt that much, much more never surfaced. Schlesinger fired about one thousand CIA officers, then left the agency in July 1973 to take over at the Pentagon. Colby succeeded him as DCI, regarded as a traitor, possibly even a Soviet mole, by much of the old guard. Certainly James Angleton thought so, and Colby wasted no time in firing the CIA's longtime counterintelligence expert.[13]

Classified information spilled out throughout 1973. People learned that the FBI actually wiretapped reporters and White House officials. Former White House staffer John Dean squawked first about the burglary of Ellsberg's psychiatrist's office, then about Nixon's Enemies List. Nixon henchmen began to resign. The national security apparatus suddenly looked vulnerable, and the president most of all.[14]

UFOs in the Early 1970s

UFOs may have been old news in the early 1970s, but they had not gone away altogether. While there were few reports of strange craft, there were interesting reports of crop circles, as well as unexplained animal mutilations. Several cases described large, circular impressions within a grassy area, often after a witness claimed to see a large craft descend in the field the night before.[15]

Some landing reports were fairly well documented, such as the Delphos case of November 2, 1971. At a farm near Delphos, in northern Kansas, a sixteen-year-old boy, out with his dog in the evening, saw a mushroom-shaped object with multicolored lights, hovering low over the ground about seventy-five feet away. It was about nine feet in diameter and sounded like "an old washing machine." The young man became temporarily blind but regained his sight and called his parents. All three saw the object high in the sky, about half the apparent size of the full moon. It then vanished. On the ground was a glowing ring, about a foot wide, and several trees glowed. A month later, UFO researcher Ted Phillips investigated the site. He found the ring and noticed that the soil felt strange, "like a slick crust, as if the soil was crystalized." UFO researcher Michael Swords wrote that the soil was "hydrophobic [resistant to wetting], luminescent, and anaesthetic," and could not attribute this to anything known. In the late 1980s, Erol Faruk, a British chemist, wrote a series of articles about Delphos, concluding that the evidence pointed to an unconventional aerial object as "the most tenable explanation—despite its implications."[16]

In 1972, a man from Eganville, Ontario, took aerial photographs of perfect circles burned into the grass at the time of UFO reports in the area, then showed his slides at an Experimental Aircraft Association meeting. Ten years later, the effects of the circles remained visible.

Many crop circles were reported in South Australia, including the following three cases. In December 1971 at Tooligie Hill, a crop circle about ten feet in diameter was discovered in a wheat field. During the previous night, a local farmer had seen a large ball of red light descending on the field where the rings were found. In Bordertown in 1973, seven crop circles were discovered in an oat field, ranging in size from about eight feet to fifteen feet in diameter, all swirling counterclockwise. In December 1973, in Wokurna, South Australia, another crop circle was found in a wheat field, with counterclockwise swirls and bare soil patches.[17]

On June 28, 1973, a closely observed landing case was reported from Columbia, Missouri. At half past midnight, a man and his sixteen-year-old daughter looked out the window of their home to see two bright, silvery-white light beams about five feet apart and fifty feet away. The objects tapered to about two feet in diameter at the bottom. As the beams faded, a twelve- to fifteen-foot bright oval object appeared close to the ground, lighting up the area "as bright as day." They heard a "thrashing sound," and the trees swayed so much that a large limb snapped off. As the father reached for his gun and called for help, the UFO moved away to the north, passed beneath some tree limbs, rose, and hovered. Blue and orange bands of light were now visible on the surface of the craft. It moved silently to its original position, but disappeared before police arrived at 1:45 A.M. The police took a quick look, then left. Later searches uncovered broken tree limbs, damaged foliage, scorched leaves up to height of thirty-five feet, and impressions in the ground as deep as two feet.[18]

Animal mutilations became widespread throughout the American West during the 1970s, especially Colorado, Nebraska, Kansas, Minnesota, Iowa, and Wisconsin. They also occurred in such eastern states as Pennsylvania and Florida. But the phenomenon was global, reaching Canada, Mexico, Panama, Puerto Rico, Brazil, parts of Europe, the Canary Islands, and Australia.

As mutilations became common, cases arose which defied simple explanations. Frequently, the anal area of the animal was bored out and the reproductive organs removed. The cuts seemed to be precise, very smooth, and in a few cases, a near perfect circle of hide was removed from the belly. Often the eyes, tongue, ears, and reproductive organs were missing. Usually there were no signs of struggle, nor of blood—either in the victim's body or anywhere at the site—and predators often avoided the carcass. Even more strange, there were frequently no tracks around the animal other than its own.

Many mutilations appeared to coincide with sightings of nearby UFOs, as well as mysterious, unmarked, black helicopters. Inevitably, the UFO connections prompted claims that aliens were performing the mutilations, perhaps with a focus on the reproductive system. Skeptics claimed the mutilations were probably the work of predators and perhaps cults. Still, several veterinarians could not determine what killed the animals, in some cases claiming the removal of organs was made by instruments that were not available to them. Other investigators doubted that predators were capable of performing the precise incisions found on mutilated carcasses.

Beyond question, the phenomenon of mutilated cattle was real. In Minnesota, twenty-two cases of mutilated cattle carcasses were reported between 1970 and 1974. In Iowa, so many reports emerged that U.S. Attorney General Alan Donielson asked the FBI in 1973 to make "an intensive investigation." Between 1973 and 1975, the state of Colorado confirmed more than 130 cattle mutilations. In the following decades, there have been approximately ten thousand mutilation reports.

The primary official study of mutilations, analogous to the Condon Report in its study and conclusions, was undertaken by retired FBI agent Kenneth M. Rommel, Jr., for the state of New Mexico in 1979. Rommel concluded that "the vast majority of mutilations are caused by predators and scavengers." During the course of his study, unfortunately, reports of mutilations dropped off. He personally investigated only fifteen cases and analyzed twelve more cases investigated by local law enforcement officials. Rommel declined to request on-the-scene participation from the various experts he consulted with. Nor was he interested in the cause of death, per se, for any animal. If there was evidence of scavenger activity, that was enough to move on. Rommel also re-investigated, such as was possible, 117 "classic" mutilation cases that had occurred since 1975; each of these, he concluded, could be explained conventionally. He quoted one physician who stated, that "surprising as it may seem to the uninitiated, many of the scavengers make as clean a cut as might be done by a surgeon. . . ."

Rommel's report was thorough and sober, but inadequate to persuade many ranchers and some investigators. Alleged cases of mutilations, numbered in the many thousands, continued to appear. John Altshuler, who had examined Lady in 1967, later examined many such cases during the 1990s and found lesions "consistent with electrosurgical excision." Other researchers continued to find abnormally high radiation levels near the dead animals.

Some of the most active researchers believe not in aliens, but covert human activity, as the key to the mutilation mystery. The theory is that the mutilations are occurring as part of a covert, random sampling of cattle to test for excessive levels of radiation contamination. The area of northern New Mexico, which was the hotspot of mutilation activity during the 1990s, happens to be downwind from the nuclear test site in Nevada, possesses several active uranium mines, was the scene of many nuclear detonations in past decades, and also has two major nuclear research laboratories. Over the years, an estimated 1,000 kilotons of radioactive dust fell on New Mexico, Nevada, and Colorado. Perhaps, in order to carry out necessary, albeit illegal, monitoring of dangerous levels of radiation, a covert operation is behind the phenomenon. As to the technologies required to undertake the job, they could be well within human means. The air force possesses an in-house surgical laser probably able to make the cuts described in so many cases of mutilated cattle. The device was developed by Phillips Laboratories, located in northern New Mexico, to conduct medical surgery in the field of battle.

The mutilation mystery, like the UFO mystery, is real enough. Moreover, it, too, receives no official acknowledgment from authorities. The National Livestock and Agricultural Association, the New Mexico Livestock Board, and similar official bodies deny the phenomenon exists at all. Whether the cause of the mystery derives from UFOs, covert ops, or some other source, has yet to be determined conclusively.[19]

AN UNDERWATER THESIS

Neither the decline of UFO reports nor the results of the Condon Report prevented UFO authors from continuing to publish their books. As in all fields at all times, much was disposable; other works were more valuable. One of the most intriguing, original, and intelligent of the books has also been among the most forgotten. In 1970, biologist Ivan Sanderson published his second and last UFO book *Invisible Residents*. His subtitle, a charming archaism, read *A Disquisition upon Certain Matters Maritime, and the Possibility of Intelligent Life under the Waters of This Earth*. Sanderson obtained several degrees in the biological sciences, taught zoology at Cambridge University, went into field work on behalf of the British Museum and other such institutions, and mounted nine expeditions to collect specimens.

Sanderson developed an interest in UFOs during the 1950s, and even reported a personal sighting to Project Blue Book (unexplained). He was also an ex-navy man, a fact of some significance, considering his thesis: that the UFO problem is not necessarily one dominated by the appearance of mysterious *aerial* objects. Indeed, the term unidentified flying object was misleading, he argued, as a great deal of strange activity was going on beneath the waters. He offered the perhaps startling claim that, "by actual count, over 50 percent of all so-called 'sightings' of UFOs have occurred over, coming from, going away over, or plunging into or coming out of water." He not only described scores of intriguing water-related UFO sightings, but offered the opinion that these need not involve the presence of extraterrestrial intelligence, but possibly an indigenous intelligence that evolved independently in the oceans. Or perhaps, he suggested, there were many reasons why others arriving here might choose the oceans as more hospitable than dry land.

To Sanderson the biologist, the idea of an indigenous, possibly ocean-based, intelligence behind UFOs was not really so outlandish as might seem to those untrained in his field. The Earth itself has "more than enough 'environment' available for the evolution of an almost endless variety of intelligent life-forms." To those who think smugly that it would be impossible for an intelligent life-form to have developed independently on this world without our knowledge, Sanderson wrote:

> We really know very little about our world or its environmental setup. What is more, the world that we *do* know, or think we know, is extremely limited. . . . We have only the vaguest notion of what lies more than a hundred feet under *our* feet, on land, though geologists are doing pretty well, at least in general terms, down to a few miles. We are fairly good under water down to about five hundred feet around the periphery of the continental land masses and islands, but we know practically nothing of the great body of . . . "hydrospace," which includes all seas and oceans from the surfaces down to their bottoms.

Moreover, "we know that the nature of living things on this planet alone ranges from man to ultra-filterable viruses that may produce inanimate generations. So why should we balk at the suggestion that elsewhere it could range much further?"

Sanderson speculated that "aliens" operating UFOs could be artificially intelligent, or perhaps that even some of the machines among UFOs "might also be 'alive,' having been constructed along biological rather than mechanical principles." Machines, he wrote, need not be made only of metal or ceramics. May they not be of "plastics and colloids; or colloids and gases; or even . . . 'nonmaterial' altogether?" Machines patterned on life-forms would always be better, more efficient, and more reliable than anything we can think up and construct with metal, nuts, and bolts. Such creatures could range from having a very high order of intelligence, to being a type of drone. Interestingly, in the early 1990s, Manuel de Landa, a writer on artificial intelligence and warfare, argued that we were perhaps not far away from creating machines that would blur the distinction between "real" and "artificial" intelligence.

Sanderson's collected evidence made it "painfully obvious" to him that, at the very least, these intelligences were "either acting in consort or along parallel lines of endeavor . . . surveying and studying our planet and its life-forms." Quite possibly, there are whole masses of aliens "either muscling in here or sharing in the enterprise."

Sanderson shopped his ideas and reports throughout U.S. Naval Intelligence during the late 1960s. Apparently visiting quite a few departments, he

learned that most of the topmost individuals had not read any of the extraordinary underwater UFO reports he had come across. Most thought it was all
nonsense until he would make some remark that seemed to get through. The
typical result of his meetings, he said, was that officials begged him to send them
the reports he had collected.[20]

THE DEATH OF JAMES MCDONALD

Following the disaster of 1968 and 1969, James McDonald and Allen
Hynek tried to keep the UFO issue alive. On January 21, 1970, the UFO Subcommittee of the American Institute of Aeronautics and Astronautics
sponsored a panel in New York City, and Hynek, McDonald, Thornton Page,
Gordon Thayer, and Philip Klass attended. The subcommittee, led by Joachim
P. Kuettner, consisted of scientists with no previous position on UFOs and
reached several middle-of-the-road conclusions. It criticized the NAS position
that extraterrestrials were the least likely explanation for UFOs and rejected
McDonald's position that it was the "least unsatisfactory." The subcommittee
determined there was no scientific basis for assessing such probabilities. It criticized the Condon Report, which retained a "small residue of well-documented
but unexplainable cases which form the hard core of the UFO controversy."
The Condon Report's conclusions, said the subcommittee, did not match its
data. It recommended a moderate-level, ongoing scientific study of UFOs.[21]

Despite the appearance that UFOs were completely debunked, many people remained skeptical of the official truth as handed down by Condon and the
air force. In April 1971, an engineering research magazine, *Industrial Research*,
published the results of a poll in which 80 percent of its members rejected the
Condon Report; 76 percent believed that the government was concealing UFO
facts; 32 percent believed that UFOs were extraterrestrial. Poll or no poll, however, the CIA continued to lie about its UFO interests. An internal memo dated
July 29, 1970, suggested a response to a U.S. citizen who had accused it of using
the Colorado University Project and Robertson Panel to "whitewash" UFOs.
The memo suggested to say that "we have had no interest in the UFO matter
for many years, have no files or persons knowledgeable on the subject. . . ."[22]

The worst story of 1971 was the demise of James McDonald. As far as
anyone could tell, McDonald was fine all through 1970 and into 1971. On
March 2, 1971, he testified as an expert in atmospheric physics at the House
Committee on Appropriations regarding the supersonic transport (SST) and
its potentially harmful atmospheric effects. McDonald's opponents questioned his credentials and ridiculed him as someone who believed in "little
men flying around the sky." Laughter broke out several times.

Shortly after this incident, McDonald shot himself in the head and became blind. He was committed to the psychiatric ward of the VA Medical Center in Tucson. In June, he signed himself out. On Sunday morning, June 13, a woman in south Tucson, identifying herself as a doctor, said a deranged blind man had taken a cab to the area. She wanted to know where the driver had dropped him off, and she made several calls. Meanwhile, a married couple and their children, walking along a shallow creek, found McDonald's body under a bridge at 11:40 A.M. A .38 caliber revolver was in the sand, near his head. A brief note attributed his suicide to marriage and family problems.[23]

The reader who has made it this far, and through several unproven conspiracy theories will, it is hoped, endure one more. Did James McDonald commit suicide, or did he not? Most UFO researchers say that he did. Let us look at the other possibility. We know that many intelligence agencies were skilled in "creating" suicides. But, one might ask, wasn't McDonald's mental condition already deteriorating? Jerome Clark stated that McDonald was ready to "crack" in the aftermath of the SST hearings. But what caused this? Embarrassment at the SST hearings? His marriage? Perhaps, one supposes, but both of these explanations feel flimsy. Without exception, those who knew McDonald described him as possessing great integrity and courage. Was he really the type of person to commit suicide? UFO researcher Val Germann wrote this about McDonald in an Internet essay:

Biographical Information: Dr. James E. McDonald [as of 1968]
Born: Duluth, Minnesota, May 7, 1920.
B.A., Chemistry, University of Omaha, 1942.
M.A., Meteorology, M.I.T., 1945.
Ph.D., Physics, Iowa State University, 1951.
U.S. Navy, Intelligence & Aerology, 1942–45.
Instructor, Physics, Iowa State University, 1946–49.
Assistant Professor, Physics, Iowa State University, 1950–53.
Research Physicist, Cloud Physics, University of Chicago, 1953–54.
Associate Professor, Physics, University of Arizona, 1954–56.
Full Professor, Physics, University of Arizona, 1956–57.
Senior Physicist, Institute of Atmospheric Studies, 1958–present.
Member, Weather Modification Panel, NAS, 1965–present.
Member, Navy Stormfury Advisory Panel, 1966–present.
Member, NSF Weather Modification Panel, 1967–present.
Member, AAAS, American Meteorological Society, Sigma Xi, American Geophysical Society, American Society of University Professors.
Married, Six Children.

Yes, I would say this is a candidate for suicide, wouldn't you? . . . He was at the top of his field by the late 1950s and . . . left no stone unturned once he set his mind to a project. It has been said that genius is the capacity for infinite pains, and by that standard James E. McDonald certainly qualified.

Even if McDonald had been targeted by some dark force in the U.S. intelligence community, one may ask, *how* could his "suicide" have been arranged, and *why*? After all, why fear McDonald when UFOs had become irrelevant? To answer this question, we need to remember that, while UFOs were a non-issue within mainstream culture, things were different in the classified world. There, it was understood that UFOs would not go away simply because of Edward U. Condon. Looking back, we can see the early 1970s as a lull, not the end, of the UFO problem. Those on top of the problem at the time probably understood this. Therefore, James McDonald, only fifty-one years old, could well have been perceived as a nuisance, and even a threat.

The *how* part was really no matter at all. By the early 1970s, there were already means available to alter the moods of unsuspecting persons. A pocket-sized transmitter generating electromagnetic (EM) energy at less than 100 milliwatts could do the job. This is no pie-in-the-sky theory. In 1972, Dr. Gordon J. F. McDonald testified before the House Subcommittee on Oceans and International Environment on the issue of electromagnetic weapons used for mind control and mental disruption. He stated:

> [T]he basic notion was to create, between the electrically charged ionosphere in the higher part of the atmosphere and conducting layers of the surface of the Earth, this neutral cavity, to create waves, electrical waves that would be tuned to the brain waves. . . . About ten cycles per second. . . . You can produce changes in behavioral patterns or in responses.

The following year, Dr. Joseph C. Sharp, at Walter Reed Hospital, while in a soundproof room, was able to hear spoken words broadcast by "pulsed microwave audiogram." These words were broadcast to him *without* any implanted electronic translation device. Rather, they reached him by direct transmission to the brain.[24]

Thus, we ask, could McDonald have been the victim of a program using technology such as described above? The answer is yes. Whether or not he was may never be answered. Some will claim this account of McDonald's death is little more than conspiracy mongering. Not so. It is no better willfully to ignore such unpleasant realities and pretend that McDonald died, unprovoked, of his own hand—a practice that is the rule among UFO researchers today. No one is in a position to state whether McDonald's suicide was real or not. Both scenarios are possible. It is an unsatisfying and all-too-common position, unfortunately, within the UFO field.

THE RETURN OF UFOS

UFO reports of the early 1970s were sparse. Those that surfaced, however, continued to baffle. Puerto Rico was the scene of much reported UFO activity throughout 1972, and several interesting cases came from Europe and South Africa. On September 14, 1972, an unknown object was sighted at West Palm Beach International Airport. Two FAA air traffic controllers tracked the object, as well as FAA operators at Miami International Airport and radar men at Homestead AFB. It was seen through binoculars by an FAA supervisor at West Palm Beach. Two F-106 interceptors were scrambled, and one pilot saw the glowing object, which disappeared as he closed. The story received only local coverage, and the air force explained the object as the planet Venus. On January 11, 1973, a UFO was filmed in color for twenty seconds in Cuddington, Buckinghamshire, England.[25]

In October 1973, an intense UFO wave hit the United States, coinciding with some critical developments in the American and international scenes. On October 10, Vice President Spiro Agnew resigned from office. Ten days later, a spate of resignations and firings spread through the Nixon administration. On the twenty-fourth, U.S. nuclear forces, in response to Middle East war and possible Soviet intervention, went on DEFCON 3 alert, the highest possible. Fifteen thousand troops of the 82nd Airborne Division were mobilized, and fifty B-52 bombers were readied. In this context, UFOs made their reappearance in American skies.

Most of the activity occurred in the southeastern U.S. On October 11, two men fishing in Pascagoula, Mississippi, claimed they had been abducted by horrific robot-like creatures that floated out of a hovering UFO and brought them inside the craft. Crazy as the story was, the men seemed sincere. On the seventeenth, a photograph of a UFO "occupant" was taken in Falkville, Alabama, by a local chief of police. A woman had reported a UFO landing to the police, and police chief Jeff Greenhaw investigated. He saw no craft, but on his way back noticed in his headlights a tall figure wearing a silvery suit and helmet. Greenhaw failed to communicate with it, then took four photos, two within ten feet. The figure turned and ran away, awkwardly but quickly. Most people dismissed the photos as a hoax, but Greenhaw stood by them, despite a ruined career. On the same night as Greenhaw's experience, a bedroom visitation and abduction was reported in the Midwest. It involved levitation, sophisticated instrumentation, a physiological exam on table, a human being working with aliens, and what was later termed the "mindscan" procedure.[26]

Perhaps the most amazing UFO report came the following night. Just after 11 P.M. on October 18, a U.S. Army reserve crew was flying a helicopter from Columbus to Cleveland, Ohio. They included Capt. Lawrence Coyne (nineteen years flying experience), Lt. Arrigo Jezzi, Sgt. John Healey, and Sgt. Robert Yanacsek. At 2,500 feet and good visibility, the crew noticed a red light to the west, slowly moving south. They assumed it was probably an F-100 out of Mansfield. Very abruptly, however, the light changed course and began to head right at them. Captain Coyne put the helicopter into emergency evasion in a controlled descent. When he tried to confirm the existence of a craft out of Mansfield, his UHF and VHF frequencies went dead (Mansfield later confirmed there were no aircraft in the area). The red light continued to close, becoming brighter, while the helicopter descended at the rapid speed of two thousand feet per minute.

At 1,700 feet above the ground, the crew saw the object streak in front of, then above, the helicopter. It stopped dead for about ten seconds, filling the entire windscreen. All four crew members saw it clearly: it looked like a gray cigar with a small dome on top. One member thought he saw windows. The red light was still there, in the front of the object, and there was a white light on the side and green one on the bottom. The green light swung around like a searchlight and shone into the cabin, bathing it in green light. The object then accelerated to the west, soon appearing as nothing more than a white light. It made a sharp turn and moved northwest, where it was lost above Lake Erie.

Meanwhile, the helicopter's magnetic compass had been spinning at a rate of four revolutions per minute. More seriously, and for no clear reason, the altimeter showed an altitude of 3,500 feet and a *climbing* ascent of one thousand feet per minute. Yet the stick (for descent) still pointed down. Coyne had not attempted to ascend, but his aircraft climbed to the dangerous altitude of 3,800 feet before he regained control. A few minutes later, radio frequencies returned. A complete inspection the next day found nothing wrong, and the event received a thorough investigation.

By itself, it was an amazing story. It was strengthened, however, by the presence of ground witnesses. A woman, while driving with her four children, claimed to have seen the entire encounter, including the green beam, which she said lit the ground around her.

Philip Klass said the crew misidentified a meteor or fireball and suggested the ground witnesses were lying. Jerome Clark dismissed Klass's theory as "fantastic," since none of the testimony was even remotely consistent with it. "By any standard," wrote Clark, "it is one of the most important UFO events ever recorded." Agreed.[27]

To those willing to look at it, the wave of 1973 effectively refuted the conclusions of the Condon Report. Although it had more "high strangeness" cases than most previous waves, they were reported by credible people. As odd as the cases were, they could not easily be dismissed. Of course, committed skeptics such as Condon remained steadfast. On October 21, he debunked the current sightings to the press and declared his own study of UFOs "was a waste of government money." For the public, however, five years after Condon's study was supposed to have ended fascination with UFOs, such was not the case. A November 1973 Gallup poll revealed that 51 percent of Americans believed UFOs were "real," as opposed to 27 percent who thought they were "imaginary." More startling still, 11 percent claimed to have seen one (the 1966 figure was 5 percent), translating roughly into the astonishing total of *15 million people*. Around this time, it was found that only one out of every twelve "technically trained" UFO witnesses had notified the air force of their sighting—presumably this was while Blue Book was still active. In other words, the UFO phenomenon was many times greater than the official numbers suggested. That much had remained constant since the 1940s.[28]

SUMMARY

In 1969, and into the early 1970s, the American national security state was at its most expansive. This belied a losing effort in Southeast Asia. But while the Vietnam front was being lost and domestic dissent remained widespread, the UFO front appeared to be won. Flying saucers were relegated to a remote corner of cold war history as a curiosity in cultural paranoia and mass hysteria.

The UFO phenomenon, however, did not go away after the Condon Report debunked it. Odd, unexplained, and even fantastic events continued to be reported by sober, reliable people. Although the intense media fixation of 1940s or 1960s was no longer the rule in the 1970s, evidence for the reality of UFOs as something extraordinary, and even alien, did not escape the public.

Nor, it appears, the classified world. JANAP-146 and CIRVIS remained in effect, for example, indicating that UFO reports were still being routed through those channels. Moreover, journalist Howard Blum noted that since 1972, the NSA had been "secretly monitoring and often assessing worldwide allegations of UFO activity." It was mandatory, Blum wrote, to "Flash-report" Fort Meade on all intercepted flying objects; "and these installations are required to track and Flash-report on any signals or electronics intelligence that might have an extraterrestrial origin." In February 1974, the French Defense Minister, Robert Galley, confirmed in a radio interview that his department was very interested in UFO reports and "that it had been interested since the great wave of 1954. . . ." His department's records contained "some baffling radar/visual incidents." The UFO phenomenon was global, Galley said, and he expressed his conviction that "we must regard these phenomena with an attitude of completely open mind. . . . It is undeniable that there are facts that are unexplained or badly explained."[29]

The great advantage to UFO secrecy henceforth was the official deniability that the military now possessed. Previously, those who disbelieved air force denials about UFOs always replied with the unanswerable question: then why investigate UFO reports through Project Blue Book? Now, however, the air force no longer officially investigated UFOs. With Blue Book gone, the last link to official sanction was removed from the UFO problem, and it was taken *in toto* to where the national security elite had always wanted it to be: deep within the classified world.

Conclusion

> Our acceptance of any new concept always seems to pass through three phases: At first, it is declared impossible. Then, as supporting facts accumulate, their interpretation is said to be erroneous. But finally, everybody says blandly, "We knew it all the time."
>
> —Arthur Schopenhauer

From the 1940s to the 1970s, military personnel from the United States and many other nations encountered unidentified flying objects, visually and on radar, sometimes at close range. These instances happened not scores of times, but hundreds of times, perhaps even thousands. Sometimes the encounter was nothing more than a solid radar return of an object moving at an incomprehensible speed, performing impossible maneuvers. Sometimes it included the violation of sensitive airspace. Often it involved the dispatch of one or more jets to intercept the object. At times, crew members claimed to see a metallic, disc-like object, sometimes with portholes, sometimes with lights, frequently engaged in what appeared to be intelligent, evasive maneuvers. In a very few cases, it involved the crash and military retrieval of a UFO. In a few others, it involved injury and even death to military personnel. In the large majority of instances recorded in this book, military personnel who encountered UFOs were adamant that they did not see a natural phenomenon.

This is clearly a serious development, and it was treated as such by those groups we may call the national security state. The CIA, NSA, and all branches of military intelligence received UFO reports and discussed the matter as something of serious concern. There is also evidence, provided by former Blue Book chief Edward Ruppelt, of an "Above Top Secret" group with access to all UFO data, a group that straddled the worlds of government, military, and industry.

At the same time, the military created the fiction, for public consumption only, that the UFO problem was nothing to be concerned about—certainly not the result of little green men. Aided by a heavy-handed official media and culture, it tried to convince the public that the air force's Project Blue Book was the appropriate tool for looking into this purely academic concern. Blue Book was fundamentally a public relations tool, not an investigative body. Throughout its existence, it was under orders to debunk. After 1953, the public had no idea that the best UFO cases usually went elsewhere.

I have tried to show that the cover-up of UFO information is nothing unique. A state capable of conducting terminal mind-control experiments, biological spraying of American cities, illegal mail and cable interceptions, nationwide domestic surveillance by its military, human plutonium and syphilis injections, sundry coups and assassinations, ongoing media manipulation and flat-out public lying on a continual basis, would surely be capable of lying about UFOs, too. Indeed, it was the very institutions involved in such unsavory and subterranean activities that were most interested in maintaining UFO secrecy.

What could they have been so concerned about? As everyone likes to ask, why the secrecy? Surely, if the military truly believed what it said for years about UFOs—that they are usually misidentifications of natural phenomena—it would hardly be interested in the problem. But that is not the case. As we have seen, *objects* have violated restricted airspace, and objects were seen by thousands of witnesses.

The core of the UFO problem comes down to two possible answers. Both are startling, and both difficult to accept, in their own way. The first possibility is that UFOs are the product of a revolutionary, *human*, technological breakthrough. Such rumors have existed for a long time, several of which even trace the development to Hitler's Germany. Without denying the sophistication of the German scientific establishment, such a claim cannot shake the aura of absurdity. The Germans, acknowledged by all to have done the most advanced work during the war in the field of aerodynamics, barely figured out how to reach England with their V-2 rockets. A breakthrough to create flying saucer technology would have involved much more than propulsion technology, materials, and aerodynamics. It would have meant the creation of a viable antigravity craft with nearly unlimited maneuverability and speed. There has never been the slightest shred of evidence, either in the realm of fact or common sense, that points to a German flying saucer.

Could flying saucers have been invented after the war by the Americans, or possibly someone else? As we have seen, this was a distinct possibility mulled over by various groups in the early years. During the wave of 1947, several classified documents expressed the belief that the objects were a secret American, or possibly Soviet, technology. Following the Schulgen memo of late 1947, American military intelligence seriously investigated the Soviet angle and came up empty. The group assigned to the problem in 1948, Project Sign, rejected both explanations. If Soviet, why fly these things over the American heartland? If American, why fly them over cities, where everyone could see them, or over sensitive installations, where they were harassed by our own aircraft? Add on top of this the amazing production levels that would have been necessary to fly so many of these objects, which were seen all over the world. After all, even if one discounts the Foo Fighters of World War Two, what about the sightings over Scandinavia and the rest of Europe in 1946? Were these the result of revolutionary American or Soviet technology?

Looking back from some distance, we can see that the problems of creating a flying saucer were no easier for the Americans or Soviets than they had been for the Germans. Such a breakthrough, so soon after the war, makes no sense. Moreover, it is supported by no evidence. Indeed, even as late as the mid-1950s, research into the creation of artificial gravitational fields, based on electromagnetic principles, was in its infancy. By then, UFOs had been part of the public scenery for a decade. What type of classified project could have been responsible for those sightings?

It is this very issue that makes a study of the early period of UFOs so important. Few people doubt that twenty-first-century aviation technology is capable of awesome feats, some of which might be able to produce "flying saucers." The point is, was such a technology in existence at the mid-twentieth century? All indicators point to a definitive *no*.

That brings us to the second possibility: that UFOs are the product of an alien technology. Without devising *a priori* arguments, let us simply look at the evidence, both historical and technological.

First, the phenomenon has always produced believers among those who have bothered to investigate it. For decades, every official study of UFOs followed the same pattern: extended analysis of the data persuaded researchers that aliens were the most likely explanation, a conclusion that was inimical to those in charge of the study. As early as 1948, Project Sign concluded that flying saucers were probably extraterrestrial. After the UFO project at Wright-Patterson AFB was revitalized in 1952, matters again reached the critical point, and most project members favored an extraterrestrial solution. This, too, ended in failure and dispersion. After 1966, when the air force carefully selected a university to solve the problem once and for all, a near mass resignation ensued, and UFO believers were fired midway through the project.

Within the military, as this study shows, believers in the ET thesis seem to have been widespread, but almost never discussed their views openly. The same can be said for the world of science, at least among those scientists who took the time to familiarize themselves with the problem. Aviation legends Hermann Oberth and William Lear both stated unequivocally their belief that UFOs were extraterrestrial. Navy hero Adm. Delmar Fahrney concurred, and former CIA Director Roscoe Hillenkoetter all *but* stated this. Air Force General Nathan Twining acknowledged in a classified document that the objects were "real, not visionary or fictitious."

There is no lack of important personages who attested to the reality of the UFO phenomenon, nor of the belief that aliens were behind it. But what else is there? Unfortunately, there is no authorized piece of a UFO craft to analyze, although several ought to exist. We know, for example, that objects were recovered as early as 1946, during the Swedish Ghost Rocket wave. Something must also have been recovered near Las Vegas in 1962, most likely at Roswell in 1947, and several other places over the years. None of these pieces are available, however, for obvious reasons.

What remains is photographic evidence, radar/visual evidence, and an enormous mass of witness testimony. Bearing in mind that UFOs *are* objects, they must be explained. Unless one is Philip Klass, how does one explain the Bentwaters-Lakenheath radar/visual encounter of 1956, in which a British fighter was followed by a UFO, seen visually, and tracked on multiple radars? A UFO which, incidentally, was tracked on reliable instrumentation to have traveled in excess of 4,000 mph? How does one explain the McMinnville photographs of 1950? Or police officer Lonnie Zamora's sighting of two aliens in Socorro, New Mexico, in 1964? Or the sighting of a flying saucer by U.S. Senator Richard Russell in 1955? How on Earth to explain the bizarre wave of late 1954, when hundreds of people from Britain to Iran claimed to see diminutive aliens with large heads taking soil samples, and who paralyzed them with beams of light?

The easy thing to do with UFO evidence is to ignore it. Much harder is to confront it, study it, and ask, "Just what does this mean?" If we look at the evidence with no prior positions, no expectations of what are the limits of the possible—if we are purely empirical about the matter—then we can easily conclude that alien visitation is the most probable explanation. Others have found us, or our world, and continue to find this world of interest.

Why should this be so difficult to understand? In fact, it is not. No one doubts our own ability, perhaps soon, to find another planet somewhere that supports life. Nor do most scientists doubt the existence of intelligent life elsewhere. Despite the supposedly impenetrable nature of interstellar space, there are people currently working on breakthroughs in propulsion technology, and even a few qualified scientists who believe that the speed of light may not be the ultimate barrier.

Could it be that others have already found us? I believe they have. How they arrived, I do not know, but I can speculate that they may not be able simply to walk about on our planet's surface and that they may have good reasons for making themselves scarce. I can speculate that others might find the Earth's immense resources and biodiversity to be of great value, something that, despite the possibilities of life in this universe, may yet be special in important ways. These others, whatever they are, could well be genetically engineered, or even to some extent artificially intelligent. They may not, after all, be natural biological organisms. Looking into the next fifty years of our own future, it is not so difficult to imagine things in this way.

Such are some of the possibilities and speculations inherent in the second alternative, that of alien visitation.

What is not speculation is the inability of civilian groups to get anywhere with this issue. NICAP was, by far, the world's most significant civilian UFO organization. It had prominent and active members, connections to Congress and the military, and a director who was determined to end UFO secrecy. The effort lasted a little more than ten years and failed. Perhaps, however, it is unfair to focus on the failures of NICAP. Although it fell short of its ultimate goal—government acknowledgment of the reality of UFOs—NICAP's extended fight for UFO congressional hearings kept the issue alive for another day. Moreover, NICAP, along with other organizations such as APRO, developed the core of serious UFO researchers who continued in their work for decades afterward.

A few words about Donald Keyhoe are in order. There is no question that Keyhoe was the most important UFO researcher, ever. Only James McDonald came close, but even McDonald's impact fell short when compared to that of the Major. It is not simply that Keyhoe wrote five books, along with various articles, about flying saucers and cover-ups. It is not simply that he was the driving force behind the world's most important civilian UFO organization. It is that Keyhoe, nearly by himself, opened up the field of UFO research and made it possible for others to follow. Consider the situation of the 1950s had there been no Donald Keyhoe. In 1949, his article in *True* magazine not only brought the issue of flying saucers into the public domain but introduced the idea of a military cover-up. His books in 1950, 1953, 1955, 1960, and 1973 provided an enormous amount of information, much of which was either leaked or even declassified solely for his use. In 1952, the year that UFOs seemingly engulfed America, Keyhoe was there, writing about events and forcing out information. He described the outlines of the Robertson Panel within months of its occurrence.

When Edward Ruppelt produced what some think is the best book ever on UFOs in 1956, much of what he wrote followed the path that Keyhoe had laid out. It is hard to imagine Ruppelt even writing his book at all, had not Keyhoe already written *three*. Would the conservative Ruppelt have been the first to describe the military concern about UFOs if Keyhoe had not already done so? Unlikely. To some extent, it is even possible to imagine Ruppelt's book as a kind of corrective, or even damage control, to the information that Keyhoe had placed in the public domain. Had there been no Donald Keyhoe, the UFO problem would have taken many more years, if ever, to reach a significant level of public acknowledgment.

Considering his importance to the field of UFO research, it is remarkable that Keyhoe has become, in the years since his death, almost a forgotten entity. His books are long out of print, so the general public knows nothing of him. Even UFO researchers, while giving him lip service as an important figure, almost never footnote his books, which indicates that they probably do not read them. Indeed, several writers have criticized, and therefore dismissed, Keyhoe as sensationalistic or gullible. As I mentioned at various points in this book, part of that had to do with Keyhoe's style as a writer. The tone of his books made it appear that the tension around the UFO problem was such that the walls could come down at any moment. But this is a forgivable fault, especially considering the culture of 1950s America, fraught with real cold war fears, and a legitimate concern about UFOs. It is the content of his books, however, that make him so important. It is not possible to do justice to the UFO problem of the 1950s and 1960s without a detailed study of Keyhoe, and yet this is what the vast majority of UFO writers have failed to do. The day will come when Keyhoe's reputation is reestablished for what it ought to be: as the man who pried open the UFO problem for the public and ended the military monopoly.

Despite Keyhoe, of course, it is within the national security apparatus, and not among civilians, where most of the pieces to this puzzle exist. UFOs have national security implications, if for no other reason than that they have involved the military personnel of many nations. The subject is therefore subject to secrecy protocols, a situation that has existed for over fifty years, and is unlikely to end any time soon. During the period under review in this volume, the military struggled to submerge its involvement with the UFO problem. The existence of Project Blue Book until 1969, however, had prevented this from being complete, and NICAP used Blue Book, with some success, as a kind of wedge to obtain more information. That wedge was gone after 1969, but for a period of about ten years (1975 to 1985), the Freedom of Information Act also provided an effective tool to get at the UFO problem. Unfortunately, changes during the Reagan era have since limited its usefulness, and the military dimension to the UFO problem remains locked away within the classified world.

Some believe this is as it ought to be. Can the public really handle the truth about aliens? If the presence of others constitutes a threat to humanity, for example, what could the average person even do about it? There are those who believe that secrecy about UFOs is in the public's best interest. Whatever the value of this sentiment—which I do not share—the "public interest" has never been the main concern of those making the decisions. Ultimately, a national security apparatus exists not to protect the public but itself. The attachment of Americans to the fiction of a representative government, or— God forbid—a democracy, has clouded their ability to see their society for what it is: an oligarchy that uses the forms of democracy to appease and distract the public. Whether or not this is the best solution to organizing millions of people into a body politic, it remains folly to imagine that an oligarchy is not concerned with maintaining its position, to the exclusion of all else.

If we accept the reality of an alien presence, as the UFO evidence suggests, we must be willing to consider that presence as a threat. The record of military encounters with UFOs suggests that this is the case. Since the public is completely unprepared to meet this threat, one can only hope that those groups which have been dealing with it will act in the public interest. During the period under review in this study, those groups did not always work in the public interest when it came to other matters. There is little reason to believe it was, or is, any different regarding an alien presence.

Since the 1970s, the subject of UFOs has become more complex. Encounters are as widespread as ever, and even more plentiful than in the early years. At the same time, UFOs have received a thoroughly schizophrenic cultural treatment. Within popular culture, UFOs and aliens possess a caché they never had during the cold war. Yet, the bastions of "official culture"— academia, mainstream media, government, and the elements of national security—continue to ignore the subject or else treat it as a joke. One can plainly see that neither *ABC Nightly News* nor the *American Historical Review* deems the subject worthy of analysis.

Among organizations studying UFOs, the situation is one of extreme division, far more so than in the simple days of NICAP, APRO, and Blue Book. Throughout most of the century's last three decades, very little effort was expended by the larger organizations either to end government UFO secrecy or, it appears, to reach the public with a coherent message. Instead, they have spent their efforts squirreling away huge amounts of data for . . . who knows what end?

In addition to these, there now exist organizations that serve in a kind of professional debunking capacity. The military and intelligence community continue to show myriad connections with UFO organizations, and several instances of UFO disinformation planted by intelligence personnel are known. The result has been three decades of fragmentation and perennial wheel-spinning. How can one make sense out of such confusion?

One way is by remembering that UFOs have continued to intersect with the militaries of the world. Unauthorized airspace violations by unknown vehicles continue to occur; attempted interceptions continue to take place; secrecy orders are as severe as ever. For all of our sophisticated, secret, technology (yet another element to the confusion), these objects do not appear to be under our control. Through the cultural static, that signal is clear.

But that is the subject for another book.

Appendix

TABLE OF MILITARY UFO ENCOUNTERS

This table is by no means comprehensive. Most likely, it describes only a small fraction of encounters between military personnel and UFOs, and only those that appear in this book. It does not include the many additional UFO sightings that were investigated by military or intelligence personnel. The sharp drop-off in reported military encounters during the 1960s probably has as much to do with improved control over the release of information as anything else.

Sightings designated by an asterisk (*) indicate encounters by the military of countries other than the U.S. Of the 285 military encounters in this table, 244 were American, 41 non–American. Of course, several of the sightings were officially explained, although many of the explanations were threadbare.

Abbreviations: R/V—radar/visual cases; EM—electromagnetic effects; ASV—Air Space Violation.

DATE	PLACE	DESCRIPTION
*9-41	Indian Ocean	Greenish globe
2-25-42	Los Angeles, CA	Multiple UFOs; anti-aircraft fire.
*2-26-42	Timor Sea	Illuminated disk; terrific speed.

DATE	PLACE	DESCRIPTION
*3-42	Zuiter Zee, Holland	Luminous object closely following plane; fired rounds.
8-12-42	Pacific Ocean	Large formation; no wings; not Japanese planes.
8-29-42	Columbus, MS	Two round reddish objects; extreme maneuverability.
3-44	Carlsbad, NM	Fast, glowing green object; lit cockpit.
8-44	Sumatra	Pulsing spherical object paces bomber, maneuvers.
11-44	Austria	Amber-color disc paces bomber.
1-45	Germany	Three red-white lighted objects pace fighter.
1-45	France	Pilot paced by object that zooms into sky.
3-45	Aleutian Islands	Object rises from ocean, circles ship, departs.
8-28-45	Iwo Jima	Three bright objects pace transport; EM effects.
1-16-47	North Sea	Long chase of UFO; evasive maneuvers.
2-28-47	Lake Meade, NV	Formation of discs.
6-47	Oak Ridge Nuc. Fac.,TN	ASV; photographs confiscated.
6-28-47	Lake Meade, NV	F-51 pilot sees formation of five or six circular objects.
6-28-47	Maxwell AFB, AL	Four AF officers see fast, bright, zigzagging light in sky.
6-29-47	White Sands, NM	Silvery disc seen by three scientists.

DATE	PLACE	DESCRIPTION
6-30-47	Grand Canyon, AZ	Navy pilot sees two fast, gray objects, possible landing.
7-4-47	Seattle, WA	Coast Guard personnel photographs UFO.
7-4-47	Roswell, NM	Possible UFO crash/retrieval.
7-8-47	Muroc Air Field	Four separate sightings of metallic, disc-shaped craft.
Sum. 47	Pittsburg, KS	Navy commander sees disc-shaped craft.
8-47	Media, PA	AF pilot sees disc hover and speed away.
8-4-47	Bethel, AK	Large, smooth object seen by pilot and copilot; forwarded to ADC.
8-14-47	Guam U.S.	Personnel see small, fast, zig-zagging crescent-shaped object.
Late 8-47	Rapid City AFB, SD	AF major sees twelve glowing, elliptical silent objects.
10-20-47	Wright-Patterson AFB, OH	Two cigar-shaped craft seen near the base.
1-8-48	Near Godman AFB, KY	AF captain dies while chasing UFO; possible balloon.
4-5-48	White Sands, NM	Navy personnel track disc with extreme maneuvers.
5-48	—	AF C-47 transport plane buzzed by three objects.
Sum. 48	Goose Bay, Labrador	Multiple radar tracking of target; extreme speed, etc.
10-1-48	Fargo, ND	F-51 pilot "dogfight" with small, flat circular UFO.

DATE	PLACE	DESCRIPTION
10-15-48	Cache, Japan	R/V; F-61 aircraft encounters multiple UFOs.
11-1-48	Goose Bay, Labrador	Army radar tracking of high-speed object.
11-6-48	Japan	Radar tracking of UFOs in "dogfight."
11-18-48	Near Andrews AFB, MD	Dogfight with AF pilot; extreme maneuverability.
11-23-48	Fursten-Felbruck AFB, Ger	R/V; attempted intercept; evasive action.
12-5-48	Near Albuquerque, NM	C-47 pilot sees huge green fireball appear to maneuver.
12-12-48	Near Los Alamos, NM	Silent green fireball seen by Dr. La Paz; not meteor.
1-30-49	Near Kirtland AFB, NM	Green fireball; hundreds of witnesses.
4-6-49	White Sands, NM	Several apparent sightings.
4-24-49	White Sands, NM	Metallic, elliptical object, extreme speed, tracked, etc.
5-22-49	Hanford Nuc. Fac., WA	R/V ASV; F-82 scrambled; evasive action
6-49	Oak Ridge Nuc. Fac.,TN	ASV
6-10-49	White Sands, NM	Two round white UFOs maneuver around a missile.
7-3-49	Longview, WA	Navy commander, others, see disc pass above air show.
9?-49	"Key atomic base," (NM?)	Radar of five objects at tremedous speed and altitude.
11-11-49	Straits of Hormuz	USN commander, others, see "light wheel" in water.

DATE	PLACE	DESCRIPTION
1-22-50	Kodiak, AK	Multiple R/V by Navy personnel; near collision; EM.
2-1-50	Tucson, AZ	B-29 pilot follows fireball near Monthan AFB.
2-22-50	Boca Chica Naval AS, FL	R/Vs of two glowing objects; failed intercept.
3-8-50	Dayton, OH	R/Vs of bright metallic disc; failed intercept.
3-9-50	Selfridge AFB, MI	Multiple radar, no visuals, of object at extreme speed.
3-16-50	Naval AS, Dallas, TX	Disc approaches B-36 from below, hovers, speeds away.
4-27-50	White Sands, NM	Inconclusive photograph of object streaking across sky.
5-29-50	White Sands, NM	Object tracked by two theodolite stations; movie footage.
6-24-50	Near Los Angeles, CA	Navy transport plane sees UFO pace airliner.
7-11-50	Osceola, AR	R/V of domed disc passing in front of Navy personnel.
7-30?-50	Hanford Nuc. Fac., WA	Objects seen over facility.
9-21-50	Near Otis AFB, MA	Object tracked on radar, overtakes two F-86s; no visuals.
10-12-50	Oak Ridge Nuc. Fac., TN	Wave of at least sixteen sightings in three weeks begins now.
11-7-50	—	Dogfight with light that circles aircraft several times.
12-50	Near Inchon, Korea	Navy crews see two fast, smoke-trailing objects hit water.

DATE	PLACE	DESCRIPTION
12-50	Cheyenne, WY	AF officer reports metallic UFO.
12-6-50	Laredo, TX	Possible UFO crash/retrieval.
1951	Germany	UFOs outmaneuver pilot/future astronaut Gordon Cooper.
1-51	Korea	Twenty-four UFO cases reported by military in next fifteen months.
1-16-51	Artesia, NM	Gen. Mills-Navy personnel see two disc-shaped objects.
2-10-51	Near Iceland	Near collision between Navy plane and large UFO.
2-14-51	Alamogordo, NM	AF pilots see flat, round, white object hovering.
6-1-51	Wright-Patterson AFB, OH	Base official sees disc-shaped object turn sharply.
7-9-51	Dearing, GA	F-51 pilot sees fast, disc-shaped object approach.
7-14-51	Near White Sands, NM	R/V of fast-moving UFO; probable movie footage, lost.
8 & 9-51	Sandia AFB, NM	Several ASVs by "large wing" craft.
8-26-51	Washington State	AF radar tracks object at 900 mph on two sets.
9-10-51	Fort Monmouth, NJ	R/V of metallic, disc-shaped object at 900 mph.
9-23-51	March AFB, CA	Four F-86s attempt intercept metallic, high-altitude UFO.
10-51	Korea	Fourteen ships track object circling fleet; extreme speed, etc.
10-10-51	Near Minneapolis, MN	Gen. Mills-Navy personnel track fast UFOs for two days.

DATE	PLACE	DESCRIPTION
*1-1-52	North Bay, Canada	Large object circles, maneuvers over RCAF base.
1-20-52	Fairchild AFB, WA	Large, spherical object approaches at tremendous speed.
1-21-52	Mitchell AFB, NY	Navy pilot chases dome-shaped object, outdistanced.
1-22-52	North Alaska	Multiple radar UFO; three F-94s intercept; near collision.
1-29-52	Korea	Two B-29s paced by "huge ball of fire."
3-29-52	Misawa, Japan	Small disc maneuvers between two F-86s and T-6.
4-52	Near Hawaii	UFOs circle planes carrying Navy Sec. & Adm. Radford.
4-17-52	Nellis AFB, NV	Base personnel see large group of circular objects.
5-1-52	Davis-Monthan AFB, AZ	B-36 crew, others, see two round objects overtake aircraft.
5-1-52	George AFB, CA	Five witness five daylight discs; extreme maneuverability.
5-52	Near Alexandria, VA	UFO sighting by "one of the top people" in CIA.
5-31-52	Chorwon, Korea	Object descends, climbs, reverses course; failed intercept.
6-18-52	California	Object paces B-25 for thirty minutes.
6-19-52	Goose Bay, Labrador	R/V of red-lighted object approach, climb, disappear.
6-21-52	Oak Ridge Nuc. Fac., TN	R/V ASV, intercept and near collisions.

DATE	PLACE	DESCRIPTION
6-22-52	Korea	Small object low over airstrip; extreme maneuverability.
7-1-52	Fort Monmouth, NJ	R/V of two objects hovering and speeding away.
7-2-52	Tremonton, UT	Naval aviation photographer captures UFOs on 16mm.
7-5-52	Hanford Nuc. Fac.,WA	ASV; round, flat object hovers over WA facility.
7-12-52	Montrose Beach, CA	AF officer, others, see large red object reverse course.
7-12-52	Hanford Nuc. Fac., WA	ASV; two yellow globes over facility.
7-16-52	Salem, MA	U.S. Coast Guard seaman photographs four brilliant lights.
7-18-52	Patrick AFB, FL	Four lights near field; exceptional maneuverability.
7-19-52	Washington, DC	R/Vs of UFOs over Capitol; attempted intercepts.
7-20-52	Washington, DC	AF tracks objects at 900 mph; extreme maneuvers, etc.
7-20-52	Alexandria, VA	Army officer sees red, cigar-shaped object hover, depart.
7-23-52	Near Boston, MA	Bluish-green object easily evades pursuing F-94.
7-24-52	Sierra Nevada	Two AF colonels in B-25 see three metallic craft at 1,000 mph.
7-26-52	California	Jet chases unidentified light.
7-26-52	Naval AS, Key West, FL	Hundreds see UFO with red light; ship follows it to sea.

DATE	PLACE	DESCRIPTION
7-26-52	Washington, DC	R/Vs of dozen UFOs over the Capitol; F-94s scrambled.
7-29-52	Los Alamos, NM	ASV; metallic object, 360E turn; evades interceptors.
7-29-52	Albuquerque, NM	AF officer sees rapid, elliptical light.
7-29-52	Walker AFB, NM	Weather officer, others, see fast UFOs through theodolite.
7-29-52	Michigan	F-94s attempt intercept of fast-moving UFO; R/Vs.
8-1-52	Yaak, MT	R/Vs at Air Defense Command radar station.
8-1-52	Bellefontaine, OH	R/Vs; two F-86s scrambled, out maneuvered; movie film.
8-3-52	Near Hamilton AFB, CA	R/V of two huge discs; F-86s scrambled; zoom away.
8-5-52	Haneda AFB, Japan	R/V; hovers over base, extreme speed; divides into three units.
8-20-52	Congeree AFB, SC	Air Defense Command radar tracks UFO at 4,000 mph.
8-22-52	Elgin, IL	AF jets chase pulsating yellow light.
8-24-52	Hermanas, NM/El Paso, TX	F-84 pilot sees two disc-shaped objects in both regions.
*9-19-52	Topcliffe Airfield, UK	ASV by silver, spherical UFO; jet scrambled; visuals.
*9-20-52	North Sea	Silver, spherical UFO appears during NATO exercises.
*9-21-52	North Sea	Silver, spherical UFO tracked by RAF jets; failed intercept.

DATE	PLACE	DESCRIPTION
*9-24-52	North Sea	RAF pilot gets close to silver, spherical, rotating UFO.
9-26-52	Azores	USAF personnel report strange green lights approaching.
9-30-52	Edwards AFB, CA	Two discs hovering and darting, multiple witnesses.
10-13-52	Oshima, Japan	AF pilot and engineer see UFO in clouds speed away.
10-29-52	Hempstead, NY	UFO seen by pilots of two F-94s; extreme acceleration.
11-25-52	Panama Canal Zone	Air Defense Command radar tracks two UFOs.
11-26-52	Goose Bay AFB, Labrador	F-94 chases disc-shaped UFO.
12-4-52	Laredo, TX	F-51 near collision with lighted UFO; extreme speeds.
12-6-52	Near Galveston, TX	B-29 near collision with UFO; converges with "mother ship."
12-15-52	Goose Bay AFB, Labrador	Ground crews track UFO near base.
12-29-52	Japan	USAF personnel; ground and airborne R/Vs of UFO.
1-9-53	Japan	F-94 attempted interception of UFO tracked on radar.
1-9-53	Santa Ana, TX	B-29 pilots see rapid, unidentified lights in formation.
1-28-53	Moody AFB, GA	R/V; F-86 pilot sees light change color/shape and divide.
1-29-53	Conway, SC	AF intelligence officer sees gray disc; fires shots.

DATE	PLACE	DESCRIPTION
1-29-53	Presque Isle, ME	F-94, two other fighter aircraft, see dark gray, oval UFO.
2-1-53	Terre Haute, IN	T-33 pilot reports UFO.
2-6-53	Rosalia, WA	B-36 pilot sees unknown object circling and flashing light.
2-7-53	Korea	R/V; F-94 pilot sees bright object change speeds, pull away.
2-11-53	North Africa	C-119 paced by unknown object.
2-13-53	Fort Worth, TX	R/V by B-36 of several UFOs.
2-16-53	Anchorage, AK	Reddish UFO paces USAF transport plane.
5-21-53	Kingman, AZ	Possible UFO crash/retrieval.
7-19-53	Oak Ridge Nuc. Fac., TN	Silent black object; great acceleration; joined by two others.
7-26-53	Perrin AFB, TX	Sixteen-minute sighting of seven UFOs.
Sum. 53	Ernest Harmon AFB, Can.	Two F-94s pursue UFO; one crashes; unconfirmed.
8-1-53	Sequoia-Kings National Park., CA	USAF fighters try to force disc-shaped UFO to land.
8-5-53	Rapid City, SD-Bismarck, ND	R/V; extended encounter; F-84s scrambled.
8-6-53	Naval Air Station, HI	R/V; seventy-five lighted objects, hovering, maneuvering.
8-9-53	Moscow, ID	Large glowing disc; three F-86s scrambled, outmaneuvered.
8-20-53	Castle AFB, CA	TB-29 crew sees gray oval object; buzzes plane; separates.

DATE	PLACE	DESCRIPTION
8-27-53	Greenville, MS	AF pilot, others, see "meandering light" for fifty minutes.
8-28-53	San Rafael, CA	Report to JCS, CIA, NSA of fourteen silent oval objects.
*11-11-53	London, UK	R/V of large, metallic object; failed intercept; near collision.
11-23-53	Soo Locks, MI	F-89 pursues UFO over Lake Michigan, disappears.
12-7-53	Fort Meade, MD	Army personnel see UFO.
12-24-53	El Cajon, CA	Two navy jet pilots see ten silver, oval objects for five minutes.
12-31-53	Quantico Marine Base, VA	USMC personnel see unidentified object land and take off.
2-11-54	Near Carswell AFB, TX	R/V; silent "mystery aircraft"; report to JCS, CIA, NSA.
3-8-54	Laredo AFB, TX	Pilot reports glowing red object at tremendous speed.
3-24-54	Florida	USMC pilot pursues object with extreme maneuverability.
4-22-54	San Nicholas Island, CA	American military personnel see cigar-shaped object land.
4-29-54	Fort Meade, MD	Large, bright object moves straight, shoots straight up.
5-6-54	Washington, DC	Radar tracking of UFOs; fighters scrambled.
5-13-54	Washington, DC	R/V of object fifteen miles high; exceptional maneuverability.
5-13-54	Washington, DC	Two large glowing oval objects approach airport.

DATE	PLACE	DESCRIPTION
5-24-54	Dallas, TX	Four Nat'l. Guard pilots out-maneuvered by sixteen UFOs.
5-24-54	Wright-Patterson AFB, OH	Photograph of UFO from RB29 aircraft.
6-12-54	Baltimore, MD	Jets scrambled, cannot reach large, hovering craft.
6-14-54	Washington-Baltimore area	Jets scrambled, cannot reach large, hovering craft.
6-23-54	Near Dayton, OH	F-51 pilot paced by "brilliant white light."
6-26-54	AEC Plant, ID	ASV; hovering object; intense light; rises at great speed.
6-26-54	Near Columbus, OH	ADC tracks UFO, seen by sixty airline passengers.
6-29-54	Near Goose Bay, Labrador	Airliner sees six small objects, "mother" craft; jet scrambled.
6-30-54	Brookley AFB, AL	R/V UFO sighting.
7-1-54	Walesville, NY	F-94 pursues UFO; intense heat forces ejection; fatalities.
7-3-54	Near Albuquerque, NM	R/V of nine green spheres.
8-12-54	Maxwell AFB, AL	ASV by "saucer-like" object; reported to NSA.
8-28-54	Oklahoma City, OK	Fifteen UFOs tracked on radar; jets scrambled, outdistanced.
*9-17-54	Rome, Italy	Italian AF radar tracks disc-like object on radar.
9-21-54	Azores Islands U.S.	Guard sees UFO land, human occupant, vertical take-off.

<u>Date</u>	<u>Place</u>	<u>Description</u>
*10-4-54	England	RAF Meteor jet buzzed by UFO.
*10-5-54	Behnay, Egypt	Egyptian military officer photographs "rotating saucer."
*10-14-54	Southend, U.K.	RAF Meteor near collision with silver disc-shaped object.
*11-21-54	Santa Maria, Brazil	Air base operator, others see hovering, dark object.
*12-15-54	Australia	R/V; Royal Australian Navy pilot paced by two UFOs.
1-14-55	California	Unknown object hits wing of B-47; plane lands safely.
6-4-55	Melville Sound, Canada	R/V; RB-47 tracks silver, metallic object; movie footage.
6-7-55	Elison AFB, AK	RB-47 tracks UFO on radar; experiences radar jamming.
7?-55	Pepperell AFB, Canada	Forty-nine-minute R/V of UFO; CIA report.
8-23-55	Cincinnati, OH	Three white spheres; jets scrabled; objects depart rapidly.
10-4-55	Near Kiev, USSR	U.S. Senator Richard Russell, two aides see two UFOs from a train.
10-55	Near Lovington, NM	Unknown object hits B-47; one survivor.
11-20-55	Oak Ridge Nuclear Facility, TN	ASV by two shiny, elliptical objects.
12-11-55	Near Jacksonville, FL	Navy jets in dogfight with round, reddish UFO.
1-15-56	Pusan, Korea	Glowing object sinks into sea; seen by U.S. military police.

DATE	PLACE	DESCRIPTION
4-8-56	Near Syracuse, NY	R/V; military orders commercial pilot to pursue UFO.
7-19-56	Naval AS, Hutchinson, KS	R/V of teardrop-shaped UFO.
7-22-56	Pixley, CA	C-131-D hit by object; pilot radioes it is a "flying saucer."
*8-13-56	Bentwaters & Lakenheath, UK	R/V sightings over NATO bases; intercept attempts.
*9-4-56	—	Danish radar tracks several objects at 1,800 mph.
10-26-56	Near Okinawa	Two American jets collide in process of tracking UFOs.
late 56	Castle AFB, CA	R/V of disc-shaped UFO; two jets attempt intercept.
12-56	"Far East"	R/V of round UFO by two USAF jet pilots; radar jamming.
11-24-56	Pierre, SD	Several days; jets scrambled; police chase of UFO.
1-21-57	APO	Army Base Intelligence personnel see large shiny object over base.
3-23-57	Long Beach, CA	R/V of several UFOs; F-89 pursues; many witnesses.
7-17-57	Mississippi to Oklahoma	R/V; RB-47 followed by UFO for 800 miles.
*7-24-57	Kouril Islands	Soviet anti-aircraft batteries fire on luminous UFOs.
*9-4-57	—	Four Portuguese jet pilots report bright maneuvering UFOs.
9-19-57	—	R/V by B-25 and ground crew; radar jamming.

DATE	PLACE	DESCRIPTION
*11-57	Near Alice Springs, Australia	RAF team has fifteen-minute, close-up UFO sighting.
*11-1-57	South Africa	South African jet pilot pursues high, hovering, craft.
11-2-57	Canadian, TX	Military witnesses see submarine-shaped object on ground.
11-3-57	White Sands, NM	Army patrol sees bright UFO descend to ground level.
*11-4-57	Fort Itaipu, Brazil	Circular UFO badly burns two sentries; U.S. investigation.
11-4-57	Alamogordo, NM	Elliptical UFO stalls car of White Sands engineer.
11-5-57	Gulf of Mexico	R/V by Coast Guard of high-speed UFO; stops in midair.
11-13-57	Crownsville, MD	Army confiscates exploded pieces of possible UFO.
12-12-57	Tokyo, Japan	R/V of multicolored UFO; jets scrambled.
*1-16-58	Trindade Isle, Brazil	Members of Naval survey ship photograph UFO.
3-8-58	Korea	USAF radar tracks slowly descending UFO.
*4-11-58	Jutland	Danish pilot sees UFO formation which takes evasive action.
Sum. 58	Unnamed AFB in SW	Two maneuvering UFOs evade jet interceptors.
9-8-58	Offut AFB, NB	AF Major, others, see rocket-like UFO with satellites.
11-3-58	Minot, ND	Sergeant & medic see two maneuvering UFOs; one explodes.

DATE	PLACE	DESCRIPTION
*3-59	Kolobreg, Poland	Polish soldiers see triangular object emerge from water.
4-1-59	Near Tacoma, WA	C-118 collides with unknown object, no survivors.
*6-59	Buenos Aires, Argentina	Navy traps a large object in harbor; not a sub.
9-24-59	Redmond, OR	Six jets attempt intercept of UFO; near collision; witnesses.
*7-1-60	Canada	Canadian authorities possibly recover "very strange metal."
Sum. 60	Orbit of the Earth	"Mystery satellite" tracked, photographed by Grumman.
1-10-61	Cape Canaveral, FL	UFO follows Polaris missile during launch.
1-22-61	Eglin AFB, FL	Metallic UFO approaches, makes U-turn, speeds away.
*1-29-62	Netherlands	Royal Dutch AF pilot in F-86 fires on UFO.
4-18-62	Near Las Vegas, NV	Probable crash/retrieval of UFO.
4-30-62	Low Earth Orbit	X-15 pilot photographs five or six UFOs at fifty-mile altitude.
*5-12-62	Argentina	Two Navy pilots see illuminated object rise, split in two sections.
7-17-62	Low Earth Orbit	X-15 pilot, 58 miles high, sees gray object forty feet away.
6-15-63	Off Venezuelan coast	Navy crewman sees luminous disk.
*11-12-63	Off Argentine coast	UFO follows Argentine naval vessel; electronic interference.

DATE	PLACE	DESCRIPTION
*11-21-63	North Sea	R/V of flashing red light passing near Scottish vessel.
*12-63	England	Two RAF airmen see dome-shaped object appear to land.
4-30-64	Holloman AFB, NM	Possible landing of UFO at the base, unconfirmed.
5-22-64	White Sands, NM	Radar tracking of UFO.
5-29-64	White Sands, NM	R/V of two "football shaped" UFOs.
1-5-65	Wallops Island, VA	Large disc over NASA station; radar tracks at 6,000 mph.
1-5-65	Naval Air Test Center, MD	Two UFOs on radar; one makes sharp turn at 4,800 mph.
1-11-65	Washington, DC	Army R/V of twelve to fifteen oval UFOs; jets outdistanced.
1-12-65	Near Blaine AFB, WA	Radar tracks thirty-foot object that buzzes car of gov. official.
2-11-65	North Pacific Ocean	F-169 paced by three huge objects; R/V; extreme speed.
6-4-65	Outer space	*Gemini 4* mission sighting of "weird object" with "arms."
*6-19-65	Antarctica	Chilean military sees large, lens-shaped UFO.
*7-2-65	Antarctica	English base reports UFO for eight to ten minutes.
*7-3-65	Antarctica	Argentine base reports large UFO; radio interference.
*7-14-65	Australian space station	Object descends, interfering with tracking of *Mariner IV*.
8-2-65	Several midwestern states	Many UFO visuals and radar, including several AFBs.

Date	Place	Description
*9-65	Argentina	Argentine navy reports fifteen UFO incidents since 1963.
1965	Unnamed AFB	R/V of object; hovers over base; extreme acceleration.
1965	Portsmouth Naval Base, NH	Object hovers over base before extremely fast departure.
12-9-65	Kecksburg, PA	Possible crash/retrieval of UFO.
3-14-66	Selfridge AFB, MI	Radar tracking of objects; extreme speed & maneuverability.
3-23-66	Temple, OK	Employee of Sheppard AFB sees UFO blocking road.
4-17-66	Ohio and Pennsylvania	Possible jet interception of UFO; long police chase.
6-23-66	Albuquerque, NM	Apollo space project engineer, others, see fast UFO.
8-20-66	Donnybrook, ND	Border officer sees domed UFO maneuver, zoom away.
8-24-66	Minot AFB, ND	R/V of landed UFO; strike team inspects; four hours.
*9-21-66	Prince Edward Is., Canada	Eight RCAF members see bright object stop, land, ascend.
3-5-67	Minot AFB, ND	R/V of UFO over missile site; NORAD; strike team; jets.
3-20-67	Malmstrom AFB, MT	Disruption of missile circuitry by UFO.
3-21-67	Brazil	Brazilian military craft paced by red, glowing object.
3-24-67	Near Malmstrom AFB, ND	Reported UFO landing, investigation.

DATE	PLACE	DESCRIPTION
*3-67	Cuba	Two Cuban jets attempt UFO intercept; one "disintegrates."
*6-24-67	Argentina & Uruguay	Thousands of witnesses, including military, of UFOs.
9-1-67	Edwards AFB	Possible base UFO sighting; official obstruction and denials.
9-6-67	Lake Superior	Multiple radar of twenty targets, 2,000 mph; right angles; denials.
*10-4-67	Shag Harbor, Nova Scotia	Bright object enters water; RC Navy investigation.
9-14-72	West Palm Beach, FL	Two F-106s scrambled to intercept glowing UFO.
10-18-73	Mansfield, OH	U.S. Army reserve helicopter crew; near collision; EM effects.

Endnotes

Introduction

1. The Learning Channel 1996.
2. U.S. Air Force Fact Sheet 95–03.
3. Hall 1964, 44, 138; Keyhoe 1960, 255; 1973, 40–44.
4. See McCoy 1991, Dinges 1991, U.S. Senate 1989, Mills 1986, and Cockburn and St. Clair 1998. See also Webb 1998. Webb's 1996 expose on the subject, published in the *San Jose Mercury News*, essentially got him run of town. Within a year, he had lost his job and was working in the nonprofit sector. (On this sad topic, see Osborn 1998.)
5. See Bernstein 1977, 55, 67, Overbeck n.d., and Saunders 2000.
6. On this topic, see Hansen's very excellent *The Missing Times* 2000.
7. Gillmor 1969, 26.
8. Haines 1997.
9. Steiger 1976.
10. http://www.ibmpcug.co.uk/~irdial/bluebook.htm and http://www.parascope.com/articles/0697/bluelist.htm

Chapter 1

1. Anyone interested in the long history of UFOs can consult several useful sources. See Fort 1941; 1997, especially *The Books of Charles Fort* (1941), Vallee 1969, and Tomlinson 1993.
2. Edwards 1966, 38–39.
3. Probably the best account of this remains chapter one of Jacobs's *UFO Controversy* (1975).
4. Roerich 1929.
5. Weiner 1990, 19–20.
6. Cole 1988, 33–34; Thomas 1989, 160; Bamford 1982, 236–241; Donner 1980, 7, 244, 292; Summers 1994, 168–170; Wise 1976, 145–151.

7. Wise and Ross 1964, 97–98; Dulles 1966; Marks 1979, 5.
8. Germann 1995.
9. Clark 1992, 153.
10. Good 1988, 15–17; Fawcett and Greenwood 1984, 238.
11. LePoer Trench 1966, 69; Clark 1992, 153.
12. Clark 1992, 153.
13. Hall 1964, 19.
14. Hall 1964, 19, 30.
15. Stringfield 1977, 9–10.
16. See Jacobs 1975, 35–36; Friedman and Berliner 1992, 2–3; Good 1988, 18–19, 329; Keyhoe 1955, 22; 1960, 39; Clark 1992, 153–154; and Chamberlain 1945. See also UFO Folklore Website, (http://www.qtm.net/~geibdan/newse/foo/index.html).
17. Keyhoe 1955, 22, 182–183.
18. Clark 1992, 168.
19. Department of State 1946; Good 1988, 20; Clark 1992, 170.
20. See Thompson, "The Ghost Rockets of Sweden," at Parascope Website, http://www.parascope.com/nb/cautionarytales03.htm.
21. Vallee 1965, 82–84; Clark 1992, 171; Sanderson 1970, 55.
22. Vallee 1965, 83–84; Flammonde 1976, 128.
23. Flammonde 1976, 129.
24. Good 1988, 20–21; Clark 1992, 171.
25. Clark 1992, 171; Flammonde 1976, 131; Good 1988, 21.
26. Department of State 1946; Good 1988, 21–22.
27. Vallee 1965, 86–88.
28. Good 1988, 22–23; Clark 1992, 169.
29. *Sydney Sun* 1967; Good 1988, 23; Fowler 1981.
30. Clark 1992, 171; *New York Times* 1946; Good 1988, 23; Flammonde 1976, 132.
31. *New York Times* 1946; Clark 1992, 172.
32. Indeed, some writers still hold to the idea that foo fighters were German experimental craft, even though many sightings occurred in the Pacific. See, for example, Birdsall 1992, 32–34.
33. Powers 1979, 28, 46; Wise and Ross 1964, 134.
34. Hunt 1991, 19, 97, 149.
35. Hunt 1991, 22–25, 28–33, 58, 113–115.
36. Wise and Ross 1964, 98; Powers 1979, 31–32.
37. Weiner 1990, 114; Wise and Ross 1964, 98; Powers 1979, 32.
38. Powers 1979, 32; Hunt 1991, 26, 37; Wise and Ross 1964, 98.
39. Powers 1979, 34; Bamford 1982, 242–244; Donner 1980, 276.
40. Keyhoe 1973, 45–46; Hall 1964, 19.
41. U.S. Army 1947a, 151, 154; Keyhoe 1950, 24; Vallee 1965, 89–90.

Chapter 2

1. Randle 1997a, 11; Keyhoe 1950, 24; Vallee 1969, 191; 1965, 24; Hall 1964, 129; *St. Louis Post-Dispatch* 1947; United Press 1947.

2. Strategic Air Command 1949; Hynek 1977, 142–143; Fawcett and Greenwood 1984, 171.

3. See Johnson letter from Project Blue Book files; Arnold and Palmer 1952; Randle 1997, 11–13; Keyhoe 1950, 24; 1953; Jacobs 1975, 36–38; Hynek 1977, 99; Ruppelt 1956, 18, 36–38; Lorenzen and Lorenzen 1976, 238; Friedman 1996, 4–5; and Clark 1992, 216–219; 1998, 58–62.

4. FBI Report from Project Blue Book files; Randle 1997a, 13–15.

5. Keyhoe 1950, 24; Ruppelt 1956, 35–36; Hall 1964, 20; Randle 1997a, 52–53.

6. *St. Louis Post-Dispatch* 1947, Hall 1964, 129.

7. Vallee 1969, 191.

8. *St. Louis Post-Dispatch* 1947; United Press 1947.

9. Keyhoe 1960, 89; Associated Press 1947; United Press 1947.

10. Smith 1947; Good 1988, 253; Hall 1964, 129.

11. *St. Louis Post-Dispatch* 1947; Jacobs 1975, 42.

12. Ruppelt 1956, 19; Randle 1997a, 52; Keyhoe 1960, 39–40.

13. The following do not constitute the sum of Roswell literature but are certainly most influential works and the logical starting point for most readers. Uneven in quality, they are: *The Roswell UFO Crash: What They Don't Want You to Know* (Korff 1997); *UFO Crash at Roswell: The Genesis of a Modern Myth* (Saler, Ziegler, and Moore 1997); *The Day after Roswell* (Corso and Birnes 1997); *The Real Roswell Crashed Saucer Cover–up* (Klass 1997); *The Roswell Report: Case Closed* (McAndrew 1997); *Top Secret/MAJIC* (Friedman 1996); *The Truth About the UFO Crash at Roswell* (Randle and Schmitt 1994); *Roswell in Perspective* (Pflock 1994); "The Naked Truth" (Zechel 1994 [http://www.rmdavis.demon.uk/ufos/nathen/nat22.txt]); *Crash at Corona* (Friedman and Berliner 1992); *UFO Crash at Roswell* (Randle and Schmitt 1991); and *The Roswell Incident* (Berlitz and Moore 1980).

14. Friedman and Berliner 1992, 65; Good 1988, 260; Randle 1997a, 17–50; Randle and Schmitt 1994, 164.

15. Friedman and Berliner 1992, xiii.

16. *Roswell Daily Record* 1947.

17. *St. Louis Post-Dispatch* 1947; Associated Press 1947.

18. FBI 1947a; Randles 1988, 19–20.

19. Randle and Schmitt 1994, 171.

20. Friedman and Berliner 1992, 102–103.

21. Randle 1997a, 38–39.

22. Friedman and Berliner 1992, 84–85

23. Friedman and Berliner 1992, 114–120.

24. Friedman and Berliner 1992, 75.

25. Friedman and Berliner 1992, 76–77.

26. Friedman and Berliner 1992, 121–123.

27. Bitzer 1995.

28. McAndrew n.d.

29. U.S. Air Force 1995; McAndrew 1997.
30. Ruppelt 1956, 37; Hall 1964, 130.
31. Palmer 1967, 179, 185–188.
32. U.S. Army 1947b, Vallee 1965, 91; 1969, 191, Clark 1992, 256–257, Keyhoe 1953, 41; 1960, 89, Ruppelt 1956, 37, Hynek 1977, 95–97, and Hall 1964, 20, 130.
33. Randle 1997a, 51.
34. FBI 1947b.
35. See George A. Filer, "Latest UFO Sightings on Worldwide Upswing" at http://www.jeffrense.com/ufo/flyers112098.htm
36. FBI 1947c; Fawcett and Greenwood 1984, 149–150.
37. From Air Force Base Intelligence Report, "Flying Discs," AFBIR–CO, 30 July 1947, Randle 1997, 52, and UFO Briefing Documents at the International Space Sciences website, http://isso.org/inbox/ubd/case/1947.htm.
38. Air Defense Command 1947; FBI 1947d; Fawcett and Greenwood 1984, 156–158.
39. Jacobs 1975, 41.
40. Hall 1964, 130.
41. Alaska Communication System 1947.
42. U.S. Air Force 1947a.
43. Hynek 1977, 36–41; Vallee 1965, 91.
44. Ruppelt 1956, 39.
45. Randle 1997a, 55.
46. For an unusual and insightful analysis of the Maury Island incident, see Val Germann, "Premonitions of the Future, Support for 'New Revelations' in Early Material: The Arnold Case" (Usenet article [22 April 1996], http://www.alt.paranet.ufo).
47. Palmer 1967, 160.
48. FBI FOIA letters are available from Fair-Witness Project, 4219 W. Olive Street, Suite 247, Burbank, California 91505.
49. See "The Investigation of the Assassination of President John F. Kennedy," Hearings Before the Select Committee on Assassinations of the United States House of Representatives, 95th Congress, 2nd Session. Vol I, 120–121; vol IV, 22–26, 376–383; and vol VI, 257–273. For more information on Crisman and Maury Island, see Thomas 1999; Extractions from CIA file: CRISMAN, Fre Lee, Number OSS/CIA 4250ece, located at Control Records Dispatch, Davenport, Iowa (cited in Marrs 1997, 129; Halbritter n.d.; Covington n.d.); "The Secret Life of Fred Crisman," UFO Magazine 8 (5); Keel 1971, 103–105; and Don Ecker's Crisman Story at the Paranormal Research Primer,
    http://www.tje.net/para/documents/ crisman1.htm.
50. Jacobs 1975, 38; Clark 1992, 246.
51. Fuller 1980, 40–41.
52. Fitch 1947; Thomas 1999, 185.
53. Weaver 1994.
54. Covington n.d.
55. Hoopes and Brinkley 1992, 357.

56. Powers 1979, 38.
57. Air Material Command 1947; Good 1988, 476–478. (Many sources have reprinted the letter in its entirety.)
58. Kevin Randle discusses this point in *Conspiracy of Silence* (1997a, 55).
59. Friedman and Berliner 1992, 59–60.
60. Korff 1997, 171.
61. Hesemann and Mantle 1997, 96.
62. Randle 1997b.
63. Friedman 1990.
64. Friedman 1996, 78–80; Randle 1997b, 36–37.
65. Randle 1997b, 34; Hesemann and Mantle 1997, 97.
66. See Hesemann and Mantle 1997, 100.
67. Friedman 1996, 86–102. See also Greenwood n.d.
68. National Archives, Washington, D.C. 20408, Reply to attention of Military Reference Branch, Subject: Reference Report on MJ-12, To: The Record (22 July 1987). http://madasafish.com/~coscon/cosmicmaj2.htm.
69. Friedman 1996, 96.
70. Keyhoe 1960, 89.
71. U.S. Air Force 1947b.
72. Counter Intelligence Corps 1947; Berlin Command 1947.
73. Ruppelt 1956, 45–46, 49.
74. Jacobs 1975, 44; Randles 1988, 23; Flammonde 1976, 327.
75. Ruppelt 1956, 23.
76. Keyhoe 1973, 82.
77. Jacobs 1975, 40, 46; Ruppelt 1956, 47.

Chapter 3

1. U.S. Army 1948; Jacobs 1975, 44–46; Hall 1964, 130; Hynek 1977, 33; 1972, 169.
2. I am indebted to journalist Leslie Kean and aerial phenomenon researcher Clifford Stone for forwarding to me air force files on the Mantell case. See also Ruppelt 1956, 52, Jacobs 1975, 44–45, Clark 1992, 240–244, Keyhoe 1973, 15–16, Edwards 1966, 90, and Good 1988, 262–263.
3. U.S. Air Force 1948a.
4. Scientific Advisory Board 1948.
5. Keyhoe 1973, 46–47; Hall 1964, 130; Vallee 1965, 92; Ruppelt 1956, 101; Good 1988, 265–266.
6. Hall 1964, 83–84.
7. Keyhoe 1960, 88; Vallee 1965, 94.
8. See Hall 1964, 44, 130, McDonald n.d., Jacobs 1975, 46, 309, Good 1988, 264, Keyhoe 1960, 87–88; 1973, 46; 1953, 33, Edwards 1966, 90, Ruppelt 1956, 61, Randles 1988, 28, and Clark 1992, 82–84.
9. See Aldrich n.d., Ruppelt 1956, 62–63, 67, Keyhoe 1973, 16–17, Hall 1964, 110; 1988, 172, Clark 1992, 138–139, Good 1988, 264, Jacobs 1975, 47, and Randle 1998, 60–61.
10. Aldrich n.d.

11. Fuchs 1974.
12. Hall 1964, 130; 1988, 173, 234–235; Vallee 1965, 94–95; Randles 1988, 28; Clark 1992, 180–182.
13. Hynek 1977, 134–136; Ruppelt 1956, 68; Hall 1964, 130; 1988, 173, 235–236.
14. Hall 1964, 130; 1988, 173, 236–237; Vallee 1965, 95.
15. Ruppelt 1956, 68–69; Hall 1964, 130; 1988, 174, 237; Keyhoe 1953, 34.
16. Keyhoe 1953, 204; Ruppelt 1956, 75–76, 81; Hall 1988, 173–174l Clark 1992, 182–191; Good 1988, 266.
17. Good 1988, 30, 264–265; Friedman and Berliner 1992, 27.
18. Ruppelt 1956, 83–84, 87; Jacobs 1975, 50; Hynek 1977, 33.
19. Keyhoe 1955, 182; Clark 1992, 116–117.
20. Powers 1979, 53; Saunders and Harkins 1968, 129; Winks 1987, 396–397.
21. Cole 1988, 6.
22. Good 1988, 265.
23. Clark 1992, 184.
24. FBI 1949a; Fawcett and Greenwood 1984, xiv, 159–161; Good 1988, 267; Randles 1988, 30.
25. Mandelkorn 1949; Good 1988, 265; Clark 1992, 184–185.
26. Hynek 1977, 17–18; 1972, 179; Jacobs 1975, 47–48.
27. FBI 1949b; CIA 1949; Fawcett and Greenwood 1984, 113–114, 161.
28. Bowers 1949; Good 1988, 330.
29. Clark 1992, 185.
30. Moore n.d., Fawcett and Greenwood 1984, 114–115, Ruppelt 1956, 101, Hall 1964, 2–3, 130; 1988, 174, 238, 324–325, Wilkins 1955, 226, Edwards 1966, 239, Keyhoe 1950, 14, Hynek 1977, 104–105, and Vallee 1965, 96. Keyhoe learned of this event quickly, got the essentials correct, and incorrectly placed it at April 29. He also noted that "two other discs, smaller types, were watched from five observation posts on hills on the proving ground. Circling at incredible speed, the two discs paced an army high–altitude rocket that had just been launched, then speeded up and swiftly outclimbed the projectile." Hall 1988 reprinted the full CIA Report in his appendix.
31. U.S. Air Force 1948b; Hall 1964, 130; Ruppelt 1956, 89–90; Jacobs 1975, 50.
32. Keyhoe 1950, 7–9, 19, 22.
33. Keyhoe 1953, 35–36.
34. Clark 1992, 187–188.
35. Jacobs 1975, 51; Ruppelt 1956, 91–92.
36. See Rogow 1963, 1–7, 16–18, 48, 290–307, 314, 344, Hoopes & Brinkley 1992, 368, 376–378, 406, 413–417, 423, 427, 438–440, 447, 449, 454, 460–467, Borklund 1966, 63, and Simpson 1966, 1–44.
37. Hynek 1977, 141.
38. Hall 1964, 130; 1988, 174–175, 238–239; LePoer Trench 1966, 177.
39. See Flammonde 1976, 329–330, Jacobs 1975, 52, and Hynek 1977, 17, 46, 253, 260. As Hynek pointed out, of the more than 12,000 total UFO reports collected through the end of 1969, only 63 cases were labeled

"Psychological" and only 116 were hoaxes, "most of which were quite easily detected and dismissed."

40. Clark 1992, 188–189; Ruppelt 1956, 76; Flammonde 1976, 330.
41. Rees 1950; Good 1988, 267; Clark 1992, 189.
42. Hall 1988, 176–177; 1964, 130.
43. Jacobs 1975, 53–54; Randle 1997a, 4; Friedman and Berliner 1992, 27; Ruppelt 1956, 94–95; Hall 1964, 130; Keyhoe 1950, 5–6; 1953, 28; 1955, 92; Hynek 1977, 18–19, 260; Flammonde 1976, 330.
44. FBI 1950a; Fawcett and Greenwood 1984, 165–166; Randles 1988, 30–32.
45. Ruppelt 1956, 19, 99–100.
46. Hall 1988, 74–75.
47. Fawcett and Greenwood 1984, 167; Blum 1990, 210.
48. Keyhoe 1950, 13.
49. Fawcett and Greenwood 1984, 170; Howe 1989, 393; Hall 1988, 326.
50. Keyhoe 1950, 10.
51. Keyhoe 1950, 10–12; 1960, 41; Hall 1964, 130.
52. McLaughlin 1950; Ruppelt 1956, 100, 103; Hall 1964, 130; Jacobs 1975, 57; Keyhoe 1960, 41.
53. Keyhoe 1950, 12; Ruppelt 1956, 105–106; Hall 1964, 130.
54. Ruppelt 1956, 106; Hall 1964, 30, 44, 130.
55. Ruppelt 1956, 109; Hall 1964, 131; Hynek 1977, 67–68; *UFO Magazine* 1990.
56. Clark 1992, 238–240; Hynek 1977, 284; Hall 1964, 131; Randles 1988, 157–158.
57. Hynek 1977, 54–55.
58. Hynek 1977, 57.
59. Hall 1964, 31, 131; Keyhoe 1955, 37.
60. Quoted in Good 1988, 267.
61. FBI 1950b; Fawcett and Greenwood 1984, 167–168.
62. CIA 1950; Fawcett and Greenwood 1984, 115–116; Good 1988, 340–341.
63. Ruppelt 1956, 286–287; Hall 1964, 88, 131; Randle 1997a, 117–118; Hynek 1977, 252–253; Clark 1992, 244–246, 253–254.
64. Scully 1950.
65. Lorenzen 1976, 169; Clark 1992, 115, 301–302.
66. From private notes of Wilbert Smith, reprinted with permission from his widow in Good 1988, 397, and letter to William S. Steinman from Dr. Robert I. Sarbacher, Washington Institute of Technology (Oceanographic & Physical Sciences), Palm Beach, Florida 33480 (29 November 1983). See also Good 1988, 413–414 and Clark 1992, 115–116.
67. Keyhoe 1953, 130; Clark 1992, 309–310.
68. Smith 1950; Fawcett and Greenwood 1984, xv; Friedman and Berliner 1992, 47–52.
69. FBI 1950c; Hynek 1977, 68–69, 139–140; Hall 1964, 131; Fawcett and Greenwood 1984, 171–175.
70. FBI 1950d; Fawcett and Greenwood 1984, 175.

71. Friedman and Berliner 1992, 67–68; Hall 1988, 78; Randle 1995, 192–193.
72. Hall 1964, 23, 131.
73. U.S. Air Force 1951; Hall 1988, 239, 328–330; 1964, 131.
74. Keyhoe 1953, 48; Hall 1964, 131; LePoer Trench 1966, 28.
75. Hall 1964, 131; Jacobs 1975, 63.
76. Ruppelt 1956, 133–150; Clark 1992, 230–237; Hall 1964, 131; Vallee 1965, 99; Randle 1997a, 86. Also see Kevin Randle's article in *UFO Magazine* (1993a).
77. Ruppelt 1956, 134–135, 148–149.
78. Ruppelt 1956, 127–129, 155; Jacobs 1975, 64–65; Hall 1964, 131; Clark 1992, 161–163; Good 1988, 269; Wilkins 1955, 226.
79. Keyhoe 1953, 48–49, 256; Ruppelt 1956, 130–132; Hall 1964, 131.
80. Hall 1964, 56, 131; 1988, 240–241; Keyhoe 1953, 49, 255–256.
81. Ruppelt 1956, 154–160; Flammonde 1976, 330–331.

Chapter 4

1. Ruppelt 1956, 26, 162–163; Keyhoe 1953, 128; Hall 1964, 131.
2. Ruppelt 1956, 169–170; Hall 1964, 131.
3. Ruppelt 1956, 174; Hall 1964, 131; Vallee 1965, 100.
4. Ruppelt 1956, 175–176, 182; U.S. Air Force 1952.
5. Ruppelt 1956, 178, 217; Jacobs 1975, 68–69; Flammonde 1976, 331–332; Clark 1992, 272; 1996, 408.
6. Keyhoe 1953, 50–51; Ruppelt 1956, 177; Edwards 1966, 317; Jacobs 1975, 69–71; Hall 1988, 176.
7. Keyhoe 1953, 257; Hall 1964, 5, 132.
8. Hall 1988, 145, 241–242.
9. Keyhoe 1953, 50; 1960, 85–86; 1973, 80.
10. Ruppelt 1956, 184.
11. Hynek 1977, 107, 111–112.
12. Ruppelt 1956, 181.
13. Keyhoe 1953, 51; Ruppelt 1956, 185; Flammonde 1976, 332; Bryan 1956.
14. Ruppelt 1956, 225; Hynek 1977, 87–90.
15. Ruppelt 1956, 190, 192; Jacobs 1975, 72.
16. Keyhoe 1953, 52–53; Flammonde 1976, 332; Hall 1964, 132; Jacobs 1975, 73.
17. Ruppelt 1956, 196–199; Flammonde 1976, 332.
18. Hall 1964, 132; Keyhoe 1953, 52; *UFO Magazine* 1990.
19. Ruppelt 1956, 202–203, 205; Jacobs 1975, 74; Vallee 1965, 100.
20. Ruppelt 1956, 288–289; Keyhoe 1973, 81–82; Hynek 1977, 235–236; Clark 1992, 387–389; Randle 1997a, 112–114.
21. Keyhoe 1953, 54; Hall 1964, 132; *UFO Magazine* 1990; Hynek 1977, 53.
22. Hall 1964, 132; 1988, 146.
23. Keyhoe 1953, 57–58, 257; Hall 1964, 132.
24. Ruppelt 1956, 205.
25. Ruppelt 1956, 209–210.

26. Keyhoe 1953, 62–66; Ruppelt 1956, 211–216; Hall 1964, 132; 1988, 332–335; Good 1988, 270; Randle 1997a, 93; Randles 1988, 37; Flammonde 1976, 38; Clark 1992, 396–403.
27. Keyhoe 1953, 68; Hall 1964, 132.
28. Ruppelt 1956, 24; Hall 1964, 132 ; Edwards 1966, 12; Keyhoe 68.
29. Keyhoe 1953, 54–71; Ruppelt 1956, 218–222; Jacobs 1975, 77; Good 1988, 270–271; Randle 1997a, 98, 105; Randles 1988, 37–38; Clark 1992, 399–400.
30. Randles 1988, 189.
31. Jacobs 1975, 74, 77; Clark 1992, 402.
32. Edwards 1966, 87–88.
33. Ruppelt 1956, 244; Keyhoe 1953, 75–89.
34. Ruppelt 1956, 34, 230; Jacobs 1975, 78; Randles 1988, 38–39; Flammonde 1976, 332–333; Friedman and Berliner 1992, 30; Edwards 1966, 65; Clark 1992, 400–401.
35. Keyhoe 1953, 256; Hynek 1977, 61–63, 114–115; Hall 1964, 132.
36. Ruppelt 1956, 256; Hall 1964, 132; Keyhoe 1953, 256.
37. Keyhoe 1953, 256; Ruppelt 1956, 257; Hall 1964, 132; Wilkins 1955, 226; Edwards 1966, 14.
38. Hall 1964, 132; Keyhoe 1953, 255–257; Sanderson 1970, 194.
39. Ruppelt 1956, 247.
40. Friedman and Berliner 1992, 30–31.
41. Burgess 1953.
42. FBI 1952a; Fawcett and Greenwood 1984, 175–177; Good 1988, 272.
43. In 1997, the CIA's official historian, Gerald K. Haines, argued that the U-2 spy plane was the cause of many UFO sightings. I rejected this argument in "The CIA, Official History, and You: A Study of Gerald Haines and UFOs," *UFO Magazine* (December/January 2001), http://keyholepublishing.com/Haines.htm.
44. Fawcett and Greenwood 1984, 119–122.
45. From CIA reports, "Flying Saucers over Belgian Congo Uranium Mines," "Flying Saucers in East Germany," "Luminous Object Seen over Port Gentil," "Strange Objects Seen in Sky over Algeria," "Saucers Observed in Two Areas of Oran," "Disks Appear over Marrakech," etc. See Edwards 1966, 174–176, Hynek 1977, 204–205, Fawcett and Greenwood 1984, 117–118, and Vallee 1969, 198.
46. Clark 1952; Good 1988, 330.
47. Tauss 1952; Fawcett and Greenwood 1984, 123; Good 1988, 330–331; Randle 1997a, 107–109.
48. CIA 1952; Good 1988, 268, 331–334.
49. Computer UFO Network 1952; Jacobs 1975, 82; Clark 1992, 272.
50. Lorenzen and Lorenzen 1976, 1–2, 248–251; 1968, 187.
51. Donner 1980, 269, 275; Wise 1976, 184; Keith 1997, 74.
52. Sanderson 1967, 39–51; Lorenzen and Lorenzen 1976, 169–170; Barker 1956, 7–26; Keyhoe 1953, 116–118; Clark 1992, 145–146.
53. Ruppelt 1956, 253.

54. Randles 1988, 43–44; Wilkins 1955, 119, 135–136; Hall 1964, 133; Vallee 1965, 101.
55. Vallee 1965, 102; Keyhoe 1953, 256.
56. Chadwell 1952a; Good 1988, 31, 328–329; Randle 1997a, 108; Fawcett and Greenwood 1984, 123–126; Clark 1992, 402.
57. Ruppelt 1956, 252, 256; Flammonde 1976, 333.
58. Keyhoe 1973, 82.
59. Weiner 1990, 120.
60. Fawcett and Greenwood 1984, xvi.
61. Fawcett and Greenwood 1984, 189.
62. Keyhoe 1953, 3–7, 17–18, 255; Hall 1964, 133.
63. Keyhoe 1953, 161–167, 255; 1955, 40–41; Hall 1964, 133.
64. Fawcett and Greenwood 1984, 122–123, 128–129; Hall 1964, 133.
65. Keyhoe 1953, 255–256; Hall 1964, 133.
66. Keyhoe 1953, 5–6, 255; Hall 1964, 133.
67. Keyhoe 1973, 84; Flammonde 1976, 333.
68. FBI 1952b; Ruppelt 1956, 285; Randle 1997a, 109; Fawcett and Greenwood 1984, 177; Randles 1988, 41.
69. Ruppelt 1956, 298.
70. Durant 1953, Ruppelt 1956, 264.
71. Chadwell 1952b.
72. Good 1988, 335; Fawcett and Greenwood 1984, xiv; Randles 1988, 35; Hall 1988, 336–337.
73. Hynek 1977, 20; Randle 1997a, 109.
74. Cross 1953; *UFO Magazine* 1993.
75. Keyhoe 1973, 85.
76. Lorenzen and Lorenzen 1976, 249–250.
77. Page 1992.
78. For additional useful information on the Robertson Panel, see Ruppelt 1956, 286–294, Flammonde 1976, 334–340, Clark 1992, 289–291, Jacobs 1975, 91–97, Lorenzen and Lorenzen 1976, 249–250; 1968, 227–241, Randles 1988, 44–45, Fawcett and Greenwood 1984, 127, and Randle 1997a, 119–125.
79. Robertson 1953.
80. Jacobs 1975, 90; Randles 1988, 40; Friedman and Berliner 1992, 31.
81. Stringfield 1977, 137–138; Randle 1997a, 129–130.
82. Hynek 1977, 236–238.
83. Ruppelt 1956, 297; Keyhoe 1973, 85–86; Clark 1992, 273.
84. Hynek 1977, 21–22; Keyhoe 1955, 40.
85. Ruppelt 1956, 298; Jacobs 1975, 98–99; Randle 1997a, 129.
86. Keyhoe 1953, 242, 246.

Chapter 5

1. Thomas 1989, 89.
2. Marks 1979, 60–62, 141–145, 214; Thomas 1989, 123; Keith 1997, 79.

3. Cole 1988, 64.

4. Hall 1964, 134; Clark 1992, 310–311.

5. Keel 1971, 207; Stringfield 1977, 141; Wilkins 1955, 186.

6. Stringfield 1977, 179–186; Randles 1988, 21; Hall 1988, 78; Randle 1995. A concise description of Stancil's experience is "UFO Crashes and Retrievals," Skywatch International Website, http://www. .home.earthlink.net/~skywatcher22/UFOCRASH.htm.

7. CIA 1953a; Fawcett and Greenwood 1984, 128–130; Hall 1964, 133.

8. Ruppelt 1956, 298.

9. Atomic Energy Commission 1953; Hall 1988, 361–363.

10. Hall 1988, 359–360.

11. Ruppelt 1956, 304–306 is the source of the August 12-13 date, which Keyhoe 1973 and NICAP followed; Hynek and Vallee 1965, 103–104 give the earlier date. See also Hall 1964, 4, 133 and Hynek article in the *Saturday Evening Post* (December 17, 1966), cited in David 1967, 218.

12. U.S. Air Force 1954b; Computer UFO Network n.d.; Keyhoe 1955, 24; Hall 1964, 22, 133; Jacobs 1975, 104; Flammonde 1976, 340–341; Randle 1997a, 128–132.

13. Keyhoe 1973.

14. Keyhoe 1955, 63; 1973; Hall 1964, 133.

15. Blue Book Case No. 2686.

16. Blue Book Case No. 2692, 2840, and 2844.

17. U.S. Air Force 1953; Good 1988, 278.

18. Vallee 1965, 204.

19. Hall 1964, 133.

20. Hall 1964, 134; LePoer Trench 1966, 32–33; Wilkins 1955, 62.

21. Hall 1964, 134; Keyhoe 1955, 14; 1960, 42; Good 1988, 273; Vallee 1965, 237; Clark 1992, 222–224.

22. Miller 1953; CIA 1953b; Good 1988, 280; Fawcett and Greenwood 1984, 130; Hall 1964, 134.

23. Wilkins 1955, 221.

24. Stringfield 1977, 142.

25. Keyhoe 1955, 24.

26. Keyhoe 1955, 55.

27. *Library Journal* 1953; *New York Times* 1953; *Springfield Republican* 1953.

28. Barker 1956, 53–106; Keyhoe 1973, 106.

29. Bender 1963. For excerpts of Bender's book, see http://www.peg.apc.org/~nexus/meninblack.html.

30. Clark 1992, 74.

31. Menzel 19953b; Good 1988, 278.

32. Perry 1953; Good 1988, 279; U.S. Air Force 1955.

33. Complete text of "JANAP 146(C) Communication Instructions for Reporting Vital Intelligence Sightings from Airborne and Waterborne Sources , 10 March 1954" available at CUFON, The Computer UFO Network, http://www.cufon.com/cufon/janp146c.htm. See also Jacobs 1975, 105 and Keyhoe 1955, 8R.

34. U.S. Air Force 1954a.
35. Jacobs 1975, 106.
36. Keith 1997, 211.
37. Marks 1979, 79–89; Thomas 1989, 160–162.
38. Summers 1994, 409.
39. Marks 1979, 195, 200; Keith 1997, 118.
40. Lorenzen and Lorenzen 1976, 2; Edwards 1966, 276.
41. Randles 1988, 45.
42. Edwards 1966, 249; Clark 1992, 117.
43. Keyhoe 1955, 88–90; Hall 1964, 134.
44. Keyhoe 1955, 98–100.
45. Hall 1964, 134; Wilkins 1955, 67; Edwards 1966, 253–254; Good 1988, 283.
46. Hall 1964, 134.
47. Keyhoe 1955, 99; Hall 1964, 134.
48. Clark 1992, 79.
49. Keyhoe 1955, 230; Hall 1964, 134; Wilkins 1955, 64, 119.
50. Keyhoe 1955, 101; Jacobs 1975, 138.
51. Keyhoe 1955, 108.
52. Jacobs 1975, 133; Keyhoe 1955, 116–120, 134; Hall 1964, 134; *True* 1954.
53. Keyhoe 1955, 231.
54. Stringfield 1977, 10.
55. Stringfield 1977, 85.
56. Donner 1980, 245; Wise 1976, 153.
57. Wilkins 1955, 65, 119, 123.
58. CIA n.d.; Fawcett and Greenwood 1984, 132–133; Hall 1964, 134; Edwards 1967, 80–81; Blue Book Cases No. 2926 and 2937.
59. Classified message from the Commander, Carswell AFB, Texas, to the directorate of intelligence; Commander, Air Defense Command, Ent AFB, Colorado; and ATIC 8th Air Force, Carswell AFB. See Good 1988, 281–282.
60. CIRVIS 1954a; Keyhoe 1955, 110; Hall 1964, 134; Good 1988, 284.
61. Clark 1992, 117–118.
62. Kabus 1954; Edwards 1966, 68–69; Good 1988, 281–282; Vallee 1969, 206; Keyhoe 1955, 133–134.
63. Keyhoe 1955, 138–139, 143; Wilkins 1955, 233–234.
64. Keyhoe 1955, 144; Edwards 1967, 84; Hall 1964, 134.
65. Keyhoe 145–146; Edwards 1967, 85.
66. Edwards 1967, 86; Ruppelt 1956, 310–311; Hall 1964, 134; Keyhoe 1955, 149.
67. Stringfield 1977, 85; Edwards 1967, 86; Keyhoe 1955, 158.
68. Keyhoe 1955, 162.
69. Fawcett and Greenwood 1984, 134.
70. Keyhoe 1955, 167–168.
71. Keyhoe 1955, 168–169.
72. Keyhoe 1955, 170–173; Randles 1988, 46–47; Good 1988, 189–191; Leoer Trench 1966, 34–36; Clark 1992, 80–81. Tolstoy quote is from *War and Peace*, Book Four, Part Nine.

73. Hall 1964, 134; Keyhoe 1955, 174–175; 1973; Edwards 1966, 56–57; Vallee 1965, 238.
74. Ruppelt 1956, 308; Hall 1964, 134; Edwards 1967, 86.
75. Clark 1992, 293.
76. CIA n.d.; Fawcett and Greenwood 1984, 134.
77. Wilkins 1955, 237; Sanderson 1970, 32.
78. Edwards 1966, 250; Keyhoe 1955, 192–193; Clark 1992, 137.
79. Keyhoe 1955, 188–189. (Navy order reprinted in Keyhoe 1955, 309–311.)
80. See U.S. Air Force 1954, Keyhoe 1955, 194, and Good 1988, 280. Clark 1992, 273 writes that Keyhoe interpreted this order as evidence of cover-up but that others who knew about the Robertson Panel believed it was just the implementation of debunking. What was the difference?
81. CIRVIS 1954b; Good 1988, 284–285.
82. Keyhoe 1955, 25–26; Hall 1964, 134.
83. Vallee 1965, 105; 1979, 31; Lorenzen and Lorenzen 1976, 143–144.
84. Vallee 1969, 68; Clark 1992, 96.
85. CIA 1954; Fawcett and Greenwood 1984, 134; Vallee 1969, 208; 1965, 105–106.
86. Vallee 1969, 17–18, 209; Lorenzen and Lorenzen 1976, 116–118; Stringfield 1977, 77.
87. Vallee 1969, 209; 1965, 106, 110.
88. Lorenzen and Lorenzen 1976, 119–120.
89. Vallee 1969, 212; Stringfield 1977, 77; Lorenzen and Lorenzen 1976, 120.
90. Wilkins 1955, 57.
91. Vallee 1969, 214.
92. Vallee 1969, 215.
93. Vallee 1969, 215–216.
94. Lorenzen and Lorenzen 1976, 28–29; Vallee 1965, 71; 1969, 217.
95. Vallee 1969, 218; Lorenzen and Lorenzen 1976, 121.
96. Vallee 1969, 219.
97. Hall 1964, 134.
98. Stringfield 1977, 77; Lorenzen and Lorenzen 1976, 121.
99. Vallee 1969, 223.
100. Stringfield 1977, 77–78; Vallee 1969, 224–225.
101. Lorenzen and Lorenzen 1976, 123; Stringfield 1977, 78; Vallee 1969, 227.
102. Lorenzen and Lorenzen 1976, 33.
103. Lorenzen and Lorenzen 1976, 123; Stringfield 1977, 78; Vallee 1969, 231.
104. Hall 1964, 134; CIA 1954; Fawcett and Greenwood 1984, 134; Keyhoe 1955, 26, 198–199; Ruppelt 1956, 71–72, 310.
105. Wilkins 1955, 243.
106. Wilkins 1955, 244; Lorenzen and Lorenzen 1976, 122; Vallee 1969, 220–226.
107. Vallee 1969, 228, 237.
108. Wilkins 1955, 245.
109. Wilkins 1955, 57, 243–247.
110. Hall 1964, 134; Lorenzen and Lorenzen 1976, 121; Vallee 1969, 221; Wilkins 1955, 244–245.

111. Keyhoe 1955, 207; LePoer Trench 1966, 19–20; Bowen 1977, 1–2.
112. *Flying Saucer Review* 1962; Vallee 1969, 230, 236.
113. Vallee 1969, 18–19, 235–236.
114. Edwards 1966, 191–192; Keyhoe 1955, 212–213; Hall 1964, 134.
115. Lorenzen and Lorenzen 1976, 125–126; Vallee 1979, 164; 1969, 241, 244.
116. Keyhoe 1955, 26–27; Hall 1964, 119, 134.
117. Vallee 1969, 241, 244.
118. Lorenzen and Lorenzen 1976, 144–145; Vallee 1969, 245.
119. Lorenzen and Lorenzen 1976, 146; Vallee 1969, 246–247.
120. Edwards 1966, 177–178; Lorenzen and Lorenzen 1976, 145–146; Vallee 1969, 247.
121. Vallee 1969, 244–246; Ruppelt 1956, 310; Hall 1964, 135; Wilkins 1955, 257.
122. Chalker 1996, 63–65.
123. Randles 1988, 94.
124. Keyhoe 1955, 205.
125. U.S. Air Force 1954c, 12–13; Jacobs 1975, 134.
126. Stringfield 1977, 11; Clark 1992, 321. Clark gives the year 1955 for this.
127. Keyhoe 1955, 214–215.
128. Powers 1979, 120; Wise and Ross 1964, 130.
129. Keyhoe 1955, 236; Edwards 1966, 12; Jacobs 1975, 137; LePoer Trench 1966, 176; Wilkins 1955, 257.
130. Keyhoe 1955, 238.
131. Second Commission on Organization of the Executive Branch of the Government, chaired by former President Herbert C. Hoover, established by act of July 10, 1953 (67 Stat. 142) and extended by act of May 23, 1955 (69 Stat. 64). Cited in *IC21: The Intelligence Community in the Twenty-First Century.* Staff Study, Permanent Select Committee on Intelligence, House of Representatives, One Hundred Fourth Congress. Appendix C. CRS Report: Proposals for Intelligence Reorganization 1949–1996. (A Report Prepared for the Permanent Select Committee on Intelligence, House of Representatives.) Richard A. Best, Jr., Analyst in National Defense, and Herbert Andrew Boerstling, Research Assistant, Foreign Affairs and National Defense Division, February 28, 1996. http://www.fas.org/irp/congress/1996_rpt/ic21/ic21018.htm.
132. U.S. House 1996, 6–7.
133. Powers 1979, 98.
134. Marks 1979, 147, 159.
135. Cole 1988, 18.
136. De Landa 1991, 192, 197–199.
137. ATIC 1955; Ruppelt 1956, 297; Flammonde 1976, 341.
138. Jacobs 1975, 134–135.
139. U.S. Air Force 1955; Jacobs 1975, 135.
140. U.S. Air Force 1955b.
141. Ruppelt 1956, 310.
142. Stringfield 1977, 169–170.
143. See Keyhoe 1955, 250–251, 258, and *New York Herald-Tribune* 1955. Thirty-two years later, Lear's son, John Lear, one of the world's most

accomplished pilots with strong CIA connections, made even more detailed statements about aliens.

144. Talbert 1955.
145. *Interavia* 1956, 373–374.
146. For more information, see the Thomas Townsend Brown Site, which includes detailed information and many primary articles on Brown's work. http://soteria.com/brown/.
147. Keyhoe 1955, 165, 192; Edwards 1966, 163.
148. Keyhoe 1955, 253.
149. Walters 1962, 140.
150. LePoer Trench 1966, 141–142; Hall 1988, 178; Clark 1992, 122.
151. Wilkins 1955, 268.
152. Keyhoe 1955, 269.
153. *New York Times* 1956, 25; *Library Journal* 1955, 2766.
154. Hall 1964, 107; *UFO Magazine* 1993b; Jacobs 1975, 139–143; Keyhoe 1960, 43; Friedman and Berliner 1992, 31–32; Clark 1992, 274.
155. Keyhoe 1955, 247–250, 260; Hall 1964, 135; Vallee 1969, 248.
156. Vallee 1969, 248–250; Hall 1964, 135; Stringfield 1977, 87–92.
157. Lorenzen and Lorenzen 1976, 174–175; Vallee 1969, 251; Stringfield 1977, 86–87; Clark 1992, 214–216.
158. Good 1988, 285–286.
159. Good 1988, 34; Hall 1988, 338–339.
160. Powers 1979, 120; Wise and Ross 1964, 130.
161. Hall 1964, 135; Stringfield 1977, 12–14.
162. Stringfield 1977, 138–139.
163. Sanderson 1970, 33; Hall 1964, 135; Vallee 1969, 250–251.
164. Clark 1992, 303–304; *Focus* 1985.
165. Keyhoe 1960, 43; 1955, 206.
166. Keel 1971, 207.
167. Hall 1964, 135.
168. Weiner 1990, 35.
169. Wise n.d., 21; Donner 1980, 20, 181–195.
170. Hall 1964, 107; Jacobs 1975, 135–137, 143–144.
171. *New York Times* 1956.
172. Fawcett and Greenwood 1984, 135.
173. Stringfield 1977, 14, 165; Edwards 1966, 163.
174. Sanderson 1970, 33.
175. Keyhoe 1960, 167–184; Hall 1964, 135.
176. Good 1988, 269.
177. Hall 1964, 135; Vallee 1969, 253; Edwards 1966, 72–73; Randles 1988, 190; Clark 1992, 225–227.
178. Gillmor 1969, 163–164, 248–256; Good 1988, 44–46; Clark 1998, 333–336.

Chapter 6

1. Keyhoe 1973, 91.

2. Hall 1964, 107; Flammonde 1976, 341; Clark 1992, 274; Keyhoe 1960, 49–50.
3. Keyhoe 1960, 20–21, 44–45, 48; Jacobs 1975, 146–148; LePoer Trench 1966, 177; Hynek 1977, 239; 1972, 189; Stringfield 1977, 15.
4. Keyhoe 1960, 57, 62–63.
5. Keyhoe 1960, 58–62, 96; 1973.
6. Keyhoe 1960, 266–267.
7. Keyhoe 1960, 64–68.
8. Wise and Ross 1964, 220–225.
9. Marks 1979, 110, 146; Thomas 1989, 159, 162–163; Keith 1997, 91, 102.
10. Barron 1974, 434–424.
11. Hall 1964, 136; Vallee 1965, 238.
12. Hall 1988, 243.
13. Sanderson 1970, 34.
14. Keyhoe 1960, 103–105, 111.
15. Hall 1964, 136; Sanderson 1970, 34; Lorenzen and Lorenzen 1968, 51.
16. Vallee 1969, 254; Keyhoe 1960, 54–56; Good 1988, 282.
17. Keyhoe 1960, 58–61; Hall 1964, 136.
18. Hall 1964, 136; Sanderson 1970, 34; Vallee 1969, 255.
19. Lorenzen and Lorenzen 1976, 126–127; *Flying Saucer Review* 1965; Vallee 1969, 255–256.
20. Keyhoe 1960, 70–79.
21. Keyhoe 81–82, 91, 96; Randles 1988, 54.
22. Clark 1992, 274; Jacobs 1975, 150–151; Keyhoe 49–50.
23. Clark 1992, 285–286; 1998, 505–508.
24. Good 1988, 283.
25. U.S. Air Force n.d.a; Keyhoe 1973, 232–238, 280–281; Vallee 1969, 237.
26. Hall 1964, 136; Vallee 1969, 257–258; Gillmor 1969, 138–143; Edwards 1966, 78; Clark 1992, 331–333.
27. Saunders and Harkins 1968, 126–127.
28. Lorenzen and Lorenzen 1976, 62–87; *Flying Saucer Review* 1966; Vallee 1969, 259–260; Clark 1992, 100, 392–395.
29. *Flying Saucer Review* 1966; Vallee 1969, 260; Lorenzen and Lorenzen 1976, 150.
30. Edwards 1966, 57–58; Hall 1964, 120, 136.
31. Keyhoe 1973; Vallee 1965, 239–240; Clark 1992, 206–207.
32. Keyhoe 1960, 128; Vallee 1969, 263.
33. Randles 1988, 94–95.
34. Keyhoe 1960, 128–129; Vallee 1969, 265–267.
35. Keyhoe 1960, 113.
36. Vallee 1969, 261.
37. Edwards 1966, 31; Hall 1964, 136; Keyhoe 1960, 114.
38. Vallee 1969, 262.
39. Vallee 1969, 262; Hall 1964, 136; Keyhoe 1960, 120.
40. Keyhoe 1960, 121; Edwards 1966, 121; Hall 1964, 136; LePoer Trench 1966, 42; Vallee 1969, 262.

41. Clark 1992, 262–264; Vallee 1969, 264; Hall 1964, 136.
42. Vallee 1969, 266; Keyhoe 1960, 129; Hall 1988, 245; 1964, 136.
43. Keyhoe 1960, 141; 1973, 52.
44. Hynek 1972, 128; Jacobs 1975, 153–155; Hall 1988, 147; Fuller 1966a, 35; Lorenzen and Lorenzen 1976, 177–180; Randles 1988, 58.
45. Keyhoe 1960, 119; Hall 1964, 107.
46. Keyhoe 1960, 126–127, 130; Randles 1988, 54–59; Hall 1988, 244–245; Vallee 1969, 262; Clark 1992, 228–229, 293.
47. Hall 1964, 136.
48. Keyhoe 1960, 132–134.
49. Vallee 1969, 267; Hall 1964, 137; Edwards 1966, 240–241.
50. Clark 1996, 95.
51. Randles 1988, 63; Jacobs 1975, 135, 155.
52. Hall 1964, 107; *Life* 1958, 16; Edwards 1966, 135.
53. Jacobs 1975, 159, 163; Clark 1992, 275.
54. Keyhoe 1960, 22–23, 155–165; Jacobs 1975, 156; Clark 1992, 69.
55. Oldenburgh 1958; Edwards 1966, 89.
56. Ayres 1958; Hall 1964, 173.
57. Keyhoe 1960, 218.
58. Jacobs 1975, 150; Clark 1992, 274.
59. Keyhoe 1960, 166–167, 182–184.
60. Keyhoe 1960, 189–190.
61. Keyhoe 1960, 191.
62. Hall 1964, 110.
63. Keyhoe 1960, 199, 232–233; Vallee 1965, 156.
64. Keyhoe 1960, 30, 208.
65. Keyhoe 1960, 219–227.
66. Jacobs 1975, 160.
67. Keyhoe 1960, 258; Clark 1992, 293; 1998, 518.
68. Vallee 1969, 270; Hall 1964, 137.
69. Hall 1964, 137; LePoer Trench 1966, 43–44; Clark 1992, 326–330.
70. Hall 1964, 137; Vallee 1969, 271; Edwards 1966, 62, 258; Lorenzen and Lorenzen 1976, 151.
71. Edwards 1966, 95–96.
72. *Flying Saucer Review* 1958; Vallee 1969, 270–272; Hall 1964, 137; Keyhoe 1960, 204; Edwards 1966, 258; Fuller 1966a, 237.
73. CIA 1958a; Vallee 1969, 273.
74. Hall 1964, 137; Vallee 1969, 272.
75. CIA 1958b; Fawcett and Greenwood 1984, 136–137.
76. Sanderson 1967, 29–32; Hynek 1977, 44; Clark 1992, 229–230; Hall 1964, 137.
77. Keyhoe 1960, 239; Jacobs 1975, 160–162; Clark 1992, 275; Flammonde 1976, 341.
78. Clark 1992, 274–275; Jacobs 1975, 163–166.
79. Jacobs 1975, 164–165.
80. Good 1988, 284.

81. Keith 1997, 91–93; Cannon 1989.
82. Weiner 1990, 36.
83. Flammonde 1976, 341; Clark 1992, 274–275.
84. I am indebted to the assistance of fellow UFO researcher Val Germann, whose insights and research were invaluable in writing this section.
85. From FBI file on J. Allen Hynek, http://www.cufon.org/cufon/fbi-hynek.htm.
86. Vallee 1992a 87, 110, 408–410.
87. Clark 1998, 395.
88. *Neues Europa* 1959; Good 1988, 370.
89. Jacobs 1975, 173–174.
90. Edwards 1966, 85.
91. Keyhoe 1960, 15, 247–248.
92. Keyhoe 1960, 27–36; Hall 1964, 137; Good 1988, 284; Tacker 1960, 233–235.
93. Fawcett and Greenwood 1984, 138; Vallee 1969, 274.
94. Edwards 1966, 117–118; Hall 1964, 137; Sanderson 1970, 34–35; Fawcett and Greenwood 1984, 138; Vallee 1969, 275.
95. Vallee 1969, 274; Edwards 1966, 70–71; Vallee 1965, 238.
96. Sanderson 1967, 227–241; Keel 1971, 174; Vallee 1965, 124; Clark 1992, 40–41, 209–210.
97. Lorenzen and Lorenzen 1968, 52–53.
98. Hall 1964, 137, Lorenzen and Lorenzen 1976, 332, Vallee 1965, 201–204; 1969, 276, Hynek 1977, 216, Edwards 1966, 183–185, Randles 1988, 171, LePoer Trench 1966, 155–158, Clark 1992, 177–180, 348.
99. Hall 1964, 138; Keyhoe 1960, 250–252; LePoer Trench 1966, 44–45; Vallee 1969, 276.
100. Edwards 1966, 258; Fuller 1966a, 237; Vallee 1969, 276–277; *APRO Bulletin* 1959.
101. Jacobs 1975, 151; Clark 1992, 273; 1996, 408.
102. Keyhoe 1973, 40–44, 48–49; Hall 1964.
103. Jacobs 1975, 168–170.
104. Keyhoe 1960, 252–254.
105. Keyhoe 1960, 258–260; Clark 1992, 293.
106. Ruppelt 1960, 243–277.
107. Clark 1992, 293.
108. U.S. Air Force 1959; Edwards 1966, 65, 315; Hall 1964, 108, 138; Good 1988, 288; Lorenzen and Lorenzen 1976, 247; Blum 1990, 65; Flammonde 1976, 341–342.
109. Weiner 1990, 5; Good 1988, 299; Wise and Ross 1964, 325.
110. Powers 1979, 184; Thomas 1989, 223.
111. Marks 1979, 150–151; Thomas 1989, 194, 228.
112. Wise n.d. 23; 1976, 223.
113. Hunt 1991, 220.
114. Summers 1994, 311; Wise and Ross 1964, 24; Powers 1979, 130; Weiner 1990, 36.

115. Lorenzen and Lorenzen 1976, 3, 251; Clark 1992, 13.
116. Clark 1996, 410; Jacobs 1975, 174; Flammonde 1976, 342.
117. Hall 1988, 179.
118. Good 1988, 289; Steiger 1976, 14.
119. LePoer Trench 1966, 45–46; Hall 1964, 138.
120. CIA 1960.
121. Keyhoe 1960, 248, 257; 1973; Keel 1971, 193; Blum 1990, 103, 106; Edwards 1966, 152–153.
122. Wise and Ross 1964, 131.
123. Wise and Ross 1964, 26–27; Powers 1979, 186–187; Summers 1994, 312–315.
124. Lorenzen and Lorenzen 1976, 152; Vallee 1969, 278.
125. Edwards 1966, 86.
126. Hall 1964, 138.
127. LePoer Trench 1966, 46.
128. Hall 1964, 138.
129. Vallee 1969, 280.
130. Jacobs 1975, 176–180; Hall 1964, 173; Clark 1996, 410.
131. Stringfield 1977, 167.
132. Edwards 1966, 229–230, 317; De Landa 1991, 199; U.S. Air Force n.d.b.; Hall 1964, 108; Keyhoe 1973, 138–139; Randles 1988, 60; Flammonde 1976, 342.
133. Jacobs 1975, 178; Hall 1964, 138; Clark 1996, 409.
134. *New York Times* 1960; Edwards 1966, 317; Hall 1964, 138. For a copy of the report itself, see http://in_search_of.com/frames/nasa_brookings/nasa_nf.shtml#summary.
135. Keith 1997, 220; Powers 1979, 184; Thomas 1989, 231; Marks 1979, 81; Wise 1976, 220.
136. Powers 1979, 142, 187; Wise and Ross 1964, 30–33.
137. Weiner 1990, 37–38.
138. *The Nation* 1961; *New York Times* 1961; *Miami Herald* 1961; Wise and Ross 1964, 34–35, 51; Powers 1979, 142–143.
139. Wise and Ross 1964, 63–71.
140. Marks 1979, 212; Thomas 1989, 232; Wise and Ross 1964, 199; Powers 1979, 167, 175, 187; Barron 1974, 201.
141. Summers 1994, 326–327, 334; Powers 1979, 186; Donner 1980, 195–203; Wise and Ross 1964, 102, 229; Blum 59.
142. Edwards 1966, 205–206.
143. Hall 1964, 138–139.
144. Clark 1996, 168–175; Vallee 1969, 24–25, 281.
145. Sanderson 1970, 35; Lorenzen and Lorenzen 1968, 51; Vallee 1969, 281.
146. Hall 1964, 139.
147. Vallee 1969, 282.
148. Vallee 1969, 282.
149. Sanderson 1970, 35–36.
150. Jacobs 1975, 178; Edwards 1966, 75.

151. Hall 1964, 108.
152. Keyhoe 1973, 92–93; Hall 1964, 139.
153. Hall 1964, 108; Flammonde 1976, 342; Jacobs 1975, 180–181.
154. Hall 1964, 139; Keyhoe 1973, 94; Jacobs 1975, 181–183.
155. Keyhoe 1973, 103; Jacobs 1975, 182–183.
156. Most of what follows derives from the detailed account of the Hill abduction in Fuller 1996. See also Fuller 1966, 192–193, Vallee 1969, 282, Clark 1996, 235–253, Hall 1964, 139, Randles 1988, 60–62, Cannon 1989, and Keyhoe 1973, 241.
157. Clark 1996, 223–227; 1998, 521–525.
158. Keyhoe 1973, 97.
159. Edwards 1966, 75, 86–88; LePoer Trench 1966, 166.
160. Blum 1990, 72; Clark 1996, 128.
161. Keyhoe 1973, 92–103; Fawcett and Greenwood 1984, 207.

Chapter 7

1. The most thorough examination of this event is Kevin Randle's excellent chapter in *History of UFO Crashes* (1995, 79–94). See also Edwards 1966, 13 and Clark 1996, 259–261.
2. Hall 1964, 108, 139; Flammonde 1976, 342; Jacobs 1975, 185.
3. NASA 1962; Hall 1964, 139; LePoer Trench 1966, 63–64; Good 1988, 366.
4. *Time* 1962; LePoer Trench 1966, 65; Good 1988, 366.
5. *APRO Bulletin* 1962; Jacobs 1975, 184; Clark 1992, 259–261.
6. *NICAP Investigator* 1962; Good 1988, 289.
7. Fuller 1966a, 63–65.
8. Good 1988, 290; Blum 1990, 66.
9. Hall 1964, 139–140; Vallee 1969, 287.
10. David 1967, 151–155; Sullivan 1964; Edwards 1966, 196.
11. Vallee 1965, 124; LePoer Trench 1966, 147.
12. Marks 1979, 108.
13. Wise 1976, 188; Thomas 1989, 249; Keith 1997, 81.
14. Lorenzen and Lorenzen 1976, 152; Hall 1964, 139; Fawcett and Greenwood 1984, 139; Vallee 1969, 284–285.
15. *Flying Saucer Review* 1964; Vallee 1969, 286; Keyhoe 1973.
16. *APRO Bulletin* 1962; Vallee 1969, 286; Clark 1996, 165–167.
17. Keyhoe 1973; Hall 1964, 140; Vallee 1969, 289.
18. *Flying Saucer Review* 1963; Vallee 1969, 288, 291; Hall 1964, 140.
19. Hall 1964, 140; Jacobs 1975, 187; Edwards 1966, 281.
20. Hall 1964, 140.
21. Edwards 1966, 120; Sanderson 1970, 36.
22. *Flying Saucer Review* 1963; Vallee 1969, 35–37, 293; Delgado and Andrews 1989, 188; LePoer Trench 1966, 50–51; Hall 1964, 140.
23. Hall 1964, 140; Vallee 1969, 293.
24. The point, admittedly, remains disputed. See Summers 1994, 354–355, 366–367, 371–372.
25. Wise and Ross 1964, 101, 277–278; Weiner 1990, 127.

26. Powers 1979, 285; Wise n.d., 22.
27. Edwards 1966, 155–156; Vallee 1975, 41.
28. Vallee 1969, 296–297; Edwards 1966, 206–207.
29. Edwards 1966, 186–190, Hynek 1977, 223–229, Good 1988, 343–345, 371–373, Jacobs 1975, 189–191, Lorenzen and Lorenzen 1976, 8–11, 182–186, 244, Fawcett and Greenwood 1984, 139–141, Friedman and Berliner 1992, 33, Hall 1988, 147, Vallee 1969, 16, 297. See also accounts published in *Flying Saucer Review* (1964) and by Coral Lorenzen in *Fate* magazine 1964, 27–38, LePoer Trench 1966, 52–53, Clark 1996, 93, 452–465, and *Studies in Intelligence* (1966).
30. Vallee 1969, 300–301; Edwards 1966, 131–133.
31. Vallee 1969, 297–298.
32. Clark 1996, 127.
33. Edwards 1966, 32–33; Vallee 1969, 298–299.
34. Lorenzen and Lorenzen 1976, 244–245.
35. LeMay 1965, 541–543; Edwards 1966, 309; Fawcett and Greenwood 1984, 211.
36. Jacobs 1975, 191; Keyhoe 1973, 115; Edwards 1966, 281.
37. Vallee 1975, 36–37.
38. Keyhoe 1973, 106–107.
39. Edwards 1966, 128–130.
40. Edwards 1966, 94–95; Keyhoe 1973; Vallee 1969, 304; Fuller 1966a, 36; Sanderson 1970, 36.
41. Vallee 1969, 304.
42. Fuller 1966a, 37; Vallee 1969, 305.
43. Fawcett and Greenwood 1984, 231–234; Hall 1988, 11, 354–358; 2001.
44. Wise 1976, 153; Donner 1980, 238–245.
45. Sanderson 1970, 37.
46. Keel 1971, 185–187.
47. Vallee 1969, 305; Hall 1988, 249–250.
48. Edwards 1966, 92–93; Keyhoe 1973; Hall 1988, 250–252; Vallee 1969, 305; Stringfield 1977, 193–194; Clark 1996, 175–177.
49. Edwards 1966, 91–92; Keyhoe 1973, 57; *Flying Saucer Review* 1965; Vallee 1969, 307; Fuller 1966a, 37–38.
50. Edwards 1966, 208; Keyhoe 1973, 111, 256–257; Randles 1988, 132–133.
51. Edwards 1966, 283–285; Keyhoe 1973, 112; Fuller 1966a, 50.
52. Berliner n.d.
53. *Flying Saucer Review* 1965; Vallee 1969, 19–21, 308; Lorenzen and Lorenzen 1976, 128–129; Bowen 1977, 57–71; Clark 1996, 534–536.
54. Sanderson 1970, 20; Vallee 1969, 308.
55. Keyhoe 1973, 112.
56. Lorenzen and Lorenzen 1976, 156–158; Edwards 1966, 121, 318; Vallee 1969, 309–311.
57. Keyhoe 1973, 113; David 1967, 221; Jacobs 1975, 193, 197–198.
58. Edwards 1966, 287–290; 1967, 94–95; Keyhoe 1973, 113–114; Vallee 1969, 311; Fuller 1966a, 19, 41–45.

59. Edwards 1966, 301–302; Good 1988, 298–299; Fuller 1966a, 49; Keel 1971, 108.
60. Vallee 1975, 42.
61. Tully 1969, 9.
62. Fuller 1966a, 201–202.
63. Fuller 1966a, 240–249.
64. Fuller 1966a; Hynek 1977, 154–160; Clark 1996, 178–182.
65. Edwards 1966, 295–296; Fuller 1966a, 44–45, 246–247; Vallee 1969, 316; Clark 1996, 146–148.
66. Edwards 1966, 259; Fuller 1966a, 237.
67. Fuller 1966a, 46–47.
68. Jacobs 1975, 198.
69. Flammonde 1976, 342–343; Steiger 1976, 16.
70. Edwards 1966, 288–289; Randles 1988, 131; Jacobs 1975, 196; Fuller 1966a, 164, 189.
71. Fuller 1966a, 205–206.
72. Vallee 1969, 42.
73. Fuller 1966a, 232–235; Edwards 1966, 259–265; Keyhoe 1973, 213–224; Keyhoe 1973, Keel 1971, 195; Flying Saucer Review 1966, Vallee 1969, 320.
74. Edwards 1966, 266; Fuller 1966a, 235–236.
75. Edwards 1966, 127–128; UFO Magazine 1991; Opatka n.d.; Cameron 1997; Randle 1995, 95–120.
76. Fawcett and Greenwood 1984, 4; Powers 1979, 8; Donner 1980, 253; Cole 1988, 65–71.
77. Thomas 1989, 252.
78. Chomsky 1989, 75.
79. Jacobs 1975, 195–200; Vallee 1979, 228.
80. Clark 1992, 137.
81. Jacobs 1975, 198–199; Randles 1988, 63–64; Flammonde 1976, 343–344.
82. Fuller 1966a, 248.
83. Delgado and Andrews 1989, 180; Randles 1988, 171; Flying Saucer Review 1966; Vallee 1969, 32–33, 322.
84. Keyhoe 1973, 117–118; Vallee 1969, 323.
85. Keyhoe 1973, 118; Vallee 1969, 323.
86. Saunders and Harkins 1968, 61; Keyhoe 1973, 118; Jacobs 1975, 200–202; Vallee 1975, 43–44; 1969, 323; Hynek 1966, 17–21.
87. Wise 1966; Newsweek 1966; David 1967, 195–197, 209–212.
88. Jacobs 1975, 203; Vallee 1975, 45–46.
89. Jacobs 1975, 204; Randles 1988, 63–64.
90. Jacobs 1975, 204–206; Vallee 1975, 44; Flammonde 1976, 345; Steiger 1976, 17.
91. Keyhoe 1973, 121; Jacobs 1975, 200.
92. Vallee 1969, 324; Clark 1996, 290–291.
93. Vallee 1969, 326–328.
94. Hynek 1972; Clark 1996, 396–406; 1998, 450–465.
95. Vallee 1969, 329; 1975, 44; Keyhoe 1973, 121–122.

96. Hynek 1977, 112; Clark 1996, 292–294; Vallee 1992a.
97. Lorenzen and Lorenzen 1976, 98.
98. Lorenzen and Lorenzen 1968, 74; Keyhoe 1973, 122.
99. Vallee 1975, 49.
100. Keyhoe 1973, 122; Vallee 1969, 332.
101. Vallee 1969, 334.
102. David 1967, 213; Hynek 1966; Vallee 1969, 334.
103. Vallee 1969, 335–336.
104. Sanderson 1970, 58–61.
105. Saunders and Harkins 1968, 129, 194; Keyhoe 1973, 152; Jacobs 1975, 208.
106. Flammonde 1976, 345.
107. Keyhoe 1973, 126.
108. Jacobs 1975, 216–217; Blum 1990, 216; *New York Times* 1966; David 1967, 158; Clark 1996, 298.

Chapter 8

1. U.S. Air Force 1966; Edwards 1967, 123.
2. Keyhoe 1973, 130–132; Jacobs 1975, 209; Flammond 1976, 345–346; Sauders and Harkins 1968.
3. Clark 1996, 294.
4. Jacobs 1975, 214–220; Clark 1996, 249.
5. Saunders and Harkins 1968, 117.
6. Keyhoe 1973, 137; Saunders and Harkins 1968, 46–47.
7. Vallee 1969, 49–50; Saunders and Harkins 1968, 60–61; Craig 1995, 189–190.
8. Saunders and Harkins 1968, 61.
9. Saunders and Harkins 1968, 64.
10. Keyhoe 1973, 131–134; Saunders and Harkins 1968, 62–63.
11. Keyhoe 1973, 136.
12. Craig 1995, 235; Randle 1997a, 150.
13. Lorenzen and Lorenzen 1976, 4; David 213–226.
14. *Flying Saucer Review* 1967; 1968; Vallee 1969, 337–338.
15. Saunders and Harkins 1968, 68–69, 73–76, 109–110.
16. Saunders and Harkins 1968, 118–119.
17. Keyhoe 1973, 137–139; Clark 1996, 295.
18. Vallee 1975, 50; 1979, 52; Randle 1997a, 149.
19. Good 1988, 345.
20. Saunders and Harkins 1968, 110.
21. Saunders and Harkins 1968, 130–133.
22. Keyhoe 1973, 142; Good 1988, 23.
23. Keyhoe 1973, 143, 147.
24. Lorenzen and Lorenzen 1968, 196.
25. Thomas 1989, 253, 258–259.
26. Valentine 1990; Powers 1979, 230–232.
27. Powers 1979, 237–241.
28. Wise n.d., 23.

29. Powers 1979, 151, 165, 198.
30. Donner 1980, 270–271; Wise 1976, 184.
31. Donner 1980, 212–232, 263, 276.
32. Jacobs 1975, 222; Lorenzen and Lorenzen 1976, 5, 98, 186–190; 1968, 22, 216; Clark 1996, 94, 293.
33. Vallee 1969, 339–340; Lorenzen and Lorenzen 1968, 59–60.
34. Randles 1988, 134.
35. Fawcett and Greenwood 1984, 237.
36. Keyhoe 1973, 10–11; Good 1988, 300–301.
37. Klotz and Salas n.d.
38. Fowler 1981, 186–187; Good 1988, 301; Vallee 1969, 341–342.
39. Fawcett and Greenwood 1984, 195–201.
40. Lorenzen and Lorenzen 1968, 60, 65; *Flying Saucer Review* 1967; Vallee 1969, 342–344.
41. Gillmor 1969, 316–324; Vallee 1969, 345; Clark 1996, 191–200.
42. Clark 1996, 297–298; Randles 1988, 65; Good 1988, 369; Crone 1967.
43. Clark 1996, 295, 298.
44. Keyhoe 1973, 147; Saunders and Harkins 1968, 117.
45. Saunders and Harkins 1968, 182.
46. Keyhoe 1973, 257; Craig 1995, 188.
47. Saunders and Harkins 1968, 81–83.
48. Saunders and Harkins 1968, 113–116.
49. Saunders and Harkins 1968, 106.
50. Saunders and Harkins 1968, 134; Jacobs 1975, 229; Craig, 196.
51. Lorenzen and Lorenzen 1968, 63.
52. Lorenzen and Lorenzen 1976, 56–58, 254; 1968, 42–43.
53. Lorenzen and Lorenzen 1961–63.
54. NICAP 1968; Vallee 1969, 348–349; Sanderson 1970, 38; Lorenzen and Lorenzen 1968, 54.
55. Sanderson 1970, 20–21.
56. Lorenzen and Lorenzen 1968, 54–55; NICAP 1968; Vallee 1969, 350; Sanderson 1970.
57. Lorenzen and Lorenzen 1968, 11; 1976, 248.
58. Vallee 1992; 1969, 346–350; 1979, 39–40; *Flying Saucer Review* 1967; 1968; *APRO Bulletin* 1967.
59. Saunders and Harkins 1968, 135. On Hynek, see FBI file on Dr. J. Allen Hynek, http://www.cufon.org/cufon/fbihynek.htm.
60. Saunders and Harkins 1968, 124–125.
61. Saunders and Harkins 1968, 123–124.
62. Saunders and Harkins 1968, 140–141, 247.
63. Saunders and Harkins 1968, 140.
64. Saunders and Harkins 1968, 141–142; Keyhoe 1973, 148–149, 255.
65. Saunders and Harkins 1968, 146.
66. Saunders and Harkins 1968, 142–143; Craig 1995, 197.
67. Lorenzen and Lorenzen 1976, 5; Keyhoe 1973, 150.
68. Howe 1989, 1–5, 104; Vallee 1969, 47; Clark 1996, 18–20.

69. Gillmor 1969, 351–353; Sanderson 1970, 38–39; Keyhoe 1973, 150; Lorenzen and Lorenzen 1968, 56; Clark 1996, 135–136.
70. Lorenzen and Lorenzen 1968, 225.
71. Saunders and Harkins 1968, 176.
72. Lorenzen and Lorenzen 1968, 197.
73. Saunders and Harkins 1968, 179, 194; Keyhoe 1973, 150–151; Craig 1995, 188.
74. Saunders and Harkins 1968, 179; Craig 1995, 190.
75. Clark 1996, 299.
76. Vallee 1975, 57–59; 1969, 356; Randles 1988, 65–70; *Flying Saucer Review* 1968; Clark 1996, 95–96.
77. Saunders and Harkins 1968, 186–200, 244–252; Keyhoe 1973, 175; Craig 1995, 200–201; Clark 1996, 296.
78. *Look* 1968; Craig 1995, 205–206, 244; Keyhoe 1973, 177; Jacobs 1975, 233.
79. Keyhoe 1973, 178–179; Criag 1995, 207–208, 211, 220; Saunders and Harkins 1968, 201–204; Clark 1996, 297, 415.
80. McDonald 1968; Keyhoe 1973, 179–186; Jacobs 1975, 233–238; Flammonde 1976, 346–347; Clark 1996, 297; Saunders and Harkins 1968, 173–174; *UFO Magazine* 1991.
81. Saunders and Harkins 1968, 202.
82. Fowler 1981.
83. It has been suggested elsewhere, including in the first edition of this book, that the author of this document was the legendary Lambros D. Callimahos, known within the NSA as "The Guru." I am grateful to Dr. Hal Puthoff for the correction of this error. The document's author remains classified information.
84. Computer UFO Network 1968; Good 1988, 423–424; Fawcett and Greenwood 1984, 185–186; Blum 1990, 80.
85. Kocher n.d.
86. Keyhoe 1973, 177; Craig 1995, 202.
87. *Flying Saucer Review* 1968; Vallee 1969, 356.
88. Sanderson 1970, 38; *Flying Saucer Review* 1968; Vallee 1969, 357; Bowen 41.
89. *Flying Saucer Review* 1968; Vallee 1969, 357–358.
90. Bowen 1977, 40–56.
91. Vallee 1979, 31; 1975, 21–25; 1969, 359; Clark 1996, 161–165.
92. Craig 1995, 213.
93. Keyhoe 1973, 250–252; 266–267; Flammonde 1976, 347; Craig 1995, 238.
94. Keyhoe 1973, 269–276; Flammonde 1976, 347; Jacobs 1975, 242, 249.
95. Jacobs 1975, 243–244; Clark 1996, 297; Keyhoe 1973, 275–277.
96. Clark 1996, 416.
97. Jacobs 1975, 252.
98. Donner 1980, 263, 274; Tully 1969, 22, 77.
99. Donner 1980, 29, 232, 287–288.
100. Powers 1979, 315; De Landa 1991, 228.
101. Thomas 1989, 272–276; Keith 1997, 60.
102. Donner 1980, 318–319.

103. Powers 1979, 255; Summers 1994, 435; Wise 1976, 55.
104. Chomsky and Hermann 1979, 116–117, 288, 340; Peck 1987, 266; Wise 1976, 88.
105. Tully 1969, 9, 11.
106. Bolender 1969.
107. Hynek 1977, 287; Keyhoe 1973, 279–280; Stringfield 1977, 156; Vallee 1975, 51, Friedman and Berliner 1992, 35–38; Flammonde 1976, 347–349; Craig 1995, 236.
108. Fawcett and Greenwood 1984, 13–14; Keyhoe 1973, 280–281.
109. Zechel 1979, 5–8; Good 1988, 351–352; Fowler 1981; Fawcett and Greenwood 1984, 207; Clark 1992, 259–261.
110. Clark 1996, 567.
111. Clark 1996, 64.
112. *Flying Saucer Review* 1970; Delgado and Andrews 1989, 183.
113. Clark 1996, 82.
114. Delgado and Andrews 1989, 179; Vallee 1979, 164.
115. Delgado and Andrews 1989, 188.
116. Vallee 1969, 56.
117. Sagan and Page 1972; Keyhoe 1973, 279; Clark 1996, 1–3.

Chapter 9

1. Powers 1979, 11, 290–300; Wise 1976.
2. Weiner 1990, 128.
3. Donner 1980, 275–277.
4. Thomas 1989, 276; Marks 1979, 218.
5. Summers 1994, 448–451; Donner 1980, 263; Wise 1976, 70.
6. Donner 1980, 265–267; Powers 1979, 318–319; Wise 1976, 154–155, 269; Summers 1994, 472.
7. Donner 1980, 181, 240; Wise 1976, 281; Summers 1994, 455–456.
8. Wise 1976, 79, 156–157; Powers 1979, 323.
9. Summers 1994, 430, 480–501.
10. Powers 1979, 309, 320, 345; Wise 1976, 158, 178; Summers 1994, 480.
11. Thomas 1989, 278–279; Donner 1980, 276; Powers 1979, 313–314, 348.
12. Powers 1979, 10–11, 352; Donner 1980, 277.
13. Powers 1979, 14, 358–361, 367; Thomas 1989, 280–281.
14. Powers 1979, 366; Wise 1976, 75, 165; Donner 1980, 248.
15. Delgado and Andrews 1989, 179.
16. Vallee 1975, 35–36; Clark 1996, 148–151.
17. Delgado and Andrews 1989, 184–185.
18. Hall 1988, 269–270; *Skylook* 1973.
19. Howe 1989; Rommel 1980; Onet n.d.; Vallee 1979, 164; The Learning Channel 1999.
20. Sanderson 1970. See also De Landa 1991.
21. Clark 1996, 3–5; 1998, 604.
22. Keyhoe 1973, 282; Fawcett and Greenwood 1984, 142.
23. Jacobs 1975, 261; Clark 1996, 299–300.

24. Keith 1997, 204, 220, 239.

25. Vallee 1975, 17; Clark 1996, 206–207; Keyhoe 1973, 3–4; Randles 1988, 160–161.

26. Vallee 1975, 15, 51–52; Clark 1996, 96, 200–202, 389–398; Hall 1988, 270–271; Randles 1988, 162–163.

27. Clark 1996, 121–126; Randles 1988, 102–105; Hall 1988, 271–272.

28. *New York Times* 1973; Flammonde 1976, 30–32; Stringfield 1977, 142; Vallee 1979, 228; 1975, 40.

29. Blum 1990, 82; Bowen 1977, vii–xi; Vallee 1975, 56.

Bibliography

Author's note. This is not exhaustive, but merely a listing of sources I have used in this study. Several sources, in particular those dealing with non-UFO matters of the intelligence community, could well have been replaced, or supplemented, by other studies. Nevertheless, the following bibliography constitutes a good foundation upon which to build.

Adler, Bill, ed. 1967. *Letters to the Air Force on UFOs*. New York: Dell.

Air Defense Command. 1947. Letter on "Cooperation of FBI with AAF on Investigations of 'Flying Disc' Incidents" (03 September).

Air Material Command. 1947. "Flying Discs." Letter to Commander of the Army Air Forces (23 September).

Alaska Communication System. 1947. "Subject: Matters of National Interest" (19 August). Signal Corps. http://www.project1947.com/fig/bethel.htm.

Aldrich, Jan L. n.d. "1948 UFO Documents: Background: Early Documents." http://www.project1947.com/fig/1948back.htm.

APRO Bulletin. 1959. Report (September).

———. 1962. Editorial (July) and Article (September).

———. 1967. Article (July).

Arnold, Kenneth, and Ray Palmer. 1952. *The Coming of the Saucers: A Documentary Report on Sky Objects That Have Mystified the World*. Amherst, Wisconsin: The Authors.

Ashpole, Edward. 1989. *The Search for Extraterrestrial Intelligence*. London: Blandford Press.

Associated Press. 1947. Stories, 04 July, 08 July.

ATIC. 1955. "Evaluation of Unidentified Flying Objects." Memorandum (15 February).

Atomic Energy Commission. 1953. "Air Space Violation at Oak Ridge, Tennessee." Nashville: Tennessee Military District (27 July).

Ayres, Congressman William H. 1958. Letter to NICAP (28 January).

Bamford, James. 1982. *The Puzzle Palace: A Report on America's Most Secret Agency*. Boston: Houghton Mifflin.

Barclay, David, and Therese Marie Barclay, eds. 1993. *UFOs: The Final Answer? Ufology for the Twenty-first Century*. London: Blandford Press.

Barker, Gray. 1956. *They Knew Too Much About Flying Saucers*. New York: University Books.

Barron, John. 1974. *KGB: The Secret Work of Soviet Secret Agents*. New York: Reader's Digest Press.

Bender, Albert K. 1963. *Flying Saucers and the Three Men*. N.p.: Neville Spearman Ltd. See also Close Encounters with Mysterious "Men in Black." http://www.peg.apc.org/~nexus/meninblack.html.

Berlin Command of Military Government for Germany (U.S.). 1947. "Subject: Horten Brothers (Flying Saucers)" (16 December). http://www.project1947.com/fig/horten1.htm.

Berliner, Don. n.d. The Blue Book Unknowns. http://www.ibmpcug.co.uk/~irdial/bluebook.htm.

Berlitz, Charles, and William Moore. 1980. *The Roswell Incident*. New York: Grosset and Dunlap.

Bernstein, Carl. 1977. The CIA and the Media: How America's Most Powerful News Media Worked Hand in Glove with the Central Intelligence Agency. *Rolling Stone*, 20 October, 55–67.

Birdsall, Mark. 1992. Nazi Secret Weapon: Foo Fighters of WWII. *UFO Magazine* 7 (4):32–34.

Bitzer, J. Barry. 1995. Schiff Receives, Releases Roswell Report. Missing Documents Leave Unanswered Questions (28 July). http://www.v_j_enterprises.com/gao.html.

Black Vault: UFOs [http://blackvault.com/ufos/]. Contains thousands of U.S. government documents pertaining to UFOs.

Bloecher, Ted. 1967. *Report of the UFO Wave of 1947*. N.p.: The Author.

Blum, Howard. 1990. *Out There: The Government's Secret Quest for Extraterrestrials*. New York: Simon and Schuster.

Bolender, Brig. Gen. Carroll H. 1969. Memorandum. CUFON Computer Info Service. Freedom of Information Act Document Files, #54. http://www.textfiles.com/ufo/foiadoc.ufo.

Bondarchuk, Yurko. 1979. *UFO Canada.* New York: Signet Books.

Borklund, C. W. 1966. *Men of the Pentagon, from Forrestal to MacNamara.* New York: Praeger Publishers.

Borosage, Robert L., and John Marks, eds. 1976. *The CIA File.* New York: Grossman Publishers. Especially, David Wise's article, "Covert Operations Abroad: An Overview."

Bowen, Charles, ed. 1977. *Encounter Cases from Flying Saucer Review.* New York: Signet Books.

Bowers, H. L. 1949. "Notes and Comments on 'Unidentified Flying Objects'—Project Sign." CIA Memorandum to Dr. Machle (31 March).

Bryan, Joseph. 1956. Letter to Edward J. Ruppelt (03 April). Cited in *Captain Edward J. Ruppelt: Summer of the Saucers—1952,* edited by Miranda Jane Emmert (Albuquerque, N.M.: Rose Press International, 2000), 100.

Burgess, Gen. W. M. 1953. Memorandum (04 December). AISS Document.

Cameron, Grant Robert. 1997. "'Special Prosecutor' for James Oberg?" Usenet article (01 March).

Cannon, Martin. 1989. *The Controllers: A New Hypothesis of Alien Abduction.* N.p.: The Author.

Central Intelligence Agency. n.d. "Unidentified Aircraft at Marignane Airfield, France;" "Unidentified Objects over Southern Rhodesia;" "Flying Saucers over the Hague, Netherlands." Reports in Lawrence Fawcett and Barry Greenwood, *Clear Intent: The Government Cover-up of the UFO Experience* (Englewood Cliffs, N.J.: Prentice-Hall, 1984).

———. 1949. Memorandum (15 March). Office of Special Investigation.

———. 1950. "Information Report." Memorandum (04 August).

———. 1952. Draft report (15 August).

———. 1953a. "Danish Defense Leaders Take Serious View of Flying Saucers." Document quoting Stockholm *Morgan-Tidningen* (13 July).

———. 1953b. "Celestial Disk Changes Form." CIA Report Describing Sighting in France (09 December).

———. 1954. "Flying Disk Sighted in Aisne Department" and Reports (September).

———. 1958a. Teletype (11 December). Cited in Lawrence Fawcett and Barry Greenwood, *Clear Intent: The Government Cover-up of the UFO Experience* (Englewood Cliffs, N.J.: Prentice-Hall, 1984), 137–138.

————. 1958b. "Reported Photographs of Unidentified Flying Objects." Memorandum (01 October).

————. 1960. Memorandum (17 March). Cited in Lawrence Fawcett and Barry Greenwood, *Clear Intent: The Government Cover-up of the UFO Experience* (Englewood Cliffs, N.J.: Prentice-Hall, 1984), 137–138.

Chadwell, H. Marshall. 1952a. "Subject: Flying Saucers." Memorandum for Director of Central Intelligence (24 September).

————. 1952b. Memorandum from Assistant Director of Scientific Intelligence to CIA Director (02 December).

Chalker, Bill. 1996. *The Oz Files: The Australian UFO Story*. Potts Point, N.S.W., Australia: Duffy and Snellgrove.

Chamberlain, Jo. 1945. "The Foo Fighter Mystery." *The American Legion Magazine*. Project 1947. http://www.project1947.com/amlfoo.html.

Chomsky, Noam. 1989. *Necessary Illusions: Thought Control in Democratic Societies*. Boston: South End Press.

Chomsky, Noam, and Edward S. Herman. 1979. *After the Cataclysm, Postwar Indochina and the Reconstruction of Imperial Ideology*. Boston: South End Press.

CIRVIS. 1954a. Operational Immediate. Report (29 March).

————. 1954b. Report from the Flight Service Center, Maxwell AFB, to Commander of Air Defense Command, Ent AFB, Colorado (12 August).

Clark, Jerome. 1992. *The UFO Encyclopedia, Volume Two. The Emergence of a Phenomenon, from the Beginning through 1959*. Detroit: Omnigraphics, Inc.

————. 1996. *The UFO Encyclopedia, Volume Three. High Strangeness: UFOs from 1960 to 1979*. Detroit: Omnigraphics, Inc.

————. 1998. *The UFO Book: Encyclopedia of the Extraterrestrial*. Detroit: Omnigraphics, Inc.

Clark, Ralph L. 1952. Memorandum from Acting Assistant Director for the Office of Scientific Intelligence to the Deputy Director of Intelligence (29 July).

Cockburn, Alexander, and Jeffrey St. Clair. 1998. *Whiteout: The CIA, Drugs, and the Press*. New York: Verso.

Cole, Leonard A. 1988. *Clouds of Secrecy: The Army's Germ Warfare Tests over Populated Areas*. Totowa, N.J.: Rowman & Littlefield.

Computer UFO Network. n.d. Library of Verified UFO Documents Released through the Freedom of Information Act. http://www.cufon.org/cufon/cufon_v.htm.

————. 1952. Special Report on Conferences with Astronomers on Unidentified Flying Aerial Objects to Air Technical Intelligence Center, Wright-Patterson Air Force Base (06 August). http://www.parapsychology.com/dossier/HardEvidence/stork1–7.txt.

————. 1968. "UFO Hypothesis and Survival Questions." Draft. http://www.cufon.org.

Corso, Col. Philip J. (Ret.) with William J. Birnes. 1997. *The Day after Roswell*. New York: Pocket Books.

Counter Intelligence Corps. 1947. "Subject: Flying Saucers" (10 November). Region VI, 970th Counter Intelligence Corps Detachment. http://www.project 1947.com/fig/cicnov47.htm.

Covington, John. n.d. *Maury Island: What Really Happened?* http://www.seanet.com/~johnso/maury.htm.

Craig, Roy. 1995. *UFOs: An Insider's View of the Official Quest for Evidence*. Denton, Texas: University of North Texas Press.

Crone, Nyla. 1967. "The UFO Phenomenon: A New Frontier Awaiting Serious Scientific Exploration." *Arizona Daily Wildcat* (06 April).

Cross, H. C. 1953. Letter to Miles E. Coll (09 January).

David, Jay, ed. 1967. *The Flying Saucer Reader*. New York: Signet Books.

De Landa, Manuel. 1991. *War in the Age of Intelligent Machines*. New York: Zone Books.

Delgado, Pat, and Colin Andrews. 1989. *Circular Evidence: A Detailed Investigation of the Flattened Swirled Crops Phenomenon*. London: Bloomsbury.

Department of State. 1946. Telegrams dated 11 July 1946, 29 August 1946.

Dinges, John. 1991. *Our Man in Panama*. New York: Random House.

Donner, Frank J. 1980. *The Age of Surveillance: The Aims and Methods of America's Political Intelligence System*. New York: Knopf.

Dulles, Allen. 1966. *The Secret Surrender*. New York: Harper & Row.

Durant, F. C. 1953. *Report on Meetings of Scientific Advisory Panel on Unidentified Flying Objects Convened by Office of Scientific Intelligence, CIA: January 14–18, 1953*. Washington, D.C.: Central Intelligence Agency.

Edwards, Frank. 1966. *Flying Saucers, Serious Business*. New York: L. Stuart.

————. 1967. *Flying Saucers, Here and Now!* New York; L. Stuart.

Fate. "UFO Lands in New Mexico." Article (August).

Fawcett, Lawrence, and Barry Greenwood. 1984. *Clear Intent: The Government Cover-up of the UFO Experience*. Englewood Cliffs, N.J.: Prentice-Hall.

Federal Bureau of Investigators. 1947a. Teletype message, 08 July.

———.1947b. Memorandum for Mr. Ladd (10 July). Freedom of Information Act Document Files. CUFON Computer UFO Network. Document 1.

———. 1947c. Memorandum from E. G. Fitch on "Flying Discs" (29 July).

———. 1947d. Memorandum on "Reports of Flying Discs" (19 September).

———. 1949a. Memorandum from Special Agent in Charge, San Antonio, Texas, to FBI Director J. Edgar Hoover (31 January).

———. 1949b. Memorandum (25 March).

———.1950a. "Unidentified Phenomena in the Vicinity of Kodiak, Alaska." Memorandum (10 February).

———. 1950b. "Summary of Aerial Phenomena in New Mexico." Memorandum (August).

———. 1950c. "Object Sighted over Oak Ridge, Tennessee." Memorandum (25 October).

———. 1950d. "Re: Flying Saucers." Memorandum (03 December).

———. 1952a. "Subject: Flying Saucers." Memorandum (29 July).

———. 1952b. Memorandum (27 October).

Fitch, E. G. 1947. "Subject: Flying Saucers." Office Memorandum to D. M. Ladd (06 August). U.S. Government.

Flammonde, Paris. 1976. *UFO Exist!* New York: Putnam.

Flying Saucer Review. 1958. Article (March).

———. 1962. Article (December).

———. 1963. Articles (April and May).

———. 1964. Articles (April and July–August).

———. 1965. Articles (January, April, and May).

———. 1966. Articles (February, April, and June).

———. 1967. Articles (January, March, and May).

———. 1968. Articles (February, April, and May).

———. 1970. Article (January–February).

Focus. 1985. "Senator Richard Russell's UFO Sighting: Top Secret!" Article (30 September).

Fort, Charles. 1941. *The Books of Charles Fort*. New York: Henry Holt and Company.

———. 1997. *Lo!* Revised by Mr. X. N.p.: John Brown Publishing.

Fowler, Raymond E. 1981. *Casebook of a UFO Investigator: A Personal Memoir.* Englewood Cliffs, N.J.: Prentice-Hall.

Friedman, Stanton T. 1990. *Final Report on Operation Majestic 12.* Mount Ranier, Md.: n.p.

———. 1996. *Top Secret/MAJIC.* New York: Marlowe & Co.

Friedman, Stanton T., and Don Berliner. 1992. *Crash at Corona: The U.S. Military Retrieval and Cover-up of a UFO.* New York: Paragon House.

Fuchs, James R. 1947. Oral History Interview with Gen. Robert B. Landry (28 February). Interview transcript, Harry S. Truman Library. http://www.sunsite.unc.edu/lia/president/TrumanLibrary/oral_histories/Landry_Robert.html.

Fuller, Curtis G., ed. 1980. *Proceedings of the First International UFO Congress.* New York: Warner Books.

Fuller, John G. 1966a. *Incident at Exeter: The Story of Unidentified Flying Objects over America Today.* New York: Putnam.

———. 1966b. *The Interrupted Journey: Two Hours Lost "Aboard a Flying Saucer."* New York: MJF Books.

Germann, Val. 1995. "Power Science and the UFO." Usenet (07 Aug). http://www.alt.paranet.ufo.

Gillmor, Daniel S., ed. 1969. *Final Report of the Scientific Study of Unidentified Flying Objects. Conducted by the University of Colorado under Contract to the United States Air Force.* New York: Bantam Books.

Good, Timothy. 1988. *Above Top Secret: The Worldwide UFO Cover-up.* New York: Morrow.

Greenfield, Irving. 1967. *The UFO Report.* N.p.: Lancer Books.

Greenwood, Barry. n.d. Majestic-12 Follies Returns. UFO Historical Revue. http://www.cufon.org/uhr/uhr3.htm.

Haines, Gerald K. 1997. A Die-Hard Issue: CIA's Role in the Study of UFOs, 1947–1990. *Studies in Intelligence* 1, no. 1.

Halbritter, Ron. n.d. Before the UFO Crash at Roswell, There was . . . Maury Island: The Hoax on You. http://www.n6rpf.com_us.net/maury-isl.html#list.

Hall, Richard, ed. 1964. *The UFO Evidence.* Washington, D.C.: The National Investigations Committee on Aerial Phenomena.

———. 1988. *Uninvited Guests: A Documented History of UFO Sightings, Alien Encounters & Cover-ups.* Santa Fe, N.M.: Aurora Press.

———. 2001. Interview in *International UFO Reporter*, 26, no. 1 (Spring).

Hansen, Terry. 2000. *The Missing Times: News Media Complicity in the UFO Cover-up*. N.p.: Xlibris Corporation.

Hendry, Allan. 1979. *The UFO Handbook: A Guide to Investigating, Evaluating, and Reporting UFO Sightings*. Garden City, N.Y.: Doubleday.

Hesemann, Michael, and Philip Mantle. 1997. *Beyond Roswell: The Alien Autopsy Film, Area 51, and the U.S. Government Cover-up of UFOs*. New York: Marlowe & Co.

Holledge, James. 1965. *Flying Saucers over Australia*. London: Horwitz.

Hoopes, Townsend, and Douglas Brinkley. 1992. *Driven Patriot: The Life and Times of James Forrestal*. New York: Knopf.

Howe, Linda Moulton. 1989. *An Alien Harvest: Further Evidence Linking Animal Mutilations and Human Abductions to Alien Life Forms*. Littleton, Colo.: L. M. Howe Productions.

Hunt, Linda. 1991. *Secret Agenda: The United States Government, Nazi Scientists, and Project Paperclip, 1945 to 1990*. New York: St. Martin's Press.

Hynek, J. Allen. n.d. *Special Report on Conferences with Astronomers on Unidentified Flying Aerial Objects to Air Technical Intelligence Center, Wright-Patterson Air Force Base (August 6, 1952)*. See Computer UFO Network, Seattle, Washington. http://www.parapsycology.com/dossier/HardEvidence/stork1_7.txt.

———. 1966. Are Flying Saucers Real? *Saturday Evening Post* (17 December), 17–21.

———. 1972. *The UFO Experience: A Scientific Inquiry*. Chicago: H. Regnery Co.

———. 1977. *The Hynek UFO Report*. New York: Dell.

Interavia. 1956. The Gravitics Situation. Gravity Rand Ltd. XI, no. 5, 373–374.

Jacobs, David. 1975. *The UFO Controversy in America*. Bloomington: Indiana University Press.

Jessup, Morris K. 1955. *The Case for the UFO, Unidentified Flying Objects*. New York: Citadel Press.

———. 1957. *The Expanding Case for the UFO*. (New York: Citadel Press.

Johnson, Loch K. 1989. *America's Secret Power: The CIA in a Democratic Society*. New York: Oxford University Press.

Kabus, Irvin. 1954. Report filed (30 April). 809th CIC Det.

Keel, John. 1970. *UFOs: Operation Trojan Horse*. New York: Putnam.

———. 1971. *Our Haunted Planet*. New York: Fawcett Publications.

Keith, Jim. 1997. *Mind Control, World Control: The Encyclopedia of Mind Control*. N.p.: Adventures Unlimited Press.

Keyhoe, Donald E. 1950. *The Flying Saucers Are Real.* New York: Fawcett Publications.

———. 1953. *Flying Saucers from Outer Space.* New York: Holt and Company.

———. 1955. *The Flying Saucer Conspiracy.* New York: Holt and Company.

———. 1960. *Flying Saucers: Top Secret.* New York: Putnam.

———. 1973. *Aliens from Space.* Garden City, N.Y.: Doubleday.

Klass, Philip. 1974. *UFOs Explained.* New York: Random House.

———. 1983. *UFOs: The Public Deceived.* Buffalo, N.Y.: Prometheus Books.

———. 1997. *The Real Roswell Crashed-Saucer Cover-up.* Amherst, N.Y.: Prometheus Books.

Klotz, Jim, and Robert Salas. n.d. *The Malmstrom AFB UFO/Missile Incident.* http://www.cufon.org/cufon/malmstrom/malm1.htm.

Kocher, George. n.d. "UFOs: What to Do." Private Paper. Official Web Site, National Investigations Committee on Aerial Phenomena. http://www.qtm.net/~geibdan/newse/July/rand.htm.

Korff, Kal K. 1997. *The Roswell UFO Crash: What They Don't Want You to Know.* Amherst, N.Y.: Prometheus Books.

The Learning Channel. 1996. Alien Secrets: Area 51. Transmedia and Dandelion Productions for Sky Television.

———. 1999. "The Cattle Files." Transmedia and Dandelion Productions.

LeMay, Curtis, and MacKinlay Kantor. 1965. *Mission with LeMay: My Story.* Garden City, N.Y.: Doubleday.

LePoer Trench, Brinsley. 1966. *The Flying Saucer Story.* London: Spearman.

Library Journal. 1953. Review (01 November).

———. 1955. Review (01 December), 80:2766.

Life. 1958. Article (06 January).

Look. 1968. Magazine Article (14 May).

Loftin, Robert. 1968. *Identified Flying Saucers.* New York: D. McKay Co.

Lorenzen, Coral E. 1966. *Flying Saucers: The Startling Evidence of the Invasion from Outer Space: An Exposure of the Establishment's Flying Saucer Cover-up.* (Original Title: *The Great Flying Saucer Hoax*) New York: William-Frederick Press).

Lorenzen, Jim, and Coral Lorenzen. 1967. *Flying Saucer Occupants.* New York: New American Library.

————. 1968. *UFOs over the Americas.* New York: Signet Books.

————. 1969. *UFOs: The Whole Story.* New York: New American Library.

————. 1976. *Encounters with UFO Occupants.* New York: Berkeley.

Mandelkorn, Cmdr. Richard S. 1949. *Report of a Trip to Los Alamos, New Mexico, 16 February 1949.* U.S. Navy. Research and Development Division. Sandia Base, Albuquerque, New Mexico.

Marchetti, Victor, and John Marks. 1980. *The CIA and the Cult of Intelligence.* New York: Knopf.

Marks, John. 1979. *The Search for the Manchurian Candidate: The CIA and Mind Control; The Secret History of the Behavioral Sciences.* New York: Times Books.

Marrs, Jim. 1997. *Alien Agenda: Investigating the Extraterrrestrial Presence among Us.* New York: Harper Collins Publishers.

McAndrew, Capt. James. 1997. *The Roswell Report: Case Closed.* (Washington, D.C.: Headquarters United States Air Force.

McAndrew, First Lt. James. n.d. *Project Mogul: Balloon Research Findings.* The Air Force Report.

McCoy, Alfred W. 1991. *The Politics of Heroin: CIA Complicity in the Global Drug Trade.* Brooklyn, N.Y.: Lawrence Hill Books.

McDonald, James E. n.d. Letter to Richard Hall.

————. 1968. "In Search of Scientific Legitimacy." Statement to Congress (29 July).

————. 1972. Science in Default: Twenty-Two Years of Inadequate UFO Investigations. In *UFOs: A Scientific Debate*, edited by Carl Sagan and Thornton Page. Ithaca, N.Y.: Cornell University Press, 52–122.

McLaughlin, Cmdr. R. B. 1950. "How Scientists Tracked a Flying Saucer." *True* (March).

Menzel, Donald H. 1953a. *Flying Saucers.* Cambridge: Harvard University Press.

————. 1953b. Letter to Maj. Gen. John A. Samford, Air Technical Intelligence Center, Dayton, Ohio (16 October).

Menzel, Donald H., and Lyle G. Boyd. 1963. *The World of Flying Saucers: A Scientific Examination of a Major Myth of the Space Age.* Garden City, N.Y.: Doubleday.

Menzel, Donald H., and Ernest H. Taves. 1977. *The UFO Enigma: The Definitive Explanation of the UFO Phenomenon.* Garden City, N.Y.: Doubleday.

Miami Herald. 1961. Report (11 January).

Michel, Aimé. 1956. *The Truth about Flying Saucers*. New York: Criterion Books.

———. 1958. *Flying Saucers and the Straight-Line Mystery*. New York: Criterion Books.

Miller, Lt. Col. W. 1953. U.S. Army Intelligence Report from Director, Counterintelligence Division, to the Assistant Chief of Staff, G-2 (10 December).

Mills, James. 1986. *The Underground Empire: Where Crime and Governments Embrace*. Garden City, N.Y.: Doubleday.

Moore, C. B. n.d. "Object Report." CIA document. General Mills Aeronautical Research.

NASA. 1962. Letter to *Flying Saucer Review* (22 May).

The Nation. 1961. Report (07 January).

Neues Europa. 1959. Article (01 January).

New York Herald-Tribune. 1955. "Space-Ship Marvel Seen If Gravity Outwitted." Article (21 November).

New York Times. 1946. Article, 11 October.

———.1953. Review (22 November), 50.

———. 1956. Review (22 January).

———. 1960. Article (15 December).

———. 1961. Report (10 January).

———. 1966. Article (23 August).

———. 1973. Article (21 October).

Newsweek. 1966. "Pie in the Sky". Article (04 April).

NICAP. 1968. *UFO Investigator*. Article (March).

NICAP Bulletin. 1962. Report (August).

Oberth, Hermann. 1957. *Man into Space: New Projects for Rocket and Space Travel*. Translated by G. P. H. DeFreville. New York: Harper.

Oldenburgh, Capt. G. H. 1958. Letter (23 January).

Onet, George E., D.V.M., Ph.D. n.d. "Animal Mutilations: What We Know, and Don't Know." National Institute for Discovery Science. http://www.accessnv.com/nids/animal1-1.html.

Opatka, Kim. n.d. Kecksburg Crash Controversy Remains Unsolved. http://www.cninews.com.

Ordway, Frederick I. and Mitchell R. Sharpe. 1979. *The Rocket Team*. Foreword by Wernher von Braun. New York: Crowell.

Osborn, Barbara Bliss. 1998. "Are You Sure You Want to Ruin Your Career?" *FAIR* 11 (2) http://speech.scun.edu/ben/news/cia/index.html.

Overbeck, Ashley. n.d. *Spooky News: A Report on CIA Infiltration and Manipulation of the Mass Media.* http://www.mprofaca.cro.net/mainmenu.html.

Page, Thornton. 1992. Letter to James L. Klotz (03 October). http://www.cufon.com/cufon/tp_corres.htm.

Palmer, Raymond. 1967. *The Real UFO Invasion.* N.p.: Greenleaf Classics.

Peck, James, ed. 1987. *The Chomsky Reader.* New York: Pantheon Books.

Perry, Col. George. 1953. Letter to Brig. Gen. W. M. Burgess, Deputy for Intelligence, Air Defense Command, Ent AFB, Colorado (23 December).

Pflock, Karl T. 1994. *Roswell in Perspective.* N.p.: Fund for UFO Research.

Powers, Thomas. 1979. *The Man Who Kept the Secrets: Richard Helms and the CIA.* New York: Knopf.

Randle, Kevin D. 1995. *A History of UFO Crashes.* New York: Avon Books.

———. 1997a. *Conspiracy of Silence.* New York: Avon Books.

———. 1997b. *The Randle Report: UFOs in the '90s.* New York: M. Evans.

Randle, Kevin, and Donald R. Schmitt. 1991. *UFO Crash at Roswell.* New York: Avon Books.

———. 1994. *The Truth about the UFO Crash at Roswell.* New York: M. Evans.

Randles, Jenny. 1988. *The UFO Conspiracy: The First Forty Years.* New York: Blandford Press.

Rees, Lt. Col. Doyle. 1950. Memorandum to Brig. Gen. Joseph F. Carroll, Director of Special Investigations (25 May).

Robertson, H. P. 1953. Letter to H. Marshall Chadwell (20 January).

Roerich, Nicholas. 1929. *Altai—Himalaya: A Travel Diary, with Twenty Reproductions from Paintings.* New York: Frederick A. Stokes Company.

Rogow, Arnold A. 1963. *James Forrestal, a Study of Personality, Politics, and Policy.* New York: Macmillan.

Rommel, Kenneth M., Jr. 1980. Operation Animal Mutilation: Report of the District Attorney First Judicial District, State of New Mexico (June). http://www.site034145.primehost.oom/articles/0597/romindex.htm.

Roswell Daily Record. 1947. Article, 08 July.

The Roswell Report: Fact versus Fiction in the New Mexico Desert. 1995. Washington, D.C.: Headquarters U. S. Air Force.

Ruppelt, Edward J. 1956. *The Report on Unidentified Flying Objects*. Garden City, N.Y.: Doubleday.

———. 1960. *The Report on Unidentified Flying Objects*. 2d ed. Garden City, N.Y.: Doubleday.

Sagan, Carl, and Thornton Page, eds. 1972. *UFOs—A Scientific Debate*. Ithaca, N.Y.: Cornell University Press.

St. Louis Post-Dispatch. 1947. Articles, 03 July, 08 July.

Saler, Benson, Charles A. Ziegler, and Charles B. Moore. 1997. *UFO Crash at Roswell: The Genesis of a Modern Myth*. Washington, D.C.: Smithsonian Institution Press.

A Sampler of Items in Seven Parts. The 4602nd Air Intelligence Service Squadron. Ent Air Force Base, Colorado Springs, Colorado. http://www.cufon.org/cufon/cufon_v.htm.

Sanderson, Ivan. 1967. *Uninvited Visitors: A Biologist Looks at UFOs*. New York: Cowles Education Corp.

———. 1970. *Invisible Residents: A Disquisition upon Certain Matters Maritime, and the Possibility of Intelligent Life under the Waters of This Earth*. New York: World Pub. Co.

Saunders, David R., and R. Roger Harkins. 1968. *UFOs? Yes! Where the Condon Committee Went Wrong*. New York: World Pub. Co.

Saunders, Frances Stoner. 2000. *The Cultural Cold War: The CIA and the World of Arts and Letters*. New York: New Press.

Scientific Advisory Board. 1948. "Utilization of Technical Intelligence" (17–18 March). Washington, D.C.: The Pentagon. http://www.project1947.com/fig/afsab.htm.

Scully, Frank. 1950. *Behind the Flying Saucers*. New York: Holt and Company.

Sheaffer, Robert. 1981. *The UFO Verdict: Examining the Evidence*. Buffalo, N.Y.: Prometheus Books.

Simpson, Cornell. 1966. *The Death of James Forrestal*. Boston: Western Islands.

Skylook. 1973. Article (September), no. 70. (Now *MUFON UFO Journal*).

Smith, Capt. E. J. 1947. Interview by District Intelligence Officer, Thirteenth Naval District. Seattle, Washington (09 July).

Smith, W. B. 1950. "Memorandum to the Controller of Telecommunications." Top Secret Confidential Department of Transport, Intradepartmental Correspondence (21 November). Ottawa, Ontario.

Springfield Republican. 1953. Review (01 November).

Steiger, Brad, ed. 1976. *Project Blue Book: The Top Secret UFO Findings Revealed*. New York: Ballantine Books.

Strategic Air Command. 1949. Memorandum to Director of FBI (10 January). SAC Knoxville. Subject: "Flying Saucers" Observed over Oak Ridge Area.

Stringfield, Leonard H. 1957. *Saucer Post . . . 3-0 Blue*. N.p.: The Author.

———. 1977. *Situation Red: The UFO Siege*. Garden City, N.Y.: Doubleday.

Studies in Intelligence. 1966. vol. 10, no. 4.

Sullivan, Walter. 1964. *We Are Not Alone*. New York: McGraw-Hill.

Summers, Anthony. 1994. *Official and Confidential: The Secret Life of J. Edgar Hoover*. New York: Pocket Star Books.

Sydney Sun. 1967. Article, 25 February.

Tacker, Lawrence. 1960. *Flying Saucers and the U.S. Air Force*. Princeton, N.J.: Van Nostrand.

Talbert, Ansel E. 1955. "Work to Break Gravity Barrier"; "Future Planes May Defy Gravity and Air Lift in Space Travels"; "Engineers Aiming to Flout Gravity." Articles in *Miami Herald* (November 30 to December 2).

Tauss, Edward. 1952. Letter from Acting Chief of the Weapons and Equipment Division of the Office of Scientific Intelligence to the Deputy Assistant Director of OSI (01 August).

Thomas, Gordon. 1989. *Journey into Madness: The True Story of Secret CIA Mind Control and Medical Abuse*. New York: Bantam Books.

Thomas, Kenn. 1999. *Maury Island UFO: The Crisman Conspiracy*. Lilburn, Ga.: IllumiNet Press.

Time. 1962. Magazine article (27 July).

Tomlinson, Arthur. 1993. Look Back in Astonishment. In *UFOs, The Final Answer? Ufology for the Twenty-first Century*, edited by David Barclay and Therese Marie Barclay. London: Blandford Press.

True. 1954. "What Our Air Force Found Out about Flying Saucers." (April).

Tully, Andrew. 1969. *The Super Spies: More Secret, More Powerful Than the CIA*. New York: Morrow.

UFO Magazine. 1990. vol. 5, no. 3.

———. 1991. Articles (vol. 6, nos. 1 and 2).

———. 1993a. vol. 8, no. 2.

———. 1993b. vol. 8, no. 3.

———. 1993c. vol 8, no. 5.

United Press. 1947. Story, 04 July.

U.S. Air Force. n.d.a. Fact Sheet 95-03. "Unidentified Flying Objects and Air Force Project Blue Book." Air Force Link. The Official Site of the U.S. Air Force. http://www.af.mil.

———. n.d.b. *Introductory Space Science, Vo. II.* Chapter 33: Unidentified Flying Objects. Department of Physics, for course Physics 370, 1968–1970. http://www.cufon.org/cufon/afu.htm.

———. n.d.c. Air Force Information Policy Letter for Commanders, Vol. XIV, no. 12. Issued by Office of Secretary of the Air Force.

———. 1947a. "Subject: Re Flying Disc" (27 August). Headquarters Fourth Air Force. Office of the Assistant Chief of Staff. A-2 Intelligence. Hamilton Field, Calif. http://www.project1947.com/fig/guam47.htm.

———. 1947b. "Intelligence Requirements on Flying Saucer Type" (30 October). At Project 1947—The Schulgen Memo. http://www.project 1947.com/fig/schulgen.htm.

———. 1948a. "Flying Discs" (03 March). Director of Intelligence. http://www.project1947.com/fig/anderson.htm.

———. 1948b. "Memorandum for Mr. Forrestal: Publicity on Flying Saucer Incidents." Memorandum for Record (24 November). Office of the Secretary. http://www.project1947.com/fig/1948d.htm and http://www.project1947.com/fig/1948f.htm.

———. 1951. "Incoming Classified Message" (10 July). Staff Message Division. OSI Robins AFB Macon to CS, USAF, Washington, D.C.

———. 1952. Historical Data for 4602nd Air Intelligence Service Squadron (01 July to 30 July). Ent Air Force Base. Colorado Springs, Colorado.

———. 1953. Classified message from Hamilton AFB, California, to Headquarters (31 August).

———. 1954a. *A Summary of the Second Commander's Conference, 13–16 January 1954.* Headquarters 4602nd Air Intelligence Service Squadron, Ent AFB, Colorado, 83–84.

———. 1954b. Air Force Regulation AFR 200-2 (12 August).

———. 1954c. *Squadron History.* 4602nd Air Intelligence Service Squadron. Air Defense Command (01 July to 31 December).

———. 1955a. 4602nd Squadron 200-2. Air Intelligence Service Squadron Document (15 March).

———. 1955b. *History of the 4602nd Air Intelligence Service Squadron, 01 January 1955 to 30 June 1955, Volume II.* Ent AFB, Colorado.

———. 1959. Operations and Training Order from the Inspector General of the Air Force to Base Commanders (24 December).

———. 1966. Air Force Regulation 80-17 (19 December).

U.S. Army. 1947a. Memorandum to the FBI (08 August). Cited in Lawrence Fawcett and Barry Greenwood, *Clear Intent: The Government Cover-up of the UFO Experience.* (Englewood Cliffs, N.J.: Prentice-Hall, 1984), 151, 154.

———. 1947b. Subject: Investigation of "Flying Discs" (14 August). Headquarters Muroc Army Air Field. Office of the Commanding Officer. http://www.project1947.com/fig/muroc47.html.

———. 1948. "Unconventional Aircraft" (21 January). General Staff, U.S. Army Intelligence Division. http://www.project1947.com/fig/hort1.htm.

U.S. House. 1966. Committee on Armed Services. *Unidentified Flying Objects.* Hearings, Eighty-Ninth Congress, Second Session (April 5). Washington, D.C.: Government Printing Office.

U.S. House. 1968. Committee on Science and Astronautics. *Symposium of Unidentified Flying Objects.* Hearings, Ninetieth Congress, Second Session (July 29). Washington, D.C.: Government Printing Office.

U.S. House. 1996. Permanent Select Committee on Intelligence. *IC21: The Intelligence Community in the Twenty-first Century.* Hearings Before the Permanent Select Committee on Intelligence, House of Representatives, One Hundred Fourth Congress.

U.S. General Accounting Office. 1995. *Report to the Honorable Steven H. Schiff, House of Representatives: Results of a Search for Records Concerning the 1947 Crash Near Roswell, New Mexico.* Washington, D.C.: General Accounting Office.

U.S. Senate. 1989. Committee on Foreign Relations. Subcommittee on Terrorism, Narcotics, and International Operations. *Drugs, Law Enforcement, and Foreign Policy.* Washington, D.C.: Government Printing Office.

Valentine, Douglas. 1990. *The Phoenix Program.* New York: Morrow.

Vallee, Jacques. 1965. *Anatomy of a Phenomenon: Unidentified Objects in Space—A Scientific Appraisal.* Chicago: H. Regnery Co.

———. 1969. *Passport to Magonia: From Folklore to Flying Saucers.* Chicago: H. Regnery Co.

———. 1975. *The Invisible College: What a Group of Scientists Has Discovered About UFO Influences on the Human Race.* New York: Dutton.

———. 1979. *Messengers of Deception: UFO Contacts and Cults.* Berkeley, Calif.: And/Or Press.

———. 1992a. *Forbidden Science: Journals 1957–1969.* Berkeley, Calif.: North Atlantic Books.

———. 1992b. *UFO Chronicles of the Soviet Union: A Cosmic Samizdat.* New York: Ballantine Books.

Vallee, Jacques, and Janine Vallee. 1966. *Challenge to Science: The UFO Enigma.* Chicago: H. Regnery Co.

Volkmann, Ernest, and Blaine Baggett. 1989. *Secret Intelligence: The Inside Story of America's Espionage Empire*. Garden City, N.Y.: Doubleday.

Walters, Helen B. 1962. *Hermann Oberth: Father of Space Travel*. New York: Macmillan.

Weaver, Col. Richard L. 1994. *Report of Air Force Research Regarding the "Roswell Incident."* Executive Summary. U.S. Air Force Security and Special Program Oversight.

Webb, Gary. 1998. *Dark Alliance: The CIA, the Contras, and the Crack Cocaine Explosion*. New York: Seven Stories Press.

Weiner, Tim. 1990. *Blank Check: The Pentagon's Black Budget*. New York: Warner Books.

Wilkins, Harold P. 1954. *Flying Saucers on the Attack*. New York: Citadel Press.

———. 1955. *Flying Saucers Uncensored*. New York: Citadel Press.

Winks, Robin W. 1987. *Cloak and Gown: Scholars in the Secret War, 1939–1961*. New York: Morrow.

Wise, Bill, 1966. "The Week of Flying Saucers." *Life* (01 April).

Wise, David. n.d. The CIA Files. n.p., 21.

———. 1976. *The American Police State: The Government against the People*. New York: Random House.

Wise, David, and Thomas Ross. 1964. *The Invisible Government*. New York: Bantam Books.

———. 1967. *The Espionage Establishment*. New York: Random House.

Zechel, W. Todd. 1979. NI-CIA-AP or NICAP? *Just Cause* (January), 5–8.

———. 1994. The Naked Truth: Crashed Saucers, Covert CIA Cover-ups, UFO Cover-ups. Associated Investigators Group. http://www.rmdavis.demon.uk/ufos/nathen/nat22.txt.

Index

200, 217-218, 264, 294-295, 305-306, 358, 363, 369
investigation of, 102
Special Report #14, 122, 125, 178, 329. *See also* Battelle Report
staff, 100, 113, 130, 220, 239, 249, 306, 314
Blum, Howard, 258, 309, 385, 421, 432-434, 437, 439, 441, 444
Boca Chica Naval Air Station, 81, 399
Boeing Corporation, 22, 40, 318, 323
Boggs, Jere, 66
Bolender, Brig, General Carroll H., 362, 369, 440, 444
Bolster, Admiral Calvin, 70, 99
Bos, Capt, Jan P., 155
Bowen, Charles, 333, 427, 435, 439, 441, 444
Bowie, Robert R., 46
Boyd, Cmdr, Randall, 110-111, 154, 450
Boyd, Lee, 154
Brazel, Mac, 21, 23, 25-26
Brazel, William, 25
Brazil, 42, 166, 200-203, 215-216, 232, 243, 268, 331, 365, 376, 408, 410, 413
Brazilian Army, 203
Brent, George, 258-259
British Air Ministry, 10, 115, 147
British Air Ministry's Directorate of Intelligence (Research), 10
British Army, 163
Bronk Detlev, 45
Brookings Institution, 239
report, 245
Brooks, Overton, 245, 249-250
Brothers, Dave, 303
Brown, Captain Tom, 18
Brown, Harold, 300-301
Brown, Lt. Frank M., 36
Brown, Thomas Townsend, xiii, 175, 429
Bryan, III, Colonel Joseph J., 100-101, 191, 239, 364-365, 422, 444
Buffalo Evening News, 186
Bulebush, Bill, 295
Burgess, General, 128, 143
Burgess, John, 281
Burns, Haydon, 203, 270, 281, 305, 316, 325, 410
Bush, Dr. Vannevar, 3-4, 44-48, 88, 175, 224, 336
Butler, William, 217
Byrd, Senator Harry, 185

Cabell, General Charles P., 61, 92-94, 134, 194, 247
Cahn, J. P., 86-87
California, 102, 105, 178, 236, 243, 401-402, 408
Bakersfield, 17
China Lake, 238
Culver City, 105
Fullerton, 187
Long Beach, 149, 197, 236
Mojave Desert, 31
Monterey, 280
Panorama City, 187
Pine Crest, 270
Pixley, 187
Rio Vista, 277
San Jose, 99
San Nicholas Island, 174
San Rafael, 137
Santa Ana, 286
Santa Maria, 181
Sequoia-Kings National Park, 136
Cambridge Research Laboratory, 78
Cameron, Ewen, 133, 171, 194-195, 238, 267, 374, 436, 445
Camp Drum, 115
Canada, 18-19, 51, 87, 141, 178, 195, 294, 296, 308, 338, 376, 401, 408, 411, 413, 444
Canadian Aerial Phenomena Research Organization (CAPRO), 325
Canine, Julian, 194
Capen, Charles, 207
Capitol, the, 105-106, 116, 152, 188, 373, 402-403
Carlan, Major U. G., 84
Carlborg, Herbert A., 211
Carter, Jimmy, ix, 365
Carter, Launor, 297
Carvalho, Bernard J., 191
Castro, Fidel, 220, 242, 245-247
Cavitt, Captain Sheridan, 21-22, 24, 28-29
CBS, 210-211, 300
correspondents, 373
Laboratories, 238
News, xxvi
representatives of, 209
television, 209
Center for UFO Studies (CUFOS), 24, 365
Central Intelligence Agency. *See* CIA

Cross, H. C., x, 121-122, 249, 424, 446
Cruttwell, Norman E. G., 231
Cuban Jet incident, 323
Cummings, Lt. Jerry, 92
Cutler, Robert, 49-50
Cybulski, Captain, 143, 171
Czechoslovakia, 164

da Silva, Rivalino, 268
Dahl, Harold A., 35-42
Daily Telegraph, 10, 243
Davidson, Capt. William, 36-41
Davis, Isabel, 146
Dean, John, 375
Dean, Sergeant Oliver, 234
Defense Intelligence Agency (DIA), 245
Delaware, 16, 152
Delgado, Jose, 219, 360, 434, 436, 440, 446
Dempster, Derek, 173
Denmark, 7, 116, 204
Dennis, Glenn, 25-26
Denver Post, 313, 328
Department of Justice, United States, 212, 279
Department of State, United States, 80, 416, 446
Detrick, Fort. *See* Maryland
Dewey, Thomas, 60, 71-72, 101, 106, 108, 120, 184, 191, 209, 212
Dewilde, Marius, 158-159, 161
DIA. *See* Defense Intelligence Agency
Discoverer, 146, 244
Dodge Corporation, 63, 223, 331
Dominican Republic, 242
Donielson, Alan, 377
Donner, Frank, 361, 415-416, 423, 426, 429, 433, 435-437, 439-440, 446
Donovan, William "Wild Bill," 4, 7
Doolittle, General James, 6, 9, 170
dos Santos, Raimondo, 243
Doty, Richard, 45, 48
Douglas Aircraft Corporation, 85
Douglass, Earl, 191
Dowding, Lord, 173, 185
Downing, Thomas, W., 249
Drake, Frank, 241
Dugger, Barbara, 26
Dulles, Allen, 12, 42, 132, 173, 194, 238, 244-246, 416, 446

Dunn, Colonel Frank, 92, 94, 100
Durant, Frederick, 113, 120, 123-124, 126, 365, 424, 446
Dussia, Captain, 294
Dustman, Ross, 304
Dutch East Indies, 2

Eastern Air Lines, 36, 59, 61, 206, 210
Eberstadt, Ferdinand, 13
Edgewood Arsenal, 195, 219, 238
Edwards, Frank, 123, 138, 145, 147, 151-152, 155, 176-177, 191, 235, 241, 264, 297, 319, 446
Efron, Ruben, 181
Egypt, 163, 408
Egyptian Army, 163
Ehrlichmann, John, 372-373
Eickhoff, Thomas B., 147, 173
Einstein, Albert, 229
Eisenhower, Dwight D., xxiv-xxv, 45-46, 49-50, 117, 122-123, 128, 142, 146, 149, 169-170, 183, 220, 238, 242, 245-246
Ellsberg, Daniel, 373, 375
Elmira Star-Gazette, 317
Emerson, Colonel Robert B., 191-192
Estabrooks, George, 360-361
Estimate of the Situation, The, xviii, 35, 60-61, 65, 93, 184, 209, 212
Eton Range, 281
Exon, General Arthur, 25, 58

FAA. *See* Federal Aviation Administration
Fahrney, Admiral Delmar, 70, 84, 191-194, 225, 258, 310, 389
Falcon Lake, 324
Faraday, Michael, 229
Fawcett, Lawrence, 118, 127, 280, 330, 445-446, 454
FBI, xviii, 3, 20, 23, 78, 115, 144, 183-184, 267, 296, 321, 372
  field offices, 17, 39, 184, 280, 373
  files, 4, 93, 184, 271. *See also* FBI, memos
  interviews by, 18, 33, 39, 83, 324
  investigations by, 14, 19, 31, 41, 89, 183, 360, 377
  memos, 17, 32, 41, 67-68, 88, 110, 120, 207. *See also*, FBI, files
  surveillance by, 4, 40, 71, 148, 271, 373, 375
Federal Aviation Administration (FAA), xxii-xxiii, 233, 292

Gottlieb, Sidney, 133, 144, 194, 238, 245, 267, 296, 372, 374
Goudsmit, Samuel A., 4, 123
Gray, Gordon, 45, 170, 174, 220
Great Falls. *See* Montanna
Greece, 4, 7, 10, 319-320
Green Fireballs, 63-64, 66-67, 70, 78, 162, 179
Greene, Clarence, 184
Greenhaw, Jeff, 383
Greenland, 169
Greenwood, Barry, 33, 49, 118, 127, 185, 280, 323, 416-427, 429, 431-432, 434-436, 438-440, 445-446, 448, 454
Gregory, Captain George T., 185, 218
Ground Observer Corps (GOC), 135, 137, 152, 155, 168, 180
Grumman Aircraft Corporation, 240, 243, 411
Guam, 34, 51, 397
Guatemala, 123, 242, 246
Guevara, Ernesto "Che", 320
Gulf of Tonkin, xxv

Haines, Gerald K., xxviii, 169, 415, 423, 448
Haldeman, H. R., 372-373
Hall, Richard, 79, 138, 195, 213, 239, 253, 273, 275, 279, 283, 291, 314-315, 328, 334, 432, 448, 450
Hall, Robert L., 347
Hammit, Frank, 243
Harder, James A., 347
Hardin, Captain Charles, 147, 152, 168, 185
Harkins, R. Roger, 308-309, 338-340, 344, 359, 420, 430, 436-439, 452
Harris, Waldo, 256-257
Harrison, Jr., Robert Wayne, 74
Hart, Carl, 90-91
Hart, Major C. R., 263, 265
Hartman, William K., 355
Hartranft, J. B., 191
Harvey, Luis, 268, 271, 361
Hathaway, Lt. Colonel E. U., 181
Haut, Lt. Walter, 22
Hawaii, 99, 232, 282, 401

Headrick, Lt. Colonel Richard T., 234
Healey, Sergeant John, 198, 204, 212, 383
Hearst Newspapers, xxvi
Heflin, Rex, 286-287
Helms, Richard, 16, 62, 170, 184, 247, 267, 272, 296, 320, 372, 374, 451
Henderson, John E., 214
Hess, Seymore, 349
Hill Abduction Case, 250
Hill, Barney, 251, 256, 321
Hill, Betty, 251-253, 256, 321
Hillenkoetter, Rear Admiral Roscoe H., 14-15, 45, 47, 54, 62, 117, 190-191, 198, 210, 212, 225-226, 240, 249-250, 258-260, 262, 264, 310, 390
Hines, Richard, 243, 249-250
Hippler, Lt. Colonel Robert, 316
Hitler, Adolf, 12, 132, 388
Hogan, Captain B.W., 73
Hogg, A. R., 204
Hohman, Robert, 253-254
Holcomb, Lt., 108
Holland. See Netherlands, 6, 164, 396
Hoover Commission, 170
Hoover, Herbert, 170, 428
Hoover, J. Edgar, 3, 23, 39, 81, 242, 271, 372-373, 447, 453
Horner, Richard, 209-211
Horten brothers, 12, 53, 444
Hottel, Guy, 81
Howard, James, 58, 154, 258, 309, 373, 385, 444
Howe, Linda Moulton, 337, 421, 438, 440, 448
HT Lingual, 115
humanoid sighting. *See* alien sightings
Hungary, 167
Hunsaker, Jerome, 45
Hunt, David, 288
Hunt, E. Howard, 373
Hunter, Harriet, 346
Huston, H. Wayne, 302
Huston, Tom, 372-373
Hutchinson, Edward, 187, 309, 409
Hynek, J. Allen, ix, xiii, xxvii, xxx-xxxi, 60, 67, 77, 92, 101, 114, 121, 124-128, 130, 136, 143,

Saucedo, Pedro, 204
Saunders, David, 66, 314, 316, 359, 452
Sawyer, James H., 234
Schiff, Steven, 27-28, 444, 455
Schirmer, Herb, 341-342
Schlesinger, James, 374-375
Schmitt, Donald, 24, 417, 451
Schopenhauer, Arthur, 387
Schulgen, Brig. General George F., xiii, 32-33, 35, 43-44, 51-53, 56, 388, 454
Sciacca, Jr., Thomas P., 275
Scotland, 197, 204, 271
Scott, William, 316
Scripps-Howard Newspapers, xxvi
Scully, Frank, 65, 86-87, 89, 140, 421, 452
Seamans, Robert B., 345, 361, 363
Seattle Times, 286
Sebago, 205-207
Seitz, Frederick, 317, 346
Shag Harbor, 337, 357, 414
Shallett, Sydney, 69-70
Shandera, Jaime, 44, 46, 49
Sharp, Joseph, 382
Sharpe, Mitchell R., 176, 451
Shea, Major David J., 359
Sheaffer, Robert , 289, 366, 452
Sheehy, Monsignor Maurice, 73-74
Sheldon, Charles, 365
Sherrill, Colonel John, 213
Shipco, Paul, 294
Shirkey, First Lt. Robert, 27
Signal Security Agency, 13, 40
Simon, Benjamin, 254
Simonton, Joe, 247-248
Skyhook Balloons, 56-57
Slusher, Robert, 27
Smart, Richard, 243
Smith, Captain Edward J., 19
Smith, Captain Harry, 124
Smith, Colonel Weldon, 120, 129
Smith, E. J. "Smithy", 33, 37-40
Smith, General Sory, 140
Smith, Robert, 27
Smith, Walter Bedell, 116, 121-122, 124
Smith, Wilbert, 87, 107, 133, 176, 225, 243, 257, 266, 421
Society for the Investigation of Human Ecology, 171, 194
Souers, Rear Admiral Sidney, 13, 45, 72

South Africa, 169, 203, 383, 410
South Dakota, 35, 135, 196, 285
Soviet Union. *See* Union of Soviet Socialist Republic
Spaatz, General Carl, 21, 61
Spain, 111, 167, 178, 232
Spaulding, Lt. Colonel John, 304
Spaur, Dale F., 302-304
Spellbinder, 296
Sperry-Rand Corporation, 174
Sprinkle, R. Leo, 298, 341
Sputnik, 171, 200-201, 203-204, 207-208, 217
SR-71. *See* aircraft, classified
Stalin, Joseph, xxi
Stancil, Arthur G., 134, 425
Stanford, Ray, 275
Stanton, William, 24, 26, 46, 88, 182, 304, 323, 447
Steiner, Lt. Colonel Harold A., 297
Stenvers, Major Mervin, 187
Stevens, Ralph, 19
Stevenson, Adlai, 122
Stevenson, David B., 123
Stockey, George, 214
Stokes, James, 205
Stone, Captain Edward, 66
Stone, Clifford, xv, 57, 419
Stowe, David, 46
Strategic Air Command, xxiv, 23, 180, 183, 246, 289
Strategic Services, Office of, 4
Strieber Whitley, 158
Stringfield, Leonard, 6-7, 134, 147-148, 152, 168, 179-181, 185, 191, 193, 416, 424-430, 433, 435, 440-441, 453
Strong, Philip G., 123
Struve, Otto, 241
Stuart Cook, 344
Students for a Democratic Society, 360
Styles, Chris, 338
Summers, Anthony, 373, 453
Sweden, 7-12, 139, 164, 227, 240, 416
Swett, Captain Ben, 254
Switzerland, 216
Swords, Michael, 126, 375
Sylvester, Arthur, 266
Symington, Stuart, 71, 75, 374

About the Author

Richard M. Dolan studied at Alfred University and Oxford University before completing his graduate work in history at the University of Rochester, where he was a finalist for a Rhodes scholarship. Prior to his interest in UFOs, Dolan studied U.S. Cold War strategy, Soviet history and culture, and international diplomacy. He lives in Rochester, New York, where he is at work on volume 2 of his study.

Hampton Roads Publishing Company

. . . for the evolving human spirit

HAMPTON ROADS PUBLISHING COMPANY publishes books on a variety of subjects, including metaphysics, spirituality, health, visionary fiction, and other related topics.

For a copy of our latest trade catalog, call toll-free, 800-766-8009, or send your name and address to:

HAMPTON ROADS PUBLISHING COMPANY, INC.
1125 STONEY RIDGE ROAD • CHARLOTTESVILLE, VA 22902
e-mail: hrpc@.hrpub.com • Internet: www.hrpub.com